EYEWITNESS HISTORY

The 1970s

Neil A. Hamilton

Facts On File
An imprint of Infobase Publishing

To my mother, my brother, and
my Aunt "Cider"

The 1970s

Copyright © 2006 by Neil A. Hamilton
Maps and graphs copyright © 2006 by Infobase Publishing

Facts On File, Inc.
An imprint of Infobase Publishing
132 West 31st Street
New York NY 10001

Library of Congress Cataloging-in-Publication Data
Hamilton, Neil A., 1949–
    The 1970s / Neil A. Hamilton.
        p. cm. — (Eyewitness history)
    Includes bibliographical references and index.
    ISBN 0-8160-5778-8
    1. United States—History—1969—Juvenile literature. 2. Nineteen seventies—Juvenile literature. I. Title: Nineteen seventies. II. Title. III. Series.
    E855.H365 2006
    909.82'7—dc22   2005016808

Text design by Joan M. McEvoy
Cover design by Cathy Rincon
Maps and graphs by Sholto Ainslie

Printed in the United States of America

VB JM 10 9 8 7 6 5 4 3 2 1

This book is printed on acid-free paper.

CONTENTS

ACKNOWLEDGMENTS

In the writing of this book, I owe a special debt of thanks to Nicole Bowen, executive editor for American history at Facts On File. Her guidance has been invaluable in seeing this manuscript through to publication. My thanks go also to Laura Shauger, for her attention to numerous details in pulling together the complete work, especially the many photographs, and to Joan Nichols, for her expertise in line editing the manuscript.

I would like also to thank Bret Heim, the Government Documents and Reference Librarian at Spring Hill College in Mobile, Alabama, for helping to uncover and acquire numerous sources. Finally, I would like to thank my family for their support and encouragement.

INTRODUCTION

THE 1960s COUNTERCULTURE AS A BACKDROP TO THE 1970s

The 1970s were preceded by one of the greatest periods of social and political upheaval in American history: the 1960s counterculture. *Counter* means "against," and in this instance, the counterculture was a movement against mainstream culture. It consisted of a widespread, largely uncoordinated array of people and groups who were rebelling against societal standards and practices—everyone from hippies, who wanted to create an alternative society that was founded on psychedelic enlightenment and communal relations, to New Leftists, who wanted to overthrow the existing political system and replace it with a populist one that was rooted in socialism or, even more extreme, Marxism or anarchy.

The counterculture had its roots in the 1950s, a decade when the cold war—with its emphasis on a foreign enemy that had to be confronted and contained—gripped America and encouraged conformity. Suburbia displayed this sameness: look-alike houses, cars with big tail fins, television shows that were whiter than white. And it appeared in the harsher, starker forms of racism, censorship, and blacklists.

Conformity, however, was shaken by an expanding youth culture that was evident in the rise of rock and roll and more so by the Civil Rights Movement. For the counterculture generation—mainly those who reached their teens in the 1960s—a transcendent moment came in 1960 when black college students in Greensboro, North Carolina, staged a sit-in at a segregated lunch counter. The television and newspaper coverage of the event stirred African-American and white youths across America. To these young people, the reaction of white segregationists to the sit-in made society seem undemocratic and cruel. Consequently, they decided to take the lead in making America live up to its professed ideals. With this upsurge, there emerged the Student Nonviolent Coordinating Committee, under whose direction college-age activists traveled to Mississippi and other southern states to work for black voting rights. These volunteers experienced oppression and reactionary violence firsthand. In their effort, they learned tactics and strategies for fighting injustice, such as marches, sit-ins, and boycotts. Thus the Civil Rights movement propelled America into the counterculture.

The Vietnam War reinforced the sense of injustice, of a country gone astray from its professed democratic and humanitarian ideals. To the massive number of young people who populated America amid a post–World War II "baby boom," the Vietnam War may have been the strongest influence in creating the counterculture. The deaths from the war and the government lies connected to it made society's oppression and corruption naked, or so young people believed. Moreover, television provided unparalleled exposure to the war's violence and bloodshed, thus further fomenting discontent, while the draft made young people see the war as a palpable threat to their lives.

To many of these youths, the anvil of American industry and the brainpower of American technocrats who created ever-greater prosperity produced an impersonal machine that was concerned more with maintaining cold-war social stability than correcting society's deficiencies. "This is the time when the operation of the machine becomes so odious, makes you so sick at heart, that you can't take part," said student protest leader Mario Savio. He continued:

> You've got to put your bodies upon the levers, upon all the apparatus, and you've got to make it stop. And you've got to indicate to the people who run it, to the people who own it, that unless you're free, the machine will be prevented from working at all.[1]

Machine, apparatus, odious—the words fell on receptive ears, young people who felt oppressed and restive. So the counterculture emerged—hippies and college-based political activists who were tied to a New Left; black activists; female activists; those with serious agendas and those with frivolous ones; those aiming for political change; those aiming for cultural change.

Music changed. At first, young people flocked to folk music with its social and political consciousness; then they turned to the early Beatles with their innocent lyrics and upbeat outlook; they listened to psychedelic rock with its hallucinogenic imagery; they finally switched to harsher, politicized rock as antiwar protests grew heated and the gulf between counterculture and straight society widened.

Artists experimented. They used happenings, performance art, psychedelic images, posters. They produced movies with no plot, with little plot, with amateur actors, with rock soundtracks. Nudity appeared in Broadway shows; musicals declared the Age of Aquarius.

Politics, cultural influences, social practices all tumbled together. All cascaded in a countercultural rush and a tremendous challenge to authority. In the late 1960s, the political activists hardened, and some radicals, such as a group called Weatherman, sought a violent overthrow of the government.

Some historians believe that the counterculture went through stages: an early stage, prior to 1968, when the Civil Rights movement worked its greatest influence and young people expressed optimism about change; a middle stage, from 1968 to 1970, when society polarized and the core within both the counterculture and society at large no longer held; and a late stage, after 1970, when new activist groups came to the fore, stirred by the previous developments.

Thus, the counterculture of the 1960s continued past 1969 and into the 1970s, although in different form, with some elements in retreat and others advancing. For example, women's liberationists emerged from the counterculture and embraced its spirit and drive in the early 1970s to push for reform.

As the counterculture expanded, the lines between it and mainstream society both widened and blurred. Mainstream society railed against "unwashed," "drug-crazed," and "long-haired" "hippies" and against the decline of moral values. Yet, movies and television changed to reflect countercultural values; middle-aged Americans wore bell bottoms, and commercials promoted products through psychedelic images.

The counterculture's pervasive influence, the discontent, and the extensive questioning of givens, of authority, of what those in power handed down as wisdom appeared in comments made in 1968 by a high school student. He said:

> The main thing that's taught us in school, is how to obey rules, dress in our uniforms, play the game, and no, don't be uppity! Oh, we're trained for participating in the democratic process—we have our student governments—they can legislate about basketball games and other such meaningful topics. Don't mention the curriculum. They'll tell us what to learn.[2]

In challenging mainstream ideas and practices, the counterculture—hippies, New Leftists, and assorted others—challenged authority and the basic premises of what the United States stood for. In *The Movement and the Sixties,* author Terry H. Anderson states: "The counterculture believed that the nation had become a Steppenwolf, a berserk monster, a cruel society that made war on peasants abroad and at home beat up on minorities, dissidents, students, and hippies. America the Beautiful was no more; it had been replaced by America the Death Culture."[3]

The questions and challenges that were raised by the counterculture continued into the 1970s, but given the view that America represented a "Death Culture," out to destroy dissidents, the counterculture became splintered, harsher, less willing to compromise, and less optimistic. For its part, mainstream society saw in the counterculture an invading horde about to destroy the values and institutions that had made America great. A deeply divided, polarized country entered the 1970s.

THE 1970s AS A FORGOTTEN DECADE

The 1970s sometimes have been called the forgotten decade, squeezed between the more tumultuous and exciting sixties and the more economically expansive and nationalistic eighties. At other times, the 1970s have been called the decade better forgotten.

It was, the argument goes, a terrible period filled with everything the 1960s could offer as backwash: the defeat in Vietnam with the horrible scenes of Vietnamese refugees trying desperately to flee their country; Watergate with the resignation of President Richard Nixon and the subsequent distrust of government that came from it and from the lies surrounding the Vietnam War; economic problems that ranged from an oil embargo (and escalating oil prices) to stagflation (the debilitating combination of high inflation and high unemployment); polarized views as conservatives derided the countercultural excesses and liberals derided mainstream hypocrisy; presidential ineptitude as Jimmy Carter struggled mightily and with much failure to deal with a demoralized society; war in the Middle East as Arabs and Israelis went to battle and nearly dragged the United States and the Soviet Union into a military conflict; embarrassment and rage as revolutionaries in Iran held Americans hostage; fear as a nuclear power plant in Pennsylvania almost collapsed into meltdown; even pop-culture decay as disco seemed to make music vacuous and mindless.

There were, however, many positive accomplishments: manned journeys to the Moon and to the *Skylab* space station; reforms that advanced women's rights;

treaties between the United States and the Soviet Union that addressed the spread of nuclear weapons; a decrease in tension between the United States and Communist China; provocative books and artful movies; and the everyday accomplishments of people who were holding their families together, enjoying their personal relationships, and taking satisfaction in doing their jobs.

Although the 1960s counterculture continued deep into the 1970s, at least from the mid-1970s onward, there was a pronounced movement away from the more idealistic features of the counterculture, especially its emphasis on harmony and community. To use the somewhat shopworn but still perceptive observation of novelist and essayist Tom Wolfe, the 1970s became the "Me Decade." Wolfe wrote:

> One only knows that . . . great religious waves have a momentum all their own. Neither arguments nor policies nor acts of the legislature have been any match for them in the past. And this one has the mightiest, holiest roll of all, the beat that goes . . . *Me* . . . *Me* . . . *Me* . . . *Me* . . .[4]

Dividing the 1970s into several broad categories helps to summarize some of the decade's more notable developments. Those categories follow below.

Militancy

Both peaceful and violent protests shaped the decade and thus directly continued the spirit of the 1960s counterculture. Antiwar protests, for example, captured nationwide attention with the tragic shooting of college students by the national guard at Kent State University in Ohio and the terrorist bombing by radicals at the University of Wisconsin in Madison. But two groups more than any others kept alive the countercultural protests into the 1970s: Native Americans and women. Both determined they would fight for the rights long denied them.

Radical Indians turned to the American Indian Movement (AIM), which was organized in 1968. AIM modeled itself after the militant Black Panthers and, at first, focused on monitoring police actions in urban Indian ghettos to prevent false arrests, harassment, and brutality. It then expanded its efforts to Indian reservations and sought to protect Native American treaty rights. AIM's protests included a "countercelebration" in 1971 atop Mount Rushmore in South Dakota to expose what the group called the forcible and illegal taking of the mountainous terrain from the Oglala Lakota in the 19th century; a march in 1972 in Gordon, Nebraska, to publicize the refusal of the local authorities to file charges against two white men who were implicated in the murder of an Oglala Lakota; and, in 1973, a standoff with federal agents at Wounded Knee, on the Pine Ridge Reservation in South Dakota, to prevent the granting of concessions to white ranchers on the reservation and the expansion of uranium mining that would likely contaminate the land.

For women, the fight for rights that had been long denied them dated back to the 19th and early 20th centuries, a crusade that resulted in the Nineteenth Amendment to the Constitution, which granted women suffrage when it was ratified in 1920. The suffrage amendment, however, left many discriminatory laws and practices in place. Consequently, women were denied equal educational and job opportunities, equal pay, and equal justice. In reaction to this oppression, in the late 1960s, women activists began what became called a second wave of feminism, to extend the first wave of feminism that was embodied in the suffrage movement. The second wave ranged from moderates, who emphasized equal rights, to radicals, who emphasized dismantling the male-dominated capitalist economic system along with traditional family structures that supported male supremacy and placed women in a subservient position. The second wave took form in a diverse array of protests, some advocating passage of the Equal Rights Amendment, others advocating lesbian rights. As with so many of the protest movements rooted in the 1960s, the women's movement of the 1970s displayed the tumult and controversy characteristic of a society shaped by the pervasive counterculture.

Politics

When Richard Nixon ran for the presidency in 1968, he tried to distance himself from the lies of the outgoing president, Lyndon Johnson. He promised: "Let us begin by committing ourselves to the truth—to see it like it is, and tell it like it is—to find the truth, to speak the truth, and to live the truth."[5] But on June 17, 1972, operatives for the Nixon reelection campaign broke into the Democratic party headquarters in Washington, D.C., at an apartment and office complex that was called Watergate. Their capture unraveled the secrets and lies that permeated the Nixon administration; moreover, it weakened trust in the country's political system and leaders, a weakening that had been underway since the mid-1960s. In his book *Time of Illusion,* Jonathan Schell likened Nixon's politics to the performance of an evil magician: The president appeared to be open, compassionate, and truthful while, in actuality, he was secretive, hateful, and deceitful. Americans now applied this description to nearly every politician.

When Gerald Ford followed Richard Nixon into the White House, he seemed to be operating with the same deceit when he pardoned his predecessor. While Jimmy Carter projected a benevolent and open image, he found himself hampered by the distrust that had grown so extensive (and was burdened by his own incompetence). That distrust and, with it, Americans turning their backs on politics characterized the politics of the decade.

Economics

An editorial cartoon drawn in 1976 showed the oversize face of an Arab sheik with the acronym *OPEC* (for Organization of Petroleum Exporting Countries) affixed to his forehead and his cavernous mouth swallowing whole a huge automobile emblazoned with the caption *American Lifestyle.* To many Americans, it appeared as if the Arab oil nations, through a yearlong embargo of oil shipments to the United States that was followed by increased oil prices, had combined with other bewildering forces to devour a once-prosperous economy.

By the middle of 1974, prices for heating oil and gasoline had risen as much as 33 percent. By 1980, the price of crude oil was nearly seven times higher than it had been 10 years earlier. Although Americans still paid less for oil than did people in other industrialized countries, the crisis worsened an already intense feeling of despair and decline that flowed from the debacle in Vietnam and the Watergate scandal.

Caused in part by the problems with oil, and more by long-term developments, such as increased foreign competition, factories reduced their workforces or shuttered their doors. Chrysler, for example, closed 13 plants and cut 31,000 jobs. While the Northeast "Rust Belt" suffered the most, every region experienced losses, and although 27 million new jobs were created in the 1970s, laid-off factory workers watched and worried as America's shift to a service economy forced many of them to flip burgers in low-pay, fast-food eateries or stock shelves in discount stores.

Inflation added to the miseries, reaching double digits by the end of the 1970s and contributing to a decline in living standards. By 1980, the typical family had only 7 percent more real purchasing power than a decade earlier—and that increase came in 1970–73, before OPEC's oil embargo and the cavernous mouth that swallowed the economy whole.

The Environment

Two events served as symbols for the nation's environment, one a symbol of hope, the other of despair. The hope: On April 22, 1970, millions of Americans celebrated the first Earth Day, showing their support for environmental reform. At about the time of this event, Congress passed several clean air and water acts, and many states passed similar legislation. In December 1970, President Nixon created the Environmental Protection Agency (EPA). The Endangered Species Act of 1973 pledged the federal government to protect species and their habitats threatened with extinction.

Between 1974 and 1977, clean-air laws reduced the number of unhealthy days in 25 major cities by 15 percent and the number of highly unhealthy days by 35 percent. In the late 1970s, President Jimmy Carter and Congress established a $1.6 billion superfund to clean up abandoned chemical-waste sites. By executive order, he protected about 100 million acres of land in Alaska as national parks, forests, or wildlife refuges. The accomplishments amounted to what some historians have called the golden age of environmentalism.

The despair: In 1979, the near meltdown of the Three Mile Island nuclear power plant near Harrisburg, Pennsylvania, reinforced the threat that had been posed by modern technology and confirmed long-held environmentalist views about the danger of using nuclear energy to generate electricity. And with the economy being so weak, Congress lowered many environmental standards to promote manufacturing and employment. Even President Carter deserted his strong environmentalism and relaxed the enforcement of federal antipollution standards.

Nuclear Arms

Throughout the 1950s and 1960s, the United States and the Soviet Union engaged in an enormous buildup of nuclear weapons as part of their cold-war strategy. The 1970s produced efforts to control the spread of those weapons, efforts the leaders of both countries, especially President Richard Nixon and Communist Party Secretary Leonid Brezhnev, sought to expand through a spirit of cooperation, or détente.

In 1972, prolonged negotiations led to the Strategic Arms Limitation Treaty, or SALT I, which set a ceiling on intercontinental ballistic missiles (ICBMs), while a related agreement limited both nations' employment of antiballistic missile systems. SALT I, however, said nothing about multiple independently targetable reentry vehicles (MIRVs), where one missile carried several nuclear warheads, each programmed to a different target, and, as a result, both nations added more of them to their arsenals. Although in 1973 Brezhnev and Nixon signed a statement called the Prevention of Nuclear War, Henry Kissinger spoke hard politics when he said privately: "The way for us to use [SALT] is for us to catch up."[6] Soon, the United States had 10,000 nuclear warheads; the Soviet Union, 4,000.

In 1979, President Jimmy Carter signed SALT II with the Soviet Union. The treaty restricted the number of MIRVs and froze the number of delivery systems. The U.S. Senate rejected it, however, and the decade ended at best with a mixed record on containing the spread of nuclear weapons and the threat of nuclear war.

Education

Schools in the 1970s bore the brunt of reform campaigns that were meant to correct failures from the 1960s or to change traditional practices. Reform came on the heels of disturbing news: Between 1970 and 1974, the verbal score on the average Scholastic Aptitude Test (SAT) fell 16 points; in just one year, from 1974 to 1975, it dropped another 10. Additionally, the average math score, which had dropped eight points from 1970 to 1974, plunged another eight.

Although part of the decline could be attributed to the increased number of students taking the test, the trouble went deeper. Experts blamed the results on family instability, youthful alienation, declining attention spans, and poor teaching.

In several localities, busing raised a tremendous fury and harmed race relations. In 1971, the Supreme Court issued its landmark decision in *Swann v. Charlotte-Mecklenburg Board of Education* whereby the justices ruled unanimously that federal courts could require busing to desegregate schools.

In Boston, white parents, mainly Irish-American, vehemently fought busing. They used marches and sit-ins and chanted "Hell, no! We won't go!" Nationally, as busing and other desegregation measures took effect, middle-class whites fled public schools for private ones, or they fled to the suburbs, creating a racial imbalance the court decision had intended to correct.

Racial controversy enveloped colleges, too, as the federal government pursued affirmative-action programs to boost black-student enrollment. In a court case involving Alan Bakke, a white student, the Supreme Court in a divided vote ruled that schools could consider race as one factor in setting admissions standards.

Federal programs and regulations raised the specter of communities losing control over their public schools. Between 1965 and 1977, such regulations increased from 92 to nearly 1,000. A Gallup poll found that, by a two-to-one margin, adults believed the national government should allow school districts to spend federal monies as local officials saw fit. Yet, the trend toward more federal regulations, unleashed in the 1970s, continued to accelerate, reaching a much higher level in the early 2000s.

Popular Culture

Nostalgia, pessimism, escapism—these characterized 1970s popular culture. People in their twenties especially looked longingly back to the 1950s and early 1960s, the supposedly tranquil and happy decade when they grew up. They flocked to the movie *American Graffiti* in 1973, whose story told about a group of small-town teenagers the night after they graduated from high school, in 1962, in a world untouched by the Vietnam War, the tumultuous developments of the counterculture years, or the hardships of the 1970s.

According to a survey conducted by the University of Michigan, the "level of worry" among young people 21 to 39 years old climbed from 36 percent in

1967 to 50 percent in 1976. This worry and pessimism could be seen in the popularity of such books as *The Closing Circle* (1971) by Barry Commoner, which portrayed a country and a world facing collapse from environmental degradation, and in *An Inquiry into the Human Prospect,* by Robert L. Heilbroner, which presented high birthrates, excessive armaments, and an unbalanced distribution of wealth as threats to human survival. "Is there hope for man?" Heilbroner asked. He provided his own answer: a sharp, unequivocal "no."

Escapism could be found at discos, first appearing in the late 1960s in New York City's black and Latin neighborhoods. Unlike rock and roll, disco made the audience important, making the dancers the center of attention. One music historian has called discos narcissistic; as to why people flocked to them, one culture analyst commented: "They are depressed by taxes and inflation. They want to party. . . . I call it 'The music that fiddles while Rome burns.' "[7]

Self-indulgence commanded the decade. Americans immersed themselves in self-actualization programs, such as EST, as never before. Wolfe's "Me . . . Me . . . Me . . . Me" dominated social relationships. Whatever the self-indulgence, however, in many ways America seemed exhausted in the 1970s, economically prostrate, politically bankrupt, and socially spent. For many, life had been reduced from pursuing ideals to, as the Bee Gees sang, "staying alive."

1

Divided America
January 1970–December 1970

It was as if tear gas from the 1968 Democratic National Convention at Chicago had wafted into the year 1970, bringing with it the residue from all the tumult, violence, and distrust of the 1960s. As January lurched into February, the trial of several antiwar defendants for inciting a riot at the convention—the Chicago Seven, as they were called—was nearing an end. The nation had followed the courtroom proceedings for nearly four months and now awaited a jury verdict. Looking back today, the event reveals a bridge between the 1960s and 1970s, with the spirit of the earlier decade continuing into the next.

THE 1960S ON TRIAL IN THE 1970S

When the delegates gathered for the Democratic National Convention on August 26, 1968, they did so in a most unconventional atmosphere. American society was reeling from a series of shocks: the communist-led Tet Offensive that beleaguered U.S. troops in Vietnam in January and made it clear that the war was far from over; the decision by President Lyndon Johnson in March to not run for reelection; the assassination of civil-rights leader Martin Luther King, Jr., in April during a strike by sanitation workers in Memphis, Tennessee; the takeover of several campus buildings, also in April, by student protesters at Columbia University in New York; and the assassination of presidential candidate Robert Kennedy in June, just minutes after he addressed supporters who had gathered in Los Angeles to cheer his victory in the California Democratic primary.

Add to these developments disputes between those in the counterculture mounting an assault on America's mainstream and those rallying to the defense of the mainstream, between moderates in the Civil Rights movement and radicals who advocated black power, and between those who supported the Vietnam War and those who opposed it, and the setting appeared ripe for a divisive political gathering. Little wonder, then, that violent clashes erupted at the Democratic National Convention in late August 1968.

At one point, the police used clubs, tear gas, and mace to repulse protesters as they tried to march peacefully to the amphitheater where the convention delegates were meeting. Television cameras broadcast the melee and with it the chant

1

of the crowd: "The whole world is watching! The whole world is watching!" Some of the tear gas drifted into the amphitheater, choking delegates in a painful awareness of the fighting that was continuing outside.

The mayhem in Chicago split the country. Mainstream America applauded the police, while many young dissidents equated the law enforcement with Gestapo tactics—another layer of oppression added to Vietnam and racism.

Early in 1969, Richard Nixon, the newly inaugurated president, and John Mitchell, his attorney general, decided to have the justice department prosecute the eight leaders involved in the protests. The authorities leveled conspiracy charges against Jerry Rubin and Abbie Hoffman of the protest group the Yippies; Dave Dellinger, a long-prominent figure in social-justice movements; Tom Hayden, who had earned his dissenter's credentials in the Civil Rights movement and with the leftist Students for a Democratic Society (SDS); Rennie Davis of the Mobilization Committee to End the War in Vietnam (MOBE); Bobby Seale of the militant Black Panthers; and two lesser-known activists who had worked as MOBE protest marshals, John Froines and Lee Weiner.

The trial of the Chicago Eight, as they were first called, began in October 1969 before Julius Hoffman, a graying magistrate and a conservative, who valued tradition and decorum. He often derided the defendants' testimony, while the Chicago Eight shouted obscenities. At one point, Seale so strenuously objected to Hoffman refusing to let him act as his own defense counsel that the judge ordered him gagged and chained while in the courtroom. Judge Hoffman eventually declared a mistrial for Seale, which resulted in a separate trial for the Black Panther and left the Chicago Eight as the Chicago Seven. Clearly, the early conflict between Judge Hoffman and the defendants displayed the dichotomy between mainstream America and its attackers, the countercultural protesters.

At best, the government had contradictory evidence to support its claim, and the indictments appeared to be aimed at cowering the protesters and making them look disreputable. In this atmosphere, Vice President Spiro Agnew called the defendants "kooks" and "social misfits."

The tumultuous trial continued into 1970. On February 4, the *New York Times* reported that federal marshals and defendants scuffled "in the well of the court" in reaction to Judge Hoffman revoking bail for Dellinger and ordering him to remain locked up for the remainder of the proceedings. The judge said that he was doing so because Dellinger "has disrupted sessions of the court with the use of vile and insulting language."[1] Amid the pandemonium, Abbie Hoffman, his head shaking with emotion, his scraggly long hair flying about, shouted at the judge: "You are a disgrace to the Jews, runt! You should have served Hitler better!"[2]

In his summation for the prosecution, Assistant United States Attorney Richard G. Schultz claimed that the defendants had come to Chicago intending to incite a riot and unleash a leftist revolution. The defense attorney, Leon I. Weinglass, however, insisted that the government had contrived the entire case to cover for the police violence at the convention. Weinglass said: "Some explanation had to be offered for the police charges into peaceful demonstrators. They had to pick scapegoats. History always has its scapegoats."[3]

On February 18, the jury acquitted all the defendants on the conspiracy charge, but it found Rubin, Hoffman, Dellinger, Hayden, and Davis guilty on a lesser count of rioting. They appealed, and in 1972, a higher court vacated the convictions, charging Judge Hoffman with flagrant bias in the case.

EXPLOSIVE ACTIONS, DIVIDED THOUGHTS

In late February 1970, in the wake of the Chicago Seven trial, riots erupted in Isla Vista, California, a village of about 11,000 people near Santa Barbara, populated largely by students attending the University of California. For three nights, youths battled local, county, and state police. The protesters hurled rocks and firebombs; the police dropped tear gas from helicopters and yelled through bullhorns for the crowds to disperse.

Then on February 25, about 1,500 rioters stormed a shopping center and set fire to the local branch of the Bank of America. Flames shot into the nightime sky as the mob watched, their figures silhouetted against the flickering light. The violence caused Governor Ronald Reagan to declare a state of emergency and to put the National Guard on alert. The authorities announced a dusk-to-dawn curfew. As it turned out, the rioting resulted in 36 arrests, along with injuries to 25 sheriff's deputies.

In the speculation surrounding what or who had set off the riots, Reagan suspected William Kunstler, an attorney for the Chicago Seven. He had spoken to a gathering just hours before the first attack, and, following his speech, students rallied at Perfect Park, where police arrested one of them. The crowd reacted to the arrest in anger, and the rioting ensued. Yet, several protesters later denied that Kunstler had incited them. He had, they said, spoken only about the Chicago Seven.

One student leader claimed that the riots had stemmed from a long trail of abuses by the local police, but clearly there was also seething anger over the treatment of protesters at the 1968 Democratic National Convention, a treatment punctuated by the guilty verdict against the Chicago Seven. The riots at Isla Vista most likely erupted to attack middle America and the cheers mainstream society had expressed for the police in the Chicago streets and the judge in the city's courtroom.

Moreover, the rioting expressed discontent with other larger influences that still permeated daily life from the 1960s: materialism, greed, and the cruelty produced by a corporate war machine. According to one protester, the students had attacked the Bank of America because "it was the biggest capitalist thing around."[4]

The chairman of the bank reacted to the assault by calling it "an outrageous act of violence." He labeled it "an insurrection against the democratic process of the kind that leads to further violence, bloodshed, and anarchy."[5]

A morally inspired attack on a citadel of capitalism or an anarchistic threat to democracy—the opposing opinions, like the polarized actions, expressed the divide . . . the deep and ever deepening divide . . . in American society. The rage continued: Angry protesters targeted other bank branches, and by the end of 1970 the Bank of America reported two dozen fires at or bombings of its buildings.

THE TRULY RADICAL

For the truly radical, and for anyone in mainstream society looking to demonize the counterculture, there existed Weatherman. The group evolved from Third World Marxists, a faction within the New Left organization Students for a Democratic Society, led by James Mellen, Bernardine Dohrn, and Mark Rudd. Third World Marxists despised American imperialism and called for a rearguard action to weaken it and coincide with revolutions then under way in underdeveloped, or Third World, nations. At an SDS convention in 1969, Third World Marxists presented a position paper whose title, "You Don't Need a Weatherman to Know Which Way the Wind Blows," echoed lyrics from a song by Bob Dylan. Thus the song gave the dissident group its name, Weatherman, while the paper expressed the desire for violent revolutionary tactics.

In their most sensational action, the Weathermen launched their days of rage in Chicago in October (the second anniversary of the death of Cuban revolutionary hero Ernesto "Che" Guevara). "The pigs are the capitalist state, and as such define the limits of political struggles," declared Weatherman. For three days, several hundred of the dissidents took to the streets, smashing windows and burning cars.

But for all their bodily sacrifice and turgid doctrinal pamphlets, the Weathermen failed to gain many recruits or ignite the group's much-desired revolution. Consequently, about 100 Weathermen decided at their national war council in December 1969 to go underground. The Weather Underground turned inward, determined to weaken the federal government through terrorist acts. Rudd, Dohrn, and others disappeared from view. They lived a clandestine existence marked by furtive looks in rearview mirrors, fake identifications and nervous suspicions about police whom they encountered at restaurants, code names and tapped phones, and secret summits and rooms in fleabag hotels. A couple of years later, a book titled *Prairie Fire* in which the Weathermen connected themselves to prominent dissidents in American history, including Cochise, Nat Turner, Marcus Garvey, and Emma Goldman, contained songs and poems and sported a red cover. As one Weatherman said, it was meant to be a book that people would *want* to hold.

Then on March 6, 1970, a vintage four-story row house in New York City, built in a modified Greek Revival style and located in an exclusive neighborhood at number 18 West 11th Street (near Fifth Avenue), collapsed in a massive explosion, caused when Weathermen living there accidentally detonated a bomb. Imagine the scene: a blast so powerful that it severely damaged two other row houses attached to number 18, including one owned and occupied by actor Dustin Hoffman, and shattered window panes in several nearby buildings; a wailing convoy of fire trucks and police cars arriving while flames continued to shoot into the noontime air and glass popped and shattered in the burning building.

Three of the Weather Underground radicals died in the explosion; others, including Cathlyn Wilkerson, wearing tattered blue jeans (her father, who owned several radio stations also owned the townhouse), and Kathy Boudin, naked, her body covered with soot, ran from the flames. A neighbor gave Wilkerson and Boudin clothes before they vanished.

The Weathermen had been in the basement making pipe bombs and crude antipersonnel bombs, loaded with roofing nails, for their terrorist attacks. (They apparently intended to detonate one device at a military dance at Fort Dix, New Jersey.) Someone crossed a wire, and the house blew up. (Initial newspaper reports inaccurately attributed the explosion to a faulty gas main—no one could fathom that bombs were being made in such a high-class neighborhood.)

The Weathermen involved in the explosion exemplified the group's membership: privileged white youths who had developed an uncompromising anger toward the U.S. government. Those killed were two men, Theodore Gold and Terry Robbins, and a woman, Diana Oughton. Their bodies were discovered by investigators sorting through the rubble. Oughton's body was so badly mutilated that its identity could be determined only by the fingerprints from a severed hand. Weatherman Bill Ayers later wrote: "The smoking ruin was a catastrophe of the exotic and the everyday—a gym shoe lying alongside a box of lead pipes, an open copy of *Catch-22* with a blasting cap for a page marker."[6]

Gold's background reads like a template for the members of Weatherman. Like so many other young activists, he first became involved in the Civil Rights movement. Before his entry into Columbia, New York City's Ivy League college, he collected food for blacks in Mississippi; later, he joined the Congress of Racial Equality (CORE). It was in the Civil Rights movement that he learned about injustice in an American society that prided itself on its democratic qualities.

Gold served as vice chairman of the campus SDS chapter and helped to lead the disruptive strike at Columbia in spring 1968. He once wrote: "We need a red party so we can learn to struggle."[7] Shortly before the bomb blast, he reportedly told a friend, "I've been doing a lot of exciting underground things, and I know I'm not afraid to die."[8]

In its brief existence, the Weather Underground took credit for some 20 bombings. They bombed the Pentagon, the U.S. Capitol, the headquarters of the New York City Police Department, the New York Board of Corrections, and the offices of corporations that were doing business in Chile and Puerto Rico.

THE ENVIRONMENTAL DECADE

Urban America faced a tremendous environmental crisis in the 1970s. Chemicals polluted water. Smog from industries, power plants, and cars blackened skies and endangered health.

Like so many other developments in the early part of the decade, environmental concerns were linked closely to the 1960s. Rachel Carson's book *Silent*

Pollution from a coke plant clouds the air near Clairton, Pennsylvania. *(National Archives and Records Administration)*

Spring, published in 1962, revealed the dangers of pesticides and herbicides, how certain types of them could be found in nearly all living things, and how they were killing fish and wildlife and endangering human beings. "For THE FIRST TIME in the history of the world," Carson wrote in the chapter titled Elixirs of Death, "every human being is now subjected to contact with dangerous chemicals, from the moment of conception until death. In the less than two decades of their use, the synthetic pesticides have been so thoroughly distributed throughout the animate and inanimate world that they occur virtually everywhere."[9]

Environmental awareness and demands for action in the pollution crisis had been expressed by everyone from hippies to young people who were associated with the Sierra Club and similar groups. Some activists even proposed establishing an Earth People's Park for New Mexico or Colorado.

Others searched for a statement and an accomplishment on a big scale, and they obtained it with Earth Day, which was first staged on April 22, 1970. The idea for Earth Day originated with Senator Gaylord Nelson of Wisconsin, a Democrat, who envisioned the concept in 1969. He was joined by Representative Pete McCloskey of California, a Republican. Together they cochaired an Earth Day campaign committee in Washington, D.C., and worked to establish a special day for people to meet and discuss environmental issues. Helping them was Denis Allen Hayes, a young antiwar activist. He had a bachelor's degree from Stanford University and left his graduate studies at Harvard to supervise Earth Day.

Earth Day celebrations took many forms and went well beyond talk. Girl Scouts in canoes removed garbage from along the Potomac River; thousands of citizens picked up roadway trash in Vermont; blacks in St. Louis conducted street theater, dramatizing health problems caused by lead paint; people in San Francisco attended teach-ins; and 5,000 activists gathered at the Washington Monument to sing along with folk artists Pete Seeger and Phil Ochs and to stage a march on the Interior Department.

National Educational Television canceled its regular programs to devote an entire day to the environmental crisis. The commercial television networks ABC, CBS, and NBC also broadcast special programs to promote Earth Day.

In New York City, a huge crowd jammed Fifth Avenue. Thousands of other people strolled along 14th Street and through Union Square under colorful banners that hung from lampposts in front of the Consolidated Edison Company— the giant utility that had been roundly criticized for years by environmentalists— while, against the backdrop of the Vietnam War, balloons drifted overhead, bearing such slogans as "War Is the Worse Pollution." Indeed, the pervasiveness and the divisiveness of the still controversial Vietnam conflict appeared in comments that were made by mayor John Lindsay: "Pure water will not wash away the stain of an immoral war."[10]

"If the environment had any enemies they did not make themselves known," declared the *New York Times.* "Political leaders, governmental departments and corporations hastened to line up in the ranks of those yearning for a clean, quiet, fume-free city."[11] In an editorial published the following day, the *Times* insisted that Earth Day signified a lasting concern with the environment, though the newspaper noted: "Fifth Avenue . . . is again just another noisy, congested, exhaust-poisoned traffic artery."[12]

Earth Day and the environmental movement directly affected political institutions. Shortly before and after the observance, Congress passed a record number of environmental acts, and many states passed legislation promoting reform. Congress produced the Federal Water Pollution Control Act amendments, the Marine Mammal Protection Act, the Safe Drinking Water Act, and the Toxic Substances Control Act, among others. The politicians had apparently counted heads: Public-opinion surveys showed the environment to be a leading issue, and more than 20 million people had picked up the trash, dramatized the problems, sung the songs, and otherwise participated in Earth Day activities.

Earth Day energized a decadelong focus (which had accelerated in the 1960s) aimed at threats posed by environmental degradation, leading up to the Three Mile Island nuclear accident in 1979. These concerns and fears surfaced in several books, most notably *The Closing Circle: Nature, Man, and Technology,* published by Barry Commoner in 1972. An urbanite by birth and upbringing, Commoner was a botany professor who had previously written several scholarly and popular articles and, in 1963, a book in which he discussed the damage to the environment from increased use of nitrogen fertilizers and gas-guzzling, air-polluting automobiles.

In *The Closing Circle,* Commoner wrote: "We are in an environmental crisis because the means by which we use the ecosphere to produce wealth are destructive of the ecosphere itself."[13] If Americans pursued development friendly to the environment and thus saved the world from destruction, if they followed policies friendly to nature rather than those at war with it, he said, they could maintain their high standard of living. Drawing on his botanical background, he said: "The first photosynthetic organisms transformed the rapacious, linear course of life into the earth's first great ecological cycle. By closing the circle they achieved what no living organism, alone, can accomplish—survival."[14] That lesson, he said, must be learned by everyone. "Human beings have broken out of the circle of life, driven not by biological need, but by the social organization they have devised to 'conquer' nature . . . the end result is the environmental crisis, a crisis of survival. Once more, to survive, we must close the circle."[15]

Gaylord Nelson later claimed that Earth Day reflected a time when "Americans made it clear that they understood and were deeply concerned over the deterioration of our environment and the mindless dissipation of our resources. . . . That day . . . forcibly thrust the issue of environmental quality and resource conservation into the political dialogue of the nation. . . . In short, Earth Day launched the Environmental Decade with a bang."[16]

Yet, corporate lobbyists decried excessive governmental regulation, and real-estate developers played on the traditional mentality that land could serve no more vital function than as private property for private proprietary interests. Moreover, the cost of cleaning up the environment presented a constant obstacle to reform.

CAMPUS PROTEST

In the 1960s, America's traditionally quiet college campuses exploded in rebellion. Unlike the 1950s character Dean Moriarity, who in Jack Kerouac's novel *On the Road* declared his generation's "noble function" to be simply moving—to go, man, go—the baby-boomer generation found its meaning in protest. Students marched for civil rights and against the Vietnam War; they called for more democracy and less hatred; they wanted women liberated and the power of college administrators curtailed. In loco parentis (whereby colleges acted as surrogate parents toward their students) gave way to personal autonomy.

For baby boomers in the late 1960s and 1970s, college had become a rite of passage, so much so that by 1973, the number of college students reached 10 million. Consequently, public universities became monoliths: By 1970, more than 50 colleges had enrollments topping 15,000; eight of them had enrollments exceeding 30,000. Prior to World War II, no such large-size campuses existed, and college life prompted an idyllic image of select high school graduates congregating beneath shady oaks to drink from a benevolent fountain of knowledge—*alma mater* meaning nourishing mother.

Now the university—17,000 students at North Carolina in Chapel Hill, 27,000 at Texas in Austin, 35,000 at Wisconsin in Madison, 27,000 at California in Berkeley—developed complex bureaucracies and placed students in classes where enrollment numbered in the hundreds. Historians Irwin Unger and Debi Unger insist that with its attachment to economic growth and corporations, "The University of California . . . by its president's own assertion, was no ivory tower but a part of the establishment and a bastion of the system."[17]

Universities were seen by both administrators and students as thought factories. They were seen as places where data could be analyzed rationally and coldly and applied to a scientific and economic world. For administrators, the emphasis was on controlling the hordes of students and funneling them into society so that they could be contributive, productive, and economically sated. For students, the approach meant confinement and conformity—a stifling, oppressive atmosphere.

Student activism dating from the 1960s pulsated into 1970. Although some school administrators and journalists reported a decline in campus protests during the year, the Urban Research Corporation of Chicago, a private group committed to monitoring college activities, reported more campus unrest from January into March than for the same period in 1969. The group's survey of mainstream and underground newspapers and of official college reports found that campus protests had erupted in all sections of the country, with Ohio, New York, Michigan, Massachusetts, and California topping the list.

The protests appeared at public and private colleges, large ones and small ones, liberal arts schools and technical institutes. Most of the protests involved student demands for more power in campus decision making or called for more minority representation, either in governance or in courses offered, such as the entreaties for black studies classes and African-American teachers. War-related demonstrations accounted for 22 percent of the protests.

The Urban Research Corporation found increasing efforts by Mexican-American and Puerto Rican students for "minority recognition." Other controversies centered on such time-honored student concerns as tuition, grading systems, dormitory rules, and food service.

In all, student protests occurred at a rate of more than one per day. Violence, the research group said, was "uncommon," evident in only one out of every five protests.

KENT STATE

Shortly after the report appeared, America experienced its most shocking encounter with campus violence when national guardsmen killed four students

President Nixon points to a map of Cambodia as he explains the U.S. invasion of that country. *(National Archives and Records Administration)*

at Ohio's Kent State University. Kent State erupted in the wake of President Nixon's decision to send U.S. combat troops into Cambodia, a country adjoining Vietnam.

Nixon said that the communist enemy had established bunkers in Cambodia and was using the country as a launching point for attacks against American forces in South Vietnam. The bunkers, he insisted, and most especially the central headquarters of the North Vietnamese army in Cambodia had to be destroyed. This was crucial, he claimed, if the United States were to withdraw more troops from Vietnam safely and provide protection for those troops remaining. On April 30, in a nationwide television address, the president proclaimed:

> Tonight, American and South Vietnamese units will attack the headquarters for the entire Communist military operation in South Vietnam. The key control center has been occupied by the North Vietnamese and Vietcong for five years in blatant violation of Cambodia's neutrality. . . .
>
> The future of 18 million people in South Vietnam and seven million people in Cambodia is involved; the possibility of winning a just peace in Vietnam and in the Pacific is at stake.[18]

Nixon wanted to enact, as he had called it on more than one occasion, his "madman" theory. As several historians have noted, including Stephen Ambrose in *Nixon: The Triumph of a Politician, 1962–1972,* he wanted the communists in Vietnam, and communists in Russia and China, to see his dark, brooding scowl as a demonic force. He wanted them to believe that he would use force under any and all circumstances to achieve his objectives, with no guilt about violating humanitarian standards. He wanted them to think that he was a loose cannonball in a nuclear world.

A U.S. Army sergeant clears away brush near Da Nang in Vietnam. *(National Archives and Records Administration)*

But Nixon had another agenda too. He wanted to show antiwar protesters that he would use force where and when *he* wanted it used. He would out-tough them. Also, he would use the invasion to rally mainstream America around him—another toss of political lye at unwashed hippiedom. Cognizant that his action would likely cause protests on college campuses, he embraced the challenge and sought to use the invasion to crush the dissidents. In a nationwide speech announcing the attack on Cambodia, he declared:"It is *not our power but our will that is being tested tonight.*"[19] (Many years later, Nixon's national security advisor, Henry Kissinger, called the president's speech "delusional.") The invasion accomplished little. Several thousand bunkers were destroyed, but the central headquarters were never found. In the long run, Cambodia was destabilized, and America was polarized.

Nixon's approach to the seemingly endless war in Vietnam—the "quagmire," as reporter David Halberstam called it—was to turn over the bulk of the fighting to South Vietnam's army (ARVN, or the Army of the Republic of Vietnam), while gradually withdrawing U.S. troops. He called this Vietnamization. He withdrew more than 100,000 troops from 1969 to early 1970.

For Nixon, though, Vietnamization did not mean that U.S. troops would simply pack their duffel bags and head home; rather, the United States would pound the enemy harder in an attempt to gain concessions at peace talks that were then underway.

Thus, the winding down meant a ratcheting up. The ground war would be widened into Cambodia. (Nixon had previously, and secretly, begun to bomb enemy encampments there. He withdrew U.S. troops from Cambodia at the end of June.) This angered college students who had scaled back their antiwar protests in response to the first withdrawals of U.S. troops. The National Student Association reacted to Nixon's speech by calling for his impeachment and proclaiming:"We plan to rally students throughout the country" in an effort to make sure that the power to declare and make war be "put back where the Founding Fathers meant them to be—in the hands of the Congress elected by the people."[20]

So the students took to protesting more. They demonstrated in New York, Pennsylvania, Maryland, California, and elsewhere. An article in *Time* magazine presented a roll call:

At Yale University in New Haven, where Cambodia was . . . a last-minute addition to a broad May Day protest over judicial and police treatment of Black Panthers, some 4,000 U.S. Marines and paratroopers were deployed for quick response to any violence.

At Berkeley . . . another ROTC protest made that campus look as chaotic as ever. For two days, groups of up to a thousand demonstrators, many of them off-campus "street people," including high school students, smashed windows and fought police.

A protest against ROTC activities at Stanford turned into two nights of clashes between demonstrators and police in which dozens of officers and 16 students were injured.

Science-oriented Caltech experienced its first antiwar demonstration when about 250 students rallied to hear professors assail the new U.S. involvement.

An angrier mood prevailed at the University of Maryland, where some 500 students charged into the campus Air Force ROTC. . . . They burned uniforms, smashed typewriters, [and] threw files out of windows. . . .[21]

Vice President Spiro Agnew called colleges "circus tents or psychiatric centers for overprivileged, under-disciplined, irresponsible children of the well-to-do permissivists."[22] President Nixon called protesting students "bums blowing up the campuses." But his words galvanized more students. Quiet campuses came alive; quiet students came alive as stunned baby boomers stirred themselves into staging the most massive protests yet.

Thousands of citizens from all walks of life joined them. More than 200 state department workers resigned to protest Nixon's invasion, while others marched in the streets. The *New York Times, Wall Street Journal,* and *Washington Post* excoriated Nixon. The president, furious at his critics, told his staff that they should treat congressional opponents harshly. "Don't worry about divisiveness," he insisted. "Having drawn the sword, don't take it out—stick it in hard. . . . Hit 'em in the gut. No defensiveness."[23]

As students at college campuses went on strike, violence erupted at Kent State in northeastern Ohio. Kent was an old town, with an old train station, with old, big trees lining quiet streets—"the original Tree City"—and with a lively college bar scene. Historian Milton Viorst later wrote:

The 1960s ended in . . . Kent. It happened on May 4, 1970, in the bright sunshine, just after midday, at a campus demonstration which was like so many others except that, in thirteen crackling seconds of gunfire, four students were killed. . . . What passion remained of the 1960s was extinguished in the fusillade.[24]

Before the fusillade, students had protested in the streets. "We took these big garbage cans from the side of the road, wheeled them into the middle of the

National Guard troops march amid clouds of tear gas during the protest at Kent State. *(Kent State University Libraries and Media Services, May 4 Collection)*

street, and set them on fire. It was an awesome sight," one student later recalled.[25] They attacked businesses, smashing windows in downtown Kent, and they set fire to the campus ROTC building, an aging structure scheduled to be torn down. (According to some evidence, an undercover government agent may have participated in setting fire to the building; other evidence indicates that authorities let the building be destroyed to create a reason for calling in the National Guard.) As firefighters attempted to douse the flames, a crowd cut their fire hoses.

At the same time, it was election season, and the state's primary vote loomed just two days away. Seeking to make political capital, Ohio's governor James Rhodes, a Republican candidate for the U.S. Senate (a race he eventually lost), visited Kent on the morning of May 3 and gave a provocative speech. He played to conservative voters, those snarling or cringing in fear at the demonstrators and the hippies and the counterculture in general, by claiming that the demonstrations at Kent resulted from revolutionaries who were out to "destroy higher education in Ohio." These protesters, Rhodes declared, were "the worst type of people we harbor in America, worse than the brown shirts and the communist element . . . we will use whatever force necessary to drive them out of Kent!"[26]

Rhodes reacted to the demonstrations on and off campus and to the clashes between students and police by sending the National Guard to Kent State—soldiers tired and edgy from just having finished patrolling a violent strike involving the Teamster's Union. Rhodes ordered them to act "quickly" and "firmly," in line with comments he made earlier to an FBI agent about the way in which he would deal with those who wanted to "subvert our government." By May 3, the Kent State campus was teeming with guardsmen and armored personnel carriers.

On that fateful May 4 at 11 A.M., about 200 students gathered on the college commons. By noon, the crowd had increased to roughly 1,500; some were spectators, and others were protesters there to criticize the invasion of Cambodia and the presence on campus of the National Guard. Because the guard was under orders to disperse any gatherings, they proceeded to do so. Consequently, about 120 men carrying M-1 rifles formed a line and fired tear gas. Most students ran; a few lobbed the tear-gas canisters back at the guardsmen.

The guardsmen then congregated on a practice football field. They stayed there for about 10 minutes while they fired more tear gas at a small group of students that was located in a nearby parking lot, next to Prentice Hall; some students again threw the canisters back. At one point, several guardsmen, members of Troop G, knelt down and aimed their rifles as if ready to fire. Other students watched the confrontation from a veranda at Taylor Hall. The tension seemed to ease when Adjutant General Robert Canterbury declared that the protesters had been dispersed, and the guardsmen marched away, up Blanket Hill.

Then, as students began to leave the scene for their classes, about 12 members of Troop G, who had reached the crest of the hill and had their backs toward the dispersing crowd, suddenly turned and fired into the students standing in and near the Prentice Hall parking lot. Smoke from the rifles puffed into the air, and echoes from the bullets reverberated among the buildings of higher learning. In all, the guardsmen fired a total of 67 shots in a 13-second period.

When the shooting ended, the National Guard insisted that the soldiers had come under attack from a sniper and that they had fired in self-defense. The claim lacked any validity. The guardsmen who fired shouted no warning, nor did they give any warning shots. They failed to use official procedures of crowd control. The students they shot were 71 to 730 feet away. Some guardsmen later admitted that they fired their rifles indiscriminately and because their fellow guardsmen were doing so.

Many analysts say that it was highly unlikely that the guardsmen would have acted as they did, nearly in unison, without an order being given or some prior arrangement having been made. Indeed, some eyewitnesses later said the men had plotted their move several minutes earlier.

A protester jumps in a puddle of blood following the shootings at Kent State. *(Kent State University Libraries and Media Services, May 4 Collection)*

Those killed were Allison Krause, 19 years old; Jeffrey Miller, 20; Sandra Scheuer, 20; and William Schroeder, 19. Two of the four dead (11 others had been wounded, including one who was permanently paralyzed by a shot in the back) were passersby, walking to class. White middle-class blood had been spilled; white middle-class lives had been lost at a college that was seen by middle-class parents not as one of Agnew's "circus tents" or "psychiatric centers" but as the route to advancement for their sons and daughters. One African-American student at the university recalled: "Really, Kent was no bastion of liberalism. It was a fairly conservative campus. Ohio had a conservative governor. No one knew what Kent was. That's why it was so incredible. It wasn't Columbia or Berkeley."[27]

Despite the killings, Nixon and Agnew showed no sympathy for the students; indeed, Nixon shifted all blame to the protesters. He said about the shooting: "This should remind us all once again that when dissent turns to violence it invites tragedy."[28] The New York Times looked at his comment and condemned it for lacking compassion. For his part, Agnew called the deaths "predictable," given the "traitors and thieves and perverts in our midst."[29]

The administration's position caused Nixon's secretary of the interior, Walter J. Hickel, to voice an unusual protest. In a letter to the president, Hickel charged Nixon with alienating America's youth. He said that the president, in refusing to communicate with young people, was contributing to anarchy and revolt. (Shortly thereafter, Nixon fired Hickel.)

With the shock from Kent State, campuses across the nation careened toward complete chaos. In the following seven days, students at 350 universities went on strike, including those at Whittier College, Nixon's alma mater, and protests forced the closing of 500 campuses. Classes were canceled at Wellesley College and at the universities of Oregon, Washington, Montana, and throughout the entire 27-campus Georgia University system, along with the University of Miami, where 300 students blockaded the main administration building. Rallies against the invasion of Cambodia and against the killings at Kent State resulted in tear gas being used on protesters at the University of Kentucky, the University of Illinois, and the University of Alabama. Several buildings at the University of Wisconsin were firebombed; firebombs damaged ROTC facilities at the University of Nevada in Reno and Ohio University in Athens. Fire damaged an administration building at Valparaiso University in Indiana, a student center at Fordham University, and a bookstore at Marietta College in Ohio.

Someone, most likely police, fired birdshot pellets on the campus of the University of Buffalo. Students at the University of Missouri and at Syracuse University held rallies where they burned effigies of President Nixon. Antioch College, in Ohio, offered "sanctuary" to any of the state's college students "evicted" from their campuses and to national guardsmen who were "unwilling to follow the orders of their commanders in repressing the students of Ohio."[30] Even administrators joined in expressing outrage, with 35 university presidents calling for the withdrawal of U.S. troops from Cambodia.

In all, violence erupted between students and police at 24 colleges, even a few in the typically tranquil conservative South, and ROTC buildings came under attack at 30 universities, while 100 possible bombings or acts of arson were reported on campuses. The severity of the outbreaks caused the governors of Ohio, Michigan, Kentucky, and South Carolina to declare states of emergency on their college campuses, and the National Guard was called out in 16 states to quell rioting at 20 universities. The nation appeared to be trying to keep its college youths in line by resorting to soldiers, tear gas, and bayonets and closing its ears to their complaints.

A special federal commission that was appointed to investigate Kent State condemned the killings, saying that the National Guard had no reason to act the way it did. An FBI report concluded that none of the guardsmen had faced a life-threatening situation.

In Ohio, though, the National Guard took no disciplinary action against the men involved. On the contrary, it promoted them. For its part, the state not only refused to indict any guardsmen, but a grand jury instead indicted 25 students, faculty members, and others. This same grand jury had issued a report absolving the guardsmen of all blame, but a federal judge reacted to the absurdity of the claim by ordering the report destroyed.

In November 1971, the jurors in the trial of one of the 25 defendants, Jerry Rupe, visited the site of the shooting—cold, snow-covered ground by then, with all traces of the burned ROTC building gone and only a small knot of student protesters on hand to greet them. As it turned out, the state failed to get any significant convictions. Rupe was found guilty only of a misdemeanor, a second defendant pleaded guilty to first-degree riot charges, and in December, charges against the other defendants were dismissed for lack of evidence.

Mainstream America sided with the National Guard and with the massive authority used to quell the many campus demonstrations (though parents of college students worried about the safety of their children who might be subjected to excessive law-enforcement tactics). For older Americans, especially, authority could do no wrong. "I feel terrible about those children getting killed," said one woman, "but they must have provoked the Guard."[31] While this reaction came in part as a direct result of Kent State, it came, too, from everything that mainstream America hated about its wayward countercultural youth: their clothes, hair, music, hippie behavior, and radical activism. Kent State was democracy Latin American–style—a referendum held to the beat of soldiers' boots and victims' blood. One student, Alan King, recalled many years later: "Kent was in middle America. And the Ohio National Guard rioted, killed, and wounded its children."[32]

VIOLENCE AT JACKSON STATE COLLEGE

Unlike Kent State, Jackson State was in the heart of black America. Little more than a week following the shootings at Kent State, police opened fire at Jackson State College, a predominantly African-American school in Jackson, Mississippi. They killed two students. During the years, the tragedy at Jackson State has received much less attention than the one at Kent State. Some historians attribute this to the killings having involved black students rather than white ones, others because Vietnam and the invasion of Cambodia were less significant influences than they had been at Kent State.

The Jackson State carnage actually resulted from several issues. Students on the campus were incensed by the shooting at Kent State. They were also angered by continuing tension between them and white residents in Jackson. On the night of May 14, rumors spread that the mayor of Fayette, Mississippi, Charles Evers, the brother of slain black civil rights leader Medgar Evers, had been shot and killed, along with his wife.

Students subsequently rioted. They set several fires and overturned a dump truck located at a construction site on the campus. White motorists traveling along Lynch Street, which bisected the campus, reported they had been pelted by rocks.

When Jackson firefighters, sent to the scene of the blazes, encountered a hostile crowd, they asked the police to back them up. About 75 city and state police blockaded Lynch Street and sealed off 30 blocks around the campus. Nearby, National Guard members stood ready to act if needed.

The police protected the firefighters and then, for reasons unclear, marched along Lynch Street toward a women's dormitory, Alexander Hall. A crowd numbering about 100 had gathered in front of the dorm. As the police approached, the students hurled obscenities and bricks.

Confusion then erupted. Someone threw or dropped a bottle to the pavement, and it shattered with a loud pop. At the same time, a police officer, hit by an object, fell to the ground. The police later claimed that they had encountered a shot fired from the third floor of the dorm. Two television news reporters at the scene said that they had heard a shot being fired, though they were unsure from where it had come. A radio reporter claimed to have seen someone with a pistol in a dorm window, but a federal investigative commission later stated that it could find "no evidence of small arms fire" from the dormitory.

Whatever the circumstances, just past midnight on May 15, the police opened fire. The shots lasted for about 30 seconds. Students ran; some huddled behind trees in front of the library. Others headed for the dorm, and as they struggled with the glass double doors, the shots continued; some of the students were trampled in the crowd; others fell from bullet wounds.

Two students lay dead. Phillip Lafayette Gibbs, 21 years old, was killed 50 feet from the door of Alexander Hall, his head pierced by buckshot. Earl Green, 17, a senior at nearby Jim Hill High School, was shot in front of the college dining hall. He had been walking home but stopped to watch the confrontation. Twelve other Jackson State students were wounded by gunfire.

FBI investigators later estimated that more than 460 rounds of gunfire had struck the dorm. They found at least 160 bullet holes in the outer walls of the stairwell. *Time* magazine said about the shooting:

> No tear gas was used; there was no warning given to the crowd. [Police] shotguns were loaded with deadly 00 buckshot rather than anti-riot birdshot.... The five-story building was spattered indiscriminately with gunfire from top to bottom. Every window on that end of the dorm was shattered. No effort had been made to fire warning shots or shoot over the crowd's heads.[33]

The shooting at Jackson State worsened racial tension in the city and brought the entire community to the brink of complete upheaval. Blacks boycotted white businesses, and black public-school students left their classes to join in picket lines. Before the crisis cooled, whites and blacks flocked to gun shops and armed themselves. Jackson State students threatened to burn down Capitol Street.

No arrests resulted from the tragedy. The shooting reinforced a harsh view held by many young people, especially countercultural youths, that mainstream society intended to use the police to kill college students. Lethal force against dissidents had become the modus operandi of America.

Under increasing pressure from the campus demonstrations and the violence, on June 13, Richard Nixon appointed the President's Commission on Campus Unrest, led by former Pennsylvania governor William Scranton. The commission held 13 days of public hearings in Jackson, Mississippi; Kent State, Ohio; Washington, D.C.; and Los Angeles, California, and concluded that while some students acted provocatively and even criminally, the authorities used excessive force. Vice President Spiro Agnew belittled the report and said that it promoted permissiveness.

A BOMBING AT THE UNIVERSITY OF WISCONSIN

While the commission was at work, radicals bombed the Army Mathematics Research Center (AMRC), located in Sterling Hall at the University of Wisconsin in Madison. The August 24 blast killed one postdoctoral student, Robert Fassnacht, age 33, and injured four other people. The bomb, made from ammonium nitrate and fuel oil and planted in a station wagon parked next to the hall, sent debris flying up to three blocks away and damaged 26 other campus buildings.

As with many colleges, the University of Wisconsin had experienced a surge in enrollment with the arrival of the baby boomers, an increase from 14,000 students in the late 1950s to 34,000 in 1970. With the deepening of the Vietnam War, student protests had roiled the campus. In 1967, students picketed job recruiters for Dow Chemical to protest the corporation's manufacture of napalm, and Nixon's Cambodian invasion caused several hundred students to take to the streets of Madison and smash storefront windows.

The bombing of the AMRC was staged by four militants who called themselves the New Year's Gang. In a printed statement, they made clear their hatred for the center as a place linked to the military complex. They claimed:

The AMRC, a think-tank of Amerikan militarism, was a fitting target for such revolutionary violence. As the major U.S. Army center for solving military mathematical problems, it bears full responsibility for Amerikan military genocide throughout the world. While hiding behind the façade of academic "neutrality," the AMRC plays a vital role in doing the research necessary for the development of heavy artillery, conventional and nuclear bombs and missiles, guns and mobile weapons, biological weapons, chemical weapons, and much more.[34] [Radicals typically spelled *America* with a *k* to replicate Germanic lettering as a symbol for a Nazilike nation, and one they considered to be racist, fascist, and oppressive.]

The New Year's Gang turned out to be Karleton Armstrong, age 23; his brother Dwight, 19; David Fine, 18; and Leo Burt, 22. The first three were eventually caught and sentenced to prison; Leo Burt remains at large.

A two-week hearing in 1973 to consider mitigation of Karleton Armstrong's sentence brought out the frustration and anger among radicals and placed the bombing in the context of the Vietnam War. Along with the trial lawyers, several historians, scientists, soldiers, and political activists argued that the bombing was justified, given the illegal and immoral nature of the war.

"I feel a lot more criminal than him," said Samuel R. Schoor, an Army enlistee about Armstrong. "I killed a lot more people [in Vietnam]. I'd go to jail with him."[35]

"You knew, and I knew, and we were cowards," said defense attorney William Kunstler to the judge. "We did not do what Karl Armstrong did because we were middle aged, perhaps, or because our positions were secure and we didn't want to jeopardize them."[36]

"People must act to stop a government when it runs wild, as it is clear that our government was running wild," said defense attorney Melvin Greenberg. "That is our true basis of democracy."[37]

Outside the courtroom, Armstrong's supporters kept a vigil. Armstrong had earlier pleaded guilty to second-degree murder and four counts of arson involving the attack on the AMRC and several military installations. On November 1, Judge William J. Sachtjen sentenced him to 23 years in state prison. In the book *Rads,* author Tom Bates describes the closing scene:

> Before the spectators could react, Sachtjen was gone from the room, and a phalanx of Paul Bunyan-sized deputies had ushered Karl out. The stunned prisoner managed only a perfunctory salute as he disappeared from sight. The shock was broken by a lone voice crying from the back of the courtroom, "Long live the revolution!"[38]

That night, several hundred Armstrong sympathizers marched to protest the sentence. Some broke windows in downtown Madison and on campus.

WOMEN'S RIGHTS

Women's protests had been surging ever since a demonstration outside the Miss America Pageant in 1968, an event targeted for its racism and sexism. These protests, which continued into the 1970s, were part of "the second feminist wave," a continuation of the "first wave" that encompassed the 19th- and early 20th-century suffrage movement and were thus part of a long, hard fight by women against sexist discrimination and oppression. They were also a continuation of the countercultural efforts at reform. In 1970, the National Organization for Women (NOW) sponsored a nationwide women's strike for equality as a tactic to build support in Congress for an equal rights amendment to the Constitution, spotlight discriminatory practices against women in the workplace, and promote equal educational opportunities, day-care centers, and abortion rights.

NOW set August 26, 1970, the 50th anniversary of the granting of the vote to women in the United States, as the date for the strike and proclaimed: "Don't Iron While the Strike Is Hot!" The group urged women across the country to leave their jobs for the day, give up their household chores, and demonstrate.

Many women, along with men who were sympathetic to the call, responded in support, and protesters, totaling perhaps 100,000, appeared in nearly every large American city and in many smaller ones. Thousands marched in Boston, San Francisco, Los Angeles, Washington, and Chicago. The biggest demonstration took place in New York City, where about 50,000 protesters joined activist Betty Friedan in a march down Fifth Avenue. In fact, the idea for the women's strike for equality was first promoted by Friedan, who was renowned for her 1963 book *The Feminine Mystique*. This book did much to stimulate the second wave of the women's movement with its discussion of how society restricted women to traditional feminine roles. In a speech to the gathered throng behind the New York Public Library, Friedan urged women to overcome their racial and class differences to fight oppression. Conservatives criticized the demonstrators for weakening family values, but Congress intensified its work on an equal rights amendment, businesses and government agencies moved to reduce their discriminatory practices, and many women felt bonded in solidarity.

In September 1970, Robin Morgan declared *Sisterhood Is Powerful* as the title to a book that she edited. That her work contained more than 600 pages of writings from the women's liberation movement testified to both the momentum that the protest had gained in just a few years and to its diversity. Writings dealt with women in the professions, psychological and sexual repression, and emerging ideologies. One section, with the topic of changing consciousness, revealed the ethnic variety in the movement and its attraction to young people by offering views from black liberationists, Chicanos, and high school women. Suburban schools could no longer subsist as mere cookie-cutter factories for female homemakers. "Now, with awakened eyes, I could see all the brainwashing of my sisters that goes on at school," wrote one young feminist. "It starts almost the instant they are born, by their mothers, and by fathers encouraging the boys to take an interest in cars, baseball, etc., and discouraging girls."[39]

Women acted also to correct the humiliation and mistreatment they suffered from doctors who approached the practice of medicine from a male perspective, with inadequate concern for the female anatomy. In *The World Split Open,* Ruth Rosen recounts how women were treated as "ignorant" or "hysterical" patients and subject to an "arrogant attitude" from the medical establishment. The experience, she says, could be "humiliating" and "enraging."

This led a group of women in 1969 to convene a women's health workshop at Emanuel College in Boston. They studied and discussed anatomy, physiology, sexuality, venereal disease, birth control, abortion, and childbirth. From this meeting came the formation, in 1970, of the Boston Women's Health Book Collective. Members of the collective began to teach about women's bodies; they held their classes in homes, churches, and other neighborhood locations. The movement contained to grow, and in 1971, the Women's Health Conference, held in New York City, attracted 800 participants.

Presently, the members of the Boston Health Collective published their findings and ideas in a booklet, and in 1973, an expanded version appeared as the book titled *Our Bodies, Ourselves.* Immediately popular, it offered medical information, personal stories by women, and a critique of how the economic system affected women's health.

The health activists began to question many types of medical practices, such as the frequency with which doctors recommended mastectomies for breast cancer when less radical measures could be pursued. And they criticized the power that doctors had over women's bodies in dispensing the pill or deciding when a condition necessitated a therapeutic abortion. Women, they insisted, needed to exert more control over their bodies.

APOLLO 13

In the 1970s, the United States moved forward with its exploration of the Moon. But it came with the near tragic loss of three astronauts who flew the *Apollo 13* mission.

Americans had been riveted by the Moon program on July 20, 1969, when astronaut Neil Armstrong radioed Earth, "The *Eagle* has landed," and then set foot on the "fine and powdery" lunar surface. *Apollo 13* lost the glamour of that first landing; indeed, by 1970, many Americans were questioning whether the Earth really need more boxes of Moon rocks added to the four collected on previous missions.

Yet, *Apollo 13* had a different agenda: Whereas formerly astronauts had landed on the Moon's "seas," or plains, this time, astronauts were to land on a highland region. Their exploration of the hilly terrain might give a fuller picture of the Moon's geological history. Consequently, the astronauts were to launch experiments designed to tell more about the Moon's interior, whether it was hot and molten or cold and dead. One science writer called the landing an especially difficult challenge. He said: "The mission can by no means be described as routine."[40]

Apollo 13 lifted off on April 11, 1970, with *Odyssey,* the command module, and *Aquarius,* the lunar module, attached to each other. Except for a minor engine problem, the first two days of the flight went smoothly. Astronauts Jack Swigert, Fred Haise, and James Lovell even heard mission controllers jest about how they were "bored" by the flight. But a few minutes shy of 56 hours into the mission, *Odyssey*'s number-two oxygen tank exploded, causing the number-one tank to also fail. Suddenly, the astronauts had lost their normal supply of electricity, light, and water, which depended on the operation of the two tanks. Swigert, who had heard a loud bang, radioed the ground: "Houston, we have a problem."

In short order, Lovell reported looking from his window and seeing something "venting" into space; it looked like "a gas." But the "gas" turned out to be oxygen, and the discharge meant that *Odyssey* would soon lose all power, and the astronauts would freeze to death, some 200,000 miles from Earth where no other vessel could rescue them.

With just minutes of electrical power remaining aboard *Odyssey,* mission control decided to have the astronauts power down the command module (putting it into a sleep mode) and relocate to *Aquarius.* There, they would have sufficient oxygen but limited electrical power and water; in fact, they would be restricted to six fluid ounces each per day. Most unnerving, a vessel built to take care of two men for two days for exploration of the lunar surface would now have to take care of three men for four days in deep space.

The crisis necessitated a change in course: *Apollo 13* had to execute an engine burn so that the craft could swing behind the Moon and back toward Earth. The astronauts completed the burn and then endured abysmal cold as temperatures in *Aquarius* plunged to 38 degrees and made sleep all but impossible.

As *Apollo 13* neared Earth, the astronauts had to reenter *Odyssey* and power it up. They found its insides covered with cold water droplets and worried that the moisture might cause a short circuit. Fortunately, *Odyssey* held together, and the astronauts successfully jettisoned *Aquarius* and limped back to Earth. They

landed as planned, in the Pacific Ocean on April 17, four miles from the recovery ship *Iwo Jima,* located about 600 miles south of tropical Pago Pago.

JIMI AND JANIS

To some music fans, 1960s rock ended in 1970 with the deaths of Jimi Hendrix and Janis Joplin.

Hendrix and his band, the Experience, made their American debut on June 18, 1967, at the Monterey International Pop Festival in California. There, and at other performances, he presented an electrifying soul and psychedelic sound. The way Hendrix commanded his guitar led Mike Bloomfield of the Butterfield Blues Band to remark about a Hendrix concert: "In front of my eyes, he burned me to death. . . . I didn't even get my guitar out. . . . He was getting every sound I was ever to hear him get right there in that room."[41]

In 1970, Hendrix told an interviewer for *Melody Maker,* a British pop newspaper, "You know the drug scene . . . was opening up things in people's minds, giving them things that they just couldn't handle. Well, music can do that, you know, and you don't need any drugs."[42] A short time later, on September 18, Hendrix was found dead in his London apartment. The official coroner's report ruled out suicide and said that his death had resulted from "an inhalation of vomit due to barbiturate intoxication."[43] One music critic said that Hendrix had

President Nixon greets the *Apollo 13* astronauts on their arrival in Hawaii from their harrowing mission. *(National Archives and Records Administration)*

brought to life "a wider palette of sound than any other performing instrumentalist in the history of music."[44]

Janis Joplin brought into the 1970s her flailing, wailing, blues style. Before excited audiences, she sang encores into early morning hours, fueled by booze, pills, and hyperkinetic energy. Joplin and her band, Big Brother and the Holding Company, had earned a gold record with the album *Cheap Thrills* in 1968, and in 1969, her LP *Got Dem Ol' Kozmic Blues Again Mama!* also went gold. She then began to record *Pearl* but never completed it: She died on October 4, 1970, from a heroin overdose.

For Joplin, drugs and alcohol numbed loneliness and boredom and kept her demons fitfully, and dangerously, at bay. Her unstable emotions had, for years, fed her addiction. *Pearl* was released posthumously, and "Me and Bobby McGee," a single from the album, written by Kris Kristofferson, reached the top 10.

Rock music attracted a more diverse audience as the 1970s began. The Who, a British band, released the album *Tommy* in 1969, and with its songs "Pinball Wizard" and "See Me, Feel Me," it became the first successful rock opera. On June 7, 1970, the Who performed *Tommy* at the Metropolitan Opera House in New York City.

At the same time, rock morphed into heavy metal, whose fans embraced the thrills of louder chords and heavier riffs or what one observer called a "mutant strain" of music. Led Zeppelin epitomized and perfected this form; they were among its founders and crafted it in close relationship with their followers. "Led Zeppelin communed with their fans through esoteric signs and symbols," said music analyst Donna Gaines, "creating a secret society that excluded the profane world."[45]

A BASEBALL CONTROVERSY

For baseball players, 1960s activism led to 1970s independence. For years, players had been bound by the "reserve clause," which required a player to stay with one team for life unless the team chose to trade or release him. The arrangement left players with little bargaining power. In October 1969, the St. Louis Cardinals decided to trade center fielder Curt Flood, a 12-year veteran, and send him against his wishes to the Philadelphia Phillies. Flood, an African American who may have been motivated in part by the Civil Rights movement to fight for his rights (though this was clearly not a racial issue), decided to get the reserve clause overturned. He told baseball commissioner Bowie Kuhn that he would refuse to be treated simply as a "piece of property."

So in 1970, the trial of *Flood v. Kuhn* began, with Flood charging that the reserve clause violated antitrust laws. Flood lost when the federal court ruled against him. He appealed, but in 1973, the U.S. Supreme Court dealt him a 5-3 defeat. Yet, Flood's action represented part of a larger player activism evident in a strike in 1972, one instrumental in eventually weakening the reserve clause and revolutionizing the way baseball players would be treated and paid.

FUTURE SHOCK AND THE GREENING OF AMERICA

Two widely best-selling books in 1970 addressed the future as shaped by recent events. *Future Shock* by sociologist Alvin Toffler foretold great technological advances and likened the experiences that people were having with emerging technologies to the confusion encountered on entering a strange culture, an alien land. Society, he said, was undergoing a revolutionary movement from an industrial age to a "super-industrial" age. According to Toffler, technological change would accelerate other changes, making the world more confusing and difficult to grasp. This, in turn, would overwhelm people and leave them disconnected and suffering from "shattering stress and disorientation," or, in other words, future shocked.

Yale professor Charles A. Reich's *The Greening of America* found in the 1960s counterculture a much different meaning for society than the one expounded by Toffler. According to Reich, the counterculture had created a new era, Consciousness III, in which spiritual community was transcending technology.

In *Greening,* Reich saw rock music, marijuana, and communes as representing a shift in how people perceived reality. With Consciousness III led by young people, he said, society would overcome war, violence, poverty, and individual powerlessness. "The extraordinary thing about this new consciousness," he insisted, "is that it has emerged out of the wasteland of the Corporate State, like flowers pushing up through the concrete pavement. Whatever it touches, it beautifies and renews: A freeway entrance is festooned with happy hitchhikers, the sidewalk is decorated with street people, the humorless steps of an official building are given warmth by a group of musicians."[46]

The counterculture offered hope for a better future. Rather than fear the change, mainstream America should embrace it. Reich insisted: "For one who thought the world was irretrievably encased in metal and plastic and sterile stone, it seems a veritable greening of America."[47] For Reich, there wafted in the air from the 1960s more than the tear gas brought from protest. More than turmoil, violence, and distrust would shape the 1970s; a clear and rarefied air would produce an age of Aquarius. The 1970s, so it appeared, would be molded by the 1960s into an age of peace and harmony and understanding.

CHRONICLE OF EVENTS

1970

January 2: Federal Bureau of Investigations (FBI) director J. Edgar Hoover issues a report in which he decries increased militancy among college students and warns that "extremist, all-Negro" groups such as the Black Panthers are spreading hate and violence, leading to the killing of police.

January 22: President Richard Nixon presents his State of the Union address in which he says he will commit himself to fighting crime and inflation and to improving the environment. In addition, he says there is a greater likelihood of peace in Vietnam.

January 24: The Defense Department widens its investigation of the My Lai massacre, bringing to 33 the number of men either charged with crimes or suspected of having committed crimes. The massacre occurred in March 1968, when U.S. soldiers went on a rampage and shot to death more than 200 unarmed Vietnamese civilians, most of them women and children. The military covered up the atrocity for more than 18 months.

February 3: Pandemonium erupts at a pretrial hearing in New York City for 13 Black Panthers charged with attempted murder and with plotting to bomb public sites. The accused disrupt the hearing with shouts of "pig" directed at the judge and with cries of "all power to the people."

February 5: Senator John Stennis (Dem., Miss.) proposes that an education funding bill be amended to prohibit the busing of students to enforce school desegregation.

February 10: Richard Nixon submits to Congress a far-ranging plan for environmental reform, including a request for $4 billion to help in building municipal waste treatment plants.

February 16: Joe Frazier defeats Jimmy Ellis to become world heavyweight boxing champion and to fill the title vacated when it was stripped from Muhammad Ali for Ali's refusal to be inducted into the military.

February 18: A federal grand jury finds the defendants in the Chicago 7 trial not guilty of conspiring to incite riots during the 1968 Democratic National Convention. But five of the group—David T. Dellinger, Rennie C. Davis, Tom Hayden, Abbie Hoffman, and Jerry Rubin—are found guilty of crossing state lines to incite riots.

February 23: Laws take effect in Georgia and Louisiana that prohibit the busing of children to integrate public schools.

February 25: Hundreds of students at the University of California at Santa Barbara take their protest against the Vietnam War and other issues into the adjoining town of Isla Vista, where they burn down a branch of the Bank of America. Governor Ronald Reagan calls out the national guard to restore order after 25 police are injured and 36 people arrested.

February 26: The U.S. Marine Corps announces the arrest of five members of a combat patrol for murdering 11 Vietnamese civilians near Sonthang village.

March 6: A four-story townhouse in New York City's Greenwich Village explodes when members of the revolutionary Weatherman accidentally detonate a bomb on which they were working. Three Weathermen are killed in the explosion.

March 24: A widespread strike by federal postal workers begins to collapse when Congress indicates its willingness to vote pay increases. President Nixon had ordered troops to move the mail in New York City, and more than 30,000 national guardsmen and others had begun to do so.

April 8: The U.S. Senate rejects President Nixon's Supreme Court nominee, G. Harrold Carswell, a federal appellate judge from Florida heavily opposed by civil rights groups and roundly criticized as a mediocre jurist.

April 14: The *Apollo 13* spacecraft limps around the Moon after an explosion destroys equipment and nearly all of the oxygen supply needed by the three astronauts aboard, Fred W. Haise, Jr., John L. Swigert, Jr., and the commander, James A. Lovell, Jr. The astronauts survive by using the oxygen and water supply in the lunar module *Aquarius* attached to the command module, *Odyssey. Apollo 13* returns to Earth on April 17.

April 22: Millions of Americans celebrate Earth Day as part of a burgeoning environmental movement. They participate in activities that range from protest rallies to cleaning up litter.

April 30: President Nixon announces that he has ordered more than 50,000 troops to invade Cambodia and destroy bases used by the communists in attacking South Vietnam. Nixon promises that the troops will advance no more than 20 miles into Cambodia and that they will be quickly withdrawn. Although he says he is not seeking to widen the Vietnam War, many Americans interpret his actions as doing so, and the invasion touches off numerous antiwar protests.

May 4: National guard members fire into a crowd of antiwar protesters at Kent State University in Ohio, killing four young people. Eleven others are injured. The shooting, which follows several days of protests on the campus, ignites a wave of student demonstrations at colleges around the country. With many campuses on the brink of violent eruptions, more than 400 colleges and universities suspend classes. Several days later, about 100,000 antiwar demonstrators converge on Washington.

May 8: Construction workers in Manhattan attack and beat up student antiwar protesters outside city hall.

May 12: The U.S. Senate confirms President Nixon's nominee for the Supreme Court, Minnesota jurist Harry A. Blackmun.

May 15: Police fire into a women's dormitory at predominantly black Jackson State College in Mississippi, killing two young people and wounding 12 others. Prior to the shooting, tension had been building among the police, students, and the surrounding community in part over protests against the Vietnam War but more so due to racial problems.

May 29: The conviction of Black Panther leader Huey Newton for fatally shooting an Oakland, California, police officer in 1968 is overturned. A state appeals court rules that the trial judge had failed to give the jury proper instructions.

June 7: The Who perform their rock opera *Tommy* at the Metropolitan Opera House in New York City.

June 13: President Nixon appoints a commission to study the causes of violent protests on the nation's college campuses.

June 21: A court-martial in Danang, South Vietnam, sentences Pvt. Michael A. Schwartz to life in prison for the killing of 12 Vietnamese civilians in Sonthang the previous February. The court concludes that Schwartz had committed premeditated murder and rejects his claim that he had been defending himself and his men against enemy fire.

July 1: President Nixon warns that clashes between Israeli and Russian planes over the Suez in the Middle East could escalate into a larger war between the United States and the Soviet Union. He states that he is committed to protecting Israel's existence as a nation.

July 13: An FBI report calls the Black Panthers the most dangerous group in America and criticizes the Weathermen for their violent tactics.

July 23: A federal grand jury in Detroit indicts 13 members of Weatherman on charges of conspiracy to commit bombings as part of terrorist attacks on public buildings.

July 29: Cesar Chavez, the head of the United Farm Workers organizing committee, signs contracts with 26 grape growers in Delano, California. The signings follow five years of strikes and a nationwide boycott of grapes and are hailed as a victory in Chavez's effort to organize long-oppressed migrant workers and improve their economic condition.

July 29: Alvin Toffler's book *Future Shock* is published and raises new questions about the effects of technology on society.

August 7: A gunman, Jonathan Jackson, barges into the trial of James McClain, who is being held in San Rafael, California, and distributes guns to McClain and three convicts, who are present as witnesses. The five men then take Superior Court Judge Harold J. Haley hostage, but as they try to flee in a van, a gun battle erupts between them and the police, killing Haley and three of the five abductors. It turns out that Jackson, only 17 years old, is the brother of George Jackson, a convict accused of helping to murder a white guard at Soledad State Prison the previous January and that two of the guns carried by him came from Angela Davis, a militant black activist, fired from her teaching position at UCLA for espousing marxist views. The FBI quickly puts Davis, who disappears from view, on its list of 10 most-wanted fugitives.

August 11: The FBI captures Reverend Daniel Berrigan in Block Island, Rhode Island. Berrigan, a Catholic priest, had been convicted of destroying draft records in Cantonsville, Maryland, in 1968 but had fled and was wanted as a fugitive.

August 24: A bomb explodes at the University of Wisconsin in Madison, destroying the Army Mathematics Research Center. A scientist is killed in the explosion, and shortly thereafter, the FBI begins a hunt for four persons suspected of committing the terrorist attack.

September 10: Vice President Spiro Agnew begins a campaign tour to help Republican senate candidates by viciously attacking liberal Democrats. Among his charges: The liberals engage in "pusillanimous pussyfooting" on law and order.

September 16: President Nixon tells an audience of 15,000 at Kansas State University that violence has no place in America, a country where political change can be brought about peacefully.

September 26: The President's Commission on Campus Unrest, headed by William W. Scranton, issues a report that distributes the blame for campus violence among students, police, and political leaders.

October 1: The President's Commission on Campus Unrest concludes that the police assault at Jackson State College in Mississippi the previous May, in which two black youths were killed and 12 others wounded, was "unwarranted," "unreasonable," and "unjustified." Three days later, the same commission describes the shootings by National Guard members at Kent State University, also in May, in the same terms. But it adds that student protesters must share the blame for the four deaths there because they had engaged in destructive activities.

October 7: President Nixon offers the communists in Vietnam a new peace plan that includes a truce under international supervision; an international conference to discuss armed conflict throughout Indochina; an offer to negotiate a timetable for the complete withdrawal of U.S. troops; a commitment to a political settlement for South Vietnam; and the immediate release of prisoners of war. Critics call the timing of the plan politically motivated, given that congressional elections are just a few weeks away, but the Senate adopts a resolution praising it. The proposal is rejected by the communists.

October 16: A Portage County (Ohio) grand jury investigating the shootings at Kent State University the previous May clears the National Guard members involved of any wrongdoing and accuses the university administration of having been too permissive in its treatment of campus radicals.

October 29: Youths throw rocks and eggs at Richard Nixon's motorcade in San Jose, California. Two days later, the president refers to the assault as an example of "thugs and hoodlums" who have acquired too much prominence in American society.

November 3: Richard Nixon fails in his bid to gain an unequivocal Republican triumph in the off-year elections. The GOP does pick up two seats in the Senate, but it loses nine in the House, while the Democrats pick up 11 governorships to bring their lead in the state houses to 29–21 over the Republicans.

November 10: A grand jury in Marin County, California, indicts militant black leader Angela Davis for

President Richard Nixon and rock star Elvis Presley shake hands in the Oval Office. *(National Archives and Records Administration)*

murder, kidnapping, and conspiracy connected to the violent courtroom escape of James McClain the previous August.

December 16: Senator Sam J. Ervin, Jr. (Dem., N.C.), chairman of the Senate Subcommittee on Constitutional Rights, charges that Army intelligence agents have spied on political leaders and numerous other civilians.

December 21: Rock star Elvis Presley visits President Nixon at the White House. Presley wants recognition as a leader in the fight against drugs and obtains, through Nixon's intercession, a special badge making him a "federal agent at-large." During the meeting in the Oval Office, Presley criticizes the Beatles for spreading "un-American" messages, states that he wants to restore respect for the American flag, and receives from Nixon a presidential tie clasp and cuff links.

December 22: Militant black leader Angela Davis is transported under heavy guard from New York City to the Marin County (California) jail after her indictment the previous month for her involvement in the violent courtroom escape of James McClain.

EYEWITNESS TESTIMONY

Chicago Seven Trial

MR. KUNSTLER: I will get down to the evidence in this case. I am going to confine my remarks to showing you how the Government stoops to conquer in this case.

The prosecution recognized early that if you were to see thirty-three police officers in uniform take the stand that you would realize how much of the case depends on law enforcement officers. So they strip the uniforms from those witnesses, and you notice you began to see almost an absence of uniforms. Even the Deputy Police Chief came without a uniform.

Mr. Schultz said, "Look at our witnesses. They don't argue with the judge. They are bright and alert. They sit there and they answer clearly."

They answered like automatons—one after the other, robots took the stand. "Did you see any missiles?"

"A barrage."

Everybody saw a barrage of missiles.

"What were the demonstrators doing?"

"Screaming. Indescribably loud."

"What were they screaming?"

"Profanities of all sorts."

I call your attention to James Murray. That is the reporter, and this is the one they got caught with. This is the one that slipped up. James Murray, who is a friend of the police, who thinks the police are the steadying force in Chicago. This man came to the stand, and he wanted you to rise up when you heard "Vietcong flags," this undeclared war we are fighting against an undeclared enemy. He wanted you to think that the march from Grant Park into the center of Chicago in front of the Conrad Hilton was a march run by the Vietcong, or have the Vietcong flags so infuriate you that you would feel against these demonstrators that they were less than human beings. The only problem is that he never saw any Vietcong flags. First of all, there were none, and I call your attention to the movies, and if you see one Vietcong flag in those two hours of movies at Michigan and Balbo, you can call me a liar and convict my clients.

Mr. Murray, under whatever instructions were given to him, or under his own desire to help the Police Department, saw them. I asked him a simple question: describe them. Remember what he said? "They are black." Then he heard laughter in the courtroom because there isn't a person in the room that thinks the Vietcong flag is a black flag. He heard a twitter in the courtroom. He said, "No, they are red."

Then he heard a little more laughter.

Then I said, "Are they all red?"

He said, "No, they have some sort of a symbol on them."

"What is the symbol?"

"I can't remember."

When you look at the pictures, you won't even see any black flags at Michigan and Balbo. You will see some red flags, two of them, I believe, and I might say to you that a red flag was the flag under which General Washington fought at the Battle of Brandywine, a flag made for him by the nuns of Bethlehem.

I think after what Murray said you can disregard his testimony. He was a clear liar on the stand. He did a lot of things they wanted him to do. He wanted people to say things that you could hear, that would make you think these demonstrators were violent people. He had some really rough ones in there. He had, "The Hump Sucks," "Daley Sucks the Hump"—pretty rough expressions. He didn't have "Peace Now." He didn't hear that. He didn't give you any others. Oh, I think he had "Charge. The street is ours. Let's go."

That is what he wanted you to hear. He was as accurate about that as he was about the Vietcong flag, and remember his testimony about the whiffle balls. One injured his leg. Others he picked up. Where were those whiffle balls in this courtroom?

You know what a whiffle ball is. It is something you can hardly throw. Why didn't the Government let you see the whiffle ball? They didn't let you see it because it can't be thrown. They didn't let you see it because the nails are shiny. I got a glimpse of it. Why didn't you see it? They want you to see a photograph so you can see that the nails don't drop out on the photograph. We never saw any of these weapons. That is enough for Mr. Murray. I have, I think, wasted more time than he is worth on Mr. Murray.

Now, I have one witness to discuss with you who is extremely important and gets us into the alleged attack on the Grant Park underground garage.

This is the most serious plan that you have had. This is more serious than attacking the pigs, as they tried to pin onto the Yippies and the National MOBE. This is to bomb. This is frightening, this concept of bombing an underground garage, probably the most frightening concept that you can imagine.

By the way, Grant Park garage is impossible to bomb with Molotov cocktails. It is pure concrete garage. You won't find a stick of wood in it, if you go there. But, put that aside for the moment. In a mythical tale. it doesn't matter that buildings won't burn. . . .

We are living in extremely troubled times. . . . An intolerable war abroad has divided and dismayed us all. Racism at home and poverty at home are both causes of despair and discouragement. In a so-called affluent society, we have people starving, and people who can't even begin to approximate the decent life.

These are rough problems, terrible problems, and as has been said by everybody in this country, they are so enormous that they stagger the imagination. But they don't go away by destroying their critics. They don't vanish by sending men to jail. They never did and they never will.

To use these problems by attempting to destroy those who protest against them is probably the most indecent thing that we can do. You can crucify a Jesus, you can poison a Socrates, you can hang John Brown or Nathan Hale, you can kill a Che Guevara, you can jail a Eugene Debs or a Bobby Seale. You can assassinate John Kennedy or a Martin Luther King, but the problems remain. The solutions are essentially made by continuing and perpetuating with every breath you have the right of men to think, the right of men to speak boldly and unafraid, the right to be masters of their souls, the right to live free and to die free. The hangman's rope never solved a single problem except that of one man.

I think if this case does nothing else, perhaps it will bring into focus that again we are in that moment of history when a courtroom becomes the proving ground of whether we do live free and whether we do die free. You are in that position now. Suddenly all importance has shifted to you—shifted to you as I guess in the last analysis it should go, and it is really your responsibility, I think, to see that men remain able to think, to speak boldly and unafraid, to be masters of their souls, and to live and die free. And perhaps if you do what is right, perhaps Allen Ginsberg will never have to write again as he did in "Howl," "I saw the best minds of my generation destroyed by madness," perhaps Judy Collins will never have to stand in any Courtroom again and say as she did, "When will they ever learn? When will they ever learn?"

Closing remarks by defense attorney William Kunstler at the trial of the Chicago Seven, February 13, 1970, available online at http://www.law.umkc.edu/ faculty/projects/ftrials/Chicago7/Closing.html, downloaded January 25, 2004.

I want to say that sending us to prison, any punishment the Government can impose on us, will not solve the problems that have gotten us into trouble with the Government and the law in the first place, will not solve the problems of this country's rampant racism, will not solve the problems of economic justice. It will not solve the problems of the foreign policy and the attacks upon the underdeveloped people of the world. . . .

Our movement is not very strong today. It is not united, it is not well organized. But there is the beginning of an awakening in this country which has been going on for at least the last fifteen years, and it is an awakening that will not be denied. Tactics will change, people will err, people will die in the streets and die in prison. But I do not believe that this Movement can be denied, because however falsely applied the American ideal was from the beginning, when it excluded Black people and Indians and people without property, nonetheless there was a dream of justice and equality and freedom and brotherhood. And I think that dream is much closer to fulfillment today than it has been at any time in the history of the country. . . .

I salute my brothers and sisters in Vietnam, in the ghetto, in the women's liberation movement, all the people all over the world who are struggling to make true and real for all people the ideals on which this country was supposed to be founded, but never, never lived up to.

David Dellinger's statement to the court in December 1973 after he was found guilty for incitement to riot (but before he was sentenced) as a result of his activities at Chicago in 1968, in David Dellinger, From Yale to Jail *(1993), pp. 382–383.*

Invasion of Cambodia

Tonight, American and South Vietnamese units will attack the headquarters for the entire Communist military operation in South Vietnam. This key control center has been occupied by the North Vietnamese and Vietcong for 5 years in blatant violation of Cambodia's neutrality.

This is not an invasion of Cambodia. The areas in which these attacks will be launched are completely occupied and controlled by North Vietnamese forces. Our purpose is not to occupy the areas. Once enemy forces are driven out of these sanctuaries and once their military supplies are destroyed, we will withdraw.

These actions are in no way directed to the security interests of any nation. Any government that chooses to use these actions as a pretext for harming relations with the United States will be doing so on its own responsibility, and on its own initiative, and we will draw the appropriate conclusions.

Now let me give you the reasons for my decision.

A majority of the American people, a majority of you listening to me, are for the withdrawal of our forces from Vietnam. The action I have taken tonight is indispensable for the continuing success of that withdrawal program.

A majority of the American people want to end this war rather than to have it drag on intermittently. The action I have taken tonight will serve that purpose.

A majority of the American people want to keep the casualties of our brave men in Vietnam to a minimum. The action I have taken tonight is essential if we are to accomplish that goal.

Soldiers in the South Vietnamese Army (ARVN) move along a trail during an assault operation in 1970. *(National Archives and Records Administration)*

We take this action not for the purpose of expanding the war into Cambodia but for the purpose of ending the war in Vietnam and winning the just peace we all desire. We have made—we will continue to make every possible effort to end this war through negotiation at the conference table rather than through more fighting on the battlefield. . . .

My fellow Americans, we live in an age of anarchy, both abroad and at home. We see mindless attacks on all the great institutions which have been created by free civilizations in the last 500 years. Even here in the United States, great universities are being systematically destroyed. Small nations all over the world find themselves under attack from within and from without.

If, when the chips are down, the world's most powerful nation, the United States of America, acts like a pitiful, helpless giant, the forces of totalitarianism and anarchy will threaten free nations and free institutions throughout the world.

It is not our power but our will and character that is being tested tonight. The question all Americans must ask and answer tonight is thus: Does the richest and strongest nation in the history of the world have the character to meet a direct challenge by a group which rejects every effort to win a just peace, ignores our warning, tramples on solemn agreements, violates the neutrality of an unarmed people, and uses our prisoners as hostages?

If we fail to meet this challenge, all other nations will be on notice that despite its overwhelming power the United States, when a real crisis comes, will be found wanting.

President Richard Nixon's "Address to the Nation on the Situation in Southeast Asia," April 30, 1970, in Public Papers of the Presidents of the United States: Richard Nixon, 1970 *(1971), pp. 407–409.*

Cambodia was misperceived in America as a separate "war" that we must avoid. But it was not any such thing. The enemy was the same as in Vietnam. North Vietnamese troops shifted back and forth across the border as if the concept of sovereignty did not exist. They did with impunity for years what produced for us in 1970, over eight weeks, a national crisis.

Henry Kissinger presenting in his memoirs a defense of Richard Nixon's decision to send U.S. ground troops into Cambodia during the Vietnam War, in Henry Kissinger, Years of Upheaval *(1982), p. 337.*

Kent State

The FBI has conducted an extensive search and has found nothing to indicate that any person other than a Guardsman fired a weapon. As a part of their investigation, a metal detector was used in the general area where Lieutenants Kline and Fallon indicated they saw bullets hit the ground. A .45 bullet was recovered, but again nothing to indicate it had been fired by other than a Guardsman. Students and photographers on the roofs of Johnson and Taylor Halls state there was no sniper on the roofs. . . .

Of the 13 Kent State students shot, none, so far as we know, were associated with either the disruption in Kent on Friday night, May 1, 1970, or the burning of the ROTC building on Saturday, May 2, 1970.

On the day of the shooting, Jeffrey Miller and Allison Krause can be placed at the front of the crowd taunting the National Guardsmen. Miller made some obscene gestures at the Guardsmen and Krause was heard to shout obscenities at them. Victims Grace, Canfora and Stamps were, we believe, active in taunting the Guard. Grace and Canfora probably had flags and were encouraging the students to throw rocks at the Guardsmen. Dean Kahler admitted to the FBI that he had thrown "two or three" rocks at the Guardsmen at some time prior to the shooting. Joseph Lewis at the time of the shooting was making an obscene gesture at the Guard.

As far as we have been able to determine, Schroeder, Scheuer, Cleary, MacKenzie, Russell and Wrentmore were merely spectators to the confrontation.

Aside entirely from any questions of specific intent on the part of the Guardsmen or a predisposition to use their weapons, we do not know what started the shooting. We can only speculate on the possibilities. For

The remains of the burned-down ROTC building at Kent State University smolder on the tense campus. *(Kent State University Libraries and Media Services, May 4 Collection)*

example, Sergeant Leon Smith of Company A stated that he saw a man about 20 feet from him running at him with a rock. Sergeant Smith then says he fired his shotgun once in the air. He alone of all the Guardsmen does not mention hearing shooting prior to the time he fired. He asserts that "at about the same time" he fired, others fired. Some Guardsmen claim that the first shot sounded to them as if it came from a M-79 grenade launcher—a sound probably similar to that made by a shotgun.

It is also possible that the members of Troop G observed their top non-commissioned officer, Sergeant Pryor, turn and point his weapon at the crowd and followed his example. Sergeant Pryor admits that he was pointing his weapon at the students prior to the shooting but claims he was loading it and denies he fired. The FBI does not believe he fired.

Another possibility is that one of the Guards either panicked and fired first, or intentionally shot at a student, thereby triggering the other shots.

Quoted from the Justice Department's Summary of FBI Reports, undated, available online at http://dept. kent.edu/may4/justice_fbi_summary.htm, downloaded January 25, 2004.

Mr. Nixon and his advisors very likely knew that the Cambodia decision would evoke an outcry from the academic world. What was not anticipated, and probably could not have been, were the events at Kent and Jackson and that instead of a predictable reaction from the radical and activist 5 percent of the academic community, there would be an outpouring of opposition embracing perhaps half of the total college population (students, faculty, and staff). By the end of the second week of May, and after some 500 colleges had shut down temporarily or until the end of the term, the White House realized that it must, in some degree, improve relations with the campuses. This stance of solicitude lasted approximately a month—through the appointment of the Scranton Commission on June 13. The White House then resumed its critical attitude toward the colleges. During the ensuing five months, as the November election drew near, the public utterances from the White House and many Republican (and Democratic) candidates about college students, the "situation on the campuses," and law and order grew increasingly condemnatory and divisive. In California, for example, the choice, according to the Senate incumbent, was between "law and order" and "anarchy."

The major turning point in this brief history came with the November elections. Law-and-order candidates generally failed to win election, and it became clear to most observers that the politics of divisiveness and fear had, for the most part, been counterproductive.

Richard E. Peterson and John A. Bilorusky reacting to campus protests in a report sponsored by the Carnegie Commission on Higher Education, May 1970: The Campus Aftermath of Cambodia and Kent State *(1971), p. 7.*

We're seeing at, uh, the city of Kent, especially, probably the most vicious form of campus oriented violence yet perpetrated by dissident groups and their allies in the state of Ohio. For this reason most of the dissident groups have operated within the campus. This has moved over to where they have threatened and intimidated merchants and people of this community. Now it ceases to be a problem of camp—of the colleges in Ohio. This now is the problem of the state of Ohio, and I want to assure you that we are going to employ every force of law that we have under our authority, not only to get to the bottom of the situation here at Kent, on the campus, in the city, and we have asked the complete cooperation of the district attorney of the federal government because federal supplies were burned and destroyed in the ROTC building and these people after we can find them, after a complete investigation, will be turned over to the federal government.

We have asked the county prosecutor for a complete and comprehensive investigation and there's some people now out on probation that there has been a strong word to the fact that they have participated in this. And we're going to put a stop to this for this reason: the same group that we're dealing with here today, and there's three or four of them, they only have one thing in mind, that is to destroy higher education in Ohio. And if they continue this, and continue what they're doing, they're going to reach their goal for the simple reason: that you cannot continue to set fires to buildings that are worth five and ten million dollars because you cannot get replacement from the high general assembly. And last night I think that we have seen all forms of violence, the worst, and when they start taking over communities, this is when we're going to use every part of the law enforcement . . . of Ohio to drive them out of Kent.

We're going to make two recommendations to the High General Assembly. Now we've had this in Miami, in Oxford, Ohio, also Ohio State University, and we've had thirty-two police officers injured and a couple very severe. We have these same groups going from one campus to the other and to use a university, state-supported by the taxpayer of Ohio, as a sanctuary. And in this they make definite plans of burning, destroying, and throwing rocks at police and at the national guard and the highway patrol. We're asking the legislature that any person throwing a rock, brick, or stone at a law enforcement agent of Ohio, a sheriff, policeman, highway patrol, national guard, becomes a felony.

And, secondly, we're going to ask for legislation that . . . if these people are convicted, whether a misdemeanor or a felony, of participating in a riot, they're automatically dismissed, there's no hearing, no recourse, and they cannot enter another state university in the state of Ohio. We are going to eradicate the problem. We're not going to treat the symptoms. And as long as this continues, higher education in Ohio is in jeopardy. And if they are continued to give permissive consent, they will destroy higher education in this state.

Remarks by Ohio governor James A. Rhodes at the Kent firehouse in Kent, Ohio, on May 3, 1970, available online at http://dept.kent.edu/may4/ rhodes_speech_05031970.htm, downloaded January 28, 2004.

I could have sworn the shooting lasted thirty seconds or a minute. As soon as it stopped, there was a moment of silence. After that, you could hear screams of pain and a lot of screams of people horror-stricken and anguished.

Kent State student Alan Canfora describing at a later date the shootings at Kent State University on May 4, 1970, and quoted in Viorst, Fire in the Streets *(1979), p. 539.*

This should remind us all once again that when dissent turns to violence, it invites tragedy. It is my hope that this tragic and unfortunate incident will strengthen the determination of all the Nation's campuses—administrators, faculty, and students alike—to stand firmly for the right which exists in this country of peaceful dissent and just as strongly against the resort to violence as a means of such expression.

Statement of President Richard M. Nixon read by Press Secretary Ronald I. Ziegler at a news briefing on May 4, 1970, in Public Papers of the Presidents of the United States: Richard Nixon, 1970 *(1971), p. 411.*

I believe this Administration finds itself, today, embracing a philosophy which appears to lack appropriate concern for the attitude of a great mass of Americans—our young people.

Addressed either politically or philosophically, I believe we are in error if we set out consciously to alienate those who could be our friends.

Today, our young people, or at least a vast segment of them, believe they have no opportunity to communicate with government, regardless of Administration, other than through violent confrontation. But I am convinced we—and they—have the capacity, if we will but have the willingness, to learn from history.

During the Great Depression, our youth lost their ability to communicate with the Republican party. And we saw the young people of the 1930's become the predominant leaders of the 40's and 50's—associated not with our party, but rather with those with whom they felt they could communicate. What is happening today is not unrelated to what happened in the 30's. Now being unable to communicate with either party, they are apparently heading down the road to anarchy. And regardless of how I, or any American, might feel individually, we have an obligation as leaders to communicate with our youth and listen to their ideas and problems. . . .

I suggest . . . that you meet with college presidents, to talk about the . . . situation that is erupting, because before we can face and conquer our enemies, we must identify them, whether those enemies take physical or philosophical form. And we must win over our philosophical enemies by convincing them of the wisdom of the path we have chosen, rather than ignoring the path they propose.

In this regard, I believe the Vice President [Spiro Agnew] initially has answered a deep-seated mood of America in his public statements. However, a continued attack on the young—not on their attitudes so much as their motives—can serve little purpose other than to further cement those attitudes to a solidity impossible to penetrate with reason.

Finally, Mr. President, permit me to suggest that you consider meeting, on an individual and conversational basis, with members of your Cabinet. Perhaps through such conversations, we can gain greater insight into the problems confronting us all, and most important, into the solutions of these problems.

Excerpts from the letter sent on May 6, 1970, by Secretary of the Interior Walter J. Hickel to President Nixon in reaction to the administration's treatment of student dissent, in the New York Times, *May 7, 1970, p. 18.*

Mrs. Dickerson [Nancy H. Dickerson, NBC News]. Q. After you met with these eight university presidents yesterday, they indicated that you had agreed to tone down the criticism within your administration of those who disagree with you, Then tonight Vice President Agnew is quoted all over the news programs as making a speech which includes these words, "That every debate has a cadre of Jeremiahs, normally a gloomy coalition of choleric young intellectuals and tired, embittered elders." Why?

THE PRESIDENT: Mrs. Dickerson, I have studied the history of this country over the past 190 years. And, of course, the classic and the most interesting game is to try to drive a wedge between the President and the Vice President. Believe me, I had 8 years of that, and I am experienced on that point. Now, as far as the Vice President is concerned, he will answer for anything that he has said. As far as my attempting to tone him down or my attempting to censor the Secretary of the Interior because he happens to take a different point of view, I shall not do that. I would hope that all the members of this administration would have in mind the fact, a rule that I have always had, and it is a very simple one: When the action is hot, keep the rhetoric cool.

President Richard M. Nixon responding to a question at a press conference on May 8, 1970, in Public Papers of the Presidents of the United States: Richard Nixon, 1970 *(1971), p. 416.*

Jackson State

Well, of course, you know that the Mississippi Highway Patrol, and for that matter the Jackson police—although I am not saying Jackson police fired, because I didn't see them fire—these men are going to be infuriated by Negro students yelling, "You white sons-of-a-bitches" and "you white pigs." Now I can imagine that—and this is strictly opinion now—it's my opinion that this would make a Mississippi highway patrolman really tense up, and really feel like he wanted to fire. . . .

Why? I asked myself that a thousand times. And what I always come back to—my own personal belief—and this is nothing more than opinion. I believe that the whole shooting thing was triggered by one bottle being thrown, a bottle that was tossed right into the middle of us and that I felt sprinkle my leg, and I think probably hit highway patrolmen also. I know I heard one say that it did. My own theory—my own

opinion is—that was enough in that tense atmosphere to touch off one guy shooting. Others followed.

Comments by television news anchorman Bob Case of WJTV at a meeting of the Jackson, Mississippi, mayor's biracial committee in May 1970 and about 10 years after the shooting, in Tim Spofford, Lynch Street: The May 1970 Slayings at Jackson State College *(1988), pp. 122–123.*

The Bombing at the University of Wisconsin

The killing [in Vietnam] had to be stopped, and the thing that we could do specifically in Madison, Wisconsin was to eliminate the Army Mathematics Research Center as not only symbol but real presence of death and killing and genocide in our midst. And this was the task of the day.

Student Max Elbaum's statement in 1973 defending the actions of Karl Armstrong, who was found guilty of bombing the Army Mathematics Research Center at the University of Wisconsin in 1970, in Tom Bates, Rads *(1992), p. 254.*

Imagine the society we'd have if every time a person felt morally committed to a cause he could throw around one-ton bombs.

Wisconsin Attorney General Michael Zaleski's statement in 1973 regarding the bombing of the Army Mathematics Research Center at the University of Wisconsin in 1970, in Tom Bates, Rads *(1992), p. 254.*

Student Dissent

Far more important than the particular recommendations of this Commission are the underlying themes that are common to all:

*Most student protestors are neither violent nor extremist. But a small minority of politically extreme students and faculty members and a small group of dedicated agitators are bent on destruction of the university through violence in order to gain their own political ends. Perpetrators of violence must be identified, removed from the university as swiftly as possible, and prosecuted vigorously by the appropriate agencies of law enforcement.

*Dissent and peaceful protest are a valued part of this nation's way of governing itself. Violence and disorder are the antithesis of democratic processes and cannot be tolerated either on the nation's campuses or anywhere else.

*The roots of student activism lie in unresolved conflicts in our national life, but the many defects of the universities have also fueled campus unrest. Universities have not adequately prepared themselves to respond to disruption. They have been without suitable plans, rules, or sanctions. Some administrators and faculty members have responded irresolutely. Frequently, announced sanctions have not been applied. Even more frequently, the lack of appropriate organization within the university has rendered its response ineffective. The university's own house must be placed in order.

*Too many students have acted irresponsibly and even dangerously in pursuing their stated goals and expressing their dissent. Too many law enforcement officers have responded with unwarranted harshness and force in seeking to control disorder.

*Actions—and inactions—of government at all levels have contributed to campus unrest. The words of some political leaders have helped to inflame it. Law enforcement officers have too often reacted ineptly or overreacted. At times their response has degenerated into uncontrolled violence.

*The nation has been slow to resolve the issues of war and race, which exacerbate divisions within American society and which have contributed to the escalation of student protest and disorder.

*All of us must act to prevent violence, to create understanding, and to reduce the bitterness and hostility that divide both the campus and the country. We must establish respect for the processes of law and tolerance for the exercise of dissent on our campuses and in the nation.

We advance our recommendations not as cure-alls, but as rational and responsive steps that should be taken. We summarize here our major recommendations, addressed to those who have the power to carry them out. . . .

The Causes of Student Protest

In and of itself, campus unrest is not a "problem" and requires no "solution." The existence of dissenting opinion and voices is simply a social condition, a fact of modern life; the right of such opinion to exist is protected by our constitution. Protest that is violent or disruptive is, of course, a very real problem, and solutions must be found to such manifestations of it. But when student protest stays within legal bounds, as it typically does, it is not a problem for government to cope with. It is simply a pattern of opinion and expression.

Campus unrest, then, is not a single or uniform thing. Rather it is the aggregate result, or sum, of hundreds and thousands of individual beliefs and discontents, each of them as unique as the individuals feel them. These individual feelings reflect in turn a series of choices each person makes about what he will believe, what he will say, and what he will do. In the most immediate and operational sense, then, it is these choices—these commitments, to use a word in common usage among students—which are the proximate cause of campus unrest, and which are the forces at work behind any physical manifestation of dissent or dissatisfaction.

These acts of individual commitment to certain values and to certain ways of seeing and acting in the world do not occur in a vacuum. They take place within, and are powerfully affected by, the conditions under which students live. We will call these conditions the contributing causes of campus unrest. Five broad orders of such contributing causes have been suggested in testimony before the Commission. They are:

The pressing problems of American society, particularly the war in Southeast Asia and the conditions of minority groups;

The changing status and attitudes of youth in America;

The distinctive character of the American university during the post war period;

An escalating spiral of reaction to student protest from public opinion, and an escalating spiral of violence; and

Broad evolutionary changes occurring in the culture and structure of modern Western society. . . .

The New Youth Culture

No one who lives in contemporary America can be unaware of the surface manifestations of this new youth culture. Dress is highly distinctive; emphasis is placed on heightened color and sound; the enjoyment of flowers and nature is given a high priority. The fullest ranges of sense and sensation are to be enjoyed each day through the cultivation of new experiences, through spiritualism, and through drugs. Life is sought to be made as simple, primitive, and "natural" as possible, as ritualized, for example, by nude bathing. . . .

An important theme of this new culture is its oppositional relationship to the larger society, as is suggested by the fact that one of its leading theorists has called it a "counter culture." If the rest of the society wears short hair, the member of this youth culture wears his hair long. If others are clean, he is dirty. If others drink alcohol and illegalize marijuana, he denounces alcohol and smokes pot. If others work in large organizations with massively complex technology, he works alone and makes sandals by hand. If others live separated, he lives in a commune. If others are for police and the judges, he is for the accused and the prisoner. By these means, he declares himself an alien in a large society with which he fundamentally is at odds.

An evaluation of student protests in The Report of the President's Commission on Campus Unrest *(1970), pp. 7–8, 54–56, 63, and 67.*

You think of those kids out there. I say "kids." I have seen them. They are the greatest.

You see these bums, you know, blowing up the campuses. Listen, the boys that are on the college campuses today are the luckiest people in the world, going to the great universities, and here they are burning up the books, I mean storming around this issue—I mean you name it—get rid of the war; there will be another one.

Out there we've got kids who are just doing their duty. I have seen them. They stand tall, and they are proud. I am sure they are scared. I was when I was there. But when it really comes down to it, they stand up and, boy, you have to talk up to those men. And they are going to do fine; we've got to stand back of them.

Statement by President Richard M. Nixon during a visit to the Pentagon on May 1, 1970, in Public Papers of the Presidents of the United States: Richard Nixon, 1970 *(1971), p. 417.*

In several recent speeches I have called attention to the grave dangers which accompany the new politics of violence and confrontation and which have found so much favor on our college campuses. The time has come to recognize that the only way to bring us—the participating citizens of a great country—together is to forthrightly declare our rejection and contempt for

those who practice subversion, lawlessness, and violence.

Vice President Spiro Agnew reacting on May 4, 1970, to the shooting that day at Kent State, in the New York Times, *May 5, 1970, p. 17.*

Mr. Philip Potter [*Baltimore Sun*]. Q. Mr. President, do you believe that the use of the word "bums" to categorize some of those who are engaged in dissent—and I know that you meant it to apply to those who are destructive, but it has been used in a broader context—do you believe that is in keeping with your suggestion that the rhetoric should be kept cool?

THE PRESIDENT. I would certainly regret that my use of the word "bums" was interpreted to apply to those who dissent. All the members of this press corps know that I have for years defended the right of dissent. I have always opposed the use of violence. On university campuses the rule of reason is supposed to prevail over the rule of force. And when students on university campuses burn buildings, when they engage in violence, when they break up furniture, when they terrorize their fellow students and terrorize the faculty, then I think "bums" is perhaps too kind a word to apply to that kind of person. Those are the kind I was referring to.

President Richard M. Nixon responding to a question at a press conference on May 8, 1970, in Public Papers of the Presidents of the United States: Richard Nixon, 1970 *(1971), p. 417.*

Earth Day

Earth Day planners scheduled stunts to dramatize various aspects of the environmental crisis. As a warning of impending famine caused by the world's rising population, San Fernando State College students were organized to prepare tea and rice to give people a taste of a "hunger diet." Students at several other colleges and schools were ready to collect bottles and aluminum cans cluttering the landscape—and then to conduct "dump-ins" on the steps of city halls or manufacturers' plants.

The biggest target of all was the automobile. In Danbury, Conn., students made ready to perform the now popular ritual of burying an internal-combustion engine. At Wayne State University they marshaled pickets for General Motors' headquarters. Alternate modes of nonpolluting transportation called for "bike-ins," balloon ascensions, and pedestrian parades. Even cities joined the act. New York announced a ban on cars and the creation of pedestrian malls along 14th Street and a 45-block stretch of Fifth Avenue. Miami, never to be outdone, promised prizes to the "most polluted" floats in a huge, car-free "Dead Orange Parade," supposed to symbolize the effects of local pollution.

> From "The Dawning of Earth Day," Time, April 27, 1970, in Time Magazine Multimedia Almanac, Softkey International (1995).

Then there is another view of the future which in a sense is what Earth Day is all about. This view suggests calamity lies ahead if we don't stop doing some of the things we seem to be insistently doing, things like polluting the air, destroying our rivers, killing our oceans, and jamming our cities. Such a view is circular like the whole Earth. A circular future means that we cannot escape from whatever it is we do here and now. Life is not linear, it is round. If we pollute the Earth and others do the same, the pollution will come up over the horizon one day and destroy us.

> Artist Alan Gussow commenting in 1970 about Earth Day, in Earth Day—The Beginning (1970), pp. 3–4.

I would say that if you are a serious movement you must be prepared to take on the giant corporations who are the primary polluters and perpetrators of some of the worst conditions that affect the environment of the country and indeed the world.

> George Wiley, director of the National Welfare Rights Organization, addressing the Earth Day movement in 1970, in Earth Day—The Beginning (1970), p. 217.

A disease has infected our country. It has brought smog to Yosemite, dumped garbage in the Hudson, sprayed DDT in our food, and left our cities in decay. Its carrier is man.

Earth Day is a commitment to make life better, not just bigger and faster; to provide real rather than rhetorical solutions. It is a day to re-examine the ethic of individual progress at mankind's expense. It is a day to challenge the corporate and governmental leaders who promise change, but who shortchange the necessary programs.

It is a day for looking beyond tomorrow. April 22 seeks a future worth living. April 22 seeks a future.

> From an ad for Earth Day in the New York Times, on January 18, 1970, in Bill Christofferson, The Man from Clear Lake (2004), pp. 306–307.

I was satisfied that if we could tap into the environmental concerns of the general public and infuse the student anti-war energy into the environmental cause, we could generate a demonstration that would force this issue onto the national political agenda. It was a big gamble, but worth a try.

> Senator Gaylord Nelson reflecting in 2002 on plans for the first Earth Day in 1970, in Gaylord Nelson, Beyond Earth Day (2002), p. 7.

Women's Rights

He looked at me as if I were a rare species of caterpillar. Like a little boy whose toy had been taken away, he said, "You had no business doing that!" It really was scary to see what happened when his "omnipotence" was threatened.

> A woman describing the reaction of her doctor in the 1970s to her telling him that she had learned to examine herself with a speculum and a mirror, in Ruth Rosen, The World Split Open (2000), p. 177.

Three things have been difficult to tame. The ocean, fools, and women. We may soon be able to tame the ocean, but fools and women will take a little longer.

> Newscaster Howard K. Smith of ABC television reporting on the women's strike for equality march in New York City, August 1970, in Susan Douglas, Where the Girls Are (1994), p. 163.

DON'T COOK DINNER!
STARVE A RAT TODAY!!
HOUSEWIVES ARE UNPAID SLAVE LABORERS!
UP AGAINST THE WALL MALE CHAUVINIST PIG DOCTORS, EVE WAS FRAMED

> Slogans displayed on banners carried by marchers in New York City supporting the Women's Strike for Equality, August 26, 1970, in Judith Hennessee, Betty Friedan: Her Life (1999), p. 139.

Abortion is our right—our right as women to control our bodies. . . . Some strong and concerned people have changed a few state laws and started some good abortion-referral services and humane clinics, but for too many American women legal abortions are hard to get, hard to pay for, and once gotten, are alienating and lonely experiences. . . . Childbirth preparation means educating ourselves about what is likely to happen to our bodies, our minds, and our lives during the childbirth experience. It also means finding someone—husband, friend, or relative—to share this period with us. . . .

In stark contrast to women's numerical superiority as workers and consumers is that fact that only about 7 percent of the physicians in the United States are women. . . . It is evident that women as workers and patients occupy the wide base of a pyramid, with white male doctors at the narrow top controlling everything and everyone below them for their own interests.

Excerpts from the book published by the Boston Women's Health Book Collective, Our Bodies, Ourselves *(1973), pp. 138, 182, and 237.*

Our movement is not growing up in a vacuum. Since World War II, there has been a change in perspective on the part of people who are opposed to the destructiveness of the capitalist system. Prior to World War II, Marxists saw the main force for revolution as being the American working class. This perspective has to be broadened in the light of the anti-imperialist revolutions which have grown up since that time. The peoples of the Third World are rebelling against the economic superexploitation and caste oppression imposed on them by capitalism. Increasing numbers of American black people are seeing their own position in the United States in the same manner. And now women in the Movement are beginning to see many symptoms of oppression in common with both groups. These symptoms derive from the fact that all three are exploited to a greater extent than white, male, American workers. . . . Just as the people of the imperialized nations must destroy the source of their exploitation and oppression, capitalism, so too must we. . . .

Perhaps for the first time in human history we are faced with the possibility of a pan-human, non-exploitative society. Abundant production is possible given our technology, and there is a real need for all peoples, women and men, to unite, if we are to defeat the numerically tiny, but very powerful forces in opposition to our needs.

From "Social Bases for Sexual Equality: A Comparative View," by Karen Sacks in Robin Morgan, ed., Sisterhood Is Powerful *(1970), pp. 525–526.*

Apollo 13 *Mission*

Since *Apollo 13* many people have asked me, "Did you have suicide pills on board?" We didn't, and I never heard of such a thing in the eleven years I spent as an astronaut and NASA executive.

I did, of course, occasionally think of the possibility that the spacecraft explosion might maroon us in an enormous orbit about the Earth—a sort of perpetual monument to the space program. But Jack Swigert, Fred Haise, and I never talked about that fate during our perilous flight. I guess we were too busy struggling for survival. . . .

At 55 hours 46 minutes, as we finished a 49-minute TV broadcast showing how comfortably we lived and worked in weightlessness, I pronounced the benediction: "This is the crew of Apollo 13 wishing everybody there a nice evening, and we're just about ready to close out our inspection of Aquarius (the LM) and get back for a pleasant evening in Odyssey (the CM). Good night. . . ."

Nine minutes later the roof fell in; rather, oxygen tank No. 2 blew up, causing No. 1 tank also to fail. We came to the slow conclusion that our normal supply of electricity, light, and water was lost, and we were about 200,000 miles from Earth. . . .

The message came in the form of a sharp bang and vibration. Jack Swigert saw a warning light that accompanied the bang, and said, "Houston, we've had a problem here." I came on and told the ground that it was a main B bus undervolt. The time was 2108 hours on April 13.

Next, the warning lights told us we had lost two of our three fuel cells, which were our prime source of electricity. Our first thoughts were ones of disappointment, since mission rules forbade a lunar landing with only one fuel cell. . . .

Thirteen minutes after the explosion, I happened to look out of the left-hand window, and saw the final evidence pointing toward potential catastrophe. "We are venting something out into the—into space," I reported to Houston. . . .

It was a gas—oxygen—escaping at a high rate from our second, and last, oxygen tank. I am told that some amateur astronomers on top of a building in Houston could actually see the expanding sphere of gas around the spacecraft.

Undated excerpt form astronaut James Lovell's account of the Apollo 13 *mission, available online at http://www. hq.nasa.gov/office/pao/History/SP-350/ ch-13-1.html, downloaded January 29, 2004.*

The original *Apollo 13* crew, Commander James A. Lovell, command-module pilot Thomas K. Mattingly, and lunar-module pilot Fred W. Haise, sits behind a table on which are positioned a sextant, the *Apollo 13* insignia, and a model of an astrolabe. Mattingly was exposed to German measles prior to the mission and was replaced by his backup, John L. "Jack" Swigert, Jr. *(National Aeronautics and Space Administration)*

Jimi Hendrix

We spent most of the time just talking and reminiscing. I was surprised to see him in somewhat of a funk. He was not happy with the way his music had developed. He felt stultified somehow. . . .

We were standing outside, alone, in a lobby, and I felt a great deal of compassion for him. As he stood there, his eyes kind of drifted off, and I could see him trying to come to terms with some devil or something in his own head. And he said, "you know, I think I'm gonna start an R&B band. I gotta do something. I think I'm gonna work with some horns and put together something like Otis [Redding], cause that's really where it's at." I put my arm around him and said, "Jimi, don't you understand, man, you invented psychedelic music. Nobody ever played this before you came along. Why are you going through this crisis of self-confidence right now?"

> *Musician Mike Nesmith recounting a conversation he had with Jimi Hendrix at a party on September 10, 1970, in Johnny Black,* Jimi Hendrix: Eyewitness *(1999), p. 243.*

I never used to dream about Jimi, but one night I had a dream and Jimi came into the room. I said, "But you're dead," and he said, "It's cool. I just wanted to see you again."

> *Musician and Jimi Hendrix friend Noel Redding commenting shortly after Hendrix died on September 18, 1970, in Johnny Black,* Jimi Hendrix: Eyewitness *(1999), p. 249.*

Janis Joplin

The thing about Janis is that she just looked so unique, an ugly duckling dressed as a princess, fearlessly so. Seeing her live (Blossom Music Center, Richfield, Ohio, 1970) was like watching a boxing match. Her performance was so in your face and electrifying that it really put you right there in the moment. There you were living your nice little life in the suburbs and suddenly there was this train wreck, and it was Janis.

> *Undated statement by Chrissie Hynde of the rock group the Pretenders, available online at http://www. janisjoplin.net/kozmic/quotesll.html, downloaded January 30, 2004.*

A couple of days before Janis died, we were roaring down Sunset Boulevard in her multicolored Porsche and we headed for Barney's Beanery. Remember that place? And God, she seemed so happy. We had the top down, we were *roaring* on the road like crazy and it just felt good to be with her. When we got to the Beanery, there were a whole bunch of people, and Janis didn't know them personally. They were fans, though, and we just hung out. It was interesting to see her talk to the people because she was real open. She would talk to *anybody*. And two days later, she was dead.

> *Clark Pierson, a friend of Janis Joplin's, on the last hours before Joplin's death, in an undated comment in Myra Friedman,* Buried Alive: The Biography of Janis Joplin *(1992), pp. 339–340.*

I had a real hard time facing it. I liked Janis a lot. She was real generous, intelligent, funny, and kind. I was glad that she was a success. . . . I liked her because she was real, even to the point of dying like she did in LA. She lived and died the blues life.

> *Singer and songwriter Nick Gravenites in an undated comment about his friend Janis Joplin, in Ellis Amburn,* Pearl: The Obsessions and Passions of Janis Joplin *(1992), pp. 304–305.*

People were coming over to that house and walking around and taking shit! You know, I want this and I want that. I couldn't *believe* it. People came over and took things, people I thought would be *above* that. Hell, I know she would have given that stuff away.

Actor Peter Coyote commenting in 1970 on the scene at Janis Joplin's house in the days after Joplin died, in Myra Friedman, Buried Alive: The Biography of Janis Joplin *(1992), p. 323.*

Future Shock *and* The Greening of America

As a teacher on her 47th year of teaching young people, I cannot thank you enough. . . . I've always had beautiful students but today's are something else! I have a feeling it's truly spectacular I should have lived long enough to know these fine children!

From a letter by college teacher Mary Gwen of St. Paul, Minnesota, written in 1970 or 1971 to Charles A. Reich, author of The Greening of America, *and quoted in Charles A. Reich,* Greening *(1971), p. i.*

The parallel term "culture shock" has already begun to creep into the popular vocabulary. Culture shock is the effect that immersion in a strange culture has on the unprepared visitor. Peace Corps volunteers suffer from it in Borneo or Brazil. . . .

Future shock is the dizzying orientation brought on by the premature arrival of the future. It may well be the most important disease of tomorrow. . . .

Future shock is a time phenomenon, a product of the greatly accelerated change in society. But its impact is far worse. For most Peace Corps men, in fact most travelers, have the comforting knowledge that the culture they left behind will be there to return to. The victim of future shock does not.

Excerpt from Alvin Toffler's Future Shock *(1970), pp. 10–11.*

Curt Flood

Twelve years of my life. I spent the rest of the day in the chair right next to the telephone, answering none of the calls. *Twelve years of my life.*

I said to Marian, "There ain't no way I'm going to pack up and move twelve years of my life from here. No way at all."

Curt Flood recalling in 1970 his reaction to the decision by the St. Louis Cardinals to trade him to the Philadelphia Phillies, in Curt Flood, The Way It Is *(1970), pp. 185–186.*

2

Polarized America
January 1971–December 1971

As with the previous year, Americans in 1971 focused on a prominent court case that was indicative of the tremendous turmoil and tension in their society. This time, it was the murder trial of Charles Manson, dubbed by some newspapers the "hippie killer." Manson and three of his followers were accused of killing the actress Sharon Tate and six others. (They faced a total of 27 counts of murder and conspiracy.)

Manson described himself as a person who projected onto people what they wanted to see. But most Americans saw him as evil wrapped in lunacy—a madman who represented the darker depths of a permissive youth culture. They looked at him and trembled with horror as to what their country had become. Journalist Steven V. Roberts said the Manson family, as Manson and his followers were called, stoked a fear that "things are out of control; that all the old assumptions and values don't count anymore;" that not only is it true that "the center cannot hold" but also that "the center isn't there anymore."[1] In short, society had become completely unglued; it had become helter-skelter.

MANSON'S REIGN OF TERROR

Charles Manson had a troubled childhood. He was born in 1934, the illegitimate son of a 16-year-old girl who served prison time for robbery. He wound up being raised in a school for boys and by age 13 was deep into a life of crime. He eventually was placed in a high-security prison in Chillicothe, Ohio, and was granted parole in 1954, at age 19.

Crime, however, continued to attract him, and in California, he stole cars, worked as a pimp, and forged checks, leading to yet another arrest. In 1960, he began to serve time at a federal penitentiary in Washington State. While in prison, he became obsessed with a rock-and-roll band, the Beatles, whose songs permeated his thoughts and eventually became entwined in his murder spree. In 1967, the authorities released him.

By then, the hippie counterculture had gained media attention, and Manson started hanging out at Haight-Ashbury, the hippie capital in San Francisco. The district, originally envisioned by its young residents as an alternative society that embraced love and peace in contrast to the cruelties of the mainstream world, had become overrun with drugs, tourists, and con artists. Manson soon found there vulnerable youths who were looking for someone and something to believe in, and through his pseudoreligious babble, spoken among the bell-bottom and love-bead crowd, he put together the Manson family, so tightly under his control that, in time, it would carry out his orders to kill. Consequently, Manson never had to wield a murder weapon against his victims (though he did tie up two of them, Leno LaBianca and his wife).

The family, numbering more than 20, fell victim to Manson's hypnotic ability to break down his followers' values and replace them with his own. Joined together in part by drugs and more so by sex, the Manson family developed a tight bond.

In the early morning of August 9, 1969, four Manson family members—Charles "Tex" Watson, Susan Atkins, Patricia Krenwinkel, and Linda Kasabian—entered a house that was rented by Sharon Tate, a movie actress. Nestled in a secluded canyon, the location behind privacy gates on Cielo Drive provided a stunning view of Los Angeles below and gave Tate the quietude she wanted while avoiding isolation—a neighbor lived just 100 yards away.

Sometime around midnight, the Manson family members entered through the gates and across the property's immaculate green lawn; they shot a teenage boy, Steve Parent, who was on the grounds and had seen them. Then they entered the house and shot, stabbed, and killed Tate, Jay Sebring (an internationally renowned hair stylist), Voytek Frykowski, and Abigail Foster (heiress to a coffee empire), after putting them through sadistic torture, with more than 100 stab wounds. They hanged the pregnant Tate from a rafter before stabbing her to death. The next day, police officers found a gruesome scene, with the word *PIG* scrawled on a wall in blood.

The Manson family—this time Manson, along with Watson, Krenwinkel, and Leslie Van Houten—attacked again the next night. In the early morning hours of August 10 (while three other family members waited in a car), they murdered Leno LaBianca and his wife at their home. He was the president of a Los Angeles supermarket chain. Again, the police found a grisly scene, with the bodies bound and mutilated. Leno LaBianca's body had a fork protruding from it and the word *WAR* carved into its stomach; his wife's body had 41 stab wounds. On a refrigerator door, the phrase *Helter Skelter,* the title of a Beatles song, had been written in blood.

Manson claimed that he wanted people to believe that the murders had been committed by blacks. This, in turn, would lead to a race war. Blacks would win the war, Manson thought, but they would prove to be incapable leaders through their innate inferiority, and he and his followers would then emerge from hiding, take power, persecute blacks, and rule the world.

But in the first attack, Manson may also have acted out of anger because the owner of the Tate house, Terry Melcher, the son of actress Doris Day, had rejected his request to record his music. Manson may possibly have wanted to scare Melcher with the murders.

Manson's arrest caused a nationwide furor, and newspapers portrayed him as a demented hippie. Those references, however, distorted the meaning of *hippie,* making it appear as if some hippies promoted violence. Far from being a hippie, Manson was an incorrigible, disturbed convict, pulled into an alternative social scene that he exploited for his own ends.

Yet a few political radicals contributed to the middle-class dislike for the counterculture by identifying with Manson as a persecuted victim. They believed that his attacks, no matter how much corrupted by a warped political outlook, showed a true commitment to revolution.

At Manson's trial, Deputy District Attorney Vincent T. Bugliosi handled the prosecution. He faced the task of proving that Atkins, Krenwinkel, and Van Houten, all on trial with Manson, had carried out the killings and that Manson had ordered them. Charles "Tex" Watson was tried separately and found guilty of murder and conspiracy to commit murder in the slayings at the Tate and LaBianca homes. Linda Kasabian was granted immunity for her testimony against the family. Bugliosi said about Manson's demeanor: "He frequently played to the always-packed court-room, not only to the Family faithful but to the press and spectators as well. Spotting a pretty girl, he'd often smile or wink. Usually they appeared more flattered than offended."[2] Beneath the smiles, Manson turned out to be unstable; at one point, he lunged at the judge and screamed: "Someone should cut your head off!"[3]

Angered with the way Leslie Van Houten's lawyer, Ronald Hughes, was handling her defense, members of the Manson family kidnapped him and, as later admitted to by one family member, killed him. Although his body went undiscovered until after the trial ended, his disappearance disrupted the proceedings and forced the court to appoint a new defense attorney.

In late January 1971, a jury handed down death sentences for Manson, Atkins, Krenwinkel, and Van Houten, but when the California Supreme Court abolished capital punishment in 1972, the sentences were commuted to life terms. Manson and family members Robert Beausoleil, Charles Watson, Bruce Davis, and Steve Grogan were later tried and convicted for the murders of two other people.

Manson was denied his 10th request for parole in 2002. He said in 1971: "Mr. and Mrs. America—you are wrong. I am not the King of the Jews nor am I a hippie cult leader. I am what you have made me and the mad dog devil killer fiend leper is a reflection of your society. . . . Whatever the outcome of this madness that you call a fair trial or Christian justice, you can know this: In my mind's eye my thoughts light fires in your cities."[4]

VIETNAMIZATION AND THE MY LAI MASSACRE

While the Manson trial unfolded, the Vietnam War continued under President Nixon's Vietnamization plan, intended to turn over more of the fighting to South Vietnam's army. In February, South Vietnamese troops invaded Laos, supported by American air power, with the goal of disrupting communist supply lines that were connected to South Vietnam by capturing the town of Tchepone. This action, the Americans expected, would show the effectiveness of the South Vietnamese army and, by extension, the success of Vietnamization. The invasion, however, failed. North Vietnamese troops routed the South Vietnamese, who, panic-stricken, tried desperately to board American helicopters that had been sent in to evacuate the wounded. Nixon's National Security Advisor, Henry Kissinger, later said that "the operation, conceived in doubt and assailed by skepticism, proceeded in confusion."[5]

The following month, Weatherman, the domestic revolutionary group that was committed to overthrowing the U.S. government, reappeared when it exploded a bomb at the Pentagon. In *Fugitive Days,* Weatherman Bill Ayers describes his own role in the attack. "Everything was absolutely ideal on the day I bombed the Pentagon," he recalls. "The sky was blue. The birds were singing. And the bastards were finally going to get what was coming to them."[6] The bomb, detonated in a toilet, did minimal damage and hurt no one.

To a Weatherman, Vietnam said everything about American oppression. "In that same time, the Pentagon spent millions of dollars and dropped tens of thousands of pounds of explosives on Vietnam, killing or wounding thousands of human beings, causing hundreds of millions of dollars of damage," writes Ayers. "Because nothing justified their actions in our calculus, nothing could contradict the merit of ours."[7]

Henry Kissinger speaks on the phone. *(Courtesy Gerald R. Ford Library)*

That same month, on March 29, a court-martial convicted Lieutenant William Calley, Jr., of premeditated murder in the deaths of 22 men, women, and children at the South Vietnamese hamlet of My Lai. The My Lai Massacre and Calley's ensuing trial, along with accusations and court-martial proceedings against other officers and soldiers, had occupied national attention for nearly three years.

On March 16, 1968, a U.S. army platoon, Charlie Company, led by Calley, entered My Lai, a hamlet of 700 people who lived in red-brick homes and thatch-covered huts. The soldiers in the platoon had previously engaged in beating civilians, burning hamlets, poisoning wells, and raping women. Furthermore, in the brutal guerrilla war between the Americans and their communist enemy, the area around My Lai had been declared a "free-fire zone" by the United States, making all Vietnamese there subject to attack. In addition, American military leaders had established body counts, tallying dead bodies and using the numbers as evidence of progress in the war. This tactic encouraged soldiers to kill noncombatants to show their effectiveness as fighting units.

When Charlie Company entered My Lai, the soldiers were accompanied by an army photographer, Ronald Haberle. He later told how he saw about 30 different GIs kill about 100 civilians and how he tried to take the picture of a five-year-old standing amid the chaos of shots and burning buildings, but before he could do so, the American soldiers killed the child.

A member of Charlie Company recalled: "People began coming out of their hooches and the guys shot them and burned the hooches—or burned the hooches and then shot the people when they came out."[8] One soldier shot at a baby lying on the ground; he missed his target twice but killed the infant with his third shot. Other soldiers raped women. Army helicopter pilot Hugh Thompson reported seeing children being shot at point-blank range.

At one point, the soldiers marched about 80 old men, women, and children to a ditch. Calley ordered his men to push the Vietnamese into it and shoot them. Some of his men refused, but others obeyed. When a two-year-old child tried to run away, Calley grabbed the child, threw him back into the ditch, and shot him. Thompson rescued some of the Vietnamese with his helicopter, including a baby who had been clinging to her dead mother.

By noon, My Lai was no more. The Americans had destroyed it. They killed more than 350 Vietnamese in the hamlet. Twenty months later, army investigators discovered mass graves at the site.

Shaken by the massacre, Hugh Thompson filed a complaint, but the army declared the assault on My Lai a victory and covered up what had happened. (The suppression of evidence was undertaken at every level of command.)

But in March 1969, Ronald Ridenhour, a former GI, investigated stories that he had heard from fellow GIs and sent letters to several members of Congress. An inquiry followed, and that September, the army charged Calley with several crimes, including premeditated murder. Two months later, journalists, led by Seymour Hersh and his Pulitzer Prize winning stories, began to report on My Lai, and *Life* magazine published Haberle's photos.

Ultimately, the army charged 25 officers and enlisted men with crimes. In January 1971, however, it dropped charges against four officers who had been accused of concealing the massacre. That same month, a court-martial cleared a sergeant of intent to kill six civilians in the hamlet. The army eventually dismissed charges against five other soldiers on the grounds of insufficient evidence. When the charges involving the various officers and soldiers were all settled, Lieutenant William Calley was the only one found guilty.

Calley insisted at his court-martial: "I felt then—and still do—that I acted as directed. I carried out my orders, and I did not feel wrong in doing so."[9] His conviction ignited controversy. Both supporters and opponents of the war thought that Calley had been made a scapegoat. The supporters believed that he had been unfairly targeted at a time when excesses had been committed by both sides in combat; in effect, he was a victim of the war's barbarity and only acted in line with its viciousness. The opponents (joined by many of the war's supporters on this point) insisted that Calley had been targeted to let other higher-ranking officers escape punishment.

Calley was sentenced to life imprisonment, but pressure from those who called him a hero led President Nixon to intervene in the case. Nixon was preparing in 1971 to run for reelection and wanted to solidify his conservative base; thus, in what historian William H. Chafe has called a "pernicious appeal to the right," the president ordered Calley released from a military stockade and placed under house arrest at the soldier's apartment at Fort Benning, Georgia.[10] There, Calley watched TV, learned gourmet cooking, and entertained his girlfriend. He was later imprisoned for four months at Fort Leavenworth, Kansas. Meanwhile, he appealed his conviction in the civilian courts, and in September 1974, a federal judge ordered him released because his hearing had been prejudiced by pretrial publicity. On October 30, while an appeals court considered the case, the army paroled Calley, effective November 19, 1974.

Journalist Neil Sheehan, writing in his book *A Bright Shining Lie,* concludes: "The military leaders of the United States, and the civilian leaders who permitted the generals to wage war as they did, had made the massacre inevitable."[11] To that can be added other massacres, as well.

The army called My Lai an aberration, but the army was wrong, for numerous other killings occurred both before and after My Lai. From May through November 1967, Tiger Force, an elite platoon attached to the army's 101st Airborne Division, roamed through Vietnam's Central Highlands, murdering hundreds of civilian men, women, and children. The soldiers mutilated and tortured some of their victims; others they shot while the victims begged for their lives. They collected ears, teeth, and scalps as souvenirs. As with My Lai, the army covered up the atrocities. An investigation that began in 1971 and lasted more than four years led to six suspects resigning from the army but no convictions for war crimes.

One member of Tiger Unit said years later: "The story that I'm not sure is getting out is that while they're saying this was a ruthless band ravaging the countryside, we were under orders to do it."[12] By 1971, government and military leaders knew fully the rampage committed by Tiger Force.

One historian claims: "I can safely, and sadly say, that the Tiger Force atrocities are merely the tip of the iceberg in regard to U.S.-perpetrated war crimes in Vietnam."[13] And David Hackworth, a retired colonel who created Tiger Force in 1965, said in 2003: "Vietnam was an atrocity from the get-go. It was that kind of war, a frontless war of great frustration. It was out of hand very early. There were hundreds of My Lais. You got your card punched by the numbers of bodies you counted."[14]

According to the *New York Times,* besides the My Lai massacre, only 36 cases involving possible war crimes from Vietnam resulted in army court-martial trials, and from those, there resulted only 20 convictions.[15]

In the 1970s, the American public knew little about atrocities in Vietnam beyond My Lai. Yet, the My Lai massacre itself undermined support for the war, for the military, and for the government, and it contributed to the widening lack of faith in the political system that was so characteristic of the decade.

J. Edgar Hoover poses for his official portrait. *(National Archives and Records Administration)*

DOMESTIC SPYING

In a stunning move, on April 5, 1971, longtime Democratic representative Hale Boggs of Louisiana stood on the floor of the House and demanded the resignation of FBI director J. Edgar Hoover. Few politicians had previously challenged Hoover in any way, let alone so forwardly. The 76-year-old director had been in charge of the FBI since 1924. He had made it *his* bureau, a personal fiefdom shaped by him and mythologized by him from the 1930s right into the 1960s when the hit TV show *The FBI* used scripts of which he approved to present his agents, and society, as he preferred them: orderly, white, middle-class, male-dominated. Hoover and the FBI had become inseparable. President Lyndon Johnson even waived a mandatory retirement provision in 1965 that enabled the director to remain in office. During the years, states historian Athan G. Theoharis, "Hoover had enjoyed virtual immunity from criticism and congressional scrutiny."[16]

Although according to Hoover biographer Richard Gid Powers the director was "in less control of the FBI" in the late 1960s, he had accumulated power so vast that it may well have ranked second only to the president of the United States. Hoover, in fact, could break, or at least seriously damage, any politician he wanted. "He's got files on everybody, God damn it," Richard Nixon once said about him with a touch of admiration.[17]

Thus, Boggs entered dangerous terrain with his demand, but he made it because he concluded that Hoover had tapped the telephones of members of Congress and had planted spies on college campuses. His words resonated with other members of Congress who had long chafed under Hoover's power and privately expressed the view that their offices had been bugged by the FBI. Boggs said:

The country cannot survive under a man who in his declining years has violated the Bill of Rights of the United States. . . . In private conversations and communications, numerous members of congress have reported to me their firm conviction that their telephone conversations and activities are the subject of surveillance by the FBI.[18]

His accusation ignited a sharp exchange between the FBI's defenders and attackers:

"[Boggs is] either sick or not in possession of his faculties," said Deputy Attorney General Richard Kleindienst.

"Stolen FBI files have shown us that the agency routinely maintains large and inaccurate dossiers on special groups and individuals . . . whose politics the director finds personally offensive," said congresswoman Bella Abzug (Dem., N.Y.).

"I think there is a good bit of imagination here. If [Boggs] has good substantial bona fide evidence he should reveal it," said Senator Robert C. Byrd (Dem., W.Va.).[19]

Senator Edmund Muskie (Dem., Maine) raised more suspicions about the FBI when he complained about participants in the environmental Earth Day celebration, held in 1970, having been placed under surveillance by government agents. Muskie even displayed an FBI intelligence report to support his accusation. "Is there any political activity in the country which the FBI does not consider a legitimate subject for watching?" he asked.[20]

President Nixon defended Hoover, calling the attacks against him unfair. Vice President Spiro Agnew, usually Nixon's point man, rallied to Hoover's defense. In a long speech (which the White House insisted that it had not cleared), he offered the most likely reason for the attacks on the FBI director: "the fact that he is anathema to the New Left and extremists of every stripe, and he doesn't mince words in calling attention to them as dangerous to the country."[21] Agnew ridiculed the assertion by Senator George McGovern (Dem., S.Dak.) that "virtually every political figure, every student activist, every leader for peace and social justice is under the surveillance of the FBI."[22]

Hoover vehemently denied that any member of Congress had been bugged and "went into a frenzy calling congressional leaders to assure them that [Boggs's] charges were untrue."[23] When Kleindienst asked him if a rogue agent could have done some bugging, Hoover called it unlikely, "although you can't ever tell as we used to have so few employees and now have about 20,000 today, but I seriously doubt it because it would have had to be done by the Washington Field Office and that is under pretty close contact and control here at headquarters because of its location."[24] (In terms of agents, the FBI had 7,600 of them, compared to 441 when Hoover first became director.)

Boggs died in a plane crash in 1972 without substantiating the charges that he had made. Yet, Muskie's and McGovern's portrayal of the FBI as an agency that was deeply involved in illegal taps and in widespread spying on political leaders, activists, and others, proved to be accurate. For one, Boggs possessed dossiers that had been compiled by the FBI on critics of the Warren Commission, the official government group that had investigated the assassination of President John Kennedy (and of which Boggs was a member). The FBI kept a close watch on the political affiliation of the critics; the dossiers "dealt with the left wing organizations these people belonged to."[25]

On a much larger scale, beginning in the mid-1950s and continuing through the 1960s and into 1971, the FBI aimed a powerful secret counterintelligence program, or COINTELPRO, at dissidents—militants, leftists, peace groups, antiwar activists, women's rights advocates, environmentalists, and anyone else who appeared to challenge what the federal government and Hoover deemed to be acceptable ideology and behavior. Hoover founded COINTELPRO and staffed it with 2,000 FBI agents. Working undercover, they infiltrated groups and even incited some of them to commit criminal acts. COINTELPRO agents neither minced words nor restrained their actions in using numerous dirty tricks, such as leaking false information to newspapers (what it called disinformation) and breaking into homes and offices. "As it blocked dissidents from speaking, turned them against one another, and used rumor and slander to discredit them and their causes," Richard Gid Powers writes in *Secrecy and Power*, "the Bureau attempted to restrict the political choices available to Americans."[26]

Although few Americans in the 1960s knew about COINTELPRO, activists suspected its existence. The actions by COINTELPRO were joined by other government undercover activities that were conducted by army intelligence and also the CIA, through its illegal domestic spy program called Operation Chaos.

When Boggs, Muskie, and McGovern leveled their charges, they helped to unravel the secrecy surrounding the government's domestic spying. In 1975, a Senate committee, led by Idaho Democrat Frank Church, exposed the excesses and abuses committed by the FBI and other government agencies in the name of national security. The startling revelations coalesced with the deceit that was used in fighting the war in Vietnam and with the lies that were involved in Watergate (which began to appear as a major story in 1973) to undermine public faith in the government.

PROTESTS IN WASHINGTON, D.C., AND CALIFORNIA

Wearing their military uniforms and medals, members of Vietnam Veterans Against the War came to Washington, D.C., from as far away as California. About 1,000 of these committed dissidents met at Arlington National Cemetery and then marched to the White House and on to the Capitol, where they gathered on the west lawn.

Thus, on April 19, they began a week of protest, adding their distinction as former soldiers to the previous demonstrations by people from other walks of life. There ensued a legal battle when the Justice Department sought to prevent the veterans from camping out on the Mall, only to be rebuked by a federal judge. It was, in fact, a sensitive situation for the Nixon administration because some of the veterans were crippled from their war wounds, a few were even in wheelchairs, and any attempt to break up the protest would likely generate more sympathy for the dissidents and lead to severe criticism of the president. Consequently, when about 100 veterans were arrested for demonstrating on the steps of the Supreme Court building and charged with obstructing justice, the government intervened to have the charges reduced.

On April 23, the chief spokesperson for the protesters, John Kerry, a former naval officer (later a U.S. senator from Massachusetts and, in 2004, the presidential nominee of the Democratic Party), appeared before the Senate Foreign Relations Committee. Wearing his uniform and his medals (three Purple Hearts, a Bronze Star, and a Silver Star), he condemned the war and Nixon's policy of gradually withdrawing from it. He wanted a more rapid end to the fighting, and he criticized the senators for failing to take a firm stand to bring that about. "How do you ask a man to be the last to die in Vietnam?" he said. "How do you ask a man to be the last to die for a mistake?"[27]

A founder of the Vietnam Veterans Against the War, Jan Barry, expressed in an article the frustration and anger among his colleagues. He said:

> We were not prepared to go to Vietnam to uphold a tragicomic (but nonetheless sickening) series of warlord dictatorships. . . . Nevertheless, many of us did. Now every last one of us is guilty, along with Calley, of committing war crimes. Because a "free-fire zone"—where anything that moves can be shot—is by definition a violation of the Geneva Convention of 1949 with respect to the treatment of civilians; because a "search-and-destroy mission"—where anything living is destroyed or removed—is also a violation of the Geneva Conventions; because massive defoliation, "recon by fire," saturation bombing, "mad minutes," and forcibly relocating villagers are all violations of international law, and therefore, war crimes.[28]

On April 23, about 700 veterans marched solemnly in front of the Capitol and threw away their medals. Purple Hearts and Silver Stars lay on the ground. Many of them had been given to the veterans by the parents of dead soldiers.

During the last days of April, Washington became a city under siege by protesters, mainly antiwar activists, but also others who demanded civil rights legislation, welfare reform, and women's liberation. On April 24, thousands of protesters staged a huge but peaceful antiwar rally. Then several hundred dissidents undertook an unauthorized march to the White House. In a show of civil disobedience, others crowded the sidewalk in front of the Selective Service building. On April 30, members of the Peoples' Coalition for Peace and Justice blocked the entrance to the Justice Department, and the police arrested them.

An increasingly tense and confrontational atmosphere overtook the city. The dissidents expected support from workers in the bureaucracy but usually received only derisive epithets. On May 1, about 50,000 protesters showed up for an antiwar rally, a number that surprised officials who expected a much smaller turnout, and who now felt that the situation might get out of hand.

The following day, the police decided to revoke a permit that they had granted for protesters to encamp along the Potomac River; instead, they forced them to disperse. The 30,000 or so dissidents stumbled in an early morning daze from their tents and sleeping bags as police rousted them. Most decided to leave the grounds, but a few subjected themselves to arrest. When some of them staged a march, the police charged into them and without provocation brandished their nightsticks.

The chief of police later said that the protesters had to be removed because their actions during the previous few days had become more violent. Indeed, there circulated among the dissidents literature calling for the use of force. Protest leaders, however, including Rennie Davis of Chicago Seven fame, insisted that it was the Nixon administration with its police-state tactics that was discrediting those who preferred peace. Ratcheting up the tension, the government sent federal troops into the city, including a convoy of more than 50 trucks carrying soldiers from the Sixth Armored Calvary.

On May 3, the May Day Tribe tried to disrupt the federal government by barricading streets and preventing workers from arriving at their jobs. Battles broke out between the protesters and the police, and 7,000 of the tribe were arrested and held behind wire fences at a temporary restraining center located near Robert F. Kennedy Stadium. (A few hundred others were held indoors at the Washington Coliseum.) The mass arrests and the show of force by the police kept the protesters from office buildings, and the May Day Tribe failed to shut down the government. Tear gas, however, drifted along streets, debris slowed traffic, and, in general, the city struggled to function.

On May 4, thousands more demonstrators gathered outside the Justice Department. With Attorney General John Mitchell looking from a balcony above, puffing on a pipe like an unfazed potentate, the police again resorted to arrests. The following day, May 5, protesters rallied near the Capitol steps and called for a peace treaty with communist North Vietnam. Moreover, they wanted the release in the United States of all political prisoners.

The arrests from the several days of protests totaled about 12,000, but May 5 brought a reprimand from a three-judge panel of the Court of Appeals. The police, the judges ruled, had acted wrongfully when they arrested protesters en masse without charging each one with specific illegal acts.

John Mitchell likened the protesters to Nazi Brown Shirts; those who took to the streets in the footsteps of the Vietnam Veterans Against the War, he claimed, had connections to communists. Much of the protest leadership, he said, and much of the money for the demonstrations came from the Reds. One public poll conducted by the Opinion Research Corporation of Princeton, New Jersey, found widespread support in the nation for the police crackdown; fully 76 percent called the arrests of the more than 12,000 protesters "justified." As it turned out, the government obtained only 63 guilty verdicts from the thousands they had charged with crimes.

A different protest ended on June 14, when 15 Native Americans vacated Alcatraz Island in California. Nearly two years before, 80 Indians had taken over the site, formerly the location of a federal prison, basing their action on an old treaty whose provisions gave the Sioux (Dakota, Lakota, Nakota) tribe the right to claim unused federal land. They wanted the U.S. government to surrender Alcatraz and provide money for an Indian cultural center.

In response to the protest, newspapers and magazines around the country ran stories detailing life on Indian reservations, where unemployment exceeded 50 percent, most people lacked running water, and disease and alcoholism ran rampant. The Indians who occupied Alcatraz drew the connection between their actions and conditions elsewhere, when, with a touch of satire, they said that the island fortress resembled most reservations in its isolation, inadequate sanitation facilities, unemployment, nonproductive land, and lack of schools. Further, they said those who had once lived there had "always been prisoners and kept dependent on others."[29] In taking over the island, the Indians displayed a banner bearing a broken peace pipe on a field of blue. With their evacuation, their objective remained unfulfilled, and the peace pipe remained broken.

STATE SECRETS AND PUBLIC CONTROVERSY

When it came to Vietnam, Daniel Ellsberg was at first a hawk. In 1959, he joined the RAND Corporation, a prestigious, California-based think tank. In the mid-1960s, he began to work for the federal government on the staff of the assistant secretary of defense for international security affairs. There, he helped to shape President Lyndon Johnson's decision to escalate the American military fight in Southeast Asia.

But he grew disillusioned with the civilian deaths in Vietnam and with the corrupt South Vietnamese government. Then, in 1967, Secretary of Defense Robert S. McNamara requested an official history of the Vietnam War, and Ellsberg joined a team of 30 to 40 civilian and military analysts in compiling one. They worked for a year in an office next to McNamara's, poring over documents that were in part provided through the defense secretary's connections. As Ellsberg dug into the past, his findings only deepened his disillusionment. American entry into the war, he concluded, had resulted from excessive presidential power and devious tactics.

In 1969, Ellsberg decided to convince government leaders that the United States should withdraw its troops. For the most part, the leaders resisted. Consequently, he made a monumental decision in 1971: He would photocopy the written history on which he had been working, soon called the *Pentagon Papers,* and leak it to the *New York Times.* He did so at great personal risk, for the government had labeled the *Papers* "top secret."

The *Times* published the first excerpts from the *Pentagon Papers* on June 13 in what *Time* magazine called a "sensational affair" that "began quietly with the dull thud of the 486-page [newspaper] arriving on doorsteps and in newsrooms."[30]

In their entirety, the *Papers*—some 40 volumes in all—comprised 3,000 pages of analysis and 4,000 pages of supporting documents, including cablegrams, memorandums, and draft proposals. The account covered U.S. policy in Southeast Asia from near the end of World War II to the late 1960s. In publishing the secret history, the *Times* cautioned its readers about the report's many gaps, a result of the researchers having been unable to access certain documents, such as confidential presidential material.

The *Papers* revealed the nearly constant drumbeat of the domino theory as a rationale that had been given to the public for the war, the belief that if South Vietnam fell to the Communists, all of Southeast Asia would fall and perhaps other regions too. Ellsberg and the research staff presented evidence of internal debates within the government about policy in Vietnam, and they showed how some policymakers worried about dissent within the United States. Writing in the spring of 1967, Assistant Secretary of Defense John T. McNaughton said: "The feeling is that we are trying to impose some U.S. image on distant peoples we cannot understand (anymore than we can the younger generation here at home), and that we are carrying the thing to absurd lengths. Related to this feeling is the increased polarization that is taking place in the United States with the seeds of the worst split in our people in more than a century."[31]

The decision by the *New York Times* to publish the *Pentagon Papers* polarized the nation even more. Attorney General John Mitchell issued a warning: If the *Times* continued to print the secret history, it would cause "irreparable injury to the defense of the United States."[32] The Nixon administration subsequently obtained an injunction to prevent further publication, the first time the government had sought such a measure based on "national security." The effort to impose censorship of a news story prior to its appearance was interpreted by many observers as a grave threat to the First Amendment freedom of the press.

A debate erupted between those supporting the government and those supporting the *Times*. On the one side:

"The government of the United States is treading upon the most dangerous of grounds in taking legal action to prevent publication of information by The New York Times," said the Associated Press Managing Editors Association in a letter. "Once information has been made available to editors, through whatever means, and they have had opportunity to judge it as not being crucial to security, it becomes their responsibility to resist . . . any attempt to interfere with their constitutional responsibility to publish that information for their readers."

"[The government's] action might, indeed, herald the end of American civil liberties," said a group of nine college newspaper editors and officials.

On the other side:

"The New York Times should be brought immediately to account [for their action]," said H. R. Rainwater, the national commander of the Veterans of Foreign Wars. "If there was no contingency plan on the war, then everyone in the Pentagon would be wrong. There must be a contingency plan, and that's the plan the *New York Times* is trying to reveal while we are in the middle of a war. It's very close to the thin edge of treason, if not treason itself."[33]

The *Times* published the secret history for three days before the federal courts issued restraining orders and halted the printing; shortly thereafter, other restraining orders stopped the *Washington Post* and the *Boston Globe* from printing the *Papers*. While legal hearings continued, the FBI issued an arrest warrant for Daniel Ellsberg, charging him with "unauthorized possession of top-secret documents" and failing to return them.

The Supreme Court dealt the Nixon administration a severe defeat on June 30 when it ruled, 6-3, that the government could not block publication of the *Pentagon Papers*. According to the court majority, the First Amendment placed a burden on the government to prove that extremely extenuating circumstances warranted prior censorship. The government, the majority said, had failed to meet such a standard.

The justices grouped themselves in three blocks for the decision. Three of them thought that the government had absolutely no authority to prevent prior publication under any circumstances; three of them thought that the government could prevent publication but only where the information involved presented dire harm to the nation's security; the three dissenting justices thought that the executive branch should be able to determine when such harm existed, and they said that the publication of the *Pentagon Papers* had presented such a threat.

At the end of its nine-part *Pentagon Papers* series, the *New York Times* concluded:

> The public claim that the United States was only assisting a beleaguered ally who really had to win his own battle was never more than a slogan. South Vietnam was essentially the creation of the United States. The American leaders . . . hired agents, spies, generals, and presidents where they could find them in Indochina. They thought and wrote of them in almost proprietary terms as instruments of American policy. Ineluctably, the fortunes of these distant, often petty men became in their minds indistinguishable from the fortunes of the United States.[34]

As for Daniel Ellsberg, in 1973, a judge dismissed all the charges against him because the government had engaged in duplicitous acts: Ellsberg's phone had been illegally wiretapped, the office of his former psychiatrist had been burgled by secret agents, and the judge himself had been offered the directorship of the FBI in an attempt by President Nixon to affect the outcome of the trial.

The controversy over the publication of the *Pentagon Papers* and the content of the secret history itself further undermined the public's confidence in the government and in the country's political leaders. Perhaps Nixon's chief of staff, H. R. Haldeman, grasped this meaning when, amid the airing of the *Papers,* he said to the president: "Out of the gobbledygook comes a very clear thing: . . . you can't trust the government; you can't believe what they say; and you can't rely on their judgment; and . . . the implicit infallibility of presidents, which has been an accepted thing in America, is badly hurt by this because it shows that people do things the president wants to do even though it's wrong, and the president can be wrong."[35]

CHINA RECONSIDERED

An unexpected turn in America's relationship with communism began on April 10, 1971, when, at the invitation of the Chinese government, nine American Ping-Pong players arrived in Beijing to play several exhibition matches against Chinese opponents. On April 14, Premier Zhou Enlai (Chou Enlai) met with the Americans. Taken together, the games and the meeting signaled a thawing of relations between the United States and China.

The thaw deepened on April 26, when a report commissioned by President Nixon recommended that Communist China be admitted into the United Nations. For years, the United States had prevented China's admission. Nixon himself had been a strident critic of Communist China throughout his political career and had stood firmly against allowing it into the UN.

The Ping-Pong games and the report set the stage for a stunning announcement by President Nixon on July 15: He would travel to Communist China in 1972 to meet its leaders. Numerous conservatives denounced him for going soft on communism, but Democratic and Republican congressional leaders praised his plan.

JESSE JACKSON AND PUSH

In 1971, civil rights advocate Jesse Jackson founded People United to Save Humanity (PUSH) to overcome racial and ethnic barriers and advance civil rights and opportunities for an array of disadvantaged people.

In the late 1960s, Jackson emerged as a leading figure in Dr. Martin Luther King, Jr.'s, Southern Christian Leadership Conference (SCLC). Soon after, on April 4, 1968, a gunman assassinated King as he stood on a balcony at the Lorraine Hotel in Memphis, Tennessee. Jackson said that on that tragic day, he held King in his arms and heard his last words as the fallen leader's blood stained his shirt. Others disputed the account and said that Jackson exaggerated the story to make it appear as if the SCLC leadership should be handed to him.

Although Ralph Abernathy, rather than Jackson, became the group's new leader, Jackson, who was ordained a Baptist minister in 1968, continued to work for the SCLC. At the same time, in 1969 and 1970, he led marches on the Illinois state capital at Springfield to demand programs to help fight hunger. The legislature subsequently agreed to fund school lunch programs. When Chicago mayor Richard Daley resisted Jackson's reform efforts, Jackson decided to unseat him, and in 1971, he ran for mayor. Jackson lost, but his campaign may have paved the way for the city to elect its first black mayor in 1983, when Harold Washington won the office. Moreover, Jackson's defeat made it possible for Jackson to devote his efforts to Operation PUSH.

As tension mounted within the SCLC between Jackson and Abernathy, and as some SCLC staffers criticized Jackson for being overly aggressive and antagonistic, he quit the organization in 1971 and founded PUSH. Jackson was proud of his heritage, which was one of black blood mixed with Cherokee and Irish, and he intended PUSH to help people of many different colors and nationalities, though it focused on African Americans. In the early 1970s, he obtained agreements with Burger King and Kentucky Fried Chicken to employ more blacks. Soon, other companies signed similar agreements, and PUSH chapters appeared in several cities.

In the mid-1970s, Jackson established PUSH EXCEL to encourage minority students to stay in school. He said in 1976 that African Americans needed to accept a larger share of responsibility for their lives and to rebuild their communities with "moral authority." He called on parents, teachers, superintendents, and school boards to impose more discipline among young African Americans to assure their success.

TIME TO DIE

Violence at a prison near Buffalo, New York, at the town of Attica—where dairy farms, open fields, and verdant hills melted into a square of 30-feet-high, six-feet-thick concrete walls and turrets—reminded Americans that the turmoil born of the 1960s still pulsated in the 1970s. In fact, the trouble at the Attica State Penitentiary, a 40-year-old maximum-security prison, showed how even inmates were influenced by the social upheaval.

Conditions at Attica had bred anger among the prisoners. As the prison became overcrowded, the predominantly African-American and Puerto Rican population felt degraded. They complained about poor food, cramped housing, and cruel guards.

Then, on the morning of September 9, the guards hauled to isolation cells two inmates involved in a fight. Some prisoners thought the two inmates were being tortured, and the anger in the penitentiary escalated. The following day a group of prisoners attacked several guards with iron pipes, chains, and baseball bats. One of the injured guards died a couple of days later from injuries suffered when he had been thrown from a window.

The ranks of the rioters quickly grew to more than 1,000. They gained control of the prison, smashed furniture and windows, and set fire to six buildings, including the school, a metalworking shop, and the chapel. Later in the day, state police forced the inmates to retreat, but they still held some of the cellblocks, along with 40 hostages, a leverage they used to made demands. Those ranged from realistic to preposterous (or some might say, 1960s-style outrageous) and included an end to censorship of reading materials; more recreation and less cell time; better doctors; religious freedom; the firing of the prison superintendent; complete amnesty; and speedy and safe transportation to a "non-imperialistic country."

Leaders for the inmates began to negotiate with state officials, including State Corrections Commissioner Russell G. Oswald, whom they distrusted. The inmates demanded that they be allowed to meet with several people of their own choosing, among them William M. Kunstler, the lawyer who defended the Chicago Seven, and Bobby Seale, chairman of the Black Panther Party. State officials allowed Kunstler into the cellblocks, but they barred Seale's entry.

With the hostages still being held (the number fluctuated due to releases and the discovery by the prisoners of other guards in hiding), and a gloomy, intermittently heavy rain moving across the hills, the talks continued. At the same time, state troopers fired tear gas into one of the captured cellblocks. State officials eventually agreed to many of the inmates' demands, but they adamantly refused to grant a full amnesty from criminal prosecution for the rioters or to fire the prison superintendent. The inmates wanted Governor Nelson Rockefeller to meet with them at Attica, but he refused. "I do not feel that my physical presence on the site can contribute to a peaceful settlement," Rockefeller said.[36]

An observer committee appointed to oversee the negotiations said the governor's refusal to appear could bring greater trouble. The prisoners and the hostages, they warned, might be massacred.

Such fears soon came to pass. Oswald wanted further negotiations on neutral ground and not within the prison. For the inmates, it was an impossible condition: If they left the prison, they would expose themselves to arrest. Rockefeller remained adamant about his decision to stay away from Attica, and the inmates interpreted his stand as a sign that he considered them unimportant.

On the morning of September 13, state troopers assaulted Attica with tear gas dropped from helicopters, along with a barrage of gun fire. Troopers on the ground encountered trenches filled with burning gasoline, and they dodged booby traps and Molotov cocktails. "Place your hands on top of your head . . .," boomed a loudspeaker from one of the helicopters circling above. "Do not harm the hostages. Surrender peacefully. Sit or lie down. You will not be harmed. Repeat, you will not be harmed."[37] The shooting continued. "You murdering bastards," William Kunstler said to one guard, and then in reference to the assault by the troopers: "They're shooting them. They're murdering them."[38]

The assault resulted in the deaths of 32 inmates and nine guards and civilian employees. The authorities reported a gruesome scene: Some of the guards had been beaten to death, others had their throats cut by the inmates.

Medical examiners, however, reported that the hostages had died not from beatings or from cut throats but from gunshot wounds that had been fired, as it turned out, from imprecise shotguns. "Some were shot once; some as many as five, 10, 12 times," reported one medical examiner.[39] He did say that the guards had been beaten and that their hands had been tied behind their backs.

The hostages had, in fact, been killed by the state troopers. (None of the rioting inmates had guns.) A relative of one of the dead guards blamed Governor Rockefeller for the bloodshed. The governor, however, defended himself against his critics. "There was no alternative but to go in," he insisted.[40] In agreeing to many of the inmates' demands, he said, the state had committed itself to substantial reform at the prison. He called the other demands unrealistic and reiterated that it would have been futile for him to attend the negotiations. The governor insisted the state troopers had done a "superb job."

Inmates at the Attica State Correctional Facility in Attica, New York, raise their fists in a sign of solidarity for their demands and their ongoing protest. (© Bettmann/Corbis)

Rockefeller blamed the uprising on revolutionaries among the inmates. He claimed that if he had conceded anything more, he would have sent a message to radicals both inside and outside of prisons that they could succeed through violence.

In the aftermath of the riot, guards at Attica forced inmates there to strip and then beat them with clubs in the prison yard. They tortured one of the rebellion's leaders.

In 1972, an investigative commission criticized Rockefeller. The assault by the state troopers, the commission said, had been poorly planned, poorly executed, and likely to have been unnecessary, and in staying away from Attica, the governor had shirked his responsibilities. The commission said that he should have been "present at the scene of the critical decision involving great risk of loss of life."[41]

Back in September 1971, a member of the crisis observer team, state representative Herman Badillo, said: "We wanted the governor to come [to the prison] to talk with us to get the benefit of our experience before he made a final and irrevocable decision. As far as I'm concerned, there's always time to die."[42]

ECONOMIC WOES

Throughout most of the post–World War II era, Americans had been accustomed to economic growth. From 1945 through the 1960s, the Gross National Product increased more than 100 percent, and in the 1960s, unemployment dipped to 4 percent while inflation remained under control.

But President Lyndon Johnson had insisted on fighting the Vietnam War without raising taxes, and, in July 1971, President Richard Nixon announced one of the highest budget deficits ever: $23.2 billion, a revelation that mocked the prediction made 18 months earlier of a modest budget surplus. One analyst said the entire country was paying heavily in inflated dollars "for the Johnson Administration's reluctance to properly fund the Vietnam War."[43]

The fiscal deficits weakened the dollar and came amid unusual trade deficits and a slide in the stock market. At the same time, previously high consumer spending caused the inflation rate to hit 4.5 percent, and unemployment reached 6 percent, presenting a disturbing combination of higher prices and dwindling jobs.

On August 15, President Nixon addressed these problems by taking measures to strengthen the dollar and reduce federal spending and by asking Congress to cut taxes. Most notable, however, was his imposition of a 90-day freeze on wages and prices to be supervised by a Cost of Living Council. Nixon had previously ignored calls for a freeze from congressional critics, led by Democrats, so his turnabout caught people by surprise. "We must create more and better jobs," Nixon said. "We must stop the rise in the cost of living; we must protect the dollar from the attacks of international money speculators."[44]

Congressional leaders generally supported Nixon's proposals:

"The measures to bolster the dollar are particularly gratifying to me," said Senator Jacob Javits (Rep., N.Y.). "I expect to be able to support the president in most of his recommendations."

"The President has not only changed his game plan, but he has also reversed his field," said Senator William Proxmire (Dem., Wis.). "I support his program."

"I am delighted that his patience has finally run out," said Senator Mike Mansfield (Dem., Mont.) about the president's policy reversal.[45]

Nixon followed his August decision with "phase two" of his "economic stabilization program" that he announced in October. He proposed, and Congress eventually approved, several supervisory agencies under the aegis of the Cost of Living Council to review wage and price increases to protect against inflation. Nixon wanted to more than halve the existing inflation rate and to move the country from a freeze to a restraint while deflating the psychology of inflation. In time, his policies failed; during the 1970s, the United States sank into greater economic troubles.

WOMEN'S RIGHTS

In 1971, women continued their fight for equal rights by breaking through the barriers that were intended to keep them from holding political office. The credit for much of this effort went to the National Women's Political Caucus (NWPC), which was founded in July largely by members of the National Organization for Women (NOW) but inclusive of other activists. Among NWPC's members were United Auto Workers organizer Olga Madur, civil rights leader Fannie Lou Hamer, and Elly Peterson of the Republican National Committee.

Prior to the formation of NWPC, the vast majority of activist Republican and Democratic women held only low-level positions in their parties. NWPC dedicated itself to providing publicity, organizational support, and money to elect to office women who embraced equal pay, the ERA, prochoice, an end to the war in Vietnam, environmental reform, and measures to improve income for the poor. The creation of the Women's Campaign Fund in 1974 especially boosted the moneys needed to back such candidates.

Throughout the 1970s, more women won prominent political positions. The Democratic Party acceded to demands by the NWPC and promoted gender equality within its ranks to the point that, whereas in 1968 women held 13 percent of the seats at the national convention, they held 40 percent of the 1972 national convention seats. Furthermore, a woman, Jean Westwood, became chair of the Democratic National Committee. Similar changes occurred in the Republican Party where women's share of convention seats went from 17 percent in 1968 to 30 percent in 1972. Many of those who became convention delegates benefited from educational meetings held by the NWPC around the country with the goal of making women better informed than their male counterparts.

At the same time, women's share of local offices and the seats they held in state legislatures more than doubled. Two women won governorships: Ella Grasso in Connecticut and Dixie Lee Ray in Washington, both without having to rely on taking over offices vacated by dead husbands, the more traditional route for the few women who held public office previously. Mary Anne Krupsak won the lieutenant governorship in New York with the slogan "She's Not One of the Boys," and Bella Abzug won a congressional seat from the same state.

Jane Byrne became mayor of Chicago as a Democrat, and Kathy Whitmire became mayor of Houston as a Republican. Although the number of women in Congress remained small, they nevertheless helped call national attention to sex discrimination and promoted legislation to correct such abuses.

As women fought to obtain their rights, opponents charged them with being too masculine and even lesbian. Many men admired assertiveness in men; they disdained it in women, and so labeled it an aberrant behavior. The charges of lesbianism caused NOW to distance itself from those women fighting for lesbian rights. That action, in turn, caused a group of lesbian feminists in 1971 to split from NOW.

These lesbians and many others in the 1970s identified less with the gay rights movement and more with the feminist movement. To them, lesbianism was not so much a sexual declaration as it was a declaration of pure feminine identity; that is, it represented women who relied only on other women for their identity rather than on men or on institutions that had been shaped by men.

This was expressed by the radical lesbians who left NOW when, at about the time of their departure, they issued an essay titled "The Woman-Identified Woman." In it, they said that "As long as woman's liberation tries to free women without facing the basic heterosexual

In 1970, Bella Abzug won election to Congress as a Democrat from New York. She was among the strongest advocates for women's rights and was an ardent promoter of the Equal Rights Amendment (ERA), as evident by the slogan she scrawled on this photograph shortly after it was taken. *(Library of Congress)*

structure that binds us in one-to-one relationship with our oppressors, tremendous energies will continue to flow into trying to straighten up each particular relationship with a man, into finding how to get better sex, how to turn his head around—into trying to make the 'new man' out of him, in the delusion that this will allow us to be the 'new woman.' "This, they claimed, would split women's "energies and commitments." Women must realize that "It is the primacy of women relating to women, of women creating a new consciousness of and with each other, which is at the heart of women's liberation, and the basis for the cultural revolution."[46]

TO THE MOON . . . TWICE

America's economy remained vigorous enough and its people determined enough to continue the country's manned exploration of the Moon. On January 31, astronauts Edgar D. Mitchell, Stuart A. Roosa, and Alan B. Shepard, Jr., blasted off from Cape Kennedy, Florida. Their Saturn 5 rocket cut into a sky pockmarked with storm clouds and headed for the Moon on the *Apollo 14* mission, budgeted at $400 million. Vice President Spiro Agnew, National Security Advisor Henry Kissinger, Prince Juan Carlos and Princess Sophia of Spain, and Neil Armstrong, the first man to set foot on the Moon during the *Apollo 11* flight in 1969, watched the launch from a spectator's stand. Three hours later, a serious problem arose: The command module encountered difficulties linking with the lunar module. "We're unable to get capture," reported commander Mitchell. The astronauts struggled for two hours to complete the procedure and narrowly avoided causing damage to the docking ring that would have made a lunar landing impossible.

Shepard and Mitchell set down their craft on the Moon five days later in a valley in the Fra Mauro highlands, whose mountains reached 8,000 feet. Scientists had chosen the crater-strewn site because they believed that it contained rocks that were 4.6 billion years old, as old as the Moon itself.

The astronauts made two moonwalks. On the first walk, they collected rocks and soil (part of the 108 pounds for the mission as a whole) and set up a seismograph to record moon quakes and a small nuclear-powered station to conduct scientific experiments. On the second walk, they planned to journey to Cone Crater but failed to find it. The crater's ridges melted into the Moon's grey sameness and undulating surface. Mitchell later described the scene as "a cold black sky" with extremely "sharp horizons" amid desolate, stark, but also magnificent terrain. Shepard and Mitchell spent about nine hours on the Moon, considerably more than the two-and-a-half hours spent by the *Apollo 11* astronauts. The Apollo mission ended on February 9, when the capsule carrying the three astronauts splashed into the Pacific.

On July 29, the *Apollo 15* astronauts—David R. Scott, James B. Irwin, and Alfred Worden—began to orbit the Moon in their vehicle *Endeavour* as they prepared for a lunar landing. The following day, Scott and Irwin embarked on a three-day stay on the Moon's surface. In July 31, they used a lunar rover, resembling a beach buggy, to explore near the Apennine Mountains.

By the time the astronauts returned to Earth on August 7, scientists connected to the mission were calling it "man's greatest hours in the field of exploration" and describing it as one of the most productive scientific expeditions ever.[47] The

Astronaut Jim Irwin sets up the first lunar roving vehicle to be used on the Moon. *(National Space Science Data Center)*

astronauts brought back with them about 175 pounds of moon rocks and soil. They had taken photos of canyon walls to gain important clues about the Moon's formation and had planted numerous scientific instruments on the surface. Additionally, *Endeavour* dispensed a small satellite in lunar orbit to record information about the Moon's gravitational and magnetic fields. The mission had been nearly flawless, except for the failure of one of *Endeavour's* landing parachutes to open.

TELEVISION CHANGED

On January 12, 1971, the television sitcom, and television in general, experienced an unprecedented assault on its formulaic shows when *All in the Family* premiered on the CBS network. The show intruded on such escapist fluff as *Petticoat Junction; Gomer Pyle, U. S. M. C.;* and *Green Acres.* (These shows all aired on CBS, earning the network a reputation for rural, some said hayseed, humor.)

Created and produced by Norman Lear, *All in the Family* dove into topical political and social issues and used language previously unheard on TV. The impact was perhaps even greater than what we might imagine today because television then consisted almost exclusively of the three major networks (ABC, CBS, and NBC). There were few independent stations (especially outside major cities), and cable broadcasts were limited.

The show's story line revolved around a family that is torn by conflict between a middle-aged father, Archie Bunker (played by Carroll O'Connor), and his son-in-law, Mike Stivic (played by Rob Reiner). Mike, an antiwar college student (and later teacher) who hated Richard Nixon, did battle with Archie, a conservative and bigoted blue-collar worker. Caught in between the warring sides were Mike's wife, Gloria (played by Sally Struthers), and Archie's wife, Edith (played by Jean Stapleton). Struthers was torn between her love for Mike and her general agreement with his views and her love for her father. Archie often ridiculed Edith for being scatterbrained, or, as he put it, a "dingbat." But Edith loved her entire family, could never do anyone any harm, and through her compassion and insight kept the family united. She even grew as women's liberation grew and, although still shaped by her upbringing in a traditional world which said that the wife should obey her husband, Edith showed moments of independence from Archie.

All in the Family broke with the prevailing mainstream comedies where the father of the family was all-knowing, or at least the commanding voice around the hearth. As Archie struggled to make a living in a society that was undergoing deep social change and economic stress, the program presented his frailties and prejudices, those of the other characters, and, by reflection, America itself in a sharply humorous way.

Archie used words previously banned by network censors, such as *spade, spic,* and *hebe.* The show covered controversial topics, even flash points for the cultural and political wars that were emerging between the right and the left, topics such as race, Watergate, homosexuality, and abortion. *All in the Family* paved the way for other shows to present topical comedy and explore the edge of acceptable TV behavior.

Yet another show changed television in 1971: *Soul Train,* a syndicated black dance program. To a certain extent, it resembled *American Bandstand.* But where *Bandstand* presented mainly white teens dancing to rock music in a strict dress-code environment, *Soul Train* let its teens wear what they wanted, and it followed black standards in a standardized white world. "At the beginning we were determined that if *American Bandstand* was going right, we would go left," said the show's founder, Don Cornelius.[48] In short, the show tapped into black soul and garnered a fervent audience of young African Americans who tuned in for the latest dance moves and songs by black artists.

A BOXING HERO BLOODIED

Many blacks looked up to the boxer Muhammad Ali as a hero, someone who ruled his sport while defying white authority. Ali dominated professional boxing by floating, as he said, like a butterfly and stinging like a bee. But on March 8, 1971, Ali, who was trying to win back the world heavyweight title, which had been stripped from him when he defied the military draft, fell to the canvas and to defeat at the hands of Joe Frazier in a 15-round decision at New York's Madison Square Garden.

Ali's jaw was swollen so much from Frazier's fists that it had to be x-rayed at a hospital. Ali had predicted that Frazier's end would come in the sixth round. But the sixth round came and went, and Frazier remained standing; he even began to taunt Ali with his body, leaving it, at times, unprotected to receive Ali's blows as if to say that they meant nothing and that he could take anything.

"Ali, Ali," and "Joe, Joe," the crowd of 20,455 chanted alternately. In the 15th round, Frazier landed the blow that sent Ali momentarily, and dazedly, to the canvas, only the third time Ali had been knocked down in 10 years of professional fighting. "When I heard the decision I had no feeling," Ali said the following day. "Just go home, we lost, that's all." [49]

JIM MORRISON'S DEATH

In rock music, Jim Morrison and the Doors tied many of their songs to the themes of psychological neuroses and death. Morrison's own neuroses led to self-destructive behavior, and his death, attributed to "natural causes," may well have resulted from his alcoholism.

The Doors emerged as a psychedelic band that was tied to dark themes and deep introspection, and, beginning with their first album in 1967, they attracted a large following. Critics parsed the meanings of their songs while teenagers screeched at Morrison's leather-clad figure. Morrison adopted shamanistic tendencies, and in the 1968 album *Waiting for the Sun* presented himself as the Lizard King.

By 1971, Morrison was emotionally drained and decimated by drugs and alcohol. He took a leave from the band and traveled to Paris. There, he and his wife lived in seclusion. Despite his attempt to reinvigorate himself, he died on July 3.

In the years following, and most especially in the 1980s and 1990s, a Morrison cult emerged, propelled by strange circumstances surrounding his death. Rumors spread that he had never died, that he had instead followed his long-expressed desire to drop out of society, assumed a new identity, and started life over. His biographers state in *No One Here Gets Out Alive:* "He was gripped by the fact that [the writer Arthur] Rimbaud had written all of his poetry by the age of nineteen and then disappeared into North Africa." [59]

NEW RECREATION

For years, South Florida tourism officials had dreaded the opening of Disney World in Orlando. They feared that visitors who had once trekked to the sun-baked beaches around Miami and Fort Lauderdale would bypass them to take their families to the grandiose amusement park, built at a cost of $400 million and sprawled across 100 acres. The *New York Times* reported:

> The stirrings of dust from the rising Disney World have made the past year a period of serious introspection and some worry 230 miles to the south in the established resort world of Miami, Miami Beach, and all the other resort communities in southern Florida and on both the peninsula's east and west coasts. The question: what will this vast Disney-promoted amusement park-resort-tourist center do to Florida's major industry, tourism, and especially to that part of it situated south of Orlando? [51]

In terms of numbers, however, the opening of Disney World on October 1, 1971, proved inauspicious. Amid predictions that a crowd of 30,000 would jam the park's gates, only 10,000 showed up. Stories about possibly crowded roads and impossible parking may well have kept the crowd total down. Still, the future boded well for the new business. "Let's face it," said one visitor from nearby

Tampa. "I'm going to be back here whether I like it or not—the kids will see to that. And at Christmas, I have relatives visiting from North Carolina, and all they're talking about already is Disney World."[52]

The Strange Mystery of D. B. Cooper

On November 24, a strange event unfolded in the Pacific Northwest when, in the afternoon, a middle-aged man, described as cool and calm and dressed in a business suit and wearing sunglasses, boarded a Northwest Airlines Boeing 727 jet in Portland, Oregon. As the plane headed for Seattle, he opened his briefcase and showed a flight attendant two red cylinders, perhaps sticks of dynamite, with wires connected to them. He then threatened to blow up the plane unless he were given $200,000 and four parachutes. (The hijacker apparently wanted the authorities to think that he might force one or more other people to jump with him, this way he would avoid being given a faulty parachute.)

When the plane landed in Seattle, the FBI, who called the man D. B. Cooper, loaded the money and the parachutes onto the aircraft. The hijacker allowed all the passengers and two of the three flight attendants to debark. The plane then took off, with permission from Cooper to refuel at Reno, Nevada.

During the flight, Cooper ordered the plane to fly below 10,000 feet and the exit door to the cabin be opened. He then locked the flight attendant in the cockpit with the crew. When the plane landed at Reno, Cooper was nowhere to be found.

Cooper had apparently jumped, sight unseen, into the clear night sky, despite two planes trailing behind the passenger jet. The FBI and other law-enforcement agencies began a massive search covering four states. Neither Cooper nor any trace of the money or the parachute that he used has ever been found. Authorities doubt that he could have survived the jump, but of all the airliners, the 727 offered the best hope of a person accomplishing such a feat. Cooper's heist contained nothing of the tragedy of the Manson crime, but the element of mystery surrounding it has, during the years, intrigued many.

CHRONICLE OF EVENTS

1971

January 6: The army drops charges against four officers accused of covering up the 1968 assault on My Lai. Later in January, a court-martial will clear a sergeant of intent to kill six civilians in the hamlet, and the army will dismiss charges against five other soldiers, saying that there is insufficient evidence to prosecute them. This will leave charges pending against only three men, all of them officers, with the most prominent of them being Lieutenant William Calley.

January 22: In his State of the Union address, President Nixon calls for a "new revolution" in government to reform welfare, health care, the economy, and the way that the federal government and the states share power.

January 26: Charles Manson and three of his followers are found guilty of murdering actress Sharon Tate and six others in 1969.

January 28: U.S. District Judge William K. Thomas rules illegal a report by the Portage County (Ohio) grand jury that placed much of the blame for the shooting at Kent State University in 1970 on the college's administrators and students.

February 5: Commanded by Captain Alan Shepard, the *Apollo 14* mission successfully lands on the Moon. Shepard and navy commander Edgar D. Mitchell explore the surface of the Moon during two lunar walks. They will return to the Earth four days later.

February 8: Six hundred National Guard troops arrive in Wilmington, North Carolina, to quell four days of riots between whites and blacks in which two people have been shot to death.

February 26: The army orders a court-martial for Colonel Oran K. Henderson for covering up the My Lai massacre.

March 1: The Weather Underground explodes a bomb in a restroom of the Capitol building in Washington, D.C., causing damage but no bodily harm.

March 8: The army announces its court-martial of Captain Ernest L. Medina for premeditated murder in the March 1968 attack by U.S. troops on civilians at My Lai in Vietnam.

March 29: In one of the most controversial and divisive cases in American history, a court-martial jury convicts Lieutenant William L. Calley, Jr., of premeditated murder in the deaths of 22 men, women, and children killed in the South Vietnamese hamlet of My Lai on March 16, 1968. The verdict touches off protests for and against the Vietnam War and causes a divide between those who wave the American flag as a symbol for support of the U.S. military and those who believe that Calley's actions symbolize a shameful episode in American overseas intervention.

April 5: In an unusual criticism from a leading politician against the powerful director of the FBI, J. Edgar Hoover, Democratic Representative Hale Boggs of Louisiana demands that Hoover be fired because the FBI has tapped the telephones of members of Congress. Others, however, defend Hoover, who has been holding the directorship for 46 years; Representative Gerald Ford (Rep., Mich.), for one, says Americans have been fortunate to have Hoover at the helm.

April 10: In a thawing of relations between Communist China and the United States, nine American Ping-Pong players arrive in Beijing at the invitation of the Chinese. Three days later, they play their Chinese opponents in exhibition matches, and on April 14, Premier Chou Enlai meets with the American players, along with those from England, Canada, Nigeria, and Colombia.

April 19: Vietnam Veterans Against the War begins an antiwar protest in Washington, D.C., during which about 1,000 members of the group throw their combat ribbons, helmets, and uniforms onto the steps of the Capitol.

April 24: About 200,000 protesters gather in Washington, D.C., where they march for peace. The protest includes a rock music show at the Washington Monument.

April 26: A high-level study group put together by President Nixon recommends that Communist China be admitted into the United Nations.

May 1: The new rail system, Amtrak, begins operation in an attempt to preserve passenger service on the nation's tracks.

May 3: The Washington police begin to arrest thousands of antiwar protesters in an effort to prevent a militant assault on the nation's capital. In a two-day period, the protesters are detained in station houses and makeshift facilities, most notably a football field ringed by chain-link fencing. Later, courts will rule the detentions a violation of constitutional rights.

May 13: A jury of eight whites and four blacks acquits 13 Black Panthers on counts of conspiring to bomb several sites in New York City, including police stations and department stores. The defendants include Afeni Shakur, who will continue her commitment to black activism and who will become the mother of Tupac Shakur, a rap singer who will be shot to death in the 1990s.

May 25: Judge Harold H. Mulvey dismisses all charges against Black Panthers Bobby G. Seale and Ericka Huggins, who are on trial for the murder of Alex Rackley, a former Panther. Mulvey makes his decision after a jury declares itself deadlocked.

June 2: General John Donaldson, a former brigade commander in South Vietnam, is charged with killing six Vietnamese and assaulting two others in Quang Ngai Province in 1969. He is the highest-ranking officer who is accused of killing civilians in the Vietnam War.

June 12: In a ceremony at the Rose Garden of the White House, President Nixon's daughter, Tricia Nixon, weds Ed Cox. Four hundred guests attend what is the first outdoor wedding at the White House.

President Nixon escorts his daughter Tricia during the White House ceremony at which she married Ed Cox. *(Library of Congress, Prints and Photographs Division)*

June 13: The *New York Times* begins to publish the *Pentagon Papers,* government documents that are labeled top secret and reveal the decisions that were made in widening the U.S. involvement in Vietnam. The papers are damning; they show how governments officials lied and distorted information to get the United States into the Vietnam War and to deepen the country's involvement.

June 15: The Justice Department seeks an injunction against the *New York Times* for the newspaper's publishing of the *Pentagon Papers.*

June 30: The U.S. Supreme Court votes 6-3 that any attempt by the government to prevent the *New York Times* and the *Washington Post* from publishing the *Pentagon Papers* is unconstitutional.

June 30: Ohio becomes the 38th state to ratify the Twenty-sixth Amendment to the Constitution, thus making effective the lowering of the voting age in elections to age 18.

July 1: Founded by feminist Gloria Steinem, *Ms.* magazine begins to publish monthly. A sample edition had appeared in *New York* magazine the previous December, and another issue followed in January 1972, containing a petition to legalize abortions.

July 15: President Nixon goes on national television to announce that he will, within the next year, travel to Communist China to meet with that country's leaders. It is a stunning announcement, partly because it indicates a willingness to normalize relations with a country that the United States heretofore considered illegitimate and a menace to world peace, and partly because Nixon had made strident anticommunism a reoccurring theme in his political career. Many conservatives denounce the move as a sellout, but Democratic and Republican congressional leaders praise the initiative.

July 30: The astronauts of *Apollo 15* land on the Moon and the next day begin to explore its surface. While Major Alfred Worden remains aloft in the command module, Colonel David Scott and Lieutenant Colonel James Irwin land the lunar module, *Falcon,* near the rim of a deep canyon close to a lunar mountain range that is called the Apennine Front. Scott and Irwin spend a total of 18 hours and 37 minutes on the lunar terrain and travel more than 17 miles in their moon vehicle. They are the seventh and eighth men to set foot on the Moon's surface. They will return safely to Earth on August 7.

August 2: Secretary of State William P. Rogers announces that the United States will support the

Gloria Steinem is caught in an unguarded moment. *(Copyright © 1978 Diana Mara Henry)*

membership of Communist China in the United Nations.

August 15: President Nixon reveals a new economic program that includes a 90-day wage, price, and rent freeze in an attempt to control inflation. In addition, he orders a 5 percent cut in federal jobs and asks Congress to reschedule a pending income tax cut so it will take effect earlier than planned.

August 20: The army announces that Lieutenant William Calley's life sentence for murdering 22 Vietnamese civilians at My Lai is being reduced to 20 years.

August 21: George Jackson, an inmate whose younger brother, Jonathan, had tried to free him during a shootout in Marin County in August 1970, is shot and killed when he tries to escape from San Quentin prison in California. Jackson had managed to let 20 inmates out of their cells and was fired on as he ran across the prison yard during the melee.

September 13: More than 1,000 New York state troopers and police end a four-day old rebellion by inmates at Attica state prison by attacking the facility; 32 inmates die in the attack, which includes the use of shotguns, notorious for their lack of accuracy. Initially, reports state that the hostages were killed by the prisoners, but it is later revealed that they were killed by troopers. New York governor Nelson Rockefeller is widely criticized by civil rights groups for approving the attack and for failing to come to the site to seek a compromise with the inmates.

September 22: A court-martial jury acquits Captain Ernest L. Medina of murdering more than 100 Vietnamese civilians at My Lai in 1968.

October 7: President Nixon announces additional policies to restrain wages and prices and to hold inflation to no more than 2–3 percent annually.

October 10: London Bridge, designed by John Rennie and completed in 1831, opens as a tourist attraction at Lake Havasu City, Arizona. The bridge had been bought by entrepreneur Robert P. McCulloch in 1968 and was shipped piece by piece to the United States. It will become second only to the Grand Canyon as Arizona's biggest tourist site.

October 25: The United Nations General Assembly votes to seat Communist China and to expel Nationalist China (Taiwan).

November 12: President Nixon orders the withdrawal of 45,000 troops from Vietnam by February 1 to lower the number of troops there to 139,000, a sharp reduction from the more than 500,000 three years earlier.

December 6: The U.S. Senate confirms President Nixon's nomination of Lewis F. Powell to the Supreme Court. Powell, a Virginian, is the first conservative Southerner to be confirmed to the court since 1941.

December 10: The U.S. Senate confirms President Nixon's nomination of William H. Rehnquist to the Supreme Court, although liberals vote against him to protest his civil rights record.

December 11: For yet a third time, prosecutors fail to obtain a guilty verdict against Black Panther leader Huey P. Newton on the charge of killing an Oakland, California, police officer in 1967. The jury deadlocks on a 6-6 vote.

December 17: A military court acquits Colonel Oran K. Henderson of covering up the My Lai massacre that had occurred in Vietnam in 1968.

December 23: Teamster union boss Jimmy Hoffa is released from prison after President Nixon commutes Hoffa's 13-year sentence for jury tampering. Hoffa served

London Bridge was dismantled and moved to the middle of the Arizona desert. *(National Archives and Records Administration)*

slightly less than five years for his crime; he is prohibited from managing any labor organization until 1980.

December 26: The United States begins an intense five-day air assault on North Vietnam in response to what it calls increased communist aggression. The bombing ignites antiwar protests in and outside of Congress.

December 26: Several Vietnam War veterans take over the crown of the Statue of Liberty from whence they fly a U.S. flag upside down. They end their protest two days later.

December 30: A federal grand jury in Los Angeles reindicts Daniel J. Ellsberg for making the *Pentagon Papers* public.

EYEWITNESS TESTIMONY

Charles Manson

"We climbed over a fence and then a light started coming toward us and Tex told us to get back and sit down.... A car pulled up, in front of us and Tex leaped forward with a gun in his hand and stuck his hand with the gun at this man's head. And the man said, 'Please don't hurt me, I won't say anything.' And Tex shot him four times."

"Did you actually see Tex point the gun inside the window of the car and shoot the man?"

"Yes, I saw it clearly."

"About how far away were you from Tex at the time that he shot the driver of the car?"

"Just a few feet."

"After Tex shot the driver four times what happened next?"

"The man just slumped over. I saw that, and then Tex put his head in the car and turned the ignition off. He may have taken the keys out, I don't know, and then he pushed the car back a few feet and then we all proceeded toward the house and Tex told me to go in back of the house and see if there were open windows and doors, which I did."

"Did you find any open doors or windows in the back of the house?"

"No, there was no open windows or doors."

"What is the next thing that happened, Linda?"

"I came around from the back, and Tex was standing at a window, cutting the screen, and he told me to go back and wait at the car, and he may have told me to listen for sounds, but I don't remember him saying it."

"While you were down by the car do you know where Tex, Sadie, and Katie were?"

"No, I didn't see them."

"Did either of those three come down to the car?"

"Yes, Katie came down at one point."

"Did Katie say anything to you?"

"Yes, she asked for my knife, and I gave it to her, and she told me to stay there and listen for sounds, and I did, and she left."

"When she left, did she walk in the direction of the residence?"

"Yes."

"Did you see either Patricia Krenwinkel or Susan Atkins or Tex walk into the residence?"

"No, I didn't."

"Were you all alone by the car?"

"Yes...."

"I heard a man scream out 'No. No.' Then I just heard screams. I just heard screams at that point. I don't have any words to describe how a scream is. I never heard it before."

"How long did the screaming continue?"

"Oh, it seemed like forever, infinite. I don't know."

"Was the screaming constant or was it in intervals?"

"It seemed constant, I don't know."

"Now, what did you do when you heard these screams?"

"I started to run toward the house."

"Why did you do that?"

"Because I wanted them to stop."

"What happened after you ran toward the house?"

"There was a man just coming out of the door and he had blood all over his face and he was standing by a post, and we looked into each other's eyes for a minute, and I said, 'Oh, God, I am so sorry. Please make it stop.' And then he just fell to the ground into the bushes. And then Sadie came running out of the house, and I said, 'Sadie, please make it stop.' And then I said, 'I hear people coming.' And she said, 'It is too late.' And then she told me that she left her knife and she couldn't find it, and I believe she started to run back into the house. While this was going on the man had gotten up, and I saw Tex on top of him, hitting him on the head and stabbing him, and the man was struggling, and then I saw Katie in the background with the girl, chasing after her with an upraised knife, and I just turned and ran to the car down at the bottom of the hill."

"Now, when you told Sadie that people were coming, was that the truth?"

"No."

"Why did you tell her that?"

"Because I just wanted them to stop."

"You said you saw Katie. That is Patricia Krenwinkel?"

"Yes."

"Was she chasing someone?"

"Yes."

"Was it a man or a woman?"

"It was a woman in a white gown."

Testimony by Manson family member Linda Kasabian at the murder trial of Charles Manson in November 1970. Here she describes the murders at the Tate house. She was the star witness for the prosecution; available online at http://www.law.umkc.edu/faculty/ projects/ftrials/manson/mansontestimony-k.html, downloaded February 13, 2004.

There has been a lot of charges and a lot of things said about me and brought against the co-defendants in this case, of which a lot could be cleared up and clarified....

I never went to school, so I never growed up to read and write too good, so I have stayed in jail and I have stayed stupid, and I have stayed a child while I have watched your world grow up, and then I look at the things that you do and I don't understand....

You eat meat and you kill things that are better than you are, and then you say how bad, and even killers, your children are. You made your children what they are....

These children that come at you with knives. They are your children. You taught them. I didn't teach them. I just tried to help them stand up....

Most of the people at the ranch that you call the Family were just people that you did not want, people that were alongside the road, that their parents had kicked out, that did not want to go to Juvenile Hall. So I did the best I could and I took them up on my garbage dump and I told them this: that in love there is no wrong.... I told them that anything they do for their brothers and sisters is good if they do it with a good thought....

I was working at cleaning up my house, something that Nixon should have been doing. He should have been on the side of the road, picking up his children, but he wasn't. He was in the White House, sending them off to war....

I don't understand you, but I don't try. I don't try to judge nobody. I know that the only person I can judge is me . . . But I know this: that in your hearts and your own souls, you are as much responsible for the Vietnam war as I am for killing these people....

I can't judge any of you. I have no malice against you and no ribbons for you. But I think that it is high time that you all start looking at yourselves, and judging the lie that you live in. I can't dislike you, but I will say this to you: you haven't got long before you are all going to kill yourselves, because you are all crazy. And you can project it back at me . . . but I am only what lives inside each and everyone of you.

My father is the jailhouse. My father is your system . . . I am only what you made me. I am only a reflection of you. I have ate out of your garbage cans to stay out of jail. I have wore your second-hand clothes . . . I have done my best to get along in your world and now you want to kill me, and I look at you, and then I say to myself, You want to kill me? Ha! I'm

Charles Manson heads to court in Los Angeles where he takes the witness stand during the Tate–LaBianca murder trial to complain about conditions at the county jail. *(© Bettmann/Corbis)*

already dead, have been all my life. I've spent twenty-three years in tombs that you built.

Sometimes I think about giving it back to you; sometimes I think about just jumping on you and letting you shoot me . . . If I could, I would jerk this microphone off and beat your brains out with it, because that is what you deserve, that is what you deserve....

If I could get angry at you, I would try to kill everyone of you. If that's guilt, I accept it . . . These children, everything they done, they done for the love of their brother....

If I showed them that I would do anything for my brother—including giving my life for my brother on the battlefield—and then they pick up their banner, and they go off and do what they do, that is not my responsibility. I don't tell people what to do....

These children [indicating the female defendants] were finding themselves. What they did, if they did whatever they did, is up to them. They will have to explain that to you. . . .

It's all your fear. You look for something to project it on, and you pick out a little old scroungy nobody that eats out of a garbage can, and that nobody wants, that was kicked out of the penitentiary, that has been dragged through every hellhole that you can think of, and you drag him and put him in a courtroom. You expect to break me? Impossible! You broke me years ago. You killed me years ago. . . .

I have killed no one and I have ordered no one to be killed. I may have implied on several different occasions to several different people that I may have been Jesus Christ, but I haven't decided yet what I am or who I am. . . . Guilty. Not guilty. They are only words. You can do anything you want with me, but you cannot touch me because I am only my love. . . . If you put me in the penitentiary, that means nothing because you kicked me out of the last one. I didn't ask to get released. I liked it in there because I like myself.

Mr. Bugliosi is a hard-driving prosecutor, polished education, a master of words, semantics. He is a genius. He has got everything that every lawyer would want to have except one thing: a case. He doesn't have a case. Were I allowed to defend myself, I could have proven this to you. . . . The evidence in this case is a gun. There was a gun that laid around the ranch. It belonged to everybody. Anybody could have picked that gun up and done anything they wanted to do with it. I don't deny having that gun. That gun has been in my possession many times. Like the rope was there because you need rope on a ranch. . . . They put the hideous bodies on [photographic] display and they imply: If he gets out, see what will happen to you. . . .

[Helter Skelter] means confusion, literally. It doesn't mean any war with anyone. It doesn't mean that some people are going to kill other people . . . Helter Skelter is confusion. Confusion is coming down around you fast. If you can't see the confusion coming down around you fast, you can call it what you wish. . . . Is it a conspiracy that the music is telling the youth to rise up against the establishment because the establishment is rapidly destroying things? Is that a conspiracy? The music speaks to you every day, but you are too deaf, dumb, and blind to even listen to the music. . . . It is not my conspiracy. It is not my music. I hear what it relates. It says "Rise," it says "Kill." Why blame it on me? I didn't write the music. . . .

Danny DeCarlo . . . said that I hate black men, and he said that we thought alike. . . . But actually all I ever did with Danny DeCarlo or any other human being was reflect him back at himself. If he said he did not like the black man, I would say 'O.K.' So consequently he would drink another beer and walk off and say 'Charlie thinks like I do.' But actually he does not know how Charlie thinks because Charlie has never projected himself. I don't think like you people. You people put importance on your lives. Well, my life has never been important to anyone. . . .

[Linda Kasabian] gets on the stand and she says when she looked in that man's eyes that was dying, she knew that it was my fault. She knew it was my fault because she couldn't face death. And if she can't face death, that is not my fault. I can face death. I have all the time. In the penitentiary you live with it, with constant fear of death, because it is a violent world in there, and you have to be on your toes constantly. . . .

[I taught the Family] not to be weak and not to lean on me. . . . I told [Paul Watkins] "To be a man, boy, you have to stand up and be your own father. . . . I do feel some responsibility. I feel a responsibility for the pollution. I feel a responsibility for the whole thing. . . . To be honest with you, I don't recall ever saying "Get a knife and a change of clothes and go do what Tex says." Or I don't recall saying "Get a knife and go kill the sheriff." In fact, it makes me mad when someone kills snakes or dogs or cats or horses. I don't even like to eat meat—that is how much I am against killing. . . .

I haven't got any guilt about anything because I have never been able to see any wrong. . . . I have always said: Do what your love tells you, and I do what my love tells me. . . . Is it my fault that your children do what you do? What about your children? You say there are just a few? There are many, many more, coming in the same direction. They are running in the streets—and they are coming right at you!

[Cross-examination by Vincent Bugliosi:]

Q. You say you are already dead, is that right, Charlie?

A. Dead in your mind or dead in my mind?

Q. Define it any way you want to.

A. As any child will tell you, dead is when you are no more. It is just when you are not there. If you weren't there, you would be dead.

Q. How long have you been dead? . . . To be precise about it, you think you have been dead for close to 2,000 years, don't you?

A. Mr. Bugliosi, 2,000 years is relative to the second we live in.

Charles Manson's direct testimony to the court on November 20, 1970, at his murder trial. The testimony was heard without the jury present. When asked if he wanted to testify in front of the jury, he said no, that he no longer felt the pressure that he had been feeling. Available online at http://www.law.umkc.edu/faculty/projects/ftrials/manson/mansontestimony-m.html, downloaded February 13, 2004.

William Calley and the My Lai Massacre

Now, everybody that went through that village said there was shooting. A man could not sit back there with the command post in a place that is not over five hundred to three hundred yards away in area and not know what is going on. The evidence shows that Captain Medina had been a good company commander, but somehow or other self preservation got into Captain Medina's life at that time and it was necessary for him to take some defensive efforts to protect that. So, when you start to measure the interest, and I will be frank to say that on behalf of both of them, it's terrific; but between he and Lieutenant Calley, because they are both running the last yards, probably to a life or death sentence, and when the stakes are that high, somebody has got to try to escape responsibility.

Medina used a phrase that he was guilty of misprision of a felony by not reporting. Of course, Captain Medina can afford to make that sort of an admission now because he cannot be prosecuted on that charge, the statute of limitations having barred it. Now, gentlemen, for the life of me, I cannot understand why we could take a group of twenty or thirty men out of the United States Army, all good men, all good citizens, at the time they were picked up, put them over there, and have an incident like this happen unless it had been suggested, ordered, or commanded by somebody upstairs. I will leave that up to you good gentlemen to figure out. Why a lieutenant, the lowest man on the totem pole, would be issuing orders like that without having some directive or orders from on high. . . .

Captain Medina was a man, a disciplinarian. He wanted orders obeyed. He said that and he didn't brook any denial or disobedience of orders. It may well be that the niceties of the military require that if I have a question about an order, I go to my company commander and say, "Captain, I think this is an illegal order, and I don't think I should obey it," but the other philosophy is that they were saying here, "Obey it first and then go back and find out what about the legality of it," because if you take the former in this situation, your troops might be dead; and if you don't follow out a combat order, then you sacrifice your troops. What a horrid choice to place upon anybody.

The court is also going to instruct on the legality and illegality of orders. You will have it in written form so there is no point in my doing anything more or less than this; that he will define an illegal order and what is an illegal order and he may tell you, in this case, that the killing of civilians—in certain situations, a given order to kill those might be an illegal order, but he also will tell you that that does not end the subject.

That is just a commencement. For, on top of it a man that is involved, whether he uses the subjective or objective test, it must be known to the individual involved that the order and the circumstances—when, where, and why it was given and the facts that control that decision as to whether a person should know whether it's legal or illegal—flow out of his environment, flow out of many things that you have heard in this case, including these things that were bothering this unit on 16 March 1968; and he will tell you that if an ordinary, reasonable person would have done what Lieutenant Calley did, in this case, and obeyed the order; if it was given to him, then, of course, you cannot find Lieutenant Calley guilty because the test that you apply and the measuring rod you use is colored by the facts and circumstances surrounding the giving of the order and if you adopt the philosophy, you obeyed first and asked after in this situation, no one would take that kind of an order and do that, because if they didn't and there was some kind of counterattack here, something happened, then it would be too late.

It may be the difference between winning and losing and so, as you look back on the situation—I could hardly stand here and tell you in good conscience that people, like at Nuremberg, could be excused or justified—but I think when you put untrained troops out in areas and they are told to do certain things, they have a right to rely on the judgment and the expertise, then you are bound to give credence in effect to orders from their company commander; and so when you take that background, the laws of war were tailored in certain respects to meet this very situation, then you will understand that the Congress of the United States and other bodies feel that leeway and latitude should be given to people who were far from home and trying to save the United States of America.

I do not believe that history records another incident when the United States of America ever had a similar situation, nor do I believe that we have taken collectively a group of people who were engaged in a combat mission and what they believed to be a combat mission and put them up before a court for trial. So, you gentlemen are in a situation where you must chart a course for what should be done. You are in a situation where I believe that if ever a presumption of innocence, the personal rights and obligations that are available to protect the men of the armed services ought to be extended in favor of this accused.

They cannot be prosecuted. Sure, they can then come forward with witnesses. They can disclose anything that happened. It's too late to help them, but the man that is in the service, the man that stays in the service and tries to build the morale and efficiency of the United States Army, does not have that protection. To me, I think if I were—if it were possible for me to do it, somehow or other I would give weight to the fact that a man who wanted to make the army a career, who was not told—never a word said to Lieutenant Calley that I can recall, about any of his problems in this case until he had extended in Vietnam and was ordered back to the United States believing he was coming back to a new assignment. There was nothing said to him. All the time, apparently, the finger pointing to Captain Medina, who himself stated that he would probably get twenty years and all of a sudden, times change. Who becomes the pigeon—Lieutenant Calley, the lowest officers. . . .

Summation by defense attorney George Latimer at the court-martial of Lieutenant William Calley, March 1971, available online at http://www.law.umkc.edu/ faculty/projects/ftrials/mylai/defense.html, downloaded February 14, 2004.

Now, we have shown that when C Company landed on 16 March 1968, they did in fact land on the western side of the village of My Lai. All of the testimony is in agreement on that fact. We have also shown that the accused was in the platoon, a headquarters group, and a mortar platoon. We showed that when they landed, the accused's platoon assumed the position on the south side of the village. He had two squads and a platoon and a headquarters element for this operation. One squad was commanded by Sergeant Bacon. The first lift

arrived at 0730 hours and it carried, as you will recall, after the first lift landed, elements of the First Platoon then secured portions of the LZ [landing zone] for the second lift to come in. Before the second lift landed, the First Platoon moved into the village. They received no fire from that village. None. The witnesses are in agreement on that fact.

Now the accused's platoon had Sergeant Mitchell's squad on the south side of the village, and it had Sergeant Bacon's squad on the north side of the village. And when they entered the village, the platoon, as you will recall, found no armed VC [Vietcong]. All they found were old men, women, children, and babies. They began to gather up these thirty to forty unarmed, unresisting men, women, children, and babies, because they weren't receiving any fire. Meadlo and Conti moved them out on the trail, and they made them squat down on the north-south trail.

Lieutenant Calley returned fifteen minutes later and said to Meadlo, "Why haven't you taken care of this group?" "Waste them." "I want them dead." "Kill them." The versions differ here slightly between the testimony of Sledge, Conti, and Meadlo regarding the actual words that Lieutenant Calley spoke. But, nonetheless, Lieutenant Calley then issued an order to Meadlo, and in fact Calley and Meadlo shot those people on the north-south trail.

Jim Dursi had gathered another group of people and he moved this other group of civilians along the southern edge of the village until he came to an irrigation ditch. And when he arrived at the irrigation ditch with his people, he was joined by Lieutenant Calley. And what happened there? Lieutenant Calley directed that those individuals, those groups of people, be placed into that irrigation ditch, and that they all would be shot by Meadlo and Dursi.

You recall the testimony of Paul Meadlo to Jim Dursi, "Why don't you shoot?" "Why don't you fire?" "I can't." "I won't." Dennis Conti approached from the south and came up and observed Calley and Meadlo and Mitchell firing into that ditch and killing those people. And Conti moved north and set up a position. Robert Maples was in the area. He observed ten to fifteen people being put in that irrigation ditch by Lieutenant Calley. He observed Lieutenant Calley and Meadlo place the people in the irrigation ditch and fire into the people, but he didn't see the people come out.

Thomas Turner, you recall, testified that he, while he assumed the position to the north of the ditch, observed over a hundred people placed in that ditch during an hour to an hour-and-a-half period. These people were screaming and crying and that he passed Meadlo and Calley firing into that ditch he moved forward.

And then you recall the testimony of Charles Sledge, that after that they moved north of the ditch where there was a man dressed in white, a fact which the accused admits, that Calley interrogated this individual; when the man refused to speak, Calley butt-stroked him with his rifle and then shot him. And then Charles Sledge testified that when he returned someone yelled out, "There's a child getting away, a child getting away!" Lieutenant Calley returned to that area, picked up the child, threw the child in the ditch, and shot him.

Many of the facts which we have related to you as having been proved by this evidence beyond any reasonable doubt have not in fact been disputed by the defense and were in many cases supported by the defense's own evidence, including the testimony of the accused. . . .

A lot of people testified concerning their estimates of how many people died and the bodies. Some would say five, some would say ten, some would say fifteen to twenty. But what's the best evidence that you have as to how many people died? The best evidence you have, gentlemen, is prosecution exhibit 12A of the numbers. Look at that photograph when you go back into your deliberation. How many people are shown in that photograph? If you count the number of people in that photograph, you will find not less than twenty-five actually shown in the photograph, nine of which are clearly identified as children, and three of which are clearly identified as infants. Can there be any question about the fact that photograph has been well identified? You've heard twenty people testify, before you that they saw that group of bodies on the north–south trail. Twenty out of that company.

There can be no doubt about the fact that those people were on the north–south trail and they were in fact dead. Would they be there that long and observed by that many people over that period of time with the wounds that they had and be alive? There is no doubt at all gentlemen, about the fact that Lieutenant Calley shot the people in prosecution exhibit 12A and that they are in fact dead and died as a result of his acts on 16 March 1968. . . .

You will be told as a matter of law that the obedience of a soldier is not the obedience of an automaton.

When he puts on the American uniform, he still is under an obligation to think, to reason, and he is obliged to respond not as a machine but as a person and as a reasonable human being with a proper regard for human life, with the obligation to make moral decisions, with the obligation to know what is right and what is wrong under the circumstances with which he is faced and to act accordingly.

We submit to you in this case that the accused received in fact no order to have done what he did in My Lai on 16 March 1968. He cannot rely upon an order in the first instance, because there was no order to round up all those men, women, and children and summarily execute them. There was an order, yes, to meet and engage the Forty-eighth VC Battalion in My Lai. We submitted to you all the evidence regarding the pre-operational planning for this operation. You heard what the mission of this operation was—to meet and engage the armed enemy unit that they expected to be there. Is there anything unlawful about that order? On the night of 15 March, do you think that they anticipated or intended when they got to the village the next day there would be no one there with weapons, and all they would find would be old men, women, children, and babies, and that the mission was to go in and gather those people up and take them out on that trail and that ditch and shoot them? Do you think that those were the orders on the night of 15 March? Do you think that that was the order that emanated in those task force briefings?

There is no evidence to show that any order was given to summarily execute. There is no evidence to show that there was an order given not to take prisoners. There was an order given to meet and engage an armed enemy unit, and this is the order that Captain Medina relayed to his men, to meet and engage the forty-eighth VC Battalion, and the defense's own witnesses testified to this, as have the government's. . . .

The reasonable man, gentlemen, is an objective standard. You represent the reasonable men under the law. The reasonable man charged with knowledge of the law to apply in a given situation. The reasonable man would know and should know, without any doubt, that under the circumstances in which he found himself on the sixteenth of March, 1968, that any order to gather up over thirty people on that north–south trail, and to summarily execute those people is unlawful. It can't be justified. A reasonable man would know that to put over seventy people in that irrigation ditch, like a bunch of cattle—men, women, children, and babies—that to do that is unlawful. A reasonable man not only would know it, he should know it, and he could not rely upon any order to commit that, to absolve himself of criminal responsibility for that conduct.

There can be no justification, gentlemen, and there is none under the law, or under the facts of this case. We have established beyond reasonable doubt every element of every offense that we have charged, and the facts clearly demonstrate that those acts were unjustifiable and without excuse. We have carried our burden, and it now becomes your duty to render the only appropriate sentence, punishments, and adjudications you can make in this case, and that is to return findings of guilty of all of the charges and specifications.

Summation of Aubrey Daniels for the prosecution at the court-martial of William L. Calley, Jr., Fort Benning, Georgia, March 1971, available online at http:// www.law.umkc.edu/faculty/projects/ftrials/mylai/closing argument.html, cited February 13, 2004.

It is evident that efforts to suppress and withhold information concerning the Son My [known as My Lai] incident were made at every level in the Americal Division. These efforts . . . were successful in containing the story of Son My within the division. It is evident to this Inquiry, after interviewing most of those who witnessed the events at Son My, that any serious attempt to interrogate such individuals immediately following the incident would have resulted in full disclosure of the event. Many testified in a manner which showed an eagerness to express what had apparently caused them great concern. If there had been real concern in the chain of command, if anyone had taken action to ask questions, they would have had full and complete answers.

One matter which casts further suspicion on the Americal Division is the almost total absence of files and records of documents relating to the Son My incident and its subsequent investigation. With few exceptions the files have been purged of these documents and records of their removal or destruction have not been maintained. The single notable exception to this has been the copy of Col Henderson's 24 April report, and this document was found in the files . . . where it would not normally have been filed. The files of U.S. advisory teams which had knowledge of the Son My incident were similarly barren.

Another factor which may have contributed to suppression was the manner in which information concern-

ing the Son My incident was handled in Vietnamese circles. Such information was apparently not discussed to any extent in GVN [Government of Vietnam] channels, as witnessed by the number of U.S. personnel who worked closely with Province, District, and ARVN authorities and yet had no knowledge that the incident had occurred. Even on the Vietnamese civilian side, a measure of silence fell over the community. Without exception, Americans who worked and lived closely with Vietnamese in both official and social circles in Quaug Ngai Province stated that they had not obtained an inkling of the incident.

Excerpt from Report of the Department of the Army Review of the Preliminary Investigations into the My Lai Incident, *more popularly called* The Peers Report *(1974), p. 313.*

You should be stripped of your stripes, you chicken-livered traitor, for the trouble you have caused our country and our military. What do you think war is? A game of ping-pong? The village was a threat to our own men. Would you rather see our men moved down by the enemy? Your kind is our worst enemy, the rat commie within our country.

From a postcard sent in the early 1970s by an anonymous writer to army helicopter pilot Hugh Thompson, who helped expose the My Lai massacre, in Trent Angers, The Forgotten Hero of My Lai *(1999), p. 178.*

How shocking it is if so many people across this nation have failed to see the moral issue which was involved in the trial of Lt. Calley: that it is unlawful for an American soldier to summarily execute unarmed and unresisting men, women, children, and babies.

From a letter written in 1971 by Aubrey M. Daniel III, prosecutor in the Calley case, to President Richard Nixon to protest Nixon's intervention in the case, in Trent Angers, The Forgotten Hero of My Lai *(1999), p. 183.*

Imagine that the troops of some other nation massacre the inhabitants of a village. Several soldiers are tried and acquitted. Silence. One [Lt. William Calley] is charged with personally murdering 102 persons; he is convicted of murdering 22. Immediately the country is in an uproar. The capitol is flooded with protests, the convicted man with pledges of support. Regional legislatures petition for his release, and important regional officials order flags flown at half mast or other symbolic gestures of solidarity. . . .

At the same time another soldier, convicted of premeditated murder, of twelve villagers in a separate incident, is released after serving less than ten months in jail. . . .

If all this happened in Germany, we would declare a resurgence of Nazism. If it happened in Israel, the whole world would denounce it. If it happened in Egypt or among the Palestinians, there would be talk of the cruelest barbarism. But when it happens in America?

From a commentary in Commonweal *magazine on April 12, 1971, by Peter Steinfels, in James S. Olson and Randy Roberts,* My Lai *(1998), pp. 189–190.*

COINTELPRO

The FBI jeopardizes the whole system of freedom of expression which is the cornerstone of an open society. . . . At worst it raises the specter of a police state . . . in essence the FBI conceives of itself as an instrument to prevent radical social change in America . . . the Bureau's view of its function leads it beyond data collection and into political warfare.

Yale law professor Thomas I. Emerson commenting in 1971 on secret domestic surveillance by the FBI through COINTELPRO, in Ward Churchill and Jim Vander Wall, The COINTELPRO Papers *(1990), p. 1.*

Daniel Ellsberg and the Pentagon Papers

By 1956, peace in Vietnam was plainly less dependent upon the Geneva Settlement than upon power relationships in Southeast Asia—principally upon the role the U.S. elected to play in unfolding events. In 1957 and 1958, a structured rebellion against the government of Ngo Dinh Diem began. While the North Vietnamese played an ill-defined part, most of those who took up arms were South Vietnamese, and the causes for which they fought were by no means contrived in North Vietnam. In 1959 and 1960, Hanoi's involvement in the developing strife became evident. Not until 1960, however, did the U.S. perceive that Diem was in serious danger of being overthrown and devise a Counterinsurgency Plan.

It can be established that there was endemic insurgency in South Vietnam throughout the period 1954–1960. It can also be established—but less surely—that the Diem regime alienated itself from one after another of those elements within Vietnam which might have offered it political support, and was grievously at fault in its rural programs. That these conditions engendered animosity toward the GVN [government of Vietnam] seems almost certain, and they could have underwritten a major resistance movement even without North Vietnamese help.

It is equally clear that North Vietnamese communists operated some form of subordinate apparatus in the South in the years 1954–1960. Nonetheless, the Viet Minh "stay-behinds" were not directed originally to structure an insurgency, and there is no coherent picture of the extent or effectiveness of communist activities in the period 1956–1959. From all indications, this was a period of reorganization and recruiting by the communist party. No direct links have been established between Hanoi and perpetrators of rural violence. Statements have been found in captured party histories that the communists plotted and controlled the entire insurgency, but these are difficult to take at face value. . . .

Three interpretations of the available evidence are possible:

Option A—That the DRV [Democratic Republic of Vietnam; that is, communist north Vietnam] intervened in the South in reaction to U.S. escalation, particularly that of President Kennedy in early 1961. Those who advance this argument rest their case principally on open sources to establish the reprehensible character of the Diem regime, on examples of forceful resistance to Diem independent of Hanoi, and upon the formation of the National Liberation Front (NLF), alleged to have come into being in South Vietnam in early 1960. These also rely heavily upon DRV official statements of 1960–1961 indicating that the DRV only then proposed to support the NLF.

Option B—The DRV manipulated the entire war. This is the official U.S. position, and can be supported. Nonetheless, the case is not wholly compelling, especially for the years 1955–1959.

Option C—The DRV seized an opportunity to enter an ongoing internal war in 1959 prior to, and independent of, U.S. escalation. This interpretation is more tenable than the previous; still, much of the evidence is circumstantial.

The judgment offered here is that the truth lies somewhere between Option B and C. That is, there was some form of DRV apparatus functioning in the South throughout the years, but it can only be inferred that this apparatus originated and controlled the insurgency which by 1959 posed a serious challenge to the Diem government. Moreover, up until 1958, neither the DRV domestic situation nor its international support was conducive to foreign adventure; by 1959, its prospects were bright in both respects, and it is possible to demonstrate its moving forcefully abroad thereafter. . . .

Excerpt from the Pentagon Papers, *published in 1971, showing a more complex situation in South Vietnam than the simplistic public statements by the United States that North Vietnam was the sole aggressor in the war, available online at http://www.mtholyoke.edu/acad/ intrel/pentagon/pent11.htm, downloaded February 14, 2004.*

If the government would agree that if Ellsberg appeared today he could be released in his own recognizance . . . there would be no difficulty in having him appear today. If any of you are ready to contribute to a bail fund, maybe we'll produce him today.

Leonard B. Boudin, lawyer for Dr. Daniel Ellsberg, answering reporters' questions on June 26, 1971, as to when Ellsberg will surrender to federal authorities in the Pentagon Papers *case, in the* New York Times, *June 27, 1971, p. 1.*

Mr. Justice Black, with whom Mr. Justice Douglas joins, concurring

I adhere to the view that the Government's case against the *Washington Post* should have been dismissed and that the injunction against the *New York Times* should have been vacated without oral argument when the cases were first presented to this Court. I believe that every moment's continuance of the injunctions against these newspapers amounts to a flagrant, indefensible, and continuing violation of the First Amendment. Furthermore, after oral argument, I agree completely that we must affirm the judgment of the Court of Appeals for the District of Columbia Circuit and reverse the judgment of the Court of Appeals for the Second Circuit for the reasons stated by my Brothers DOUGLAS and BRENNAN. In my view it is unfortunate that some of my Brethren are apparently willing to hold that the publication of news may sometimes be enjoined. Such a holding would make a shambles of the First Amendment.

Our Government was launched in 1789 with the adoption of the Constitution. The Bill of Rights, including the First Amendment, followed in 1791. Now, for the first time in the 182 years since the founding of the Republic, the federal courts are asked to hold that the First Amendment does not mean what it says, but rather means that the Government can halt the publication of current news of vital importance to the people of this country.

In seeking injunctions against these newspapers and in its presentation to the Court, the Executive Branch seems to have forgotten the essential purpose and history of the First Amendment. When the Constitution was adopted, many people strongly opposed it because the document contained no Bill of Rights to safeguard certain basic freedoms. They especially feared that the new powers granted to a central government might be interpreted to permit the government to curtail freedom of religion, press, assembly, and speech. In response to an overwhelming public clamor, James Madison offered a series of amendments to satisfy citizens that these great liberties would remain safe and beyond the power of government to abridge. Madison proposed what later became the First Amendment in three parts, two of which are set out below, and one of which proclaimed, "The people shall not be deprived or abridged of their right to speak, to write, or to publish their sentiments, *and the freedom of the press, as one of the great bulwarks of liberty, shall be inviolable.*" (Emphasis added) The amendments were offered to *curtail* and *restrict* the general powers granted to the Executive, Legislative, and Judicial Branches two years before in the original Constitution. The Bill of Rights changed the original Constitution into a new charter under which no branch of government could abridge the people's freedoms of press, speech, religion, and assembly. Yet the Solicitor General argues and some members of the Court appear to agree that the general powers of the Government adopted in the original Constitution should be interpreted to limit and restrict the specific and emphatic guarantees of the Bill of Rights adopted later. I can imagine no greater perversion of history. Madison and the other Framers of the First Amendment, able men that they were, wrote in language they earnestly believed could never be misunderstood, "Congress shall make no law abridging the freedom of the press." Both the history and language of the First Amendment support the view that the press must be left free to publish news whatever the source, without censorship, injunctions, or prior restraints.

In the First Amendment the Founding Fathers gave the free press the protection it must have to fulfill its essential role in our democracy. The press was to serve the governed, not the governors. The Government's power to censor the press was abolished so that the press would remain forever free to censure the Government. The press was protected so that it could bare the secrets of government and inform the people. Only a free and unrestrained press can effectively expose deception in government. And paramount among the responsibilities of a free press is the duty to prevent any part of the government from deceiving the people and sending them off to distant lands to die of foreign fevers and foreign shot and shell. In my view, far from deserving condemnation for their courageous reporting, the *New York Times,* the *Washington Post,* and other newspapers should be commended for serving the purpose that the Founding Fathers saw so clearly. In revealing the workings of government that led to the Vietnam war, the newspapers nobly did precisely that which the Founders hoped and trusted they would do. . . .

The Government argues in its brief that in spite of the First Amendment, the authority of the Executive Department to protect the nation against publication of information whose disclosure would endanger the national security stems from two interrelated sources: "[t]he constitutional power of the President over the conduct of foreign affairs and his authority as Commander-in-Chief. . . .'

The word "security" is a broad, vague generality whose contours should not be invoked to abrogate the fundamental law embodied in the First Amendment. The guarding of military and diplomatic secrets at the expense of informed representative government provides no real security for our Republic. The Framers of the First Amendment, fully aware of both the need to defend a new nation and the abuses of the English and Colonial governments, sought to give this new society strength and security by providing that freedom of speech, press, religion, and assembly should not be abridged. This thought was eloquently expressed in 1937 by Mr. Chief Justice Hughes—great man and great Chief Justice that he was—when the Court held a man could not be punished for attending a meeting run by Communists:

"The greater the importance of safeguarding the community from incitements to the overthrow of our institutions by force and violence, the more imperative is the need to preserve inviolate the constitutional rights of free speech, free press and free assembly in order to maintain the opportunity for free political discussion, to the end that government may be responsive to the will of the people and that changes, if desired, may be obtained by peaceful means. Therein lies the security of the Republic, the very foundation of constitutional government."

Opinion of Justice Hugo Black, June 30, 1971, in the case of New York Times Co. v. the United States, *available online at http://usinfo.state.gov/usa/infousa/facts/democrac/48.htm, downloaded November 17, 2004.*

The Court has performed its most valuable service for many a year. . . . This is a great day for freedom in the land.

Statement by Senator Hubert H. Humphrey (Dem., Minn.) on June 30, 1971, in reaction to the U.S. Supreme Court decision in the Pentagon Papers *case, in the* New York Times, *July 1, 1971, p. 16.*

I started [the process of copying the *Pentagon Papers*] with what seemed the most important, most useful material, on the assumption the whole thing would come out in a matter of weeks. . . . If I'd had one of those fast machines, the kind that just go zip, zip, zip for each copy, that would have been marvelous; I could have given a copy to every member of Congress. But as it was, I had a rather slow machine. In fact, I started out wanting to make four copies, and within an hour, we switched to two because it just took too long—we couldn't afford the time. . . .

In a general way, what I did could be seen as a classic Gandhian dream, to suppose that such an act of nonviolent truth-telling—and taking responsibility for it, publicly—is precisely what it took to disturb this government profoundly.

Their policy and administrative framework had been based for a whole generation on secrets and lying. The notion that the Ship of State is leaking truth is as frightening and unstabilizing as anything could possibly be.

Comments by Daniel Ellsberg in 1973 about his purloining and releasing the Pentagon Papers, *in "Leaking the Truth" by Jann S. Wenner, in Ashley Kahn, Holly George-Warren, and Shawn Dahl,* Rolling Stone: The Seventies *(1998), p. 43.*

Women's Rights

What is a lesbian? A lesbian is the rage of all women condensed to the point of explosion. She is the woman who, often beginning at an extremely early age, acts in accordance with her inner compulsion to be a more complete and freer human being than her society—perhaps then, but certainly later—cares to allow her.

From "The Woman-Identified Woman," an essay by the group Radicalesbians, released in 1970 and part of the controversy surrounding the departure of lesbians from NOW in 1971, available online at http://www. cwluherstory.com/CWLUArchive/womidwom. html, downloaded April 16, 2005.

Someone had to do it first. In this country everybody is supposed to be able to run for President, but that's never really been true. I ran *because* most people think the country is not ready for a black candidate, not ready for a woman candidate.

African-American congresswoman Shirley Chisholm explaining why she sought the Democratic presidential nomination in 1972, in Shirley Chisholm, The Good Fight *(1973), p. 3.*

Moon Missions

Shepard: (From the foot of the ladder) While Ed is loading up the ETB . . . (Listens) While Ed is loading up the ETB (with film mags and cameras), (as per checklist) I'll describe the general landing site. We are, in fact, in a low area. (Looking east and south) There seems to be a general swale or a wide valley between the Triplet Craters and the Doublet Craters. And we are on the downhill side at this particular point. (Turning slowly toward the west) It levels off at a lower elevation to the left of the LM (south), approximately 15 feet lower there, and then it starts back up to the rim of Doublet. It's a very uneven landing area here. And, of course, like all of the sections of the Moon, it's pockmarked by [a] tremendous amount of craters. The surface here, as we pointed out, is mostly fines and I hate to discuss any kind of lineations here in the immediate vicinity of the LM, because I can see very definite indications of the radial dust pattern caused by the descent engine. And I don't see any other lineal pattern, as such, right here in the area.

Observations of astronaut Alan Shepard on February 5, 1971, as he prepared to set foot on the surface of the moon during the Apollo 14 *mission, from a flight transcript, available online at http://www.hq. nasa.gov/alsj/a14/a14-prelim1.html, downloaded February 15, 2004.*

Scott: Well, in my left hand, I have a feather; in my right hand, a hammer. And I guess one of the reasons we got

here today was because of a gentleman named Galileo, a long time ago, who made a rather significant discovery about falling objects in gravity fields. And we thought where would be a better place to confirm his findings than on the Moon.

And so we thought we'd try it here for you. The feather happens to be, appropriately, a falcon feather for our Falcon. And I'll drop the two of them here and, hopefully, they'll hit the ground at the same time. (Pause)

Scott: How about that!

[Ground communicator Joseph P.] Allen: How about that! (Applause in Houston)

Scott: Which proves that Mr. Galileo was correct in his findings.

Apollo 15 *Astronaut David R. Scott describing on August 1, 1971, an experiment by which he released a hammer and feather simultaneously; they fell side by side and hit the ground at the same time. Galileo had postulated that a feather and a stone released in the Moon's airless environment would strike the lunar surface at the same time because the gravitational pull on each would be identical. From a flight transcript available online at http://www.hq.nasa.gov/ alsj/a15/a15.clsout3.html, downloaded February 15, 2004.*

Vietnam Veterans against the War

When asked during the televised interview how he felt about the results of [the antiwar protest in Washington], Kerry replied: "Hopeful, because a lot of people listened to us; depressed, because so many people who couldn't be bothered with us before suddenly became our friends and joined the bandwagon." Later, when [Morley] Safer asked him flat out, "Do you want to be president of the United States?" Kerry answered, "No. That's such a crazy question when there are so many things to be done and I don't know whether I could do them."

An account of a 1971 interview with John Kerry, then spokesperson for Vietnam Veterans Against the War, conducted by Morley Safer of the CBS television program 60 Minutes, *in Douglas Brinkley,* Tour of Duty: John Kerry and the Vietnam War *(2004), p. 381.*

Jim Morrison and the Doors

He was drinking twice as much as anybody else. At the end of the meal they came with two bottles of cognac and asked him which one he wanted. And he just grabbed one of them, tore off the top and raised the neck to his mouth.

Jim Morrison's friend Herve Muller describing how Morrison acted at a lunch in Paris just a few weeks before Morrison died. An undated comment in Jerry Hopkins and Danny Sugerman, No One Here Gets out of Here Alive *(1980), p. 358.*

All in the Family

I didn't swear. GD. The first word is God. How can that be a swear word? It's the most popular word in the Bible. The second word, damn, that's a perfectly good word, you hear it all the time, like they dam the river to keep it from flooding. And you read in the Bible that some guy was damned for cheating or stealing or having sex in the family. And who damned him? Who else? God. God damned him. Edith, beautiful words right out of the Bible.

Archie Bunker (played by Carroll O'Connor) explaining to his wife Edith (played by Jean Stapleton) in a 1971 episode of the TV show All in the Family *how his use of the phrase "God damn" was not swearing. Available online at http://www.imdb.com/title/tt0066626/ quotes, downloaded February 16, 2004.*

Muhammad Ali

It's a good feeling to lose. The people who follow you are going to lose, too. You got to set an example of how to lose. This way they can see how I lose. It'll be old news a week from now. Plane crashes, a President assassinated, a civil rights leader assassinated, people forget in two weeks. Old news.

Muhammad Ali commenting immediately after his failure, on March 8, 1971, to defeat Joe Frazier and recapture the world heavyweight boxing crown, in New York Times, *March 10, 1971, p. 49.*

It was the most vicious fight I've ever seen. I've never seen so many good punches thrown so often.

Arthur Mercante, the referee in the fight between Muhammad Ali and Joe Frazier, commenting in March 1971 on the battle between the two men, in Mark Kram, Ghosts of Manila *(2001), p. 147.*

[Referee Arthur] Mercante tried to hush us up. But this [Ali] was a talking machine. No way this fight would be waged in silence.

But for all his talk, and for all the playacting he did for the crowd, he was no longer the fighter that razzle-dazzled the folks in those first couple of rounds. Now he was down off his toes, and had taken to leaning up against the ropes and jiving. Sometimes he shook his head to the crowd to discount the damage of my punches. Sometimes he looked toward the ringside press and told them, "Noooooo connnteessst." Sometime he threw these pittpat punches against my gloves or against my forehead, as though testing for termites, joke punches, as if he was goofing on me.

But the joke was on him. I was fighting in earnest, and he was just trying to disguise the fact that he was stalling—that he couldn't do what he used to and dance for fifteen rounds. Not that he *couldn't.* I wouldn't let him. I was pounding the body and the head, and making those nimble legs of his say whoaaa, what's happening here.

Joe Frazier recalling in 1996 the fourth round of his fight with Muhammad Ali at Madison Square Garden in New York City in 1971, in Joe Frazier, Smokin' Joe *(1996), p. 109.*

Disneyworld

Here in Florida we have something special we never enjoyed at Disneyland . . . the blessing of size. There's enough land here to hold all the ideas and plans we can possibly imagine.

Walt Disney, founder of Disneyland, reflecting in the late 1960s on the building of his giant amusement park near Orlando that opened in 1971, in Jeff Kurtii, Since the World Began *(1996), p. 179.*

Can we do it without Walt? We don't know—but let's try. And remember, we're not going to spend one penny over $125 million.

Walt Disney's brother, Ray Disney, commenting in the late 1960s on the prospects of completing Disneyworld in the wake of Walt Disney's death, in Eve Zibart, The Unofficial Disney Companion *(1997), p. 36.*

3
Restless America
January 1972–December 1972

Vietnam, the fight for women's rights, Richard Nixon's dramatic trips to Communist China and the Soviet Union, the presidential election, and the almost invisible unfolding of Watergate, working like a phantom hand to shape politics and further erode faith in government—these were the events that more than any other defined 1972. In them appeared the tension between old and new, between truth and lies, between values that had been shaped in the 1960s and the realities of the 1970s.

VIETNAM AND THE TORTUROUS ROAD TO PEACE

The year began with First Lady Pat Nixon in Monrovia, Liberia, on the start of an eight-day goodwill tour through West Africa. On her return, President Nixon observed, "We have a very good, friendly, government-to-government relationship with the countries of Africa. But we, in America, also have a very deep personal interest in those countries, and by Mrs. Nixon going there, she was demonstrating what I know every person in this country would want to: that we have a feeling of friendship and affection for the millions of people that live in this very old continent, but with many new countries and with great, great hopes for the future."[1]

Monrovia, however, was no Saigon, and goodwill tours held no likeness to hardball diplomacy. On the international scene, Vietnam still took center stage—a dogged crisis, spilling seemingly endless quantities of blood while peace talks between the United States and communist North Vietnam dragged on.

President Nixon continued his Vietnamization policy, in which he ordered the turning over of the ground fighting from American troops to ARVN, the Army of the Republic of South Vietnam. On January 13, Nixon announced that he would withdraw 70,000 additional U.S. combat troops by May 1, reducing the troop level to 69,000, the lowest since President Lyndon Johnson escalated the fighting in 1965.

But many doubted that Nixon's policy would enable South Vietnam to withstand the communist rebellion. After all, the main reason why Americans began to fight in Vietnam, taking the offensive under Johnson, was because ARVN

An American B-52 returns to an air base in Thailand from deployment over South Vietnam. *(National Archives and Records Administration)*

proved incapable of doing so. In reality, Vietnamization was Nixon's way of ending the U.S. troop commitment while he avoided having to admit defeat. Through this policy, he sought to sidestep an obstacle that he had seen destroy other politicians and had even used himself against his opponents, namely, that to lose a country to communism, as China had been "lost" in 1949, displayed weakness, even disloyalty, on the part of the political leaders involved.

Historian Stanley Karnow concludes in his book *Vietnam* that Nixon, early in his administration, "ruled out victory in Vietnam" but refused also "to contemplate defeat." Consequently, he wanted a "durable peace agreement" rather than an indecisive Korean-style armistice.[2] The president's National Security Advisor, Henry Kissinger, however, wanted a more limited treaty, one designed simply to give the Saigon government some time to establish itself and perhaps survive. Even the most optimistic intelligence analysts, though, believed that it would take at least eight years for Saigon to gain the allegiance of those people living in Communist-controlled regions, and they made their estimates when American troop support was much higher than in 1972.

While Vietnamization provided an "out" for Nixon from the war, it left him in a precarious position. His effort to withdraw all American forces reduced his leverage over the communists and may have even encouraged them to think that they could win.

On January 25, the president took the unusual step of publicly announcing that he had, in October 1971, made considerable concessions to the enemy at peace talks in Paris. Nixon claimed that he had proposed three initiatives: the withdrawal of all U.S. forces within six months of an agreement on principles; a cease-fire of hostilities throughout Indochina; and the resignation of President Nguyen Van Thieu of South Vietnam, to be followed a month later by elections there to choose a new leader. In exchange, the North Vietnamese would have to release all prisoners of war and withdraw their forces from South Vietnam. The proposal, Nixon said, "has not been rejected, but it has been ignored. I reiterated [the] peace offer tonight. It can no longer be ignored."[3]

Nixon made it clear, as well, that Kissinger had engaged in several secret meetings with North Vietnamese leaders from August 1969 to August 1971. Both sides, he said, made proposals, and both sides rejected them.

Why Nixon was now making his October proposal public remained unclear. He may have been trying to put pressure on the Communists to consider his latest offer more seriously, or he may have been trying to silence his domestic critics who had been deriding him for failing to tender anything meaningful. Whatever the case, he shifted the blame for the continued fighting to the Communists. "We are publishing the full details of our plan tonight," he said. "It will prove beyond doubt which side has made every effort to make these negotiations succeed. It will show unmistakably that Hanoi—not Washington or Saigon—has made the war go on."[4]

Nixon insisted that he had made an offer "fair to North Vietnam and fair to South Vietnam." Yet in his announcement, he left unclear what would be the status of America's powerful air force, and its airfields and aircraft carriers, during any cease-fire. Furthermore, Nixon stipulated that Thieu's resignation and the subsequent elections must be preceded by the cease-fire, in effect leaving the Communists with having to restart the war and receive criticism for doing so should the election process break down. And Thieu's resignation would leave in place South Vietnam's other officials (except the vice president, who would also resign), the very ones who would oversee any elections (though Nixon said the vote would be under international supervision).

Interestingly, the president made reference to the widespread distrust toward politicians in America when he said: "Some of our citizens have become accustomed to thinking that whatever our Government says must be false . . . as far as this war is concerned."[5] The *Pentagon Papers* and the lies and deceit committed by presidents since the 1950s had clearly taken their toll.

Congressional leaders expressed differing views about Nixon's proposal, even though they almost uniformly appeared surprised that the president had gone as far as he had in making concessions. Representative Gerald R. Ford of Michigan, the House Republican leader, said, "the president has set the record straight by revealing his efforts to end the war through broad and comprehensive negotiations." John Stennis of Mississippi, the Democratic chairman of the Senate Armed Service Committee, said, "this shows that the president has done all that he could reasonably and honorably do as the chief executive of our nation." But Senator Frank Church of Idaho, a leading Democratic opponent of the war, demurred and said that the president's offer "would require the North to stop fighting and settle instead for elections in the South under a caretaker government. This has been suggested before and rejected."[6]

The North Vietnamese, in fact, criticized Nixon's public announcement and his proposals; they particularly disliked the idea of leaving Thieu in power until shortly before elections could be held. "How can we accept an election," one of the North Vietnamese delegates, Xuan Thuy, questioned, "when Thieu's forces, including a million-man army, pacification forces, civil guards, and police are operating down to the hamlet level?"[7] Nevertheless, the North Vietnamese stopped short of completely rejecting the U.S. ideas, and representatives on both sides realized that the American willingness to jettison Thieu had been a shift damaging to the South Vietnamese leader's standing.

Thieu, meanwhile, worried that Nixon might pressure him to make more concessions. He especially fretted—and even fumed—when Secretary of State William Rogers indicated that the U.S. negotiators would be "flexible." Thieu thought that he might be abandoned. On February 10, he warned: "The American government cannot act as a representative of the Vietnamese government in discussions with the other side about internal politics without first consulting Saigon."[8]

While the exchanges among the governments continued, the communists prepared for a massive military offensive. They wanted to influence the peace talks and the fall elections in the United States by delivering a severe blow to the Americans. Intelligence officials in Washington received news of the impending attacks, but they greatly underestimated their intensity. Secretary of Defense Melvin Laird told Congress that any Communist assault would be limited; Army Chief of Staff William Westmoreland said it would be of short duration.

Those assessments proved wrong. On March 30, the Communists threw 120,000 troops into battle, striking in three regions in South Vietnam: the northern provinces, the central highlands, and the provinces just north of Saigon. The most intense attacks occurred in the northern provinces, where the Communists sent ARVN reeling. They captured the provincial capital of Quang Tri in May and held it until September.

The offensive helped the Communist guerrillas in the Mekong Delta. As ARVN repositioned itself to meet the onslaught, its troop strength in the delta declined. More than 100 government posts consequently fell to the Communists.

American officials put on a false front about the combat: ARVN, they said, had fought well. Actually, ARVN had performed miserably. While the Communists had suffered huge casualties and had failed to completely annihilate ARVN, they accomplished their objective to embarrass U.S. policy by exposing Vietnamization as a failure. The White House news summaries given to Nixon vividly revealed the truth by describing ARVN's retreat with the words *rout, disarray,* and *crushing.*[9] Karnow says, "By puncturing the illusion of Vietnamization, [the attacks] clouded the period ahead with uncertainties."[10]

Nixon reacted in May to the communist offensive with a strategy that he had long favored and used previously: sending B-52s to bomb North Vietnam into oblivion and devastate Communist troops in the south. If peace were to come, Nixon wanted it to emerge through the smoke of a smoldering landscape, one so devastating that it would show that the United States had not lost the war but instead had pounded the Communists to their knees. He called it peace with honor.

Also in May, Nixon took another step when he ordered the mining of the main North Vietnamese port, Haiphong. Such action had been rejected previously for fear that the mines would sink a Soviet ship and produce a dangerous crisis with the USSR. Indeed, a Soviet freighter did strike one of the mines, but by then Soviet leaders were so anxious to have a summit with Nixon, they issued only a mild protest about the incident.

NIXON IN CHINA

On February 17, while the controversy over the Vietnam peace talks continued, President Nixon and his wife boarded a marine-corps helicopter on the lawn of the White House to begin their historic trip to the People's Republic of China. Several thousand people cheered as the couple waved from the open doorway of the helicopter. The crowd consisted of the vice president, the cabinet, office workers, and more than a thousand children bused in from nearby schools to stand behind a rope barrier, with a cold wind swirling about, for what Nixon hoped would be a much warmer future. He wanted those children, he said, to live in a "safer world" so that they could grow up in a "world of peace."[11]

Officials confiscated a sign the children spontaneously displayed. "Be a Nice Guy to Chou En-lai [Zhou Enlai]," it said good-humoredly in reference to the Chinese premier, but the White House wanted only that which had been planned and packaged. Presently, the helicopter lifted into overcast skies. Snow began to fall. A stop in Hawaii and Guam beckoned before the presidential party would reach Shanghai in China, 20,000 miles from Washington.

Preparations for the trip had begun several months earlier and followed a series of delicate discussions that included a July 1971 secret trip by Henry Kissinger to China. The trip embodied all the elements that were contained in the stereotype of the inscrutable Oriental (though Zhou Enlai disagreed with Kissinger's secrecy) and all the contents of a political thriller: Kissinger claiming during a visit to Pakistan that he had developed a stomachache and would have to stay in bed; the Pakistanis then helping him sneak his way out of their country by flying him on a jet over the snow-covered mountains to China; Kissinger and Nixon agreeing on a code name for the mission, Marco Polo, and a secret code word, "Eureka!"—to be communicated to the White House should Kissinger consider his trip a success. On July 11, Nixon received a cable with the word for which he had hoped: "Eureka!"

The planning for the China trip—indeed, the entire trip itself—reflected Nixon's preference to surprise and to make big decisions with little input from others and with little outside consultation. One Nixon biographer, Richard Reeves, sees it all as part of the president's "scheming to bypass the checks and balances built into the United States Constitution and the scrutiny of the people, the Congress, and the press."[12]

When Nixon pursued his visit to China, he left himself open to possible setbacks. Although Kissinger's trip had laid the groundwork for a consensus with the Chinese on several issues, there remained the possibility that a final communiqué could become clouded in acrimonious disputes. The trip could worsen relations with the Soviet Union or complicate matters with the war in Vietnam. More worrisome, it could expose the president to domestic critics—conservatives, in particular—who might feel betrayed and accuse him of dancing with the devil.

Yet, the trip deepened a "triangular relationship" intended by Nixon to play on a flaring distrust between China and Russia. The two countries looked at each other suspiciously across the tense Sino-Soviet border where the Russians were engaging in a huge military buildup and the Chinese were reacting by bolstering their own ground forces. (Indeed, while in China, Nixon made a revealing comment: The "whole world is watching," he said in reference to an audience that included the Soviet Union.) The showdown between the two countries made it possible that the Chinese would welcome an overture for improved relations from the Americans. The Chinese, Kissinger said, "wanted strategic reassurance, some easing of their nightmare of hostile encirclement."[13]

At the same time, a warming relationship between the Americans and the Chinese could not only worry the Soviets but also worry the North Vietnamese, who might suspect that China would lose its ardor for the fight against the Americans in southeast Asia. In a speech before a group of newspaper editors and publishers in Chicago in 1970, Kissinger acknowledged the Chinese-Russian tension (and by implication its importance to American foreign policy):

> The deepest rivalry which may exist in the world today is . . . that between the Soviet Union and Communist China. Along a frontier of 4,000 miles, there are territorial claims on one side and a military buildup on the other. This is made more severe by the dispute between the two great Communist states as to which of them represents the center of Communist orthodoxy, which gives a quasi-religious connotation to their conflict.[14]

For Nixon, a trip to China, while a bit of a gamble, held the prospect of tremendous domestic political benefits. He could be hailed as a man of vision and peace. He could divert attention from the Vietnam War. He could strengthen his standing for the 1972 presidential election.

Imagine how the American people riveted their attention on Nixon's trip. Here he was traveling to a country whose ancient non-Western civilization held a fascinating appeal; a country with whom the United States had not had diplomatic relations since the late 1940s and from which there had been few photographs for 20 years; a country labeled, amid a long and unnerving cold war, as an enemy . . . no, as evil incarnate . . . a country so hated by some that Nixon himself had refused until recently to call it by its proper name, the People's Republic of China, instead electing to call it Red China. On this ground, as much as any foreign soil, trod Richard Nixon.

The president planned to play the domestic impact to the hilt. So Kissinger made sure that the bulk of the press corps in the White House entourage consisted of television reporters. The visual impact they would provide, he correctly surmised, would far outdistance the print medium. Fortunately for Nixon, the time difference between China and most of the United States worked to his advantage too. Events occurring in the morning in China would be broadcast live on American television during prime time. Those occurring in the evening would be shown during the morning talk and news shows.

Nixon later described his first impression of Beijing:

> I looked out the window. It was winter, and the countryside was drab and gray. The small towns and villages looked like pictures I had seen of towns in the Middle Ages.[15]

His plane stopped at the terminal, the door opened, and out he stepped with his wife, Pat. Nixon observed:

> Chou En-lai [Zhou Enlai] stood at the foot of the ramp, hatless in the cold. Even a heavy overcoat did not hide the thinness of his frail body. When we were half way down the steps, he began to clap. I paused for a moment and then returned the gesture, according to the Chinese custom.

I knew that Chou had been deeply insulted by [Secretary of State] John Foster Dulles's refusal to shake hands with him at the Geneva Conference in 1954. When I reached the bottom step, therefore, I made a point of extending my hand as I walked toward him. When our hands met, one era ended and another began.[16]

The *New York Times* called the encounter "the end of a generation of hostility" and the beginning of a "new but still undefined relationship."[17]

An eerie atmosphere permeated the president's arrival at Beijing. A huge portrait of Communist Party chairman Mao Zedong (Mao Tse-tung) decorated the airport, as did posters bearing slogans about the "proletariat and the oppressed people" of the world. But while television cameras carried the event live to the United States via satellite, the wintry streets in the city stood desolate. Only silence greeted Nixon's motorcade. No crowds. No signs. No bands. The setting bespoke an official stand: no elaborate public ceremony for a country that had no diplomatic relations with China.

Yet on the afternoon of February 22, Nixon was granted an unexpected meeting with Mao Zedong—an opening audience rarely given to foreign visitors. Mao's power had declined since his halcyon days as the leader of his country's revolution, and he was old and sick and had difficulty speaking, but he remained, symbolically, an important figure. That he and Nixon would even share the same room together said much about the diplomatic shift underway. Nixon and Kissinger were surprised by Mao's articulate manner and awed by his commanding personality. Kissinger later said the revolutionary "dominated the room . . . by exuding in almost tangible form the overwhelming drive to prevail."[18]

President Nixon shakes hands with Chinese Communist Party leader Mao Zedong. *(National Archives and Records Administration)*

There followed in the evening a festive banquet staged by Zhou Enlai in a huge dining hall that was filled with 800 guests who were entertained by a band playing "America the Beautiful" over and over again. Shark was eaten—an unintended symbol of the dangerous diplomatic waters—and Zhou expressed the hope that the issue which had for so long prevented better relations between the United States and China, mainly the U.S. backing and recognition of Taiwan (Nationalist China) as the legitimate government for all of China, soon would be surmounted, given recent American movement on the issue.

Nixon followed his Chinese host's comments by stating that he saw no reason for the United States and China to be enemies since neither desired to conquer the other's territory. It was as if he had erased his cold-war vehemence toward the Chinese communists, leaving all those over whom he had demonized for the years with his red-baiting baffled, if alive, and turning over in their graves, if dead.

Beijing's hitherto becalmed streets soon buzzed with the news of Nixon's visit. Few Chinese owned televisions, but they flocked to newsstands to buy the latest editions of the *People's Daily,* which contained pictures of the American president and rarely seen pictures of Mao Zedong in his study.

During the next several days, Nixon and Kissinger engaged in lengthy talks with their Chinese counterparts. In between the talks, they attended a variety of events. Nixon's walk along the Great Wall of China received worldwide coverage, with photos spread across newspapers of the president and his communist hosts clad in heavy overcoats and pointing to features at the site. Nixon drew an analogy to the Great Wall and the international scene. "As we look at this wall," he said, "what is most important is that we have an open world."[19] (He was accused by the press for often being banal with his comments, such as when he said that the city of Hangzhou (Hangchow), with its gorgeous lakes and gardens and old palace, "looks like a postcard.")[20]

Three days later, on a visit to a factory in Shanghai, the analogies kept coming, but they were a bit more strained, a result of talks into the early morning

Chinese workers prepare to labor in the streets during President Nixon's trip. *(National Archives and Records Administration)*

hours having tired the participants. Standing before a printing press, Nixon said: "This is a machine operated by a single button. You must be careful when you push the button that you push the right button. Sometimes when we push the button, it doesn't turn out all right." To which Zhou responded: "We must push the button for constructive purposes."[21]

In the communiqué issued at the end of Nixon's visit, the president said that he wanted Communist China and Taiwan to settle their differences without outside interference, and he pledged the ultimate withdrawal of all U.S. troops and military installations from Taiwan "as tension in the area diminishes," a reference to the war in Vietnam and a prod to the Chinese to help resolve the conflict. Zhou agreed to increased scientific, technological, cultural, and athletic exchanges with the United States and to expanded trade. Furthermore, the communiqué implied that neither the United States nor China would allow their relationships with the Soviet Union to interfere with their mutual contacts. Finally, in a veiled reference to Soviet expansionist desires, both countries said that they stood against hegemony by any country in the Asia Pacific region.

Overall, Nixon and Zhou had reached a compromise. The *New York Times* reported: "The President had wanted an even faster pace of diplomatic and private communications and exchanges. The Premier had wanted a firmer recognition of Peking [Beijing] as the sole and legal government on [meaning to rule over] Taiwan."[22] Irrespective of this, the communiqué paled in importance to the thaw underway between the United States and China as a result of the Nixon visit. Although it offered little in the way of concrete, immediate changes—no diplomatic recognition of Communist China, for example, which would await another six years; and no American desertion of Taiwan, an issue which Nixon said could not be resolved at the time ("We could only agree to disagree," he said), or Chinese abandonment of North Vietnam—it laid the groundwork for a normalized relationship, more pragmatic than ideological.

On returning to Washington, President Nixon reassured Taiwan that no secret deals had been made in Beijing. He said, "We will not negotiate the fate of other nations behind their back;" and, he insisted, "there were no secret deals of any kind."[23]

An enthusiastic crowd greeted Nixon and cheered when he and the first lady descended the steps from *Air Force One.* But a small knot of protesters carried black umbrellas to mock Nixon by equating his diplomacy with that of British Prime Minister Neville Chamberlain's 1930s appeasement of Adolf Hitler—Chamberlain having often been portrayed with umbrella in hand.

Nixon faced numerous attacks from right wingers. The John Birch Society asserted that the president's visit to China had "humiliated the American people and betrayed our anti-communist allies."[24] Conservative commentator William F. Buckley claimed that Nixon had "sold out" to Communist China in a crass effort to boost his domestic political standing. In doing so, he said, the president had undermined America's treaty relationships in Asia and had passed a death sentence on Taiwan's survival as a free nation.

But writing in the *New York Times,* moderate political commentator James Reston praised Nixon for trying to step back from the deep abyss of the cold war. He called the president's trip "Mr. Nixon's finest hour."[25] While Reston recognized that Nixon was engaging in a time-honored tactic of boosting the weaker of two rivals to the United States, in this case China over Russia, he saw in the policy a bigger vision of seeking a less-stressful world. Reston concluded: "[The president] has shown foresight, courage, and negotiating skill. He has changed his direction, his policy, and the tone of his diplomacy, and there are few people in [Washington] today who don't welcome the change."[26]

In remarks to Zhou in Beijing, President Nixon indicated he well recognized his pioneering direction. He said:

> We look at each country in terms of its own conduct rather than lumping them all together and saying that because they have this kind of philosophy they are all in utter darkness. I would say in honesty to the Prime Minister that my views, because I was in the Eisenhower administration, were similar to those of Mr. Dulles at the time. But the world has changed since then, and the relationship between the People's Republic and the United States must change too. As the Prime Minister has said in a meeting with Dr. Kissinger, the helmsman must ride with the waves or he will be submerged with the tide.[27]

POLITICAL TROUBLES

Around the time Nixon returned from China, a political dispute erupted over the president's nomination of Assistant Attorney General Richard Kleindienst to replace John Mitchell as attorney general (who was leaving the administration to direct Nixon's reelection campaign). The Senate Judiciary Committee had already held hearings and cleared Kleindienst for the post, but in late February, newspaper columnist Jack Anderson reported that Nixon had pressured Kleindienst to drop an antitrust suit against ITT (International Telephone and Telegraph) in return for the corporation's donation of $400,000 to the upcoming Republican National Convention.

The suit went back to 1969, when Richard McLaren, head of the antitrust division of the Justice Department, charged ITT with restraint of trade and sought to force it to give up ownership of three companies that it had recently acquired. McLaren lost the case but announced that the government would appeal. Mitchell then negotiated a compromise, whereby ITT was allowed to keep one of the three companies and, at the same time, promised to provide money for the Republican Convention. Kleindienst was supervising the ITT cases and thus was involved in the deal.

When Anderson published the information, Kleindienst protested that he had maintained his independence in the cases, and he asked the Senate Judiciary Committee to reopen his confirmation hearing so that he could clear his name. As Democrats pilloried Nixon for underhanded dealings, a strange twist developed: Dita Beard, an ITT lobbyist who claimed that she had written a memo revealing the connection between the donation to the Republicans and Mitchell's intervention, disappeared. Anderson claimed that Beard had said to him: "ITT has told me to get out of town."[28] Beard was later discovered in a hospital room in Denver. She was visited by a Nixon operative, E. Howard Hunt, disguised in a red wig, who pressured her to state publicly that the memo that she had written was a forgery.

Meanwhile, Kleindienst marched back to the hearing room. To the committee, he admitted that he had helped to arrange a meeting between ITT officials and government lawyers. But, he claimed, "I was not interfered with by anybody at the White House. I was not importuned. I was not pressured. I was not directed."[29]

In fact, Nixon had telephoned Kleindienst in mid-April 1969 and told him: "I want something clearly understood, and, if it is not understood, McLaren's ass is to be out in one hour. The ITT thing—stay the hell out of it. Is that clear? That's an order."[30] Still, the Senate, unaware of this conversation, confirmed Kleindienst.

Nixon, who at a press conference in March defended Kleindienst and the way that the Justice Department had dealt with ITT, said at Kleindienst's swearing-in ceremony in June that the new attorney general had shown "loyalty and devotion" to America. "There is no question," Nixon insisted, "that here is a man who is strong in character and who is at his best when the going is roughest. He will be a great attorney general."[31]

Shortly before the ceremony, Mitchell, in part motivated by the aggressiveness of the Democrats in the Kleindienst controversy, approved a plan to have members of the Committee for the Reelection of the President (also called the Committee to Reelect the President), or CREEP, illegally break into the Democratic National Headquarters at the Watergate complex. The cancer in the presidency became ever more malignant. In 1974, all the deceit caught up with Kleindienst, and his Senate statement came back to haunt him when he admitted that he had failed previously to testify fully and accurately. By then, the Watergate crisis was roiling the country, and the trail of lies tied to it was bringing down a president.

AN EQUAL RIGHTS AMENDMENT ROOTED IN THE SIXTIES

In *The Unfinished Journey,* historian William H. Chafe writes: "Of all the social movements of the 1960s, the one that retained the most strength in the 1970s was the struggle for women's liberation and women's rights."[32] In March, the struggle appeared to move forward when the U.S. Senate voted 84-8 to approve an equal rights amendment (ERA) to the Constitution. Coupled with the earlier approval by the House of Representatives in October 1971, the vote sent the amendment to the states for consideration.

The action followed intense lobbying by the activist National Organization for Women (NOW) in both houses of Congress but especially with members of the Senate Judiciary Committee. Those who supported the amendment, however, also agreed to let it expire if it were not ratified within seven years. The heart of the amendment read: "Equality of rights under the law shall not be abridged by the United States or by any state on account of sex."

Passage of the ERA occurred while women were experiencing massive changes in their social and economic standing. More than 50 percent of working women had children age six to 16, meaning that these "working moms" were breaking down the old societal rules about a mother's proper place being in the home, taking care of the kids. At the same time, the greatest increase in employment for women was occurring among those aged 20 to 24, and these women, who included a much larger number of college graduates than even before, were entering fields that were traditionally dominated by men: business, medicine, engineering, and law.

Women no longer wanted to have large families, nor did they feel as compelled to marry. Both men and women pursued self-fulfillment to the point where they were less willing to work at keeping marriages together. The divorce rate increased 82 percent in the 1970s, and, by 1980, those living in "single households" reached 23 percent, as compared to 10.9 percent in 1964.

As the role of women changed, their desire for rights that had been denied them expanded. A majority of women wanted equal career opportunities, day-care centers, and more liberal abortion laws. Yet, there was far from gender unity on these issues; conservative women disagreed with the majority, and a wide range of women thought that feminists had become too extreme.

By 1973, 30 states had ratified the ERA, putting it only eight states short of the votes it needed. Then the drive stalled. Conservatives in particular claimed that its broad sweep would make women subject to a military draft, would weaken the standing of women in court cases involving alimony and child custody, and would end the segregation by sex of public bathrooms. At the same time, many African-American and Hispanic women failed to rally behind the amendment because they thought the fight against racial and ethnic discrimination more important. Ultimately, despite an extension of the original seven-year limitation, the ERA failed. In 1982, the amendment, passed by the Senate 10 years earlier with such high hopes, died a mere three states short from being ratified.

TITLE IX

The second wave of feminism scored victory, however, when Congress passed Title IX of the 1972 Higher Education Act. The fight for the legislation was led by Edith Green, a Democratic congresswoman from Oregon. Green wanted additional laws to attack sex bias in education. The main part of Title IX prohibited any sex discrimination in educational programs or activities that receive federal funds—a sweeping rule because it affected nearly all schools and colleges, both public and private. Title IX did, however, contain an exemption for undergraduate admissions to private colleges, allowing them to restrict the number of male or female students on campus.

While Green was promoting Title IX, she requested feminists to keep a low profile so as not to arouse opposition to the legislation. The stealth strategy worked; few people realized how far-reaching Title IX would be in terms of affecting schoolroom classes that excluded women or athletic programs that limited their participation.

In fact, once Title IX passed Congress and was signed into law, its opponents belatedly mounted a strong campaign to weaken it or to make it unworkable. Most of the opposition came from athletic departments and organizations. In particular, the National Collegiate Athletic Association argued that Title IX would bankrupt colleges financially by requiring equal expenditures for women's and men's sports. Many high schools also objected to the potential financial impact of the law.

While these challenges fell short, the Department of Health, Education and Welfare (HEW), whose Office of Civil Rights had the task of enforcing the law, dragged its feet. The department's officials, largely men influenced by bureaucratic inertia and conservative politics, considered sex discrimination to be less important than other issues and recoiled at feminist demands as threatening to male-dominated culture.

HEW withheld releasing Title IX regulations until 1974 and waited another year to revise them. One of the questions that was answered pertained to whether the law required the same athletic teams for the sexes or allowed separate ones. Some feminists had argued against separate teams; others argued, however, that separate teams were necessary to avoid having women lose out to men in most sports on the basis of physical strength. By and large, HEW sided with the "separate teams" approach. The department ruled against requiring equal funding for men and women's programs but said that single-sex teams had to be treated equally.

HEW's enforcement of Title IX remained lethargic. But the law gradually expanded its reach, largely due to a suit that had been filed by feminist groups against HEW and the Department of Labor to ensure proper enforcement of Title IX and to suits that had been filed in state courts by women. In 1974, the National Organization for Women created the Project on Equal Education Rights (PEER) to monitor Title IX enforcement.

THE TRIAL OF PHILIP BERRIGAN

Not only did the women's rights movement pulsate with the spirit of the 1960s, so, too, did a prominent trial involving 48-year-old Reverend Philip Berrigan, a Roman Catholic priest and longtime social activist. The government charges against him seemed to reveal the more radical and violent side of the previous decade. To wit: Berrigan and his followers had conspired to kidnap Henry Kissinger, blow up heating tunnels under federal buildings, and vandalize draft boards. They apparently planned to hold Kissinger in custody for a week so that they could submit him to a mock war-crimes trial.

To prosecute Berrigan along with six other antiwar activists including Sister Elizabeth McAlister and Reverend Joseph Wenderoth, the government relied heavily on the testimony of Boyd F. Douglas, Jr., a 31-year-old criminal who was purportedly so emotionally unstable that he had twice tried to commit suicide. At the time of the alleged conspiracy, Berrigan was in prison at Lewisburg, Pennsylvania, serving time for destroying draft records in Baltimore and in Catonsville, Maryland, as part of a protest against the Vietnam War.

Douglas and Berrigan met at the Lewisburg prison. Beginning in May 1970, Berrigan, the story went, used Douglas to smuggle written messages between Berrigan and his confederates outside the prison—an action facilitated by Douglas's status as a trustee who was permitted to leave his cell to attend classes at a nearby college. (Curiously, among 1,800 prisoners, he was the only inmate who had this privilege.) But Douglas was an FBI informer; having become one, he later said, shortly after he began to smuggle the letters.

Berrigan communicated extensively with Sister McAlister, a New York nun. In one such message, McAlister proposed the scheme to abduct Kissinger. Reverend Wenderoth offered the plan to blow up the tunnels, which was intended to spread panic throughout the government. The defense attorneys never denied that the messages contained the statements claimed to be in them by the government, but they called the ideas vague, far from serious, and certainly nothing resembling a conspiracy.

Former U.S. attorney general Ramsey Clark led the defense team. He showed that Douglas had demanded and received $50,000 from the government for his work as an informant. Then, after the prosecution spent five weeks and used 64 witnesses in presenting its case (at a cost exceeding $1 million), the trial took a stunning twist: The defense rested without calling a single witness.

The judge, R. Dixon Herman, infuriated the defense attorneys by presenting instructions to the jury that they called prejudicial against Berrigan and his colleagues. The jury deliberated the charges for several days before notifying the judge on April 2 that it had found Berrigan guilty of a letter-smuggling charge but that it had deadlocked on the more substantive charges. (The jury would also find Sister McAlister guilty of smuggling.) Herman told them to go back and to deliberate some more.

It did little good. The jurors again declared themselves deadlocked on the conspiracy charges. Consequently, on April 5, Judge Herman declared a mistrial. The government never pursued a retrial on the conspiracy charges, and later, an appeals court overturned the letter-smuggling convictions.

Berrigan was paroled in November 1972 and quit the priesthood in 1973, at which time, he revealed that he had secretly married Elizabeth McAlister. The couple moved to a commune in a black neighborhood of Baltimore. True to their 1960s principles, they continued to fight social injustice.

A JURY ACQUITS ANGELA DAVIS

In January 1972, an all-white jury in San Jose, California, acquitted black radical Angela Davis of murder, kidnapping, and criminal conspiracy in a trial that reached back to the turmoil of the 1960s counterculture.

A committed revolutionary who wanted nothing less than to make America communist, Angela Davis was, in the late 1960s, a member of the Black Panther Party in California and of the Communist Party. In 1970, she organized a campaign to help George Jackson and two men who were imprisoned at Soledad, a bleak prison that bears the Spanish name for solitude. Jackson had recently led his fellow inmates in condemning the racism prevalent at the prison. Their protest led to a riot, the death of a guard, and charges against Jackson and his followers. Davis believed Jackson to be innocent, the victim of a government effort to punish him for his outspoken leadership.

Then in August 1970, Jonathan Jackson, George's brother, led a radical group in raiding a courthouse during a trial in San Rafael, California. They captured Judge Harold J. Haley, a district attorney, and several jurors, whom they held as hostage. Jonathan intended to exchange them for George and thus have his brother released from jail. The plan backfired, however, when police attacked the assailants and a hail of gunfire resulted in several deaths, including Jonathan and the judge. Unfortunately for Angela Davis, two guns carried by Jonathan Jackson were registered in her name. The authorities thus labeled her an accomplice and determined to arrest her. To elude capture, Davis went into hiding, but later in the year, the FBI discovered her in New York City. She was then transported under heavy guard to Marin County in California.

There, she stood trial on charges of murder, conspiracy, and kidnapping. Throughout her confinement, she received strong support from both African-American and white radicals. Even moderate observers considered the charges against her to be weak and part of a government plan to persecute her. On June 4, 1972, the jury in San Jose acquitted her, reinforcing the view of those who believed that she had been wrongly treated because of her radicalism.

THE SHOOTING OF GOVERNOR GEORGE WALLACE

George Wallace, the governor of Alabama who gained national prominence from his fight against integration at the University of Alabama in 1963 (he briefly stood in "the schoolhouse door" in a futile effort to block federal marshals), had been a problem for Richard Nixon ever since 1968, when he and Wallace were both running for president. As an independent candidate, Wallace appealed to the conservative rage that was then taking hold and threatened to siphon enough votes from Nixon's own conservative base to deny Nixon the presidency.

Wallace tapped into the backlash against racial integration, especially the court-decreed desegregation of public schools, and he tapped into the anger over higher taxes, bigger government, rising crime, increasing permissiveness, and expanding social and political protests. He once claimed if any demonstrators lay down in front of his car, he would run them over, and his supporters hooted their approval.

Nixon thought Wallace would again run as an independent in 1972, and if he captured the South and the Democrats captured several Northern industrial states, then the Democratic nominee might win. With such concerns, Nixon decided to derail Wallace's attempt in 1970 to win back the Alabama governorship. Wallace decided to seek the office so that he would have a base from which to pursue the presidency. He ran as a Democrat against his party's incumbent, Albert Brewer.

The early polls indicated that Brewer would win the Democratic primary (and whoever won would become governor because there existed no effective Republican opposition). Wallace, however, could yet stage a comeback. Fear of losing was in Nixon's political gut; so, too, apparently, were paranoia and deceit. Consequently, the president resorted to unethical and illegal tactics.

At a meeting Nixon held with his chief of staff, H. R. Haldeman, the president decided to funnel money remaining from his 1968 presidential campaign to Brewer. Haldeman jotted down what Nixon had to say: "100 G for Brewer. Move on this."[33]

Haldeman next contacted Nixon's personal attorney, Herbert Kalmbach, to get the money and deliver it to a Brewer aide. Kalmbach filled a briefcase with hundred-dollar bills and headed for the Sherry Netherland hotel in New York City, where he met his contact person in the lobby. Kalmbach then took the money, $100,000, from his briefcase, stuffed it into a manila envelope, and handed it over. Other transfers soon followed, totaling $400,000 in all.

Nixon tried another ploy too. He pressured the IRS to audit the tax returns of Wallace's brother, Gerald. Nixon suspected that Gerald had received kickbacks from contractors who were doing business with the Alabama state government. The president had his aides leak news of the audit to newspaper columnist Jack Anderson.

Both tactics failed. Alabama voters thought the IRS story nothing more than dirty politics. Moreover, they drifted away from the lackluster Brewer to embrace Wallace's recycled rants against high taxes and an intrusive federal government.

Wallace finished second to Brewer in the first primary vote, but he beat the incumbent in the runoff.

Wallace's victory did nothing to ease Nixon's mind. Then, however, Wallace announced in August 1970 that he would seek the presidency not as a third-party candidate but as a Democrat. His decision helped Nixon in two ways: It lessened the possibility that Wallace would at any point run independently, and it promised to tear the Democratic Party asunder. Shortly after Wallace made his announcement, the Justice Department let it be known that it was dropping an ongoing investigation into Gerald Wallace for corrupt practices. No hard evidence exists to prove a quid pro quo, but at the least Nixon realized that he could now ease up on George Wallace; by avoiding to antagonize him, he could court his voters, once, of course, the governor lost the Democratic presidential contest.

Wallace entered the 1972 primaries with a less acerbic message than in 1968; he no longer talked about running people over. But he continued to appeal to those frustrated with liberals and with the general direction of the country. His criticisms of increased crime, a bloated bureaucracy, and Washington insiders who had lost touch with the common folk touched deep currents.

As Wallace traveled about the Democratic primary states, the crowds that he attracted often reflected his own intensity: Those who liked him cheered wildly, and those who disliked him taunted him, heckled him, and even threw objects at him. In Maryland, a chanting crowd of blacks forced him to cut short a speech in Hagerstown early in May. In Frederick, someone threw a rock that hit him on the shoulder.

On the morning of May 15, Wallace spoke to a crowd at a park in Wheaton. Some of the spectators tried to shout him down; others pelted him with coins, rocks, oranges, and tomatoes. These hostile acts only encouraged his supporters, who used it as evidence that America had lost its moral moorings.

Supporters of presidential candidate George Wallace stand by their campaign mule in 1972. *(Copyright © 1972 Diana Mara Henry)*

Among those in the crowd at Wheaton: Arthur Bremer, a shiftless 21-year-old who had attended a Wallace rally in Milwaukee, where he stood less than 30 feet away from the governor. At Wheaton, Bremer led cheers for Wallace.

In the afternoon, Wallace spoke to a crowd at a shopping center in Laurel. About 1,000 people listened to him with little reaction, and no hecklers appeared. As he left, several well-wishers pressed against a rope barrier and implored him to come closer. To his secret service guard, James Taylor, Wallace said, "I suppose I had better shake hands." "Don't go, governor," Taylor implored. "That's all right," Wallace said, "I'll take the responsibility."[34]

Wallace worked the crowd. As he finished and headed toward his car, he heard someone shout: "Hey, George, let me shake hands with you!"[35] The words came from Bremer. When Wallace turned to see who had called out, Bremer shot him with a .38 snub-nosed revolver. Spectators reacted: They threw Bremer down and started pummeling him. Wallace lay sprawled on his back.

Five bullets had pierced Wallace's body. The governor remained conscious on his way to a nearby hospital. "I am in pain," he said.[36] He would remain in pain for the rest of his life, for one of the bullets had cut through his spinal canal and paralyzed his lower body. He would never again walk, and no drugs or surgery could rid him of the biting ache he felt every day.

Wallace spent five hours in surgery. Three other people were wounded in the shooting.

Richard Nixon learned almost immediately about the tragedy. Once again, he responded with his penchant for illegal acts. He and an aide, Charles Colson, developed a bizarre plot: They decided to have E. Howard Hunt break into Bremer's Milwaukee apartment and plant literature issued by the campaign of Democratic presidential candidate George McGovern. Nixon believed that once the literature was discovered, the public would connect Bremer to McGovern fanatics.

His attempt to besmirch McGovern collapsed, however, when FBI agents sealed Bremer's apartment before Hunt could enter it. Further ruining the plan, news photographers had previously been allowed into the apartment and had taken pictures of the site that showed it devoid of McGovern material.

Bremer apparently had no political motivation in shooting Wallace. He had actually wanted to shoot Nixon but found it difficult to get close to the president. Bremer even expressed disappointment at having to settle on Wallace as a target. The governor, he believed, was small fry whose killing would never bring him the attention that he desired. His political thoughts seemed a jumble. In one of his scrawled writings, he said, "Happiness is hearing George Wallace singing the National Anthem, or having him arrested for a hit-and-run traffic accident."[37] Bremer was eventually sentenced to 63 years in prison.

To Americans, the shooting was another in the long line of political violence stemming from the 1960s. The assassinations of John Kennedy, Martin Luther King, Jr., and Robert Kennedy, along with physical attacks against others underscored the polarized and unsettled society. *Izvestia,* the newspaper of the Soviet Union's government, commented, "Once again an election year—once again a shooting."[38]

In the meantime, Wallace went on to win the Maryland primary and an important one in Michigan. Polls showed little connection between the tragedy at Laurel and his victories. He won votes because he had connected with concerns about crime and school busing. Wallace vowed to continue his campaign from a wheelchair, if he had to, but he eventually quit the race.

Wallace changed politics by promoting the antiliberal themes that many Americans found appealing. One Wallace biographer, Stephan Lesher, states: "From 1968 to 1992 no person was elected president without clearly embracing and articulating (though not necessarily implementing) the Wallace issues."[39] Historian Dan T. Carter states: "The politics of rage that George Wallace made his own had moved from the fringes of our society to center stage. He was the most influential loser in twentieth-century American politics."[40]

In the long run, Republicans understood Wallace's appeal more than did Democrats. By co-opting Wallace's antiliberal attacks, Republicans put the Democrats on the defensive into the 1990s and beyond.

HISTORIC TRIPS AND MEANINGFUL TREATIES

In Canada, April brings with it warming winds to break the ice. That same month, President Nixon tried his own hand at thawing troubled relations with America's northern neighbor in a trip to Ottawa. The Canadians had been complaining about American economic and political pressure, which threatened to relegate their country to a mere appendage of the United States. Nixon, though, said that in international relations, "the soundest unity is that which respects diversity, and the strongest cohesion is that which rejects coercion."[41] His statement signaled that the United States would accept recent efforts by Canada to establish closer diplomatic ties with China and the Soviet Union. Additionally, the president promised to pursue equitable trade agreements with Canada.

The biggest publicity came for an environmental pact between the two countries. Officially titled the Great Lakes Water Quality Agreement, it addressed the rapidly escalating pollution on the Great Lakes. Lakes Erie and Michigan had become dumping grounds for raw sewage, and in Lake Erie, phosphates were strangling aquatic life.

To meet the goals of the agreement, Canada acted to reduce phosphates in laundry detergents. The United States promised to continue to expand its efforts at building and improving municipal sewage plants.

While in Canada, Nixon made several statements aimed at the Soviet Union as he prepared to meet with its communist leaders in Moscow to discuss Vietnam and reach agreements on nuclear weapons. Then, in early May, he took a calculated risk to escalate the Vietnam War by mining the main North Vietnamese harbor of Haiphong. He knew his move might wreck the upcoming Moscow summit and could cost him reelection in November, but he had to respond to the communist offensive more emphatically; nothing seemed to be stopping or even seriously hampering the North Vietnamese. To his aides, Nixon said: "The summit isn't worth a damn if the price for it is losing in Vietnam. My instinct tells me that the country can take losing the summit, but it can't take losing the war."[42]

The president addressed Americans on national TV and said that the Soviet Union must accept the mining of Haiphong as a defense of U.S. interests. He was trying, he insisted, "to keep the weapons of war out of the hands of the international outlaws of North Vietnam."[43]

Coupled with massive bombing attacks against the communists, the mining displayed a determined effort to protect President Nguyen Van Thieu in South Vietnam. Both amounted to desperate measures in a desperate situation.

Yet, the Soviet Union was desperate as well, for it wanted to avoid an endless, expensive arms race with the United States. Henry Kissinger noted: "Under [Brezhnev] the Soviet Union had undertaken a colossal military buildup.... The accumulating military means create their own opportunities and an inherent threat to the global balance of power. On the other hand, the massive devotion of scarce resources to military hardware would also inhibit the modernization of Soviet society."[44] In addition, the Soviet Union wanted the prestige of being treated as an equal of the United States, an aura that a meeting in Moscow would confer. "Equality," Kissinger said, "seemed to mean a great deal to Brezhnev."[45]

So despite Nixon's escalation, the Soviet Union opted to proceed with the summit. The United States would be able to eat its cake and have it, too, or as Kissinger put it: "I think we are going to be able to have our mining and bombing and have our summit...."[46]

Nixon looked at the Moscow summit as another part of his new policy, called détente. He believed that the United States had to move beyond the simplistic response to Soviet power of building more nuclear bombs and threatening to throw them around. More bombs actually meant less security because the Soviet Union could respond in kind. In any event, with the rise of China, the world had become less bipolar—the United States versus the Soviet Union—and more tripolar. Détente meant a lessening of tension, and this arrangement, if nuclear war were to be avoided, needed to be achieved with both China and the Soviet Union.

Détente appealed to the Soviets too. A lessening of tension with the United States would free them to engage China more directly. To the Soviets, the threat from the Chinese loomed larger than the one from the Americans.

Unlike the trip to China, the one to the Soviet Union came with less mystery. Congress had been notified weeks in advance about what agreements the president expected to reach on nuclear weapons, and, indeed, delegates from both countries had been hard at work on the issue during meetings in Helsinki, Finland, at what were called the Strategic Arms Limitation Talks, or SALT. (In fact, the talks left little for Nixon and the Soviet leaders to negotiate, making the Moscow summit more ceremonial than substantive.) Furthermore, for most Americans, Russia was less enigmatic than China because the United States had more political and economic dealings with the Soviets than with the Chinese.

Yet, the trip was momentous. Henry Kissinger exuded: "This has to be one of the great diplomatic coups of all times!"[47] When Nixon landed at Vnukovo Airport on May 22, 1972, with a light rain dampening the runway, he became the first sitting American president to visit the Soviet leadership in Moscow. His welcome resembled the one in China: a polite, official greeting at the airport while the government discouraged crowds along the streets. Still, about 100,000 curiosity seekers turned out, far more than had been the case in Beijing. They gathered along side streets, behind police barricades, to watch for Nixon's motorcade as it sped along the broad main avenues beneath U.S. flags that workers had hastily attached to light poles. But they were a disappointed group, for the cars sped so quickly to the Kremlin that they saw no one inside them.

Nixon met unexpectedly in the afternoon with Soviet Communist Party leader Leonid Brezhnev. The two men had been scheduled to talk at a later time. Alone in a room (except for interpreters), they discussed nuclear arms, trade, and the war in Vietnam. Nixon described Brezhnev's appearance:

[He] looked exactly like his photographs: the bushy eyebrows dominated his face, and his mouth was set in a fixed, rather wary smile.48

Kissinger said about Brezhnev:

[He] was . . . quintessentially Russian. He was a mixture of crudeness and warmth; at the same time brutal and engaging, cunning and disarming.49

In his talks with Nixon, Brezhnev claimed that the U.S. leader's actions in Vietnam had pushed Brezhnev to the point of nearly canceling the summit.

Nixon and Brezhnev engaged in lengthy talks the following day, largely about nuclear arms, with Nixon's schedule so consumed by government activities that he had no time to venture beyond the Kremlin. During the course of Nixon's visit, the leaders exchanged sharp words about Vietnam. Brezhnev accused Nixon of being insincere about wanting to end the war; he referred to those in the United States who opposed the conflict: "Certainly I doubt that families of those who were killed or maimed or who remain crippled support the war."50 Nixon expressed his anger over the recent North Vietnamese offensive—the one that exposed Vietnamization as a sham—having been bolstered by Soviet military aid. He said that he had reduced the U.S. combat role in Vietnam, and he charged: "Since this new offensive began, 30,000 South Vietnamese civilians . . . have been killed by the North Vietnamese using Soviet equipment."51

The summit's most historic agreements came on May 26, when Nixon and Brezhnev signed two documents: an antiballistic missile (ABM) treaty that limited each country to 200 launchers for defensive missile systems (100 each at two sites each) and a five-year interim accord, known as SALT I, which froze offensive intercontinental ballistic missiles (ICBMs), both land-based and submarine-based, to

President Nixon and Soviet leader Leonid Brezhnev shake hands in Moscow. *(National Archives and Records Administration)*

their current levels. No on-site verifications were provided for; compliance would have to be checked through existing methods, such as satellite surveillance.

The agreements contained so many deficiencies that they still allowed each country to improve and even expand its nuclear arsenal. For example, there were no controls that were placed on the number of strategic nuclear bombers and no limits on the numbers of warheads that could be placed on the offensive missiles. The last point showed that neither Nixon nor Brezhnev had come to grips with a recent technology, multiple independent reentry vehicles, or MIRVs.

The two countries put the numbers of weapons involved at 1,618 land-based and 710 submarine-based ICBMs for the Soviet Union, compared with 1,054 and 656, respectively, for the United States. But the United States had 460 strategic bombers to the Soviet Union's 140, and, because of MIRVs on many of its missiles, the United States would soon have substantially more nuclear warheads than the Soviet Union, 5,700 to 2,500.

Despite the faulty agreements, Soviet Premier Aleksei Kosygin said: "This is a great victory for the Soviet and American peoples in the matter of easing international tension. This is a victory for all peace loving people because security and peace is the common goal."[52]

Henry Kissinger told reporters that Nixon and Brezhnev had gone far in stabilizing the arms race between their two countries. An American official especially praised the treaty on defensive missiles for preventing either side from gaining an advantage through a security blanket that would allow it to launch a first strike. By leaving themselves vulnerable to attack, both countries rested their security and the avoidance of a nuclear war, as they had for years, on the policy of mutually assured destruction.

Writing in *Nixon: The Triumph of a Politician, 1962–1972,* historian Stephen A. Ambrose concludes: "For all the flaws, for all that he could have driven a harder bargain, for all that he had failed to freeze, much less reduce, nuclear arsenals and delivery systems, Nixon had achieved a symbolic breakthrough, namely that the two sides could set limits on their destructive capability."[53] In August, the U.S. Senate ratified the ABM treaty.

During the rest of his trip, Nixon attended the Bolshoi Ballet—where one woman shouted from the audience "Viva Vietnam!"—and he addressed the Soviet people on television. In his 20-minute broadcast, the president spoke from the Green Room of the Grand Kremlin Palace and assured his listeners that the United States wanted peace. He added: "As great powers, we shall sometimes be competitors, but we never need be enemies."[54]

A BREAK-IN AT WATERGATE

Not long after returning from the Soviet Union, President Nixon vacationed in Key Biscayne, Florida. In his memoirs, he recounted:

On Sunday morning, June 18 . . . when I got to my house I could smell coffee brewing in the kitchen, and I went in to get a cup. There was a *Miami Herald* on the counter, and I glanced over the front page. The main headline was about the Vietnam withdrawals: *Ground Combat Role Nears End for U.S.*

There was a small story in the middle of the page on the left-hand side, under the headline: *Miamians Held in D.C. Try to Bug Demo Headquarters.*[55]

The Watergate complex in Washington was the scene of the break-in at the Democratic headquarters by Nixon campaign operatives. *(National Archives and Records Administration)*

So began the public unfolding of Watergate. The *Miami Herald* article referred to operatives from CREEP who broke into the headquarters of the Democratic National Committee at the Watergate building in Washington and were arrested. (Money for CREEP projects came from illegal fund-raising directed by John Mitchell while he was attorney general, a man whom Nixon once called "the leader of our fight against crime and lawlessness."[56]) The burglars were James W. McCord, Bernard L. Barker, Eugenio R. Martinez, Frank Sturgis, and Virgilio R. Gonzalez. McCord formerly worked for the Central Intelligence Agency (CIA) and was at the time a security agent for the Republican National Committee and CREEP. Barker owned a real-estate company and had contributed money to the Republican Party. All five men had been involved in anti-Castro activities.

The burglars were arrested in the early morning hours. Their big mistake: They had stuck tape to a door to keep it from locking, and when the security guard on duty, Frank Wills, discovered the tape and removed it, they raised his suspicions by replacing it. The guard then called the police, and they followed a trail of taped doors to the DNC headquarters on the sixth floor, where they found the Nixon operatives in an inner office.

The burglars were supposed to replace a malfunctioning bug they had planted in an earlier break-in, on May 28. What CREEP hoped to accomplish by spying on the Democrats, however, remains a mystery and may never be known. As it turned out, the burglars carried with them more than a bug; they possessed new $100 bills, tear-gas fountain pens, and walkie-talkies. The burglars had rifled through files and pried open the ceiling panels near an office. John Mitchell, the chairman of CREEP, responded to the arrests with an emphatic denial: "We want to emphasize that [McCord] and the other people involved were not operating either on our behalf or with our consent. I am surprised and dismayed at these reports."[57]

"Surprise" and "dismayed" covered up the truth. Nixon had long disliked Larry O'Brien, the chairman of the Democratic Party. Worried that O'Brien had dirt on him, and, in any event, believing that any information that he could get about Democratic political plans could only benefit his own reelection, Nixon placed pressure on his underlings to go after O'Brien. His determination probably explains why CREEP broke into the Watergate offices, and the CREEP operatives probably did so under the direction of none other than Mitchell. Nixon's own later claims that he was shocked about the break-in when he read about it and could not understand why anyone would do such a thing were most likely subterfuges. Given the pressure that he had exerted and the atmosphere he had created—along with his own political life in the dark hallways of surreptitious ventures—he likely fully understood why the break-in had occurred. What he might not have understood is why the burglars had been so stupid as to get caught.

Once the burglars were arrested, Richard Nixon resorted to the devious, paranoid, and protective side of his personality and began a cover-up. At first, he may well have wanted to guard Mitchell, his longtime political friend, although, presently, he decided on a plan to make Mitchell the fall guy. More likely, he feared that if all the facts behind those implicated in the burglary became known, other illegal activities conducted by his administration would be exposed. And that could ruin his bid for reelection.

Nixon was, more than anything else, a political animal. (As reported by one Nixon biographer, the president's closest aide, H. R. Haldeman, once insisted that Nixon was so consumed by politics and was so much a loner that he often forgot the names of his two daughters.[58]) He thrived in Washington, in the machinations connected to power, or the loss of it. He left nothing to chance in his political campaigns—he directed them, no one else—and although it can be said that many of his actions reached beyond securing power for himself, little of what he did failed to have his political future as the primary consideration, whether it

Larry O'Brien, a target of the Watergate break-in, is pictured here at the 1972 Democratic National Convention. *(Copyright © 1972 Diana Mara Henry)*

be his trip to China, his trip to Russia, his harangue against long-haired youth or liberal do-gooders, or his seething indictment of busing to achieve school desegregation.

Memos he wrote to his aides and notations he made on memos showed that he followed nearly every political development and interpreted nearly every event with his chances for reelection in mind. About the economy, he told his aides H. R. Haldeman and Bob Colson: "It is our job to get *our* issue at the top."[59]

About the *Washington Post* calling his foreign policy one of "stalemate and rhetoric," he told Haldeman: "This is where our people should be talking about our bold . . . initiatives—*never* undertaken by JFK et al."[60]

About Elliot Richardson, the secretary of Health, Education, and Welfare, being too compliant in pursuing school desegregation, he said to his domestic affairs adviser, John Ehrlichman: "I'll see the son-of-a-bitch and give him some backbone!"[61]

About the possibility that his aides could make an analogy between the solar eclipse that was scheduled to occur on the opening day of the Democratic Convention and the fate of America, he wrote to Colson: "Your people should be able to do something with this."[62]

He combined these points into a succinct statement concerning what he would have to hit in the presidential campaign: "The issues are radicalism; peace-at-any-price; a second-rate United States; running down the United States; square America versus radical America."[63]

On June 23, 1972, Nixon met with Haldeman, and they conspired to obstruct justice by agreeing to a plan that had been proposed by John Mitchell and the president's counsel, John Dean to get the CIA to tell the FBI that an investigation would jeopardize CIA operations. According to a transcribed version of their tape-recorded conversation, complete with the disjointed pattern often found in casual talk, Nixon agreed with the plan and instructed Haldeman to tell the CIA: " 'The President's belief is that this is going to open the whole Bay of Pigs [Cuban crisis] thing again. And because these people are plugging for, for keeps, and that they should call the FBI in and say that we wish for the country, don't go any further into this case,' period."[64] When Haldeman took the concocted story to CIA Director Richard Helms, Helms responded: "The Bay of Pigs had nothing to do with this!"[65] Still, Helms reluctantly agreed to tell the FBI to drop its investigation. FBI agents involved in the case, however, continued to pursue their leads.

Within a short while, Nixon approved the payment of hush money to the operatives (funds that he later called "humanitarian" payments). On August 1, 1972, Nixon and Haldeman talked about the arrests:

Haldeman: "They're all out of jail, they've all been taken care of. We've done a lot of discreet checking to be sure there's no discontent in the ranks, and there isn't any. . . . It's very expensive, It's a costly—
Nixon: "That's what the money is for."
Haldeman: "—exercise, but that's better spent than—"
Nixon: "Well, . . . they have to be paid. That's all there is to that."[66]

On September 15, Nixon, Haldeman, and Dean again met in the Oval Office. The president praised Dean for plugging the political holes and keeping

Watergate from developing into a debilitating scandal. He ranted against his enemies, threatened to ruin Edward Bennett Williams, the lawyer representing the Democrats in their $1 million invasion of privacy suit against CREEP, and said that the FBI and the justice department must be used to attack his political opponents. The rant was Nixon's vengeance and hatred raw and naked, joined by Haldeman and Dean, who added fuel to the president's toxic statements.

Also in September, John Mitchell gave a deposition in the Democrats' suit. He stuck to his previous story about having no prior knowledge of the break-in. At about the same time, Democratic presidential nominee George McGovern asserted that in May, even before Watergate, Nixon political operatives had tried to break into his headquarters. McGovern said that it indicated a dangerous trend. He said that if administration officials could do this against him, they "would have no qualms . . . about violating the privacy of the voting booth, or the church, or your home if it were necessary to carry out their purposes."[67] The next step, he warned, would be a one-party state where liberties would be trampled. He considered Watergate more than a sideshow, more than the impression that was left by the White House of a "few of the boys getting carried away."

Democrats in the House of Representatives tried to fan the Watergate flames. An investigation by the banking committee found that $100,000 that was used to finance the burglars came from moneys raised in Mexico, making it an illegal contribution. The money, delivered to Pennzoil headquarters in Texas, was stuffed into a suitcase and flown to Washington.

Just a few days after this revelation, a grand jury indicted the five burglars, along with former low-level Nixon aides G. Gordon Liddy and E. Howard Hunt, for conspiring to break into the Democratic headquarters at Watergate. Liddy and Hunt had been at the Howard Johnson Hotel, across the street from Watergate, where they had stationed themselves to supervise the break-in.

End of story, so it appeared. The Justice Department said that the indictments closed the Watergate investigation. A spokesperson insisted: "We have absolutely no evidence to indicate that any others should be charged."[68] Larry O'Brien, however, thought differently and urged the president to appoint a special prosecutor.

McGovern called the indictments a whitewash. Higher ups had to have been involved, he claimed, and big questions had yet to be answered, such as: Why the break-in? Who ordered it? Who paid for it? What happened to the information collected by such spying?

At the end of September, the *Washington Post* reported that, while serving as attorney general, John Mitchell had dipped into a secret slush fund to finance surveillance of the Democrats. Both Mitchell and CREEP denied the "lies."

Richard Nixon weighed in at a press conference in early October. He called the investigation one of the most thorough in the government's history, one he had always insisted should go wherever it might go. "I wanted every lead carried out until the end," he claimed, "because I wanted to be sure that no member of the White House staff and no man or woman in a position of major responsibility in [CREEP] had anything to do with this kind of reprehensible activity."[69]

McGovern again: Richard Nixon has "no respect for constitutional government and personal freedom." The president had directed the illegal bugging operations, he charged, and the Nixon administration "more than any other in the history of this country has undermined our personal and our constitutional rights."[70]

Yet, McGovern made no headway on Watergate. "He desperately tried to exploit the issue," says historian Stanley I. Kutler. "But the Democratic presidential candidate could not attract serious attention on more momentous matters; how, then, could he hope to arouse voter interest in what seemed to be a campaign peccadillo?"[71]

When the *Washington Post* reported that Haldeman had used secret money to finance political espionage, the White House vehemently denied the charge. Even more, it went on the offensive and accused the newspaper of working to boost McGovern in the presidential election.

Nixon's cover-up appeared to be working. The Watergate burglars maintained their silence in the weeks leading up to the November vote, and only a few newspapers devoted any significant space to the break-in. An exception: the *Washington Post* and two of its reporters, Carl Bernstein and Bob Woodward, who refused to accept Nixon's professions of ignorance. This was, after all, a president who once had said, "When I am the candidate, I run the campaign." They pursued leads, endured threats, and overcame stonewalling to produce articles in which they raised doubts about the president's story and paved the way for a much deeper investigation.

NIXON'S LANDSLIDE

George McGovern insisted that the American people would never reelect a president whose officials had been involved in spying and burglary against a political opponent. He was wrong. Nixon won by a landslide in November.

For that, McGovern had partly himself to blame. Earlier in the year, he had run well in the first Democratic primaries, winning in Massachusetts and Pennsylvania, and after George Wallace ended his campaign, McGovern won a string of primary elections, including delegate-rich California. But he appealed mainly to the party's liberals. Moderates felt left out; they even felt antagonized by his bold proposals, such as a $30 billion cut in defense spending and a $1,000 grant to every person as a way to fight poverty and redistribute income. The Democratic Convention in Miami Beach only reinforced the sense of estrangement among moderates and among the party's traditional political brokers. Platform positions on abortion and busing and the enhanced power that was given to minorities and women through new rules convinced numerous Democrats to stay away from the McGovern campaign. Even the AFL-CIO, a traditional supporter of Democratic candidates, declared its neutrality in the general election.

When reports revealed that McGovern's running mate, Missouri senator Thomas Eagleton, had been treated for manic depression and had been given electric shock therapy, McGovern added to the woes of his injured campaign. First, he insisted that he stood behind Eagleton completely. Then as the criticism of Eagleton as unfit for the vice presidency intensified, he dumped

Thomas Eagleton (left) and George McGovern clasp hands at the 1972 Democratic National Convention. *(Copyright © 1972 Diana Mara Henry)*

Sargent Shriver and George
McGovern wave to supporters in
Washington, D.C. *(Copyright ©
1972 Diana Mara Henry)*

him and replaced him on the ticket with former Peace Corps director Sargent
Shriver. McGovern thus appeared to have made a bad choice to begin with and
then seemed to be a man whose word meant little.

More than McGovern's mistakes worked in Nixon's favor. In late October, just
days before the election, Henry Kissinger entered a briefing room at the White
House and presented reporters with important news about the Vietnam War: "We
believe that peace is at hand," he said. "We believe that an agreement is in sight."[72]
As it turned out, Kissinger had said more than Nixon had wanted him to, and the
claim proved to be a bit premature. (An agreement was initialed on January 23, 1973.)
But it raised the public's hopes that the long, divisive conflict had finally been
resolved. The announcement, Kissinger later noted, "produced jubilation nationally."[73] Even the war issue had seemingly deserted McGovern.

On election day, Nixon captured 61 percent of the popular vote and won in
the electoral college, 521-17. Most tellingly, an entire region, the South, shifted
its loyalties from the Democrats to the Republicans (a shift underway in several
Southern states at least since the 1964 election), and core Democratic groups, such
as blue collar workers, went over to the Republican side en masse.

One consolation for the Democrats: They retained control of Congress. The
election results told another story too: Millions of Americans stayed away from the
polls. The low turnout indicated dissatisfaction with both candidates and a
widespread alienation from the entire political process.

VIETNAM HAMMERED AND NIXON EXPOSED

On December 13, the "peace at hand" negotiations with North Vietnam collapsed. Nixon decided to force the Communists back to the negotiating table by
launching a ferocious air attack on North Vietnam. He resumed heavy bombing

President Nixon is greeted by school children during his 1972 campaign. *(National Archives and Records Administration)*

and used B–52s "on a sustained basis for the first time over the northern part of North Vietnam."[74]

The assault, dubbed Linebacker Two by Nixon and called the Christmas Bombings by most everyone else, began on December 18. For 11 days, American planes blasted the terrain mainly from Hanoi to Haiphong. They targeted railroads, power plants, docks, and shipyards. Stray bombs hit houses and hospitals. The North Vietnamese shot down 26 U.S. aircraft, including 15 B–52s. The toll among the pilots and crews: 31 captured and 62 killed.

Critics pummeled Nixon for the attack. European governments and Pope Paul VI expressed dismay and even outrage. The *Washington Post* called the air war "savage and shameless."[75] Hanoi reacted by signaling its willingness to resume talks.

The bombing began just six days after Nixon admitted that two of his aides, David Young and Egil Krogh, Jr., had operated out of the White House as "plumbers," investigators assigned to track down the sources of news leaks. (The formal name of the group was the White House Special Investigations Unit.) The two men had a private telephone line; it circumvented the White House switchboard and allowed them to conduct business without official records being kept of their conversations. Nixon's press secretary, Ron Ziegler, insisted that none of the Watergate burglars were connected to the plumbers, nor had the burglars been directed by the plumbers. Actually, the plumbers consisted of more than two men, and Young and Krogh had indeed recruited Liddy and Hunt for various jobs early on.

In time, a more complete story of the plumbers would merge with Watergate, adding to an interlocking scandal comprising massive abuses of power and illegal and unconstitutional acts. The plumbers staged covert operations that were aimed at Nixon's critics and opponents; they operated as a secret police force. John Ehrlichman had formed the plumbers and worked with them, and Nixon himself gave them orders. The next 18 months would reveal these facts and the multitude of Nixon crimes. The unraveling had begun; the cover-up would be exposed.

MOON MISSION

On April 19, astronaut John W. Young radioed, "Hello, Houston, sweet 16 has arrived." The words referred to the *Apollo 16* Moon mission. On that date, Young, along with fellow astronauts Thomas K. Mattingly and Charles M. Duke, positioned their command module in the lunar orbit required to proceed with their landing on the Moon. On the following day, Young and Duke headed for terrain north of Descartes Crater. Their expedition was delayed by a malfunction of the guidance system aboard the command module, but otherwise, everything proceeded without a significant hitch.

Young and Duke spent 71 hours on the Moon, longer than any previous mission. They collected 214 pounds of lunar material, the first ever gathered from the Moon's mountains. The astronauts completed their $450 million mission and returned to Earth on April 27, landing in the Pacific Ocean near Christmas Island.

A delay hindered another lunar mission, *Apollo 17*, as well, this time on December 7 when the rocket carrying the space capsule attempted to lift off from Earth. A malfunction set the flight back more than two hours. Then *Apollo 17* roared into space, made up its lost time, and headed for the Moon. The astronauts on board, Eugene A. Cernan, Harrison H. Schmitt, and Ronald E. Evans, were making the sixth and last U.S. manned flight to the Moon, part of a program which, since the 1960s, cost $25 billion.

Cernan and Schmitt walked on the Moon. They dedicated a rock to the young people of Earth, took it with them for their return trip, and planted a plaque that said:

Here man completed his first
explorations of the moon
December 1972, A.D.
May the spirit of peace in
   which we came
Be reflected in the lives of
   All mankind

John Ehrlichman gained enormous power as President Nixon's domestic adviser. *(National Archives and Records Administration)*

THE GODFATHER AND PONG

Mario Puzo's novel *The Godfather* came to the big screen in March 1972 in a movie adaptation that was directed by Francis Ford Coppola. Critic Pauline Kael called it a "vivid" portrayal of the Mafia, one that presented the underworld crime organization as a twisted extension of American business practices and, in the process, offered a critique of both.

The movie attracted large audiences, and those who saw it would long remember Marlon Brando as Don Vito Corleone, his voice changed into a whisper and his facial image puffed out by balls of cotton that were stuffed into his cheeks for the part. The cast included Al Pacino, James Caan, Robert Duvall, Abe Vigoda, Talia Shire, and Diane Keaton. *The Godfather* won Academy Awards for Best Picture and Best Screenplay, and Brando won an Academy Award for Best Actor.

A customer entering a bar in Sunnyvale, California, in September 1972 would have noticed a coin-operated device that was causing a much bigger sensation than the old pinball machine. The device was the first video arcade game, *Pong,* an electronic version of Ping-Pong. About a year earlier, California engineer Nolan Bushnell took a few hundred dollars from his savings and founded a company called Atari, which manufactured *Pong.*

So many people played *Pong* in the Sunnyvale bar that within a few weeks, the overused machine needed repairs. By 1974, more than 100,000 *Pong* games, most made by Atari, some by other companies, were stationed in arcades and bars across the country.

HARDSHIPS IN BASEBALL

In baseball, for the first time ever, a players' strike delayed the start of the major league season. The dispute involved the players' demand to increase the pension fund, but it involved something else, too: getting to the bargaining table team owners who hated the thought of sitting down and talking to their employees. Union leader Marvin Miller observed: "They [the owners] haven't negotiated yet in their whole lives and they're not about to."[76]

The owners' reluctance plus a dispute over whether the players should be paid for any games missed because of the strike threatened to make the walkout a long one. But on April 13, the two sides agreed on a figure for the pension fund, and they agreed that the missed games would be jettisoned and the season would be shortened. On April 15, the familiar cry of "play ball!" could be heard in 12 major-league ballparks across the country.

The season began as the 18th for Roberto Clemente, the Pittsburgh Pirates right fielder who was considered to be one of the most talented players in the history of the sport. The year ended in his tragic death. Clemente, 37 years old, had won four batting championships and entered the season with a .318 average, second-highest among active major leaguers at the time. He had earned a reputation for playing outstanding defense and had won 12 gold gloves.

He had also earned a reputation for speaking his mind on subjects that most ballplayers thought best left untouched. A native of Puerto Rico, he complained that African Americans and Latinos were discriminated against in product endorsements, receiving far fewer of them than Anglo ballplayers. He criticized baseball's reserve clause for keeping players chained to one ball club. He charged U.S. newspapers with misunderstanding Hispanic players, and he openly complained about being given little acclaim for his athletic accomplishments. He once said: "Nobody does anything better than me in baseball."[77]

Clemente played for the Pirates when they won the World Series in 1960. He hit safely in each of the games and compiled a .312 average. But he made a much bigger impact in 1971 when the Pirates upset the Baltimore Orioles four games to three to again win a world championship. In the series, Clemente batted .414, hit two home runs, made two difficult running catches, and was named Most Valuable Player.

As much as Clemente spoke out, he acted to help others. When an earthquake devastated Nicaragua, he volunteered to lead Puerto Rico's efforts in providing aid to the victims. One of those involved in the project said about Clemente: "He did not just lend his name to the fund-raising activities the way some famous personalities do. He took over the entire thing, arranging for collection points, publicity and the transportation to Nicaragua."[78]

On the night of December 31, Clemente boarded a four-engine DC-7 plane at San Juan International Airport. The plane was loaded with supplies, perhaps overloaded according to some reports. Shortly after takeoff, it crashed into rough seas. Clemente's body was never found.

The way in which Clemente died caused the National Baseball Hall of Fame to waive its rule of waiting five years from the end of a player's career before inducting him. He was inducted on August 5, 1973.

Back in January, President Nixon hailed Clemente for his playing abilities and "for his splendid qualities as a generous and kind human being."[79] The world needed people such as him in a time of political lies and continuing war.

CHRONICLE OF EVENTS

1972

January 2: First Lady Pat Nixon arrives in Monrovia, Liberia, to begin an eight-day goodwill tour that will take her through West Africa.

January 5: President Richard Nixon signs a bill authorizing $5.5 billion to be spent on developing a space shuttle that will be lifted into space aboard a rocket but return like an airplane.

January 10: A U.S. district judge orders the merger of the predominantly black schools of Richmond, Virginia, with the nearly all-white schools in neighboring Henrico and Chesterfield counties. The merger is aimed at forcing racial integration.

January 13: President Nixon announces that 70,000 additional U.S. combat troops will be withdrawn from South Vietnam by May 1. This will reduce the troop level to 69,000, the lowest since President Lyndon Johnson's escalation of the fighting in 1965.

January 17: The New Jersey Supreme Court rules that the state's death penalty violates the Fifth Amendment of the U.S. Constitution. The decision makes New Jersey the 13th state where there is no death penalty.

January 25: President Nixon reveals that, during the previous October, he presented a secret plan to officials of communist North Vietnam who were meeting with American officials in Paris to discuss an end to the Vietnam War. Under the terms of the plan, the United States would withdraw all of its forces in South Vietnam within six months in exchange for a cease-fire throughout Indochina and the release of all American prisoners of war. The plan included a proposal to hold an election in South Vietnam to choose a new president there. Nixon reports that to date, the communists have ignored his plan.

January 29: Newspaper columnist Jack Anderson publishes an internal memo from International Telephone and Telegraph that shows a direct link between the government's decision to drop antitrust action against the company in exchange for ITT contributing money to the Republican Party. An investigation by the U.S. Senate fails to result in any charges of wrongdoing.

February 18: California ends its death penalty after the state's supreme court rules that it violates the California constitution.

February 21: The trial of Reverend Philip Berrigan and six other antiwar activists, collectively known as the Harrisburg Seven, begins in Harrisburg, Pennsylvania. They are accused of plotting to kidnap President Nixon's foreign policy adviser Henry Kissinger and of conspiring to blow up heating tunnels connected to office buildings and to raid draft offices in Washington, D.C.

February 21: President Richard Nixon begins his historic visit to Communist China when he arrives in Beijing. The visit ends the U.S. isolation of China and paves the way to American diplomatic recognition of the Communist government. Those accompanying the president include First Lady Pat Nixon, Secretary of State William Rogers, and National Security Advisor Henry Kissinger. The eight-day trip involves banquets, sightseeing, the acceptance of two panda bears as a gift to the United States, and long negotiating sessions, with Nixon holding meetings with Premier Zhou Enlai [Chou En-lai] and Chairman Mao Zedong (Mao Tse-tung). In a communiqué issued on February 27, Nixon and Zhou pledge that they will strive for a normalization of relations between their two countries, will seek to lessen the danger of war, and will oppose the efforts by any nation to establish a hegemony in the Asia-Pacific region.

February 23: Black activist and communist Angela Davis is released from jail on $102,500 bail. Her trial on charges of furnishing guns and helping to plot an escape

Newspapers throughout the country carried photos of President Nixon as he toured the Great Wall of China. *(National Archives and Records Administration)*

of black inmates in Marin County, California, will begin on February 28.

February 24: Reverend Daniel Berrigan, a Jesuit antiwar activist, is released from jail after serving 18 months of a three-year term for burning draft records in Cantonsville, Maryland. He says that he will now journey to Harrisburg to witness his brother Philip's trial.

February 28: President Nixon goes on national television to discuss his trip to China. He says that he entered into no secret deals and that the visit has paved the way for more peaceful relations with the Chinese government.

March 2: Acting Attorney General Richard Kleindienst reacts to charges of corruption against him by asking the Senate Judiciary Committee to reopen hearings that it had just concluded in considering his nomination to become attorney general. The committee had approved the nomination, but shortly thereafter, charges surfaced that Kleindienst had been involved in settling an antitrust suit against the International Telephone and Telegraph Company in exchange for that corporation's helping to defray the costs of the Republican National Convention scheduled for 1972 in San Diego. The Judiciary Committee heard new evidence but stood by its earlier decision to recommend Kleindienst's nomination. In June, the Senate voted 64-19 to confirm his appointment as attorney general.

March 6: Jack Nicklaus becomes the leading money winner in professional golf when he wins the Doral Eastern Open Title. At this point, his career earnings exceed $1.4 million.

March 7: Senator Edmund Muskie of Maine wins the New Hampshire Democratic presidential primary, outdistancing South Dakota senator George McGovern by a margin of 46 percent to 37 percent. Muskie had been considered the frontrunner in the race, and the results reaffirmed his status.

March 13: Author Clifford Irving and his wife admit that they defrauded book publisher McGraw-Hill by presenting his book about multimillionaire Howard Hughes—with information allegedly provided by Hughes—as truthful when it was, in fact, a hoax.

March 14: Alabama governor George C. Wallace stuns moderates by winning the Florida Democratic presidential primary. The conservative's tally of 42 percent of the vote far outstrips the 18 percent won by Minnesota senator Hubert Humphrey and the votes won by eight other candidates.

March 15: The movie *The Godfather* premieres. An adaptation for the screen of Mario Puzo's novel of the same name by Francis Ford Coppola, it stars Al Pacino, Robert Duvall, James Caan, and Marlon Brando.

March 17: President Nixon announces that he will send to Congress legislation prohibiting the federal courts from ordering busing to integrate public schools. He acts as an increasing number of whites express their opposition to busing.

March 22: The U.S. Senate votes to approve an equal rights amendment. The margin is 84-8, and, coupled with the measure's earlier approval by the House of Representatives, the amendment now goes to the states for ratification.

March 22: The National Commission on Marijuana and Drug Abuse recommends the end to all criminal penalties for the private use and possession of marijuana. The commissioners say that marijuana does not pose any major threat to the nation's public health.

March 23: U.S. officials walk out of the Paris peace talks to protest the failure of the communist North Vietnamese to negotiate in earnest. They will decide to return, however, on April 27.

March 27: An all-white jury in San Francisco acquits two black convicts of killing a prison guard at California's Soledad prison.

April 4: Senator George McGovern of South Dakota wins the Wisconsin Democratic presidential primary with 30 percent of the vote. His victory propels him to prominence in the presidential campaign, while the former front runner, Senator Edmund Muskie of Maine, falls farther behind.

April 5: The trial of Reverend Philip Berrigan and six others, known as the Harrisburg 7, for plotting to kidnap presidential adviser Henry Kissinger and blow up heating systems attached to federal office buildings ends in a mistrial when a jury deadlocks at 10-2 in favor of acquittal. Earlier, the jury found Berrigan and Sister Elizabeth McAlister guilty of smuggling letters to and from Lewisburg Federal Penitentiary where Berrigan is serving a six-year sentence for destroying draft records in Baltimore and Catonsville, Maryland.

April 5: For the first time, the opening of the major league baseball season is delayed by a players' strike. The delay, however, lasts only one week when the team owners agree to changes in pension plan payments.

April 15: On a visit to Canada, President Nixon signs a treaty with Prime Minister Pierre Elliott Trudeau providing for the governments of Canada and the United States to act together in eradicating pollution in the Great Lakes. The treaty especially aims at ridding Lake Erie of a two-foot-thick coating of algae that covers several hundred miles of its surface in summer. The algae forms as a result of phosphorous carried by detergents and other sewage that flows into the lake.

April 25: Minnesota senator Hubert H. Humphrey wins the Pennsylvania Democratic presidential primary with 35 percent of the vote. Nevertheless, Senator George McGovern of South Dakota wins enough delegates to boost him into the lead for the nomination.

April 25: The Ford Motor Company recalls all 1972 Torinos and Mercury Montegos to correct a problem that causes the rear wheels to fall off. The recall involves a total of 436,000 cars.

April 27: Maine senator Edmund Muskie announces that he will withdraw from the remaining Democratic presidential primaries, although he will remain a candidate for his party's nomination.

April 27: The *Apollo 16* Moon mission ends when astronauts John W. Young, Charles M. Duke, Jr., and Thomas K. Mattingly successfully guide their space capsule to a landing in the Pacific Ocean. While on the Moon, Young and Duke collected 214 pounds of rocks and soil and set up a $40 million science station.

May 1: Quang Tri, the capital city of South Vietnam's northernmost province, falls to communist forces in a major blow to the U.S. program of Vietnamization (turning the fighting over to the South Vietnamese army, or ARVN). Soldiers in ARVN's 3rd Division flee Quang Tri in a panic, leaving behind tanks, armored cars, and artillery.

May 2: J. Edgar Hoover, the 77-year-old director of the FBI, dies in his sleep in his Washington, D.C., home. Hoover had served as director for 48 years under eight presidents. His body lay in state on May 3 in the Capitol.

May 2: Minnesota Senator Hubert H. Humphrey scores a narrow win in the Indiana Democratic presidential primary, edging out Governor George C. Wallace of Alabama.

May 4: Alabama governor George C. Wallace wins the Tennessee Democratic presidential primary with an impressive 70 percent of the vote. His victory is partly based on his strong stand against busing to achieve racial integration in public schools.

May 8: President Nixon launches Operation Linebacker when the U.S. mines Haiphong and other ports in North Vietnam. The mining effectively closes the ports and disrupts the flow of military supplies to Communist forces.

May 11: A federal appeals court overturns the contempt sentences issued against the Chicago Seven antiwar activists during their trial in 1970 before Judge Julius Hoffman.

May 15: Alabama governor George C. Wallace is shot while campaigning for the Democratic presidential nomination at a shopping center in Laurel, Maryland. The police arrest 21-year-old Arthur Bremer for the shooting that also injures three other people. Bremer was wearing Wallace campaign buttons and had been sighted at other Wallace rallies in Wisconsin, Michigan, and Maryland. On May 16, the governor recovers from five hours of surgery. One of the bullets that struck him near his spinal cord leaves him permanently paralyzed from the waist down.

May 16: Alabama governor George C. Wallace wins the Democratic presidential primary in Michigan with 51 percent of the vote. His victory shows his strong appeal outside of the South. The same day, he also wins the primary in Maryland with 39 percent of the vote.

May 22: President Nixon visits the Soviet Union, going to Moscow for a discussion with Kremlin leaders about nuclear arms and other pressing issues. He asks Communist Party General Secretary Leonid I. Brezhnev and Premier Aleksei Kosygin for restraint in the Soviet support of North Vietnam and expresses the hope that the United States and the Soviet Union will never go to war. Two days later, Nixon signs an agreement with Kosygin for a joint U.S.-Soviet space flight in 1975. But the highlight of the visit will come on May 26 when Nixon and Brezhnev sign two documents, known as the strategic arms limitation, or SALT, accords, dealing with nuclear weapons. (Talks between the United States and the Soviet Union about limiting nuclear weapons had begun in 1969.) One of them, an ABM treaty that will later be ratified by the U.S. Senate, limits the number of each country's antiballistic missiles; the other, an Interim Agreement on Certain Measures With Respect to the Limitation of Strategic Offensive Arms (to be of five-year duration), freezes the number of intercontinental ballistic missiles and submarine-launched missiles to roughly their existing numbers.

June 3: The Peers Panel, which is investigating the My Lai massacre, charges the entire command structure of the U.S. Army's American Division with misconduct. The panel, headed by Lieutenant General William R. Peers, claims that the division's two top generals committed 43 acts of misconduct or omission in an investigation of the atrocity.

June 4: An all-white jury in San Jose, California, acquits black radical Angela Davis of murder, kidnapping, and criminal conspiracy relating to a 1970 shootout in which a judge and three others were killed.

June 12: Major General John Lavelle tells a House Armed Services subcommittee that he ordered some 20 unauthorized air raids on targets in North Vietnam between November 1971 and March 1972. Lavelle had been fired as commander of the U.S. 7th Air Force in Vietnam the previous March as a result of his action.

June 14: The Environmental Protection Agency makes illegal nearly all uses of the pesticide DDT.

June 17: Five men are arrested for breaking into the offices of the Democratic National Committee at the Watergate complex in Washington, D.C. The men had with them cameras and bugging devices.

June 20: Senator George McGovern wins the New York Democratic presidential primary, giving him a near lock on his party's nomination.

July 1: Former attorney general John N. Mitchell quits as chairman of Richard Nixon's Committee to Reelect the President. He states that he wants to spend more time with his family, but his resignation comes just two weeks after the Watergate break-in.

July 10: The Democratic National Convention opens in Miami Beach. During the session that lasts four days, the delegates select South Dakota senator George McGovern as their presidential nominee.

July 25: The Associated Press reveals that the U.S. government had engaged in a 37-year study of syphilis that denied treatment for the disease to 400 black men at Tuskegee Institute.

July 25: Missouri senator Thomas F. Eagleton, the Democratic nominee for vice president, confirms reports that during a six-year period, he had undergone treatment for depression, nervous exhaustion, and fatigue that included electric shock therapy. His admission raises questions about whether he has the mental stability to serve in the vice presidency. Presidential nominee George McGovern insists that he will not abandon Eagleton and that he is confident that the American public will be compassionate and understanding enough to support the nominee. On July 29, McGovern will state that he is standing behind Eagleton "1,000 percent."

July 31: Democratic presidential candidate George McGovern announces that Senator Thomas Eagleton is withdrawing as his vice presidential running mate. McGovern says that the move is not motivated by Eagleton's health but by the continuing controversy over Eagleton's suitability for the vice presidency, a controversy that threatens to detract from the campaign. As it turns out, McGovern's choice of Eagleton and then his indecisiveness in removing him greatly damages McGovern's standing in the presidential race.

August 3: The Senate ratifies the ABM treaty that limits the United States and the Soviet Union to two antiballistic missile sites each.

August 4: A jury of six men and six women finds Arthur H. Bremer guilty of shooting Alabama governor George C. Wallace and three bystanders at a shopping center in Laurel, Maryland. At the time of the shooting, Wallace had been campaigning for the Democratic presidential nomination. The charges against Bremer—four counts of assault to murder, four counts of assault with a firearm, and one count of carrying an illegal gun—result in a 63-year prison sentence.

August 8: A special session of the Democratic National Committee in Washington chooses R. Sargent Shriver, former ambassador to France and director of the Peace Corps under President John Kennedy, to succeed Thomas Eagleton as the party's vice presidential candidate.

August 11: The last U.S. ground combat troops leave Vietnam. The first combat troops, a contingent of marines, had landed at Danang in 1965. The war continues, however, as U.S. planes bomb North Vietnam and 43,500 service personnel remain in South Vietnam.

August 21: The Republican National Convention convenes at Miami Beach. During the session, which lasts until August 23, the delegates nominate President Richard Nixon and Vice President Spiro Agnew for reelection.

August 26: U.S. swimmer Mark Spitz wins seven gold medals at the XX Olympic Games that open on this date. The Olympics become best known, however, for the attack by the Palestinian group Black September on the Israeli athletic team when the terrorists break into the team's lodgings and kill two athletes while taking nine hostages. The games are suspended, and a gun battle between West German police and the terrorists results in the deaths of four Palestinians, all nine hostages, and one police officer.

August 29: President Nixon announces that he has investigated the break-in at the Democratic National Headquarters at Watergate and has found no connection between his staff and the burglary.

Vice President Spiro Agnew is seen here campaigning in 1972; only months later, he would face criminal charges and be forced to resign. *(National Archives and Records Administration)*

September 1: President Nixon and Premier Kakuei Tanaka of Japan end a two-day summit conference in Hawaii with an agreement by Japan to import more than $1 billion in U.S. goods during the next two years. The move is praised by Nixon as a way to lessen the American trade deficit with Japan.

September 2: The army ends its review of the 1968 My Lai massacre. The only punishments are reprimands of a colonel and a captain and the discharge of an infantry sergeant.

September 5: The Reverend Philip F. Berrigan is sentenced to four concurrent two-year terms for his role in smuggling letters at the federal penitentiary in Lewisburg, Pennsylvania. Sister Elizabeth McAlister is also sentenced to a one-year term for the crime. The sentences will later be overturned on appeal.

September 14: By an 88-2 vote, the Senate ratifies the Interim Agreement from the SALT talks, freezing the number of offensive nuclear missiles in the United States and the Soviet Union to their current amount.

September 15: A federal grand jury indicts seven men on charges of breaking into the Democratic national headquarters at the Watergate complex. Those indicted include E. Howard Hunt, a consultant to President Nixon, and G. Gordon Liddy, former counsel on finances to the Committee to Reelect the President. Former attorney general John Mitchell, who had recently resigned as chairman of the committee, says that the men who broke into the headquarters were not operating with the consent of Nixon campaign officials.

September 29: Carl Bernstein and Bob Woodward of the *Washington Post* reveal that former attorney general John Mitchell maintained a slush fund to pay for "dirty tricks" against Democratic candidates. Their investigation leads the White House to admit in late October that the slush fund had indeed existed.

October 3: President Nixon and Soviet Foreign Minister Andrei Gromyko sign the documents implementing the SALT treaty and a nuclear missile pact. The treaty limits the numbers of antiballistic missile sites in the United States and the Soviet Union; the pact limits the number of land-based and submarine-housed nuclear missiles held by each country.

October 16: A small plane carrying Representatives Hale Boggs (Dem., La.) and Nick Begich (Dem., Ark.), crashes on a flight from Anchorage to Juneau. An extensive search fails to find any survivors.

October 22: The Oakland Athletics, boosted by Gene Tenace's four home runs, win the World Series by defeating the seemingly invincible Cincinnati Reds in seven games.

October 24: Baseball great Jackie Robinson dies of a heart attack. Robinson was the first African American to play major league baseball when he appeared on the field for the Brooklyn Dodgers in 1947.

November 7: Republican candidate Richard Nixon wins reelection as president in a landslide, defeating Democratic candidate George McGovern with more than 60 percent of the popular vote and by winning every state except Massachusetts. (McGovern won in Washington, D.C.).

November 16: Two black students are killed by buckshot during violence on the campus of Southern University in Baton Rouge, Louisiana. The predominantly African-American school had experienced weeks of student protests over academic and housing issues. In December, a state investigation concludes that the buckshot came from a single shotgun blast originating from an area where sheriff's deputies were stationed.

November 27: President Nixon announces that he will shake up his cabinet to avoid stagnation in his administration. He says that he wants to make sure that his second term avoids going "downhill." During the next several days, he accepts the resignations of cabinet members and shifts the assignments of others among the departments. Included in the changes: Melvin Laird is replaced by Elliot Richardson as secretary of defense.

November 29: The Reverend Philip Berrigan, who was serving a prison term for destroying draft board records, receives parole.

December 4: Judge John Sirica begins hearing pretrial motions in the Watergate criminal trial.

December 7: Apollo 17 lifts off from Cape Canaveral headed for the Moon. Astronauts Eugene Cernan and Harrison Schmitt are scheduled to walk on the lunar surface.

December 12: The White House admits to the operation of "the plumbers," a group assigned to break into the offices of political opponents.

December 18: President Nixon orders massive air attacks on North Vietnam. The destruction of civilian targets in Hanoi and Haiphong raises a storm of international protest. In raids that will last until December 30, the United States will admit to losing more than 25 aircraft, while about 100 airmen will be reported as missing, killed, or captured.

December 26: Former president Harry S. Truman dies at age 88 at his home in Independence, Missouri.

December 28: Whitman Knapp, chairman of the Knapp Committee that is investigating wrongdoing in the New York City police department, concludes that most police are corrupt. The malfeasance committed by the officers includes working for organized crime, picking the pockets of dead people, and participating in the drug trade.

December 31: Roberto Clemente, who had risen from poverty in Puerto Rico to become an outstanding baseball player with the Pittsburgh Pirates, dies when the cargo plane in which he is flying crashes in the Atlantic shortly after taking off from San Juan. Clemente had been helping to transport food and other supplies to the victims of an earthquake in Nicaragua.

EYEWITNESS TESTIMONY

President Nixon's Vietnam Peace Proposal

Good evening:

I have asked for this television time tonight to make public a plan for peace that can end the war in Vietnam.

The offer that I shall now present, on behalf of the Government of the United States and the Government of South Vietnam, with the full knowledge and approval of President Thieu, is both generous and far-reaching.

It is a plan to end the war now; it includes an offer to withdraw all American forces within 6 months of an agreement; its acceptance would mean the speedy return of all the prisoners of war to their homes. . . .

For 30 months, whenever Secretary Rogers, Dr. Kissinger, or I were asked about secret negotiations we would only say we were pursuing every possible channel in our search for peace. There was never a leak, because we were determined not to jeopardize the secret negotiations. Until recently, this course showed signs of yielding some progress.

Now, however, it is my judgment that the purposes of peace will best be served by bringing out publicly the proposals we have been making in private. Nothing is served by silence when the other side exploits our good faith to divide America and to avoid the conference table.

Nothing is served by silence when it misleads some Americans into accusing their own government of failing to do what it has already done. Nothing is served by silence when it enables the other side to imply possible solutions publicly that it has already flatly rejected privately. . . .

We are being asked publicly to respond to proposals that we answered and, in some respects, accepted months ago in private.

We are being asked publicly to set a terminal date for our withdrawals when we already offered one in private.

And the most comprehensive peace plan of this conflict lies ignored in a secret channel, while the enemy tries again for military victory.

That is why I have instructed Ambassador Porter to present our plan publicly at this Thursday's session of the Paris peace talks, along with alternatives to make it even more flexible.

We are publishing the full details of our plan tonight. It will prove beyond doubt which side has made every effort to make these negotiations succeed. It will show unmistakably that Hanoi—not Washington or Saigon—has made the war go on.

Here is the essence of our peace plan; public disclosure may gain it the attention it deserves in Hanoi.

Within 6 months of an agreement:

—We shall withdraw all U.S. and allied forces from South Vietnam.

—We shall exchange all prisoners of war.

—There shall be a cease-fire throughout Indochina.

—There shall be a new presidential election in South Vietnam.

President Thieu will announce the elements of this election. These include international supervision and an independent body to organize and run the election, representing all political forces in South Vietnam, including the National Liberation Front.

Furthermore, President Thieu has informed me that within the framework of the agreement outlined above, he makes the following offer: He and Vice President Huong would be ready to resign one month before the new election. The Chairman of the Senate, as caretaker head of the Government, would assume administrative responsibilities in South Vietnam, but the election would be the sole responsibility of the independent election body I have just described.

There are several other proposals in our new peace plan; for example, as we offered privately on July 26 of last year, we remain prepared to undertake a major reconstruction program throughout Indochina, including North Vietnam, to help all these peoples recover from the ravages of a generation of war.

We will pursue any approach that will speed negotiations.

We are ready to negotiate the plan I have outlined tonight and conclude a comprehensive agreement on all military and political issues. Because some parts of this agreement could prove more difficult to negotiate than others, we would be willing to begin implementing certain military aspects while negotiations continue on the implementation of other issues, just as we suggested in our private proposal in October.

Or, as we proposed last May, we remain willing to settle only the military issues and leave the political issues to the Vietnamese alone. Under this approach, we would withdraw all U.S. and allied forces within 6 months in exchange for an Indochina cease-fire and the release of all prisoners.

The choice is up to the enemy.

This is a settlement offer which is fair to North Vietnam and fair to South Vietnam. It deserves the light of public scrutiny by these nations and by other nations throughout the world. And it deserves the united support of the American people.

We made the substance of this generous offer privately over 3 months ago. It has not been rejected, but it has been ignored. I reiterate that peace offer tonight. It can no longer be ignored.

The only thing this plan does not do is to join our enemy to overthrow our ally, which the United States of America will never do. If the enemy wants peace, it will have to recognize the important difference between settlement and surrender.

This has been a long and agonizing struggle. But it is difficult to see how anyone, regardless of his past position on the war, could now say that we have not gone the extra mile in offering a settlement that is fair, fair to everybody concerned.

By the steadiness of our withdrawal of troops, America has proved its resolution to end our involvement in the war; by our readiness to act in the spirit of conciliation, America has proved its desire to be involved in the building of a permanent peace throughout Indochina.

We are ready to negotiate peace immediately.

If the enemy rejects our offer to negotiate, we shall continue our program of ending American involvement in the war by withdrawing our remaining forces as the South Vietnamese develop the capability to defend themselves.

If the enemy's answer to our peace offer is to step up their military attacks, I shall fully meet my responsibility as Commander in Chief of our Armed Forces to protect our remaining troops.

We do not prefer this course of action.

We want to end the war not only for America but for all the people of Indochina. The plan I have proposed tonight can accomplish that goal.

Some of our citizens have become accustomed to thinking that whatever our Government says must be false, and whatever our enemies say must be true, as far as this war is concerned. Well, the record I have revealed tonight proves the contrary. We can now demonstrate publicly what we have long been demonstrating privately—that America has taken the initiative not only to end our participation in this war, but to end the war itself for all concerned.

This has been the longest, the most difficult war in American history.

Honest and patriotic Americans have disagreed as to whether we should have become involved 9 years ago; and there has been disagreement on the conduct of the war. The proposal I have made tonight is one on which we all can agree.

Let us unite now, unite in our search for peace—a peace that is fair to both sides—a peace that can last.

Thank you and goodnight.

Text of President Richard Nixon's address to the nation on January 25, 1972, that made public his plan for peace in Vietnam, in Public Papers of the Presidents of the United States: Richard Nixon, 1972 *(1974), pp. 100–105.*

The issue is to us: We are prepared, in all conscience and in all seriousness, to negotiate with them immediately any scheme that any reasonable person can say leaves open the political future of South Vietnam to the people of South Vietnam, just as we are not prepared to withdraw without knowing anything at all of what is going to happen next. So we are not prepared to end this war by turning over the Government of South Vietnam as part of a political deal.

We are prepared to have a political process in which they can have a chance of winning which is not loaded in any direction.

Comments by Henry Kissinger at a news conference on January 26, 1972, in which he refers to the October 1971 U.S. peace proposal, as reported in the New York Times, *January 27, 1972, p. 14.*

The Government of the [Democratic Republic of North Vietnam] is of the view that the substance of the negotiations between [it and the United States] should be made known to the public. However, as wished by the U.S. party, the Government of the DRVN agreed to the decision that the parties would refrain from publicizing the private meetings, yet President Nixon, in his Jan. 25, 1972 statement, and Mr. H. Kissinger at his Jan. 26 press conference, unilaterally divulged the substance of the private meetings between the U.S. and the DRVN; they even distorted the fact.

The U.S. Government had broken its engagements and created serious obstacles to the negotiations. For its part, the DRVN party has always shown goodwill. . . .

In deciding now to unilaterally make public the substance of the private meeting between the DRVN and the U.S., the Nixon Administration has further laid bare its fallacy. This way of doing so is aimed at deceiving public opinion in the U.S. and in the world, at serving Mr. Nixon's political objectives in this election year, and at allowing him to pursue "Vietnamization" of the war, and not "to serve in the best way the cause of peace," as he claims.

Excerpt from the text of a North Vietnamese communiqué issued on January 31, 1972, in answer to Richard Nixon's disclosure of peace negotiations, as translated into English and printed in the New York Times, *February 1, 1972, p. 12.*

Richard Nixon and Attorney General John N. Mitchell

As you have requested in your letter of February 15, I accept your resignation as Attorney General effective March 1, 1972. I do so on a note of the utmost regret—but a regret compensated by a sense of personal and heartfelt gratitude on behalf of myself and all Americans.

As chief legal advisor to the President, and as the leader of our fight against crime and lawlessness, you have left a permanent imprint for the better on our Nation of which I am immensely proud. You have made this a time of historic accomplishment in expanding and intensifying the Federal Government's anti-crime efforts in launching new and more effective efforts to combat drug abuse, in improving the system of justice for all, and, not least, in developing greater public support for the forces of law and justice throughout the country. You have given the American people new—and newly justified—confidence in their ability to halt the spiral of crime, and to restore domestic peace.

Your consistently wise advice and counsel have been of immense value to me throughout the course of our Administration, and I know I can speak for all of your colleagues in saying we shall greatly miss you around the Cabinet table.

President Nixon's letter accepting the resignation of Attorney General John N. Mitchell, February 15, 1972, in Public Papers of the Presidents of the United States: Richard Nixon, 1972 *(1974), pp. 363–364.*

President Nixon in China

I know of no Presidential trip that was as carefully planned nor of any President who ever prepared himself so conscientiously. . . . Nixon read all of the briefing books with exquisite care, as we could tell by his underlining of key passages throughout. As was his habit, he committed the talking points to memory and followed them meticulously in his meetings with Chou En-lai while seeking to cultivate the impression that he was speaking extemporaneously.

Henry Kissinger commenting in 1979 on President Richard Nixon's 1972 trip to the People's Republic of China, in Henry Kissinger, White House Years *(1979), p. 1,051.*

THE PRESIDENT. I can only say to the media, who, like myself, have never seen the Great Wall before, that it exceeds all expectations. When one stands there and sees the Wall going to the peak of this mountain and realizes that it runs for hundreds of miles, as a matter of fact thousands of miles, over the mountains and through the valleys of this country, that it was built over 2,000 years ago, I think that you would have to conclude that this is a great wall and that it had to be built by a great people.

Many lives, of course, were lost in building it because there was no machinery or equipment at the time. It had to all be done by hand. But under the circumstances, it is certainly a symbol of what China in the past has been and of what China in the future can become. A people who could build a wall like this certainly have a great past to be proud of and a people who have this kind of a past must also have a great future.

My hope is that in the future, perhaps as a result of the beginning that we have made on this journey, that many, many Americans, particularly the young Americans who like to travel so much, will have an opportunity to come here as I have come here today with Mrs. Nixon and the others in our party, that they will be able to see this Wall, that they will think back as we think back to the history of this great *People,* and that they will have an opportunity, as we have had an opportunity, to know the Chinese *people,* and know them better.

What is most important is that we have an open world. As we look at this Wall, we do not want walls of any kind between peoples. I think one of the results of our trip, we hope, may be that the walls that are erected, whether they are physical walls like this, or whether they are other walls, ideology or philosophy, will not divide peoples *in the world;* that peoples, regardless of their differences and backgrounds and their philosophies, will have an opportunity to communicate with each other, to know each other, and to share with each other those particular endeavors that will mean peaceful progress in the years ahead.

So, all in all, I would say, finally, we have come a long way to be here today, 16,000 miles. Many things that have occurred on this trip have made me realize that it was worth coming, but I would say, as I look at the Wall, it is worth coming 16,000 miles just to stand here and see the Wall.

Do you agree, Mr. Secretary?

SECRETARY ROGERS. I certainly do, Mr. President. It really is a tremendous privilege we have all had to be here today.

THE PRESIDENT. And I really didn't need the coat.

TRANSLATOR. No, this is great weather.

THE PRESIDENT. It's marvelous. And nobody is ever going to see the hat that I brought. I didn't need it. And my ears are not nearly as cold as they get when I walk

sometimes on the streets of New York—in those side streets that go, you know, through the middle of Manhattan and down through those tall buildings—and the wind blows. It's much colder than this.

TRANSLATOR. The Vice Premier says that Mr. President has given a very good speech. [Laughter]

THE PRESIDENT. I was supposed to just say a word. The Vice Premier has climbed to the top. But we both decided that this was a job really for Foreign Ministers and not for the Vice Premier and myself.

But I would simply conclude, because I know we have to go on, that while we will not climb to the top today, we are already meeting at the summit in Peking.

An exchange between President Nixon and reporters at the Great Wall of China on February 24, 1972, in Public Papers of the Presidents of the United States: Richard Nixon, 1972 *(1974), pp. 370–372.*

The Equal Rights Amendment

I've never seen anything like it in all my years here. In their hearts, many of those guys out there don't really believe in this amendment. But they were getting so much heat from the women, they didn't have any choice.

Statement by an unidentified U.S. senator in 1971 about the Senate's passage of the Equal Rights Amendment, quoted in Flora Davis, Moving the Mountain *(1991), p. 134.*

Title IX

We've got a boys gym and a girls' gym. Before, we could use the girls' gym for wrestling and B team basketball a lot more than we can now. I think girls have a right to participate but to a lesser degree than boys. If they go too far with the competitive stuff, they lose their femininity.

Ron Weld, a coach at a Wisconsin high school, commenting in 1973 on the impact of Title IX, in Flora Davis, Moving the Mountain *(1991), p. 215.*

The historic passage of Title IX was hardly noticed. I remember one or two sentences in the Washington papers.

It would be another three years before the regulations of Title IX would be issued, and then another year before it would take effect. By then, higher education and the country understood that Title IX was

President and Mrs. Nixon visit the Great Wall of China. *(National Archives and Records Administration)*

going to change the landscape of higher education forever.

Bernice R. Sandler, senior scholar, Women's Research and Education Institute, and leading advocate in the early 1970s of Title IX, recalling in 1997 the initial impact of the legislation, available online at http://www.bernicesandler.com/id44.htm, downloaded April 23, 2005.

We find in the Book of Genesis . . . "God created man in His own image. . . . Male and female created He them." . . . The law should make such distinctions as are reasonably necessary for the protection of women and the existence and development of the race. When He created them God made physiological and functional differences between men and women. . . . Some wise people profess the belief that there may be psychological differences.

The physiological and functional differences . . . empower men to beget and women to bear children. . . . From time whereof the memory of mankind runneth not to the contrary, custom and law have imposed upon men the primary responsibility for providing habitation and a livelihood . . . to enable their wives to nurture, care, and train their children.

Senator Sam Ervin (Dem., N.C.) explaining in 1972 why he opposed the Equal Rights Amendment, in Joan Hoff-Wilson, ed., Rights of Passage *(1986), p. 83.*

The laws of every one of the 50 states now require the husband to support his wife and children. . . . This Equal Rights Amendment will remove this sole obligation from the husband, and make the wife equally responsible to provide a home for her family, and to provide 50 percent of the financial support of her family.

Phyllis Schlafly speaking out in November 1972 against ratification of the Equal Rights Amendment, in Jane J. Mansbridge, Why We Lost the ERA *(1986), p. 90.*

Philip Berrigan

The group plans to blow up underground electrical conduits and steam pipes serving the Washington, D.C. area in order to disrupt Federal operations. The plotters are also concocting a scheme to kidnap a highly placed Government official. The name of a high White House staff member has been mentioned as a possible victim. If successful, the plotters would demand an end to U.S. bombing operations in Southeast Asia and the release of all political prisoners as ransom. Intensive investigations are being conducted concerning this matter.

Statement by FBI Director J. Edgar Hoover in November 1970 before a closed session of the Senate Appropriations Committee discussing supposed plans by Philip and Daniel Berrigan and others to disrupt the U.S. government, in Richard Curtis, The Berrigan Brothers *(1974), p. 132.*

I became concerned about the goals of these people. I am a Catholic, and I am a product of a very strict Catholic upbringing. . . . I became concerned about what I was hearing from Father Philip Berrigan. . . . I felt that if I had enough evidence to produce at the time, the authorities would believe in what I was telling them . . . and they would realize the threats of these people to the United States government.

Statement by Boyd Douglas, a fellow inmate of Philip Berrigan, at the 1972 trail of Berrigan, in Richard Curtis, The Berrigan Brothers *(1974), p. 145.*

President Nixon in the Soviet Union

Dobryy vecher [Good evening]

I deeply appreciate this opportunity your Government has given me to speak directly with the people of the Soviet Union, to bring you a message of friendship from all the people of the United States and to share with you some of my thoughts about the relations between our two countries and about the way to peace and progress in the world. . . .

In the 3 years I have been in office, one of my principal aims has been to establish a better relationship between the United States and the Soviet Union. Our two countries have much in common. Most important of all, we have never fought one another in war. On the contrary, the memory of your soldiers and ours embracing at the Elbe, as allies, in 1945, remains strong in millions of hearts in both of our countries. It is my hope that that memory can serve as an inspiration for the renewal of Soviet–American cooperation in the 1970's.

As great powers, we shall sometimes be competitors, but we need never be enemies.

Thirteen years ago, when I visited your country as Vice President, I addressed the people of the Soviet Union on radio and television, as I am addressing you tonight. I said then: "Let us have peaceful competition not only in producing the best factories but in producing better lives for our people.

"Let us cooperate in our exploration of outer space. . . . Let our aim be not victory over other peoples but the victory of mankind over hunger, want, misery, and disease, wherever it exists in the world."

In our meetings this week, we have begun to bring some of those hopes to fruition. Shortly after we arrived here on Monday afternoon, a brief rain fell on Moscow of a kind that I am told is called a mushroom rain, a warm rain, with sunshine breaking through, that makes the mushrooms grow and is therefore considered a good omen. The month of May is early for mushrooms, but as our talks progressed this week, what did grow was even better: a far-reaching set of agreements that can lead to a better life for both of our peoples, to a better chance for peace in the world.

We have agreed on joint ventures in space. We have agreed on ways of working together to protect the environment, to advance health, to cooperate in science and technology. We have agreed on means of preventing incidents at sea. We have established a commission to expand trade between our two nations.

Most important, we have taken an historic first step in the limitation of nuclear strategic arms. This arms control agreement is not for the purpose of giving either side an advantage over the other. Both of our nations are strong, each respects the strength of the other, each will maintain the strength necessary to' defend its independence.

But in an unchecked arms race between two great nations, there would be no winners, only losers. By setting this limitation together, the people of both of our nations, and of all nations, can be winners. If we continue in the spirit of serious purpose that has marked our discussions this week, these agreements can start us on a new road of cooperation for the benefit of our people, for the benefit of all peoples. There is an old proverb that says, "Make peace with man and quarrel with your sins." The hardships and evils that beset all men and all nations, these and these alone are what we should make war upon.

As we look at the prospects for peace, we see that we have made significant progress at reducing the possible sources of direct conflict between us. But history tells us that great nations have often been dragged into war without intending it, by conflicts between smaller nations. As great powers, we can and should use our influence to prevent this from happening. Our goal should be to discourage aggression in other parts of the world and particularly among those smaller nations that look to us for leadership and example. . . .

Speaking for the United States, I can say this: We covet no one else's territory, we seek no dominion over any other people, we seek the right to live in peace, not only for ourselves but for all the peoples of this earth. Our power will only be used to keep the peace, never to break it, only to defend freedom, never to destroy it. No nation that does not threaten its neighbors has anything to fear from the United States.

Soviet citizens have often asked me, "Does America truly want peace?"

I believe that our actions answer that question far better than any words could do. If we did not want peace, we would not have reduced the size of our armed forces by a million men, by almost one-third, during the past 3 years. If we did not want peace, we would not have worked so hard at reaching an agreement on the limitation of nuclear arms, at achieving a settlement of Berlin, at maintaining peace in the Middle East, at establishing better relations with the Soviet Union, with the People's Republic of China, with other nations of the world. . . .

I would like to take this opportunity to try to convey to you something of what America is really like, not in terms of its scenic beauties, its great cities, its factories, its farms, or its highways, but in terms of its people.

In many ways, the people of our two countries are very much alike. Like the Soviet Union, ours is a large and diverse nation. Our people, like yours, are hard working. Like you, we Americans have a strong spirit of competition, but we also have a great love of music and poetry, of sports, and of humor. Above all, we, like you, are an open, natural, and friendly people. We love our country. We love our children. And we want for you and for your children the same peace and abundance that we want for ourselves and for our children.

We Americans are idealists. We believe deeply in our system of government. We cherish our personal liberty. We would fight to defend it, if necessary, as we have done before. But we also believe deeply in the right of each nation to choose its own system. Therefore, however much we like our system for ourselves, we have no desire to impose it on anyone else.

As we conclude this week of talks, there are certain fundamental premises of the American point of view which I believe deserve emphasis. In conducting these talks, it has not been our aim to divide up the world into spheres of influence, to establish a condominium, or in any way to conspire together against the interests of any other nation. Rather we have sought to construct a better framework of understanding between our two nations, to make progress in our bilateral relationships, to find ways of insuring that future frictions between us would never embroil our two nations, and therefore the world, in war.

While ours are both great and powerful nations, the world is no longer dominated by two super powers. The world is a better and safer place because its power and resources are more widely distributed. . . .

Some of you may have heard an old story told in Russia of a traveler who was walking to another village. He knew the way, but not the distance. Finally he came upon a woodsman chopping wood by the side of the road and he asked the woodsman, "How long will it take to reach the village?"

The woodsman replied, "I don't know."

The traveler was angry, because he was sure the woodsman was from the village and therefore knew how far it was. And so he started off down the road again. After he had gone a few steps, the woodsman called out, "Stop. It will take you about 15 minutes."

The traveler turned and demanded, "Why didn't you tell me that in the first place?"

President Nixon and his National Security Advisor Henry Kissinger take a stroll between meetings with Soviet leaders in Moscow. (*National Archives and Records Administration*)

The woodsman replied, "Because then I didn't know the length of your stride."

In our talks this week with the leaders of the Soviet Union, both sides have had a chance to measure the length of our strides toward peace and security. I believe that those strides have been substantial and that now we have well begun the long journey, which will lead us to a new age in the relations between our two countries. It is important to both of our peoples that we continue those strides. . . .

Through all the pages of history, through all the centuries, the world's people have struggled to be free from fear, whether fear of the elements or fear of hunger or fear of their own rulers or fear of their neighbors in other countries. And yet, time and again, people have vanquished the source of one fear only to fall prey to another.

Let our goal now be a world free of fear—a world in which nation will no longer prey upon nation, in which human energies will be turned away from production for war and toward more production for peace, away from conquest and toward invention, development, creation; a world in which together we can establish that peace which is more than the absence of war, which enables man to pursue those higher goals that the spirit yearns for.

Yesterday, I laid a wreath at the cemetery which commemorates the brave people who died during the siege of Leningrad in World War II. At the cemetery, I saw the picture of a 12-year-old girl. She was a beautiful child. Her name was Tanya. The pages of her diary tell the terrible story of war. In the simple words of a child, she wrote of the deaths of the members of her family: Zhenya in December. Grannie in January. Leka then next. Then Uncle Vasya. Then Uncle Lyosha. Then Mama. And then the Savichevs. And then finally, these words, the last words in her diary: "All are dead. Only Tanya is left."

As we work toward a more peaceful world, let us think of Tanya and of the other Tanyas and their brothers and sisters everywhere. Let us do all that we can to insure that no other children will have to endure what Tanya did and that your children and ours, all the children of the world, can live their full lives together in friendship and in peace. *Spasibo y do svidaniye.* [Thank you and goodbye.]

President Nixon's radio and television address to the people of the Soviet Union, broadcast from the Green Room at the Grand Kremlin Palace in Moscow on May 28, 1972, in Public Papers of the Presidents of the United States: Richard Nixon, 1972 *(1974), pp. 629–632.*

THE UNITED States of America and the Union of Soviet Socialist Republics,

Guided by their obligations under the Charter of the United Nations and by a desire to strengthen peaceful relations with each other and to place these relations on the firmest possible basis,

Aware of the need to make every effort to remove the threat of war and to create conditions which promote the reduction of tensions in the world and the strengthening of universal security and international cooperation,

Believing that the improvement of US–Soviet relations and their mutually advantageous development in such areas as economics, science and culture, will meet these objectives and contribute to better mutual understanding and business-like cooperation, without in any way prejudicing the interests of third countries,

Conscious that these objectives reflect the interests of the peoples of both countries,

Have agreed as follows:

First. They will proceed from the common determination that in the nuclear age there is no alternative to conducting their mutual relations on the basis of peaceful coexistence. Differences in ideology and in the social systems of the USA and the USSR are not obstacles to the bilateral development of normal relations based on the principles of sovereignty, equality, non-interference in internal affairs and mutual advantage.

Second. The USA and the USSR attach major importance to preventing the development of situations capable of causing a dangerous exacerbation of their relations. Therefore, they will do their utmost to avoid military confrontations and to prevent tile [sic] outbreak of nuclear war. They will always exercise restraint in their mutual relations, and will be prepared to negotiate and settle differences by peaceful means. Discussions and negotiations on outstanding issues will be conducted in a spirit of reciprocity, mutual accommodation and mutual benefit.

Both sides recognize that efforts to obtain unilateral advantage at the expense of the other, directly or indirectly, are inconsistent with these objectives. The prerequisites for maintaining and strengthening peaceful relations between the USA and the USSR are the recognition of the security interests of the Parties based on the principle of equality and the renunciation of the use or threat of force.

Third. The USA and the USSR have a special responsibility, as do other countries which are permanent members of the United Nations Security Council, to do everything in their power so that conflicts or situations will not arise which would serve to increase international tensions. Accordingly, they will seek to promote conditions in which all countries will live in peace and security and will not be subject to outside interference in their internal affairs.

Fourth. The USA and the USSR intend to widen the juridical basis of their mutual relations and to exert the necessary efforts so that bilateral agreements which they have concluded and multilateral treaties and agreements to which they are jointly parties are faithfully implemented.

Fifth. The USA and the USSR reaffirm their readiness to continue the practice of exchanging views on problems of mutual interest and, when necessary, to conduct such exchanges at the highest level, including meetings between leaders of the two countries. The two governments welcome and will facilitate an increase in productive contacts between representatives of the legislative bodies of the two countries.

Sixth. The Parties will continue their efforts to limit armaments on a bilateral as well as on a multilateral basis. They will continue to make special efforts to limit strategic armaments. Whenever possible, they will conclude concrete agreements aimed at achieving these purposes.

The USA and the USSR regard as the ultimate objective of their efforts the achievement of general and complete disarmament and the establishment of an effective system of international security in accordance with the purposes and principles of the United Nations.

Seventh. The USA and the USSR regard commercial and economic ties as an important and necessary element in the strengthening of their bilateral relations and thus will actively promote the growth of such ties. They will facilitate cooperation between the relevant organizations and enterprises of the two countries and the conclusion of appropriate agreements and contracts, including long-term ones.

The two countries will contribute to the improvement of maritime and air communications between them.

Eighth. The two sides consider it timely and useful to develop mutual contacts and cooperation in the fields of science and technology. Where suitable, the USA and the USSR will conclude appropriate agreements dealing with concrete co-operation in these fields.

Ninth. The two sides reaffirm their intention to deepen cultural ties with one another and to encourage fuller familiarization with each other's cultural values. They will promote improved conditions for cultural exchanges and tourism.

Tenth. The USA and the USSR will seek to ensure that their ties and cooperation in all the above-mentioned fields and in any others in their mutual interest are built on a firm and long-term basis. To give a permanent character to these efforts, they will establish in all fields where this is feasible joint commissions or other joint bodies.

Eleventh. The USA and the USSR make no claim for themselves and would not recognize the claims of anyone else to any special rights or advantages in world affairs. They recognize the sovereign equality of all states.

The development of U.S.-Soviet relations is not directed against third countries and their interests.

Twelfth. The basic principles set forth in this document do not affect any obligations with respect to other countries earlier assumed by the USA and the USSR.

Text of the "Basic Principles of Relations Between the United States of America and the Union of Soviet Socialist Republics," signed May 29, 1972, in Public Papers of the Presidents of the United States: Richard Nixon, 1972 *(1974), pp. 633–635.*

The Soviet leaders were psychologically too insecure and insensitive to intangibles to trust themselves in theoretical discussion. . . . They could hardly trust a capitalist statesman more than they trusted one another. . . . Soviet leaders therefore reinsured themselves over and over again by documents and written interpretations. Philosophical discussions made them visibly nervous; they considered them either a trick or a smokescreen; they maneuvered them as rapidly as possible in the direction of some concrete result that could be signed. The result was that even written agreements were achieved by so much haggling along the way that they stood alone and on their own terms; they left little residue of goodwill.

Henry Kissinger commenting in 1979 on President Nixon's 1972 trip to the Soviet Union, in Henry Kissinger, White House Years *(1979), p. 1,210.*

The Mining of Haiphong

While working in communications as a civilian employee of the U.S. Army, who provided communica-

tions support for the Defense Civil Preparedness Agency (now FEMA), I served as Assistant Communications Officer . . . I believe I can speak for many when I say that I am relieved this period in our history is over. . . .

And never will I forget the day about five years earlier at Coast Guard Hqtrs. when we received CONFIDENTIAL traffic that a USAF aircraft sank one of our 95-footers, killing several Coasties and the South Vietnam advisor on board. The aircraft pilot reported to his ground controller a "target" and provided the position. He was advised the vessel must be an enemy, and permission was given to fire.

With its white hull and "U S COAST GUARD" boldly painted on its sides, the 95-footer was fired upon and sunk-an easy target.

Further investigation after the "accident" revealed that the USN had widely disseminated a notice in country, which the USAF should have absolutely been aware of, that reported the 95-footer was in a well-marked "safe" area where the U.S. Coast Guard was operating with the South Vietnamese. The USAF disagreed, claiming the 95-footer was in a target area.

War is especially hell when you kill your own!

Don Gardner, describing his experience of the mining of Haiphong in 1972 as a civil employee of the U.S. Army. Available online at http://www.jacksjoint. com/warishell.htm.

This is to advise you that I am planning tomorrow night to drive my Pontiac Station Wagon up onto the curb of Pennsylvania Avenue in front of the White House and run over all of the hippies who are lying there. My plan is to do this while they are asleep sometime between 2 and 3 A.M. Would you please let me know what coordination you would like to arrange?

A memo from presidential aide Charles Colson to aide John Dean, written in May 1972 in the wake of protests over the president's decision to mine the North Vietnamese harbor of Haiphong, in Richard Reeves, President Nixon: Alone in the White House *(2001), 476.*

I think there is no question but that the mining has been effective. We sat out here in the Tonkin Gulf and saw ships going into Haiphong for all these years and there aren't any going that way now and they aren't coming out.

The ones that are in there are behind the minefields, the ones that are not there aren't going to get in. So we have shut off the support of third country sources by mines.

Admiral Bernard A. Clarey, commander in chief of the U.S. Pacific Fleet, justifying the mining operations of 1972 in an interview aboard the USS Oklahoma City, *May 25, 1972, "Admirals Agree: Mining Effective,"* Stars and Stripes. *Available online at http://www.ussokcity.com.*

The 1972 Presidential Election

About ten days before the 1972 election I asked George McGovern, the Democratic nominee for president, whether he thought the American people had been given an accurate picture of him. McGovern already had come to terms with the prospect of a landslide defeat by President Richard M. Nixon. But he responded vehemently. "Accurate?" he shouted, pounding the table. "I'm running against Richard Nixon and people think I'm the dishonest one! How can that be accurate?"

Newspaper reporter Jack W. Gemond recounting in an issue of the Columbia Journalism Review *of November/December 1999 an interview he had in 1972 with Democratic presidential nominee George McGovern, available online at http://www.cjr.org, downloaded April 27, 2005.*

Apollo Moon Missions

The Apollo 16 landing area, termed the Descartes region, is situated in the southern highlands of the Moon (latitude 9°00'01" South, longitude 15°30'59" East). For this landing, we have selected a relatively smooth area nestled in the picturesque and rugged lunar highlands.

Since prehistoric times, man has known that the Moon, as seen with the unaided eye, has both light areas and dark areas. The dark areas look smooth, the light areas more rugged. The dark areas are called maria (plural of mare) from the mistaken belief, now centuries old that they were once seas. (*Mare* is the old Latin word for *sea*.) We visited such areas on Apollo 11, 12, and 14. Then on Apollo 15 we landed just at the edge of a dark area and during the exploration that followed climbed part way up the initial slopes of the Apennine Mountains, a light area.

The light areas are termed highlands, a name carried over from the days when it was believed that they stood higher than the lunar seas. That they indeed stand higher than the maria is now well established by measurements made on previous Apollo flights. On Apollo 16, we will visit the highlands and examine two different kinds of rock that together cover about 11 1/2 percent of the front side of the Moon.

A description of the lunar landing site for the upcoming Apollo 16 *mission, written by Gene Simmons for NASA, in* On the Moon with Apollo 16: A Guidebook to the Descartes Region *(1972), available online at http://history.nasa.gov/ EP-95/ep95.htm, downloaded April 8, 2004.*

Cernan: Jack, I'm out here. Oh, my golly! Unbelievable! Unbelievable; but is it bright in the Sun. [Pause] Okay! We landed in a very shallow depression. That's why we've got a slight pitch-up angle. [It's a] very shallow, dinner-plate-like, dish crater just about the width of the struts [meaning the total span of the landing gear]. How you doing, Jack? Schmitt: Fine. Getting the circuit breakers verified. . . .

Cernan: The LM [landing module] looks beautiful. [Pause] Oh, do we have boulder tracks coming down [the side of North Massif]. Let me see exactly where we are. I think I may be just in front of Punk.

Mission Control: Okay. We copy that, Gene, and are the boulder tracks . . .

Cernan: I'm beginning to . . .

Mission Control: . . . to both the north and south?

Cernan: Okay. On the North Massif we've got very obvious boulder tracks. A couple of large boulders come within 20 or 30 feet of the [break in slope] . . . Looks like where we can get to them; there's a couple I know we can get to. Well, the Sun angle is such that, what I saw on the South Massif earlier, I can't see very well. But, I know there were boulder tracks over there. Bear Mountain . . . Boy, it's hard to look to the east [toward the Sculptured Hills]. Bear Mountain and the Sculptured Hills have a very, very similar texture on the surface. The Sculptured Hills' [texture] is like the wrinkled skin of an old, old, 100-year-old man. [That] is probably the best way I could put it. Very, very hummocky, but smoothly pockmarked. I do not see any boulders up on the Sculptured Hills from here. But it's awful hard to look to the east and to the southeast.

A conversation among astronauts Harrison "Jack" Schmitt, Eugene Cernan, and mission control as Cernan set foot on the lunar surface, on December 11, 1972, available online at http://www.hq.nasa.gov/ alsj/a17/a17j.html, downloaded April 8, 2004.

The Godfather

Michael Corleone: My father made him an offer he couldn't refuse.

Kay Adams: What was that?

Michael: Luca Brasi, held a gun to his head, and my father assured him, that either his brain or his signature would be on the contract.

A conversation between Michael Corleone, played by Al Pacino, and Kay Adams, played by Diane Keaton. The conversation refers to the Godfather, Don Corleone, played by Marlon Brando. From the movie The Godfather *(1972), available online at http://www.fiftiesweb.com/movies/godfather.htm, downloaded April 27, 2005.*

I must have interviewed two thousand people. We videotaped every old Italian actor in existence. But it became apparent that the role called for an actor of such magnetism, such charisma, just walking into a room had to be an event. We concluded that if an Italian actor had gotten to be seventy years old without becoming famous on his own, he wouldn't have the air of authority we needed.... We finally figured that what we had to do was lure the best *actor* in the world. It was that simple. It boiled down to Laurence Olivier or Marlon Brando, who *are* the greatest actors in the world. [Robert Evans, who was in charge of production at Paramount, and I] went back and forth on it, and . . . he told me that, ironically enough, he'd been thinking of Brando as the Godfather all along and had, in fact, written him a letter to that effect over two years before. Brando seemed too young, even to me, but sometimes when you go out on a limb and connect with someone—Mario, in this case—you say, "It's God signaling me." So we narrowed it down to Brando. He had turned down the role in *The Conversation* some months earlier, but after he'd had a chance to read *The Godfather,* he called back and said he was interested, that he thought it was a delicious part—he used that word, delicious.

Director Francis Ford Coppola recalling in 1975 how Marlon Brando was selected for the role of the godfather in the movie The Godfather, *in Gene D. Phillips and Rodney Hill, eds.,* Francis Ford Coppola Interviews *(2004), pp. 20–21.*

Roberto Clemente

We lead different lives in America. The language barrier is great at first and we have trouble ordering food in restaurants. Even segregation baffles us. . . .

Once we're at peace with the world, we can do the job in baseball. The people who have never experienced these problems don't know what it's like.

Pittsburgh Pirates outfielder Roberto Clemente commenting in 1964 about the difficulties facing Latin baseball players in the major leagues, in Baseball: 100 Classic Moments in the History of the Game *(2000), p. 216.*

4

Watergate America— Crisis of Conscience
January 1973–August 1974

The period from the beginning of January 1973 to the resignation of President Richard Nixon on August 9, 1974—19 months in all—can rightfully be called the Era of Watergate. True that during this time Americans dealt with much more than Watergate. The U.S. Supreme Court handed down its historic ruling on abortion in the case of *Roe v. Wade;* the United States and North Vietnam signed a peace agreement; those Arab nations that were within the Organization of Petroleum Exporting Countries (OPEC) suspended their shipments of oil to the United States; the economy deteriorated as inflation intensified; war in the Middle East threatened to bring the United States and the Soviet Union into a direct military conflict; Nixon held two summits with Soviet leaders and embarked on an overseas tour that included stops in Egypt and Israel; and the Symbionese Liberation Front kidnapped newspaper heiress Patricia Hearst.

But Watergate overwhelmed nearly everything else (and in doing so went beyond domestic developments and influenced foreign policy). With Watergate, more than a constitutional crisis took hold, and more than Richard Nixon stood exposed. Watergate uncloaked an American society at war with itself; split by distrust, even hatred; given to imperial ventures waged by an imperial, even imperious, presidency; and too often preoccupied with images over substance and with ambition over principle.

For Richard Nixon, the irony about Watergate was that it surfaced as a dominant issue—one so deep that it paralyzed his presidency—while he was most popular: within weeks of his landslide victory in November 1972 and his second inauguration in January 1973. With the exception of some Washington insiders who knew more about Nixon than did the general public, nothing had seemed seriously amiss with the president's White House morals. In 1971, one of Nixon's aides, William Safire, went so far as to propose in a memo to another aide: "Why don't we make more of the fact that ours is a scandal-free Administration?"[1]

AN INAUGURATION AND AN END TO WAR

For his inauguration on January 21, 1973, Richard Nixon stood on a temporary portico beside the Capitol. A U.S. Marine Band, its members wearing scarlet

President and Mrs. Nixon wave to spectators during the inaugural motorcade in Washington in 1972. *(National Archives and Records Administration)*

tunics in contrast to the gray, cold day, spread out before him, and a crowd of 20,000 gathered in the bandstand. A stiff wind carried the chants of distant protesters: "Nixon, Agnew, you can't hide; we charge you with genocide." The president indirectly answered them in his speech, when he said about Vietnam: "As America's longest and most difficult war comes to an end, let us again learn to debate our differences with civility."[2]

Civility took leave from the inaugural parade. In spite of Nixon's popularity, a small group of protesters threw eggs, oranges, and apples at the president's open car. None of them struck him, and he kept waving, smiling, and flashing the victory sign.

This inauguration was indeed Nixon's great triumph. It followed one of the biggest landslide victories in presidential history when he defeated Democrat George McGovern the previous November. No more governing with a razor-thin margin on his mind, as he had to after the 1968 election. He now claimed a mandate. His second term seemed destined for greatness. "From this day forward," he said, "let each of us make solemn commitment in his own heart to bear his responsibility, to do his part, to live his ideals so that together, we can see the dawn of a new age of progress for America, and together, as we celebrate our 200th anniversary as a nation, we can do so proud in the fulfillment of our promise to ourselves and to the world."[3]

But 11 days before Nixon again took office, the trial of the Watergate burglars had begun in the Washington court of 69-year-old Judge John Sirica. Called Maximum John for the severity of the sentences that he handed down, Sirica had a controversial reputation. Many observers thought him too arbitrary, as evident by the numerous decisions of his that were overturned on appeal for violating constitutional rights. His personal probity, though, won him admirers.

For all the later importance of Watergate, the event went as lightly noticed in January 1973 as the faint voices of the protesters during Nixon's inaugural speech. The president's support overwhelmed such negative issues, particularly one that Nixon's press secretary, Ron Ziegler, had labeled a "third-rate burglary."

Historian Stanley I. Kutler observes: "When the burglars' trial began, newspaper reports treated it as a commonplace criminal event."[4]

Within the inner offices of the White House, however, there had been worries aplenty; even in 1972, "The President and several close aides . . . had cause for concern. They realized that an inquiry into the Watergate affair might link [them] to the burglary and its aftermath, and expose a pattern of unethical and illegal conduct condoned and encouraged by the President himself."[5] Clearly, the president's inaugural call—for Americans to be " 'proud in the fulfillment of our promise to ourselves and to the world"—could well be buried under an avalanche of scandal.

The day after Nixon's inauguration, attention shifted to Paris, where National Security Advisor Henry Kissinger arrived to meet with Le Duc Tho, the chief negotiator for North Vietnam, amid reports that the two men would sign a peace treaty. One week earlier, they had completed negotiations setting the conditions for an end to the war.

Kissinger and Tho initialed the agreement on January 23, 1973. Under its terms, the United States pledged to withdraw its remaining troops, numbering 23,700, from South Vietnam, while North Vietnam was allowed to keep its troops there. The North Vietnamese promised to release all American POWs. That evening, President Nixon addressed Americans for 10 minutes on national television and said that a cease-fire would go into effect within days. He called the agreement "peace with honor" and stressed that the United States would still back South Vietnam with supplies and would stand by its diplomatic position that Nguyen Van Thieu's government represented the "sole legitimate government" in South Vietnam.

In the negotiations, Nixon was able to extract some concessions from the communists, mainly that Thieu could remain in power and Hanoi would release the POWs. The peace provisions, though, practically guaranteed a communist takeover of South Vietnam. The agreement did not draw a national boundary line between North and South Vietnam. Importantly, the United States failed to get accepted the principle of mutual troop withdrawal that it had long demanded. Instead, the article that allowed communist troops to remain in South Vietnam made it nearly impossible for Thieu's government to survive and for the main U.S. war goal, to turn back the communists, to be met. Historian Larry Berman concludes: "Comparing the [Communist's] ten-point program of 1969 and the 1973 final agreement, it is striking how much of the former remained intact in the latter; in fact, the wording is almost identical on key points."[6]

Furthermore, the agreement brought no immediate peace. Fighting between North Vietnamese and South Vietnamese troops quickly resumed, and men and supplies continued to make their way from the North to the South.

Nixon fumed about the fighting, for it belied his claim of peace, and he fumed about Kissinger grabbing so much credit for the treaty. In a memo, he said to his chief of staff, H. R. Haldeman, that Kissinger needed to get across to the public the image of a president "lonely" and possessing "heroic courage."[7]

ROE v. WADE

Beginning in the late 1960s, feminists within the women's liberation movement began to call for the repeal of all laws that limited a woman's right to abortion.

They engaged in an intense campaign that included testimony before state legislative committees and staged "speak-outs" at which women explained the reasons for their having had illegal abortions. At the same time, public support for abortion grew. Whereas 91 percent of the respondents to a poll in 1965 said that they opposed any loosening of existing restrictions on abortions, 64 percent said in a 1972 poll that the decision to have an abortion should be left to the woman and her doctor.

Then in January 1973, the U.S. Supreme Court under Chief Justice Warren Burger handed down a momentous decision in the case of *Roe v. Wade* when it ruled unconstitutional all state laws that prohibited a woman's right to an abortion during the first three months of pregnancy. The court went on to instruct that during the next six months of pregnancy a state could regulate abortion procedures to protect "maternal health" and that during the last 10 weeks, a state could prohibit abortions altogether (except where necessary to protect the life of the mother).

The ruling fulfilled a goal of women's rights activists who promoted freedom of choice, but it enraged conservatives. Justice Harry Blackmun recognized the intensity of the issue when he wrote the opinion of the court, joined by Chief Justice Burger and five other justices. Blackmun wrote:

> We forthwith acknowledge our awareness of the sensitive and emotional nature of the abortion controversy, of the vigorous opposing views . . . and of the deep and seemingly absolute convictions that the subject inspires. One's philosophy, one's experiences, one's exposure to the raw edges of human existence, one's religious training, one's attitudes toward life and family and their values, and the moral standards one establishes and seeks to observe, are all likely to influence and to color one's thinking and conclusions about abortion.[8]

While women were fighting for equal rights in the 1970s, they were also entering the job market in increasing numbers; here, office workers take a lunch break at Fountain Square in downtown Cincinnati. *(National Archives and Records Administration)*

The chief justice of the United States, Warren Burger, meets the press. *(National Archives and Records Administration)*

He added: "Our task, of course, is to resolve the issue by constitutional measurement, free of emotion and of predilection."[9] Emotion, though, had pervaded the issue from the start and would continue to do so for decades to come. To many conservatives, the decision personified liberal efforts to destroy America's morals. *Roe v. Wade* energized a right-wing fight, both secular and religious, to protect traditional values, unborn children, and families.

WATERGATE BECOMES A CRISIS

In late January and February, three developments in the Watergate scandal jeopardized the cover-up orchestrated by President Nixon and his aides. First, a jury found James W. McCord and G. Gordon Liddy guilty in the Watergate break-in. But the trial left Judge Sirica in doubt: He said that there was likely to be more to the story than had been revealed. That observation added fuel to rumors in Washington about the case and justified its further exploration.

Second, on February 7, the Senate voted 73-0 to establish a committee to investigate Watergate, formally titled the Senate Select Committee on Presidential Campaign Activities. The senators turned to Sam Ervin (Dem., N.C.) to head it, and it soon became popularly called the Ervin committee or the Watergate committee. Traditional in his values and uncompromising in his integrity, Ervin was widely respected in Washington, and his southern manners and avuncular features added calmness and dignity to the proceedings. Nixon reacted to the committee with the strategy of publicly stating his cooperation but actually hindering access to materials and witnesses and portraying its work as a partisan attack.

Finally, on February 28, L. Patrick Gray, the acting director of the FBI, revealed to a Senate committee then considering whether to confirm his appointment as permanent director, that he had given the president's counsel, John Dean, full access to reports dealing with the bureau's Watergate investigation and had even allowed Dean to sit in on interviews with suspects. His admission confirmed the scrutiny given Watergate by Nixon's closest aides and implied Nixon's own interest in the investigation.

Gray's statement caused the White House to back away from its support of his nomination. Nixon's domestic adviser, John Ehrlichman, told Dean to let Gray "twist slowly, slowly in the wind."[10]

For Nixon, Watergate was becoming more than another problem: It was becoming a crisis. Nixon well knew the meaning of such an event. In 1962, he wrote a book, *Six Crises,* in which he told about his own experiences with serious challenges, such as the Alger Hiss case, President Dwight Eisenhower's heart attack, and the presidential campaign of 1960. His words bore relevance to what he now faced. He wrote:

> Reaction and response to crisis is uniquely personal in the sense that it depends on what the individual brings to bear on the situation—his own traits of personality and character, his training, his moral and religious background, his strengths and weaknesses.[11]

MILITANT INDIANS

In late February, there also occurred a militant protest that was reminiscent of the 1960s counterculture: Members of the American Indian Movement (AIM) rallied at Wounded Knee on the Pine Ridge Reservation in South Dakota. AIM had been founded in the late 1960s and modeled itself after the Black Panthers. As such, it sought to protect urban Indians from abuses such as police brutality. Now, AIM had arrived at Wounded Knee, a cluster of weathered buildings exposed to the windswept plains, to protest an alliance between Sioux tribal president Richard "Dickie" Wilson and the federal government that threatened to result in white ranchers receiving more rights to reservation lands and the government acquiring access to uranium deposits. For Indians, the Wounded Knee site held special meaning: It was where, in 1890, the U.S. Army massacred many Sioux, largely children, women, and elderly men.

Wilson's police force reacted to the protesters by surrounding them, whereupon AIM activist Russell Means and some 200 Indians confiscated weapons from a trading post, rounded up hostages, and erected barricades, thus creating a standoff. The federal government reacted by sending in marshals and enormous firepower, including helicopters and grenade launchers. In the early days of the showdown, shots rang out (no one knows who fired first), and the government forces assaulted AIM. An AIM spokesperson declared: "We will occupy this town until the government sees fit to deal with the Indian people, particularly the Oglala Sioux tribe in South Dakota. We want a true Indian nation, not one made up of Bureau of Indian Affairs puppets."[12]

During the occupation, which lasted until early May, sporadic fighting left two Indians dead and one FBI agent wounded. The standoff ended when Means and six other AIM protesters signed an agreement with federal officials, sealed with a traditional peace-pipe ceremony, that called for a government investigation into the reservation leadership but provided no amnesty for the insurgents. Means then surrendered to U.S. marshals and was arraigned before being released on bond so that he could attend meetings with the Nixon administration in Washington.

Means called the agreement "a small victory, a preliminary victory, in our war with the U.S. over treaty rights." Nothing, however, came of the AIM demand that the government fully enforce the 1868 Fort Laramie Treaty, whose violation had led to the Indians losing large tracts of land.[13]

In October, Means stood trial in St. Paul, Minnesota, for his role at Wounded Knee. He won his case when the judge threw out the charges against him and against another AIM leader, Dennis Banks, on grounds that the FBI had violated the wiretap law and that the federal government had engaged in illegal activities. Several years later, Means still defended Wounded Knee as a worthwhile protest. He said: "Wounded Knee woke up America. We're still here, and we're resisting. John Wayne did not kill us all."[14]

A CANCER CLOSE TO THE PRESIDENCY

Nixon took two measures in March 1973 to battle inflation. Early in the month, he announced mandatory price controls on crude oil, gasoline, heating oil, and other refinery products. Later in the month, he announced a ceiling on wholesale and retail prices for beef, pork, and lamb.

In between those economic bookends, Watergate crept ever more forcefully into the national consciousness. What had been a largely obscure story received much greater media coverage. On March 24, the *New York Times* ran a front-page, right-column headline: WATERGATE SPY DEFENDANTS WERE UNDER 'POLITICAL PRESSURE' TO ADMIT GUILT AND KEEP SILENT. The revelation came from James W. McCord, Jr., chief of security for Nixon's campaign organization, the Committee to Reelect the President, or CREEP, who sent a letter to John Sirica that the judge read in court on the day that he handed down sentences for the Watergate defendants. The *Times* called the letter "one of the most remarkable documents to surface throughout the nine-month Watergate affair."

The spectators in the packed courtroom listened to the letter in astonishment, as did McCord's attorneys, from whom he had kept the letter secret. McCord went so far as to say that his family feared for his life should he tell what he knew. He asserted that the defendants had committed perjury during the trial and had all been under "political pressure to plead guilty and remain silent."[15] Clearly, Watergate had expanded beyond a break-in; the investigation now began to delve into obstruction of justice. The big question became one of who had applied the pressure and why.

The judge handed down stiff sentences while keeping McCord's pending, to be determined by the extent of his cooperation. Bernard L. Barker, Eugenio R. Martinez, Frank A. Sturgis, and Virgilio R. Gonzalez received 40-year maximum prison terms; E. Howard Hunt received 35 years; and G. Gordon Liddy received six-to-20 years. (Sirica later reduced the sentences for everyone except Liddy.) All but McCord and Liddy had pleaded guilty to various charges; they had been convicted by a jury.

In the White House, Nixon brooded. On March 21, when he knew about McCord sending a letter to Sirica (he had earlier received indications that McCord would break ranks) but had yet to know of its contents, the president met in the Oval Office with John Dean. Dean told Nixon: "I think I know more about Watergate than you do." He warned:

> We have a cancer within, close to the Presidency, that is growing. It is growing daily. It's compounded, growing geometrically now, because it compounds itself.[16]

Nixon might have been able to change course at this point, to tell Dean it was time to find out who had done wrong and to take whatever consequences there might be. But the pressure to keep Watergate covered up so that other illegal acts would continue to be covered up, coupled with Nixon's penchant for duplicity and secrecy, continued their grip. Thomas Jefferson had once said about slavery that it was like holding "a wolf by the ears." Watergate had become Nixon's wolf (and maybe his master). Hold on to the cover-up, and it will grow meaner and ever more dangerous; let it go, and it will attack you.

Dean told Nixon that the Watergate defendants wanted more money to maintain their silence, that Hunt was threatening to tell everything unless paid. Nixon responded: "We could get that. . . . you could get a million dollars, and you could get it in cash. I, I know where it could be gotten."[17] H. R. Haldeman then entered the room, and Nixon again stated that a million dollars could be gotten to pay the defendants. He asked Dean to find a way to continue the cover-up so that Watergate would not destroy his presidency.

Nixon and his aides hoped that John Mitchell would take full blame for Watergate. If he would fall on his sword, then the investigation, they believed, would end. Or, as Nixon put it, Mitchell would be the "hell of a big fish" that was thrown to the president's enemies.

The next morning, Nixon told Dean, Haldeman, and John Ehrlichman in the Oval Office what they should do if asked to testify: "I want you all to stonewall it, let them plead the Fifth Amendment, cover-up or anything else if it'll save the plan. That's the whole point."[18]

Nixon had written in *Six Crises:* " 'Selflessness' is the greatest asset an individual can have in a time of crisis. 'Selfishness' . . . is the greatest liability."[19]

McCord linked Watergate closer to the White House when he testified before the Ervin committee on March 28. While reporters and photographers waited anxiously outside closed doors, he told the committee that Mitchell, the former attorney general and director of CREEP, knew of the Watergate break-in plot beforehand. McCord implicated others too: John Dean; Jeb Stuart Magruder, deputy manager of the Nixon reelection campaign; and Charles W. Colson, the president's former special counsel. Mitchell later called the statements about him "slanderous" and insisted: "I have previously denied any prior knowledge of or involvement in the Watergate affair and again reaffirm such denials."[20]

Secrecy begets more secrets, and lies, often cultivated by secrecy, beget more lies. In the Nixon administration the secrecy and lies became so extensive that the politicians—Nixon, Haldeman, Ehrlichman, Dean, and others—often lost track of which stories they had concocted to perpetuate whatever deceit in which they were involved, and all the participants realized that the stories depended on an unbreakable conspiracy, a solid wall, a stone wall, as Nixon had said.

The stone wall, already showing chinks, suffered a tremendous blow on April 2 when John Dean told prosecutors that he would talk to them about the Watergate break-in, the break-in at the office of Dr. Daniel Ellsberg's psychiatrist (in the *Pentagon Papers* case), and the payment of hush money to the Watergate defendants. Clearly, Dean's decision displayed desperate measures among the president's aides, an increasing number of whom were now maneuvering to strike the best deal they could with prosecutors to protect themselves.

Just eight days later, Jeb Magruder sought his own deal. He told prosecutors that he would admit to having perjured himself before the grand jury in 1972 and

Presidential advisers John
Ehrlichman and H. R. Haldeman
became known as the Berlin Wall.
*(National Archives and Records
Administration)*

would reveal how Liddy, Dean, and Mitchell had prior knowledge of the
Watergate break-in. In his capacity as deputy manager at CREEP, Magruder was
Mitchell's aide; he thus had intimate knowledge of campaign tactics.

On April 15, Dean told President Nixon that he had started to talk to the
Watergate prosecutors. The news convinced the president that the cover-up
would unravel, and it convinced him that he must let go of his two closest and
trusted aides, Haldeman and Ehrlichman. Nixon met again with Dean the following day and said to him: "Nothing is privileged that involves wrongdoing, on
your part or the wrongdoing on the part of anybody else. I am telling you that
now I want you when you testify, if you do, to say that the President told you that.
Would you do that? Would you agree to that?"[21] Dean said yes. Nixon, though,
had not converted to openness. Haldeman had earlier told him to make sure that
the White House tape machine was working when he talked to Dean, and it was.
The president's comments were obviously meant only to give the appearance of
forthrightness.

On April 17, the president announced to the press new developments in the
Watergate case and said that he was directing his aides to cooperate with the Ervin
Committee. He said that his own investigation had produced "major developments" and added: "I condemn any attempts to cover up in this case, no matter
who is involved."[22] Nixon's press secretary, Ron Ziegler, offered his own startling
admission: The president's previous statements, ones denying that his top aides had
been connected to a cover-up, no longer could be supported; as Ziegler said in
one of the more famous statements during the scandal, his previous comments
about Watergate were "inoperative."[23]

Writing in the *New York Times,* William Safire, by then a former Nixon staffer,
admitted that he was wrong to have thought that no one at a high level in the
White House could have been so "stupid" as to have staged the Watergate break-
in and then covered it up. He added that Nixon's commitment to finding the

guilty parties means "the world's leading expert [on political comebacks] has just made his appearance on the right side of the Watergate investigation."[24]

Nixon demanded the resignations of Haldeman and Ehrlichman on April 29 and said that the dismissals, which he would announce along with those of John Dean, and the resignation of Attorney General Richard Kleindienst (also demanded by the president) were the "toughest things I've ever done in my life." To Haldeman, he said, "I am the guilty one."[25] Dean later recalled how he could barely contain his anger at the president:

> When he announced the resignations of Haldeman and Ehrlichman, "the two finest public servants it has been my privilege to know," I steeled myself. He removed Kleindienst with faint praise. Then he shoved a ten-sword sentence into me, twisted it with a brief pause, and quickly stepped away so that all could see whom the President had stuck it to: "The counsel to the President, John Dean, had also resigned."[26]

Nixon announced the shake-up in a national address on April 30 but admitted no wrongdoing on his part and, in a blatant lie, said he had only recently learned the full extent of the Watergate cover-up. Before going to bed that night, a despondent Nixon told his daughter Julie that he hoped that he would not wake up in the morning.

Nixon had written in *Six Crises:* "The easiest period in a crisis situation is actually the battle itself. The most difficult is the period of indecision—whether to fight or run away."[27]

In addition to the dismissals, Nixon had on his mind a report in the *New York Times* that revealed how, in June 1972, Dean had given L. Patrick Gray papers from E. Howard Hunt's office safe that Gray then burned. The report showed how Gray had perjured himself before the Senate Judiciary Committee. With the revelation, Gray, who had withdrawn his name from consideration as permanent FBI director, resigned.

Amid the trials and tribulations of a nation that was undergoing both Watergate and the last throes of the Vietnam War, Americans still enjoyed traditional pastimes; in this photo, people are enjoying the Memorial Day holiday at Battery Park in lower Manhattan. *(National Archives and Records Administration)*

An "Unparalleled Intrusion": The Daniel Ellsberg Trial Ends

Wrapped into the escalating controversy surrounding White House tactics, the trial of Daniel Ellsberg and his co-defendant, Anthony J. Russo, Jr., on charges of conspiracy, theft, and espionage in the *Pentagon Papers* case, which had begun in January, came to a sudden end on May 11. Judge William Byrne dismissed the charges because of improper conduct by the federal government.

The *New York Times* offered a succinct summation of what had transpired:

> In the last week of the trial, in a series of disclosures no novelist could invent, the Government admitted, chapter by chapter, the intrusion of the executive branch into the judicial process to a degree possibly unparalleled in American history.[28]

The disclosures:

1. The break-in at the office of Ellsberg's psychiatrist had been conducted by five men, including Watergate conspirators E. Howard Hunt and G. Gordon Liddy.

2. The break-in stemmed from President Nixon's order to John Ehrlichman to investigate the leak of the *Pentagon Papers*.

3. In violation of its charter, the CIA was conducting spy operations in the United States against domestic targets.

4. The Nixon administration met with Judge Byrne during the trial to discuss the possibility of his becoming director of the FBI.

In charging Ellsberg with espionage, the government was making an unusual case. The crime, it said, had been committed even though the defendant had not given any secret information to a foreign government. But without specific laws dealing with the release of classified information—for Congress had passed none—the charge was a stretch.

Ironically, in prosecuting Ellsberg, the government caused to be released more information about national security procedures than the defendant ever had. For example, the trial showed how agents operated in the field, how they conducted wiretaps, and how secret diplomacy worked.

Ultimately, the way Judge Byrne dismissed the charges made a retrial impossible. The government, he said, had polluted the proceedings. "The conduct of the Government," Byrne concluded, "has placed the case in such a posture that it precludes the fair, dispassionate resolution of these issues by a jury."[29] In short, big brother had seriously violated Ellsberg's constitutional rights.

Nixon's Changed Course on Watergate

In another of the myriad Watergate twists and turns, President Nixon did an about face on May 22, 1973, when he broke with his long-held position that the White House had no involvement with the affair. Moreover, in a 4,000-word statement he admitted to having ordered wiretaps to determine leaks of information that were injurious to national security. He said: "Fewer than 20 taps, of varying duration were involved. They produced important leads that made it possible to tighten the security of highly sensitive materials."[30]

He admitted that in the face of domestic violence, including "rioting . . . on college campuses," he sought to create a secret superintelligence system that would combine the FBI with the CIA and other agencies and that would involve breaking and entering into businesses and residences to protect national security. The plan failed when FBI director J. Edgar Hoover objected to it.

Nixon also admitted to having formed the "plumbers"—"A small group at the White House," he said, "whose principal purpose was to stop security leaks and to investigate other sensitive security matters." He directed the group to "find out all it could" about Daniel Ellsberg's "associates and his motives."[31]

Concerning Watergate, he admitted having thought the CIA was somehow involved in the operation, and he had told Haldeman and Ehrlichman "to ensure that the FBI would not carry its investigation into areas that might compromise . . . covert national security activities." But, he said, he never intended to stop the investigation into Watergate. He claimed: "I had no prior knowledge of the . . . bugging operation," nor "did I know until the time of my own investigation of any efforts to provide [the Watergate defendants] with funds."[32]

BREZHNEV'S VISIT TO THE UNITED STATES

The Watergate storm subsided briefly when Leonid Brezhnev, the head of the Soviet Communist Party's politburo and thus the leader of the Soviet Union, arrived for a visit to the United States, landing at Andrews Air Force Base, near Washington, on June 16, 1973. Much as the weather had been rainy when Nixon arrived in Russia back in 1972, rain greeted Brezhnev; and much as Nixon had been told by the Russians that the rain was a good omen, the Americans told the Russians the same. Omen or not, during Brezhnev's visit, the Ervin Committee, acting in deference to the Russian leader but against those who wanted the pursuit of Watergate to continue unabated, suspended its hearings.

Brezhnev spent nine days in the United States and met with Nixon at the White House and at the president's home in San Clemente, California. The summit produced little, partly because Watergate distracted Nixon. The man who had vigorously pursued foreign policy in 1972 seemed spent. The Americans and the Russians failed to bridge their differences over the testing and deployment of multiple independent reentry vehicles on land-based missiles and so failed to make progress on a SALT II treaty. They did, however, sign a basic-principles document in which they renounced the use of force between the United States and the Soviet Union and between themselves and third countries.

Late in the night of June 23, Nixon and Brezhnev engaged in a long and heated discussion over the Middle East. The Soviet leader wanted Nixon to join him in persuading Israel to withdraw to the borders it had before the 1967 war. Nixon refused, but Brezhnev kept pushing the point. He said that if they failed to act, Egypt would be forced to attack Israel. Nixon paid no heed to the threat, but it proved to be a warning that was to be fulfilled in the months ahead.

Nixon and Brezhnev signed several modest agreements covering transportation, agriculture, and oceanic studies, among other issues, but the most notable result of the summit was the continuation of détente. Before Brezhnev left, he invited Nixon to visit the Soviet Union in 1974.

NIXON AND CONGRESSIONAL FUNDING

Nixon had complained to Brezhnev about a communist offensive then underway in Cambodia. He wanted the Soviet leader to use his influence to end it but got nowhere. Nixon thought the House of Representatives would join the Senate in passing a bill to end funds for bombing in Cambodia. Congress indeed did so on June 25. Nixon vetoed the bill two days later, and the House upheld him. But the proposal to override fell just 35 votes short of the two-thirds required. Clearly the antiwar forces were stronger than ever, and Congress was reasserting the authority in foreign affairs that it had relinquished under Lyndon Johnson and Richard Nixon.

Presently, with another cut-off bill looming, Nixon and Congress reached an agreement whereby he could have funds for bombing but only until August 15. After that date, the United States would have to end its military activity in Indochina. Nixon bitterly recalled in his memoirs:

> The effect of [the cut-off] was to deny me the means to enforce the Vietnam peace agreement. We were faced with having to abandon our support of the Cambodians who were trying to hold back the Communist Khmer Rouge, who were being supplied and supported by the North Vietnamese in violation of the peace agreement.[33]

Many historians believe that Nixon was forced to make a deal debilitating to his power because of Watergate. Henry Kissinger later said: "Surrender would have been inconceivable had not the John Dean testimony drained all [the president's] inner resources."[34]

ANOTHER BOMBSHELL: TAPES IN THE WHITE HOUSE

John Dean appeared before the Senate Watergate Committee on June 25. The press and public had been anticipating his testimony. He was the closest of Nixon's aides to testify to date, and a large crowd turned out for his appearance; some spectators even camped out overnight to be first in line for admission.

Dean sat down in the caucus room of the Old Senate Office Building, whose windows had been blackened for the television lights. He looked dapper in a tan suit, blue shirt, and green tie. He appeared calm, even grave, his young, bespectacled face showing little emotion, and read a 245-page statement in a nearly ceaseless monotone. Silence otherwise enveloped the room; a reporter for the *New York Times* recalled how one observer said wryly: "It's so quiet, you could hear a guillotine drop."[35]

The monotone, Dean's very lack of passion, carried with it a sense of inner resolve and truth, and what Dean had to say intensified the seriousness of Watergate: He told how the Watergate break-in resulted from a deep climate of suspicion and distrust in the White House; he said that he left a meeting with Nixon and Haldeman on September 15, 1972, believing that the president knew all about the cover-up; he described cash payments to the burglars and to Hunt

Americans may have been driven apart by protests and political differences, but they also came together for social events, such as this quilting bee in New York City's Central Park in June 1973, sponsored by the New York Parks Administration Department of Cultural Affairs. *(National Archives and Records Administration)*

and how the president had said that a million dollars could be gotten; and he recalled how he and Nixon discussed plans to continue the cover-up during the Senate hearings. Two days later, he revealed how the White House kept an "enemies list," with the intent to attack those who opposed the president and his policies. The attacks "ranged from starting IRS audits to banning the enemies from White House social functions."[36]

The questioning of Dean went on for days, and for hours each day, a grinding, grueling experience. Dean displayed an incredible memory with an impressive recollection for detail, but he later admitted: "I was weary, and when you're tired you can make mistakes, I kept reminding myself. It was three o'clock. Four o'clock. Five o'clock. And the questions kept coming."[37]

As Dean testified, a national television audience watched. Richard Nixon did not. He remained isolated, having contact only with Ziegler; his new chief of staff, Alexander Haig; and a couple of other aides. He built no bridges to other political leaders, sought no communion with anyone in Congress.

It was at the June 25 committee hearing that Senator Howard Baker (Rep., Tenn.) posed the question on nearly everyone's mind: "What did the president know and when did he know it?" Cracking that enigmatic nut would crack open the case. As much as the situation had worsened for Nixon, Dean's testimony had yet to be fully corroborated (despite his having provided 47 documents), and there were doubts that it ever would be.

But on July 13, Alexander Butterfield, a former deputy assistant to the president, appeared before the Watergate committee's staff, and when they asked him if the White House had a taping system, he responded: "I was hoping you fellows wouldn't ask that." Then he described the system, installed in the Oval Office, at Camp David, in the White House cabinet room, and at a couple of other locations. In the Oval Office, it was a voice-activated device, he said, and the tapes had been stored in the Executive Office Building by the Secret Service. Three days later, Butterfield presented his information to the full committee, and newspapers called the revelation "a bombshell."

The committee's chief counsel, Samuel Dash, asked him: "If one, therefore, were to reconstruct the conversations at any particular date, what would be the best way to reconstruct these conversations, Mr. Butterfield, in the president's Oval Office?"

"Why in the obvious manner, Mr. Dash," he responded. "To obtain the tape and play it."[38]

Historian Stanley I. Kutler claims that Butterfield's testimony "changed the course of the hearings and redirected the conflict between Congress and Nixon."[39] It did so by shifting the focus to a fight over the tapes. On July 17, Ervin said he wanted the Watergate tapes. On July 18, special prosecutor Archibald Cox also demanded them. Nixon refused; he said they were part of his confidential presidential materials, and they would only confirm that he was telling the truth. On July 23, Ervin issued a subpoena for the tapes, the first one issued by a congressional committee on a president since 1807. When, on July 26, Judge Sirica issued a subpoena in response to Cox's request for the tapes, Nixon took the position that the separation of powers provided for in the Constitution meant that the courts had no power to force him to respond.

Nixon, meanwhile, had been hospitalized with viral pneumonia. While he was bedridden, his aides and advisers came to see him, and there ensued a debate over whether or not to destroy the tapes. His chief lawyer, Fred Buzhardt, recommended they be burned before the subpoena was officially served; so, too, did Kissinger and New York governor Nelson Rockefeller. The tapes were Nixon's private property, they asserted, for the president to do with as he pleased.

White House counsel Leonard Garment disagreed. Nixon would be destroying evidence, he insisted, be it the tapes that were about to be subpoenaed or be it the tapes in general. Haldeman sided with Garment but for the selfish reason of thinking that the tapes might help clear him of any wrongdoing. In the end, Nixon decided to preserve the tapes, partly because, like Haldeman, he thought there might be enough on them to clear him (if used selectively) and partly, probably largely, because he thought he would win any court fight to hold onto them. Years later, Nixon said he made the wrong decision; he should have destroyed them.

From July 24 to August 1, Ehrlichman and Haldeman testified before the Watergate committee. Ehrlichman treated the senators with contempt and tried to place the blame for Watergate on Dean while portraying him as a liar. Stanley I. Kutler says that "Ehrlichman offered a maze of detail, contradiction, evasion, and confrontation."[40] Haldeman portrayed Nixon as one who delegated so much authority (an audacious assertion given Nixon's hands-on treatment of his campaigns) that the president knew little about the Watergate break-in.

At one point, Haldeman commented about the taping system and revealed that he even took some of the tapes home to listen to them. This outraged the senators. Sam Ervin remarked: "The United States Senate can't have those tapes but you, a private citizen, can?"[41]

Nixon's woes were worsened by Bob Woodward and Carl Bernstein at the *Washington Post*. The two reporters continued to probe the cover-up. They received leaks from the Justice Department and congressional investigators and from an informant in the White House, whom they called Deep Throat. In May

2005, the *Washington Post* confirmed that W. Mark Felt, assistant director of the FBI during the Nixon administration, was Deep Throat.

A BLOODY COUP IN CHILE

Richard Nixon's devious dealings extended beyond Watergate and into foreign affairs when he determined to change the government of Chile. Back in 1970, Chileans elected Salvador Allende, a Marxist, as their president. A people willingly electing a Marxist went against the assertion by the United States that communists could gain power only through force, and it rankled Nixon, who believed that communism might soon extend from Chile to other Latin American countries. "I believed," he later wrote, "that a Communist regime in Cuba exporting violence, terrorism, and revolution throughout Latin America was dangerous enough."[42]

As a result, Nixon and Kissinger decided to circumvent the State Department, which was willing to accept the election results, and use the CIA to destroy Allende. At a meeting with John Mitchell, Kissinger, and CIA Director Richard Helms, Nixon approved doing whatever it took to topple Allende. He implied that he wanted Allende "eliminated."

The CIA then began to recruit agents, at first to prevent Allende from being inaugurated and later to foment a coup against him. Using $10 million, Kissinger funneled arms and money to two factions opposed to Allende. On August 16, 1973, the CIA told its agent in Chile that Allende must be overthrown. A few days later, one of the Chilean factions killed a general who opposed a coup.

Then on September 11, 1973, a military junta led by General Augusto Pinochet overthrew Allende. During the assault, Allende was killed, either from dying in the attack or by committing suicide.

The Nixon White House denied any involvement in the coup, and the CIA has since denied that it orchestrated it, although the agency has admitted knowing that it would be staged. Only the complete release of classified documents will give an accurate picture of what transpired, but the desire of Nixon and the CIA for a coup undoubtedly sent signals to Chileans who were discontented with Allende and told them that the United States would applaud his removal. Indeed, on the day of the overthrow, the U.S. naval attaché in Chile called the event America's "D-day."

The coup and the end to a Marxist government, though, actually reduced freedom in Chile. A brutal military dictatorship began under Pinochet, thus making for one less democratic country in Latin America.

WAR IN THE MIDDLE EAST AND OIL EMBARGOED

The statement by Brezhnev at the June 1973 summit with Nixon that Egypt might attack Israel became reality on October 6, when Egyptian forces crossed the Suez Canal to battle the Israelis on the Sinai Peninsula. At the same time, Syrian troops fought the Israelis in the Golan Heights.

Yet another Middle East conflict had begun, this one called the Yom Kippur War. The Arabs sought to push Israel back to its pre-1967 borders, and, in attacking when they did, they caught their enemy off guard. The Israelis had also become overconfident. In their view, the Arabs lacked the temerity to attack them, and if they did attack, they would face the same fate that they had in 1967: a quick defeat. These factors, along with Arab planning, commitment, and bravery, resulted in Syria and Egypt advancing rapidly, with the Syrians pushing through the Golan Heights and the Egyptians driving several miles into the Sinai.

With the cold war going on, the fighting in the Middle East involved the prestige and influence of the United States and the Soviet Union. The Arabs were using Soviet weapons; the Israelis, American ones. Thus, success for the Arabs meant a blow to the reputation of U.S. armaments. Beyond that, an Arab victory would expand Soviet influence in the Middle East.

Amazingly, when the war erupted, Secretary of State Henry Kissinger kept President Nixon in the dark about it for more than two hours. Kissinger believed that Nixon had become incapacitated to act, or at least crippled, by Watergate. Furthermore, Kissinger wanted to take charge of the crisis. Before he even talked with Nixon, he had contacted the United Nations, Israel, Egypt, Syria, Jordan, and the Soviet Union.

Nixon, though, soon involved himself fully in the war. He told Israel that he would replace any weapons they lost, and, on October 13, he began an airlift. The Soviets responded in kind for the Arabs, and for the next week, American and Soviet planes flew hundreds of missions. The Russians, however, could not keep up with the Americans in this arms race, and a replenished and regrouped Israeli army drove the Syrians back from the Golan Heights and encircled the Egyptian troops in the Sinai.

Richard Nixon may well have saved the day for Israel. Historian Stephen Ambrose observes that the president "made it possible for Israel to win. . . . He showed that despite the buffeting he was taking over Watergate, he was still in command. . . . He knew that his enemies, who included some of Israel's best friends, would never give him credit for saving Israel. He did it anyway."[43]

Nixon's decision to rearm Israel risked Arab retaliation, and it came on October 19, when Saudi Arabia announced that it was ending oil shipments to the United States. Meanwhile, Nixon had sent Kissinger to meet with Brezhnev in Moscow to arrange a settlement in the Yom Kippur War. Kissinger wanted a cease-fire; Nixon wanted a comprehensive treaty involving Egypt, Syria, Israel, the United States, and the Soviet Union to establish a permanent peace in the Middle East. But Kissinger thought such a treaty impossible to obtain and ignored the president's wishes. Nixon put no pressure on Kissinger to obey.

On October 22, the UN Security Council adopted a resolution sponsored by the Soviets and the Americans that imposed a cease-fire in the Middle East. It was, however, quickly violated when Israel ignored it, and full disengagement of the Egyptian and Israeli armies awaited another round of negotiations by Kissinger in January 1974.

Just two days after the resolution passed, Brezhnev sent a proposal to Nixon: He wanted the United States and the Soviet Union to send troops to the Middle East to enforce the cease-fire. In a thinly veiled warning, he added: "I will say it straight that if you find it impossible to act jointly with us in this matter, we should be faced with the necessity urgently to consider the question of taking appropriate steps unilaterally."[44] Nixon opposed the joint mission, in part because he thought it could lead to increased cold-war tension in the Middle East. Yet, he feared that if the Soviets went in alone, Israeli and U.S. interests would be gravely threatened.

Kissinger then presided at a meeting with the chairman of the Joint Chiefs of Staff, the director of the CIA, the secretary of defense, and Nixon's chief of staff Alexander Haig. Early on the morning of October 25, U.S. forces around the world were placed on DEFCON III, meaning Defense Condition 3, a high-alert preparatory to war.

Nixon was unaware of this action until he awoke later in the morning. It remains unclear whether he told Haig to get Kissinger moving on an alert. Later, Kissinger claimed that Nixon had been too "distraught" to participate in the meeting; other aides said Nixon had been drunk. (Maybe he was; a recently released tape from the Nixon White House shows Kissinger telling an aide on October 11, shortly after the Yom Kippur War began, "When I talked to the president, he was loaded."[45])

Whatever the case, the alert heightened the possibility of a nuclear war with the Russians. Had the Soviet Union responded in kind, the conflict indeed could have occurred. But the Russians held back. Instead, the UN Security Council reaffirmed the cease-fire resolution, and Kissinger told the Israelis that they must no longer ignore it. On October 27, the United Nations agreed to send an international peacekeeping force to the Middle East.

At that time, the public thought that Nixon had been in full command of the decision to go to DEFCON III, and most people thought he had done so to divert attention from his Watergate troubles. Stephen Ambrose observes: "Nixon was right to say the President needed support in a crisis, but for him it was too late. All his actions and statements had become suspect."[46]

Nixon was quite willing to use the entire Middle East turmoil for his own domestic political benefit. He especially looked forward to receiving the support of Jewish leaders, and, indeed, a number of them began to pressure Democrats to

A gas station in Oregon displays a sign of the times during the gasoline shortage. *(National Archives and Records Administration)*

back away from any effort to impeach the president, a friend of Israel.

Also in October, the Saudi oil embargo spread to other Middle Eastern oil nations, members of OPEC. Ever since the 1960s, Americans had become more dependent on foreign oil. In 1960, 19 percent of the oil Americans consumed came from abroad; in 1972, 30 percent did so—and Americans used wasteful amounts in homes, in industries, and in large, gas-guzzling cars. Few Americans knew the phrase *energy efficiency,* and fewer cared about applying it.

The embargo damaged the U.S. economy, which was already hurt by government instability and the winding down of the Vietnam War. During the year that the embargo was in effect, gasoline and home-heating-fuel prices rose by 33 percent. The embargo panicked people, and they crowded service stations to keep their car tanks full. This only made the crisis worse. Besieged by customers and shorted by suppliers, gas stations often ran out of fuel. Stuck in long lines as they waited to get gas, drivers sometimes lost their temper and engaged in shouting matches, even fistfights, with one another. Some states resorted to gas rationing, restricting motorists to obtaining fuel only on certain days based on their license tag numbers. The oil shortage caused many Americans to shift to smaller, more fuel-efficient cars and placed pressure on Detroit to improve automobile gas mileage.

A miner finishes his shift at the Virginia–Pocahontas Coal Company near New Richlands, Virginia. From mining to manufacturing to service and office jobs, workers were experiencing difficult times in the 1970s as inflation and unemployment, coupled with lagging wages, adversely affected incomes. *(National Archives and Records Administration)*

The oil price rise may have helped boost inflation into the double digits, while industrial productivity rose hardly at all. Moreover, the embargo damaged the sense of American superiority, the sense that no country or group of countries could really hold the powerful United States hostage.

THE RESIGNATION OF VICE PRESIDENT SPIRO AGNEW

For Americans seeking stability in a time of countercultural and postcountercultural upheaval, October was one of the worst of months. Nixon's Watergate troubles nearly paralyzed the presidency; war in the Middle East escalated the tension in the cold war; the oil embargo threatened to destroy the economy. And then Vice President Spiro Agnew was forced to resign.

For months, Agnew had been under criminal investigation by the Justice Department. He was suspected of extortion, bribery, and tax evasion. A Baltimore grand jury was also investigating Agnew, looking into whether he (and other political leaders) had been paid kickbacks by contractors while he was governor of Maryland.

As newspapers reported the charges, Agnew denied them. He called them "damned lies." Publicly, Nixon supported his vice president; privately, his aides told him the evidence against Agnew was mounting.

Spiro Agnew was the only vice president who was forced to resign the office because of criminal charges. *(Library of Congress, Prints and Photographs Division)*

At a meeting with Nixon on September 25, Agnew insisted that he would fight any charges against him and that he would push to have his case heard by Congress through impeachment proceedings. The process, he claimed, would allow him to gain a national audience for his defense and a true "jury" of his peers, fellow politicians who would be more sympathetic to his plight than would a courtroom jury.

But the House speaker, Carl Albert, a Democrat, rejected Agnew's plea for an impeachment inquiry. Albert said that he would not act while the matter was "before the courts."

In late September, Agnew appeared more defiant than ever. In a speech before the National Federation of Republican Women, he shouted: "I will not resign if I am indicted! I will not resign if I am indicted!"[47] His perverse declaration rang hollow to most people, but his audience cheered.

Agnew soon changed his mind. On October 9, he again met with Nixon, this time to tell him about a deal to which he had agreed with the Justice Department. He would resign the vice presidency and plead nolo contendere (no contention) to one count of having failed to report income for tax purposes. In return, he would be sentenced to three years probation, fined $10,000, and be granted immunity from further prosecution. October had taken yet another toll on Nixon's administration.

GERALD FORD AND PRESIDENTIAL POWER

Under the terms of the Twenty-fifth Amendment, Nixon nominated Agnew's replacement: Republican congressman Gerald Ford of Michigan, the House minority leader. He chose Ford in part to win support from Congress for his own Watergate problems. By picking Ford, he thought that the House would look on him more favorably. Ford's critics thought that Nixon had taken out an insurance policy—the House, they believed, would never impeach Nixon, knowing that next in line for president would be a man whose abilities, they thought, made him an effective congressman but were too limited for the requirements of the White House. Nixon made his selection public on October 12. Congress quickly confirmed the appointment, and Ford was sworn in on December 6.

In a bid to limit the type of presidential power that had involved the United States in the Vietnam War and, under Richard Nixon, had expanded the war into Cambodia, Congress passed the War Powers Act. Under its terms, the president was prohibited from sending troops to fight overseas or putting them in situations where hostilities appeared imminent for more than 60 days unless Congress authorized otherwise.

Nixon vehemently opposed the act as crippling the presidency, and on October 24, he vetoed it. He called it "unconstitutional" and "dangerous," but in

President and Mrs. Richard Nixon meet with Representative and Mrs. Gerald R. Ford in the Blue Room of the White House after Nixon nominated Ford to succeed Spiro Agnew as vice president. *(Courtesy Gerald R. Ford Library)*

November both the House and the Senate overrode his veto. Ultimately, it did little to limit presidential power. In fact, by allowing a president to send troops anywhere for up to 60 days, the act provided a stamp of approval for overseas intervention by the executive. It became clear that Congress would probably never vote to remove troops from hostilities and risk seeing them, and American interests, harmed.

A POLITICAL FUROR: THE SATURDAY NIGHT MASSACRE

At the time of the DEFCON III alert, Henry Kissinger claimed, he had thought that Nixon was too "distraught" to handle the crisis because of the battle over the Watergate tapes. Everyone suspected that the tapes could prove who was telling the truth, Nixon or his accusers. Nixon knew, however, that if Congress got hold of them, he would be ruined, so the fight over them had to be a fight to the finish.

On August 15, he again insisted that he must hold onto the tapes. "It is absolutely necessary," he insisted, "if the President is to be able to do his job as the country expects, that he be able to talk openly and candidly with his advisers about issues and individuals."[48]

One week later, Judge Sirica ordered Nixon to turn over to him some of the subpoenaed tapes so that he could review them. Nixon appealed Sirica's decision, but in October, he lost. Rather than continue his appeal to the Supreme Court, Nixon decided to contain the investigation by getting rid of Watergate special prosecutor Archibald Cox.

Nixon had long disliked, even hated, Cox. He thought Cox's Harvard credentials and friendship with the Kennedy family made Cox part of the Eastern elite, a group that, Nixon believed, was determined to destroy him.

The president decided to make Cox an offer that the public would see as a compromise but that the special prosecutor would never accept. Nixon said that he would give transcripts of the tapes and the tapes themselves to a third party, Mississippi senator John Stennis, to verify and pass along to Cox. In return, Cox would be forbidden to subpoena any additional tapes.

Cox strenuously objected to the proposal and said that it would cripple his investigation. Nixon then ordered Attorney General Elliot Richardson to fire Cox. Richardson refused and instead resigned, saying that he had vowed to protect the independence of the special prosecutor. Nixon said in private about Richardson: "I'm not surprised that the pious bastard cares more for his ass than for his country."[49]

The assistant attorney general, William Ruckleshaus, also refused to fire Cox, and so Nixon fired Ruckleshaus. Nixon finally found someone who would do the deed: the solicitor general, Robert Bork.

The turmoil occurred on Saturday night, October 20 (five days before the DEFCON III alert) and was thus called the Saturday Night Massacre. People around the country watched on TV as reporters labeled the event the most serious constitutional crisis in America's history, and they watched as FBI agents, acting under orders from the White House, sealed the special prosecutor's office.

Telegrams flooded the White House and Congress—150,000 of them on Sunday, the greatest number ever for a 24-hour period—and 450,000 within 10 days. Nearly all of them condemned the firing of Cox, and many insisted that Nixon should be impeached. The president's approval rating plummeted to 17 percent; newspapers called for his resignation or impeachment (the *Atlanta Constitution,* the *Salt Lake City Tribune,* the *Boston Globe,* the *Detroit News,* among them). Even traditionally Republican-friendly *Time* magazine, in its first-ever editorial, called for Nixon to quit.

Nixon had blundered and blundered badly. Stephen Ambrose says: "Nixon did not fire Cox to protect the principle of executive privilege and confidentiality, but to protect himself from his own words."[50] As it turned out, the firing made people more distrustful of Nixon and more willing to believe that the president was fast becoming a tyrant.

Nixon had said in *Six Crises:*

> The public likes to glamorize its leaders, and most leaders like to glamorize themselves. We tend to think of some men as "born leaders." But I have found that leaders are subject to all the human frailties: they lose their tempers, become depressed, experience the other symptoms of tension. Sometimes even strong men cry.[51]

The public's anger over the Saturday Night Massacre led Nixon to appoint a new special prosecutor, one who would have complete independence, and it led him to tell Judge Sirica on October 23 that he would turn over to him the subpoenaed tape-recorded conversations. But this, too, came with a shocking development: On October 30, White House lawyer, J. Fred Buzhardt, Jr., informed Sirica that two of the subpoenaed conversations had never been recorded; hence the tapes for them did not exist. Buzhardt said that for one of the conversations, Nixon's phone had been disconnected from a recording device, and that for the other conversation, a tape recorder had malfunctioned. The news only buttressed the view that Nixon was being deceitful. Judge Sirica said later: "Here it was the end of October, and the White House was making the first public admission that the two critical tapes didn't exist."[52] In fact, Nixon had known about the missing tapes for at least a month before he made their status public.

October closed with a straight party-line vote of 21-17 by which the House Judiciary Committee gave its chairman, Peter Rodino (Dem., N.J.), subpoena powers to conduct an impeachment inquiry. Nixon named Leon Jaworski as the new Watergate special prosecutor. Jaworski turned out to be even more aggressive than Cox with the investigation.

"I Am Not a Crook"

Nixon thought he could escape his critics at least for a few days by taking a trip to the Deep South, the most conservative region of the country and one still supporting him. His first stop, ironically, was at a place known for producing entertaining fiction: Walt Disney World in Orlando. There, on November 17, 1973, he answered questions from members of the Associated Press Managing Editors Association. Many of the questions dealt with the president's finances, with the reports that he had avoided paying income taxes in 1970 and 1971 by illegally backdating a gift of his vice presidential papers to the National Archives. And then came this statement:

> I made my mistakes, but in all my years of public life, I have never profited, never profited from public service—I have earned every cent. And in all of my years of public life, I have never obstructed justice. And I think, too, that I could say that in my years of public life, that I welcome this kind of examination, because people have to know whether or not their President is a crook. Well, I am not a crook.[53]

This, then, was how far distrust had gone—the president having to deny directly: "I am not a crook."

A few days later, a problem surfaced with another tape. On November 21, Nixon revealed that it contained an 18½-minute gap. Later, electronics experts concluded that an erasure had been caused by someone purposefully moving the tape back and forth through a recording machine. To this day, no one is sure who erased the tape, but the evidence points heavily to Nixon.

Meanwhile, Leon Jaworski presented to the House Judiciary Committee 800 pages of documents, several tape recordings, and a 60-page report. When Jaworski first listened to the tapes, he advised the White House to hire a good attorney, for he believed that the president had committed crimes.

The year ended with reports circulating about a number of additional questionable financial dealings by the president. Among the accusations: He had spent more than $10 million in government money on improving his houses in Key Biscayne, Florida, and San Clemente, California. Nixon called the amount "exaggerated," but said that whatever money was spent was necessary to ensure security. A later investigation found that while much money indeed went into legitimate security measures, other funds went into luxuries.

Nixon had written in *Six Crises:*

> When a man has been through even a minor crisis, he learns not to worry when his muscles tense up, his breathing comes faster, his nerves tingle, his stomach churns, his temper becomes short, his nights are sleepless.[54]

MORE TAPES ARE SUBPOENAED

While the House Judiciary Committee continued its work, so, too, did a Washington grand jury, and on March 1, 1974, it indicted several former Nixon aides for their roles in the Watergate cover-up. They included such "big fish" as John Mitchell, H. R. Haldeman, John Ehrlichman, and Charles Colson. The jury reached to the highest office when it named Richard Nixon an unindicted coconspirator.

In mid-April, the House Judiciary Committee subpoenaed 42 additional tapes, and Jaworski subpoenaed 64. Nixon reacted as he had with the first subpoenas from the Senate Watergate Committee and from Cox: He refused to release them. Instead, he said he would provide the House committee with edited transcripts of the tapes.

But Judge Sirica, acting at the request of the special prosecutor, rejected the president's plan and ordered that the actual tapes be given to Jaworski. This time, Nixon appealed to the Supreme Court, and the justices agreed to hear his case on the basis of "imperative public importance," a rare act, used only in emergencies.

A TRIUMPHAL TRIP ABROAD

As these events unfolded, Nixon sought some solace and political redemption in foreign affairs, where he had accomplished so much in the past. He thought, too, that by making a trip abroad and meeting with foreign dignitaries, he would divert attention from Watergate and show his countrymen that he was indispensable. On June 12, he arrived at Cairo, and more than 1 million people wildly cheered him as he rode in an open convertible. Later, he and Egyptian President Anwar Sadat rode in a railroad car to Alexandria. Six million people turned out to see them along the route. The two leaders signed documents pledging greater cooperation between their nations on several matters. But the real importance was the easing of long-strained relations.

Nixon flew to Saudi Arabia and then to Syria. If there was to be peace in the Middle East, he believed, he must improve contacts with the leaders of those countries. From Syria, he flew to Israel. There, he urged the Israelis to take the courageous step of seeking peace through statesmanship. He unsuccessfully tried to get the Israeli prime minister, Yitzhak Rabin, to commit to negotiations with the Arabs.

Later in June, Nixon traveled to Moscow to meet with Brezhnev (despite suffering from the same painful case of phlebitis that he had endured during his trip to the Middle East). They discussed a possible nuclear test ban treaty, continuing tension in the Middle East, and Soviet restrictions on Jewish emigration. In the end, the two men signed accords dealing with economic, technical, and industrial cooperation. They agreed to limit each of their countries to just one antiballistic missile site. But nothing in the summit would cause it to be labeled a breakthrough.

TOWARD IMPEACHMENT

Nixon flew back to the United States on July 3. Five days later, James St. Clair argued for the president before the Supreme Court in the case involving the release of the additional Watergate tapes. He stated that the constitutional separation of powers gave the president immunity from having to reveal his private conversations or to abide by a subpoena from the judicial branch. He stated also that national security was at risk.

Leon Jaworski argued that the Constitution made no claim for executive privilege and that, further, the public interest overrode any such claim. He added that, in any event, Nixon could no longer make such a claim because he had released edited transcripts of the tapes.

On July 24, the Court issued its ruling in the case of *United States v. Nixon*. The justices agreed with St. Clair that executive privilege existed in principle, but they denied that it existed for Nixon because his case involved a criminal prosecution. Thus, the Court ruled, the president had to give up the tapes. Nixon considered disobeying the Court, but the unanimity of the justices convinced him that he would find no public support for such a move.

That same day, the House Judiciary Committee began six days of hearings to determine whether the president should be impeached. More than 35 million viewers watched the proceedings on TV. One public opinion poll found that Americans favored impeachment by a margin of 66 percent to 27 percent.

On July 27, the committee passed its first article of impeachment by a 27–11 vote. The tally included six Republicans, thus making it a bipartisan measure. The article accused Nixon of obstruction of justice. *Time* magazine reported the scene:

> After four garrulous days, the talking stopped. The room was silent, and so, in a sense, was a watching nation. One by one, the strained and solemn faces of the 38 members of the House Judiciary Committee were focused on by the television cameras. One by one, their names were called. One by one, they cast the most momentous vote of their political lives, or of any representative of the American people in a century. . . .
>
> Thus six Republican Congressmen joined all 21 Democrats to recommend that the House of Representatives impeach Richard M. Nixon and seek his removal from the presidency through a Senate trial. And thus the Judiciary Committee climaxed seven months of agonizing inquiry into the conduct of Richard Nixon as President by approving an article of impeachment that charges he violated both his oath to protect the Constitution and his duty to take care that the laws be faithfully executed. By that historic rollcall vote, Richard Nixon became only the second President to stand so accused by a committee of Congress.[55]

On July 29, the committee passed another article. It dealt with abuse of power. On July 30, a third article dealt with contempt of Congress.

Republican senators, including Barry Goldwater (center) meet with the press after discussing Watergate with President Nixon. *(National Archives and Records Administration)*

An emotional President Nixon says farewell to his cabinet and members of the White House staff just moments before boarding his helicopter and heading to his home in California. *(National Archives and Records Administration)*

Nixon's end drew ever closer. Then it came, on August 5, when the president released the transcripts of the meeting that he had with Haldeman on June 23, 1972, when Nixon and Haldeman plotted to use the CIA to block the FBI investigation of Watergate; when Haldeman told Nixon of John Dean's plan to have the CIA tell the FBI to back away, to which Nixon replied: "All right. Fine"; and when Haldeman explained, "We're set up beautifully to do it," to which Nixon responded: "Good deal. Play it tough." Nixon then provided the story whereby the CIA should tell the FBI that an investigation of Watergate would "open the whole Bay of Pigs thing up again."[56]

This was called the smoking-gun tape because it clearly showed the president obstructing justice. The reaction was a swift, nearly universal condemnation of Nixon. The 10 Republican members of the House Judiciary Committee who had opposed his impeachment now moved to support it. Gerald Ford said: "The public interest is no longer served by repetition of my previously expressed belief that . . . the President is not guilty of an impeachable offense."[57]

Even the most conservative Republicans deserted the president. Privately, Arizona senator Barry Goldwater said, "There are only so many lies you can take and now there has been one too many. Nixon should get his ass out of the White House—today."[58]

Nixon knew that the House would vote for his impeachment and that the Senate would convict him. He well knew what this would cost him financially— the loss of his considerable yearly pension ($60,000) and money for staff support ($100,000). He felt exhausted and depressed. He decided to resign.

Nixon had written in *Six Crises:* "Meeting crises involves creativity. It engages all a man's talents. When he looks back on life, he has to answer the question: did he live up to his capabilities as fully as he could?"[59]

The night of August 7, Nixon called Kissinger to the White House. They met in the Lincoln Sitting Room, where they talked about their accomplishments. Then, as they walked down the hall, Nixon asked Kissinger to kneel down with him in the Lincoln Bedroom and pray, which they did.

Nixon had written in *Six Crises:* "One man may have opportunities that others do not. But what counts is whether the individual used what chances he had."[60]

The morning of August 8, Richard Nixon told Gerald Ford about his decision to quit. He told the leaders of Congress early that night. At 9 P.M. he told the American people. "I have always tried to do what was best for the nation," he said to his television and radio audience. He said that he no longer had the support of Congress. "Therefore, I shall resign the Presidency effective at noon tomorrow."[61]

He was the first president to resign, and his resignation came just 10 months after the vice president had resigned. In such a short span of time, the country's two top executive officeholders had been changed; the landslide victory of 1972 had been erased. The *New York Times* reported:

> Mr. Nixon, in a conciliatory address on national television, said that he was leaving not with a sense of bitterness but with a hope that his departure would start a "process of healing that is so desperately needed in America."[62]

President Nixon hugs his daughter Julie after announcing his resignation. *(National Archives and Records Administration)*

GRUESOME MURDERS

In August 1973, details unfolded in the largest multiple murder case in American history to that time when 17-year-old Elmer Wayne Henley and 18-year-old David Owen Brooks confessed to their role in the slaying of 27 young men over a period of three years. Henley and Brooks had procured the victims between 1970 and 1973 in Houston, Texas, for 32-year-old Dean Corll, a one-time candy-store clerk (hence his nickname, "the candy man").

Henley and Brooks enticed the young men, generally in their mid- to late teens, to Corll's Houston home with promises of drugs. Henley later said that Corll paid him and Brooks $200 for each young man they procured. Once Corll had his victims inside his house, he shackled them to a board with handcuffs, sodomized them, and killed them.

Corll's murder spree came to an end when he and Henley had a falling out. Henley had brought a male friend and a girl to Corll's house. Angered by the presence of the girl, Corll handcuffed Henley and his two friends to the boards while they were passed out from sniffing glue. When Henley awoke, he convinced Corll to set him free. He then grabbed Corll's gun and demanded that Corll free the other two. When Corll refused, Henley fired six shots, hitting Corll in the chest and killing him.

The police found 17 bodies in a boat shed that was rented to Corll and 10 more at two other sites. Henley and Brooks had helped bury the bodies, wrapping them in plastic bags and covering them with lime. Brooks received a life term for his role in the murders, and Henley received concurrent 99-year terms for each murder.

PATRICIA HEARST AND THE SYMBIONESE LIBERATION FRONT

The radical Symbionese Liberation Army (SLA) gained national attention in February 1974 when it kidnapped Patricia Hearst, the 19-year-old daughter of newspaper publisher Randolph A. Hearst. Patty Hearst, a student at the University of California in Berkeley, was abducted from her off-campus apartment. The SLA demanded that the elder Hearst distribute free food to the Bay area's poor. Hearst did so, spending $2 million on the project. The kidnappers later demanded an additional $4 million ransom.

The SLA had taken credit for the murder in November 1973 of Marcus Foster, the black superintendent of the Oakland city schools. They acted in protest of his plan to require identification cards for all students, a "fascist" policy, they said. As their grand goal, the SLA sought to ignite an uprising by the masses against the U.S. government. They used the term *Symbionese* to mean the coming together, or symbiosis, of all people. Their motto: "Death to the fascist insect that preys upon the life of the people."

In April, though, Hearst's kidnapping took a bizarre twist. In a recorded message, she told how she had become a member of the SLA to "fight for the freedom of all oppressed people." A few days later, she and several other members of the group robbed a San Francisco bank.

The next month, SLA leaders William Harris and Emily Harris (known within the SLA as Tico and Yolanda) entered Mel's Sporting Goods Store in

Inglewood, California. Caught shoplifting, William Harris pointed a revolver at one of the store employees. The clerk knocked the gun from his hand and succeeded in placing a handcuff on his left wrist when Patricia Hearst—Tania to the SLA—began to shoot into the store from across the street with a rifle. Everyone on the premises took cover, and the Harrises escaped. There followed in May a shootout with the police at a house that the SLA was using as a hideout in Los Angeles. The showdown resulted in the house catching fire. Six SLA members were killed in the confrontation.

The saga of Hearst and the SLA ended in September 1975, when police arrested several of the revolutionaries and found Hearst living in a house with one of her colleagues near San Francisco. "Don't shoot," she said to the police. "I'll go with you." Hearst was later granted immunity for her testimony against several SLA members. She later claimed that she had been coerced by the SLA into committing violent acts. Many prominent psychiatrists concluded that the groups' influence caused Hearst to change her personality and become one of "them."

SPACE STATION MISSIONS

As part of the Apollo space program, on May 14, 1973, the United States launched the *Skylab* space station into orbit around Earth and readied it for a manned crew. The beginning of the project, however, proved troublesome. Vibrations during liftoff caused a meteoroid shield on *Skylab* to rip away, taking with it one of two solar panels. A piece of the shield wrapped around a second solar panel, disabling it. To maintain power to *Skylab* with the damaged panels, technicians positioned it to face the sun more directly than planned. That boosted the electrical supply but exposed the cabin of the space station to temperatures exceeding 125 degrees.

Because of the problems, the sending of astronauts to the station had to be delayed. Captain Charles Conrad, Jr., and commanders Joseph P. Kerwin and Paul J. Weitz finally entered orbit on May 25, 1973, and once at *Skylab,* they installed an exterior parasol to deflect the Sun's rays and decrease the cabin temperature, which gradually dropped to 75 degrees. Soon after, astronauts Conrad and Kerwin engaged in a space walk to restore the disabled space shield, and on another space walk, Conrad acted like a frustrated mechanic working on an old car and used a hammer to knock a battery back into operation.

Once on board, the astronauts conducted a large number of experiments, completing nearly their full agenda of duties despite other problems, such as instruments jamming. They studied the Sun with solar telescopes, conducted medical tests, and took pictures of 31 states and nine countries.

One of the mission's main objectives was to see what effects prolonged weightlessness would have on human beings. The astronauts spent 28 days in space, and when they returned, there were some worries. The *New York Times* reported that the astronauts felt "light headed" and added: "Gravity was pulling their blood into their lower extremities faster than their circulatory system could provide the necessary pressure to force the blood back up to their brains. The system had not been accustomed to pumping against gravity for so long."[63]

Commander Weitz took seven or eight hours to get back his "Earth legs" and experienced muscle soreness and a drop in blood pressure during exercise routines. Commander Kerwin suffered the worst effects. On reentry, he complained of dizziness and had to wear an inflatable device around his legs to stimulate blood circulation.

In late July, astronauts Alan L. Bean, Jack R. Lousma, and Owen K. Garriott began a mission to *Skylab* that lasted 59 days. They conducted more than 1,000 hours of solar and Earth experiments, orbited the Earth 858 times, and walked in space three times (during which they installed a new solar shield).

The last *Skylab* mission began on November 16, 1973, and ended on February 8, 1974. During it, astronauts Gerald P. Carr, William R. Pogue, and Edward G. Gibson observed and photographed the comet Kohoutek. Their four space walks totaled 22 hours and 13 minutes. The astronauts operated several experimental processes for making metal alloys and crystals for electronics, and they observed the Sun for 338 hours. On their return, they experienced fewer side effects than had the previous astronauts. Doctors attributed this to a more extensive physical-exercise program.

The *Skylab* space station cost $294 million. The entire project cost $2.5 billion. Skylab plummeted to Earth in 1979, having been occupied a total of six months.

HANK AARON'S HOME-RUN RECORD

Ever since Babe Ruth set a record in major league baseball of 714 career home runs, it was thought that the mark would stand forever. The "forever" ended on April 8, 1974, when Hank Aaron hit home-run number 715.

Unlike Ruth, Aaron set his career record not with a large number of home runs over a few years but with a longevity in the National League noted for respectable home-run numbers most years. Aaron began to play with the Milwaukee Braves (later the Atlanta Braves) in 1954. From 1957 to 1973, he hit between 24 and 47 home runs a season. As Aaron began to approach Ruth's record in the early 1970s, he received a massive number of encouraging letters but also a troubling number of hate-filled ones from people who detested the idea of an African American becoming the new home-run king. On top of that pressure, he had to withstand an immense amount of media scrutiny. He grew to dislike the constant barrage of writers, cameras, and tape recorders, the incessant questions.

At the end of 1973, his career home-run total reached 713. On April 4, 1974, the first day of the baseball season, he tied Ruth's record with number 714. Four days later, in the fourth inning, while facing Los Angeles Dodger pitcher Al Downing, Aaron hit number 715—a low-pitched ball that he sent sailing over the left-field fence. By the time he retired, he had hit 755 home runs. He later said about the day when he broke Ruth's record: "I was in my own little world at the time. It was like I was running in a bubble."[64]

A BASKETBALL SUPERSTAR CHANGES THE SPORT

Until 1967, professional basketball had been largely the domain of the National Basketball Association (NBA). But then a new league, the American Basketball Association (ABA), was formed. It had a difficult time competing with the NBA, despite trying several gimmicks such as using red-white-and-blue balls, staging slam-dunk contests, and incorporating a three-point shot.

The ABA went from gimmicks to quality in 1971 when the Virginia Squires signed Julius Erving, a junior sensation at the University of Massachusetts where he set numerous records. Erving became one of only six players in NCAA history to average more than 20 points and 20 rebounds a game. Unlike the NBA, the ABA had no rules against, or compunctions about, signing players who still had college eligibility. (In this case, Erving chose to forego his senior year at Massachusetts.) Erving, nicknamed "Dr. J.," soon gained an almost mythical reputation for his abilities on the court. During his rookie year, he scored 27 points a game. He could "blur through an entire team, softly rolling the ball off his fingertips into the hoop" and could dunk at a height "from which he was looking down at the basket."[65] He thus popularized the "airborne" and the "above the rim" style of play.

Erving's pro career really took off after August 1, 1973, when the New York Nets signed him. Exposure to the big-city market brought him more time on television and earned him bigger contracts. He was among the first basketball players to set the trend for lucrative salaries and major endorsements. He led the Nets to ABA championships in 1974 and 1976.

Erving finished his playing career in 1987 with the Philadelphia 76ers, having moved there in 1976 after the ABA and NBA merged. In 1983, he led the team to an NBA championship. Erving remains one of only three players in pro basketball history to score more than 30,000 career points.

One sports observer claims: "Today, the NBA allows the three-point field goal, remembers fondly its first years of slam-dunk contests . . . [and] regularly signs teenagers and underclassmen. . . . The greatness of the Doctor is the reason why."[66]

SCANNERS ACROSS THE COUNTRY

On June 16, 1974, consumers in Troy, Ohio, experienced an innovation that would change shopping habits for years to come. On that date, the first Universal Price Code (UPC) scanner went into operation at the Marsh supermarket. A package of chewing gum earned the honor of being the first item checked out through the new system.

The idea for using coded information to record sales originated in the 1950s with Norman Woodland and Bernard Silver, but it remained impractical until the invention of the laser in the 1960s. In 1972, RCA tested the first laser supermarket scanner. It relied on reading standard print and failed to work properly. Then George J. Laurer of IBM, working with Woodland and others, developed the UPC, a system of standardized black and white lines that encoded 12 digits.

No longer did cashiers have to read the price of each item at checkout and punch each price into cash registers. The scanner quickened the pace of service, and the bar code soon appeared everywhere in the shopper's world.

CHRONICLE OF EVENTS

1973

January 10: The trial of the Watergate burglars begins before Judge John Sirica. The following day, E. Howard Hunt pleads guilty, and a few days later, the four Cuban burglars do the same. But James W. McCord and Gordon Liddy continue to proclaim their innocence.

January 11: President Nixon ends the mandatory wage and price controls that he had imposed nearly 18 months earlier.

January 16: Steve Carlton becomes professional baseball's highest-paid pitcher when he signs a one-year, $167,000 contract with the Philadelphia Phillies.

January 21: Richard Nixon is inaugurated president to begin his second term. He claims that new domestic and foreign policy initiatives will bring peace and progress.

January 22: The U.S. Supreme Court rules unconstitutional all state laws that prohibit a women's right to an abortion during the first three months of her pregnancy. During the next six months of pregnancy, the Court rules, a state can regulate abortion procedures to protect "maternal health," and during the last 10 weeks, a state can prohibit abortions, except where necessary to protect the life of the mother.

January 23: Former President Lyndon Baines Johnson dies at age 64 after suffering a heart attack at his ranch in Johnson City, Texas.

January 23: Henry Kissinger and Le Duc Tho initial a peace agreement in Paris to end the war in Vietnam. The agreement calls for the United States to withdraw its remaining troops from South Vietnam. North Vietnam, however, is permitted to keep its troops in the South. The communists promise to release all American POWs.

January 27: Defense Secretary Melvin R. Laird announces the end to the military draft.

January 28: The Defense Department announces that Colonel William Nolde is the last U.S. casualty in Vietnam as the negotiated cease-fire takes effect.

January 30: A jury finds James W. McCord and Gordon Liddy guilty in the Watergate break-in. Judge Sirica says that he suspects that there is more to Watergate than was revealed at the trial.

February 7: The Senate votes 73-0 to establish a select committee to investigate Watergate. The Senate Select Committee on Presidential Campaign Activities is headed by Sen. Sam Ervin (Dem., N.C.) and will be more popularly called the Ervin committee or the Watergate committee.

February 28: Members of the American Indian Movement begin a siege at Wounded Knee, South Dakota, to protest the treatment of Sioux Indians on the Pine Ridge Reservation and government mistreatment of Indians in general. With AIM in control of a trading post and church, federal marshals, FBI agents, and Bureau of Indian Affairs police surround the hamlet.

February 28: L. Patrick Gray tells a Senate committee then considering whether or not to confirm his appointment as director of the FBI that as acting director he had given the president's counsel, John Dean, full access to reports dealing with the bureau's Watergate investigation and had even allowed Dean to sit in on interviews with suspects. Gray's admission causes the White House to back away from supporting his nomination, with President Nixon's domestic adviser, John Ehrlichman, telling Dean to let Gray "twist slowly, slowly, in the wind." Gray will withdraw his name from consideration in April.

March 6: President Nixon announces mandatory controls to limit price increases for crude oil, gasoline, heating oil, and other refinery products.

March 21: White House counsel John Dean warns President Nixon that the Watergate investigations were getting closer to the Oval Office and that "We have a cancer within, close to the Presidency, that is growing." Nixon responds to the information from Dean that the Watergate conspirators were seeking more money to maintain their silence by telling him: "We could get that. . . ."

March 23: One of the seven Watergate conspirators, James W. McCord, says in a letter to Judge John Sirica, read in open court by the judge on this day, that he and the other defendants had been pressured to plead guilty and remain silent. He says there are other people involved in Watergate, and he asks for a private meeting with the judge.

March 28: In a closed Senate hearing, James W. McCord says that former Attorney General John N. Mitchell had prior knowledge of the Watergate break-in.

March 29: The last U.S. troops depart South Vietnam, about eight years after President Lyndon Johnson had turned over ground combat to the U.S. army. North Vietnam releases 67 POWs, bringing to 587 the number set free.

March 29: President Nixon announces a ceiling on wholesale and retail prices for beef, pork, and lamb in an attempt to end the spiraling inflation affecting those products.

March 29: A jury in New York convicts black activist H. Rap Brown, former leader of the Student Non-violent Coordinating Committee, and three codefendants of armed robbery and assault with a deadly weapon following an October 1971 holdup of a bar in New York City.

April 2: John Dean informs the Watergate prosecutors that he is willing to talk about the Watergate break-in, the break-in at the office of Dr. Daniel Ellsberg's psychiatrist, and the payment of hush money to the Watergate defendants.

April 3: President Nixon meets with South Vietnamese president Nguyen Van Thieu at San Clemente, California. The two men agree to carry out the provisions of the Paris peace treaty, and Nixon agrees to seek economic aid for South Vietnam.

April 4: The World Trade Center is dedicated at a ribbon-cutting ceremony. Construction of the center, at the heart of which are the two 110-story World Trade Towers, was begun in 1966. The towers were designed by Seattle-born architect Minoru Yamasaki and dominate the Manhattan skyline. A 16-acre, 12-million-square-foot complex, the World Trade Center ultimately will resemble a miniature city, with a daytime population of more than 140,000 and seven buildings arranged around a plaza. Underground will be a giant mall with nearly a hundred stores and restaurants and a network of subway and other train stations.

April 17: President Nixon reveals that his own investigation into Watergate has produced "major developments." He agrees to let his aides testify before a Senate investigating committee and promises to fire any government employee who is indicted in connection with the case.

April 20: Testifying before a grand jury, former Attorney General John Mitchell recants his earlier statement that the Watergate break-in had been a surprise to him and admits that he had heard talk of illegal bugging operations during the 1972 presidential campaign.

April 23: National Security Advisor Henry Kissinger announces that the United States will seek a new working relationship with its European allies to lessen tension caused by the Vietnam War and ease differences resulting from economic development.

The World Trade Center towers pierce the sky over New York City. *(National Archives and Records Administration)*

April 26: The acting head of the FBI, L. Patrick Gray, reveals that at the suggestion of White House aides John Ehrlichman and John Dean, he burned some papers belonging to Watergate conspirator E. Howard Hunt. Gray resigns his post on April 27 and is replaced by William D. Ruckelshaus.

April 27: The judge in the *Pentagon Papers* trial reveals a justice department memo that shows two of the Watergate defendants, E. Howard Hunt and G. Gordon Liddy, had broken into the office of Dr. Daniel Ellsberg's psychiatrist.

April 30: The Watergate scandal deepens when President Nixon accepts the resignations of three of his top aides: chief of staff H. R. Haldeman, domestic affairs adviser John D. Ehrlichman, and presidential counsel John W. Dean. Privately, Nixon now senses that Watergate will cost him the presidency.

April 30: Attorney General Richard Kleindienst resigns, claiming that he can not be fair in enforcing the law because some of his friends have been involved in illegal activities.

May 1: Federal investigators report that they have evidence of a high-level cover-up in the Watergate case

September 20: Singer and songwriter Jim Croce dies in a plane crash in Louisiana. His hit single "Bad, Bad Leroy Brown" had reached number one just two months earlier.

September 21: The Senate confirms President Nixon's appointment of Henry Kissinger as secretary of state. Kissinger had been serving as the president's National Security Advisor.

September 24: E. Howard Hunt tells the Senate Watergate Committee that special White House counsel Charles Colson had ordered a diplomatic cable faked to make it look as if President John Kennedy had taken part in plans to assassinate South Vietnamese President Diem in 1963.

September 25: The *Sklyab* astronauts—Alan L. Bean, Jack R. Lousma, and Owen Garriot—return to Earth after 59 days on the space station.

October 6: The Arab-Israeli, or Yom Kippur, War erupts with Egyptian forces crossing the Suez Canal and Syrian forces battling in the Golan Heights. By October 11, the Egyptians advance into the Sinai Peninsula against Israeli troops who had been occupying it.

October 9: Vice President Spiro Agnew informs President Nixon that he will resign his office in light of a criminal investigation against him. Agnew has arranged a deal with federal prosecutors whereby he will resign and plead nolo contendere for failing to pay income taxes in return for three years' probation, payment of a $10,000 fine, and immunity from further prosecution.

October 11: General Services Administrator Arthur Sampson testifies before the House Government Activities Subcommittee that "mistakes" had been made in the spending of millions of dollars on projects at President Nixon's private homes in San Clemente, California, and Key Biscayne, Florida. A few days later, Chairman Jack Brooks (Dem., Tex.) says that money which was earmarked for security at the Nixon homes may well have been spent on luxury items.

October 12: A counterattack by Israeli troops brings them to within 18 miles of Damascus, the Syrian capital. By October 24, the Israelis surround the city of Suez on the Sinai Peninsula and, with it, the Egyptian 3rd Army.

October 12: President Nixon announces that, under the terms of the Twenty-fifth Amendment, he is nominating House minority leader Gerald Ford (Rep., Mich.) to become vice president.

October 19: John Dean pleads guilty to one count of conspiracy to obstruct justice in plotting to cover up the Watergate break-in. The plea is part of a bargain with Watergate special prosecutor Archibald Cox, according to which Dean agrees to testify for the prosecution in future Watergate proceedings in exchange for immunity.

October 19: To protest American policy in the Middle East, Arab oil-producing nations, who believe Washington too pro-Israel, ban oil shipments to the United States. The embargo lasts until March 18, 1974.

October 20: In a stunning development, Attorney General Elliott Richardson resigns and his deputy William D. Ruckelshaus, along with Watergate special prosecutor Archibald Cox, are fired by President Nixon after Cox rejects a compromise offered by Nixon in reaction to a court order to turn over the Watergate tapes. Nixon had proposed to turn over transcripts of the tapes rather than the tapes themselves. Richardson resigns rather than obey Nixon's order to fire Cox. Nixon then fires Ruckelshaus when the deputy also refuses to fire Cox. Finally, Solicitor General Robert H. Bork, who has become acting attorney general, agrees to fire Cox. Nixon's action—dubbed the "Saturday Night Massacre"—will result in massive public protests when letters and telegrams flood the White House and Congress. Many people and several prominent organizations, including the AFL-CIO, will call for Nixon to resign or be impeached.

Joblessness hit black Americans hard in the 1970s, as it did here in north Philadelphia, where a worker for the Urban Coalition talks to unemployed men. *(National Archives and Records Administration)*

March 29: President Nixon announces a ceiling on wholesale and retail prices for beef, pork, and lamb in an attempt to end the spiraling inflation affecting those products.

March 29: A jury in New York convicts black activist H. Rap Brown, former leader of the Student Non-violent Coordinating Committee, and three codefendants of armed robbery and assault with a deadly weapon following an October 1971 holdup of a bar in New York City.

April 2: John Dean informs the Watergate prosecutors that he is willing to talk about the Watergate break-in, the break-in at the office of Dr. Daniel Ellsberg's psychiatrist, and the payment of hush money to the Watergate defendants.

April 3: President Nixon meets with South Vietnamese president Nguyen Van Thieu at San Clemente, California. The two men agree to carry out the provisions of the Paris peace treaty, and Nixon agrees to seek economic aid for South Vietnam.

April 4: The World Trade Center is dedicated at a ribbon-cutting ceremony. Construction of the center, at the heart of which are the two 110-story World Trade Towers, was begun in 1966. The towers were designed by Seattle-born architect Minoru Yamasaki and dominate the Manhattan skyline. A 16-acre, 12-million-square-foot complex, the World Trade Center ultimately will resemble a miniature city, with a daytime population of more than 140,000 and seven buildings arranged around a plaza. Underground will be a giant mall with nearly a hundred stores and restaurants and a network of subway and other train stations.

April 17: President Nixon reveals that his own investigation into Watergate has produced "major developments." He agrees to let his aides testify before a Senate investigating committee and promises to fire any government employee who is indicted in connection with the case.

April 20: Testifying before a grand jury, former Attorney General John Mitchell recants his earlier statement that the Watergate break-in had been a surprise to him and admits that he had heard talk of illegal bugging operations during the 1972 presidential campaign.

April 23: National Security Advisor Henry Kissinger announces that the United States will seek a new working relationship with its European allies to lessen tension caused by the Vietnam War and ease differences resulting from economic development.

The World Trade Center towers pierce the sky over New York City. *(National Archives and Records Administration)*

April 26: The acting head of the FBI, L. Patrick Gray, reveals that at the suggestion of White House aides John Ehrlichman and John Dean, he burned some papers belonging to Watergate conspirator E. Howard Hunt. Gray resigns his post on April 27 and is replaced by William D. Ruckelshaus.

April 27: The judge in the *Pentagon Papers* trial reveals a justice department memo that shows two of the Watergate defendants, E. Howard Hunt and G. Gordon Liddy, had broken into the office of Dr. Daniel Ellsberg's psychiatrist.

April 30: The Watergate scandal deepens when President Nixon accepts the resignations of three of his top aides: chief of staff H. R. Haldeman, domestic affairs adviser John D. Ehrlichman, and presidential counsel John W. Dean. Privately, Nixon now senses that Watergate will cost him the presidency.

April 30: Attorney General Richard Kleindienst resigns, claiming that he can not be fair in enforcing the law because some of his friends have been involved in illegal activities.

May 1: Federal investigators report that they have evidence of a high-level cover-up in the Watergate case

September 20: Singer and songwriter Jim Croce dies in a plane crash in Louisiana. His hit single "Bad, Bad Leroy Brown" had reached number one just two months earlier.

September 21: The Senate confirms President Nixon's appointment of Henry Kissinger as secretary of state. Kissinger had been serving as the president's National Security Advisor.

September 24: E. Howard Hunt tells the Senate Watergate Committee that special White House counsel Charles Colson had ordered a diplomatic cable faked to make it look as if President John Kennedy had taken part in plans to assassinate South Vietnamese President Diem in 1963.

September 25: The *Sklyab* astronauts—Alan L. Bean, Jack R. Lousma, and Owen Garriot—return to Earth after 59 days on the space station.

October 6: The Arab-Israeli, or Yom Kippur, War erupts with Egyptian forces crossing the Suez Canal and Syrian forces battling in the Golan Heights. By October 11, the Egyptians advance into the Sinai Peninsula against Israeli troops who had been occupying it.

October 9: Vice President Spiro Agnew informs President Nixon that he will resign his office in light of a criminal investigation against him. Agnew has arranged a deal with federal prosecutors whereby he will resign and plead nolo contendere for failing to pay income taxes in return for three years' probation, payment of a $10,000 fine, and immunity from further prosecution.

October 11: General Services Administrator Arthur Sampson testifies before the House Government Activities Subcommittee that "mistakes" had been made in the spending of millions of dollars on projects at President Nixon's private homes in San Clemente, California, and Key Biscayne, Florida. A few days later, Chairman Jack Brooks (Dem., Tex.) says that money which was earmarked for security at the Nixon homes may well have been spent on luxury items.

October 12: A counterattack by Israeli troops brings them to within 18 miles of Damascus, the Syrian capital. By October 24, the Israelis surround the city of Suez on the Sinai Peninsula and, with it, the Egyptian 3rd Army.

October 12: President Nixon announces that, under the terms of the Twenty-fifth Amendment, he is nominating House minority leader Gerald Ford (Rep., Mich.) to become vice president.

October 19: John Dean pleads guilty to one count of conspiracy to obstruct justice in plotting to cover up the Watergate break-in. The plea is part of a bargain with Watergate special prosecutor Archibald Cox, according to which Dean agrees to testify for the prosecution in future Watergate proceedings in exchange for immunity.

October 19: To protest American policy in the Middle East, Arab oil-producing nations, who believe Washington too pro-Israel, ban oil shipments to the United States. The embargo lasts until March 18, 1974.

October 20: In a stunning development, Attorney General Elliott Richardson resigns and his deputy William D. Ruckelshaus, along with Watergate special prosecutor Archibald Cox, are fired by President Nixon after Cox rejects a compromise offered by Nixon in reaction to a court order to turn over the Watergate tapes. Nixon had proposed to turn over transcripts of the tapes rather than the tapes themselves. Richardson resigns rather than obey Nixon's order to fire Cox. Nixon then fires Ruckelshaus when the deputy also refuses to fire Cox. Finally, Solicitor General Robert H. Bork, who has become acting attorney general, agrees to fire Cox. Nixon's action—dubbed the "Saturday Night Massacre"—will result in massive public protests when letters and telegrams flood the White House and Congress. Many people and several prominent organizations, including the AFL-CIO, will call for Nixon to resign or be impeached.

Joblessness hit black Americans hard in the 1970s, as it did here in north Philadelphia, where a worker for the Urban Coalition talks to unemployed men. *(National Archives and Records Administration)*

involving John D. Ehrlichman, H. R. Haldeman, and John N. Mitchell. The three men plotted to deny all knowledge of the break-in and to provide money to the defendants, along with promises of executive clemency.

May 2: The *New York Times* reports in a front-page story that Republican espionage and sabotage in the 1972 presidential campaign was much wider than previously indicated.

May 4: A left-wing guerrilla group, the People's Revolutionary Armed Forces, kidnaps the U.S. consul general in Mexico, near his home in Guadalajara. The kidnappers demand and obtain the release of 30 prisoners in exchange for the release of the American. The prisoners are flown to sanctuary in Cuba.

May 10: President Nixon makes several changes to his cabinet and staff, including the appointment of General Alexander M. Haig, Jr., to fill the position held by H. R. Haldeman and the appointment of J. Fred Buzhardt as special counsel for Watergate matters.

May 11: Judge William Byrne dismisses all charges of conspiracy, theft, and espionage against Dr. Daniel Ellsberg and codefendant Anthony Russo, Jr., in the *Pentagon Papers* case because the conduct of the government was making a fair trial impossible. Byrne reveals that the White House had plotted the break-in at the office of Ellsberg's psychiatrist, and he states that presidential adviser John Ehrlichman tried to influence him in the case by dangling before him the possibility of appointing him FBI director.

May 15: The CIA reveals that, in 1972, presidential counsel John W. Dean had asked it to help in covering up Watergate by paying money to the arrested burglars.

May 17: The Senate Select Committee on Presidential Campaign Activities, chaired by North Carolina Democrat Sam Ervin, begins its hearings. It will meet until August 7, during which time it will hold 37 days of hearings and the television networks will broadcast more than 300 hours of testimony.

May 17: The *Washington Post* reports that Watergate was only a small part of a much larger program of illegal activities conducted by the White House.

May 22: President Nixon issues a lengthy statement in which he admits that he tried to limit the scope of the Watergate investigation to protect legitimate national security concerns. He denies that he had any involvement in the break-in or any subsequent cover-up. He says that from 1969 to 1971, he engaged in wiretaps, but these were to protect foreign policy. He admits also to the establishment of the "plumbers," but only as a way to protect national security and not as a means to engage in any illegal activities. He says that he directed the plumbers to gather information on Dr. Daniel Ellsberg, who had leaked the *Pentagon Papers* to the *New York Times.*

May 25: The *New York Times* reports that the CIA informed the White House as early as 1969 that no connection existed between foreign governments and radical groups within the United States. Despite this, the Nixon administration continued to warn about such connections.

May 29: Thomas Bradley defeats incumbent Sam Yorty to become the first black mayor of Los Angeles. Bradley is a 21-year veteran of the city police force.

June 13: As inflation accelerates, President Nixon imposes a 60-day freeze on all retail prices. He calls it a temporary measure to allow Congress time to address the issue more thoroughly.

June 14: Jeb Stuart Magruder, deputy director of the Committee to Reelect the President, testifies before the Senate Watergate Committee that he and other high-ranking Republican officials had plotted to bug the Democrats and had then tried to cover up their involvement. He claims that Nixon's chief of staff H. R. Haldeman knew about the spy plans.

June 16: Soviet Communist Party General Secretary Leonid I. Brezhnev begins a nine-day visit to the United States. On June 22, he and President Nixon will sign an agreement whereby the Soviet Union and the United States promise to enter into discussions with each other should relations between them, or between either one of them and a third country, deteriorate to the point of threatening nuclear war.

June 21: The U.S. Supreme Court rules that governments can ban works that appeal to a "prurient interest in sex." The definition of *prurient* must be based on the views of "the average person, applying contemporary community standards." Dissenters on the court criticize the 5-4 ruling as too restrictive of free speech and the press and too vague in its definition.

June 22: Three astronauts successfully complete the first mission aboard America's orbiting space station, Skylab. Charles Conrad, Jr., Joseph P. Kerwin, and Paul J. Weitz set a record for spending 28 days in space.

June 25: Former presidential counsel John W. Dean reads a six-hour statement and reveals that the Watergate cover-up had spread into the Department of Justice and into the Oval Office itself. He says that he had warned President Nixon in March 1973 of "a cancer

March 29: President Nixon announces a ceiling on wholesale and retail prices for beef, pork, and lamb in an attempt to end the spiraling inflation affecting those products.

March 29: A jury in New York convicts black activist H. Rap Brown, former leader of the Student Non-violent Coordinating Committee, and three codefendants of armed robbery and assault with a deadly weapon following an October 1971 holdup of a bar in New York City.

April 2: John Dean informs the Watergate prosecutors that he is willing to talk about the Watergate break-in, the break-in at the office of Dr. Daniel Ellsberg's psychiatrist, and the payment of hush money to the Watergate defendants.

April 3: President Nixon meets with South Vietnamese president Nguyen Van Thieu at San Clemente, California. The two men agree to carry out the provisions of the Paris peace treaty, and Nixon agrees to seek economic aid for South Vietnam.

April 4: The World Trade Center is dedicated at a ribbon-cutting ceremony. Construction of the center, at the heart of which are the two 110-story World Trade Towers, was begun in 1966. The towers were designed by Seattle-born architect Minoru Yamasaki and dominate the Manhattan skyline. A 16-acre, 12-million-square-foot complex, the World Trade Center ultimately will resemble a miniature city, with a daytime population of more than 140,000 and seven buildings arranged around a plaza. Underground will be a giant mall with nearly a hundred stores and restaurants and a network of subway and other train stations.

April 17: President Nixon reveals that his own investigation into Watergate has produced "major developments." He agrees to let his aides testify before a Senate investigating committee and promises to fire any government employee who is indicted in connection with the case.

April 20: Testifying before a grand jury, former Attorney General John Mitchell recants his earlier statement that the Watergate break-in had been a surprise to him and admits that he had heard talk of illegal bugging operations during the 1972 presidential campaign.

April 23: National Security Advisor Henry Kissinger announces that the United States will seek a new working relationship with its European allies to lessen tension caused by the Vietnam War and ease differences resulting from economic development.

The World Trade Center towers pierce the sky over New York City. *(National Archives and Records Administration)*

April 26: The acting head of the FBI, L. Patrick Gray, reveals that at the suggestion of White House aides John Ehrlichman and John Dean, he burned some papers belonging to Watergate conspirator E. Howard Hunt. Gray resigns his post on April 27 and is replaced by William D. Ruckelshaus.

April 27: The judge in the *Pentagon Papers* trial reveals a justice department memo that shows two of the Watergate defendants, E. Howard Hunt and G. Gordon Liddy, had broken into the office of Dr. Daniel Ellsberg's psychiatrist.

April 30: The Watergate scandal deepens when President Nixon accepts the resignations of three of his top aides: chief of staff H. R. Haldeman, domestic affairs adviser John D. Ehrlichman, and presidential counsel John W. Dean. Privately, Nixon now senses that Watergate will cost him the presidency.

April 30: Attorney General Richard Kleindienst resigns, claiming that he can not be fair in enforcing the law because some of his friends have been involved in illegal activities.

May 1: Federal investigators report that they have evidence of a high-level cover-up in the Watergate case

growing on the presidency" but that Nixon ignored him. He says that Nixon had personally involved himself in the cover-up for at least eight months and that the president had at one point congratulated him on helping to impede the government investigation.

June 26: John W. Dean tells the Senate Watergate committee that the White House has kept an "enemies list" containing the names of politicians, journalists, entertainers, academicians, and Democratic campaign contributors and that these people have been harassed by government investigators.

June 27: The Senate approves President Nixon's appointment of Clarence M. Kelley as director of the FBI, an organization he has served for 21 years.

June 29: President Nixon reluctantly agrees to an amendment attached to an appropriations bill that commits him to ending military activity in Cambodia by August 15.

June 29: President Nixon announces a voluntary conservation drive, led by the government, to promote the saving of energy. He appoints Colorado governor John A. Love to head a new energy office in the White House.

July 10: John N. Mitchell, the former attorney general and director of CREEP, tells the Senate Watergate committee that he helped efforts to "limit the impact" of Watergate on the president's reelection campaign. The following day, he implicates Nixon's top advisers, John D. Ehrlichman and H. R. Haldeman, in a plan to develop a cover-up.

July 16: Former presidential deputy assistant Alexander P. Butterfield surprises the Senate Watergate Committee with testimony that President Nixon had, since 1971, secretly recorded conversations in the White House and the Executive Office Building.

July 17: Herbert W. Kalmbach, formerly President Nixon's personal attorney and fund-raiser, testifies before the Senate Watergate committee that he improperly and illegally raised more than $200,000 to be paid the defendants in the Watergate break-in.

July 17: The Senate approves a bill authorizing the construction of the controversial Alaska oil pipeline, to cost $3.5 billion and traverse nearly 800 miles from the Alaska North Slope oil fields to the port of Valdez.

July 24: Appearing before the Senate Watergate Committee, former presidential adviser John D. Ehrlichman places the blame for the Watergate cover-up on another Nixon aide, John Dean. He states that neither he nor President Nixon had authorized the break-in at the office of Daniel Ellsberg's psychiatrist. The following day, he insists that he was not part of the Watergate cover-up.

July 30: Former presidential chief of staff H. R. Haldeman tells the Senate Watergate Committee that he has not participated in the Watergate cover-up, nor has President Nixon.

August 13: Five Black Muslims from St. Croix in the Virgin Islands are convicted for the murders in 1972 of eight persons at a swank golf club in Christiansted. They receive life sentences.

August 14: Elmer Wayne Henley, 17, and David Owen Brooks, 18, are indicted by a grand jury in Houston, Texas, after they confess to the sex-and-torture slayings of 27 young men during a period of three years.

September 4: A grand jury in Los Angeles indicts former presidential adviser John Ehrlichman, former Nixon administration officials Egil Krogh, Jr., and David R. Young, along with convicted Watergate conspirator G. Gordon Liddy, on charges arising from the 1971 break-in at the office of Dr. Daniel Ellsberg's psychiatrist. Another indictment charges Ehrlichman with perjury before the grand jury.

September 6: Patrick J. Buchanan, a special consultant to President Nixon, testifies before the Senate Watergate Committee that he had promoted a plan to derail Edmund Muskie's bid for the Democratic presidential nomination in 1972 and advance the candidacy of George McGovern. Buchanan denies, however, that his efforts involved anything "unethical" or "improper."

September 11: A military junta that includes General Augusto Pinochet overthrows President Salvador Allende in Chile, thus ending 46 years of civilian rule. Allende had been elected in 1970, making his administration the first freely elected national marxist government in the history of the world. The violent overthrow included the use of bombers and heavy artillery in Santiago and resulted in the death of Allende. The episode will later become an issue in American politics when evidence surfaces that the United States encouraged Allende's overthrow.

September 20: Billie Jean King and Bobby Riggs engage in a tennis match at the Astrodome in Houston, Texas, an event promoted as a "Battle of the Sexes." Riggs wants to prove male superiority in the sport. King, age 29 and the winner of five Wimbledon singles titles, soundly defeats the 55-year-old Riggs before more than 30,000 spectators, a record crowd for a tennis match.

September 20: Singer and songwriter Jim Croce dies in a plane crash in Louisiana. His hit single "Bad, Bad Leroy Brown" had reached number one just two months earlier.

September 21: The Senate confirms President Nixon's appointment of Henry Kissinger as secretary of state. Kissinger had been serving as the president's National Security Advisor.

September 24: E. Howard Hunt tells the Senate Watergate Committee that special White House counsel Charles Colson had ordered a diplomatic cable faked to make it look as if President John Kennedy had taken part in plans to assassinate South Vietnamese President Diem in 1963.

September 25: The *Sklyab* astronauts—Alan L. Bean, Jack R. Lousma, and Owen Garriot—return to Earth after 59 days on the space station.

October 6: The Arab-Israeli, or Yom Kippur, War erupts with Egyptian forces crossing the Suez Canal and Syrian forces battling in the Golan Heights. By October 11, the Egyptians advance into the Sinai Peninsula against Israeli troops who had been occupying it.

October 9: Vice President Spiro Agnew informs President Nixon that he will resign his office in light of a criminal investigation against him. Agnew has arranged a deal with federal prosecutors whereby he will resign and plead nolo contendere for failing to pay income taxes in return for three years' probation, payment of a $10,000 fine, and immunity from further prosecution.

October 11: General Services Administrator Arthur Sampson testifies before the House Government Activities Subcommittee that "mistakes" had been made in the spending of millions of dollars on projects at President Nixon's private homes in San Clemente, California, and Key Biscayne, Florida. A few days later, Chairman Jack Brooks (Dem., Tex.) says that money which was earmarked for security at the Nixon homes may well have been spent on luxury items.

October 12: A counterattack by Israeli troops brings them to within 18 miles of Damascus, the Syrian capital. By October 24, the Israelis surround the city of Suez on the Sinai Peninsula and, with it, the Egyptian 3rd Army.

October 12: President Nixon announces that, under the terms of the Twenty-fifth Amendment, he is nominating House minority leader Gerald Ford (Rep., Mich.) to become vice president.

October 19: John Dean pleads guilty to one count of conspiracy to obstruct justice in plotting to cover up the Watergate break-in. The plea is part of a bargain with Watergate special prosecutor Archibald Cox, according to which Dean agrees to testify for the prosecution in future Watergate proceedings in exchange for immunity.

October 19: To protest American policy in the Middle East, Arab oil-producing nations, who believe Washington too pro-Israel, ban oil shipments to the United States. The embargo lasts until March 18, 1974.

October 20: In a stunning development, Attorney General Elliott Richardson resigns and his deputy William D. Ruckelshaus, along with Watergate special prosecutor Archibald Cox, are fired by President Nixon after Cox rejects a compromise offered by Nixon in reaction to a court order to turn over the Watergate tapes. Nixon had proposed to turn over transcripts of the tapes rather than the tapes themselves. Richardson resigns rather than obey Nixon's order to fire Cox. Nixon then fires Ruckelshaus when the deputy also refuses to fire Cox. Finally, Solicitor General Robert H. Bork, who has become acting attorney general, agrees to fire Cox. Nixon's action—dubbed the "Saturday Night Massacre"—will result in massive public protests when letters and telegrams flood the White House and Congress. Many people and several prominent organizations, including the AFL-CIO, will call for Nixon to resign or be impeached.

Joblessness hit black Americans hard in the 1970s, as it did here in north Philadelphia, where a worker for the Urban Coalition talks to unemployed men. *(National Archives and Records Administration)*

October 22: The United States and the Soviet Union push a resolution through the UN Security Council calling for a cease-fire in the Arab-Israeli War.

October 23: Reacting to the widespread protests following the Saturday Night Massacre, President Nixon agrees to abide by a court order to turn over the Watergate tapes.

October 24: The House Judiciary Committee votes to begin proceedings to determine whether President Nixon should be impeached.

October 25: U.S. forces are placed on precautionary alert. The Americans claim that they have information showing that the Soviet Union might send troops into the Arab-Israeli War to defeat Israel. The approval on October 27 of a 7,000-member peacekeeping force to be sent to the Middle East by the United Nations ends the crisis.

October 30: The White House informs U.S. District Court Judge John Sirica that two of the Watergate tapes requested to be turned over have been lost. The announcement greatly damages President Nixon's public support and causes even some Republican leaders to call for Nixon's resignation.

November 1: The White House announces the appointment of Leon Jaworski as the new Watergate special prosecutor. Jaworski, a conservative Texas Democrat, is assured by President Nixon that there will be no restrictions placed on the investigation.

November 5: U.S. District Court Judge Gerhard A. Gesell sentences Donald H. Segretti to six months in prison for dirty tricks that he used in trying to disrupt the 1972 Democratic presidential primary in Florida.

November 7: The House and the Senate override President Nixon's veto of the war powers bill. The legislation restricts the president's ability to send armed forces to fight overseas without congressional approval.

November 7: President Nixon states in a national TV address that in the wake of an Arab oil embargo imposed on the United States, he will ask Congress for an emergency energy act. Even this crisis, however, is interrupted by the Watergate scandal when, at the end of his address, Nixon responds to those who are saying he should resign. He says: "I have no intention of walking away from the job I was elected to do."

November 9: President Nixon begins a publicity offensive to fight his eroding standings in the public-opinion polls. His efforts include meetings with leading congressional Republicans and six southern Democratic senators, along with an appearance at a convention of the National Association of Realtors.

November 9: U.S. District Court Judge John Sirica sentences six of the defendants in the Watergate break-in. The sentences handed down are: two-and-one-half to eight years to E. Howard Hunt for planning the break-in and for carrying out the burglary; one to five years to James McCord, Jr.; one to four years each for Frank A. Sturgis, Eugenio R. Martinez, and Virgilio R. Gonzalez; and 18 months to six years for Bernard L. Barker. Another of the defendants, G. Gordon Liddy, had already been sentenced to 20 years for his refusal to cooperate with the prosecution.

November 13: The Gulf Oil Corporation and the Ashland Oil Company, along with two top executives from each of the firms, plead guilty to making illegal contributions of $100,000 each to the Nixon reelection campaign. The moneys had been laundered through foreign countries to hide their origin.

November 16: President Nixon signs into law a bill to build an oil pipeline from Alaska's North Slope to the port of Valdez. He says that the pipeline will help to make the United States energy self-sufficient by 1980.

November 17: In an astonishing statement for a president, Richard Nixon tells a group of newspaper editors meeting at Disneyworld in Florida that "I'm not a crook."

November 21: In another development that greatly damages President Nixon's public standing, the White House reveals that there exists an 18½-minute gap in the tape recording of a conversation between Nixon and H. R. Haldeman from June 20, 1972, just three days after the Watergate break-in. The tape is one of those subpoenaed, and the White House is unable to explain what caused the erasure. A few days later, Nixon's personal secretary, Rose Mary Woods, testifies that she may have caused the gap when she inadvertently placed her foot on an erasure pedal while transcribing the tape and talking on the phone. Most observers consider her explanation implausible, and later tests show that the gap resulted from several intentional erasures—from back and forth motions on a tape recorder.

November 30: Egil Krogh, Jr., the former head of the White House special investigations unit called the plumbers, pleads guilty to civil rights violations connected to the 1971 break-in at the office of Dr. Daniel Ellsberg's psychiatrist.

December 4: President Nixon announces that Deputy Treasury Secretary William E. Simon will replace John A. Love as "energy czar."

December 4: Thousands of independent truckers begin a three-day protest against high fuel costs and lower highway speed limits. They block major highways in Pennsylvania, Ohio, West Virginia, Connecticut, and Delaware.

December 6: Gerald R. Ford is sworn in as the nation's 40th vice president. Both the House and the Senate had previously confirmed Ford's appointment.

December 8: President Nixon makes public his finances, including the tax returns from his first four years in the White House. He says he is doing so to clear up accusations about wrongdoings on his part. But the returns raise even more controversy when they show that the president had tripled his net worth while receiving as income only his presidential salary and funds from an expense account.

December 16: Buffalo Bills running back O. J. Simpson becomes the first professional football player to rush for more than 2,000 yards in one season. He breaks the mark by gaining more than 200 yards in the last game of the season against the New York Jets.

December 25: Two of the most popular movies in Hollywood history are released on this day and the following day: *The Sting*, starring Robert Redford and Paul Newman, and *The Exorcist*, based on a novel by William Peter Blatty.

January–August 1974

January 4: President Nixon refuses to comply with subpoenas from the Senate Watergate Committee for additional tape recordings and documents.

January 18: The mediation of Secretary of State Henry Kissinger results in Egypt and Israel signing an agreement to separate their armies along the Suez Canal to prevent further fighting.

January 23: Exxon reveals that it made huge profits during the Arab oil embargo, with earnings 59 percent higher than in the same period in 1972. The following day, Mobil announces a 68 percent increase in profits.

January 23: President Nixon proposes to Congress higher taxes on oil companies and a two-year delay in the imposition of stricter emissions standards for automobiles.

February 4: The Symbionese Liberation Army, or SLA, kidnaps Patricia Hearst, the granddaughter of publishing magnate William Randolph Hearst, from her apartment in Berkeley, California. The group demands that Patricia's father, Randolph A. Hearst, the editor and president of the *San Francisco Examiner,* distribute food to the poor.

February 6: The House of Representatives votes 410-4 to grant broad power to the Judiciary Committee to pursue its inquiry into the impeachment of President Nixon.

February 8: The *Skylab* astronauts Gerald L. Carr, William R. Pogue, and Edward G. Gibson return safely to Earth, splashing down in the Pacific Ocean. They complete the longest space flight to date, 84 days.

March 1: A grand jury indicts seven former White House and presidential campaign aides for conspiracy to cover up the Watergate scandal. The indictment includes 24 separate counts, among them making false statements and making payments to the defendants in the break-in. The grand jury decides that Richard Nixon was involved in the illegalities, and so they name him an unindicted coconspirator (concluding that they did not have the power to indict a sitting president).

March 29: One present member and seven former members of the Ohio National Guard are indicted by a federal grand jury for violating the civil rights of four Kent State University students who were killed and nine who were wounded during antiwar protests in May 1970.

April 3: President Nixon agrees to pay $432,000 in back taxes plus interest for the years 1969 through 1972.

April 3: Patricia Hearst announces in a tape-recorded message that she is joining the SLA to fight for the freedom of oppressed people. Later in the month, she is identified as one of the participants in a San Francisco bank robbery.

April 8: Hank Aaron breaks Babe Ruth's major league baseball record of 714 career home runs when he hits his 715th home-run at Atlanta–Fulton County Stadium.

April 29: President Nixon states that he is turning over to the House Judiciary Committee 1,200 pages of edited transcripts of White House conversations relating to Watergate. He claims, however, that he cannot turn over the actual tapes because they contain matters vital to the nation's security and because they are privileged conversations between himself and his aides.

May 2: The Maryland Court of Appeals orders that former Vice President Spiro Agnew be disbarred because of his plea the previous August of nolo contendere to a tax evasion charge.

May 9: The House Judiciary Committee begins its hearings to consider the impeachment of President Nixon.

May 17: Six members of the SLA are killed in a gun battle with police and a fire that breaks out at the group's hideout in Los Angeles.

June 3: Former presidential counsel Charles Colson pleads guilty to obstruction of justice and trying to influence the trial of Dr. Daniel Ellsberg. In return for the one-count indictment, he agrees to cooperate with Watergate Special Prosecutor Leon Jaworski.

July 12: Former Nixon aide John Ehrlichman and three members of the plumbers,—G. Gordon Liddy, Bernard L. Barker, and Eugenio R. Martinez—are found guilty of conspiring to violate the civil rights of Dr. Lewis Fielding, formerly the psychiatrist to Dr. Daniel Ellsberg. On July 31, the judge sentences Ehrlichman to 20 months to five years in jail.

July 24: The U.S. Supreme Court, in an 8–0 decision, rules that President Nixon has to relinquish the tapes and documents sought by Watergate Special Prosecutor Leon Jaworski. The court recognizes the existence of executive privilege but calls the right inapplicable in this instance because the materials are related to a criminal inquiry.

July 24: Beginning on this day and continuing through July 30, the House Judiciary Committee recommends to the full House three articles of impeachment against President Nixon. The articles involve obstruction of justice, abuse of power, and defiance of committee subpoenas.

August 2: Former presidential counsel John Dean is sentenced by Judge John Sirica to one to three years in prison for his role in the Watergate coverup. Dean had pleaded guilty in a special arrangement with the Watergate prosecutor, whereby he cooperated with the

A crowd stands outside the White House gate on the day of Richard Nixon's resignation. *(National Archives and Records Administration)*

prosecutor and was granted immunity from additional charges.

August 5: President Nixon releases three transcripts of a June 23, 1972, conversation which was taped in the White House and which shows that he plotted to block the FBI investigation of Watergate based on claims that the inquiry would violate national security. Furthermore, he admits that he had made "a serous act of omission" in keeping this information private. The "smoking-gun" tape shows that Nixon obstructed justice, and this causes him to lose nearly all of his support in Congress.

August 8: President Richard Nixon informs the public on national television that he will resign the presidency, effective noon the following day.

August 9: President Richard Nixon resigns as the 37th president of the United States. He is the first president ever to quit. At 12:03 P.M., Chief Justice Warren E. Burger administers the oath of office to Gerald R. Ford, making him the 38th president.

EYEWITNESS TESTIMONY

Roe v. Wade

The Constitution does not explicitly mention any right of privacy. In a line of decisions, however, going back perhaps as far as *Union Pacific R. Co. v. Botsford,* 141 U.S. 250, 251 (1891), the Court has recognized that a right of personal privacy, or a guarantee of certain areas or zones of privacy, does exist under the Constitution. In varying contexts, the Court or individual Justices have, indeed, found at least the roots of that right in the First Amendment; in the Fourth and Fifth Amendments; in the penumbras of the Bill of Rights; in the Ninth Amendment, *id.,* at 486 (Goldberg, J., concurring); or in the concept of liberty guaranteed by the first section of the Fourteenth Amendment. These decisions make it clear that only personal rights that can be deemed "fundamental" or "implicit in the concept of ordered liberty" are included in this guarantee of personal privacy. They also make it clear that the right has some extension to activities relating to marriage; procreation; contraception; family relationships; and child rearing and education.

This right of privacy, whether it be founded in the Fourteenth Amendment's concept of personal liberty and restrictions upon state action, as we feel it is, or, as the District Court determined, in the Ninth Amendment's reservation of rights to the people, is broad enough to encompass a woman's decision whether or not to terminate her pregnancy. The detriment that the State would impose upon the pregnant woman by denying this choice altogether is apparent. Specific and direct harm medically diagnosable even in early pregnancy may be involved. Maternity, or additional offspring, may force upon the woman a distressful life and future. Psychological harm may be imminent. Mental and physical health may be taxed by child care. There is also the distress, for all concerned, associated with the unwanted child, and there is the problem of bringing a child into a family already unable, psychologically and otherwise, to care for it. In other cases, as in this one, the additional difficulties and continuing stigma of unwed motherhood may be involved. All these are factors the woman and her responsible physician necessarily will consider in consultation.

On the basis of elements such as these, appellant and some *amici* argue that the woman's right is absolute

and that she is entitled to terminate her pregnancy at whatever time, in whatever way, and for whatever reason she alone chooses. With this we do not agree. At some point in pregnancy, these respective interests become sufficiently compelling to sustain regulation of the factors that govern the abortion decision. The privacy right involved, therefore, cannot be said to be absolute....

We, therefore, conclude that the right of personal privacy includes the abortion decision, but that this right is not unqualified and must be considered against important state interests in regulation....

The decision leaves the State free to place increasing restrictions on abortion as the period of pregnancy lengthens, so long as those restrictions are tailored to the recognized state interests. The decision vindicates the right of the physician to administer medical treatment according to his professional judgment up to the points where important state interests provide compelling justifications for intervention. Up to those points, the abortion decision in all its aspects is inherently, and primarily, a medical decision, and basic responsibility for it must rest with the physician. If an individual practitioner abuses the privilege of exercising proper medical judgment, the usual remedies, judicial and intra-professional, are available.

Justice Harry A. Blackmun's majority opinion for the U.S. Supreme Court in the case of Roe v. Wade, *issued January 22, 1973, available online at http:// members.aol.com/abtrbng/roefl-o2.htm, downloaded May 21, 2004.*

The speak-out [was] an unbelievably successful, and it turned out to be an incredible organizing tool. It brought abortion out of the closet where it had been hidden in secrecy and shame. It informed the public that most women were having abortions anyway. People spoke from their hearts, it was heart-rending.

Activist Irene Peslikis recalling in 1987 the role of "speak-outs" in challenging abortion laws in the early 1970s, in Ruth Rosen, The World Split Open *(2000), p. 158.*

It came like a thunderbolt—a decision from the United States Supreme Court so sweeping that it seemed to assure the triumph of the abortion movement.... The court went far beyond any of the eighteen new state laws the movement had won since

1967. . . . It climaxed a social revolution whose magnitude and speed were probably unequaled in United States history.

Lawrence Lader, an abortion reform activist, writing in 1973 about Roe v. Wade, *in Eva Rubin,* Abortion, Politics, and the Courts *(1982), p. 86.*

As the people walked out of the church afterward, the people working for Right to Life were stationed at their respective tables taking people by the arm and leading them over to the petitions—even small children (seven and nine years of age) were permitted to sign the petition.

An unidentified eyewitness reporting in May 1973 on a Catholic Mass held in Michigan City, Indiana, in Marian Faux, Roe v. Wade *(2001), p. 318.*

Many of the "pro-life" people see me as a demon. To them I'm a blasphemer and a baby-killer whose soul they have to "save." Some anti-abortion campaigners have strange ideas about how to do this. Over the years I have had hate mail sent to me, eggs thrown at my house, shotguns fired at my front door and windows, and baby clothes scattered on my front lawn. This frightens me, and on days when I am not feeling especially charitable, it makes me angry.

I take comfort and pride that many women (and men!) have supported and protected me from the pro-lifers.

Norma McCorvey, "Jane Roe" in the Roe v. Wade *case, writing in 1994 about the reaction she has received over the years from antiabortion activists, in Norma McCorvey,* I Am Roe *(1994), p. 2.*

The End to the Vietnam War

Now then, it is obvious that a war that has lasted for 10 years will have many elements that cannot be completely satisfactory to all the parties concerned. And in the two periods where the North Vietnamese were working with dedication and seriousness on a conclusion, the period in October and the period after we resumed talks on January 8, it was always clear that a lasting peace could come about only if neither side sought to achieve everything that it had wanted; indeed, that stability depended on the relative satisfaction and therefore on the relative dissatisfaction of all of the parties concerned. And therefore, it is also clear that

whether this agreement brings a lasting peace or not depends not only on its provisions but also on the spirit in which it is implemented. It will be our challenge in the future to move the controversies that could not be stilled by any one document from the level of military conflict to the level of positive human aspirations, and to absorb the enormous talents and dedication of the people of Indochina in tasks of construction rather than in tasks of destruction.

We will make a major effort to move to create a framework where we hope in a short time the animosities and the hatred and the suffering of this period will be seen as aspects of the past, and where the debates concern differences of opinion as to how to achieve positive goals. Of course, the hatreds will not rapidly disappear, and, of course, people who have fought for 25 years will not easily give up their objectives, but also people who have suffered for 25 years may at last come to know that they can achieve their real satisfaction by other and less brutal means.

The President said yesterday that we have to remain vigilant, and so we shall, but we shall also dedicate ourselves to positive efforts. And as for us at home, it should be clear by now that no one in this war has had a monopoly of moral insight. And now that at last we have achieved an agreement in which the United States did not prescribe the political future to its allies, an agreement which should preserve the dignity and the self-respect of all of the parties, together with healing

Delegates sign the Vietnam peace agreement in Paris. *(National Archives and Records Administration)*

the wounds in Indochina we can begin to heal the wounds in America.

The conclusion to a news conference statement by Dr. Henry A. Kissinger, Assistant to the President for National Security Affairs, January 24, 1973, regarding the signing of the Paris Agreement to end the Vietnam War, available online at http://www.ibiblio.org/pub/ academic/history/marshall/military/vietnam/ policies.and.politics/paris_peace_1973.txt, downloaded May 24, 2004.

Wounded Knee

Hundreds of Indians representing more than 75 different tribes supported the just demands of the Oglala Sioux people on Pine Ridge reservation at the risk of their lives and freedom. The Sioux, like every Indian tribe in the country, have ceded land to the U.S. Government; and in payment for that land the U.S. Government is supposed to provide us with certain goods and service. They don't do it. Instead of providing services, they provide tyranny.

At Wounded Knee, we finally said, "The hell with that. You are going to honor your treaty with us from now on and we are going to force you to do that because if you don't you will have to kill us." That was the point of Wounded Knee.

We have a treaty that is 105 years old and for 105 years it has been continually violated. It is time for the United States to live up to its pledges to the Indians....

We are the landlords of this country and at Wounded Knee we showed up to collect.... If the country is going to live up to its constitution, then in fact it must live up to its treaty commitments....

From a statement issued by the American Indian Movement in November 1973 concerning the Wounded Knee protest of the preceding February, available online at http://www.aics.org/WK/wk011.html, downloaded May 24, 2004.

President Nixon's Response to Watergate

RECENT news accounts growing out of testimony in the Watergate investigation have given grossly misleading impressions of many of the facts, as they relate both to my own role and to certain unrelated activities involving national security.

Already, on the basis of second- and third-hand hearsay testimony by persons either convicted or themselves under investigation in the case, I have found myself accused of involvement in activities I never heard of until I read about them in news accounts....

I will not abandon my responsibilities. I will continue to do the job I was elected to do....

With regard to the specific allegation that have been made, I can state categorically:

1. I had no prior knowledge of the Watergate operation.
2. I took no part in, nor was I aware of, any subsequent efforts that may have been made to cover up Watergate.
3. At no time did I authorize any offer of executive clemency for the Watergate defendants, nor did I know of any such offer.
4. I did not know, until the time of my own investigation, of any effort to provide the Watergate defendants with funds.
5. At no time did I attempt, or did I authorize others to attempt, to implicate the CIA in the Watergate matter.
6. It was not until the time of my own investigation that I learned of the break-in at the office of Mr. Ellsberg's psychiatrist, and I specifically authorized the furnishing of this information to Judge Byrne.
7. I neither authorized nor encouraged subordinates to engage in illegal or improper campaign tactics....

The unit operated under extremely tight security rules. Its existence and functions were known only to a very few persons at the White House. These included Messrs. Haldeman, Ehrlichman, and Dean....

WATERGATE

The burglary and bugging of the Democratic National Committee headquarters came as a complete surprise to me. I had no inkling that any such illegal activities had been planned by persons associated with my campaign; if I had known, I would not have permitted it. My immediate reaction was that those guilty should be brought to justice, and, with the five burglars themselves already in custody, I assumed that they would be.

Within a few days, however, I was advised that there was a possibility of CIA involvement in some way.

It did seem to me possible that, because of the involvement of former CIA personnel, and because of some of their apparent associations, the investigation could lead to the uncovering of covert CIA operations totally unrelated to the Watergate break-in.

In addition, by this time, the name of Mr. Hunt had surfaced in connection with Watergate, and I was alerted to the fact that he had previously been a member of the Special Investigations Unit in the White House. Therefore, I was also concerned that the Watergate investigation might well lead to an inquiry into the Special Investigations Unit itself.

In this area, I felt it was important to avoid disclosure of the details of the national security matters with which the group was concerned. I knew that once the existence of the group became known, it would lead inexorably to a discussion of these matters, some of which remain, even today, highly sensitive. . . .

It now seems that later, through whatever complex of individual motives and possible misunderstandings, there were apparently wide-ranging efforts to limit the investigation or to conceal the possible involvement of members of the Administration and the campaign committee.

I was not aware of any such efforts at the time. Neither, until after I began my own investigation, was I aware of any fundraising for defendants convicted of the break-in at Democratic headquarters, much less authorize any such fundraising. Nor did I authorize any offer of executive clemency for any of the defendants.

In the weeks and months that followed Watergate, I asked for, and received, repeated assurances that Mr. Dean's own investigation (which included reviewing files and sitting in on FBI interviews with White House personnel) had cleared everyone then employed by the White House of involvement. . . .

—It now appears that there were persons who may have gone beyond my directives, and sought to expand on my efforts to protect the national security operations in order to cover up any involvement they or certain others might have had in Watergate. The extent to which this is true, and who may have participated and to what degree, are questions that it would not be proper to address here. The proper forum for settling these matters is in the courts.

—To the extent that I have been able to determine what probably happened in the tangled course of this affair, on the basis of my own recollections and of the conflicting accounts and evidence that I have seen, it would appear that one factor at work was that at critical points various people, each with his own perspective and his own responsibilities, saw the same situation with different eyes and heard the same words with different ears.

What might have seemed insignificant to one seemed significant to another; what one saw in terms of public responsibility, another saw in terms of political opportunity; and mixed through it all, I am sure, was a concern on the part of many that the Watergate scandal should not be allowed to get in the way of what the Administration sought to achieve.

The truth about Watergate should be brought out—in an orderly way, recognizing that the safeguards of judicial procedure are designed to find the truth, not to hide the truth. . . .

Statements about the Watergate investigations by President Richard Nixon on May 22, 1973, in Public Papers of the Presidents of the United States: Richard Nixon, 1973 *(1975), pp. 547–554.*

The Trial of Dr. Daniel Ellsberg

I was sure that the Nixon administration would put me on trial and would take every effort to destroy my reputation. I did not foresee that they would actually, that Nixon's White House would actually bring agents up from Miami to Washington to "incapacitate me totally," that is, to assault, or perhaps to kill me, which did occur on May 3, 1972. I didn't think they did that. They went so far as to order physical assaults on Americans, although I knew that my government had done such things to Vietnamese in Saigon when those politicians had done things to displease them. . . .

Charles Colson, who was the counsel to the president, called Jeb Magruder, who was running the Committee to Re-elect the President (CREEP), to arrange for counter-demonstrators to disrupt physically a demonstration, a rally, at which I would be speaking on May 3. Magruder turned to Gordon Liddy and Howard Hunt, who arranged for 12 Cuban Americans, all of whom had worked for the CIA or were still on the CIA payroll, to be flown up from Miami for this purpose. They have testified that they were shown my photo, told that this was their target and that I was to be beaten up.

Daniel Ellsberg reflecting in 1999 to a reporter for CNN on developments preceding his trial for releasing the Pentagon Papers, *available online at http://www.cnn. com/SPECIALS/cold.war/guides/debate/chats/ ellsberg, downloaded May 5, 2005.*

In the courtroom, pandemonium. Cheers, hugging, crying, wild laughter. It started with a roar as soon as the judge finished his statement—in a place in which any hint of feeling from the spectators had been silenced peremptorily from the bench of the past four months—and he made little effort to stop it. He asked that the jurors be allowed to leave through the back. Then he turned around in his black robes and followed them out. The press ran to the phones; the prosecution team packed up wordlessly and left the courtroom to us. It seemed to be spinning, tilting. [My wife] Patricia and I came to each other and kissed.

When we all poured out into the sunlight on the steps of the federal courthouse, to the sea of TV cameras and flashbulbs, someone held up the headline on the morning's paper: MITCHCHELL INDICTED.

John Mitchell, the man who had indicted me. The first of my attorney generals to face prison, soon to be joined by Kleindienst, who had presided over my prosecution until his resignation nearly two weeks earlier. Presently Haldeman and Ehrlichman and Colson were indicted too. And the White House aides assigned to neutralize me, and the CIA contract agents and other Cuban-Americans ordered to incapacitate me.

Daniel Ellsberg recounting in 2002 the day the judge at his trial dismissed all charges against him, in Daniel Ellsberg, Secrets (2002), p. 456.

The Nixon-Brezhnev Summit of 1973

I. The General State Of U.S.–Soviet Relations
Both Sides expressed their mutual satisfaction with the fact that the American–Soviet summit meeting in Moscow in May 1972 and the joint decisions taken there have resulted in a substantial advance in the strengthening of peaceful relations between the USA and the USSR and have created the basis for the further development of broad area mutually beneficial cooperation in various fields of mutual interest to the peoples of both countries and in the interests of all mankind. They noted their satisfaction with the mutual effort to implement strictly and fully the treaties and agreements concluded between the USA and the USSR, and to expand areas of cooperation.

They agreed that the process of reshaping relations between the USA and the USSR on the basis of peaceful coexistence and equal security as set forth in the Basic Principles of Relations Between the USA and the USSR signed in Moscow on May 29, 1972 is progress-

ing in an encouraging manner. They emphasized the great importance that each Side attaches to these Basic Principles. They reaffirmed their commitment to the continued scrupulous implementation and to the enhancement of the effectiveness of each of the provisions of that document.

Both Sides noted with satisfaction that the outcome of the US-Soviet meeting in Moscow in May 1972 was welcomed by other States and by world opinion as an important contribution to strengthening peace and international security, to curbing the arms race and to developing businesslike cooperation among States with different social systems.

Both Sides viewed the return visit to the USA of the General Secretary of the Central Committee of the CPSU, L. I. Brezhnev, and the talks held during the visit as an expression of their mutual determination to continue the course toward a major improvement in US-Soviet relations.

Both Sides are convinced that the discussions they have just held represent a further milestone in the constructive development of their relations. Convinced that such a development of American-Soviet relations serves the interests of both of their peoples and all of mankind, it was decided to take further major steps to give these relations maximum stability and to turn the development of friendship and cooperation between their peoples into a permanent factor for worldwide peace.

II. The Prevention Of Nuclear War And The Limitation Of Strategic Armaments
Issues related to the maintenance and strengthening of international peace were a central point of the talks between President Nixon and General Secretary Brezhnev. Conscious of the exceptional importance for all mankind of taking effective measures to that end, they discussed ways in which both Sides could work toward removing the danger of war, and especially nuclear war, between the USA and the USSR and between either party and other countries. Consequently, in accordance with the Charter of the United Nations and the Basic Principles of Relations of May 29, 1972, it was decided to conclude an Agreement Between the USA and the USSR on the Prevention of Nuclear War. That Agreement was signed by the President and the General Secretary on June 22, 1973. The text has been published separately.

The President and the General Secretary, in appraising this Agreement, believe that it constitutes a histor-

Soviet Leader Leonid Brezhnev and President Richard Nixon are seen here conferring during Brezhnev's visit to the United States in 1973. *(National Archives and Records Administration)*

ical landmark in Soviet-American relations and substantially strengthens the foundations of international security as a whole. The United States and the Soviet Union state their readiness to consider additional ways of strengthening peace and removing forever the danger of war, and particularly nuclear war.

In the course of the meetings, intensive discussions were held on questions of strategic arms limitation. In this connection both Sides emphasized the fundamental importance of the Treaty on the Limitation of Anti-Ballistic Missile Systems and the Interim Agreement on Certain Measures with Respect to the Limitation of Strategic Offensive Arms signed between the USA and the USSR in May 1972 which, for the first time in history, place actual limits on the most modern and most formidable types of armaments.

Having exchanged views on the progress in the implementation of these agreements, both Sides reaffirmed their intention to carry them out and their readiness to move ahead jointly toward an agreement on the future limitation of strategic arms.

Both Sides noted that progress has been made in the negotiations that resumed in November 1972, and that the prospects for reaching a permanent agreement on more complete measures limiting strategic offensive armaments are favorable.

Both Sides agreed that progress made in the limitation of strategic armaments is an exceedingly important contribution to the strengthening of US-Soviet relations and to world peace.

On the basis of their discussions, the President and the General Secretary signed on June 21, 1973, Basic Principles of Negotiations on the Further Limitation of Strategic Offensive Arms. The text has been published separately.

The USA and the USSR attach great importance to joining with all States in the cause of strengthening peace, reducing the burden of armaments, and reaching agreements on arms limitations and disarmament measures.

Considering the important role which an effective international agreement with respect to chemical weapons would play, the two Sides agreed to continue their efforts to conclude such an agreement in cooperation with other countries.

The two Sides agree to make every effort to facilitate the work of the Committee on Disarmament which has been meeting in Geneva. They will actively participate in negotiations aimed at working out new measures to curb and end the arms race. They reaffirm that the ultimate objective is general and complete disarmament, including nuclear disarmament, under strict international control. A world disarmament conference could play a role in this process at an appropriate time.

From the joint U.S.-USSR communiqué signed at San Clemente, California, on June 22, 1973, by Richard Nixon and Leonid Brezhnev, available online at http://www.washingtonpost.com/wp-srv/ inatl/longterm/summit/archive/com1973-1.htm, downloaded May 24, 2004.

The Saturday Night Massacre

At many points throughout the nomination hearings, I reaffirmed my intention to assure the independence of the special prosecutor. While I fully respect the reasons that have led you to conclude that the special prosecutor must be discharged, I trust that you understand that I could not in the light of these firm and repeated commitments carry out your direction that this be done.

Attorney General Elliot Richardson explaining in a letter to President Richard Nixon, dated October 20, 1973, why he could not carry out Nixon's order to fire special prosecutor Archibald Cox, in an article from the Washington Post, *dated October 21, 1973, and available online at http://www.washingtonpost.com/ wp-srv/national/longterm/watergate articles/ 102173-2.htm, downloaded May 1, 2005.*

All I will say is that I carried out the president's directive.

Acting Attorney General Robert Bork commenting on his decision to carry out President Richard Nixon's order to fire special prosecutor Archibald Cox, as reported in the Washington Post, *October 21, 1973, available online at http://www.washingtonpost.com/wp-srv/ national/longterm/watergate articles/ 102173-2.htm, downloaded May 1, 2005.*

The more I thought about it, the clearer it seemed to me that public confidence in the investigation would depend on its being independent not only in fact but in appearance.

Elliot Richardson commenting in 1996 on his view of the Watergate investigation and his actions during the Saturday Night Massacre of 1973, quoted by CNN and available online at http://archives.cnn.com/1999/ ALLPOLITICS/stories/12/31/richardson, downloaded May 2, 2005.

Tapes in the White House

There was no doubt in my mind they were installed to record things for posterity, for the Nixon library. The President was very conscious of that kind of thing. We had quite an elaborate set-up at the White House for the collection and preservation of documents, and of things which transpired in the way of business of state.

White House aide Alexander P. Butterfield describing to the Ervin committee on July 16, 1973, why he believed that President Nixon installed recording machines in the White House and elsewhere, reported in the Washington Post, *available online at http://www.washingtonpost.com/wpsrv/ onpolitics/watergate/chronology.htm, downloaded May 5, 2005.*

John Dean's Testimony before the Senate Watergate Committee

Now the grave charges against the President had passed a point of no return. Carried with chilling reality into millions of American homes and spread massively on the official record of a solemn Senate inquiry, the torrential testimony of John W. Dean III fell short of proof in a court of law. But the impact was devastating. As

John Dean, counsel to the president, eventually decided to reveal the Watergate cover-up. *(National Archives and Records Administration)*

President, Richard Nixon was grievously, if not mortally wounded. . . .

As early as Sept. 15 [1972], Dean charged, the President clearly indicated his awareness that a cover-up was under way. Then and later, Dean claimed, the President talked directly to him about Executive clemency and hush money for the Wiretappers. . . . If Dean's claims are true—and his supporting details as well as some of his circumstantial documents were impressive—that would make Nixon's May 22 denials outright lies or at least render the presidential statements once again "inoperative."

Time *magazine reporting in its July 9, 1973, issue on the testimony of former White House counsel John Dean to the Senate Watergate Committee, from* Time, SoftKey Multimedia, 1995.*

The Overthrow of Salvador Allende

The Armed Forces decision to forcefully remove the Allende Government from power was made with extreme reluctance and only after the deepest soul-searching by all concerned. Even to we sideline observers, it was obvious the Chilean military were extremely reluctant to destroy over 100 years of peaceful tradition in support of their country's constitution without exhausting every other avenue of solution. Unfortunately there were no other avenues of solution. Chile was on a dead end street. Their rate of inflation was the worst in the history of the world, terrorists and weapons were being illegally introduced into Chile by the CUBANS for USE AGAINST CHILEANS, food resources were near total exhaustion, a nationwide transportation strike had paralyzed the country . . . the Armed forces had been systematically infiltrated by saboteurs who carried not patriotism for Chile in their hearts, but rather fidelity to world Marxism, Chile's children had not been to school for over two months . . . and so goes the incredible litany of tragedy that was Chile under Allende's Marxism. What perhaps history will ask in retrospect is not "Why the overthrow of the Allende Government by the Armed Forces," but rather "Why the Armed Force waited so long?"

A situation report written on October 1, 1973, by U.S. Naval attaché Patrick Ryan portrays the overthrow of Chilean ruler Salvador Allende in glowing terms, available online at http://www.gwu.edu/~nsarchiv/NSAEBB/NSAEBB8/ch21-01.htm, downloaded May 24, 2004.

On October 24 the Junta announced that summary, on-the-spot executions would no longer be carried out and that persons caught in the act of resisting the government would henceforth be held for military courts. Since that date 17 executions following military trials have been announced. Publicly acknowledged executions, both summary and in compliance with court martial sentences, now total approximately 100, with an additional 40 prisoners shot while "trying to escape." An internal, confidential report

Chilean soldiers guard members of the administration of President Salvador Allende outside La Moneda presidential palace during the coup d'état in Santiago on September 11, 1973. *(Reuters/Landor)*

prepared for the Junta puts the number of executions for the period September 11–30 at 320. The latter figure is probably a more accurate indication of the extent of this practice. . . .

The purpose of the executions is in part to discourage by example those who seek to organize armed opposition to the junta. . . . Fear of civil war was an important factor in [the Chilean military's] decision to employ a heavy hand at the outset. Also present is a puritanical, crusading spirit—a determination to cleanse and rejuvenate Chile. (A number of those executed seem to have been petty criminals.)

From a State Department memo dated November 16, 1973, that shows how the executions in Chile following the overthrow of Salvador Allende were more extensive than publicly acknowledged, available online at http:// www.gwu.edu/~nsarchiv/NSAEBB/NSAEBB8/ ch10-01.htm, downloaded May 25, 2004.

Spiro Agnew Resigns

I can't imagine anyone making such a definite statement as he did and then have this come out. Well, it's just—it's hard to believe. . . .

It's very difficult to understand why he could stand up and say categorically that he was innocent. I feel a great deal of sympathy for him, and well—disgust isn't the right word, but it's more than disappointment.

Republican Party activist Dorothy Goodnight commenting on the resignation of Vice President Spiro Agnew, as reported in the New York Times, *October 12, 1973, p. 29.*

It turns out the law-and-order administration belongs in jail. I felt sorry for Agnew, . . . but what the heck. If I did what he did, I'd be up the creek. What makes him better than me?

The reaction of Michael Terry, a high school senior in Louisville, Kentucky, to the resignation of Vice President Spiro Agnew, as reported in the New York Times, *October 17, 1973, p. 32.*

I think this is a feeling that some people may have. It was the awareness that this would be the reaction or might be the reaction, of some of my fellow citizens that led me to try to make as clear as I could, in my statement to the court . . . that the interests of justice, as well as the interests of the public, were better served in this instance by a disposition that did not involve confinement of the former Vice President in a penal institution.

Attorney General Elliot Richardson responding in October 1973 to a reporter's question that many Americans might think that Spiro Agnew was getting off lightly because of his political standing, in Richard M. Cohen and Jules Witcover, A Heartbeat Away *(1974), pp. 360–361.*

I am human, and my conduct has been no better and no worse than that of other officeholders in these United States. But I am innocent of the charges of bribery and extortion which are detailed in the Exposition of Evidence filed against me by the prosecutors in the United States District Court of Maryland. I categorically denied these allegations in open court, and I continue to deny them to this day.

Spiro Agnew writing in 1980 about the accusations that forced him from the vice presidency, in Spiro Agnew, Go Quietly *(1980), p. 9.*

President Nixon's "I Am Not a Crook" Statement

Well, I should point out I wasn't a pauper when I became a President. I wasn't very rich as Presidents go. But you see, in the 8 years that I was out of office—first, just to put it all out and I will give you a paper on this, we will send it around to you, and these figures I would like you to have, not today, but I will have it in a few days—when I left office after 4 years as a Congressman, 2 years as a Senator, and 8 years at $45,000 a year as Vice President, and after stories have been written . . . to the effect that the [Vice] President had purchased a mansion in Wesley Heights and people wondered where the money came from, you know what my net worth was? Forty-seven thousand dollars total, after 14 years of Government service, and a 1958 Oldsmobile that needed an overhaul.

Now I have no complaints. In the next 8 years, I made a lot of money. I made $250,000 from a book and the serial rights which many of you were good enough to purchase, also. In the practice of law—and I am not claiming I was worth it, but apparently former Vice Presidents or Presidents are worth a great deal to law firms—and I did work pretty hard.

But also in that period, I earned between $100,000 and $250,000 every year. So that when, I, in 1968, decided to become a candidate for President, I decided to clear the decks and to put everything in real estate. I sold all my stock for $300,000—that is all I owned. I sold my apartment in New York for $300,000—I am using rough figures here. And I had $100,000 coming to me from the law firm.

And so, that is where the money came from. Let me just say this, and I want to say this to the television audience: I made my mistakes, but in all of my years of public life, I have never profited, never profited from public service—I have earned every cent. And in all of my years of public life, I have never obstructed justice. And I think, too, that I could say that in my years of public life, that I welcome this kind of examination, because people have got to know whether or not their President is a crook. Well, I am not a crook. I have earned everything I have got.

President Richard Nixon's response to a question about his personal finances at the Annual Convention of the Associated Press Managing Editors Association in Orlando, Florida, on November 17, 1973, in Public Papers of the Presidents of the United States: Richard Nixon, 1973 *(1975), p. 956.*

President Nixon's Decision to Release Transcripts of the Watergate Tapes

Every day absorbed by Watergate is a day lost from the work that must be done—by your President and by your Congress—work that must be done in dealing with the great problems that affect your prosperity, affect your security, that could affect your lives.

The materials I make public tomorrow will provide all the additional evidence needed to get Watergate behind us and to get it behind us now.

Never before in the history of the President have records that are so private been made so public.

In giving you these records—blemished and all—I am placing my trust in the American people.

I know in my own heart that through the long, painful, and difficult process revealed in these transcripts, I was trying in that period to discover what was right and to do what was right. . . .

As for myself, I intend to go forward, to the best of my ability, with the work that you elected me to do. I shall do so in a spirit perhaps best summed up a century ago by another President when he was being subjected to unmerciful attack. Abraham Lincoln said:

"I do the very best I know how—the very best I can; and I mean to keep doing so until the end. If the end brings me out all right what is said against me won't amount to anything. If the end brings me out wrong, ten angels swearing I was right would make no difference."

President Richard Nixon's announcement, April 29, 1974, that he will release transcripts of additional Watergate tapes, but not the tapes themselves, to the House Judiciary Committee, in Public Papers of the Presidents of the United States: Richard Nixon, January 1 to August 9, 1974 *(1975), p. 397.*

The Supreme Court and President Nixon's Claim of Executive Privilege

In this case the President challenges a subpoena served on him as a third party requiring the production of materials for use in a criminal prosecution; he does so on the claim that he has a privilege against disclosure of confidential communications. He does not place his claim of privilege on the ground they are military or diplomatic secrets. As to these areas of Art. II duties the courts have traditionally shown the utmost deference to Presidential responsibilities. . . .

No case of the Court, however, has extended this high degree of deference to a President's generalized interest in confidentiality. Nowhere in the Constitution, as we have noted earlier, is there any explicit reference to a privilege of confidentiality, yet to the extent this interest relates to the effective discharge of a President's powers, it is constitutionally based.

The right to the production of all evidence at a criminal trial similarly has constitutional dimensions. . . .

In this case we must weigh the importance of the general privilege of confidentiality of Presidential communications in performance of the President's responsibilities against the inroads of such a privilege on the fair administration of criminal justice. The interest in preserving confidentiality is weighty indeed and entitled to great respect. However, we cannot conclude that advisers will be moved to temper the candor of their remarks by the infrequent occasions of disclosure because of the possibility that such conversations will be called for in the context of a criminal prosecution.

On the other hand, the allowance of the privilege to withhold evidence that is demonstrably relevant in a criminal trial would cut deeply into the guarantee of due process of law and gravely impair the basic function of the courts. A President's acknowledged need for confidentiality in the communications of his office is general in nature, whereas the constitutional need for production of relevant evidence in a criminal proceeding is specific and central to the fair adjudication of a particular criminal case in the administration of justice. Without access to specific facts a criminal prosecution may be totally frustrated. The President's broad interest in confidentiality of communications will not be vitiated by disclosure of a limited number of conversations preliminarily shown to have some bearing on the pending criminal cases.

We conclude that when the ground for asserting privilege as to subpoenaed materials sought for use in a criminal trial is based only on the generalized interest in confidentiality, it cannot prevail over the fundamental demands of due process of law in the fair administration of criminal justice. The generalized assertion of privilege must yield to the demonstrated, specific need for evidence in a pending criminal trial. . . .

We have no doubt that the District Judge will at all times accord to Presidential records that high degree of deference suggested in *United States v. Burr,* and will discharge his responsibility to see to it that until released to the Special Prosecutor no in camera material is revealed to anyone. This burden applies with even greater force to excised material; once the decision is made to excise, the material is restored to its privileged status and should be returned under seal to its lawful custodian.

The opinion of the U.S. Supreme Court as delivered by Chief Justice Warren Burger in the case of United States v. Nixon. *Issued on July 24, 1974, it mandated that the president relinquish his Watergate tapes, available online at http://www.law.umkc.edu/faculty/projects/ftrials/conlaw/separationofpowers.htm, downloaded May 24, 2004.*

President Nixon's Resignation

This is the 37th time I have spoken to you from this office, where so many decisions have been made that shaped the history of this Nation. Each time I have done so to discuss with you some matter that I believe affected the national interest.

In all the decisions I have made in my public life, I have always tried to do what was best for the Nation. Throughout the long and difficult period of Watergate, I have felt it was my duty to persevere, to make every possible effort to complete the term of office to which you elected me.

In the past few days, however, it has become evident to me that I no longer have a strong enough political base in the Congress to justify continuing that effort. As long as there was such a base, I felt strongly that it was necessary to see the constitutional process through to its conclusion, that to do otherwise would be unfaithful to the spirit of that deliberately difficult process and a dangerously de-stabilizing precedent for the future.

But with the disappearance of that base, I now believe that the constitutional purpose has been served, and there is no longer a need for the process to be prolonged.

I would have preferred to carry through to the finish, whatever the personal agony it would have involved, and my family unanimously urged me to do so. But the interests of the Nation must always come before any personal considerations.

From the discussions I have had with Congressional and other leaders, I have concluded that because of the Watergate matter, I might not have the support of the Congress that I would consider necessary to back the very difficult decisions and carry out the duties of this office in the way the interests of the Nation will require.

I have never been a quitter. To leave office before my term is completed is abhorrent to every instinct in my body. But as President, I must put the interests of America first. America needs a fulltime President and a full-time Congress, particularly at this time with problems we face at home and abroad.

To continue to fight through the months ahead for my personal vindication would almost totally absorb the time and attention of both the President and the Congress in a period when our entire focus should be on the great issues of peace abroad and prosperity without inflation at home.

Therefore, I shall resign the Presidency effective at noon tomorrow. Vice President Ford will be sworn in as President at that hour in this office.

As I recall the high hopes for America with which we began this second term, I feel a great sadness that I will not be here in this office working on your behalf to achieve those hopes in the next 2-and-a-half years. But in turning over direction of the Government to Vice President Ford, I know, as I told the Nation when I nominated him for that office 10 months ago, that the leadership of America will be in good hands.

In passing this office to the Vice President, I also do so with the profound sense of the weight of responsibility that will fall on his shoulders tomorrow and, therefore, of the understanding, the patience, the cooperation he will need from all Americans.

As he assumes that responsibility, he will deserve the help and the support of all of us. As we look to the future, the first essential is to begin healing the wounds of this Nation, to put the bitterness and divisions of the recent past behind us and to rediscover those shared ideals that lie at the heart of our strength and unity as a great and as a free people.

By taking this action, I hope that I will have hastened the start of that process of healing which is so desperately needed in America.

I regret deeply any injuries that may have been done in the course of the events that led to this decision. I would say only that if some of my judgments were wrong—and some were wrong—they were made in what I believed at the time to be the best interest of the Nation.

To those who have stood with me during these past difficult months—to my family, my friends, to many others who joined in supporting my cause because they believed it was right—I will be eternally grateful for your support.

And to those of you have not felt able to give me your support, let me say I leave with no bitterness toward those who have opposed me, because all of us, in the final analysis, have been concerned with the good of the country, however our judgments might differ.

So, let us all now join together in affirming that common commitment and in helping our new President succeed for the benefit of all Americans.

I shall leave this office with regret at not completing my term, but with gratitude for the privilege of serving as your President for the past 5 and-one-half years. These years have been a momentous time in the history of our Nation and the world. They have been a time of achievement in which we can all be proud, achievements that represent the shared efforts of the Administration, the Congress, and the people.

But the challenges ahead are equally great, and they, too, will require the support and the efforts of the Congress and the people working in cooperation with the new Administration. . . .

For more than a quarter of a century in public life, I have shared in the turbulent history of this era. I have fought for what I believed in. I have tried, to the best of my ability, to discharge those duties and meet those responsibilities that were entrusted to me.

Sometimes I have succeeded and sometimes I have failed, but always I have taken heart from what Theodore Roosevelt once said about the man in the arena, "whose face is marred by dust and sweat and blood, who strives valiantly, who errs and comes short again and again because there is not effort without error and shortcoming, but who does actually strive to do the deed, who knows the great enthusiasms, the great devotions, who spends himself in a worthy cause, who at the best knows in the end the triumphs of high achievements and who at the worst, if he fails, at least fails while daring greatly."

I pledge to you tonight that as long as I have a breath of life in my body, I shall continue in that spirit. I shall continue to work for the great causes to which I have been dedicated throughout my years as a Congressman, a Senator, a Vice President, and President, the cause of peace, not just for America but among all nations—prosperity, justice, and opportunity for all of our people.

There is one cause above all to which I have been devoted and to which I shall always be devoted for as long as I live.

When I first took the oath of office as President 5 and-one-half years ago, I made this sacred commitment: to "consecrate my office, my energies, and all the wisdom I can summon to the cause of peace among nations."

I have done my very best in all the days since to be true to that pledge. As a result of these efforts, I am confident that the world is a safer place today, not only for the people of America but for the people of all nations, and that all of our children have a better chance than before of living in peace rather than dying in war.

This, more than anything, is what I hoped to achieve when I sought the Presidency, This, more than anything, is what I hope will be my legacy to you, to our country, as I leave the Presidency.

To have served in this office is to have felt a very personal sense of kinship with each and every American. In leaving it, I do so with this prayer: May God's grace be with you in all the days ahead.

Richard Nixon's announcement, August 8, 1974, that he will resign the office of president, in Public Papers of the Presidents of the United States: Richard Nixon, January 1 to August 9, 1974 *(1975), pp. 626–629.*

5

Watergate America—
Faith No More
August 1974–1975

"Our long national nightmare is over." So declared Gerald Ford just minutes after noon on August 9, 1974, as he took over the presidency from Richard Nixon, who had just resigned. Ford had in mind the immediate nightmare of Watergate. With Nixon gone, the horrors of that scandal seemed to dissipate.

But in two significant ways, Watergate endured through the remainder of 1974 and into 1975. First, many of those involved in the scandal had yet to face justice. Top Nixon aides such as H. R. Haldeman and John Ehrlichman still awaited trial. And as for the unindicted co-conspirator, Richard Nixon, his fate, also, had yet to be decided.

Second, if by Watergate we mean more than the political scandal, if we take Watergate to mean what the scandal said about political power and authority, what it said about trust and confidence in the United States as a nation, and what it said about unity and harmony in society, then the effects of Watergate remained alive and potent through the remainder of the decade and beyond.

The United States was in a deep crisis in the mid-1970s, not simply because Nixon operatives had been caught inside the Democratic National Committee's headquarters; not simply because Nixon had tried to cover up the break-in; but because Nixon's modus operandi rested on dividing America between good guys and bad guys and exploiting a polarized society whose division had been in part caused by the Vietnam War. Nixon's actions had helped intensify a cynicism about government and had demoralized people about the nation's future.

A divided, demoralized society then encountered a declining economy that demoralized it even further, making it all the more difficult to improve conditions. In short, a crisis of leadership, attitude, and economics came together to imperil the country.

FORD TAKES CHARGE

Two hours before noon on that historic August 9, Nixon stood in the East Room of the White House to address his staff. He was sweating and trembling, and his eyes were bleary from lack of sleep. He talked about the contributions of his cabinet, about how the staff members had worked so hard without concern for personal financial gain, about how his parents meant so much to him—his father was "a great man because his did his job," and his mother was "a saint." Then he reached back to the theme of his book *Six Crises,* the theme that he thought defined his life:

> We think that sometimes when things happen that don't go the right way. . . . We think that when someone dear to us dies, we think that when we lose an election, we think that when we suffer a defeat that all is ended. We think, as [Teddy Roosevelt] said, that the light had left his life forever.
>
> Not true. It is only a beginning, always. . . . The greatness comes not when things go always good for you, but the greatness comes and you are really tested, when you take some knocks, some disappointments, when sadness comes, because only if you have been in the deepest valley can you ever know how magnificent it is to be on the highest mountain.[1]

With those words, he left the White House, boarded a helicopter for *Air Force One* and, on that plane, flew to his home in San Clemente, California. He wondered: Would he be sentenced to prison? During a sleepless night, he remarked to an aide in a phone call: "Some of the best political writing in this century has been done in jail."[2]

Gerald Ford stood in the same East Room that had been burdened with Nixon's sadness and took the oath of office that was administered by Chief Justice Warren E. Burger. Friends, the cabinet, and colleagues from Congress looked on. His wife, Betty, held the Bible on which he rested his left hand while being sworn in. "This is an hour of history that troubles our minds and hurts our hearts," he said in his speech, or what he called "just a little straight talk among friends."[3] He said he realized that the people had not elected him to the presidency, but he asked that he be confirmed "with your prayers." He said reassuringly: "Truth is the glue that holds governments together, not only our Government, but civilization itself."[4] He would be, he insisted, open and forthright and embrace brotherly love as an antidote to suspicion and hate.

Gerald Ford faces the burden of trying to restore credibility and trust in the presidency following the resignation of Richard Nixon. *(Courtesy Gerald R. Ford Library)*

The nation looked to Ford for leadership in healing the wounds inflicted by the Vietnam War, by Watergate, by economic decay. He was a decent man, a man who adhered to conservative Midwestern values, a man whose college classmates said about him in 1935: "He never smokes, drinks, swears, or tells dirty stories . . . he's not a bit fraudulent, and we can't find anything really nasty to say about him."[5]

Ford said he would quickly select a vice president, and, on August 20, he announced as his choice former New York governor Nelson A. Rockefeller. Although most members of Congress applauded Ford's selection, some conservatives grumbled. They called Rockefeller too liberal and went so far as to say that the Republican Party needed someone other than Ford, someone more in tune with conservative values, to be its standard-bearer in the next presidential election.

Questions, meanwhile, circulated about whether Ford would pardon Richard Nixon. At his vice presidential confirmation hearing, he had said that he opposed such a move, at least before any indictment. But he later dropped hints to the contrary, telling reporters and friends that the former president had suffered enough.

Then came the pronouncement: On September 8, 1974, Ford told the nation that he was granting Nixon a pardon for all federal crimes he "committed or may have committed or taken part in" while in office. The sweep of the pardon stunned many people. Ford issued the pardon *before* Nixon had been indicted for any wrongdoing; he issued it without getting the recommendation of Watergate special prosecutor Leon Jaworski; he issued it with an accompanying agreement that declared the Watergate tapes and documents to be Nixon's personal property and gave Nixon permission to destroy many of the tapes; and he issued it without requiring Nixon to admit that he had committed any crimes.

Ford said that he was acting to heal America's wounds more quickly. A trial of the former president, he said, would last months, even years, and would again divide the country and challenge "the credibility of our free institutions of government." Yet, he may have been stirred to act as well because of reports that he had received about Nixon sinking into a deep depression and suffering from deteriorating health. (Some who knew Nixon denied the reports and said more than anything else that he appeared to be relaxed. But Ford staffer Benton Becker came away from a visit with Nixon stating, "He looked terrible. He appeared to have aged and shrunken in the month since his resignation. His jowls were loose and flabby. . . . His handshake was very weak." Becker later recalled that Nixon was "an absolute candidate for suicide; the most depressed human being I have ever met.")[6] All told, Ford said, his pardon was meant to protect the public good. Ford later denied that he had been motivated to act by Nixon's personal situation. He explained in his memoirs:

> I was very sure what would happen if I let the charges against Nixon run their legal course. Months were sure to elapse between an indictment and trial. The entire process would no doubt require years: a minimum of two, a maximum of six. And Nixon would not spend time quietly in San Clemente. He would be fighting for his freedom, taking his cause to the people, and his constant struggle would have dominated the news. The story would overshadow everything else. . . . A period of such prolonged vituperation and recrimination would be disastrous for the nation. America needed recovery, not revenge. The hate had to be drained and the healing begun.[7]

Charges arose then, and have lingered ever since, that Ford and Nixon had arranged a secret deal before Nixon resigned whereby Nixon would step aside to allow Ford to become president, and Ford would then pardon Nixon. John Ehrlichman, Nixon's former domestic affairs adviser, supported the pardon as being "for the nation's good," yet wrote in his memoirs: "I *do* know Richard Nixon. I'd bet that Jerry Ford promised to pardon Richard Nixon, and that promise was made before Nixon's resignation."[8]

No evidence exists, however, to definitively prove such a deal. In fact, such an arrangement was probably unnecessary, given the work of Alexander Haig. Ford's chief of staff, Haig had served in the same position under Nixon and was an important bridge between the disgraced former president and the untried new president. Haig worked hard to get the pardon for Nixon and played on Ford's sympathy for him, even relaying reports about the former president's deteriorating mental and physical health.

Yet, if Ford thought that the pardon would heal the nation's wounds, in the short run it did exactly the opposite. A storm of criticism erupted, and Ford's press secretary, Jerald terHorst, resigned in protest over the president's action. The Watergate controversy overwhelmed Ford's administration for months. Most observers believed that the pardon, and especially the breadth of it, ruined his presidency by creating distrust. The decent man had been replaced by just another politician out to protect other politicians; a "little straight talk" had been replaced by another crooked act.

In the view of millions of Americans, the pardon worked to keep the full truth about Watergate hidden, and they objected to Nixon escaping legal punishment while his aides were standing trial and going to jail. Ford's public approval rating dropped precipitously, and no less a revered figure than Sam Ervin, chair of the Senate Watergate Committee, stated: "President Ford ought to have allowed the legal processes to take their course, and not issued any pardon to former President Nixon until he had been indicted, tried, and convicted."[9]

So intense was the controversy that, in October, Ford took the unusual step of testifying before Congress, becoming the first president since Abraham Lincoln to do so (and Lincoln had appeared informally; Ford was appearing formally). He admitted that, prior to Nixon's resignation, Alexander Haig had raised the prospect of Nixon quitting and Ford pardoning him. Ford then said he had asked Haig whether a president could pardon a person even before an indictment had been issued, and Haig said it could be done. But Ford insisted that he later told Haig that the president must make a decision about whether to resign without the prospect of a pardon.

About a week after the pardon, Nixon said to Ford in a telephone conversation: "Jerry, I know this is causing you great political difficulty and embarrassment, but I also want you to know that I'm appreciative and grateful."[10]

WATERGATE DEFENDANTS CONVICTED

In late September, Richard Nixon traveled to Sunnylands, the estate of millionaire Walter Annenberg near Palm Springs. The main house, surrounded by 220 acres of irrigated turf and 700 acres of desert, encompassed 25,000 square feet of living space. The grounds contained a swimming pool, artificial lakes, and a golf course. Nixon, however, enjoyed little; the phlebitis that had been a problem for him all year got worse. Pain wracked his body, and a blood clot developed and threatened to kill him. He was taken to a hospital in Long Beach.

Back east, the trial began for three of his top aides involved in the Watergate cover-up: John D. Ehrlichman, H. R. Haldeman, and John Mitchell, along with Mitchell's former assistant Robert C. Mardian and the attorney for CREEP, Kenneth W. Parkinson. They faced charges of conspiracy, obstructing justice, and perjury. With the pardon granted to Nixon, the way had been cleared for him to testify at the trial. Ehrlichman and Haldeman wanted him as a witness. Nixon's doctor, however, said the former president's health would prevent this; it would be at least three or four months before he could appear.

As it turned out, the presiding judge, John Sirica, who once said that he wanted Nixon in the courtroom, allowed the trial to proceed without him.

Nixon never did testify. In late October, his condition worsened, and he went into a coma and cardiovascular shock.

At the Watergate trial, Ehrlichman aggressively attacked Nixon. His lawyers blamed the former president for the cover-up, claiming that Nixon had "deceived, misled, and lied to and used John Ehrlichman to cover up his own knowledge and actions."[11] But the Watergate tapes convinced the jury of the defendants' guilt, and on January 1, 1975, it found Mitchell, Haldeman, and Mardian guilty on all charges. Parkinson was acquitted. Judge Sirica sentenced each of the guilty men to three years in prison. "If I had known Nixon was taping my conversations," Ehrlichman later said, "I would have acted differently."[12]

ECONOMIC PROBLEMS

In the 1970s, a public opinion survey asked Americans if they agreed with the statement "The land of plenty is becoming the land of want." Nearly three-quarters of the respondents answered "yes."[13]

The "land of plenty" had indeed been a defining theme in America's development. Back in the 1950s, historian David Potter had written an influential book, *People of Plenty,* with the thesis that plentitude, more than anything else, had shaped society's development from the time of the colonists onward. An abundance of natural resources, exploited by a strong work ethic, had begot material goods, reinforced the work ethic, and bred a homogeneous culture with a firm faith in progress.

Now the country's faith and progress were imperiled. This is not to say Americans were walking around in rags or that they were experiencing anything remotely akin to the 1930s depression. The expanding population, fed by a maturing baby-boomer generation, was consuming many goods. McDonald's kept building and changing its fast-food restaurants, adding a breakfast menu

In the mid-1970s, rural poverty in America remained an intractable problem. *(National Archives and Records Administration)*

Senior citizens in Chicago protest inflation, high unemployment, and high taxes in 1973, problems that continued under President Ford. *(National Archives and Records Administration)*

designed to appeal to young workers who were rushing to their jobs in the morning. Adidas sold 13 million pairs of running shoes as a jogging craze took hold. However strong youthful antimaterialism may have been in the 1960s, it faded in the seventies. *Playboy* magazine labeled the behavior a "new materialism."

Clearly, though, the government deficits of the 1960s, the OPEC oil embargo, and myriad internal problems took their toll on economic vitality. From 1970 to 1975, nearly every state recorded substantial increases in unemployment.

August 1974 especially revealed disturbing developments. The unemployment rate reached 7.4 percent; the number of jobs declined by 125,000; the gross national product was dropping; the Dow Jones industrial average lost 99 points; seasonally adjusted housing starts declined by 15 percent from the previous month; and the U.S. trade deficit hit a record $1.1 billion.

Traditionally, such an economic slowdown would be accompanied by stable or declining consumer prices. Instead, inflation took hold. A new word emerged to describe this curious, unsettling combination of high prices and slow to stagnant economic growth: *stagflation.*

Economists still debate the reasons for the crisis, but they generally emphasize increased economic competition from Western Europe and Japan; higher labor costs that made for higher production costs; burdensome government deficits; and rising prices for oil.

At the White House, President Ford scrambled to right the economy. He faced a formidable task in building political support, for although a brief honeymoon period began on his assumption of the presidency, he was a Republican dealing with a Democratic Congress and operating from an executive office that was weakened by the Watergate scandal. Furthermore, off-year elections loomed, making it difficult for members of Congress to vote for any sacrifices or hardnosed economic measures.

Intent primarily on fighting inflation, Ford spoke before a joint session of Congress in early October and requested a 5 percent income-tax surcharge on corporations and the wealthy to last one year and a $4 billion cut in federal spending. Moreover, he announced he was forming a national organization to be staffed by volunteers from across the nation who would develop ways to hold down prices. He called his program WIN for "Whip Inflation Now" and called for Americans to sign up and wear WIN lapel buttons. Within a few days, hundreds of thousands of people had requested the buttons. Yet, many derided WIN as an unrealistic propaganda ploy akin to saying that "all you have to do is think hard enough and inflation will go away."

Congress slammed Ford's plan as misguided, and while the president continued to press for the tax increase, data came rolling in to show that a recession had begun, with unemployment moving toward 6 percent. The situation had become so severe that "by the end of October the index of leading indicators reported the largest decline in any single month in twenty-three years."[14]

The economic decline converged with Watergate to produce a devastating blow to Republicans in the November 1974 elections. The Democrats added 43 House seats and 23 Senate seats, bringing their majority to 147 and 23, respectively. Tellingly, only 38 percent of all eligible voters turned out—disgust with politics and politicians might never have been greater.

Finally, in mid-November, Ford backed away from his tax-surcharge proposal and for the first time admitted that a recession had begun. He said: "We are in a recession. Production is declining, and unemployment, unfortunately, is rising." He added: "We are also faced with continued high rates of inflation greater than can be tolerated over an extended period of time."[15]

Ford reversed course and, in January 1975, advocated a measure that the Democrats in Congress had been pushing for some time: a tax cut. The temporary reduction would apply to both businesses and individuals, providing the latter with up to a $1,000 rebate on their 1974 tax returns. Interestingly, given the position of the Republican Party in the early 2000s in favor of large tax cuts even at the cost of massive deficits, conservatives in 1975 criticized Ford for favoring tax cuts over tax increases, which they thought necessary to reduce the deficit and control inflation. Many critics also felt that Ford had shown a lack of will and a dangerous inconsistency in shifting from higher to lower taxes.

Democrats in Congress responded by pushing through a much larger temporary tax cut than Ford had proposed. The president thought it too expensive; still, he signed the measure into law in March 1975.

Stagflation, though, persisted, and in October, Ford proposed a bigger, permanent tax cut, coupled with budget cuts. Economic orthodoxy called for increasing spending to stimulate a moribund economy, so Ford's proposal went in the opposite direction. He was, however, dealing with the unusual combination of stagnation and inflation.

The Democratic Congress again bucked Ford: While it approved his tax cut, it rejected his budget cuts. Ford vetoed the bill, whereupon Congress, in December 1975, passed a lower tax cut (reduced from $28 billion to $9 billion) but also promised to reduce the budget.

Near the same time, Congress passed the Omnibus Energy bill that cut domestic oil prices. The bill, however, gave the president the power to end the cost control eventually.

These measures may indeed have helped to boost the economy. While still substantial, inflation eased, dropping from 9.1 percent in 1975 to 5.8 percent in late

1976. Jobs appeared, too, with 4 million more people at work in early 1976 than in the previous year. Yet, the measures reflected less the president's efforts than those of Congress. Post-Vietnam, post-Watergate America experienced a power shift in Washington from the White House to Capitol Hill—a reaction to the excesses under Lyndon Johnson and Richard Nixon and an expression of the public distrust in the Oval Office (though clearly aimed as well at politicians in general).

NEW YORK CITY AND BANKRUPTCY

The economic downturn doomed New York City's already dangerous financial condition. So did attitudes: In fact, the economic decline and the discontent, cynicism, and pessimism about America came together to worsen New York's plight and at the same time make the city an example of what was wrong with the country.

Many in the 1970s believed that government action to fight social injustice had gone too far. Some believed, for example, that measures to advance women's rights had weakened the family, that the welfare state had grown too large and wasteful, that aid to minorities threatened to undermine the majority white culture, and that urban renewal programs had failed, producing blighted housing projects. These beliefs produced a turning inward as opposed to a New Deal–type reaching outward to help others. Middle-class Americans were hunkering down, and in doing so, the city symbolized what was wrong with the country.

Middle-class Americans fled urban decay and urban problems for the suburbs, and they fled the Rust Belt Northeast and Midwest for the Sun Belt Southeast and Southwest. From their entrenchment, they sneered at the city, with its slums, rising crime, and unruly blacks and immigrants. In leaving, they had left urban residents with fewer resources to handle their problems—a weakened tax base unable to replenish city treasuries adequately.

Thus, when New York City encountered its financial problems, many Americans opposed any government help to the metropolis. Let New Yorkers sink in the quicksand of crime, congestion, pollution, and greedy unions that they had created. Never mind that New York had borne the brunt of accepting impoverished immigrants into the United States or had been the economic engine in much of America's development.

Facing a city tottering on default, Mayor Abraham Beame acted in late July 1975 to trim the municipal budget. He abolished three city agencies and merged two others for a savings of $4 million. Moreover, he cut $32 million from the city university budget and imposed a wage freeze on all city workers. To raise money, he increased transit fees and most bridge and tunnel tolls.

But the city still faced default and with it the possibility of having to eliminate police and fire protection and other vital services. With the crisis worsening, Beame looked to Congress to provide a multibillion dollar loan guarantee. President Ford, however, opposed any such action. In late October, he sent to Congress legislation that would allow New York to file for bankruptcy and maintain vital services. At the same time, he announced: "I can tell you—and tell you now—that I am prepared to veto any bill that has as its purpose a Federal bailout of New York City to prevent default."[16]

Ford criticized the leaders of New York City and of the state for failing to do more to avert default. He said that the city and the state could invest pension funds to raise money and that they could increase taxes. He insisted that a default would neither hurt the economy nationally nor produce any loss to the federal government. His comments resulted in the *New York Daily News* printing a big bold headline: "Ford to City: Drop Dead."

Several members of Congress appeared to be more flexible than Ford or disagreed with him outright:

> "In simply proposing to make it easier for New York City to go bankrupt, the President has chosen a course that would shove New York into a tin-cup status and onto the Federal Government's back for years to come," said Senator William Proxmire (Dem., Wis.).
>
> "If more is needed [than what the president has proposed], I would be prepared to judge it on the basis of what is fair and just," said Senator Hugh Scott (Rep., Pa.).
>
> "[The president's proposal] is nothing more or less than political quackery for a financial disease that goes far beyond New York City's boundaries," said Senator Hubert H. Humphrey (Dem., Minn.).[17]

Ford declared that government deficits at all levels would bring "a day of reckoning." He asked: "When the day of reckoning comes, who will bail out the United States of America?"[18]

Both New York governor Hugh Carey and Mayor Beame denounced Ford. Beame called it a default in its own way, in this case "a default of Presidential leadership," and in alluding to the animosity of the Sun Belt to the Northeast, he said that Ford's position could revive Civil War–era sectionalism. City council president Paul O'Dwyer said that Ford's stand would never had been taken by Richard Nixon, making "one wonder whether the impeachment [drive] was really such a good idea."[19]

New Yorkers ride a graffiti-covered subway car in the mid-1970s. *(National Archives and Records Administration)*

On a cold, windy day in late November, Mayor Beame led a "United New York" rally at Times Square. "We're All Americans, Mr. Ford," read one placard. But the crowd turned out to be small and more interested in the show-business entertainers, such as actor Dustin Hoffman, who had been promised them, than in the politicians who spoke. They even booed Beame.

Some members of Congress predicted that, deep down, Ford considered New York's financial health too important for the federal government to turn its back on, and inaction or obstinacy on his part too risky politically. He would never veto a loan-guarantee bill, they said. In fact, one day after the "United New York" rally, Ford changed his mind and asked Congress to approve $2.3 billion in short-term loans for the city. The crisis ended when Congress quickly passed a bill, and the president signed it on December 9.

RIOTS IN BOSTON

To advance civil rights, the federal government issued several mandates, and the courts made several rulings on behalf of minorities. These actions generated an enormous amount of controversy and in many instances fueled the widespread distrust in government. None did so more than the forced integration of Boston's public schools through busing.

In 1971, the Supreme Court in its landmark decision *Swann v. Charlotte-Mecklenburg Board of Education* stated that the federal courts could require busing to desegregate schools. Three years later, in June 1974, federal judge W. Arthur Garrity ordered Boston to desegregate its public schools through busing. The school board protested the order: Segregation, it claimed, had evolved from housing patterns beyond its control. But Garrity said that the board had sustained and even expanded segregation through such tactics as busing black children past white schools. His desegregation plan included merging predominantly white South Boston, called Southie by its residents, and predominately black Roxbury into one school district. Each neighborhood was to have a high school that would reflect a racial mix. The plan called for 941 blacks and 1,604 whites to attend South Boston High, where there had previously been 2,178 whites and only 15 blacks.

To protest Garrity's orders, white parents, mainly Irish American, organized ROAR (Restore Our Alienated Rights), a name they picked to reflect their anger. The busing program began on September 12, 1974, and in most of the city's districts, there were few problems, but unruly whites in South Boston threw rocks at buses carrying black students. At the same time, white students boycotted classes at South Boston High School. The school sat atop Dorchester Heights, surrounded by old Victorian houses in a largely working-class neighborhood, itself worn down by high unemployment. Nearly half of South Boston's housing was so deteriorated that, in a report, the Boston Redevelopment Authority had concluded that many of the structures should be torn down. Writing recently in the *New Yorker* magazine, Susan Orlean states: "Most of the local school buildings had been erected before the turn of the century; the report called for six of the fourteen to be demolished immediately."[20] Protective of their community, however, and leery about plans for urban renewal, South Boston residents protested the report. The pressure from the redevelopment authority and the anguish over high unemployment may well have made the residents more defensive of South Boston High School and more extreme in opposing Garrity's orders.

Whatever the case, as the buses pulled up to the school on September 12, white youths began to chant "Go home, nigger" and "Turn the bus over!" One demonstrator declared: "Any white kid that goes to school out of his neighborhood should be shot, and any black kid that comes out of his neighborhood to school here should be shot."[21]

Mayor Kevin White reacted to the violence by banning public gatherings in South Boston and by ordering a police escort for the buses. Southie whites felt deserted by the mayor and besieged by the federal government. Race and attachment to their community combined to produce a potent hatred. "I was born here and Southie [high school] is my alma mater," said a truck driver. "Why should I send [my kids] to Amazonland? Its getting so the coloreds get everything."[22]

On day two of the busing, police on motorcycles escorted buses with 25 black students to South Boston High. Fewer than 100 students attended classes. Conditions remained tense but quiet until the afternoon when 300 white teenagers attacked three buses with rocks. Later that day, black youths stoned a bus carrying white students from school in Roxbury.

Black parents debated whether or not they should send their children to Southie. Many disliked tearing their children away from their neighborhood schools. Others feared for their children's safety. Addressing a highly charged meeting of black parents, Mayor White urged them to abide by the busing program and said that he would protect the students. He pleaded: "It's not the Lord's guarantee, but I'm asking for another chance, and then, if I can't produce, I'll fight along side you."[23]

Gradually, more students attended classes. But violence recurred in the Boston school districts. On October 8, 1974, clashes between white and black youths forced city transit officials to suspend the running of public buses into Roxbury and Mission Hill. On October 15, 500 members of the National Guard were called in after a black student stabbed a white student at Hyde Park High School. That December, white parents entered South Boston High and provoked their children into holding a protest in the auditorium. A few days later, a black student stabbed a white student at the school.

A black student at South Boston High later recalled:

On a normal day there would be anywhere between ten and fifteen fights. You could walk down the corridor and a black person would bump into a white person or vice versa. That would be one fight. And they'd try to separate us, because at that time there was so much tension in the school that one fight could just have the school dismissed for the entire day because it would just lead to another and another and another.

You can't imagine how tense it was in the classroom. A teacher was almost afraid to say the wrong thing, because they knew that would excite the whole class, a disturbance in the classroom. The black students sat on one side of the classes. The white students sat on the other side of the classes.[24]

In May 1975, Judge Garrity, who had established federal-court oversight of the Boston schools, issued a Phase II plan, much more comprehensive, including more school districts than had been in effect under Phase I. He wanted the city's schools to reflect the general racial mix of Boston: 51 percent white, 37 percent black, and 12 percent other minorities. He ordered 20 schools to close, and he created nine new school districts. That December, he claimed that the Boston School Committee had hindered the implementation of his desegregation orders, and so he placed South Boston High School under federal receivership.

In 1989, Judge Garrity ended the federal-court oversight of the Boston schools with the stipulation they not resegregate. The Boston School Committee developed a new plan called controlled choice. It allowed students in most instances to attend one of their top three schools of choice under a system where racial diversity was only one among several factors.

As late as 1993, racial brawls erupted at South Boston High, and police maintained a permanent presence on the school grounds. In 1999, the Boston School Committee ended all consideration of race in determining school attendance and returned to what it called a system of neighborhood schools. By that time, Boston's racial and ethnic makeup had changed. Fewer whites lived in the city, and, by-and-large, the racially divided districts had been populated by more immigrants. Coupled with white flight to the suburbs, white enrollment in the Boston public schools had declined to just 15 percent. Susan Orlean writes:

> Many people came to accept integration, but many others resolved their distaste for it by moving their kids to parochial schools—and many just left the neighborhood. This happened throughout the city. . . . But South Boston's exodus was the most dramatic. Its residents moved out of the Town, the place they had probably intended to stay forever, and into the suburbs south of Boston, such as Quincy, Weymouth, Holbrook, Brockton. The population of South Boston declined by twenty per cent.[25]

The busing violence had brought home to the North the racially charged hatred that had been usually associated with the South. Alongside the image from the 1960s of an Alabama governor standing in front of a "schoolhouse door" to prevent integration, there now appeared Stanley Forman's Pulitzer Prize–winning photograph of a black man being rammed with an American flag outside Boston City Hall.

During the crisis, the Civil Rights movement had collided with the desire of both white and black parents to maintain their community schools. Yet, often overlooked but a crucial part of the busing controversy was class—class divisions among whites and the antipathy of lower-class whites toward blacks. Harvard psychologist Robert Coles observed in 1975: "The ultimate reality is the reality of class. Having and not having is the real issue. To talk only in terms of racism is to miss the point. Lower-income whites and blacks are both competing for a very limited piece of pie."[26]

In the end, the crisis caused faith in government to drop a bit more. One parent said about the authorities: "If they can tell you where to send your kids to school, they can tell you anything, they can take anything away from you."[27]

THE DEATH OF KAREN SILKWOOD

The autumn wind was chilly and crisp when, shortly after 7:00 P.M. on November 13, 1974, Karen Silkwood left a café in Crescent, Oklahoma, got behind the wheel of her Honda Civic, and pulled onto Highway 74 bound for

Oklahoma City 30 miles away. There she planned to meet at a Holiday Inn with a reporter from the *New York Times.* She had a story to tell, a troubling one, about problems at the Kerr-McGee plutonium plant in Crescent where she worked.

At about 8:00 P.M., truck driver James Mullins noticed a glint in his headlights at the side of the highway. He stopped his truck. He and a passenger discovered Silkwood's Honda resting in the culvert, just seven miles from the café. The left front of the car was badly damaged. Karen Silkwood's lifeless arm protruded from the side window. Her death soon became controversial, and she became a cause celebre among critics of big government, big corporations, and nuclear power and among those who saw conspiracies at work behind each.

Born in Longview, Texas, in 1946, Karen Silkwood began to work for the Kerr-McGee Nuclear Corporation in August 1972 as a laboratory analyst at the Crescent plutonium plant, a box-style building sitting next to a uranium plant, both of them situated amid bucolic pastures and wheat fields. Plutonium arrived at the plant in heavily fortified vans; it was then processed into pellets and the pellets placed into stainless steel rods. The rods were to be used in a fast breeder reactor under construction in Tennessee. Silkwood's job was to check the pellets and fuel rods for any defects.

In November, Silkwood participated in a strike against the plant. The strikers, members of the Oil, Chemical and Atomic Workers Union (OCAW), wanted higher wages and improved health, safety, and training programs. Ten weeks later, a defeated and badly depleted OCAW ended the strike.

In spring 1974, Kerr-McGee sped up production. The 12-hour shifts and seven-day workweeks led to spills and to contamination that worried Silkwood. She changed from being an unobtrusive member of the OCAW to being a union activist. Hardly any of the workers, at first not even Silkwood herself, knew about the dangers of plutonium. That it could cause cancer of the liver, lungs, lymph nodes, or bones eventually made her even more worried about the shoddy training in the plant and the accidents that the corporate bosses cared little about.

For a hearing before the Atomic Energy Commission (AEC), she and other union officials compiled a damning list of transgressions:

"An employee became contaminated. As he was led out, contamination was tracked throughout the facility."

"Regular production is conducted in contaminated areas using respirators twelve hours/day up to ten days without cleanup."

"Plutonium samples are stored in desk drawers. Some were stored on a shelf for a period of two years."[28]

Going public with this information was a dangerous strategy. It invited recrimination. The risk for Silkwood intensified when she began to gather additional material that she planned to give to the *New York Times,* specific facts about unsafe fuel rods and distorted quality-control documents.

At 5:30 P.M. on November 5, 1974, Silkwood did as she had always done at the end of her workday and removed the coveralls and rubber gloves which she wore for protection from the plutonium. She checked her hands in a monitor. The clicking sound from the device indicated that she had been contaminated. Additional tests confirmed contamination to other parts of her body.

The next two days produced similar results, and a nasal smear showed that the contamination had reached beyond her skin and into her body. She asked Kerr-McGee inspectors to check her apartment. Their instruments indicated limited amounts of plutonium nearly everywhere: her furniture, bedsheets, television, and so on. They found significant contamination inside her refrigerator, a result that they found to be inexplicable.

To ease her nervousness, Silkwood took Quaaludes, which had previously been prescribed to her for sleeplessness. On November 10, she headed to Los Alamos, New Mexico, where she was tested at an AEC laboratory. The results were a bit more encouraging, showing no immediate peril.

On Wednesday evening, November 13, she met with other union officials at the café in Crescent. In *The Killing of Karen Silkwood,* author Richard Rashke describes a conversation that Silkwood had with one of them, Jean Jung, right before she left the café:

> She started to cry quietly. She told Jung she was frightened; that she had been so badly contaminated, she would eventually get cancer and die from the plutonium in her lungs. She said someone had deliberately contaminated her. . . .
>
> Karen pointed to her documents. "She then said that there was one thing she was glad about," Jung swore [later] in [an] affidavit. "That she had all the proof concerning falsification of records. As she said this she clenched her hand more firmly on the folder and notebook she was holding. She told me she was on her way to meet . . . a *New York Times* reporter . . . to give [him] this material."[29]

Then she wound up dead in the ditch along Highway 74. Curiously, the papers that she had been carrying disappeared. A state trooper reported picking up a bunch of loose sheets near Silkwood's Honda and placing them on the front seat. But when Silkwood's union friends claimed her car—after it had been checked by representatives from Kerr-McGee and the AEC—the papers were gone.

The Ohio Highway Patrol explained the car crash as accidental. Moreover, the chief medical examiner reported that Silkwood had Quaaludes in her blood, a reading of .35 mg, slightly above a therapeutic dose of .25 mg and below a toxic dose of .50 mg. Additional amounts were found in her stomach but had not been absorbed. The examiner found no trace of radioactivity during the autopsy. Given other evidence, the examiner also concluded that Silkwood's death was accidental.

A. O. Pipkin, Jr., an auto-crash expert, disagreed with these findings. He looked at dents in the rear of the car and tire tracks left on the highway. The dents indicated that the car had been hit by another vehicle; the tire tracks indicated that Silkwood had lost control of her car, perhaps from the collision.

Several magazines also disagreed with the Ohio Highway Patrol. Boldest of all, *Rolling Stone* claimed that Silkwood was murdered because of her activities against Kerr-McGee and her decision to speak with the *New York Times.* None of these publications offered definitive evidence, but they fed a widening skepticism toward government officials and big business.

Then in 1976, Bill Silkwood, Karen's father, sued Kerr-McGee, charging the company with negligence and with violating his daughter's civil rights. The civil-rights charge included accusations that Kerr-McGee had spied on Silkwood.

Moreover, the complaint charged the FBI with conspiring with Kerr-McGee officials to cover up the company's illegal activities.

On the charge of negligence, a jury in May 1979 found Kerr-McGee guilty and awarded actual damages of $550,000 and exemplary damages of $10 million. The family's victory was short-lived, however, when the Tenth Circuit Court negated both awards. Bill Silkwood then appealed to the U.S. Supreme Court, and in 1984 the judges ruled, 5-4, in his favor. Consequently, the circuit court ordered a new trial to settle the monetary damages, but rather than face another protracted struggle, Bill Silkwood reached an out-of-court settlement with Kerr-McGee for $1.85 million. Attached to the award: Both sides agreed that Kerr-McGee would not have to admit any wrongdoing.

There remained the suspicion that Kerr-McGee had sought to stop Karen Silkwood by having her killed. The company was seen as the bad guy; Karen was seen as standing up for the little person against the impersonal and cruel corporation. Added to popular motion pictures that emphasized the dangers of nuclear energy and to the catastrophe at the Three Mile Island nuclear power plant in Pennsylvania in 1979, the Silkwood case caused millions of Americans to turn against the nuclear industry and deepened the already widespread distrust toward big business and big government.

A COMMUNIST VICTORY IN VIETNAM

Vietnam returned to the news in spring 1975 to confirm the U.S. defeat in that chaotic country. As Communist forces advanced on Saigon in late April, President Nyugen Van Thieu resigned as the leader of South Vietnam. He accused the United States of abandoning his government despite the massive amount of American military aid given to his army.

Fighting on the edge of Saigon sent the sound of AK-47 rifles echoing through the city. Black smoke from a storage dump darkened the sky as communist troops seized the far side of a bridge that spanned the Saigon River. South Vietnamese helicopters fired rockets at the communists, but the South Vietnamese soldiers on the ground appeared nervous and anxious to flee.

When the communists began to assault Saigon's Tan Son Nhut airport, President Ford ordered the evacuation of Americans from the city. The assault on the airport involved more than 150 rockets smashing into planes, runways, and buildings; two U.S. Marines who were on guard there were killed. Other Communist troops severed major highways around Saigon and invaded suburban communities. One newspaper reporter said about the action around Tan Son Nhut:

> As has often happened in the Vietnam War, most of the Government soldiers simply stood in the middle of the road, making no effort to dig in, an elementary infantry tactic. A National Combat Police truck brought up a mortar and crates of ammunition, but no one moved to unload the mortar or put it into action against the Communists.[30]

Americans watched more with numbed acceptance than shock as newscasts showed workers at the U.S. embassy scrambling to board evacuation helicopters and using clubs and fists to beat back panicked South Vietnamese who were also

President Ford discusses, with Henry Kissinger (left) and Vice President Rockefeller (center), the U.S. evacuation of Saigon. *(Courtesy Gerald R. Ford Library)*

trying to flee. Meanwhile, the United States began to airlift South Vietnamese refugees to Guam; soon, 20,000 of them crowded into a refugee camp to await processing and entry into the United States. Panic and disorder marred the evacuation of South Vietnamese military officials and civilians. Several South Vietnamese helicopters landed unexpectedly on aircraft carriers of the U.S. Seventh Fleet. Two copters collided on deck, and American sailors shoved some helicopters into the ocean to make room for others to land.

Additional U.S. naval ships picked up about 22,000 Vietnamese fleeing in small boats in the South China Sea. Secretary of State Henry Kissinger informed Congress that the United States would have to accept tens of thousands of refugees.

Communist forces entered Saigon on April 30. President Duong Van Minh had announced South Vietnam's unconditional surrender, and the government's troops had begun to turn in their weapons. The victors raised the Viet Cong flag over the presidential palace and other government buildings, and Communist soldiers along the streets of Saigon shook hands with some residents, while other residents applauded the arriving convoys. Communist leaders declared that Saigon had been "totally liberated."

In the turmoil, Saigonese looted the U.S. embassy. They tore from its wall a bronze plaque bearing the names of five American servicemen killed in 1968 by Communist guerrillas. So ended some 30 years of warfare for the revolutionary Vietnamese against, first, the French, and, later, the Americans. Keyes Beech, a reporter for the *Chicago Daily News* wrote: "My last view of Saigon was through the tail door of [a] helicopter. Tan Son Nhut was burning. . . . Then the door closed—closed on the most humiliating chapter in American history."[31]

THE CAMBODIAN ATTACK ON A U.S. MERCHANT SHIP

America's involvement in Southeast Asia again escalated into a military confrontation when, on May 12, 1975, a Cambodian naval vessel attacked the U.S.

merchant ship *Mayaguez* in the Gulf of Siam and forced it into the Cambodian port of Sihonoukville (now Kompong Sum).

Only a month earlier, communist-led forces had taken control of the Cambodian government. President Ford realized that the ship seizure required a firm response by the United States to save the crew; he realized, too, that the crisis offered him an opportunity to show his mettle as commander in chief and the vibrancy of the United States at a time when his political standing was weak.

The president listened to Henry Kissinger's opinion. "At some point the United States must draw the line," the secretary of state told him. "This is not our idea of the best such situation. It is not our choice. But we must act upon it now, and act firmly."[32] Ford ordered the aircraft carrier *Coral Sea* to the site and publicly demanded the return of the *Mayaguez* and its crew.

He rejected any negotiations with the Cambodians and ordered 100 marines to land on the tiny island of Koh Tang, where the *Mayaguez* crew was being held. While American planes attacked the Cambodian mainland, the marines at Koh Tang encountered an unexpectedly fierce resistance. Within one hour, 15 of them were killed and eight American helicopters were shot down. Nevertheless, the Cambodians reacted by releasing the crew.

Ford hailed the operation as a victory, but evidence indicates the release of the captives may have resulted less from the military attack than from pressure placed on Cambodia by China. The bombing of the Cambodian mainland continued for several hours after the captives were freed, and, according to historian John Robert Greene, "The administration steered toward a plan that was less a rescue operation than a punitive mission. The bombing of the Cambodian mainland comes dangerously close to being irresponsible."[33] Furthermore, Ford violated the recently passed War Powers Act and kept Congress in the dark about his decision to launch air strikes until after he gave the order to attack. Yet, Americans often applaud military strikes, and this case was no exception; consequently, the president's action boosted his standing in the opinion polls. Most members of Congress approved, too, with Senator Jack Edwards (Dem., Ala.) stating, "I am very proud of our country and our president today."[34]

AMERICAN INVOLVEMENT IN ANGOLA AND PROBLEMS FOR FORD

Perhaps the lessons from Vietnam were limited. President Ford again showed the duplicity of executive power when he secretly involved the United States in a complex civil war in Angola, a former Portuguese colony in Africa that was scheduled to hold elections in November 1975. That summer, Ford sent money to back the rebel FNLA, or National Front for the Liberation of Angola, against the Soviet-backed MLPA, or Popular Movement for the Liberation of Angola. (These were but two of several rebel groups divided by ideology and tribal and ethnic loyalties.) Historian John Robert Greene says: "Ford wanted to use the Angolan arena to show the world—and the U.S. Congress—that the Ford administration was still in command of its foreign policy."[35] Under Operation FEATURE, the president approved $25 million for weapons and supplies, and the CIA hired mercenaries to fill the ranks of the FNLA. Ford's policy caused Fidel Castro to send Cuban troops to help the MLPA, thus igniting a wider war. Ultimately, the American aid did little good, as the MLPA captured the capital city of Luanda.

Within a short while, the *New York Times* leaked news about Ford's action, and the Senate investigated. Congress then passed a law requiring the president to end the intervention, and in February 1976, Ford signed it. He subsequently issued an executive order requiring intelligence agencies to report regularly to an oversight board and prohibiting them from participating in any plans to kill foreign leaders—a backdoor admission to what the United States had been doing overseas for years. Despite these reforms, Operation FEATURE recalled the worst in presidential covert activities from the Vietnam era and, like the Nixon pardon, damaged Ford's credibility.

THE CHURCH COMMITTEE AND POLITICAL ASSASSINATIONS

The influence of Vietnam and Watergate, of the entire national security state that had evolved during the cold war with its domestic spying and secret deals directed by an evermore powerful government, reared its head again with the revelations of the Church committee during much of 1975 and into 1976. The Senate formed the committee early in 1975 to investigate intelligence agencies; its official name was the Select Committee to Study Governmental Operations with Respect to Intelligence Activities, and it was headed by Frank Church (Dem., Idaho), an ambitious Democrat who wanted to make a name for himself and become president.

Church combined his political drive with his concern about excessive and illegal government actions to lead the committee in uncovering revealing information, some of which had been reported by a Ford-appointed commission headed by Vice President Nelson Rockefeller. Ford took a Nixonian stance in saying publicly that he would cooperate with the Church investigation while he privately resisted requests to hand over documents. In fact, he complained to his aides about the CIA cooperating more willingly than he desired with the committee.

In November 1975, the Church committee prepared to issue a damning interim report detailing American efforts to assassinate foreign leaders, among them Fidel Castro of Cuba, Patrice Lumumba of the Congo, and Rafael Trujillo of the Dominican Republic. Ford strenuously opposed making public any U.S. involvement in the assassination plots. He said the revelations would endanger national security by disrupting foreign relations. Church responded by saying that the president had for months "known of the committee's intent to publish its findings in the form of a special report."[36]

The committee report, released by Senator Church without a Senate vote formally approving its publication, detailed connections between the CIA and Mafiosi in a plot to kill Castro. Among its most bizarre findings: efforts to damage the Cuban leader's charisma by using a powder to make his beard fall out and an attempt to kill him by giving him poison cigars.

In addition, the committee investigated the overthrow of Salvador Allende in Chile and concluded that the United States had encouraged his removal, although it found no evidence of direct CIA involvement in the coup. U.S. officials, the committee said, had committed millions of dollars to removing Allende as Chile's democratically elected president.

Late in December, the committee issued a final report covering six volumes and making 183 recommendations, the most important of which called for

Congress to oversee more effectively intelligence operations. Coming from this, both the Senate and the House established permanent select committees on intelligence, and, in all, they formed six separate oversight committees. Finally, Congress would have the means (yet to be tested by the will) to keep the CIA and other intelligence agencies in line.

GOVERNMENT INVOLVEMENT IN DRUG EXPERIMENTS

Reports of secret and illegal drug experiments run by the CIA and the army further eroded public faith in the federal government. Investigations by the Rockefeller Commission and reports by the *New York Times* revealed details about a top secret CIA program called MK-ULTRA, under which LSD was administered to unsuspecting prisoners, mental patients, and even to CIA agents in the hopes of finding an effective "mind-control" drug. The program began in the early 1950s and continued for about 10 years.

The *Times* reported in July 1975 that, according to the Rockefeller Commission, the chief of the drug program, Dr. Sidney Gottlieb, destroyed records pertaining to it in 1973 to hide the details of possible illegal actions. A biochemist, Gottlieb was involved in an experiment in November 1953 in which a researcher, Frank Olson, had unknowingly been given a dose of LSD, developed anxiety attacks, and jumped to his death from a New York City hotel room. The destroyed records likely included information about the experimentation with Olson.

Also in July, the *Washington Post* reported that two projects run by the army in the late 1950s administered LSD, along with mescaline and other hallucinogens, to hundreds of soldiers and civilians. One of the projects was operated through the University of Maryland Medical School using civilian doctors. The army usually kept the subjects in the dark about the nature of the experiments.

TWO ASSASSINATION ATTEMPTS AGAINST PRESIDENT FORD

President Ford survived two assassination attempts within days of each other in 1975. The first occurred on September 5, when Lynette "Squeaky" Fromme aimed a pistol at him as he walked two feet away from her outside the California state capitol in Sacramento. Ford was on his way from a hotel to address the legislature, where, ironically, he planned to present a speech about violent crime.

As Fromme removed the pistol from her purse, Secret Service agent Larry Buendorf grabbed her arm and forced the weapon to the ground before any shots could be fired. It was later discovered that the pistol's magazine contained bullets, but there was no bullet in the chamber. Fromme, 26 years old, was a follower of Charles Manson, the deranged cult leader who had masterminded the murder of actress Sharon Tate and six others in 1969.

Ford continued to the capitol and, although shaken by the incident, spoke to the legislators. He later said in an interview: "I saw a hand coming up among several others in the front row, and obviously there was a gun in that hand."[37]

At her arraignment, Fromme appeared in a bright red robe and launched into a rambling monologue about destruction of the national parks and how young people "want to clean up the earth."[38] When the judge silenced her, she said to him, "The gun is pointed, your honor, the gun is pointed—whether it goes off is up to you."[39]

Jack and Steve Ford, the sons of President and Mrs. Ford, greet their parents on the South Lawn of the White House following the president's return from San Francisco, where Lynette "Squeaky" Fromme tried to assassinate him. *(Courtesy Gerald R. Ford Library)*

The judge then ordered her removed from the courtroom. In November, she was convicted of attempting to kill the president and sentenced to life in prison.

The second assassination attempt occurred on September 22, when Sara Jane Moore, a 45 year-old political activist, shot at Ford as he was leaving a downtown hotel in San Francisco. A bystander foiled the attempt when he deflected the .38-caliber revolver and then grabbed it from Moore.

Screams emanated from the crowd of about 3,000 people when the sound of the gunshot ricocheted from the pavement. Many ducked for cover, and the president was surrounded by Secret Service agents and immediately led to his limousine. While he, an aide, and the agents crouched on the floor, the limousine sped to the airport.

Amazingly, Moore had been arrested the day before and cited for carrying an illegal handgun, which the police confiscated along with more than 100 bullets. Secret Service agents questioned her, but they allowed her to be released. In January 1976, Moore, like Fromme, received a life sentence.

The two assassination attempts reinforced the view that American society was deeply troubled. Many believed it had become unhinged, taken over by permissiveness and selfishness.

A Religious Revival

A sense of rootless drifting, a desire to escape from society's troubles, a continuation of countercultural spiritualism—all of these contributed to a surge in religion that became pronounced by the mid-1970s. Both the New Age movement and evangelical Christianity expanded.

The New Age movement had emerged back in 1971 and had its first major prophet in 1972, when Baba Ram Dass published *Be Here Now* (Baba Ram Dass was born Richard Alpert in Boston and taught with LSD-guru Timothy Leary at Harvard in the early 1960s. He took his new name after studying Hinduism in the Himalayas.) New Age included many different beliefs and practices: Zen Buddhism, channeling, and Wicca, along with therapeutic meditation, herbalism, and holistic medicine. Baby boomers especially flocked to the New Age movement in such numbers that it appeared to be a baby-boomer phenomenon.

In general, New Age practitioners rejected traditional religions, embraced self-discovery, and sought a spiritual rebirth to a new life. Some observers have labeled New Agers "self-centered." Others, however, insist the New Age belief in self-discovery meant changing the individual as a first step before changing society. Whatever the case, New Agers generally rejected social activism.

Along with the New Age movement, a fundamentalist religious revival gained momentum. Christian fundamentalists disliked New Agers, labeling then as pagan, but they actually shared something in common: the belief that individuals needed to be infused with a holy spirit to change their lives.

Christian pop music spread, as did Christian bookstores noted for selling Christian romance stories, posters, and T-shirts. Historian Bruce J. Schulman observes: "The evangelical awakening permeated American life, giving rise to a flourishing evangelical subculture with booming churches, schools, and service organizations."[40]

PUNK

By the early 1970s, some American youths were ready for a different type of rebellion, one to replace the now receding 1960s countercultural movement. These youths were disheartened by the failures of the counterculture and by their older brothers and sisters turning to a more standardized and vacuous pursuit of money and middle-class comfort. They were dissatisfied, even dismayed, by the direction rock music was taking as society shifted gears from the 1960s—rock still being the visceral asylum through which young America expressed itself. Consequently, they turned to a cutting-edge lifestyle, a cutting-edge form of music, namely punk.

More than jilted, more than jaded, these rebellious youths felt bored. Politics, consumerism, and pop culture offered nothing challenging, nothing biting to rip at mainstream society's smug values. Rock music had gravitated in, to them, two unequally appealing directions: concert rock with its elaborate staging and instrumentation (groups such as Pink Floyd and Yes) and country rock with its soft arrangements and sentimentality (here, performers such as the Eagles and Jackson Browne).

In this environment, some rock artists offered an alternative, a prepunk assault on rock's prevailing standards. Alice Cooper, for one, appeared on stage in garish makeup and wrapped in boa constrictors. The New York Dolls used raunchy songs and an androgynous look. "Looking for a Kiss," "Lonely Planet Boy," and "Pills" presented youths whose lives revolved around little more than avoiding boredom.

The group Television embraced the essence of punk musical style when they reached back to the "garage sound" of the British bands of the mid-1960s, such as The Who, the Kinks, and the Yardbirds. They made the rhythm guitar prominent and short, frenetic, three-chord songs emblematic.

A writer for the rock magazine *Creem* first used the phrase *punk rock* in 1971, but it was the group the Dictators who first used the word *punk* on a record, 1975's *Girl Crazy.* The music, said one punk rocker, described their lives more accurately than traditional rock and roll, lives filled with "McDonald's, beer, and TV reruns." The Dictator's music led to the publication of a magazine titled *Punk* and dedicated to the alternative scene.

Head-banging youths were attracted to punk bands such as the Sex Pistols in the mid-1970s; pictured here are the group's members Sid Vicious (his faced covered with Band-Aids), Steve Jones, Paul Cook, and Johnny Rotten. *(Reuters/Landor)*

At about the same time, in 1974, came the Ramones, with their 18-minute sets of short, fast, loud songs; like bottled-up energy suddenly released raw, seemingly music that any kid could put together, amateurism rather than professionalism being an essential feature of punk. The Ramones jumped and shook and pulsated as they played, and in the audience, spike-haired kids with safety pins stuck in their skin, jumped with them. By 1975, prominent publications were paying attention to the Ramones: the *New York Times,* the *Village Voice,* and *Rolling Stone.* Patti Smith was on the scene, too, her songs often more poetic and longer, but nonetheless alive with the energy and noise that marked punk.

The American punk scene converged with the British punk scene, notably the Sex Pistols. Derided in the British press for their boorish behavior, their crude, profanity-laced language, the Sex Pistols, with their lead singer Johnny Rotten (and later with bassist Sid Vicious), took audiences to a frenzy. Head-banging, projectile-throwing, beer-spitting youths wallowed in the music and attitude—a middle-finger salute to TV and consumer culture.

But punk burned out quickly, a victim of its inability to exceed its own outrageousness or to avoid its own promotion of conformist behavior. One punk rocker said he sensed the music form's demise in 1978 when its fans all began to look like Johnny Rotten. Symbolically, the breakup of the Sex Pistols that year and charges against Sid Vicious for fatally stabbing his 20-year-old girlfriend, Nancy, announced the end to punk. Yet, punk continued to work its influence through "new-wave" artists rooted in the music (and originally punk themselves), notably the Clash, and Talking Heads, Blondie, Elvis Costello and Devo, all of whom defined rock as the 1970s came to an end.

Americans and Soviets in Space

Astronaut Vance D. Brand peered through the small window of his Apollo spacecraft and into the darkness of space. What he saw on July 17, 1975, seemed unremarkable: a small speck of light in the distance. But that speck of light was a Soyuz spacecraft launched by the Soviet Union, and the event that soon unfolded was, indeed, quite remarkable: The Apollo and the Soyuz modules docked in a historic meeting of competing, and oftentimes antagonistic, space programs. "We have capture," the American commander said, not in reference to a conquest over any enemy but in reference to the successful docking maneuver.

The U.S. crew consisted of astronauts Thomas P. Stafford (the American mission commander), Deke Slayton, and Brand. The Soviet crew consisted of cosmonauts Alexey Leonov (the Soviet mission commander) and Valeriy Kubasov. Their docking proceeded perfectly. It came after more than two years of meetings between scientists and the flight crews from both countries.

> With the docking, Soviet Leader Leonid Brezhnev sent a message: To the cosmonauts Alexey Leonov, Valeriy Kubasov, Thomas Stafford, Vance Brand, Donald Slayton. Speaking on behalf of the Soviet people, and for myself, I congratulate you on this memorable event. . . . The whole world is watching with rapt attention and admiration your joint activities in fulfillment of the complicated program of scientific experiments.[41]

In addition to ceremonial exchanges—American and Soviet crews exchanged flags—the rendezvous resulted in 44 joint activities, including four crew transfers and several scientific experiments. Importantly, the mission proved the workability of a universal docking system, and it made possible future cooperative efforts, such as projects in the early 21st century by Americans and Soviets aboard the international space station.

The Apollo and the Soyuz separated on July 19, and on July 24, Apollo splashed down in the Pacific Ocean near Hawaii. For the United States, the mission marked an end to an era: It was the last flight in the Apollo program.

LOU BROCK AND FRANK ROBINSON

Back in 1962, Maury Wills of the Los Angeles Dodgers set the record for stolen bases in a single major league season when he took 104 of them. His record fell on September 10, 1974, when Lou Brock of the St. Louis Cardinals stole second base against the Philadelphia Phillies, thus reaching number 105.

It was Brock's second steal of the game, which was played in St. Louis. He stole second in the first inning before accomplishing his record-shattering feat when he zipped from first on a 0-1 count and beat out a wide throw from the catcher to the bag. After he stole the base, the umpire stopped the game and allowed Brock to address the crowd. "The left-field fans probably knew I was going to steal 105 before I did," he later said. "They were behind me all the way."[42]

Ever since Jackie Robinson broke the racial barrier in major league baseball in the late 1940s, the number of African Americans playing the sport had increased dramatically. Yet, despite such progress, no black had ever managed a major league club.

That changed in 1975 when the Cleveland Indians selected Frank Robinson to become the club's player-manager. In his long playing career, primarily with the Cincinnati Reds and the Baltimore Orioles, Robinson was known as a home-run and RBI leader. In 1966, he became only the 13th player to achieve the Triple Crown, by leading the American League in home runs (49), RBI (122) and batting average (.316). Beginning in 1968, Robinson managed a club in the Puerto Rican winter league. He wanted to manage a major league club but was frustrated in achieving his goal until the Indians called him. On October 4, 1976, Cleveland made Robinson a full-time manager.

Although Robinson led the Indians in 1976 to their first above-500 record in eight years, his teams failed to rise above mediocrity. Still, he paved the way for other African Americans to become managers, such as Cito Gaston, who led the Toronto Blue Jays to two world championships, Dusty Baker, who managed the San Francisco Giants to playoffs, and Felip Alou, who brought the Montreal Expos a measure of success.

MUHAMMAD ALI'S BOXING CHAMPIONSHIP

At a time when black Americans were showing intense pride in their African culture, Muhammad Ali traveled to Kinshasa, Zaire, to win back his heavyweight boxing title. Ali had been stripped of his championship because he had refused to be drafted into the U.S. military. Promoter Don King put together the October 1974 title bout between Ali and the reigning champ, George Foreman, labeling it "the Rumble in the Jungle." The oddsmakers favored Foreman, known for his powerful heavy punches and agility in the ring, talents that allowed him to enter the match unbeaten in 40 previous fights.

The "rumble" was more than a prize fight. It was a cultural event, marked by the staging of a musical concert featuring African-American performers and punctuated by Ali's heroic stature in Africa and his popularity in the United States where he had become a symbol of someone who had stood up for his principles against the government and had been subsequently persecuted because of his color.

The usually brash Ali stayed true to form in winning over the crowd in Kinshasa and playing with Foreman's mind. He entered the ring wearing a white satin robe trimmed with African designs as the spectators chanted "Ali, bomaye," meaning, "Ali, kill him." Then as Foreman sat in his corner having his gloves adjusted, Ali walked by, taunting him. Ali followed a strategy of hitting Foreman in the first round with a hard punch—one that let the champ know that he was in for a tough fight—then dancing away from his opponent, avoiding his punches and tiring him out, and finally, in the sixth round, with Foreman frustrated and weary, charging forward, aggressively. In the eighth round, Ali knocked Foreman out with a left–right combination. Author George Plimpton later recounted about Ali's strategy: "In the sixth round, Ali came off the ropes. He seemed fresh, almost *titanic* in size, while Foreman before our eyes seemed to deflate, small in comparison."[43]

With his victory, Ali became only the second heavyweight boxer to win back his title, the other being Floyd Patterson who lost the championship to Ingemar Johansson in 1959 but won it back in 1960. The fight began with a full moon lighting the African landscape; it ended in the early morning with a torrential downpour, a testament to the deluge that had beaten Foreman, that wiped away Ali's critics, and that answered those who had attacked him and demoralized him by taking away his title because of his beliefs; a career righted in the stormy turbulence of a heavily divided American society.

CHRONICLE OF EVENTS

August 1974–December 1974

August 9: At 12:03 P.M. Supreme Court Justice Warren E. Burger administers the presidential oath of office to vice president Gerald R. Ford. Just minutes before, outgoing president Richard Nixon handed his resignation letter to Secretary of State Henry Kissinger and boarded a plane for his home in San Clemente, California. Ford promises an administration of "openness and candor" and states that "our long national nightmare is over." He asks Americans to put Watergate behind them.

August 20: President Ford nominates former New York governor Nelson A. Rockefeller for vice president.

August 20: The House of Representatives votes, 412-3, to accept the report compiled by its Judiciary Committee that recommended the impeachment of President Richard Nixon. Had Nixon not resigned, the action of the House would have resulted in his impeachment and placed the president on trial in the Senate. Two days later, the House publishes the committee report, 528 pages long, containing the evidence to support the three articles of impeachment the committee had approved.

September 7: The *New York Times* reports on how the CIA acted from 1970 to 1973 to undermine the presidency of Salvador Allende in Chile. Later in the month, President Gerald Ford acknowledges the CIA activities in Chile and defends them because, he says, Allende was trying to destroy freedom in that country.

September 8: President Ford announces that he is granting an unconditional pardon to Richard Nixon for any federal crimes he committed, or may have committed, or took part in while serving as president. Ford's decision unleashes a storm of protest; his press secretary, J. F. terHorst, resigns, saying that he cannot condone this action while so many of Nixon's former aides were in prison or under indictment. At a press conference a few days later, Ford denies that he had made any kind of a deal with Nixon before the former president resigned his office.

September 8: Daredevil Evil Knievel fails to complete his 1,600-foot jump over the Snake River Canyon in Idaho. Problems arose when the parachute on his steam-powered motorcycle opened too soon.

September 10: Infielder Lou Brock of the St. Louis Cardinals sets a major-league baseball record when he steals his 105th base of the season.

September 12: Violence erupts at South Boston High School in Massachusetts to protest the start of court-ordered busing to integrate the city's public schools. Only 100 of 1,500 students at the school attend classes, and Boston's mayor, Kevin H. White, is forced to provide police escorts for the schoolbuses.

September 16: U.S. District Court Judge Fred J. Nichol dismisses all charges against Dennis Banks and Russell Means for their leadership of the 1973 Indian protest at Wounded Knee, South Dakota. Nichol condemns the FBI for lying and suborning perjury at the trial.

September 25: U.S. District Court Judge J. Robert Elliott overturns the conviction of Lieutenant William Calley in the 1968 massacre of civilians at My Lai in Vietnam. Elliott rules that pretrial publicity had made it impossible for Calley to receive a fair hearing.

October 1: Five former aides to President Nixon who were officials in the Nixon reelection campaign stand trial on charges of conspiracy, obstructing justice, and perjury. The defendants are John D. Ehrlichman (domestic adviser to the president), H. R. Haldeman (chief of staff), John N. Mitchell (attorney general), Robert C. Mardian (assistant to Mitchell), and Kenneth W. Parkinson (attorney for the Committee to Reelect the President).

October 8: President Ford announces a program to "whip inflation now." He proposes a 5 percent surcharge on corporate and individual income taxes as well as restraints to keep spending below $300 billion.

October 21: U.S. District Court Judge Charles R. Richey issues a restraining order against the White House to prevent President Ford from going ahead with a previously announced agreement for the handling of the Watergate tapes. Ford had said that he would allow Nixon to destroy the tapes in three years.

October 29: Former President Richard Nixon experiences extensive internal bleeding after having surgery to prevent possible clotting in his left leg. He remains on the critical list for several days.

October 30: Muhammad Ali knocks out George Foreman in the eighth round of their boxing match in Zaire and becomes only the second fighter to ever regain the world heavyweight championship. The World Boxing Association had stripped Ali of his championship in 1967 for refusing to serve in the military.

November 4: The prosecutor at the Watergate cover-up trial discloses a memo written by E. Howard Hunt that shows that the Nixon administration had promised money and pardons to the Watergate break-in defendants. A few days later, the jury hears a Watergate tape from April 1973 in which President Nixon tells his aides that he will give full pardons to those involved in the break-in.

November 8: U.S. District Court Judge Frank J. Battisti acquits eight members of the Ohio national guard of violating the civil rights of students during the antiwar protests in 1970 at Kent State University.

November 13: Karen Silkwood, a technician for the Kerr-McGee Corporation lab and a vocal critic of safety procedures at the company's nuclear plant where she works, dies in a mysterious car accident while on her way to meet with a reporter from the *New York Times.*

December 11: President Ford says the economy has slipped into a recession, but he rejects the implementation of wage and price controls.

December 18: Congress passes legislation to fight the deepening recession. The measures include $2 billion for increased unemployment compensation and $875 million for state and local governments to create public service jobs for the unemployed.

December 19: Former New York governor Nelson A. Rockefeller is sworn in as the 41st vice president of the United States. He is the second person (Gerald Ford having been the first) to obtain the office through a vote of Congress.

December 21: The *New York Times* reports that the CIA has engaged in domestic spying in violation of its charter. The spying was aimed at antiwar and other dissident groups and included illegal break-ins and wiretapping.

December 30: President Ford pocket vetoes a bill to put stricter environmental controls on strip mining by requiring coal operators to restore the land to near its original condition.

1975

January 1: A jury in the U.S. District Court in Washington, D.C., finds John Mitchell, H. R. Haldeman, John Ehrlichman, and Robert Mardian guilty of all charges connected to the cover-up of the Watergate break-in. A fifth defendant, Kenneth W. Parkinson, is acquitted.

January 2: A federal judge rules that former Beatle John Lennon may have access to files from the Immigration Department that will shed light on why the federal government has been trying to deport him from the United States. Later in the month, Lennon files a suit, claiming that he is being persecuted for his political beliefs.

January 4: The Labor Department reports that unemployment reached 7.1 percent in December, a 13-year high. This news foreshadows more bad economic news: The Commerce Department will soon report that the real GNP for the last quarter of 1974 had dropped 9.1 percent, the worst decline in 16 years.

January 4: President Ford announces the formation of a special panel to investigate allegations of illegal CIA spying within the United States. The following day, he will appoint Vice President Nelson Rockefeller to head the investigation.

January 13: President Ford announces on national TV that he is reversing course and instead of opposing tax cuts, he will seek to have Congress enact a $16 billion tax cut that includes rebates of up to $1,000 to individual taxpayers on their 1974 taxes.

January 15: President Ford presents his State of the Union message in which he paints a dire economic picture. He predicts that the federal deficit will increase and that, by 1976, the debt will top $500 billion; he calls for a reduction in the dependence on imported oil so that by 1985, the country will no longer be vulnerable to the manipulations of foreign suppliers. Toward that end, he announces that he will raise import fees on oil.

January 21: The Labor Department reports that the consumer price index rose 12.4 percent in 1974, the highest annual rate in more than 25 years.

Mrs. Ford and Happy Rockefeller embrace in the White House while President Ford greets the recently confirmed vice president, Nelson Rockefeller, and the Rockefellers' two sons. *(Courtesy Gerald R. Ford Library)*

January 27: The Senate, by an 82–4 vote, establishes a bipartisan committee to investigate accusations of illegal activities by the CIA. Frank Church (Dem., Idaho), is named chairman, and the committee will be popularly called the Church committee.

February 5: The House, and later the Senate, passes legislation to prevent President Ford from raising the fees on imported oil for 90 days.

February 7: The Labor Department reports unemployment reached 8.2 percent in January, the highest level since 1941. Just days before, President Ford projected a nearly $52 billion deficit, the largest in the nation's history during a time of peace; and just a few days later, the Federal Reserve Board reported a steep decline in industrial production.

February 21: Judge John Sirica sentences former Nixon aides John Mitchell, H. R. Haldeman, and John Ehrlichman to two-and-a-half to eight years in prison for their roles in the Watergate cover-up and conspiracy. Robert Mardian, the former assistant attorney general, is sentenced to 10 months to three years.

February 27: Attorney General Edward Levi reveals that former FBI Director J. Edgar Hoover had compiled damaging personal information about presidents, members of Congress, and other political leaders who had opposed him. Levi's statement confirms what many observers had suspected for years: Hoover used the FBI to intimidate politicians.

March 12: Maurice H. Stans, former finance director for Richard Nixon's Committee to Reelect the President, pleads guilty to five misdemeanor charges of violating campaign laws.

March 22: Secretary of State Henry Kissinger announces that he is suspending his Middle East peace mission because of his inability to arrange compromises between Israel and Egypt.

March 26: Congress passes a compromise tax cut bill totaling $22.8 billion that gives individual taxpayers rebates on their 1974 taxes.

April 4: The Labor Department reports yet another increase in unemployment, to 8.7 percent in March. The number of unemployed, 8 million, reaches the highest level since 1940.

April 19: Van McCoy & the Soul Symphony's "The Hustle" moves up the charts as one of the first widely popular disco songs.

April 21: President Nyugen Van Thieu resigns as leader of South Vietnam as communist forces advance on Saigon. He bitterly accuses the United States of abandoning his government.

April 29: President Ford orders the evacuation of Americans from Saigon after communists assault the city's Tan Son Nhut airport.

April 30: South Vietnam announces its unconditional surrender to the communist Viet Minh. Just hours earlier, U.S. helicopters evacuated the last Americans, 395 in all, along with 4,475 South Vietnamese, from Saigon to U.S. ships offshore, in a scene characterized by panic.

May 12: A Cambodian naval ship attacks the U.S. merchant ship *Mayaguez* and forces it into port at Sihanoukville; President Ford tries to gain its release through diplomatic maneuvers.

May 14: With the failure of diplomacy, President Ford orders U.S. troops to rescue the *Mayaguez*. American planes sink three Cambodian gunboats, and 200 Marines battle Cambodian troops on Tang Island in the Gulf of Siam for 12 hours. The Americans, however, are unable to find the *Mayaguez* crew. Presently, the Cambodian government releases them. The U.S. suffered heavy casualties: 38 killed and 50 wounded.

May 16: Congress approves $405 million to resettle South Vietnamese and Cambodian refugees in the United States.

May 27: President Ford again imposes an increase in fees on foreign oil after he accuses Congress of failing to address the country's growing dependence on imported oil.

Vietnamese refugees board the USS *Durham* in the South China Sea. (*National Archives and Records Administration*)

May 27: The Alaska supreme court issues a ruling legalizing the use of marijuana in the privacy of the home. The court finds that the drug poses no significant health problem.

June 6: The government reports yet another increase in the unemployment rate, to 9.2 percent, despite an increase in the total number of people employed.

June 10: The Rockefeller Commission releases its report on CIA activities within the United States and concludes that the covert agency engaged in numerous illegal activities (although the vast majority of its actions were within the law). Those activities included operation CHAOS, a program to spy on domestic political groups, and programs to intercept phone calls to Europe and Latin America and open mail between the United States and the Soviet Union.

June 10: The New York state legislature creates the Municipal Assistance Corporation (nicknamed Big Mac) to refinance New York City's debt and prevent the municipality from defaulting on $729 million worth of notes due on June 11.

June 25: Stephen Spielberg's movie *Jaws* becomes a blockbuster and puts beachgoers on edge about predatory sharks.

June 26: Two FBI agents, Jack R. Coler and Ronald A. Williams, are killed in disputed circumstances on the Pine Ridge Reservation in South Dakota. A shootout leaves one Indian dead. The FBI claims that the agents were shot at by members of the militant American Indian Movement (AIM), but AIM disputes the allegation.

July 8: President Ford announces that he will seek the Republican presidential nomination. He says he wants to complete the job he has started.

July 17: An Apollo spacecraft from the United States and a Soyuz spacecraft from the Soviet Union link in space, and the astronauts from each country shake hands. The following day, they exchange visits and share meals. The crafts undock two days later.

July 18: The *New York Times* reports that a biochemist who headed a secret LSD program run by the CIA destroyed all the program's records in 1973 to hide details about illegal operations.

July 30: James Hoffa, the former head of the Teamsters Union, disappears outside a restaurant in Bloomfield Township, Michigan. The FBI joins the search for him on August 3.

July 31: New York City mayor Abraham Beame announces an austerity plan that will impose a wage freeze on all city workers and cut $32 million from the city university budget. Moreover, the plan increases transit fares, commuter railroad fares, and most bridge and tunnel tolls.

August 1: The Labor Department announces a drop in unemployment to 8.4 percent for July, but a few days later, it announces a sharp upward movement in consumer prices.

August 27: A federal court jury in Cleveland, Ohio, acquits Ohio Governor James Rhodes, former Kent State University President Robert White, and 27 members of the Ohio National Guard for all responsibility in the 1970 Kent State shootings. The trial was held to consider a $46 million suit against the defendants by the parents of the four students killed.

September 5: Lynette Alice "Squeaky" Fromme, 26 years old, attempts to assassinate President Ford as he enters the California capitol in Sacramento. A Secret Service agent stops Fromme when he spots her carrying a pistol.

September 10: The U.S. Fifth Circuit Court of Appeals in New Orleans reinstates the court-martial conviction of Lieutenant William Calley for the murder of 22 civilians at My Lai in Vietnam. The army, however, had previously stated that it was granting Calley parole.

September 18: The FBI captures Patricia Hearst in San Francisco, ending a 19-month search for her that began with her abduction by the Symbionese Liberation Front (SLF). She was kidnapped in February 1974 and that May announced that she was voluntarily remaining as a member of the group to help them in their fight for the "freedom of the oppressed people."

September 22: Sara Jane Moore, 45, tries to kill President Ford as he leaves the St. Francis Hotel in San Francisco. Her shot, from a .38-caliber revolver, misses its target when a civilian bystander grabs her arm. It is the second assassination attempt on the president in less than a month.

October 1: Muhammad Ali defeats former heavyweight champion Joe Frazier to retain his title in a fight in the Philippines, which is called by Ali the "Thrilla' in Manila."

October 11: The NBC comedy show *Saturday Night Live* premieres with guest host George Carlin and an ensemble cast that includes John Belushi, Chevy Chase, Dan Akroyd, and Gilda Radner.

October 20: The United States and the Soviet Union sign an agreement under which the Russians promise to purchase 6–8 million tons of American grain each year for five years.

October 29: President Ford says he opposes giving New York City federal loan guarantees and that he will veto any congressional legislation doing such. New York City Mayor Abraham Beame condemns Ford's position; he earlier noted that the city's continuing financial crisis would cause it to default by December 1 unless it received aid.

November 12: Supreme Court Associate Justice William O. Douglas retires from the court at age 77. Douglas had served since his appointment by President Franklin Roosevelt, more than 36 years ago. He had a reputation for being among the most liberal members of the court and, over the years, had earned the enmity of conservatives who labeled him an "activist."

November 17: Black militant Eldridge Cleaver is arrested in New York City after he returns from exile. Cleaver faces charges of fleeing to avoid confinement and of murder connected to a shootout between the Black Panthers and the police in Oakland, California, in 1968.

November 21: The Church committee, the Senate committee investigating CIA activities, publishes a report that says that U.S. government officials instigated assassination plots against Fidel Castro, premier of Cuba, and Patrice Lumumba, leader of the Congo, and were involved in plots that led to the deaths of Ngo Dinh Diem, president of South Vietnam; Rafael Trujillo, dictator of the Dominican Republic; and General Rene Schneider, chief of the general staff of Chile.

November 26: A federal grand jury in Sacramento, California, finds Lynette Alice "Squeaky" Fromme guilty of attempting to kill President Ford. In December, she will be sentenced to life in prison.

November 26: President Ford changes his position and asks Congress to approve $2.3 billion in short-term loans to New York City so that it can avoid default. Legislation will quickly pass, and Ford will sign it into law.

December 9: Federal District Court Judge W. Arthur Garrity places South Boston High School under federal receivership. He claims that the Boston School Committee (the school board) had hindered the implementation of his June 1974 order to desegregate the high school through busing.

By early 1975, unemployment among blacks reached 16 percent. Here, a jobless African-American man sits on a windowsill of a building on Chicago's South Side. *(National Archives and Records Administration)*

December 16: Federal District Court Judge Samuel Conti accepts the guilty plea made by Sara Jane Moore on the charge of attempting to assassinate the president. The next month, Moore will be sentenced to life in prison.

December 22: President Ford signs an energy bill that reduces the price of crude oil, and he removes a $2-per-barrel fee that he had imposed on imported crude oil.

December 22: A special state investigator releases a report on the Attica prison riot of 1971, one in which he states that the initial investigation into the riot contained "serious errors in judgment."

EYEWITNESS TESTIMONY

Gerald Ford Becomes President

Mr. Chief Justice, my dear friends, my fellow Americans:

The oath that I have taken is the same oath that was taken by George Washington and by every President under the Constitution. But I assume the Presidency under extraordinary circumstances never before experienced by Americans. This is an hour of history that troubles our minds and hurts our hearts.

Therefore, I feel it is my first duty to make an unprecedented compact with my countrymen. Not an inaugural address, not a fireside chat, not a campaign speech—just a little straight talk among friends. And I intend it to be the first of many.

I am acutely aware that you have not elected me as your President by your ballots, and so I ask you to confirm me as your President with your prayers. And I hope that such prayers will also be the first of many.

If you have not chosen me by secret ballot, neither have I gained office by any secret promises. I have not campaigned either for the Presidency or the Vice Presidency. I have not subscribed to any partisan platform. I am indebted to no man, and only to one woman—my dear wife—as I begin this very difficult job.

I have not sought this enormous responsibility, but I will not shirk it. Those who nominated and confirmed me as Vice President were my friends and are my friends. They were of both parties, elected by all the people and acting under the Constitution in their name. It is only fitting then that I should pledge to them and to you that I will be the President of all the people. . . .

Thomas Jefferson said the people are the only sure reliance for the preservation of our liberty. And down the years, Abraham Lincoln renewed this American article of faith asking, "Is there any better way or equal hope in the world?"

I intend, on Monday next, to request of the Speaker of the House of Representatives and the President pro tempore of the Senate the privilege of appearing before the Congress to share with my former colleagues and with you, the American people, my views on the priority business of the Nation and to solicit your views and their views. And may I say to the Speaker and the others, if I could meet with you right after these remarks, I would appreciate it.

Even though this is late in an election year, there is no way we can go forward except together and no way anybody can win except by serving the people's urgent needs. We cannot stand still or slip backwards. We must go forward now together.

To the peoples and the governments of all friendly nations, and I hope that could encompass the whole world, I pledge an uninterrupted and sincere search for peace. America will remain strong and united, but its strength will remain dedicated to the safety and sanity of the entire family of man, as well as to our own precious freedom.

I believe that truth is the glue that holds government together, not only our Government but civilization itself. That bond, though strained, is unbroken at home and abroad.

In all my public and private acts as your President, I expect to follow my instincts of openness and candor with full confidence that honesty is always the best policy in the end.

My fellow Americans, our long national nightmare is over.

Our Constitution works; our great Republic is a government of laws and not of men. Here the people rule. But there is a higher Power, by whatever name we honor Him, who ordains not only righteousness but love, not only justice but mercy.

As we bind up the internal wounds of Watergate, more painful and more poisonous than those of foreign wars, let us restore the golden rule to our political process, and let brotherly love purge our hearts of suspicion and of hate.

In the beginning, I asked you to pray for me. Before closing, I ask again your prayers, for Richard Nixon and for his family. May our former President, who brought peace to millions, find it for himself. May God bless and comfort his wonderful wife and daughters, whose love and loyalty will forever be a shining legacy to all who bear the lonely burdens of the White House.

I can only guess at those burdens, although I have witnessed at close hand the tragedies that befell three Presidents and the lesser trials of others.

With all the strength and all the good sense I have gained from life, with all the confidence my family, my friends, and my dedicated staff impart to me, and with the good will of countless Americans I have encountered in recent visits to 40 States, I now solemnly reaffirm my promise I made to you last December 6: to uphold the Constitution, to do what is right as God gives me to see the right, and to do the very best I can for America.

God helping me, I will not let you down.

Gerald Ford's statement on taking the oath of office as president on August 9, 1974, in the East Room of the White House, available online at http://www.ford. utexas.edu/library/speeches/740001.htm, downloaded June 28, 2004.

The Pardon of Richard Nixon

Ladies and gentlemen:

I have come to a decision which I felt I should tell you and all of my fellow American citizens, as soon as I was certain in my own mind and in my own conscience that it is the right thing to do. . . .

I have learned already in this office that the difficult decisions always come to this desk. I must admit that many of them do not look at all the same as the hypothetical questions that I have answered freely and perhaps too fast on previous occasions.

My customary policy is to try and get all the facts and to consider the opinions of my countrymen and to take counsel with my most valued friends. But these seldom agree, and in the end, the decision is mine. To procrastinate, to agonize, and to wait for a more favorable turn of events that may never come or more compelling external pressures that may as well be wrong as right, is itself a decision of sorts and a weak and potentially dangerous course for a President to follow.

I have promised to uphold the Constitution, to do what is right as God gives me to see the right, and to do the very best that I can for America.

I have asked your help and your prayers, not only when I became President but many times since. The Constitution is the supreme law of our land and it governs our actions as citizens. Only the laws of God, which govern our consciences, are superior to it.

As we are a nation under God, so I am sworn to uphold our laws with the help of God. And I have sought such guidance and searched my own conscience with special diligence to determine the right thing for me to do with respect to my predecessor in this place, Richard Nixon, and his loyal wife and family.

Theirs is an American tragedy in which we all have played a part. It could go on and on and on, or someone must write the end to it. I have concluded that only I can do that, and if I can, I must. . . .

There are no historic or legal precedents to which I can turn in this matter, none that precisely fit the circumstances of a private citizen who has resigned the Presidency of the United States. But it is common knowledge that serious allegations and accusations hang like a sword over our former President's head, threatening his health as he tries to reshape his life, a great part of which was spent in the service of this country and by the mandate of its people.

After years of bitter controversy and divisive national debate, I have been advised, and I am compelled to conclude that many months and perhaps more years will have to pass before Richard Nixon could obtain a fair trial by jury in any jurisdiction of the United States under governing decisions of the Supreme Court.

I deeply believe in equal justice for all Americans, whatever their station or former station. The law, whether human or divine, is no respecter of persons; but the law is a respecter of reality.

The facts, as I see them, are that a former President of the United States, instead of enjoying equal treatment with any other citizen accused of violating the law, would be cruelly and excessively penalized either in preserving the presumption of his innocence or in obtaining a speedy determination of his guilt in order to repay a legal debt to society.

During this long period of delay and potential litigation, ugly passions would again be aroused. And our people would again be polarized in their opinions. And the credibility of our free institutions of government would again be challenged at home and abroad.

In the end, the courts might well hold that Richard Nixon had been denied due process, and the verdict of history would even more be inconclusive with respect to those charges arising out of the period of his Presidency, of which I am presently aware. But it is not the ultimate fate of Richard Nixon that most concerns me, though surely it deeply troubles every decent and every compassionate person. My concern is the immediate future of this great country. . . .

In this, I dare not depend upon my personal sympathy as a long-time friend of the former President, nor my professional judgment as a lawyer, and I do not.

As President, my primary concern must always be the greatest good of all the people of the United States whose servant I am. As a man, my first consideration is to be true to my own convictions and my own conscience.

My conscience tells me clearly and certainly that I cannot prolong the bad dreams that continue to reopen

President Ford announces his pardon of Richard Nixon. *(Courtesy Gerald R. Ford Library)*

a chapter that is closed. My conscience tells me that only I, as President, have the constitutional power to firmly shut and seal this book. My conscience tells me it is my duty, not merely to proclaim domestic tranquility but to use every means that I have to insure it. I do believe that the buck stops here, that I cannot rely upon public opinion polls to tell me what is right. I do believe that right makes might and that if I am wrong, 10 angels swearing I was right would make no difference. I do believe, with all my heart and mind and spirit, that I, not as President but as a humble servant of God, will receive justice without mercy if I fail to show mercy.

Finally, I feel that Richard Nixon and his loved ones have suffered enough and will continue to suffer, no matter what I do, no matter what we, as a great and good nation, can do together to make his goal of peace come true.

Now, therefore, I, Gerald R. Ford, President of the United States, pursuant to the pardon power conferred upon me by Article II, Section 2, of the Constitution, have granted and by these presents do grant a full, free, and absolute pardon unto Richard Nixon for all offenses against the United States which he, Richard Nixon, has committed or may have committed or taken part in during the period from July (January) 20, 1969 through August 9, 1974.

In witness whereof, I have hereunto set my hand this eighth day of September, in the year of our Lord nineteen hundred and seventy-four, and of the Independence of the United States of America the one hundred and ninety-ninth.

President Gerald Ford's pardon of former President Richard Nixon, as presented to the American people on national television on September 8, 1974, available online at http://www.watergate.info/ford/pardon.shtml, downloaded June 28, 2004.

I have been informed that President Ford has granted me a full and absolute pardon for any charges which might be brought against me for actions taken during the time I was president of the United States.

In accepting this pardon, I hope that his compassionate act will contribute to lifting the burden of Watergate from our country.

Here in California, my perspective on Watergate is quite different than it was while I was embattled in the midst of the controversy, and while I was still subject to the unrelenting daily demands of the presidency itself.

Looking back on what is still in my mind a complex and confusing maze of events, decisions, pressures and personalities, one thing I can see clearly now is that I was wrong in not acting more decisively and more forthrightly in dealing with Watergate, particularly when it reached the stage of judicial proceedings and grew from a political scandal into a national tragedy.

No words can describe the depths of my regret and pain at the anguish my mistakes over Watergate have caused the nation and the presidency—a nation I so deeply love and an institution I so greatly respect.

I know many fair-minded people believe that my motivations and action in the Watergate affair were intentionally self-serving and illegal. I now understand how my own mistakes and misjudgments have contributed to that belief and seemed to support it. This burden is the heaviest one of all to bear.

That the way I tried to deal with Watergate was the wrong way is a burden I shall bear for every day of the life that is left to me.

Former President Richard Nixon's response on September 8, 1974, to the full pardon granted to him by President Ford, available online at http://www.watergate.info/ford/pardon.shtml, downloaded June 28, 2004.

I am concerned about what this action will do to the government's case against other accused Watergate conspirators.

I can't tell from the president's action where we will be able to stop pardoning and start prosecuting. I gather that President Ford's action had the weight of law behind it, but my concern is whether this action will hinder disclosure of the facts.

We operate under the assumption that justice delayed is justice denied. What we have here is justice suspended.

Neither Mr. Nixon nor the American people have the benefit of full airing of the facts, and there was justice for neither side.

I don't think that as governor under similar circumstances I would have taken this action. I understand the desire to put this sordid chapter behind us, and I know that there are those who feel Mr. Nixon had suffered enough. But in a case like this I think compassion must give way to law.

The reaction of Democratic Texas governor Dolph Briscoe on September 8, 1974, to President Ford's pardon of Nixon, available online at http://www.tsl.state.tx.us/ governors/modern/briscoe-nixon-1.html, downloaded June 28, 2004.

Throughout the most painful week of Gerald Ford's fledgling presidency, public protest continued to batter the White House. Far from easing after the first shock of Ford's precipitate pardon of Richard Nixon for any and all federal crimes committed during his presidency, the controversy grew. It was fed partly by Ford's refusal to explain further his mysterious reversal on his Executive intervention, partly by White House fumbling on whether all the other Watergate offenders might also be pardoned.

There was as yet no evidence that Ford's motives were other than high-minded and merciful. Indeed, some of the criticisms of his action were overwrought and hysterical. Nevertheless, Ford's first major decision raised disturbing questions about his judgment and his leadership capabilities, and called into question his competence. He had apparently needlessly, even recklessly, squandered some of that precious public trust that is so vital to every President. By associating himself so personally with the welfare of his discredited predecessor, he had allowed himself to be tainted by Watergate.

The reaction of Time *magazine to Ford's pardon of Nixon, September 23, 1974, in* Time Magazine Multimedia Almanac *(1995).*

I'm not a medical doctor, but I really have serious questions in my mind whether that man is going to be alive at the time of the [1974] election.

White House lawyer Benton Becker reporting in September 1974 to President Gerald Ford on the condition of former President Richard Nixon after having visited Nixon at San Clemente, California, in Stephen Ambrose, Nixon: Ruin and Recovery *(1991), p. 460.*

I knew when I became President that hard decisions would produce some bitter reactions. Still, I wasn't prepared for the allegations that the Nixon pardon prompted. What I intended to convince my fellow citizens was necessary surgery—essential if we were to heal our wounded nation—was being attacked as a "secret deal" that I had worked out with Nixon before he resigned. . . . Any doubts that I might have had about this were dispelled . . . [in] Pittsburgh, where I was scheduled to speak before eight hundred delegates to a conference on urban transportation. "Jail Ford, Jail Ford," some demonstrators shouted. . . . I began to wonder whether, instead of healing the wounds, my decision had only rubbed salt in them.

President Gerald Ford recalling in 1979 some of the public reaction to his decision to pardon Richard Nixon, in Gerald Ford, A Time to Heal *(1979), p. 179.*

New York City and Bankruptcy

The New York City crisis was a major social, political, and financial crisis. A bankruptcy would have major consequences in each of these areas. Socially, New York is a tale of two cities. One of them is the city of wealth and privilege, of Park Avenue and Fifth Avenue, of gala benefits for the Metropolitan Opera and of Broadway openings. The other is the city of crumbling neighborhoods, the South Bronx and Bedford-Stuyvesant, crime and poverty, large Black and Hispanic populations dependent on public assistance and on public schools, both of which were inadequate. No one knew what bankruptcy would mean to welfare or Medicaid payments, to public housing or public health, to public schools or to public safety. A judge would have to make those decisions. But what we did know was that those who lived on Fifth and Park Avenues could leave, and those who lived in Bed-Stuy and in Crown Heights could not; that the funds available for public assistance would shrink; that the business exodus from the city would accelerate and permanently affect the city's tax base; and that there was every likelihood of major social unrest.

From a speech by Felix G. Rohatyn, former chairman of the Municipal Assistance Corporation, presented on February 26, 2003, available online at http://www.sipa.columbia.edu/NEWS/ Rohatyn%20speech.pdf, downloaded May 8, 2005.

Mr. Ford's mistake was in pitching his speech not to the people but to Congressional politicians before him whose pettiness and short-sightedness know no bounds. The Congressional response, like the Congressional performance on the economy these past ten months, was a disgrace.

David Broder, a columnist for the Washington Post, *writing in October 1974 about President Ford's appeal to Congress for policies to fight inflation, in Gerald Ford,* A Time to Heal *(1979), p. 196.*

Frankly, you've got to balance your own budget before you get a great deal of sympathy or help from other levels of government.

Vice President Nelson Rockefeller reacting in 1975 to New York City's financial crisis, in Fred Ferretti, The Year the Big Apple Went Bust *(1976), p. 117.*

I think the banks have to exercise the responsibility to let the public know that New York securities are good investments, to restore confidence in their investors. I think our program should be a strong catalyst to restore confidence, because we're trying to do things to reduce our need to go into the market as often as we do now.

New York City controller Harrison Goldin answering a reporter's question in March 1975 about Mayor Abraham Beame's proposal to ease the city's financial crisis, in Fred Ferretti, The Year the Big Apple Went Bust *(1976), p. 163.*

I knew we were overextended, of course, and I expected the other shoe to drop. But I thought that would mean we would finally have to face up to service cuts if the economy or the aid picture didn't improve sharply. I never expected the crisis would be a *financing* crisis.

David Grossman, New York City budget director, commenting around 1980 on the city's financial crisis, in Charles R. Morris, The Cost of Good Intentions *(1980), p. 239.*

Conviction of John Ehrlichman

John J. Sirica lived up to his reputation when he tried the [Watergate] "cover-up" case. As a lawyer I've tried hundreds of jury cases before all kinds of judges in the seventeen years I was at the bar. I know a good judge from an inept one, and I'm compelled to say Sirica was not good. I often felt that the *Star, Post* and TV networks were having an undue influence on his conduct of the trial. Furthermore, his methods of jury selection were hasty, careless and capricious. As a result his *voir dire* failed to disclose that one juror was a close friend of the Prosecutor. Another juror wrote a note confessing her bias partway through the trial. But Sirica left her on the jury, in spite of our objections.

Nevertheless, I am not able to say I could have been acquitted under different circumstances. There is no question that I had known money was going to the burglars and I had abetted its flow.

John Ehrlichman's observation in 1979 about his trial for the Watergate cover-up, in John Ehrlichman, Witness to Power *(1982), p. 397.*

Economic Hardship

If we can't finally control inflation, we won't have an economy left to argue about.

William Simon, President Ford's secretary of the Treasury, commenting in August 1974 on the state of the economy, in John Robert Greene, The Presidency of Gerald Ford *(1995), p. 71.*

I say to you that that our inflation, our public enemy number one, will, unless whipped, destroy our country, our homes, our liberties, our property and finally our national pride as surely as will any well-armed wartime enemy. . . . The time to intercept is right now . . . my friends and fellow Americans, will you enlist now?

President Gerald Ford calling on Americans in October 1974 to support his program to fight inflation, in Gerald Ford, A Time to Heal *(1979), p. 195.*

Busing in Boston

The streets are going to be clear in South Boston. No one will be allowed to disrupt students, buses, or traffic.

Any person, or group of persons, in the area of any school must have proper identification.

No crowd, or group of three or more people, will be allowed to congregate within the immediate vicinity of any public school. If groups form near schools they will be asked to disperse and move on. And if they refuse, they will be immediately arrested.

Boston Mayor Kevin H. White announcing restrictions on September 12, 1974, in the wake of violence surrounding the busing program to achieve racial integration in South Boston's public schools, in the New York Times, *September 13, 1974, p. 1.*

It was great. It's about time the politicians felt the anger of the people. We've been good for too long. They'd pat us on the backs, and we'd go home. No more.

South Boston resident Pat Ranese reacting in September 1974 to a violent demonstration against busing, in Ronald P. Formisano, Boston against Busing *(1991), p. 77.*

They take our schools, now they take our streets. . . . This is the most degrading thing to South Boston.

Antibusing leader Ray Flynn reacting in September 1974 to the police presence in South Boston, in Ronald P. Formisano, Boston against Busing *(1991), p. 77.*

The Collapse of South Vietnam

"You fifteen people on that chopper! Run. Now. Go. Run!" We ran, through a cyclone of steaming air whipped up by the helicopter's spinning rotors. You don't think and you don't feel. With eyes gripped on that chopper, you run. Hundreds of marines in flak jackets and helmets, carrying M-16s, seemed to be bursting through space. The chopper had its tail ramp up; I threw in a bag, but couldn't make it. Someone grabbed my arm and I was dragged onboard and

Vietnamese await transportation during the evacuation from Saigon as that city fell to the communists in 1975. *(National Archives and Records Administration)*

across the floor. Seconds later, in a roar, the chopper lifted off.

Reporter Laura Palmer recounting her experience in the evacuation from Saigon in April 1975 as communist troops closed in on the city, in Ashley Kahn, Holly George-Warren, Shawn Dahl, eds., Rolling Stone: The Seventies *(1998) p. 154.*

Church Committee Investigation

I am writing to urge the Select Committee not to make public the report on the subject of assassinations, which I understand is currently in preparation. Reviews of the Select Committee's draft assassination report by officials of the Departments of State and Defense and the Central Intelligence Agency, who examined it at the request of your committee, have been submitted to me by the heads of those departments and the agency. . . .

It is my opinion that public disclosure now of information I provided to the Senate Select Committee concerning allegations of political assassination activities of the United States Government will result in serious harm to the national interest and may endanger individuals.

As I stated publicly when the allegations were published, the very idea that any person or organization within the United States Government could consider assassination as an acceptable act is abhorrent. . . .

To facilitate legitimate investigation of allegations related to assassination, I have endeavored to make available all the materials in the executive branch on this subject to the Select Committees of the Senate and the House and the Department of Justice. This was done under procedures designed to serve the national interest. . . .

I have endeavored to make all of the information available to your committee so that legislation can be proposed, if necessary, and to the Justice Department to facilitate any investigation indicated. However, we must distinguish between disclosure to the Select Committee of sensitive information and publication of the information which is harmful to the national interest and may endanger the physical safety of individuals.

There is no question about access to these materials by appropriate officials. The only issue concerns publication, which obviously cannot be limited to members of Congress and other American citizens.

Public release of these official materials will do grievous damage to our country. It would likely be exploited by foreign nations and groups hostile to the United States in a manner designed to do maximum damage to the reputation and foreign policy of the United States. It would seriously impair our ability to exercise a positive role in world affairs.

I am convinced that publication at this time will endanger individuals named in the report or who can be identified when foreign agents carefully study it. I am sure none of us want such an unfortunate result. I urge that we avoid any action that would bring it about.

I have sought to balance the competing interests involved in this matter. I made relevant intelligence information and documents available. . . . However, to protect our national defense and ability to conduct foreign affairs, as well as the traditional American right of individual privacy, I have provided most of this information in classified form.

There can be legislation, if deemed necessary, and prosecutions, if warranted. But let us do this without the damage to the United States which will occur if this information is made available to actual and potential enemies of the United States. . . .

I am sure the Select Committee will recognize the enormous responsibility it has to see to it that serious damage will not result to the United States by the publication of this report and will recognize also the duty which I have to emphasize the disastrous consequences which can occur by publication.

Letter dated November 4, 1975, from President Gerald Ford to the Church committee (the Select Committee to Study Governmental Operations with Respect to Intelligence Activities) urging the committee to keep from the public its report on the subject of assassinations, in the New York Times, *November 5, 1975, p. 18.*

The events discussed in this Interim Report must be viewed in the context of United States policy and actions designed to counter the threat of spreading Communism. Following the end of World War II, many nations in Eastern Europe and elsewhere fell under Communist influence or control. The defeat of the Axis powers was accompanied by rapid disintegration of the Western colonial empires. The Second World War had no sooner ended than a new struggle began. The Communist threat, emanating from what came to be called the "Sino-Soviet bloc," led to a policy of containment intended to prevent further encroachment into the "Free World."

United States strategy for conducting the Cold War called for the establishment of interlocking treaty arrangements and military bases throughout the world. Concern over the expansion of an aggressive Communist monolith led the United States to fight two major wars in Asia. In addition, it was considered necessary to wage a relentless cold war against Communist expansion wherever it appeared in the "back alleys of the world." This called for a full range of covert activities in response to the operations of Communist clandestine services.

The fear of Communist expansion was particularly acute in the United States when Fidel Castro emerged as Cuba's leader in the late 1950's. His takeover was seen as the first significant penetration by the Communists into the Western Hemisphere. United States leaders, including most Members of Congress, called for vigorous action to stem the Communist infection in this hemisphere. These policies rested on widespread popular support and encouragement.

Throughout this period, the United States felt impelled to respond to threats which were, or seemed to be, skirmishes in a global Cold War against Communism. Castro's Cuba raised the specter of a Soviet outpost at America's doorstep. Events in the Dominican Republic appeared to offer an additional opportunity for the Russians and their allies. The Congo, freed from Belgian rule, occupied the strategic center of the African continent, and the prospect of Communist penetration there was viewed as a threat to American interests in emerging African nations. There was great concern that a Communist takeover in Indochina would have a "domino effect" throughout Asia. Even the election in 1970 of a Marxist president in Chile was seen by some as a threat similar to that of Castro's takeover in Cuba.

The Committee regards the unfortunate events dealt with in this Interim Report as an aberration explainable at least in part, but not justified, by the pressures of the time. The Committee believes that it is still in the national interest of the United States to help nations achieve self-determination and resist Communist domination. However, it is clear that this interest cannot justify resorting to the kind of abuses covered in this report. Indeed, the Committee has resolved that steps must be taken to prevent those abuses from happening again.

The prologue to the Church committee report published November 25, 1975, outlining the context in which abuses by intelligence agencies occurred, available online at http://history-matters.com/archive/church/reports/ir/html/ChurchIR_0008a.htm, downloaded June 29, 2004.

We have found concrete evidence of at least eight plots involving the CIA to assassinate Fidel Castro from 1960 to 1965. Although some of the assassination plots did not advance beyond the stage of planning and preparation, one plot, involving the use of underworld figures, reportedly twice progressed to the point of sending poison pills to Cuba and dispatching teams to commit the deed. Another plot involved furnishing weapons and other assassination devices to a Cuban dissident. The proposed assassination devices ran the gamut from high-powered rifles to poison pills, poison pens, deadly bacterial powders, and other devices which strain the imagination.

The most ironic of these plots took place on November 22, 1963—the very day that President Kennedy was shot in Dallas—when a CIA official offered a poison pen to a Cuban for use against Castro while at the same time an emissary from President Kennedy was meeting with Castro to explore the possibility of improved relations. . . .

Efforts against Castro did not begin with assassination attempts. From March through August 1960, during the last year of the Eisenhower Administration, the CIA considered plans to undermine Castro's charismatic appeal by sabotaging his speeches. According to the 1967 Report of the CIA's Inspector General, an official in the Technical Services Division (TSD) recalled discussing a scheme to spray Castro's

Senator Frank Church, pictured with President Carter, was instrumental in uncovering abuses in the mid-1970s by the CIA. *(Courtesy Jimmy Carter Library)*

broadcasting studio with a chemical which produced effects similar to LSD, but the scheme was rejected because the chemical was unreliable. During this period, TSD impregnated a box of cigars with a chemical which produced temporary disorientation, hoping to induce Castro to smoke one of the cigars before delivering a speech. The Inspector General also reported a plan to destroy Castro's image as "The Beard" by dusting his shoes with thallium salts, a strong depilatory that would cause his beard to fall out. The depilatory was to be administered during a trip outside Cuba, when it was anticipated Castro would leave his shoes outside the door of his hotel room to be shined. TSD procured the chemical and tested it on animals, but apparently abandoned the scheme because Castro cancelled his trip. . . .

Poison Cigars

A notation in the records of the Operations Division, CIA's Office of Medical Services, indicates that on August 16, 1960, an official was given a box of Castro's favorite cigars with instructions to treat them with lethal poison. The cigars were contaminated with a botulinum toxin so potent that a person would die after putting one in his mouth. The official reported that the cigars were ready on October 7, 1960; TSD notes indicate that they were delivered to an unidentified person on February 13, 1961. The record does not disclose whether an attempt was made to pass the cigars to Castro. . . .

> *An excerpt from the Church committee report of November 25, 1975, discussing attempts by the United States to kill Cuban leader Fidel Castro, available online at http://history-matters.com/archive/church/ reports/ir/html/ChurchIR_0043a.htm, downloaded June 29, 2004.*

What's wrong with overthrowing the government of Chile? It was a commie government, wasn't it?

> *Senator James Eastland (Dem., Miss.) reacting in 1975 to the furor over the CIA's role in the overthrow of Salvador Allende's government in Chile, in LeRoy Ashby and Rod Gramer,* Fighting the Odds *(1994), p. 471.*

Ours in not a wicked country and we cannot abide a wicked government.

> *Senator Frank Church (Dem., Idaho), commenting in June 1975 about abuses by the CIA and government leaders, including their actions in Chile, in LeRoy Ashby and Rod Gramer,* Fighting the Odds *(1994), p. 492.*

Government Involvement in Drug Experiments

From its beginning in the early 1950s until its termination in 1963, the program of surreptitious administration of LSD to unwitting non-volunteer human subjects demonstrates a failure of the CIA's leadership to pay adequate attention to the rights of individuals and to provide effective guidance to CIA employees. Though it was known that the testing was dangerous, the lives of subjects were placed in jeopardy and were ignored. . . . Although it was clear that the laws of the United States were being violated, the testing continued.

> *Conclusion in 1975 by a Senate committee investigating the CIA's MK-ULTRA program, available online at http://www.meta-religion.com/Secret_societies/ Conspiracies/Mind_Control/mkultra.htm.*

The Apollo-Soyuz Rendezvous

Deke Slayton:
Hello, Valeriy. How are you. Good day, Valeriy.
Valeriy Kubasov:
How are you? Good day.
Slayton:
Excellent. . . . I'm very happy. Good morning.
Leonov:
Apollo, Soyuz. How do you read me?
Slayton:
Alexey, I hear you excellently. How do you read me?
Leonov:
I read you loud and clear.
Slayton:
Good.

> *Conversation among the U.S. astronauts and the Soviet cosmonauts as they first made voice contact on the Apollo-Soyuz mission, the morning of July 17, 1975, in Edward Clinton Ezell and Linda Neuman Ezell,* The Partnership: A History of the Apollo-Soyuz Test Project, *available online at http://www.hq.nasa. gov/office/pao/History/SP-4209/ch11-3.htm, downloaded June 26, 2004.*

Gentlemen, let me call you to express my very great admiration for your hard work, your total dedication in preparing for this first joint flight. All of us here in . . . the United States send to you our very warmest congratulations for your successful rendezvous and for your docking and we wish you the very best for a successful completion of the remainder of your mission.

President Gerald Ford's message to the astronauts and cosmonauts in the Apollo-Soyuz mission on July 17, 1975, in Edward Clinton Ezell and Linda Neuman Ezell, The Partnership: A History of the Apollo-Soyuz Test Project, *available online at http://www.hq.nasa.gov/office/pao/History/ SP-4209/ch11-3.htm, downloaded June 26, 2004.*

Lou Brock's Stolen Base Record

Once I'm on first base, I can take a modest lead and stand perfectly still, without giving away any significant information about myself. But the pitcher is obliged to move, just to deliver the pitch, and in moving he telegraphs a whole catalog of data about himself. Furthermore, he has two things on his mind: the batter *and* me. I have only one thing in mind—to steal off him. The very business of disconcerting him is marvelously complex.

Lou Brock describing in 1974 his advantage over pitchers, in Lou Brock, Stealing Is My Game *(1976), p. 182.*

In my book that record, that stolen-base record, is somethin' tremendous, but it ain't all that Lou Brock is. He's—he's just all ballplayer. When I see him run from the dugout to left field, I say, "Now that's as pretty a baseball sight—just that guy runnin' out to his position—as you'd ever want to see."

Baseball player Ernie Banks commenting in 1974 on Lou Brock, in Lou Brock, Stealing Is My Game *(1976), p. 206.*

Muhammad Ali's Heavyweight Title

Under an African moon a few hours before dawn, the 32-year-old Ali sent his 25-year-old rival crashing to the floor with a left and a chopping right. It was a bee harassing a bear, stinging incessantly until his arm-weary adversary succumbed to sheer persistence.

Reporter Dave Anderson recounting on October 30, 1974, the fight between Muhammad Ali and George Forman in Zaire, in the New York Times, *October 30, 1974, p. 1.*

6
Bicentennial America
January 1976–December 1976

On July 4, 1976, Americans staged a grand bicentennial celebration, a salute to their founders who, 200 years earlier, declared the United States to be a nation independent from Britain, and a salute to those who since that time had made their country great. Reporter Jon Nordheimer, writing on Independence Day, observed: "The American people are moving into their third century . . . with their institutions intact and with an economic and military strength beyond the visions of the courtly men who fathered the nation based on democratic principles."[1]

Yet, the tremendous travails of the 1970s (and of the 1960s), along with continuing social and economic problems, had damaged confidence. In interviews with everyday people, politicians, and academicians, Nordheimer found "self-doubts uncharacteristic for a nation that from its inception has been invigorated and enriched by great challenges."[2] He added: "Those interviewed expressed a mild disorientation about the state of American life, as though the national compass had been lost as the country moved through a confusing series of internal and external shocks."[3]

In 1976, Americans confronted those shocks through continued investigations of government actions and through a closely contested presidential election while they came to grips with issues involving minority rights and dealt with the scandals and triumphs attendant to their society at most any time.

THE REFORM OF INTELLIGENCE AGENCIES

In the preceding three years, intelligence agencies had come under scathing criticism for their unethical, illegal, and unconstitutional acts. That the Watergate burglars had once been employed by the CIA and that President Nixon's plumbers unit used CIA equipment to break into the office of Dr. Daniel Ellsberg's psychiatrist raised suspicions about the agency's involvement in the scandals. Then an internal investigation by the CIA into its own activities produced a damning 693-page report telling of illegal domestic spying, including the surveillance of newspaper columnist Jack Anderson, the wiretapping of reporters' telephones, the opening of private mail, and the monitoring of dissident groups in Washington.

The report detailed how the CIA had planned but failed to carry out successfully the assassination of three foreign leaders, the same ones later discussed in the Church committee report, namely Fidel Castro, Rafael Trujillo, and Patrice Lumumba. The report connected President John Kennedy to organized crime bosses who were hired to kill Castro. And it detailed how Operation CHAOS, a secret effort begun by President Lyndon Johnson in 1967 to uncover links between domestic antiwar groups and extremist international organizations, developed into a domestic spy operation. In 1974, the *New York Times* revealed portions of the CIA report, raising public ire about dangerous runaway bureaucrats.

With charges flying that the CIA had become a menace to individual liberties, President Ford appointed a commission in January 1975 to investigate intelligence programs. The Rockefeller Commission, as it was called after its chairman, Vice President Nelson Rockefeller, produced its own report critical of numerous activities, but in general it treated the CIA leniently and skirted the issue of political assassinations. The Senate, in the meantime, pursued its investigation through the Church committee, which resulted in Congress establishing oversight committees to supervise intelligence operations more effectively.

Then, in February 1976, President Ford announced substantial changes. He formed a new committee to prepare the budget for intelligence agencies and to allocate moneys, and he appointed CIA Director George H. W. Bush to head it. Moreover, Ford created an independent oversight board, chaired by former undersecretary of state Robert D. Murphy, to monitor intelligence operations. Finally, the president reorganized the "40 Committee," a section of the National Security Council in charge of covert operations, and changed its name to the Operations Advisory Group.

Ford said he wanted to restore public confidence in the nation's intelligence agencies; consequently, he issued a "comprehensive set of public guidelines," which he called legally binding charters that were intended to provide "stringent protections" for individual rights.[4] He especially aimed at curtailing the CIA's domestic spying.

At the same time, he sought to tighten leaks to protect intelligence secrets. He proposed a law that "would make it a crime for a Government employee who has access to certain highly classified information to reveal that information improperly."[5]

One observer called the president's actions "the most sweeping reform and reorganization of the United States intelligence agencies since 1947."[6] Yet, Ford clearly intended to protect the intelligence apparatus. Although he condemned abuses by the CIA and other agencies, in a public message, he stressed the harm caused by the leaking of secrets, and he emphatically stated: "I will not be a party to the dismantling of the CIA and the other intelligence agencies."[7] Furthermore, his turning to the CIA director to oversee all intelligence opened the door to a potentially dangerous accumulation of power by one person. When a reporter asked Ford if his legislation to stop leaks would stifle the very flow of information that had revealed the previous abuses, he answered defensively—and unrealistically—that with his reforms in place, there would be no abuses and that if there were, the abusers would be held accountable.

AN FBI SPY OPERATION REVEALED

Besides the CIA, the FBI had come under investigation by Congress and the media for its illegal activities. The story continued to unfold in March 1976, when the bureau released documents in response to a suit filed by the Socialist Workers Party charging the FBI with harassment. These documents showed that FBI agents had broken into the New York City offices of the party at least 92 times between 1960 and 1966.

Previously, the bureau had denied any break-ins against the socialists, and it had defended many of its other domestic break-ins as necessary and restricted only to obtaining information dealing with foreign espionage and protecting national security. The FBI, for example, had admitted to the Senate Intelligence Committee that it had committed 228 illegal entries against 14 organizations from 1942 to 1968, but it had not listed the Socialist Workers Party among them.

The newly released documents told how agents surveyed the layout around the party's offices—the street lighting, the foot traffic—and made keys with which to enter the buildings. Agents photographed documents and, in some cases, stole them. None of the information that was obtained revealed any attachment by the party to subversive international groups or to violent tactics. Several papers, however, dealt with party members who were involved in court cases with the government, thus compromising the defendants' right to a fair trial.

Peter Camejo, the party's presidential candidate, condemned the FBI break-ins. He said that the FBI had taken or copied "names of campaign contributors, letters on campaign strategy, political correspondence with socialists in other countries, information about legal strategy, [and] places of employment of members"—which had absolutely nothing to do with any threats to national security. He said the information "was used to get S. W. P. members fired from their jobs and to otherwise disrupt the legal political activity of the Socialist Workers party." He added: "We demand the arrest and jailing of the criminals who authorized and carried out these acts. . . ."[8] His demand was ignored.

THE SUPREME COURT AND CIVIL RIGHTS

Whatever problems government actions caused for civil liberties, the federal courts continued to advance black civil rights. Under the American practice of racial segregation that existed in the 20th century, African Americans had been denied equal employment. The Civil Rights Act of 1964 began to remove those barriers, but even as blacks acquired jobs that had been previously denied them, they still bore a serious penalty that was inflicted by the past, for they had less seniority, and thus less job security, than most whites.

The Supreme Court acted in March 1976 to rectify the situation when, in a 5-3 ruling, it held that blacks who were denied jobs in violation of Title 7 of the Civil Rights Act and then finally obtained those jobs had to be given retroactive seniority. The court said, however, that the complainant would have to prove, first, that the employer denied him or her the job because of discrimination that occurred after Title 7 went into effect and, second, that the employer used a seniority system.

The ruling meant that some whites who held seniority would now lose it to more-recently hired blacks, a particularly sensitive issue in an economy that was reeling from layoffs and slow growth. Consequently, whites complained of "reverse dis-crimination," a point on which the three dissenting justices on the court agreed. Yet, the majority showed their commitment to affirmative action, to taking proactive steps to eliminate or reduce the adverse conditions created by previous racism. A leader of the National Association for the Advancement of Colored People (NAACP), which brought the case to court, hailed the ruling, saying that it "assures that black victims of racial discrimination will be put in their rightful place."⁹

KAREN ANN QUINLAN: A QUESTION OF WHEN TO DIE

In a time when science was doing so much to change the nature of life, the ques-tion of death gripped Americans in the controversy surrounding 22-year-old Karen Ann Quinlan. During the 1970s, scientists in the United States and else-where were changing genetic codes, mixing the genes of unrelated animals, and developing in vitro fertilization. (The first "test-tube baby," Louise Brown, was born in 1978 in England.) Public values were changing, and people were begin-ning to accept many of these developments. But the shortening of life by remov-ing a person from a machine that maintained it, someone who no longer func-tioned as a human being and had no hope of ever functioning as one, remained a point of virulent controversy.

By 1975, Karen Ann Quinlan had become discontent and restless, going from job to job and hanging out with friends who drank and took drugs. In April, she went to a bar near her home in New Jersey and while partying, combined alcohol with tranquilizers. She stopped breathing, was revived, and then lapsed into a coma, suffering from what doctors diagnosed as a lesion on the upper por-tion of her brain. She had no cognitive ability at the human level; in short, she had entered a vegetative state, and there was no hope that she would ever recover.

Week after week, Karen lay in bed, oblivious to the world around her, con-nected to a respirator and feeding tubes. Her adoptive parents, Joseph and Julia Quinlan, prayed desperately for her recovery. They were devout Catholics (one photo of them during their ordeal shows them situated at home in front of a painting of the Last Supper), and they wanted Karen to live.

But by fall 1975, they realized that she would never regain consciousness. The best that she could ever have in life was to continue, in the words of one neu-rologist, as "a child without a brain." Consequently, the Quinlans decided to have their daughter removed from the respirator, and they sued to have it done.

Joseph Quinlan told the New Jersey Superior Court: "I want to put her back into a natural state. This is the Lord's will."¹⁰ The lower court denied their peti-tion, noting that the doctors tending to Karen opposed removing the respirator and that doing so might constitute murder. The Quinlans then took their case to the New Jersey Supreme Court, and on March 31, 1976, the justices handed down their decision in a 7–0 vote: The respirator could be removed, provided that Karen's doctors and a panel of hospital officials agreed that Karen stood no hope of recovery.

The justices based their decision on Karen's right to privacy, which they said exceeded any claims made by the state. They said that Karen had the right to end her attachment to the life-support system, and since she was unable to make the decision herself, her father, as legal guardian, had the right to make it for her. The justices stated: "The only practical way to prevent destruction of the right [of privacy] is to permit the guardian and family of Karen to render their best judgment, subject to the qualifications here and after stated, as to whether she would exercise it in the circumstances." They added: "We do not question the state's undoubted power to punish the taking of human life, but that power does not encompass individuals terminating medical treatment pursuant to their right of privacy."[11] The justices were confident that they knew the decision that Karen would make if she were able to:

> We have no doubt, in the unhappy circumstances, that if Karen were herself miraculously lucid for an interval and perceptive of her irreversible condition, she could effectively decide on discontinuance of the life-support apparatus, even if it meant the prospect of natural death.[12]

Joseph Quinlan said, "This decision showed courage and the will of God." Julia Quinlan said, "This is the decision we've been praying for."[13]

The ruling contained the potential for broad repercussions. A country fixated by the case hotly debated the topic of euthanasia. In an editorial, the *New York Times* stated: "What the New Jersey Supreme Court had done is nothing less than provide a formal procedure for legally ending the existence of human beings whose life has in effect already been terminated and cannot be restored."[14]

In spring, Karen Ann Quinlan was removed from the respirator. She continued to breathe, and doctors continued to feed her through tubes inserted in her nose as she lay in bed at a nursing home in Morris County. Some questioned why she remained attached to the feeding tubes. Joseph Quinlan later explained: "She is not feeling any pain or anything. We wanted the respirator removed, because it was causing her pain. Now to remove the feeding tube, that's like saying, 'I'm going to take charge again.' We know what will happen if we remove it."[15] The doctors and her parents agreed; however, she would not be given any extraordinary medical care in the event of a setback.

Karen Ann Quinlan lived for nine more years; her body weight dropped to 65 pounds, and in her emaciated state, she remained motionless, curled in a fetal position. About Joseph and Julia Quinlan at the time Karen died, the family's priest said, "They lost a daughter and they reacted as any parents would. They knew it would be forthcoming, but the moment of death was a moment of grief."[16]

A SCANDAL IN CONGRESS

Wayne Hays, a Democratic congressman from Ohio who, during 14 years, acquired enormous power in the House of Representatives once said he might be remembered as "mean, arrogant and cantankerous and tough," but he hoped he would "never be thought of as dishonest."[17] Despite his hope, a scandal in 1976 sullied his name and forced his resignation from office.

Hays served in the House as chairman of the Administration Committee, which gave him authority over numerous congressional perks, such as travel, payroll, staffing, parking, and police and, as a result, far-reaching influence over other members of Congress. In May 1976, the *Washington Post* reported that the 64-year-old Hays had on his own payroll 27-year-old Elizabeth Ray, a former Miss Virginia, who told a reporter: "I can't type, I can't file, I can't even answer the phone."[18] Ray, whose official job title was "clerk," admitted that she seldom appeared at her office. She said, "Supposedly, I'm on the oversight committee, but I call it 'the Out-of-Sight Committee'."[19] She was paid $14,000 a year.

Given her meager office skills and her lackadaisical behavior, critics said she was really being paid to serve as Hays's mistress. Hays vehemently denied the charge, but in a newspaper interview, Ray said that indeed had been the case ever since she began to work for Hays in 1974. (Ray left her job briefly later that year to become an actress in Hollywood. Later, Ray claimed that she thought that she could become a success there because of her Academy Award performances on Capitol Hill.) Ray stated that she had sexual relations with Hays once or twice a week.

Hays, who divorced his wife in 1975, apparently continued his relationship with Ray after he remarried a year later. He grew concerned, however, when Bob Woodward, a reporter for the *Washington Post,* began to ask questions; and so, according to Ray, Hays began to advise her to show up at her office for an hour or two a day. Two *Post* reporters, Marion Clark and Rudy Maxa, described Ray's office on Capitol Hill:

> [It]would be number 1506P (for Private) if the number had not been removed from the door. It is next to Rep. Bella S. Abzug's (D-N.Y.) office, in which—in only a slightly larger space—a dozen or more Abzug staffers are shoehorned into as many desks piled with office work.
>
> Ray's office is serenely empty, except for her backgammon set and collection of framed signed photographs on the wall next to her desk, from entertainers and other famous persons.
>
> On her polished wood desk is a copy of "Fear of Flying," two red telephones, and a color-coordinated red Selectric typewriter with a smoked Plexiglas top. It is unplugged because, says Ray, she doesn't know how to turn it on.[20]

Despite his power, Hays garnered little respect in Washington. Columnist Tom Wicker said "almost everyone agrees that what's happened to him couldn't happen to a more deserving fellow."[21] Another columnist, James Reston, called him "the House bully" and said, "No amount of personal arrogance, nepotism, or misuse of power had been able to bring him down, but finally he is on his way out for running a personal nightshift with public funds."[22] When Congress decided to investigate it focused on the misuse of congressional moneys.

The three-month inquiry caused Hays to resign in September. A committee put together by Speaker Carl Albert (Dem., Okla.) soon announced changes in how House operating funds would be handled. Nevertheless, the investigators kept their final report under wraps, and, by-and-large, the House resorted to its traditionally deficient practice of reforming itself behind closed doors, leaving the public skeptical about how much anything had changed, and further reinforcing its distrust in government.

THE SUPREME COURT AND THE DEATH PENALTY

> The hands turn red, then white, and the cords of the neck stand out like steel bands. . . . The prisoner's limbs, fingers, toes, and face are severely contorted. . . . The force of the electric current is so powerful that the prisoner's

eyeballs sometimes pop out on his cheeks. . . . The prisoner often defecates, urinates, and vomits blood and drool. . . . Sometimes the prisoner catches fire. . . . There is a sound like bacon frying and the sickly sweet smell of burning flesh . . . when the post-electrocution autopsy is performed the liver is so hot that doctors say it cannot be touched by the human hand. . . . The body frequently is badly burned."[23]

In those words Supreme Court justice William J. Brennan described, in 1985, a prisoner being put to death in an electric chair. Almost a decade earlier, the Court, as it had done before, addressed the constitutionality of the death penalty, particularly whether it was cruel and unusual punishment.

The Court offered its answer on July 2, 1976, when it ruled 7-2 that the death penalty did not violate the Constitution as long as judges and juries were allowed under state statutes to obtain the information and guidance necessary to consider the unique circumstances surrounding a case. In short, the justices found nothing cruel in a prisoner's eyeballs popping out from an electric charge; cruelty existed only when the sentence itself was imposed arbitrarily.

Capital punishment had been controversial for years, with its supporters insisting that it deterred murders and brought "closure" to the friends and relatives of murder victims; its opponents argued that such assertions lacked conclusive evidence, and the penalty was morally wrong, a holdover from an ignorant and barbaric past.

The Supreme Court struck down capital punishment in 1972, when it called its application too arbitrary. Several states then passed new statutes, and in its 1976 ruling, the Court considered and passed judgment on five of those.

In a separate ruling, also handed down on July 2, 1976, on a 7-2 vote, the Court struck down any statutes stipulating a mandatory death penalty. The second ruling invalidated the sentences of about half the approximately 600 prisoners on death row. Yet, the decision allowed states to continue capital punishment by modifying their laws, thus opening the way for the first executions since 1967.

The justices said that while the evidence for capital punishment as a deterrent was inconclusive, the death penalty did serve the important role of retribution. Moreover, the penalty matched the severity of the crime, in this case murder. Yet, one of the two dissenters, Justice Brennan, said that an execution "far from offering redress for the offense committed against society, adds instead a second defilement to the first."[24]

Reaction to the Court's ruling corresponded to personal views about the death penalty itself:

"The intentional killing of people by the state is barbarous in principle and violates fundamental commitments of a decent and humane society," said Aryeh Neier, executive director of the American Civil Liberties Union.[25]

"I strongly support the reinstatement of capital punishment in the Texas penal code," said Democratic Texas Governor Dolph Briscoe.[26]

"We hope that this nation's 200th year—the Bicentennial—will not . . . be marked by a resumption of official electrocutions, gassings, hangings, and shootings," said Jack Greenberg, the director counsel of the NAACP Legal Defense and Educational Fund, who argued before the court against capital punishment.[27]

AMERICA'S BICENTENNIAL

A seven-foot-tall birthday cake at the National Archives in Washington; bells ringing in all 50 states; a huge armada of sailing ships plying the waters near the Statue of Liberty—these were the sights and sounds on July 4, 1976, as Americans celebrated the bicentennial of the United States.

Although crowds generally turned out to be smaller than expected for the biggest birthday party in the nation's history, the excitement of the occasion was obvious nearly everywhere, as evident in a story in the *New York Times:*

> It began with a flag-raising atop Mars Hill Mountain in Maine, where dawn reached the continent, and moved on to Fort McHenry, in Baltimore Harbor, where it was greeted by the rocket's red glare of the national anthem. The activities were to end nearly a day later with an indigenous festival in American Samoa.[28]

The bicentennial produced numerous claims for "the biggest": in New York, the biggest gathering of sailing ships ever, more than 225 from 31 nations; in Vancouver, Washington, the biggest firework, a 165-pound skyrocket; in Washington, D.C., the biggest fireworks display, 33 tons; in George, Washington, the biggest cherry pie, 60 square feet; and in Baltimore, the biggest cake—bigger than the one at the National Archives—weighing in at 69,000 pounds.

The bicentennial produced cheese, too, in the form of commercialized products and trivial items. Celebrants could buy their beer in bicentennial cans. They could work off their calories throwing bicentennial Frisbees.

In and around Boston, the hotbed of revolutionary activity in 1776, residents who dressed as Minutemen fired a 21-gun salute over John Hancock's grave, and the U.S.S. *Constitution* fired its cannon for the first time in 95 years. John Silber, the president of Boston University, spoke at historic Faneuil Hall, though his words sounded more like an old Puritan jeremiad than a celebration as he warned about the pursuit of happiness degenerating into the pursuit of pleasure. The day ended with 500,000 people crowding a park near the Charles River and watching a massive fireworks display as Arthur Fiedler led the Boston Pops Orchestra in Tchaikovsky's stirring *1812 Overture.*

Several cities staged mass naturalization services. In Miami, 7,141 persons, mostly Cuban exiles, took the oath of citizenship. Another 2,300 did the same in Chicago, and 1,000 did so in Detroit.

Perhaps the most beautiful display was the arrival of the sailing ships at New York's harbor, accompanied by naval ships from many nations. As the sailing ships glided to their destination in the days leading up to July 4, their white canvases billowed against a clear blue sky and across the rolling waters of Long Island Sound; at night, lights glistened from the Verrazano-Narrows Bridge while the ships neared Bay Ridge.

Operation Sail attracted 6 million spectators, who viewed the parade of vessels along New York's shores while countless others watched the scene from New Jersey. The U.S. Coast Guard's three-masted *Eagle* led the procession. There followed Italy's *Amerigo Vespucci,* Japan's *Nippon Maru,* the Soviet Union's *Kruzenshtern,* Portugal's *Sagres II,* Spain's *Juan Sebastian de Elcano.* They numbered

A crowd gathers in Washington, D.C., in July 1976 to celebrate the U.S. Bicentennial. *(© Wally McNamee/Corbis)*

16 tall ships in all and numerous smaller ones, among them the *Sir Winston Churchill,* with an all–female crew, and the *Mon Lei,* a Chinese junk. Aboard the aircraft carrier USS *Forrestal,* a review party of 3,000, led by Vice President Nelson Rockefeller, watched as the crews of the sailing ships saluted while they passed by. Tugboats sprayed water into the air, adding to the spectacle.

The *New York Times* said about the holiday: "It had been a respite from worries about municipal bankruptcy, crime in the streets, and the daily realities."[29] Yet, protesters demonstrated in several cities, such as the 5,000 who marched in front of the Jefferson Memorial carrying a banner reading "Independence From Big Business." And in a speech in Philadelphia, President Ford noted the doubts that still transfixed society. "It is fitting that we ask ourselves hard questions, even on a glorious day like today," he said. Then he added:

> Are the institutions under which we live working the way they should? Are the foundations laid in 1776 and 1789 still strong enough and sound enough to resist the tremors of our times? Are our God-given rights secure, our hard-won liberties protected?[30]

He concluded by noting that for all the questions, Americans still had the liberty to raise them, pursue them, and correct what might be wrong.

Time magazine said of the Bicentennial celebration: "It was a real blast, a superbash, a party unlike any other party, ever. . . . And everywhere, the flag. Not so long ago, it was a symbol of division—burned by some or worn on the seats of their faded jeans, flaunted by others in their lapels or on their auto aerials. Last week it seemed to be back in its historic place as a loved and honored emblem of American unity."[31]

TWENTY-SIX CHILDREN ABDUCTED IN CALIFORNIA

Less than two weeks after the Bicentennial celebration, three white men, one of them carrying a sawed-off shotgun, commandeered a schoolbus near Chowchilla, California, and abducted its driver and 26 children.

Chowchilla straddles Highway 99 in the central part of the state, about 40 miles northwest of Fresno. A small farming town that is surrounded by cotton and corn fields, its population in 1976 totaled about 4,600 people, and its business district and two banks testified to a modest economy. None of the children aboard the bus came from wealthy families, and the parents of two of them were migrant workers, making the kidnapping all the more perplexing.

Nevertheless, on the afternoon of July 15, Frank Edward Ray, who had driven the local school district's buses for many years, pulled out from Dairyland School with his passengers, departing from the day's summer school classes. He made three scheduled stops; then he and the children, whose ages ranged from six to 14, traveled along a sparsely settled farm road.

A few minutes later, three masked kidnappers appeared in vans, forced the bus to stop, and drove it to a dry creek channel that was obscured by vegetation, called Bernardine Slough. The kidnappers covered the bus with foliage, then herded their captives into two vans and took them to a quarry 100 miles away, just west of Livermore near San Francisco. They forced the bus driver and the children down a ladder into a buried truck trailer, covered with dirt, brush, and gravel. They gave them a flashlight, and then removed the ladder. "We thought we were going to lose our lives right there," Ray later recalled.[32]

Fearful that the enclosure in which they were imprisoned would collapse and suffocate them, the captives began to dig their way out of the trailer. Dirt sprinkled down from the ceiling, and the heat exhausted them, but they managed to open a hole large enough for one of the boys to squeeze through, and he ran for help.

About the scene inside the truck trailer, Ray said, "There was a lot of crying and begging for momma. I had to calm 'em down, I talked to 'em and begged 'em not to holler and scream. They kept hollering and saying, 'Why did they do this to us?' "[33]

The answer appeared in a ransom note demanding $5 million. Two brothers, Richard A. Schoenfeld, 22, and James Schoenfeld, 25, along with a friend, Fred Newhall Woods, also 25, had staged the kidnapping. Woods's father was president of the company that owned the quarry. The ransom note, undelivered but discovered by police, demanded the money be in small bills and taken to a site in the Santa Cruz Mountains.

In July 1977, Woods and the Schoenfelds pleaded guilty to 27 counts of kidnapping for ransom. The three men were sentenced to life terms, and today they remain in prison.

A SOUTHERN STRATEGY FOR THE REPUBLICANS

The discord in American society that was evident since the 1960s and the widespread dismay over the country's future dovetailed with demographic changes to affect politics profoundly.

One of Richard Nixon's staffers, 29-year-old Kevin Phillips, had realized the importance of these developments back in 1969 and expressed them in an influential book titled *The Emerging Republican Majority*. Phillips perceived that Americans were moving by the hundreds of thousands from northern industrial cities, where high taxes and high crime rates predominated, to southern and southwestern locations, where sunshine, low taxes, and low crime rates prevailed. He coined the term *Sunbelt* to refer to the states from Virginia to Florida on the East Coast, and then westward from Florida through Texas and New Mexico, and finally into Arizona and southern California.

The Republicans, he claimed, had been for years slowly developing into a majority party that was poised to break the Democratic dominance of the White House and Congress that had evolved during the Great Depression. Now, he said, this Republican surge was accelerating in reaction to disgust with the counterculture and with liberal, Great Society politics. Many Sunbelt residents prized traditional values, order, and stability; they blamed the failed politics, dominated by Democrats, for the decline of the industrial cities. The Sunbelt, Phillips said, along with suburbia elsewhere, was conservative and ripe for Republican picking.

In his argument, Phillips indicated that the more extensively Democrats appealed to blacks in the South, the more extensively Democrats would drive Sunbelt whites, both long-standing residents and recent arrivals, into the Republican Party. This was similar to President Lyndon Johnson's observation about passage of the 1964 Civil Rights Act—that it doomed Democrats in the South. In his book, Phillips states: "Maintenance of Negro voting rights in Dixie, far from being contrary to G. O. P. interests, is essential if Southern conservatives are to be pressured into switching to the Republican party—for Negroes are beginning to seize control of the Democratic party in some black-belt areas."[34]

Phillips notes the peculiarity of recent urban growth and how cities could be won from the Democrats:

While urbanization *is* changing the face of America," he writes, "and the GOP must take political note of this fact . . . the new "urbanization"—sub-urbanization is often a better description—is a middle-class impetus [harmful to the Democrats]. All across the nation, the fastest-growing urban areas are steadily increasing their *Republican* pluralities, while the old central cities—seat of the New Deal era—are casting steadily fewer votes for Democratic liberalism. . . . The fastest-growing area in the nation is Southern California's staunchly conservative Orange County, and the fastest-growing cities are conservative strongholds like Phoenix, Dallas, Houston, Anaheim, San Diego, and Fort Lauderdale.[35]

Phillips concludes:

The GOP is particularly lucky not to be weighted down with commitment to the political blocs, power brokers and poverty concessionaires of the decaying central cities of the North, now that national growth is shifting to suburbia, the South and the West. The American future lies in a revitalized countryside, a demographically ascendant Sun Belt and suburbia, and new towns—perhaps mountainside linear cities astride monorails 200 miles from Phoenix, Memphis or Atlanta. National policy will have to direct itself towards this future and its constituencies; and perhaps an administration so oriented can also deal realistically with the central cities where Great Society political largesse has so demonstrably failed.[36]

Less charitable commentators agreed with Phillips's observations, but they characterized the Sunbelt in different terms. Most notably, writer Kirkpatrick Sale said the "southern rim" was characterized by "racism, rightism, and repression."[37]

To many Americans, the term *law and order* was code for "control blacks." Richard Nixon realized this when he used the phrase in his 1968 and 1972 presidential campaigns. In fact, Nixon may well have been applying Phillips's Republican majority concept to the "Southern strategy" used in his campaigns (though Phillips denied this). Under the strategy, "law and order" appealed to disgruntled northerners but also to the Sunbelt, bringing the two together into a powerful political force.

By the mid-1970s, conservatism had developed the launch pad that it needed to become a potent political force, ready to cast away the fringe image which it had inherited from 1964 when Barry Goldwater's catastrophic race for president left the movement with the reputation for kookiness. New Right leader Richard Viguerie said that the success of the revived conservative movement was based on rallying to its cause groups that were dedicated to single issues, such as the National Rifle Association (NRA) and Stop-ERA, and on mobilizing right-wing groups with broader agendas, such as the National Conservative Political Action Committee (NCPAC) and the Conservative Caucus. Moreover, it required building a tight national network of local groups that were ready to react to specific issues—such as those organized in 1974 to protest Ford's choice of Nelson Rockefeller for vice president—and ready to use direct-mail campaigns. Viguerie's direct-mail operation, based in Falls Church, Virginia, worked from a list of 15 million conservatives who could be depended on to donate time or money to right-wing causes.

GERALD FORD AND RONALD REAGAN

In the 1976 presidential race, Gerald Ford faced a challenge within his own Republican Party from former California governor Ronald Reagan. The challenger spoke the new conservative creed, one tuned into the Southern strategy. He appealed to those in the party who had been angered by Ford's turn to Rockefeller, and he appealed to the frustrated sunbelt residents and suburbanites.

At first, it appeared that Ford would do as nearly every incumbent president seeking reelection had done before him: easily defeat a challenge from within his own party. He won several early primaries with little problem and then scored a big victory in the important Illinois contest, with 59 percent of the vote to Reagan's 40 percent. *Time* magazine criticized Reagan for running a lackluster campaign that was burdened by the candidate spending too much time in obscure towns and avoiding large crowds. In contrast, Ford enthusiastically "worked the fences and the police barricades."[38]

But in the South and elsewhere in the Sunbelt, Reagan gained momentum. He beat Ford in North Carolina. He achieved a stunning victory in Texas, a landslide that embarrassed the president and provided the Californian with the credibility he needed to be considered a serious challenger. Texans warmed to Reagan's attacks against Ford for being too soft toward the Soviet Union. They liked his criticism of military base closings and his charge that Ford intended to give the Panama Canal to Panama, and in an oil-rich state, they liked Reagan's call for the end of price controls on petroleum.

Reagan won 27 of the 29 Arizona delegates chosen at a state convention, and he won 11 of 16 delegates in the Kentucky caucuses.

As the Republican National Convention approached, Reagan's delegate count in the contested primaries, boosted by a big win in California, exceeded Ford's. But the president worked the uncommitted delegates, cajoling them and making promises—or as Reagan said, "I know the president has many inducements to offer"—and in the end, Ford won the nomination, though with only 57 more delegates than the minimum 1,130 that he needed.

Clearly, Reagan had positioned himself as the emerging power within the Republican Party. *Time* magazine captured this development:

> Win or lose, his candidacy has been extraordinary. He was seen by many as shallow and simplistic and even dangerous. All but a handful of Senators and Congressmen shunned him. He was opposed by nearly every state organization. He had practically no editorial support. . . .
>
> No matter what happened, Reagan felt vindicated by the hard journey. He had not destroyed himself—or his party. He had challenged a President and made it stick.[39]

JIMMY CARTER

Meanwhile, the Democrats sensed that they could win the White House. Between Watergate and the anemic economy—recovering only fitfully in the weeks before the general election—Ford and the Republicans seemed to be faltering. As the Democratic candidates headed into the Iowa caucuses early in 1976, few people gave much of a chance to an obscure former governor of Georgia, Jimmy Carter. Yet, Carter was tremendously driven, willing to do almost anything to win, and he possessed a sense of morality, wedded to his faith as a born-again Christian, that bordered on self-righteousness. In *The Presidency of James Earl Carter, Jr.,* author Burton I. Kaufman says about the Georgian, "In him, consummate personal ambition was linked to a compelling sense of public purpose."[40]

Given the widespread disgust with politicians and with the many failures of government policies, voters listened to Carter's pleas for honesty and truthfulness in Washington. Virtue became his central message and meshed well with his appeal as an outsider, as one uncorrupted by the sleazy dealings and cozy political-club atmosphere of the nation's capital. Carter's adviser, Hamilton Jordan, said to the Georgian, "Perhaps the strongest feeling in this country today is the general distrust of government and politicians at all levels."[41] Carter took those words to heart.

Carter scored an important victory in January 1976, when he won nearly 28 percent of the vote in the Iowa caucuses, placing him in first place ahead of Indiana Senator Birch Bayh. The victory gave him momentum heading into the crucial New Hampshire primary. He finished first there, too, and gained invaluable press coverage as *Time* and *Newsweek* magazines featured his photo on their covers.

Carter took his campaign to Florida, where he recovered from a defeat in the Massachusetts primary by finishing first, ahead of former Alabama governor George Wallace, with 34.3 percent of the vote. At that point, Carter thought he would win the presidential nomination, though he forecast a tough fight with reverses ahead. He proved prescient. He won in Illinois and North Carolina but lost in New York and barely defeated Arizona congressman Morris Udall in

Democratic nominee Jimmy Carter and President Ford engage in a presidential campaign debate in Philadelphia. *(Courtesy Gerald R. Ford Library)*

Wisconsin. He finally won in a big northern industrial state when he defeated Washington senator Henry Jackson in Pennsylvania and collected enough delegates, despite losses in other primaries, to gain the Democratic nomination in July. Carter presented as his campaign slogan the rhetorical question: "Why Not the Best?" And at the Democratic convention in New York, whites and blacks stressed unity as an antidote to the country's divisiveness by holding hands and singing, "We Shall Overcome."

CARTER WINS THE WHITE HOUSE

Going into the fall, public opinion polls showed Carter leading Ford by double-digit margins. Ford had the disadvantages of never having been elected to the presidency, of having taken the unpopular move of pardoning Richard Nixon, and of presiding over a questionable economy. To make matters worse, Ford committed a gaffe in a televised debate with Carter when he denied that the Soviet Union dominated Eastern Europe.

Carter blundered, though, when in an interview with *Playboy* magazine, he used sexual slang and admitted to having "committed adultery in my heart many times."[42] More important, as the campaign edged into October, he allowed Ford to attack him effectively for "fuzziness." By November, more and more voters concluded that Carter lacked substance.

On election day, they cast their ballots not so much for Ford or for Carter as for the less objectionable candidate. Carter edged out Ford with 50.1 percent of the popular vote to the president's 48 percent. Carter would have lost except for substantial support from African Americans. Five of every six blacks voted for him.

A record number of those eligible to vote stayed home. The turnout, at only 54 percent, again bespoke an electorate that saw little value in the political system and, most likely, little difference between the two candidates. Carter would enter the White House lacking the mandate he desired and having to combat a debilitating decline in the nation's polity.

RUBIN "HURRICANE" CARTER ON TRIAL

"This is the story of the Hurricane, the man the authorities came to blame," Bob Dylan sang in a protest song in which he accused the police and courts of injustice in the arrest and conviction for murder of the professional middleweight boxer Rubin "Hurricane" Carter. The outcry over Carter's plight and the plight of his codefendant John Artis, who had also been found guilty, was considerable. The conviction was called "racist" by critics who considered the defendants to be victims of a white backlash against black civil rights activism and increased lawlessness that many whites blamed on African Americans. The outcry caused the New Jersey Supreme Court to review the case and rule that evidence had been withheld from the defense. As a result, the court said, both men, sentenced to imprisonment for life, should be retried.

Their retrial began in November and continued into December 1976. As at the original trial in 1967, testimony proved contradictory. Several prosecution witnesses placed Carter and Artis at the Lafayette Grill in Paterson, New Jersey, early in the morning of June 17, 1966, when two black men, armed with a shotgun and a pistol, gunned down three whites. The prosecution argued that Carter and Artis killed the three in an act of revenge for the killing of a friend's stepfather at a time when racial tension in the city was extraordinarily high.

But a fourth victim in the assault, who survived a bullet wound to the head, was unable at the time of the killings to identify either Carter or Artis as the shooters. He died before the retrial, but the defense entered his testimony from 1967 into the court record. Five other witnesses who testified at the retrial placed Carter elsewhere. One of them, Elwood Tuck, the owner of a bar called the Nite Spot, testified that about the time of the murder, he saw Carter "when I was closing my back room."

The trial became more complicated when several witnesses who testified against the defendants in 1967 recanted their statements, and several who testified for the defendants recanted theirs. On December 21, the jury, which included two African Americans, reaffirmed the first trial and found Carter and Artis guilty.

In 1985, however, United States District Court judge F. Lee Sarokin overturned the convictions. Suppressed evidence and racial prejudice, he concluded, had made the trial unfair. His ruling freed Carter. (Artis had been released on parole four years earlier.) In February 1988, the prosecutor filed a motion to dismiss the original indictments brought against Carter and Artis, which, when granted, resulted in all charges being dropped.

TOM WOLFE AND THE "ME DECADE"

In 1976, Tom Wolfe, a practitioner of "new journalism" who won acclaim for his analysis of the counterculture in *The Electric Kool-Aid Acid Test* (1968), wrote in *New York* magazine about a change in Americans since the 1960s: Rather than attempting to reform society, Americans were attempting to change their personalities and, in the process, doting on themselves. The 1970s, he said, had become the Me Decade.

Above all else, the Me Decade was based on a larger, more prosperous middle class (this despite the economic problems of the period). People had more money and more leisure time to indulge themselves.

The Me Decade, Wolfe said, could be found in efforts by individuals to remake their personalities. A variety of psychological programs, centered on the "me," gave each participant a chance to talk about himself or herself. For about $200 a week, a person could attend the Esalen Institute in Big Sur, California, where among other methods, psychologist Fritz Perls held lengthy encounter sessions, exposing each participant's innermost thoughts and feelings to fellow participants. Wolfe called him "A remarkable figure, a psychologist who had a gray beard and went about in a blue terry-cloth jumpsuit and looked like a great blue grizzled father bear."[43] As with Esalen, the emphasis on "me" accounts for the popularity of est (Erhard Seminars Training), a rigorous awareness program founded by Werner Erhard. He promoted est as a method to "throw away your belief system, tear yourself down, and put yourself back together again."[44]

The Me Decade could be found in the popularity of eastern mystical religions, including Hare Krishna. Numerous New Leftists, among them Rennie Davis who once advocated revolutionary social change, were now immersed in such self-exploration.

The Me Decade could be found in the rise of divorce. The increase in divorce rates between 1970 and 1979 reached 67 percent nationally. Regionally during that period, the increase hit 90 percent in New England, 91 percent in the South Atlantic states (from Delaware south through Georgia and Florida), and 113 percent in the Middle Atlantic states (New York, New Jersey, and Pennsylvania). Couples found it difficult to make sacrifices to hold marriages together. The "me" superseded the matrimonial union. Changing feelings about women's roles and women's rights may have also played into this.

Not even the presence of children kept marriages together. Many young couples, baby boomers who had been born in the late 1940s and the 1950s, rejected the idea that a bad marriage should be endured for the children's sake. This came at a time when 70 percent of the respondents to a questionnaire that was published by a leading newspaper columnist said if they had it to do all over again, they would *not* have kids. So extensive had divorce become that *Mad* magazine lampooned the trend by offering children a "Divorce Survival Badge" for doing such things as agreeing with father that the "silly young lady he is dating is 'real swell and a lot of fun.' "

The Me Decade could be found in the rising percentage of young people who were marrying late in life or were remaining single. The baby boomers stayed single longer than any other generation in the 20th century.

The Me Decade could be found in the elderly "caravaners" who traveled the country in their sleek silver Airstream trailers. As Tom Wolfe described them, they sought adventure and escape—often escape from the children who no longer wanted them—as they rolled across the interstates from the North to the South and into Mexico. Wolfe observed: "The caravaners would get deeper and deeper into a life of sheer *trailering*. They would become experts at this twentieth-century nomad life."[45] Wandering replaced community; fulfillment of the "me" dictated the movement. "It was remarkable . . . ," said Wolfe, "that ordinary folks had enough money to take it and run off and alter the circumstances of their lives and create new roles for themselves."[46]

Wolfe concluded that the common folk were doing something "only aristocrats (and intellectuals and artists) were supposed to do—they discovered and started doting on *Me!* They've created the greatest individualism in American history! . . . One only knows that the great religious waves have a momentum all their own. Neither arguments nor acts of the legislature have been any match for them in the past. And this one has the mightiest, holiest roll of all, the beat that goes . . . *Me . . . Me . . . Me . . . Me . . .* "[47]

THE APPLE COMPUTER

In the 21st century, it may be difficult to think of a time before personal computers existed, and it may be difficult to think of computers as deriving as much from a countercultural striving for liberation as from a desire to advance technology and make money.

But the birth of the personal computer, or PC, in the 1970s should be placed in the context of the countercultural influences of the 1960s. Many of those who developed early PCs saw themselves as crusaders against corporate America and for the power of the individual.

In California, the hotbed of computer development, enthusiasts formed a kind of collective, the Homebrew Computer Club, where they shared ideas and parts. One computer idealist advocated linking all knowledge together through a universal electronic world library. The general thinking about software was fully in line with the countercultural mentality: No one should pay for it; it should be shared for free.

Several developments converged in California's Silicon Valley, near Stanford University, in the mid-1970s to produce PCs as alternatives to the huge mainframes and refrigerator-sized minicomputers used by big business. For one, Intel introduced chips for calculators that were embedded with thousands of transistors. Computer hobbyists such as Steve Wozniak found that, with some modification, these chips could be used to build "microcomputers."

For another, Xerox built a desktop computer similar to a PC, complete with a mouse for navigation, icons, window graphics, and a laser printer. The company, however, failed to move quickly into manufacturing and distributing its invention.

In high school, Steve Wozniak became friends with Steve Jobs. Both of them worked part time at Hewlett-Packard, and they entered their first moneymaking venture when they manufactured a "little blue box," which they sold to college students. The box enabled callers to bypass long-distance phone charges illegally and thus served as a countercultural technological assault on big business.

Jobs, though, at first rejected the monetary path for one of self-enlightenment. He experimented with psychedelic drugs, learned the *I Ching* (a mystical book of divination), and backpacked through India, with his head shaved and his mind open to eastern mysticism.

When he returned to California, he teamed up with Wozniak, who, along with Bill Fernandez, had developed their own PC. Jobs soon suggested that they market the machine through the Homebrew Computer Club, which they did. They called their computer Apple, a name Jobs likely chose in memory of a summer that he spent in Oregon as an orchard worker.

The partnership between Jobs and Wozniak, however, was not, at first, a smooth one. While Jobs pushed to found a company revolving around the Apple, Wozniak had no desire to own a business. He feared getting bogged down in a boring corporate job in which he would have to push paper rather than be able to pursue his work as an engineer.

Nevertheless, on April 1, 1976, Jobs and Wozniak, along with Ron Wayne, a field engineer for the Atari company, founded Apple, Inc., housed in a garage in the Silicon Valley. They followed up their original PC with Apple II in 1977, a machine whose simplicity made it possible to run computer programs without the operator having to know a computer language.

At a time when few people owned their own computers, Apple grew phenomenally. The company had set as its initial goal the selling of 100 computers; in 1978, it obtained sales of $7.8 million, and in 1980, $117.9 million. Apple reached the *Fortune 500* list quicker than any other company before it.

The PC age was dawning, in large part a result of the work of Wozniak, Jobs, and others in the 1970s. These developments soon made computers accessible to teachers, students, and millions of other everyday people.

Gary Gilmore Executed

[Peter Arroyo] could see the motel manager on the floor, and the man's wife next to him with a phone in her hand, and blood all over the place. The man on the ground didn't say anything, he just made noises. His leg was moving a little. Arroyo tried to help the woman turn him over, but the footing was slippery. The man was very heavy and lying in too great a puddle.[48]

The man on the floor was the manager at the City Center Motel in Provo, Utah. His murderer (for the young man died) was Gary Gilmore, a 35-year-old who had spent more time in jail than out and who, on July 20, 1976, entered the motel office looking for money and looking to kill. He ordered the manager to lie down on the floor. Then he took a .22 automatic and shot him point-blank in the head. Gilmore was arrested, tried, found guilty, and sentenced to die.

The day before Gilmore killed the motel manager, he robbed and killed a gas station attendant. He later told an interviewer that he had entered the gas station to kill someone, to relieve the pressure that he felt in his mind. Gilmore said: "That night I knew I had to open a valve and let something out and I didn't know exactly what it would be and I wasn't thinking I'll do this or I'll do that, or that'll make me feel better."[49]

Gilmore was tried and found guilty in the death of the motel manager. His case became a national sensation when he demanded that there be no stay of his execution, no appeals, and that he be allowed to die "like a man" before a firing squad, his choice of execution. Gilmore even dismissed his court-appointed attorney when the lawyer said he would appeal the case. "I believe I was given a fair trial," Gilmore told the Utah Supreme Court, "and I think the sentence was proper."[50] On November 10, the justices agreed. Gilmore could be executed the following week.

Much to Gilmore's chagrin, the governor and the board of pardons stepped in to reconsider the sentence. Gilmore belittled the governor, calling him a "coward." He scoffed at the board: "I don't deserve anything," he said. And he mocked society: "It seems the people of Utah want the death penalty but not the execution," he said.[51] The board granted his execution request.

But Gilmore's mother halted the march to execution when she demanded and obtained a stay. The appeal failed. Gilmore was again resentenced, with his execution set for January 17.

As that date approached, the *Salt Lake Tribune* reported "a Barnum and Bailey circus atmosphere" surrounding the Gilmore execution, complete with T-shirts for sale. Bishops from the National Council of Churches staged a vigil outside the Utah State Prison.

On the morning of the 17th, Gilmore sat in a chair behind a barrier, an executioner's blind, opposite from where the riflemen stood. Fifty or so spectators watched him. "Do you have anything you'd like to say?" the warden asked. "Let's do it," Gilmore replied.[52] The jailers put a hood over Gilmore's head, a strap around his waist, and another strap over the hood. A doctor pinned a white circle, a target, on Gilmore's black shirt. The countdown began and Gilmore remained still. Then came the shots—a deafening noise for the spectators, hardly muffled by the cotton they had stuck in their ears. Writer Norman Mailer, known for his novels and

Norman Mailer wrote the revealing account of Gary Gilmore titled *The Executioner's Song.* (Copyright © 1972 Diana Mara Henry)

nonfictional accounts that studied sex, violence, and irrational impulses, wrote about Gilmore's life in *The Executioner's Song,* a book published in 1979 and winner of a Pulitzer Prize in 1980. Mailer describes the moments after the gun shots:

> The blood started to flow through the black shirt and came out onto the white pants and started to drop on the floor between Gary's legs, and the smell of gunpowder was everywhere.[53]

The doctor came up and felt Gilmore's pulse. Gilmore was still alive and lived another 20 seconds. Then the circus ended. The blood, though, still dripped, and by now it covered Gilmore's tennis shoes, the ones he liked to wear in maximum security and that he chose to wear to his death—the red, white, and blue ones.

OUTLAW COUNTRY

Imagine country music with a raw honky-tonk sound, unabashedly conveying its rural roots. Then imagine taking that music, softening its "hillbilly" flavor, and infusing it with an orchestral arrangement to broaden its appeal to an audience that would include urbanites and pop music fans. That was the direction of country music in the 1960s, a Nashville sound manufactured by record producers and performed by singers and musicians who seldom wrote their own songs. In the early 1970s, however, rebellious country artists from Texas and California began to challenge this packaged, commercialized country format. They developed progressive or "outlaw" country to move the music closer to its roots, to explore new themes, and to focus on the performers as the creators of their works, either as writers or producers.

The emergence of outlaw country paralleled a similar development in rock music. In the 1960s, Bob Dylan, the Beatles, and the Rolling Stones performed their own works with a sound quite different from the packaged product emanating from music factories in New York. They broke with the standardized formula and explored themes previously ignored or considered taboo.

The term *outlaw country* derived from the song "Ladies Love Outlaws," written by Lee Clayton and recorded by Waylon Jennings on his album of the same name. Soon the word *outlaw* was attached to singers who grew their hair long, wore leather, and sang about drinking, drugs, and sex. Their style and music dumbfounded the staid, clean-cut establishment performers and producers of the Grand Ole Opry in Nashville.

Yet, some of the outlaw artists began as traditional performers. Waylon Jennings was first signed to RCA records in 1965 by Chet Atkins, one of the producers who packaged the Nashville sound for wider audiences. But in the early 1970s, Jennings chafed at the limits on his creativity. He began to produce his own records and used his own band in the recording studio rather than the musicians provided by the record company. This rebellious approach earned him several number one hits, including "Good Hearted Woman" in 1975, "Luckenbach, Texas" in 1977 (with Willie Nelson), and "Mammas Don't Let Your Babies Grow Up to Be Cowboys," in 1978 (also with Willie Nelson). His 1976 album *Wanted! The Outlaws,* recorded with Willie Nelson, Tompall Glaser, and his wife, Jessi Colter, became the first country album ever to be certified platinum, with 1 million copies sold.

Willie Nelson also moved from traditional to outlaw country, although he established a solid record in the 1960s of recording his own songs. In 1971, Nelson left Nashville for Austin, Texas, and, influenced by the outlaw genre which was then vibrant on the local scene, began to incorporate more folk and rock elements in his music. He gained national popularity in 1973 with his album *Shotgun Willie.* His long hair and countercultural attitude made him seem more like a hippie than a country singer.

Jerry Jeff Walker, Billy Joe Shaver, and Guy Clark all contributed to the outlaw music. But by far the most controversial and iconoclastic of the outlaw artists was David Allan Coe. Born in Ohio, Coe spent part of his youth in reform school and, in the 1960s, served time in the Ohio State Penitentiary. Here was a man to whom the term *outlaw* meant more than a music rebel.

In 1967, Coe arrived in Nashville, and to gain attention from the country music establishment, he lived in a hearse that was parked in front of the Ryman Auditorium, the home of the Grand Ole Opry. Even though the country traditionalists ignored him, he soon signed a contract with an independent label, Plantation Records, and released an album in 1968.

Coe began to perform in a rhinestone suit and sometimes wore a Lone Ranger mask or covered his face in heavy makeup. He called himself the Mysterious Rhinestone Cowboy. He hung out with motorcycle gangs and would sometimes begin his concerts by driving a Harley onto the stage with a wrench tucked under his belt before singing. He dared anyone who thought him less than tough, told reporters that he had killed a man while in the penitentiary, and laced his commentary on stage and in print with expletives. His long hair and tattooed body completed his outlaw persona.

Coe's songwriting ranged from introspective, even tender, to in-your-face. While he was at first unable to move beyond a cult following for his own performances, other artists earned hit records with the songs he wrote. In 1973, Tanya Tucker recorded Coe's "Would You Lay with Me in a Field of Stone," which reached number one. In 1975, Coe finally reached the Top 10 on his own with his cover of Steve Goodman's "You Never Even Called Me By My Name." Two years later, Johnny Paycheck recorded Coe's "Take This Job and Shove It," and it became a hit. Meanwhile, Coe's album *David Allan Coe Rides Again* used the technique of moving from one song to another without interruption and included lyrics such as "if that ain't country, I'll kiss your ass," and "me and my wives have been spending our lives in a house we've been calling a home"—shocking references for that time.

By the early 1980s, outlaw country was waning. A packaged Nashville sound had again taken hold of country music, although the outlaw artists left their mark by creating a more independent environment for those who followed them.

THE VIKINGS ON MARS

"Is there life on Mars?" has long been the leading question about the mysterious red planet. In 1976, Americans sought the answer by sending aloft two unmanned spacecraft. The first, *Viking 1,* launched on August 20, 1975, took 11 months to make the 212-million-mile journey from Earth, going into orbit around Mars on July 19, 1976. The next day, the *Viking 1* landing craft separated from its octagon-shaped orbiter and followed computer-generated instructions, firing its rockets to

The *Viking I* mission produced this global mosaic of Mars. *(National Space Science Data Center)*

maneuver and slow its descent to the Martian surface. A 53-foot parachute attached to the vehicle aided in assuring a soft landing.

It took little more than three hours for the lander to travel the distance from the orbiter to the surface where it set its spindly legs on a rocky desert plain called Chryse Planitia. (Cameras aboard the orbiter, meanwhile, continued to photograph the surface, as they had done since the *Viking's* arrival.) Dr. Noel Hinners, associate administrator for space science at NASA, said about the landing: "I had tears in my eyes for the first time since—well, I guess, since I got married. It's fantastic."[54]

The landing craft contained scan cameras, an arm that could be extended to collect soil samples, meteorological measuring devices, and other scientific equipment. It was labeled "the most sophisticated vehicle ever dispatched to a neighboring world."[55] The *Viking* performed largely as planned, marred only by a balky seismometer and a stuck sampling arm that scientists loosened five days later. Within minutes of its landing, the *Viking* began to transmit black and white photographs to Earth and, later, color ones. One panoramic view showed a terrain strewn with rocks, some of them sharp edged, as if never worn down by erosion, and others smooth. The lander continued to function until 1982.

The nearly identical *Viking 2* craft left Earth on September 9, 1975, and entered orbit around Mars on August 7, 1976. The lander descended to the Martian surface on September 3 and set down at Utopia Planitia, on the edge of the planet's northern polar ice cap, about 4,000 miles northeast of the *Viking 1* site. One of the craft's legs landed on a rock, causing Viking to tilt slightly. *Viking 2* continued to operate until 1980.

The $1 billion Viking project resulted in NASA officially reporting that the Martian soil, found to be rich in iron, lacked any signs of life. But other scientists, replicating the Martian soil with information obtained from *Viking,* reached a different conclusion, leaving unsettled an answer to the question. A Mars meteorite later found in Antarctica, additional photos of Mars from another mission, and other research have all given credence to the view that Mars harbors some form of microscopic life.

Other missions followed in the 1990s and later, sending more spacecraft to the Mars surface as part of NASA's Mars Exploration Program. In 2004, land rovers continued to look for water, along with signs of past or present life. The *Viking* craft, called by one scientist "the Cadillac" of Mars missions, had led the way to these later efforts, producing a crowning technological achievement in the red, white, and blue bicentennial year.

CHRONICLE OF EVENTS

1976

January 19: President Gerald Ford presents his State of the Union address in which he calls for Congress to exercise restraint in spending while passing a tax cut. The combination, he says, will control inflation while boosting the country out of its recession.

January 26: The *New York Times* reveals the contents of a report by the House Select Committee on Intelligence that concludes that the CIA violated a 1967 presidential directive barring it from providing secret moneys to colleges and universities, that intelligence agency budgets were much higher than the figures presented to Congress, and that the National Security Agency had listened illegally to overseas telephone conversations.

February 4: The Senate subcommittee on multinational corporations reports that the Lockheed Aircraft Corporation had bribed foreign officials to secure sales of its planes. The committee states there existed widespread influence peddling in western Europe, the Middle East, and the Far East.

February 4: The federal government approves the landing of the Concorde supersonic jet airliner at JFK International Airport in New York City and Dulles Airport in Washington, D.C. The decision comes despite numerous protests by nearby residents and environmental groups about excessive noise and pollution from the plane.

February 7: The record album *Wanted! The Outlaws* enters the country-and-western charts, signaling the arrival of "outlaw country" music that will be advanced by such singers as Willie Nelson, Waylon Jennings, Jessi Colter, and David Allan Coe.

February 17: President Ford announces major changes to U.S. intelligence agencies. Among the reforms: the creation of a three-member board to oversee the management of intelligence and prepare intelligence agency budgets; legislation to protect important intelligence secrets; legislation to permit, with a judge's approval, electronic surveillance within the United States for foreign intelligence purposes; and an executive order that limits the power of intelligence agencies to intrude on the activities of U.S. citizens and sets limits on the gathering of information about them.

February 18: The Environmental Protection Agency bans the production of nearly all pesticides that contain mercury, an element linked to nervous-system disorders.

March 18: The New Jersey Supreme Court orders a new trial for boxer Rubin "Hurricane" Carter and John Artis, both of whom had been convicted and sentenced to life imprisonment for a triple murder committed in Paterson, New Jersey, in 1967. The court says the prosecutor's office had prejudiced the trial by suppressing evidence.

March 20: A federal court jury in San Francisco finds Patricia Hearst guilty on charges of armed robbery connected to the holdup of the Sunset Branch of the Hibernia Bank while she was a member of the Symbionese Liberation Front. Hearst had argued that the SLA forced her to commit the crime under the threat of death.

March 24: The U.S. Supreme Court rules 5-3 that African Americans who were denied jobs in violation of the Civil Rights Act of 1964 must be awarded retroactive seniority.

March 28: The FBI releases reports that show that it had burglarized the offices of the Socialist Workers Party 92 times between 1960 and 1966 and had stolen thousands of documents. Earlier, the justice department had denied that the burglaries had ever taken place.

March 29: The U.S. Supreme Court rules 6-3 that individual states can prosecute persons for committing homosexual acts, even if the acts are consensual and private.

March 31: The New Jersey Supreme Court rules that the respirator keeping alive Karen Quinlan, 22, can be disconnected if doctors and hospital officials agree that there is no "reasonable possibility" that she will recover. Karen's father, Joseph Quinlan, is appointed by the court as her guardian and is given the authority to consult with doctors and hospital officials to remove Karen from the respirator.

April 1: Steven Jobs and Stephen Wozniak found Apple, Inc. in a garage in California's Silicon Valley with the goal of selling 100 computers.

April 26: The Church committee issues its final report on foreign and domestic intelligence activities. It finds that the FBI knowingly and repeatedly broke laws and violated constitutional rights in its operations against domestic political groups, actions that represented excessive executive power.

May 17: Following the recommendation of the Church committee, the Senate establishes a 15-member Select Committee on Intelligence to oversee CIA activities and authorize funds for CIA operations.

May 19: Karen Ann Quinlan is removed from her respirator and breathes on her own. She lives another nine years but never regains consciousness.

May 24: The Concorde supersonic jet airliner makes its first landing at Dulles Airport in Washington, D.C., completing a flight from Paris.

May 25: Representative Wayne L. Hays (Dem., Ohio), the powerful chairman of four House committees, admits to an affair with a staff aid, Elizabeth Ray. Hays defends having Ray on his payroll, saying that she has done valuable work, but Ray admits that she hardly ever worked at her office and did not know how to type or answer the phones.

June 4: The labor department reports a drop in the nation's unemployment rate to 7.3 percent, the lowest in nearly 18 months.

June 8: Former Georgia governor Jimmy Carter wins the Ohio Democratic primary, nearly assuring his victory in the party's presidential nomination. At the same time, President Ford wins the Ohio Republican primary, but he loses to former California governor Ronald Reagan in California, leaving the two men in a close contest for the GOP presidential nomination.

June 10: Congressman Wayne L. Hays slips into a coma after taking an overdose of sleeping pills while the sex scandal with Elizabeth Ray continues.

June 14: The Supreme Court lets stand lower court rulings that uphold busing as a means of integrating public schools.

June 25: The Supreme Court rules that private nonsectarian schools cannot exclude children because of their race.

July 2: The Supreme Court rules 7-2 that the death penalty is constitutional as long as juries receive adequate information and guidance for making a decision about whether it should be administered.

July 4: Americans celebrate the U.S. Bicentennial (200th year of their country's independence) with special festivities from coast to coast. The largest and most impressive of these is Operation Sail in New York City, a display of more than 225 masted ships that includes 16 tall ships from around the world. More than 6 million people, among them President Ford, attend the event.

July 8: The New York State Supreme Court disbars former President Richard Nixon for his role in the Watergate scandal. The court finds Nixon guilty of obstructing justice.

July 12: The Democratic National Convention opens in New York City; three days later, Jimmy Carter

will accept the presidential nomination. He will select Senator Walter Mondale (Dem., Minn.) as his running mate.

July 17: Twenty-six school children and their bus driver escape their underground confinement near Chowchilla, California. They had been kidnapped two days earlier by three masked gunmen who commandeered a bus as it left a summer school session, transferred their prisoners to vans, and then held them in a quarry. Authorities will arrest the three kidnappers in late July.

July 20: The *Viking I* landing craft arrives on Mars after an 11-month journey. It transmits black-and-white and color photographs showing sand dunes, craters, and rocks. A few days later, a robotic arm will scoop up soil samples. Further tests will provide conflicting evidence as to whether there might be life on the planet.

July 21: An unidentified disease strikes a Legionnaires' convention in Philadelphia, infecting 180 people and eventually killing 29. In January 1977, the Centers for Disease Control identifies the cause of the "Legionnaires' disease" as a new bacterium.

August 8: The Labor department reports a sharp increase in the nation's unemployment rate, now reaching 7.8 percent.

August 9: A Los Angeles Superior Court jury finds two members of the Symbionese Liberation Front, William Harris and Emily Harris, guilty of kidnapping, armed robbery, and auto theft. They will later be sentenced to prison terms of 11 years for armed robbery and to life for kidnapping.

August 16: The three-day-long Republican National Convention opens in Kansas City, Kansas, and, on August 18, it will nominate President Gerald Ford and Kansas senator Robert Dole as the party's presidential and vice presidential standard-bearers.

August 21: The United States places B-52 bombers, F-4 and F-111 fighter jets and hundreds of its soldiers and those of South Korea on alert after the slaying three days earlier of two American soldiers by the North Koreans in the Korean demilitarized zone. An agreement between the U.S.-led United Nations Command and North Korea in early September will ease the tension with its provisions to avoid future clashes in the DMZ.

August 23: In a *New York* magazine article, author Tom Wolfe calls the 1970s the "Me Decade," in an allusion to its self-indulgence.

September 1: Representative Wayne L. Hays resigns the seat that he had held for 28 years in Congress. Two days earlier, the House ethics committee had voted to hold hearings into Hays's involvement in a sex scandal.

September 3: The *Viking II* landing craft puts down on Mars and transmits photographs of the surface.

October 4: Secretary of Agriculture Earl Butz resigns from office in the wake of newspaper reports disclosing that he made derogatory and racist remarks about blacks.

October 4: Cleveland Indians outfielder Frank Robinson becomes major league baseball's first black manager when he takes over that club as player-manager.

October 7: The Labor Department reports a surge in inflation. Coupled with continuing high unemployment, the economic news damages President Ford's campaign for the White House.

October 7: Convicted murderer Gary Mark Gilmore is sentenced to death in Utah and demands execution by a firing squad. A three-month legal battle follows with nationwide press coverage.

November 2: Jimmy Carter narrowly defeats Gerald Ford to become the first Deep South presidential candidate to reach the White House since before the Civil War.

December 3: President-elect Jimmy Carter announces his selection of Cyrus Vance to serve as secretary of state. Vance had previously served as deputy secretary of defense in the 1960s.

National Security Advisor Zbigniew Brezinski (left) confers with Secretary of State Cyrus Vance. *(Courtesy Jimmy Carter Library)*

December 16: President-elect Carter names Andrew Young as United States ambassador to the United Nations. Young, formerly an aide to Reverend Dr. Martin Luther King, Jr., pledges to advocate black majority rule in Africa.

December 21: A jury again finds Rubin "Hurricane" Carter and John Artis guilty of murder in a triple homicide.

EYEWITNESS TESTIMONY

The Case of Karen Ann Quinlan

It seemed to be the consensus not only of the treating physicians but also of the several qualified experts who testified in the case, that removal from the respirator would not conform to medical practices, standards and traditions.

The further medical consensus was that Karen, in addition to being comatose, is in a chronic and persistent "vegetative" state, having no awareness of anything or anyone around her and existing at a primitive reflex level. Although she does have some brain stem function (ineffective for respiration) and has other reactions one normally associates with being alive, such as moving, reacting to light, sound and noxious stimuli, blinking her eyes, and the like, the quality of her feeling impulses is unknown. She grimaces, makes stereotyped cries and sounds and has chewing motions. Her blood pressure is normal.

Karen is described as emaciated, having suffered a weight loss of at least 40 pounds, and undergoing a continuing deteriorative process. Her posture is described as fetal-like and grotesque; there is extreme flexion-rigidity of the arms, legs and related muscles and her joints are severely rigid and deformed.

From all of this evidence, and including the whole testimonial record, several basic findings in the physical area are mandated. Severe brain and associated damage, albeit of uncertain etiology, has left Karen in a chronic and persistent vegetative state. No form of treatment which can cure or improve that condition is known or available. As nearly as may be determined, considering the guarded area of remote uncertainties characteristic of most medical science predictions, she can *never* be restored to cognitive or sapient life. Even with regard to the vegetative level and improvement therein (if such it may be called) the prognosis is extremely poor and the extent unknown if it should in fact occur. . . .

She is debilitated and moribund and although fairly stable at the time of argument before us (no new information having been filed in the meanwhile in expansion of the record), no physician risked the opinion that she could live more than a year and indeed she may die much earlier. Excellent medical and nursing care so far has been able to ward off the constant threat of infection, to which she is peculiarly susceptible because of the respirator, the tracheal tube and other incidents of care in her vulnerable condition. Her life accordingly is sustained by the respirator and tubal feeding, and removal from the respirator

would cause her death soon, although the time cannot be stated with more precision. . . .

We have no doubt, in these unhappy circumstances, that if Karen were herself miraculously lucid for an interval (not altering the existing prognosis of the condition to which she would soon return) and perceptive of her irreversible condition, she could effectively decide upon discontinuance of the life-support apparatus, even if it meant the prospect of natural death. . . .

We have no hesitancy in deciding . . . that no external compelling interest of the State could compel Karen to endure the unendurable, only to vegetate a few measurable months with no realistic possibility of returning to any semblance of cognitive or sapient life. We perceive no thread of logic distinguishing between such a choice on Karen's part and a similar choice which, under the evidence in this case, could be made by a competent patient terminally ill, riddled by cancer and suffering great pain; such a patient would not be resuscitated or put on a respirator . . . and *a fortiori* would not be kept *against his will* on a respirator.

Although the Constitution does not explicitly mention a right of privacy, Supreme Court decisions have recognized that a right of personal privacy exists and that certain areas of privacy are guaranteed under the Constitution. . . .

Our affirmation of Karen's independent right of choice, however, would ordinarily be based upon her competency to assert it. The sad truth, however, is that she is grossly incompetent and we cannot discern her supposed choice based on the testimony of her previous conversations with friends, where such testimony is without sufficient probative weight. . . . Nevertheless we have concluded that Karen's right of privacy may be asserted on her behalf by her guardian under the peculiar circumstances here present. . . .

From the New Jersey Supreme Court decision in the Matter of Quinlan (70 N. J. 10, 1976), issued on March 31, 1976, available online at http://www.csulb. edu/~jvancamp/452_r6.html, downloaded July 27, 2004.

I have concluded that further judicial review of the Karen Quinlan decision is unwarranted from the standpoint of the state. . . .

Fortunately, the Supreme Court in reversing the decision of the trial court concluded that the responsible attending physicians of a comatose patient must find that there is no reasonable possibility of the patient's ever emerging from the comatose condition to a cognitive, sapient state, and that this judgment must be concurred with by an "ethics committee" of the hospital involved. Consequently, I do not see in the decision of the Supreme Court an obvious immediate danger to the public interest. . . .

We should all join together in an effort to produce in a responsible fashion the intended result of this landmark decision, for obviously it involves not only the tragic circumstances of Karen Quinlan, but possibly also the fate of countless other persons in the years ahead.

From the text of a statement by New Jersey state attorney general William F. Hyland in reaction to the ruling by the state supreme court in the matter of Karen Ann Quinlan, issued on April 6, 1976, in the New York Times, *April 7, 1976, p. 89.*

I didn't understand at first why we were going to turn off the machine. It was kind of a shock when it was first suggested. . . . They had always said to talk to her. I had called her name before and nothing happened. She had these dead eyes. But I called "Karen," and she looked at me. It just happened once. I stayed down there until 10:30 at night, but she didn't look at me again. I thought that was sad because she was my sister. But it was about the saddest thing in the world that could happen to Karen, she was always so full of life.

Karen Ann Quinlan's 19-year-old sister, Mary Ellen Quinlan, commenting in 1976 about her parent's decision to disconnect Karen's life support system and how Karen had reacted to her presence in the hospital only a few days after Karen had become comatose, in B. D. Colen, Karen Ann Quinlan *(1976), pp. 26–27.*

Whenever I thought of a person in a coma, I'd thought they would just lie there very quietly, almost as though they were sleeping. Karen's head was moving around, as if she was trying to pull away from that tube in her throat, and she made little noises, like moans. I didn't know if she was in pain, but it seemed as though she was. And I thought—if Karen could ever see herself like this, it would be like the worst thing in the world for her. It would be so hard for her to accept being so dependent on all these doctors and nurses, and the equipment and everything.

Mary Lou McCudden, one of Karen Ann Quinlan's closest friends, commenting around 1976 on her visit with Karen in 1975, soon after Karen slipped into a coma, in Joseph and Julia Quinlan, Karen Ann *(1977), p. 29.*

I felt almost exhilarated—for Karen. She was liberated now, from the machines she would have hated. And she had done something that I think benefited the whole world, and I thought she would have liked that. Been proud of that, because helping people was her way. And I kept thinking, "You're free, honey."

Julia Quinlan, Karen Ann Quinlan's mother, commenting around 1976 on the removal of her daughter from the hospital life-support system, in Joseph and Julia Quinlan, Karen Ann *(1977), p. 326.*

The Wayne Hays Scandal

Mr. Speaker, members of the House, this is the most difficult speech that I have ever made in the 28 years I have been a member of this House. . . .

Much has been said in the press, in the cloakrooms, and in gossip about Wayne Hays. I have been called more names than any member of Congress in my memory. I have been called arrogant, ruthless, cold blooded, vicious, temperamental and mean . . . just to mention a few of the ones that are printable. No one has ever said that I am also a human being . . . capable of emotions and of errors, but I am . . . and I have erred.

Six weeks ago, I was married to the woman I love more than any other person or thing in the world including the House. Prior to this time, for an extended period of time, I did have a relationship with Elizabeth Ray. I was legally separated and single. It was voluntary on her part and on mine. . . .

When I proposed to my new bride, I explained to Miss Ray that our relationship would have to end but that I would continue to help her in any way I could, so long as she continued to perform her duties as best she could.

It was at this time that Miss Ray became hysterical—threatened suicide, as she had done in the past. She also threatened blackmail and to destroy my engagement. . . .

I stand by my previous denial of Miss Ray's allegation that she was hired to be my mistress.

I further stand by my statement that Miss Ray is a seriously disturbed young lady, and I deeply regret that our relationship, and its termination, has apparently greatly aggravated both the emotional and psychological problems. . . . I stand here before you today . . . with my conscience now clear.

I sincerely hope that those responsible for this at the *Washington Post* and Miss Ray, with her forthcoming book and appearance in *Playboy* can say the same. . . .

Only time will tell whether Miss Ray will be successful in destroying my career. I pray to God she will not have destroyed my marriage.

I hope that when the time comes to leave this House, which I love, Wayne Hays will be remembered as mean, arrogant, and cantankerous and tough, but I hope Wayne Hays will never be thought of as dishonest.

From a statement by Representative Wayne L. Hays (Dem., Ohio) to the House of Representative on May 25, 1976, in the New York Times, May 26, 1976, p. 16.

You know, you're kind of cute. If you weren't a spy, I might go out with you.

A statement by Elizabeth Ray to newspaper reporter Bob Owens made while Owens was investigating Ray's relationship with congressmen on Capitol Hill, in Time, June 14, 1976, available online at http: www.time.com/ time/archive/preview/0,10987,914210,00.html, accessed June 6, 2005.

She wasn't very intelligent. If I took her out somewhere, I'd tell her not to say anything. Now and then she'd forget and call me the next day to apologize.

Attorney Charlie Schultz recalling in 1976 his own experience with Elizabeth Ray, in Time, June 14, 1976, available online at http://www.time. com/time/archive/preview/0,10987,947699,00. html, accessed June 6, 2005.

The Bicentennial

We're all so jaded, but we were able to savor each one of the ships. . . . It's really exciting because all these countries have gotten together to celebrate the Bicentennial with us.

Sharron Stein, a resident of Toledo, Ohio, commenting on the parade of ships, known as Operation Sail, during the Bicentennial celebration, in the New York Times, July 3, 1976, p. 1.

Yes it occurred to me that I could stay in New York and watch the ships. Then it also occurred to me that I could get away for three days and visit some friends. I'll watch it from [New Haven, Connecticut] on television.

Hanna Fuerst of Woodside in Queens, New York, commenting on why she decided not to attend Operation Sail for the Bicentennial celebration, in the New York Times, July 3, 1976, p. 1.

It was a real blast, a superbash, a party unlike any other party, ever. It stretched from coast to coast, from dawn to the small hours and then some—a glorious and gigantic birthday wingding that mobilized millions for a gaudy extravaganza of parades and picnics, rodeos, and regattas, fireworks and other festivities too numerous to catalogue. It was an altogether fitting celebration of the 200th anniversary of America's independence, and perhaps the best part of it was that its supreme characteristics were good will, good humor and, after a long night of paralyzing self-doubt, good feelings about the U.S.

From Time magazine, July 19, 1976, in Time Magazine Multimedia Almanac.

Twenty-six Children Abducted in California

We're all very relieved. The children were very frightened. There is no motive to this that I know of. It's a mystery. But it's over. They [the kidnappers] took the names and ages and the parents' names. Maybe they intended to demand a ransom. We don't know.

James Dumas, mayor of the town of Chowchilla, expressing relief at the rescue of the 26 children and the bus driver who were kidnapped by three local men, in the New York Times, July 18, 1976, p. 1.

It was our theory all along that whoever held the children planned to hold them for a period of time and then trade them for something.

Sheriff Ed Bates of Madera County reacting to the discovery of a ransom note in the kidnapping of 26 children and their bus driver in Chowchilla, California, in the New York Times, July 24, 1976, p. 1.

The Nomination of Jimmy Carter for President

It's a pleasure to be here with all you Democrats and to see that our Bicentennial celebration and our Bicentennial convention has been one of decorum and order without any fights or free-for-alls. Among Democrats that can only happen once every two hundred years. With this kind of a united Democratic Party, we are ready, and eager, to take on the Republicans— whichever Republican Party they decide to send against us in November.

Nineteen seventy-six will not be a year of politics as usual. It can be a year of inspiration and hope, and it will be a year of concern, of quiet and sober reassessment of our nation's character and purpose. It has already been a year when voters have confounded the experts. And I guarantee you that it will be the year when we give the government of this country back to the people of this country.

There is a new mood in America. We have been shaken by a tragic war abroad and by scandals and broken promises at home. Our people are searching for new voices and new ideas and new leaders. . . .

Guided by lasting and simple moral values, we have emerged idealists without illusions, realists who still know the old dreams of justice and liberty, of country and of community. . . .

But in recent years our nation has seen a failure of leadership. We have been hurt, and we have been disillusioned. We have seen a wall go up that separates us from our own government.

We have lost some precious things that historically have bound our people and our government together. We feel that moral decay has weakened our country, that it is crippled by a lack of goals and values, and that our public officials have lost faith in us. We have been a nation adrift too long. We have been without leadership too long. We have had divided and deadlocked government too long. We have been governed by veto too long. We have suffered enough at the hands of a tired and worn-out administration without new ideas, without youth or vitality, without vision and without the confidence of the American people. There is a fear that our best years are behind us. But I say to you that our nation's best is still ahead.

Our country has lived through a time of torment. It is now a time for healing. We want to have faith again. We want to be proud again. We just want the truth again. . . .

It is time for America to move and to speak not with boasting and belligerence but with a quiet strength, to depend in world affairs not merely on the size of an arsenal but on the nobility of ideas, and to govern at home not by confusion and crisis but with grace and imagination and common sense.

Too many have had to suffer at the hands of a political economic elite who have shaped decisions and never had to account for mistakes or to suffer from injustice. When unemployment prevails, they never stand in line looking for a job.

When deprivation results from a confused and bewildering welfare system, they never do without food or clothing or a place to sleep. When the public schools are inferior or torn by strife, their children go to exclusive private schools. And when the bureaucracy is bloated and confused, the powerful always manage to discover and occupy niches of special influence and privilege. An unfair tax structure serves their needs. And tight secrecy always seems to prevent reform. . . .

It is time for us to take a new look at our own government, to strip away the secrecy, to expose the unwarranted pressure of lobbyists, to eliminate waste, to release our civil servants from bureaucratic chaos, to provide tough management, and always to remember that in any town or city the mayor, the governor, and the President represent exactly the same constituents. . . .

My vision of this nation and its future has been deepened and matured during the nineteen months that I have campaigned among you for President. I have never had more faith in America than I do today. We have an America that, in Bob Dylan's phrase, is busy being born, not busy dying. . . .

As I've said many times before, we can have an American President who does not govern with negativism and fear of the future, but with vigor and vision and aggressive leadership—a President who's not isolated from the people, but who feels your pain and shares your dreams and takes his strength and his wisdom and his courage from you.

I see an America on the move again, united, a diverse and vital and tolerant nation, entering our third century with pride and confidence, an America that lives up to the majesty of our Constitution and the simple decency of our people.

This is the America we want. This is the America that we will have.

We will go forward from this convention with some differences of opinion perhaps, but nevertheless united in a calm determination to make our country large and driving and generous in spirit once again, ready to embark on great national deeds. And once again, as brothers and sisters, our hearts will swell with pride to call ourselves Americans.

From Jimmy Carter's acceptance speech at the Democratic National Convention in New York City on July 15, 1976, available online at http://jimmycarterlibrary. org/documents/speeches/acceptance_speech.pdf, downloaded July 27, 2004.

Gerald Ford's Nomination for President

I am honored by your nomination, and I accept it with pride, with gratitude, and with a total will to win a great victory for the American people. We will wage a winning campaign in every region of this country, from the snowy banks of Minnesota to the sandy plains of Georgia. We concede not a single State. We concede not a single vote. This evening I am proud to stand before this great convention as the first incumbent President since Dwight D. Eisenhower who can tell the American people America is at peace.

Tonight I can tell you straightaway this Nation is sound, this Nation is secure, this Nation is on the march to full economic recovery and a better quality of life for all Americans.

And I will tell you one more thing: This year the issues are on our side. I am ready, I am eager to go before the American people and debate the real issues face to face with Jimmy Carter. . . .

Something wonderful happened to this country of ours the past 2 years. We all came to realize it on the Fourth of July. Together, out of years of turmoil and tragedy, wars and riots, assassinations and wrongdoing in high places, Americans recaptured the spirit of 1776. We saw again the pioneer vision of our revolutionary founders and our immigrant ancestors. Their vision was of free men and free women enjoying limited government and unlimited opportunity. The mandate I want in 1976 is to make this vision a reality, but it will take the voices and the votes of many more Americans who are not Republicans to make that mandate binding and my mission possible.

I have been called an unelected President, an accidental President. We may even hear that again from the other party, despite the fact that I was welcomed and endorsed by an overwhelming majority of their elected representatives in the Congress who certified my fitness to our highest office. Having become Vice President and President without expecting or seeking either, I have a special feeling toward these high offices. To me, the Presidency and the Vice-Presidency were not prizes to be won, but a duty to be done.

So, tonight it is not the power and the glamour of the Presidency that leads me to ask for another 4 years; it is something every hard-working American will understand—the challenge of a job well begun, but far from finished. . . .

On a marble fireplace in the White House is carved a prayer which John Adams wrote. It concludes, "May

First Lady Betty Ford talks with a reporter while crossing Michigan during a whistle-stop campaign trip in 1976. *(Courtesy Gerald R. Ford Library)*

none but honest and wise men ever rule under this roof." Since I have resided in that historic house, I have tried to live by that prayer. I faced many tough problems. I probably made some mistakes, but on balance, America and Americans have made an incredible comeback since August 1974. Nobody can honestly say otherwise. And the plain truth is that the great progress we have made at home and abroad was in spite of the majority who run the Congress of the United States. . . .

I come before you with a 2-year record of performance without your mandate. I offer you a 4-year pledge of greater performance with your mandate. As Governor Al Smith used to say, "Let's look at the record."

Two years ago inflation was 12 percent. Sales were off. Plants were shut down. Thousands were being laid off every week.

Fear of the future was throttling down our economy and threatening millions of families.

Let's look at the record since August 1974. Inflation has been cut in half. Payrolls are up. Profits are up. Production is up. Purchases are up. Since the recession was turned around, almost 4 million of our fellow Americans have found new jobs or got their old jobs back. This year more men and women have jobs than ever before in the history of the United States. Confidence has returned, and we are in the full surge of sound recovery to steady prosperity.

Two years ago America was mired in withdrawal from Southeast Asia. A decade of Congresses had short-changed our global defenses and threatened our strategic posture. Mounting tension between Israel and the Arab nations made another war seem inevitable. The whole world watched and wondered where America was going. Did we in our domestic turmoil have the will, the stamina, and the unity to stand up for freedom? Look at the record since August, 2 years ago. Today America is at peace and seeks peace for all nations. Not a single American is at war anywhere on the face of this Earth tonight. . . .

Two years ago people's confidence in their highest officials, to whom they had overwhelmingly entrusted power, had twice been shattered. Losing faith in the word of their elected leaders, Americans lost some of their own faith in themselves. Again, let's look at the record since August 1974. From the start my administration has been open, candid, forthright. . . .

As I try in my imagination to look into the homes where families are watching the end of this great convention, I can't tell which faces are Republicans, which are Democrats, and which are Independents. I cannot see their color or their creed. I see only Americans.

I see Americans who love their husbands, their wives, and their children. I see Americans who love their country for what it has been and what it must become. I see Americans who work hard but who are willing to sacrifice all they have worked for to keep their children and their country free. I see Americans who in their own quiet way pray for peace among nations and peace among themselves. We do love our neighbors, and we do forgive those who have trespassed against us.

I see a new generation that knows what is right and knows itself, a generation determined to preserve its ideals, its environment, our Nation, and the world.

My fellow Americans, I like what I see. I have no fear for the future of this great country. And as we go forward together, I promise you once more what I promised before: to uphold the Constitution, to do what is right as God gives me to see the right, and to do the very best that I can for America.

From Gerald Ford's speech in which he accepted the Republican presidential nomination at Kansas City, Missouri, on August 19, 1976, available online at http://www.ford.utexas.edu/library/speeches/ 760733.htm, downloaded July 28, 2004.

Jimmy Carter's Presidential Campaign

Christ said, "I tell you that anyone who looks on a woman with lust has in his heart already committed adultery." I've looked on a lot of women with lust. I've committed adultery in my heart many times. This is something that God recognizes I will do—and I have done it—and God forgives me for it. But that doesn't mean that I condemn someone who not only looks on a woman with lust but who leaves his wife and shacks up with somebody out of wedlock. Christ says, "Don't consider yourself better than someone else because one guy screws a whole bunch of women while the other guy is loyal to his wife."

An excerpt from the Playboy *magazine interview in November 1976 that raised tremendous controversy during that year's presidential campaign, available online at http://www.playboy.com/world of playboy/ faq/interview.html, downloaded May 12, 2005.*

The Jimmy Carter Victory

Perhaps the strongest feeling in this country today is the general distrust of government and politicians at all levels. The desire and thrust for strong moral leadership in the nation was not satisfied with the election of Richard Nixon.

Hamilton Jordan, an adviser to Jimmy Carter, providing in 1972 what would become the outline for Carter's presidential campaign in 1976, in Burton I. Kaufman The Presidency of James Earl Carter, Jr. *(1993), p. 11.*

The 1976 election of Mr. Carter reflected, perhaps more than any other sentiment, a strong distaste for power and its misuse and support for an outsider of unquestioned integrity.

There is nothing new in the observation that the times dictate the vote. In this case . . . we must remember that the qualities sought were those actually gained. Jimmy Carter is a man of simple tastes, a bit embarrassed by pomp and circumstance. . . . He is genuinely modest; he often remarked that he hoped to be a president worthy of the American people.

Juanita Kreps, secretary of commerce under President Jimmy Carter, commenting around 1990 on Carter's election victory in 1976, in Kenneth W. Thompson, The Carter Presidency *(1990), p. 86.*

We'd lost the popular vote by almost two million votes. And as we looked at it, we saw that we had won more states by narrow margins than we had lost by narrow margins. So we knew that a challenge would not be tasteful as far as the public was concerned, and it probably would not be successful, either.

James Baker, President Ford's national campaign chairman, explaining in November 1976 why the Ford campaign decided not to challenge the outcome of that year's presidential election, in Martin Schram, Running for President 1976 *(1977), p. 358.*

The Me Decade

Encounter sessions . . . were often wild events. Such aggression! Such sobs! tears! moans, hysteria, vile recriminations, shocking revelations, such explosions of hostility between husbands and wives, such mudballs of profanity from previously mousy mommies and workadaddies, such red-mad attacks! . . .

Outsiders, hearing of these sessions, wondered what on earth their appeal was. Yet the appeal was simple enough. It is summed up in the notion: "Let's talk about *Me.*" No matter whether you managed to renovate your personality through encounter sessions or not, you had finally focused your attention and your energies on the most fascinating subject on earth: *Me.*

Tom Wolfe discussing the 1970s as the Me Decade in his essay "The Me Decade and the Third Great Awakening," in Tom Wolfe, ed., The Purple Decades: A Reader *(1982), p. 279.*

Apple Computer

I think it was my second year of college. I finally got some parts from a company that I had worked for, so I could build a computer of my own design. It was the first computer that I have ever built in my life. It was a minimal one. It couldn't do much, but it had switches and lights and it ran.

We built it down in Bill Fernandez's garage. He lived down the street, a few streets down. And Bill introduced me to Steve. That's my recollection. . . .

[Steve] was sort of a free-floating hippie who could go a lot of different ways. He ate a lot of nuts— and walked around barefoot or in sandals. He could

get a job at Atari as a technician-engineer who could take designs and finish them. And then he'd go out for a few months and work on spreads in Oregon, or go over to India, bathe in the Ganges River. Then he'd come back.

Apple Computer cofounder Steve Wozniak recounting in a 2003 interview how he first met Steve Jobs, available online at http://www.landsnail.com/apple/local/ sunspot/printstory/jsp.html, downloaded May 13, 2005.

The guy who started one of the first computer stores told us he could sell then [Apple I's] as fully stocked boards if we could make them up and deliver them. That had not dawned on us until then.

Steve Jobs, one of the founders of Apple Computer, in an undated comment recalling the suggestion that changed the way he manufactured computers, in Jeffrey S. Young, Steve Jobs *(1988), p. 93.*

The Apple was consuming all his time. I saw very little of him. He'd go off to [Hewlett Packard] and eat something at McDonald's, on the way to Jobs' house. He wouldn't get home until midnight, then he'd work some more on his stuff and leave all the parts on the kitchen table with big notes saying that nothing should be touched. I was going nuts.

Alice Robertson Wozniak, Steve Wozniak's wife, in an undated comment recalling her husband's early efforts at developing an Apple computer, in Jeffrey S. Young, Steve Jobs *(1988), p. 95.*

Steve [Jobs] got friends and relatives to call me, but I didn't want any part of running a business. I was very much the young technical nerd and thought that companies and managers were all political bullshit. It's a game that I would never want to be near. Then one of my friends telephoned me and explained that I didn't have to be a manager or a businessman. He said I could still be just an engineer for the rest of my life even if I helped start a company and got rich. That made sense to me because I didn't want something that I wasn't. It made all the difference when I realized that I could be an engineer my whole life.

Steve Wozniak in an undated comment reflecting on his decision to help Steve Jobs found Apple Computer, in Lee Butcher, Accidental Millionaire *(1988), p. 87.*

Gary Gilmore

The man I see there is not a guilty killer. He looks like a high beam to me. We Christians should turn the other cheek.

Larry Wood, a demonstrator in Salt Lake City in 1976 demanding the release of Gary Gilmore, in Time, *December 13, 1976, available online at http://www. time.com/time/archive/preview/0,10987,918554,00. html, downloaded June 6, 2005.*

I rapped on the glass. I would have to leave soon and I asked if the warden would allow us a final hand-shake. . . . He assented after Gary explained it was our final visit, on the condition I agree to a skin search. I agreed. After the search, conducted by two guards, two other guards brought Gary in. They said I would have to roll up my sleeve past my elbow, and that we could not touch beyond a handshake. Gary grasped my hand, squeezed tight, and said, "Well, I guess this is it." He leaned over and kissed my cheek. "See you in the darkness beyond."

I pulled my eyes from his. I knew I couldn't stop crying at this point, and I didn't want him to see it. . . . Gary watched me pass through [the rolling-bar doors]. "Give my love to mom," he called. "And put on some weight. You're still too skinny."

Gary Gilmore's brother, Mikal Gilmore, on his last visit with Gary Gilmore before Gilmore's execution, in Mikal Gilmore, Shot in the Heart *(1994), p. 348.*

The Trial of Rubin "Hurricane" Carter

There was silence in the wood-paneled room, broken only by the sound of sobs from women relatives. Both defendants, while obviously shaken, smiled faintly at their friends, and Mr. Artis winked at his older sister.

Reporter Leslie Maitland describing the scene in the Paterson, New Jersey, courtroom on December 21, 1976, as Rubin "Hurricane" Carter and John Artis were found guilty of murder for a second time, in the New York Times, *December 22, 1976, p. 1.*

Apology for what? He should have apologized to the State of New Jersey for all the free room and board he got [in prison]. I would have liked to have pulled the [execution] switch on him myself.

Edwin Englehardt, police commissioner in Passaic County, New Jersey, at the time of Rubin "Hurricane" Carter's arrest, responding to a reporter's question in 1988 over whether Carter was owed an apology for the time he spent behind bars, in James S. Hirsch, Hurricane *(2000), p. 306.*

After all that's been said and done—the fact that the most productive years of my life, between the ages of twenty-nine and fifty, have been stolen; the fact that I was deprived of seeing my children grow up—wouldn't you think I have the right to be bitter? Wouldn't anyone under those circumstances have a right to be bitter? In fact, it would be easy to be bitter. But it has never been my nature, or my lot, to do things the easy way. If I have learned nothing else in life, I've learned that bitterness only consumes the vessel that contains it. And for me to permit bitterness to control or infect my life in any way whatsoever, would be to allow those who imprisoned me to take even more than the twenty-two years they've already taken. Now that would make me an accomplice to their crime—and if anyone believes that I'm going to fall for that . . . then they are green enough to stick in the ground and grow!

Rubin "Hurricane" Carter reflecting in 1988 on the years he served in prison, in James S. Hirsch, Hurricane *(2000), p. 310.*

Life? That only proved to me that they still had doubts. If they had truly thought us guilty of triple murder, how in the world could they have twisted their mouths up to give us life? What life? Being abused in jail forever? It would have been more merciful to shoot me down on the spot. Mercy, my black ass! I would rather they had swung me from the courtroom rafters than for them to come in with that mercy shit. That was only a sham, and everybody had to know it.

Rubin "Hurricane" Carter recounting in 1974 his reaction to a jury finding him and John Artis guilty in 1967 of murder but recommending mercy (meaning life imprisonment rather than the death penalty), in Rubin Hurricane Carter, The Sixteenth Round *(1974), p. 307.*

7

Frustrated America
January 1977–December 1977

Americans looked forward to a new beginning in 1977, symbolized by the inauguration of Jimmy Carter as president. Carter promised to break with the deceit and political scandals of Richard Nixon. Yet, frustrations abounded: A minor scandal shook Carter's administration later in the year, and the country felt that it had yet to shake free of its economic straits when an energy crisis proved difficult for the president and Congress to resolve.

At the same time, Americans had to grapple with their legacy from the Vietnam War, namely what to do about draft resisters. They also had to deal with the question of religious sects and religious freedom; disputes over nuclear power, environmental issues, and military weapons; and the terrifying stalking and killing of young people by a murderer in New York City, who was dubbed "Son of Sam."

PRESIDENT CARTER PARDONS VIETNAM DRAFT RESISTERS

The legacy of Vietnam clung to America in attitudes about country and leadership; in the maimed bodies and shattered minds of those who had fought; in the grave markers that dotted cemeteries from Arlington to numerous small towns; and in the thousands of draft evaders who had refused to fight. What to do about the evaders generated almost as much controversy as the war itself, and the issue kept Vietnam eating away at the national psyche.

President Jimmy Carter decided to break with the past on January 21, 1977, the day following his inauguration, when he granted a pardon to nearly all the draft evaders. The pardon came from Carter's compassionate nature, and it represented his fulfillment of a campaign promise, along with his desire to heal the country's wounds. His pardon took the form of two documents, one a proclamation, and the other an executive order that put the proclamation into effect. Taken together, the documents granted an "unconditional pardon to all persons who may have committed any offense between August 4, 1964, and March 28, 1973, in violation of the Military Selective Service Act," except those who had engaged in activities "involving force or violence."[1] By omitting military deserters, the pardon applied to a relatively small number of people, about 10,000.

Carter's action drew immediate protests from both sides of the issue. On the one hand, those who had opposed the war said that the president had sold minorities short by ignoring the deserters. The draft evaders, they pointed out, were largely white and middle class; the deserters were largely African American, Hispanic, and poor.

On the other hand, those who had supported the war thought that Carter had gone too far. Senator Barry Goldwater (Rep., Ariz.) called it "the most disgraceful thing that a president has ever done," and Bill Brock, the national chairman of the Republican Party, labeled it a "slap in the face to all those Americans and their families who did their duty." T. Cooper Holt, the executive director of the Veterans of Foreign Wars, said, "This is probably one of the saddest days in the history of our country, even surpassing the Watergate days."[2]

JIMMY CARTER'S "PEOPLE'S INAUGURATION"

In the short run, the pardon failed to dent Carter's honeymoon with the public as most Americans remained confident that he would make government more effective and restore dignity to the White House while connecting to the voters who had put him in office. Carter had actually done much to raise hopes for change with the way he handled his "people's inauguration," as his staff called it.

President Carter and Rosalynn Carter walk down Pennsylvania Avenue during the 1977 inauguration. *(Courtesy Jimmy Carter Library)*

He rejected the traditional ride down Pennsylvania Avenue in an open limousine and instead walked the street, hatless, wearing a topcoat, waving and smiling broadly. The crowd loved it; they loved the change from the pomposity of the Nixon years, from the tense times when angry protesters and an angry president taunted each other. Carter's walk took him past the White House, at whose gates crowds had gathered little more than two years earlier to chant at Nixon "Jail to the Chief!" One spectator at Carter's inauguration commented: "I like the feel of this crowd. It seems benign, contented. . . . There's a soft gentleness about it."[3]

A newspaper reporter observed:

The emphasis . . . has been far more on the ordinary people than the very important people. . . .

Beginning on Tuesday, there have been—mostly for free—jazz concerts, poetry readings, horse shows, symphonies, fire-works, folk dances, tours of the city, children's programs, ethnic music, film festivals, puppet shows, bluegrass concerts, a Chinese lion dance, and all sorts of receptions by state delegations.[4]

Carter's staff likened the inauguration to Andrew Jackson's in 1829, when the "common people" poured into the streets to see their new president. Carter's inaugural crowd, however, was more restrained, and the festivities, though cloaked in simplicity, were elaborate and expensive. His inauguration cost more than $3 million; the parade alone involved 15,000 marchers in 170 units. Yet, even though no uncontrolled mob barged into the White House and stomped on the furniture with muddy boots as they had with Jackson, the inauguration stripped away the nearly royal function the ceremony had become.

Finally, as in 1829, here was a southern president, the first one elected to the presidency in the 20th century (excluding Woodrow Wilson, a Virginian who had moved to New Jersey, and Lyndon Johnson, who hailed from Texas but appeared more western than southern). Southerners took pride in the event. One spectator held a sign aloft, reading: "The South DID Rise Again."[5] Rebel yells punctuated the playing of "Dixie," and the religiosity of the region showed in Carter's inaugural address, with its pronounced (although not atypical for such speeches) reference to the Bible. He said:

Here before me is the Bible used in the inauguration of our first President, in 1789, and I have just taken the oath of office on the Bible my mother gave me just a few years ago, opened to a timeless admonition from the ancient prophet Micah: "He hath showed thee, O man, what is good; and what doth the Lord require of thee, but to do justly, and to love mercy, and to walk humbly with God."[6]

Yet, whatever traditions he reached back to, Carter would prove to be no son of the old reactionary South. He promoted a progressive agenda, albeit within his peculiar conservative limits.

The public liked what it saw. Within a few weeks, the president's public approval rating ranged in the 70th percentile. Those same polls revealed that most Americans still thought that their basic institutions could work and that they longed to "feel good about things."[7] Carter's pardon, coupled with his new approach, may well have made them feel better and may have made them think that in Jimmy Carter, they had found a president who could restore faith in their country.

THE "MOONIES" RAISE A CONTROVERSY

When the 1960s counterculture produced a surge in nontraditional religions, some young people joined the Unification Church, whose leadership under Reverend Sun Myung Moon raised concerns among more traditional Americans that it was more of a cult than a legitimate sect. Doubts about Moon's movement reached a crisis in 1977, when several parents complained that their adult children had been brainwashed into joining the church. The parents sought to reclaim custody over their offspring and in doing so raised a constitutional issue involving freedom of religion.

Moon, a Korean evangelist, founded the Unification Church in 1954 as the Holy Spirit Association for the Unification of World Christianity. Moon believed that he had been anointed by God to save humankind from the devil, and, in the intense atmosphere of the cold war, he considered Communists to be Satan's agents. That he lived in Communist North Korea and was persecuted by its government only reinforced his beliefs.

Moon fled North Korea in 1950 and built a thriving business empire in South Korea and Japan, making his money by selling weapons, machinery, and tea. He began his missionary crusade in the United States in the early 1970s, insisting that his disciples, popularly called "Moonies," refer to him as the Father and to his wife as the Mother. In 1973, he moved his world religious and business operations to Tarrytown, New York.

Critics said that Moon used fraudulent fund-raising tactics in building the Unification Church and plied the waters of popular discontent to take unfair advantage of young people who were going through personal crises and searching for an alternative to America's discordant society. (The distrust of Moon was reinforced several years later in 1982 when he was convicted of income tax evasion and sentenced to 18 months in prison.)

Some of those parents who accused Moon of "brainwashing" their adult children used the tactic of hiring "deprogrammers" to steal them away from the church and change their thinking. Deprogrammers even founded a center, called the Freedom of Thought Foundation, in Tucson, Arizona, that was aimed at Moonies, Hare Krishnas, and others who had supposedly been indoctrinated. In California, the parents of five Moonies asked the Superior Court to declare them the legal guardians of their adult offspring, claiming that the Unification Church had, through its indoctrination, made their children incompetent. In effect, the parents were likening their children, whose ages ranged from 21 to 26, to people who had become senile and could no longer make judgments on their own.

The Unification Church, however, said that the parents wanted to dictate their children's religion and thereby prevent their children from freely choosing the faith that they wanted. Church lawyers reminded the court that these were adult children, after all, who had complete independence from their parents. Neil Salomen, the president of the Unification Church, said, "We think this is a case of national significance that can decide whether the processes of the courts should be abused and whether individual decisions such as choice of religion and other minority beliefs can be practiced in this country."[8]

The trial took an unusual turn when some of the children staged musical performances to prove that they had maintained their creativity in the church. But the judge rejected their argument and the arguments of the church's lawyers and ordered that the parents be granted a 30-day guardianship over their children. He said that the parents had the best interests of their children in mind and added: "The child is the child even though a parent may be 90 and the child 60."[9] The American Civil Liberties Union joined the Unification Church in condemning the decision as an assault on freedom of religion, and many other churches agreed, despite their dislike for the Moonies.

While an appellate court stayed the lower-court's ruling and took it under advisement, the parents sent their children to deprogrammers, and two of them subsequently announced their break with the church. Appearing before the appeals court in San Francisco on April 11, 1977, attorneys for both sides presented their arguments. "There was no coercion," said the attorney for the Unification Church. "There is no shred of evidence that they were physically abused or were restrained of their liberty. The first restraint of liberty was by order of the Superior Court."[10] The attorney for the parents charged: "The change in the young people was induced by a deliberate process, controlling of somebody's mind."[11]

The appellate court sided with the Unification Church and ended the parental custody of the young adults. The ruling agreed with the extensive legal precedent that said government should distance itself from dictating religious practices or defining what might be a valid religion.

AN ENERGY CRISIS

When Jimmy Carter entered the White House, he faced an energy crisis. Severe winter cold and federal restraints placed on producer prices had taken their toll on natural gas supplies. As a result, some schools and businesses closed and with them an estimated 200,000 jobs were lost. To conserve fuel, Carter asked Americans to lower their home thermostats to 65 degrees. His advisers estimated that doing so would cut the shortage of natural gas in half.

Carter said to the country on January 21, 1977:

As many Americans know from direct experience, this Nation is confronted by near-critical shortages in natural gas supplies. This has been one of the coldest winters in our history. Electric utilities are experiencing record demand. Great stress has been placed on supplies of alternative fuels for heating.[12]

He said that even if more natural gas flowed through the nation's pipelines, "without public conservation, there may not be enough energy to allocate."[13] Yet, he realized more had to be done than simply lowering thermostats. "This nation needs a coherent energy policy," he said, "and such a program of energy action will be formulated promptly."[14]

The United States had become an energy guzzler, consuming oil and natural gas at a per capita rate far above other nations. Particularly worrisome was the increasing dependence on foreign oil, which in the previous four years had jumped from 35 percent to more than 50 percent of total supply. At the same time, the price of imported oil had more than doubled, topping $12 a barrel.

Carter wanted to avoid having the United States held hostage to developments in the oil-rich Middle East (or elsewhere, for that matter). He sought a strategy that would stimulate domestic energy production through price incentives while at the same time encourage conservation. Carter knew that he would have to maneuver carefully, for if he increased the costs of production, an economic tailspin or a financial bonanza for big oil might result, either of which would cost him public support.

During the next few weeks, Carter and his secretary of energy, James Schlesinger, worked on a plan, largely in secret. On April 18, the president preceded his announcement of it with a somber address on national television. His various comments prepared people to make sacrifices:

> "The difficult effort will be the moral equivalent of war—except that we will be uniting our efforts to build and not destroy."
>
> "The most important thing about these proposals is that the alternative may be a national catastrophe."
>
> "Those citizens who insist on driving large, unnecessarily powerful luxury cars must expect to pay more for that luxury."[15]

At the heart of Carter's energy plan: a tax on domestic oil production; a standby gasoline tax to be imposed each year that gasoline consumption exceeded government targets; a tax on automobiles with low fuel efficiency; and tax credits to encourage conservation.

Energy Secretary James Schlesinger gives a briefing to the press.
(Courtesy Jimmy Carter Library)

The plan drew some praise but also tremendous criticism. *Newsweek* magazine said, "For the first time, a strong activist President [has] seized the initiative on energy."[16] Oil executives, though, pilloried the proposal. "It's just unbelievable," said one. "In order to turn this thing around, we need a crash program of conservation, oil and natural gas production, coal development, and nuclear development. And for oil and natural gas we need to double our drilling efforts from 40,000 to 80,000 wells per year. That takes incentives and what do we get? Disincentives."[17] Jack Blanton, president of the Texas Mid-Continent Oil and Gas Producers Association, said, "It sounds very, very discouraging. We're in for one helluva dogfight."[18]

In the ensuing dogfight, Carter was his own worst enemy. First, he kept members of his administration in the dark, thus causing them to make confusing comments that gave ammunition to his critics. In a perhaps candid but damaging statement, his deputy secretary of agriculture, for example, stated that the energy plan would inflate food costs.

As it turned out, Carter had to retract his assertion about the energy plan producing economic growth when the "fact sheet" supporting him turned out to be inaccurate. Bert Lance, the president's budget director, sheepishly admitted: "There may be a temporary adverse impact [from the program]. . . ." He continued: "Over the next four years, [though,] if the impact is not favorable, it's certainly not unfavorable."[19] He said that the plan would increase the budget deficit for fiscal 1978 by some $1–3 billion, though he insisted that the administration would be committed to producing a balanced budget.

The importance of the energy plan was evident in the way the topic dominated a press conference that Carter held in late April. By then, critics had turned

President Carter and House Speaker Tip O'Neill confer aboard *Air Force One.* (Courtesy Jimmy Carter Library)

up the heat on the tax proposals. (In fact, critics began to pick apart the entire energy plan even before the president announced the details.) Carter called his plan "equitable" and said that he would steadfastly defend the proposed taxes, including the standby gasoline tax. Moreover, he warned oil companies against reaping large profits from any increases in oil prices, and, to those who worried that another crisis in the Middle East might lead to gas rationing, he said that he opposed rationing, except as a last resort, and expected his energy plan to eliminate the possibility that rationing would ever have to be imposed.

Carter received important help from the Democratic Congress when House Speaker Tip O'Neill sent the energy plan to a special committee which he put together, one loaded with its supporters—or at least those who supported most of the provisions. The members of Congress waded through five volumes of dense legislation that included arcane discussions about hydroelectric power and natural gas.

In August, the House approved nearly all of Carter's energy plan. It rejected the standby tax on gasoline as too burdensome on consumers and too politically risky, and it rejected tax rebates to the buyers of small cars because it thought that the measure would hurt the American automobile industry while benefiting foreign manufacturers.

Despite the House vote, the Senate posed the more difficult test. Oil interests who were opposed to the taxes that were meant to discourage consumption had powerful allies there, most notably Democrat Russell Long from Louisiana, a major oil and natural-gas state. Long chaired the Senate Finance Committee, and he echoed the complaints of oil executives, who insisted that the plan contained no real incentives to increase oil production. He especially disliked the wellhead tax, the money from which would go to taxpayers as a rebate rather than to the oil industry to promote expanded production.

Rather than a single bill, the Senate eventually passed several interlocked pieces of legislation that gave Carter little of what he wanted and that differed markedly from the plan passed by the House. With the Senate and the House at odds, the energy plan languished, kept in limbo by a president who failed to understand how to work with Congress.

But he learned (fitfully and, his critics say, never effectively), and he and his staff met with lawmakers, along with business, labor, and community leaders. A coalition emerged, and it rallied behind Carter's drive for an energy plan. The effort to obtain passage took several more months, and when Congress finally voted its approval in October 1978, the energy plan lacked many provisions that Carter had wanted. Still, it deregulated natural gas and equalized the cost of the product among the country's regions. Moreover, tax credits promoted energy conservation and the use of nonfossil fuels. Despite the energy plan's shortcomings, historian Burton I. Kaufman, in his book *The Presidency of James Earl Carter, Jr.,* calls it "a momentous accomplishment."[20]

THE CLAMSHELL ALLIANCE

In July 2003, a salvage company dismantled a rusted, hulking dome, the housing for the never-completed second unit of the Seabrook Nuclear Power Plant, that was situated on a marsh two miles from Hampton Beach in New Hampshire. The dismantling owed itself to a protest staged by the Clamshell Alliance 26 years earlier.

In 1968, a giant utility, the Public Service Company of New Hampshire (PSNH), announced plans to build a nuclear power plant at Seabrook. The utility, and Americans in general, thought that nuclear power was the answer to society's energy demands. Nuclear power, it was argued, would be relatively inexpensive, safe, and clean and would lessen the nation's dependence on coal and oil.

Yet, residents in the towns of Hampton and Hampton Falls objected. They decried possible nuclear contamination and questioned the plant's safety. As a result, the PSNH delayed construction. In 1971, however, the utility announced that it would build a double reactor at Seabrook. The contamination issue remained acute when the PSNH said that it would dump heated reactor water directly into the Hampton River, thus, according to biologists, endangering the nearby salt marsh and the fragile marine life, including clams.

Mollusks and clams burrow into the sand or mud. For many New Englanders, they symbolize the sea and evoke images of pristine waters. Hence, opponents to the Seabrook nuclear plant called themselves the Clamshell Alliance. Far from wanting to hide in the sand, they played on the image of purity: They were the protectors of nature against a reckless, polluting big company.

Despite a decision by the PSNH to protect the marsh by building tunnels to carry the heated water from the nuclear plant, the Clamshell Alliance—or the Clams, as they were called—said that they intended to oppose the construction. They called the tunnels insufficient, a position bolstered by the regional administrator of the Environmental Protection Agency (EPA), who rejected the tunnel system, and they called the plant unsafe. (EPA officials in Washington ultimately overruled the regional director.)

The Clamshell Alliance vowed to make the ocean front "nuclear free" and, to arouse public opinion and win their battle with the PSNH, engaged in civil disobedience. Beginning in late 1976 and continuing into 1977, more than 200 Clams were arrested for trespassing on the plant site.

The biggest protest, however, erupted in April 1977, when, for two days, 1,114 Clams were arrested in nonviolent protests. They refused to post bail and so sat in jail for days awaiting trial and clogging an already overburdened court system.

During the next several years, work on the plant continued, but so did the protests. They turned violent in 1979 when police attacked 2,000 dissidents with dogs, tear gas, and riot sticks. The protests, along with disputes between the town of Seabrook and the utility over evacuation plans to handle any possible nuclear accident and financial problems encountered by the PSNH, delayed construction. It took more than 10 years to build the plant at a cost of about $7 billion, some 6 billion over cost estimates, and the project contributed to the bankruptcy of the PSNH in 1988. When the plant began to generate power in 1990, it did so with only one reactor rather than the planned two. The Clamshell Alliance failed to prevent the Seabrook plant from operating, but its protests contributed greatly to the reduced size of the plant and to the mounting opposition to nuclear power across the nation.

In 2003, the head of the salvage company that dismantled the dome at Seabrook said that it had to be torn down rather than be left standing and beautified because "You can't put lipstick on a pig."[21] Protesters might well have said they, too, opposed camouflage—in their case, the camouflage used by the nuclear power companies to hide the dangers in their industry. At Seabrook they had exposed those dangers.

CARTER AND THE B-1 BOMBER

An opponent of the B-1 bomber called it "the most expensive white elephant ever proposed by industry and the [military] services." A supporter called it absolutely essential to counteract "the malignant growth of Soviet power" and keep "the Soviets off guard."[22] The debate roiled Congress for months, and passage of a bill to fund the bomber forced President Carter to choose sides in the controversy and either to sign or to veto the legislation.

The arguments for and against the B-1 had begun when the airplane was first proposed some 10 years earlier. Supporters of the bomber wanted it to replace the country's aging fleet of B-52s. The B-1, it was claimed, could fly much faster than the B-52 and at lower altitudes, thus enabling it to penetrate Soviet air defenses. Proponents argued that it would strengthen the triad of nuclear-equipped weapons: land-based intercontinental missiles, submarine-launched missiles, and bombers.

But opponents called the plane a boondoggle: They said it could be easily shot down by advanced Soviet air defenses. Also, they pointed to the hefty price for each plane: $100 million. They said that the money should be spent on other weaponry and on domestic programs.

Plans to deploy the B-1 advanced when, on June 28, the House, by a vote of 243-178, rejected a proposal to kill the plane's development. Most analysts expected President Carter to approve the expenditure for the aircraft, or at least a good chunk of it.

But two days later, Carter stunned Congress and the public when he announced—in what "has been one of the most difficult decisions that I have made since I've been in office"—that he would oppose deployment, although he would support money for development should other weapons systems fail and make the B-1 necessary at a later date.[23] Most U.S. Air Force officials reacted with anger at the president's decision to gut their leading bomber program. No other bomber, they said, could outwit the Soviet air defenses by flying at treetop level, below sophisticated radars. They stressed that the Soviets had improved their air defenses to include more numerous and sophisticated early-warning and control systems. Moreover, some 10,000 surface-to-air missiles at more than 1,000 sites stood poised to strike at incoming American aircraft.

Moreover, the air force officials said, the Soviet Union had deployed the Backfire bomber in Europe and Siberia, and it could fly 1,300 miles per hour as opposed to the B-52's lumbering 600 miles per hour. Although the American F-111 could fly faster than the Backfire, its bomb capacity was only 31,500 pounds, as opposed to the B-52's 60,000 pounds, and the B-1s 115,000 pounds. To them, Carter's surprising decision would cripple the air-attack part of the nuclear triad.

But Carter called the B-1 unnecessary in light of the development of the cruise missile, a jet-powered weapon able to fly at low altitudes. He said, "I think that in toto the B-1, a very expensive weapons system basically conceived in the absence of the cruise missile factor, is not necessary."[24] He noted: In the event of an attack by the Soviet Union on the United States, other American aircraft, such as the B-52, could fly close to the Soviet borders and launch cruise missiles from there, thus obviating the need for a large bomber whose flying within Soviet airspace would expose it to being shot down. The president said, "We should begin the development of cruise missiles using air-launched platforms, such as our B-52's, modernized as necessary."[25]

Carter acted on advice from his secretary of defense, Harold Brown. A former secretary of the air force, Brown had presided over development of the B-1. But he came to oppose its deployment for two reasons: the effectiveness of the cruise missile and the tremendous cost of the bomber. "The B-1 would have been a more attractive option had it been 30 percent less expensive," he admitted at a press conference. "But I believe that the technology of the cruise missile development played a larger part."[26] Recent tests, he said, had shown that the cruise missile could fly lower and with less detection than previously thought.

Other Pentagon analysts noted that each cruise missile would cost $750,000, as opposed to each B-1 costing $100 million. They expected the total overall savings from stopping deployment of the B-1 to reach into the billions of dollars.

Many hailed Carter for taking a brave stand against a wasteful program. He risked angering the air force, members of Congress whose districts encompassed thousands of workers in the program; and the Rockwell International Corporation, which had the contract to build the B-1 and which announced that it would lay off 6,000 people as a result of the president's decision. He received criticism from those who thought that his decision showed weakness toward the Soviet Union and from those who thought that he had insulted Congress in acting so soon after the House vote, one in which several members of Congress had taken political risks in announcing their stand. Better, they said, if he had made his intentions clear to Congress beforehand.

No other president had ended such an extensive military program so far along in production. Whatever the critics might say, Carter's action earned for him the reputation of being bold, a reputation that he later squandered.

"THE NIGHT OF THE ANIMALS": A BLACKOUT IN NEW YORK CITY

The lights went out in New York City at 9:34 P.M. on Wednesday, July 13, 1977, a hot, humid night punctuated by the hum of air conditioners and the voices, sometimes the irritated shouts, from thousands of open apartment windows. The blackout, the worst since a massive outage in 1965, plunged some neighborhoods into chaos when bands of blacks, Hispanics, and others took to the streets, looting and pillaging. "It's the night of the animals," said one police officer. "You grab four or five, and a hundred take their place. . . . All we can do is chase people away from a store, and they just run to the next block, to the next store."[27]

The blackout began when several lightning strikes caused a chain reaction. As a thunderstorm moved across Westchester County, just north of New York City, a bolt of lightning knocked out two power lines that were connected to the Indian Point nuclear power plant, shutting down electricity from there. About 10 minutes later, a second bolt knocked out a cable that was connected to power plants in upstate New York and New England. As the electrical grid compensated for the loss of power from those sources by reducing voltage, lights in the city flickered. Then came two more lightning strikes; one plunged parts of Westchester County into darkness; another severed the remaining connections with power plants to the north. With these failures, the lines operated by Con Edison in the

Looters take advantage of New York City's blackout to steal items from an A&P supermarket at Ogden Avenue and 166th Street in the Bronx. (©Bettmann/Corbis)

city began to shut down, a measure that was meant to protect them from a damaging overload.

The blackout caused many inconveniences, some minor and some much more serious, such as disrupted hospital services, and caused most New Yorkers to react with humor, patience, and numerous acts of kindness. Youths helped to direct traffic along streets that were devoid of lights or signals. Other New Yorkers manually moved the gears of a stuck Ferris wheel to bring its riders to the ground. Doormen at high-rise apartment buildings gave tenants flashlights so that they could see their way along the stairwells.

But on numerous streets, looters broke store windows, pried apart security bars, and set fires in an onslaught of lawlessness. Police did their best to control the violence—thousands of off-duty officers were pressed into service—but they were often overwhelmed. As fires swept through the Bushwick section of Brooklyn, looters ran around the fire trucks and continued to steal. *Time* magazine reported that in the South Bronx "Twisted [metal] grilles—some yanked from storefronts with trucks that were then filled with loot—lay across sidewalks. In the new Fedco supermarket, shelves gleamed bare and white, while several inches of mashed produce, packages of squashed hamburger, rivers of melted ice cream, and broken bottles covered the floors."[28] Looters raided about 300 stores in the neighborhood.

Protected by darkness, looters stole clothes, radios, stereos, TVs, food, furniture, and even cars. In one instance, they stole prayer shawls and Bibles. "You take your chance when you get a chance," said one. "We're poor, and this is our way of getting rich."[29] In the ghettos of Harlem, Bedford-Stuyvesant, and the South Bronx could be heard cries of "It's Christmastime! It's Christmastime!"[30]

Some store owners reacted to the violence by brandishing metal pipes and guns. At a Brooklyn supermarket, the manager, four clerks, and a security guard who wielded a machete chased away a gang of 30 youths. Also in Brooklyn, several Italian-American teenagers armed with baseball bats helped merchants guard their stores along Myrtle Avenue.

Looters even attacked other looters. One who had a pile of clothes and radios stolen from her complained: "That's just not right."[31] Many streets emptied of everyone except the looters and the police.

By morning, 3,500 people had been arrested, far exceeding the number during the previous big blackout in 1965. The suspects flooded the city's courts and jails, forcing the authorities to reopen a previously condemned prison, the Tombs. Overcrowding and the lack of air conditioning caused prisoners to complain about the heat.

Store owners had their own complaint: The looters had destroyed their businesses. *Time* reported that the Small Business Administration was making loans available for rebuilding, but despite this, many store owners said "they had been stripped bare" and "all they had worked and saved for over the years was gone," making it "financially and emotionally impossible for them to start again."[32] One Brooklyn businessman said, "Get a loan? Are you crazy? You think anybody in his rightful mind would want to get back to this neighborhood?"[33]

Experts and lay people debated why the looting had occurred and why the reaction to the blackout had been so much different from 1965. Some analysts pointed to the poverty in which people lived. Others pointed to how modern advertising had produced an insatiable desire for material goods and great frustration among those who lacked the money to buy them. But even critics of poverty said that there was no excuse for what occurred, and, in any event, it was not always clear that only poor people were doing the looting. Quite possibly the challenge to authority that had accelerated in the 1960s and continued into the 1970s found its expression in the licentious behavior of the looters. Whatever the cause of the lawlessness, the looters reinforced the view that urban America had become a jungle.

STRIP-MINING REFORM

In the early 20th century, President Theodore Roosevelt threw away a written speech when he appeared before a group of lumberers and declared, "I hate a man who skins the land."[34] During the succeeding years, numerous political leaders embraced Roosevelt's words, seized his environmental gauntlet, and sought to protect nature from human degradation and to promote resource conservation. Morris Udall, a Democratic congressman from Arizona and chairman of the House Committee on Interior and Insular Affairs, saw himself as continuing Roosevelt's fight, and in the 1960s and 1970s, he pushed for legislation to control strip mining. "People who don't respect the land don't respect themselves," he said in words that echoed Roosevelt.[35] On August 3, 1977, President Carter signed into law a strip-mining bill that was promoted by Udall and championed by several environmental groups.

The law required coal operators to restore strip-mined land to nearly its undisturbed state. This meant backfilling land, grading it, and replanting trees and grass, not simply as an aesthetic measure but to prevent the runoff of silt and dirt into streams and thus reduce the possibility of flooding. In addition, the law provided for the reclamation of old strip-mined lands, to be financed by a federal tax on coal.

Despite these provisions, the law contained several drawbacks. Most glaringly, it exempted small-sized mines; yet, these produced 100,000 tons of coal yearly in the Appalachian Highlands. Moreover, the law allowed mining companies to remove the tops of Appalachian Mountains so that they could reach the coal seams below. Environmentalists had opposed this as desecrating the land. They had wanted to restrict the companies to cutting ridges around the mountaintops and retrieving only a part of the coal.

With these limitations in mind, when President Carter signed the law he said, "in many ways this has been a disappointing effort" and added: "I would have preferred a stricter strip mine bill."[36] In fact, the law was weaker than laws that had been passed earlier by Congress, only to be vetoed by President Ford. Nevertheless, Carter said, "I found, as I campaigned around our Nation for 2 years, that there's an overwhelming, favorable sentiment among the people of our country that [strip mining] legislation be passed."[37]

The law gave the Interior Department the authority to develop environmental standards for strip mines and gave the states three years in which to implement them. Coal-mine operators said that they would comply with the law, but they insisted, as they had throughout the legislative battle over it, that it would produce fuel shortages and electrical blackouts.

Udall thought otherwise. He said, "By getting this bill passed . . . we are showing that this nation loves its land and respects it and is going to protect the land, while at the same time we increase the production of coal."[38]

THE BERT LANCE SCANDAL

As president, Jimmy Carter could ill afford a scandal. He had entered office emphasizing integrity and promising an openness that was intended to move the country beyond the malodorous Nixon years and restore trust in the White House. But he had a scandal, anyhow. It involved his close friend and adviser Bert Lance, whom he had appointed director of the Office of Management and the Budget (OMB).

The scandal began to unfold during summer 1977 and centered on Lance's complex financial arrangements as a banker in Georgia. When Carter became president, he sought to avoid improprieties by having his appointees publicly reveal their financial holdings and divest themselves of any investments that might cause a conflict of interest. Lance had headed the National Bank of Georgia (NBG) and a small neighborhood bank in Calhoun, the First National. Abiding by Carter's request, Lance placed his NBG stock, which was worth several million dollars, in a blind trust with instructions to his trustee to sell the shares by the end of 1977. He announced these plans when he appeared before the Senate for confirmation. When the value of the stock plummeted, however, Lance, who wanted to avoid selling the stock at a loss, asked Carter for help, and the president in turn asked Senator Abraham Ribicoff (Dem., Conn.), chairman of the Senate Governmental Affairs Committee, to allow Lance to keep the stock for an indefinite period beyond the end of the year.

Lance had also told the Senate that he would remove himself from any involvement in issues concerning banking regulations for as long as he held his

NBG stock. Despite this promise, he tried to influence legislation in the Senate that would help the NBG. At the same time, a newspaper columnist accused Lance of using his position to obtain a multimillion-dollar personal loan with favorable interest arrangements.

To clear up the matter, Lance appeared before the Governmental Affairs Committee with evidence that he had received no special consideration in obtaining his loan. His appearance so impressed the senators that they agreed to allow him more time to dispose of the NBG stock.

In the meantime, the government's comptroller had investigated Lance's financial dealings. He reported that the OMB director had done nothing illegal, and Carter hailed the report as vindicating his embattled friend. But the report said that Lance had stretched the law, such as when he allowed the officers at the Calhoun bank, along with several friends, to make overdrafts on their accounts and engage in unsafe banking practices.

On the heels of the comptroller's report came new accusations. On September 19, congressional staffers who were working for the Senate Governmental Affairs Committee testified before the committee that at a meeting with him in January, Lance had misled them about his finances by denying that his wife had obtained any overdrafts from the Calhoun bank and by minimizing the extent of the overdrafts obtained by members of his family. The comptroller's later investigation found that Lance, his wife, LaBelle, and their relatives, along with other bank officers, had obtained loans amounting to $450,000 and that overdrafts occurred repeatedly.

Also in September, a federal bank official claimed that he had been told by the head of the comptroller of the currency in Atlanta that Lance had asked for the strict monitoring of the Calhoun bank to end once Carter had made it known that he would appoint him to head the OMB. In Senate testimony, Lance had previously denied the accusation that he had made any such request. Curiously, the FBI closed an investigation of the Calhoun overdrafts one day before the nomination of Lance to the OMB was made public.

Amid the expanding controversy, Lance again appeared before the Senate Governmental Affairs Committee and defended himself, while charging his accusers with unfairly persecuting him. From both the committee and the public at large, his appearance received favorable reviews.

Nevertheless, political leaders on Capitol Hill told Carter that the controversy concerning Lance would likely be rejuvenated and intensify and that it would detract from the administration's agenda. In short, Carter needed to put the "Lance affair" behind him. Carter then met with Lance and advised him to resign.

When Carter announced Lance's departure at a press conference on September 21, the president's eyes became watery, and his voice faltered. Carter called his friend "a good and honorable man," and said that the allegations against him "in my opinion, have been proven false and without foundation."[39] But he said that he agreed with Lance's resignation statement in which Lance said that the price had become too high for him to remain in office.

Ultimately, the Lance affair soured Carter's relations with Congress and tarnished his mantle of integrity. "Let us create together a new national spirit of unity and trust," Carter had said in his inaugural address.[40] The Lance affair made "trust" a bit harder to come by.

SON OF SAM

By 1977, New York City had become gripped with terror as a murderer stalked its streets, shooting young people in secluded spots at night. At first called the .44-Caliber Killer and, later, the Son of Sam, the murderer, discovered to be David Berkowitz, a 24-year-old postal worker, fatally shot six victims and wounded seven others before he was captured.

It took some time for the police to link together the first attacks. Each one seemed devoid of motivation; crazy in their randomness, ugly in the way that they entered people's lives at routine moments and ripped them apart. The early attacks, at first, drew brief media attention—coverage for a day or two in the newspapers. These attacks unfolded as follows.

On July 29, 1976, two friends, 19-year-old Jody Valente and 18-year-old Donna Lauria, were sitting in a car outside Donna's apartment building in the Bronx, engaging in small talk. At about 1:00 A.M., Donna said good-bye to Jody and began to open the door of the car. At that moment, a man on the curb crouched down and fired into the vehicle, shattering the passenger's window. A bullet entered Donna's back, and her body fell from the open door onto the ground. Another bullet wounded Jody in the leg. Donna died almost instantly. The bullets came from a .44-caliber Bulldog revolver, a weapon seldom seen in the city, one known for its powerful recoil and designed to be effective at close range.

In the early morning of October 23, 1976, 18-year-old Rosemary Keenan and 20-year-old Carl Denaro were sitting in Rosemary's VW on a quiet, tree-lined street a short distance from a bar they had just left in Flushing, Queens. Suddenly gunshots shattered the driver's and passenger's windows. A bullet pierced Carl's skull. Rosemary, unhurt, frantically sought help. Carl lived, although he had to have a steel plate implanted in his head. Again the bullets came from a .44 caliber revolver.

On November 27, 1976, a blustery, cold Saturday following Thanksgiving, Joanne Lomino, age 18, and Donna DeMasi, age 16, were coming home from a movie at night. They stepped from a bus in Queens and strolled down 262nd Street. As they stood outside Joanne's house, talking for several minutes, a young man approached them and started asking for directions. Then he pulled a gun from beneath his coat and began to fire. The attack left Donna in a neck brace for months and left Joanne a paraplegic, confined to a wheelchair for the rest of her life. Police identified the bullets as coming from a .44 caliber revolver.

On Saturday, January 29, 1977, around midnight, Christine Freund, age 26, and her boyfriend, John Diel, age 30, finished a light meal and some coffee at a restaurant—they had just seen the movie *Rocky*—and got into John's car. Without warning, three .44-caliber slugs smashed the passenger's window; one passed through Christine's shoulder and lodged in her back. Four hours later, Christine died.

On March 8, 1977, 19-year-old Virginia Voskerichian, a Bulgarian immigrant and student at Columbia University, was walking home from campus at night. As she neared an apartment house on Dartmouth Street, a young man approached her on the sidewalk, and as they passed each other, he raised a gun to her face. A bullet tore through her skull, killing her instantly. The weapon used turned out to be a .44-caliber revolver.

With the Voskerichian slaying, the police began to talk about a connection among the killings. On March 10, Mayor Abraham Beame held a press conference at which he announced that there was a ballistics match between the bullets—.44-caliber slugs—used in the Lauria and Voskerichian slayings. (In truth, the police had found that although a .44-caliber gun had been used in the attacks, they could not conclude that it was the *same* gun that had been used.) Thus the public came to know the assailant as the .44-Caliber Killer. Beame and the police issued a call for help in finding the killer.

Leads, if that is the right word for them, came pouring in to the police, 7,000 in all. In many instances, they were unfounded accusations. Sometimes, angry neighbors pointed their fingers at other neighbors. Sometimes, girlfriends turned on their boyfriends. Fear spread. Amid reports that the murderer pursued women with long hair, thousands of girls cut their hair short. Others heard that he preferred brown hair, so they began to wear blond wigs or they bleached their hair. Young couples avoided deserted streets at night, and, when they heard that the murderer looked for his victims at discos, they used extra caution at those clubs or avoided them altogether.

The murderer remained quiet until April 17, 1977, when his killing spree took a bizarre turn. At 3 A.M. that day, he attacked a young couple, Valentina Suriani and Alexander Esau, who were embracing in their car. Two bullets tore through Valentina's head, two through Alexander's, killing Valentina instantly and Alexander a few hours later. This time, the .44-Caliber Killer left a letter at the murder scene, four pages long, printed in capitalized, slanted block letters. "I am deeply hurt by your calling me a wemon [*sic*] hater," he wrote. "I am not. But I am a monster." He continued:

> I am the "Son of Sam." I am a little "brat."
> When Father Sam gets drunk he gets mean. He beats his family. Sometimes he ties me up to the back of the house.
> Other times he locks me in the garage. Sam loves to drink Blood. "Go out and kill" commands Sam. . . .
> Police: let me haunt you with these words:
> I'll be back!
> I'll be back![41]

On May 30, a second ominous letter appeared, sent to Jimmy Breslin, a prominent newspaper columnist for the *New York Daily News.* When published, it sent New Yorkers into another panic. It began: "Hello from the gutters of N.Y.C., which are filled with dog manure, vomit, stale wine, urine, and blood." And in threatening words: "Tell me Jim, what will you have for July twenty-ninth?"—an obvious reference to the first anniversary of Donna Lauria's murder, a hint that he would strike again on that date.[42] He signed the letter: Son of Sam.

The Son of Sam struck again before July, shooting a young couple parked in a car in Queens. Both victims lived, with the girl making a miraculous recovery from having been shot in the head.

On July 29, New Yorkers awaited the worst—the anniversary attack by the Son of Sam. But the killer bypassed that date and struck two days later, on July 31, in an assault that provided the evidence for his capture. The victims were Stacy Moskowitz and Robert Violante, both 20 years old. Out on their first date, they went to the Kingsway Theater to see the play *New York, New York,* starring Liza Minnelli.

At about 2:30 A.M., they returned from a stroll through a park at Bay 17th Street in Brooklyn near Gravesend Bay and the Verrazano-Narrows Bridge and sat in Robert's car, parked beneath a streetlamp. Five minutes later, a hail of bullets struck them and left them both badly wounded, bleeding profusely. The next day, the *New York Post* displayed the banner headline: "NO ONE IS SAFE FROM SON OF SAM."

Robert Violante survived the shooting, though he lost sight in one eye. Stacy Moskowitz died on August 1, despite an eight-hour-long operation to remove a bullet which had torn through her brain and lodged at the base of her neck.

New Yorkers panicked. Mobs attacked suspicious young men. Newspapers, radio, and television all presented sensational stories and extensive coverage. Commercial hucksters entered the scene; some peddled T-shirts that read: "Son of Sam—Get Him Before He Gets You."

With the Violante-Moskowitz attack, Son of Sam made a mistake. He had parked his car near a fire hydrant and at about 2 A.M. received a ticket. When a witness to the attack reported having seen the cream-colored Ford Galaxie being ticketed, the police began to search their records. They retrieved a copy of the ticket and traced the car to David Berkowitz's apartment in Yonkers. In the Galaxie, they discovered a machine gun in a gunny sack and a note whose printing style resembled Son of Sam's previous letters. The note said in part:

> Because Craig is Craig, [a reference to a Westchester County deputy sheriff] so must the streets be filled with crime (death) and huge drops of lead poured down upon her head until she was dead—Yet the cats still come out at night to mate and the sparrows still sing in the morning.[43]

The police surrounded the apartment and arrested Berkowitz as he emerged from it. With his dark curly hair and husky build, he resembled the descriptions given by several witnesses. Mayor Abraham Beame, involved in a close bid for reelection and mindful of how New Yorkers, the voters, wanted closure to the case, declared: "I am very pleased to announce that the people of the City of New York can rest easy tonight because police have captured a man they believe to be the Son of Sam."[44]

Police officials revealed that Berkowitz had admitted that he was on his way to stage another attack at the time that he was arrested and intended to use the machine gun in a mass murder at a disco. They said that he provided a full confession. "Berkowitz was very cooperative," reported a police sergeant. "He was talkative and calm and answered whatever we asked."[45] Berkowitz told how he acquired the .44-caliber revolver from an old army buddy and how the color of his victims' hair had nothing to do with his attacks. He called them random and said that they were commanded by messages from a neighbor, "Sam," who "really is a man who lived 6,000 years ago" and spoke to him through a dog.

When the police arrested Berkowitz, First Deputy Police Commissioner James Taylor stated: "We have him."[46] They portrayed him as a psychopathic loner, acting on his own. Case closed.

But in *The Ultimate Evil,* investigative writer Maury Terry presents a different conclusion, one backed by exhaustive research. Terry describes how eyewitnesses to the Violante-Moskowitz attack told of *two* suspicious men at the park in *two* different vehicles. One of the men looked like Berkowitz in his creamy-white Galaxie. Another drove a yellow VW and had blond hair or perhaps was wearing a wig. One witness told how Berkowitz became so angry about being ticketed that he jumped into his car and drove away from the scene to follow the police car. His action contradicted the statement he gave to the police, that he entered the park and sat down on a bench.

Berkowitz returned to the park before the shooting, but not in time to actually do the deed himself. Terry states: "All available information demonstrates that he functioned as a lookout." Moreover, when he was ticketed, he returned to the park to see the shooter and to "argue his case for postponing" the assault. After following the police car, Berkowitz "signaled an 'all clear' to the gunman . . . the killer then approached the Violante car and fired."[47]

In later interviews with Terry and others, Berkowitz, in prison for his crimes as part of consecutive life sentences, confirmed the existence of accomplices at several of his attacks. In 1993, Berkowitz agreed once again to meet with Terry. He told the writer how he had joined a cult in 1975 because he was "lonely, looking for friends, and I'd always been intrigued by the occult."[48] In the attack on Christine Freund, he said that there were "at least five" conspirators present, and a man he called "Manson II" did the killing. The killing of Virginia Voskerichian was done by "a woman from Westchester." About the Valentina Suriani and Alexander Esau assault, he said, "I did this one, and I'm very sorry about it." The attack on Judy Placido and Sal Lupo was done by another man. The assault on Stacy Moskowitz and Robert Violante was done by other accomplices. Terry adds:

> Berkowitz explained that he confessed to sole culpability for a simple reason: he knew he was guilty. "I did two of the shootings—that's three deaths—and I played a role in the rest. So what's the difference if I said I did them all? I knew I was going to jail for life no matter what, and I deserved to. Plus I was sticking loyal to the others in the group."[49]

The "group," Terry found, was a satanic cult, called the Process. And it was involved in many more crimes than the Son of Sam shootings. Its reach extended from New York all the way to California. David Berkowitz was no loner; he was part of a conspiracy, a conclusion reached not only by Terry but also, in a renewal of the investigation in 1998, by the Yonkers Police Department. Terry calls it a "web of conspiracy" embedded in "a nationwide network of satanic cults."[50]

That same year, Berkowitz talked to ABC News and repeated what he had told Terry. He said about the Process and its role in the killings: "I mean this was not just something they were doing necessarily for any type of pleasure. It was part of an agenda, a very deep, covert, and hidden agenda, you know. They were talking about making war."[51] Whatever the validity of Terry's conclusions (and they do appear to be well founded) and Berkowitz's change of story, they have led to no further arrests in the Son of Sam case.

Women Take Back the Night and Hold a National Rights Conference

In discussing a crisis center that was established in New York City in 1977 primarily for battered women, a newspaper reporter observed that the police were usually of little help in such situations because, as a general rule, when they intervened in family disputes, the cases collapsed before they ever reached court. Women, it turned out, according to the article, were just "too ashamed to testify."

But an increasing number of women in the 1970s were tired of suffering beatings and rapes in silence. They decided to overcome their shame and fight back and change state laws that made it difficult to prosecute rapists, such as the law in New York where to gain a conviction required that the victim prove that she had been raped by force, that "penetration" had occurred, and that someone had witnessed the rapist at or near the scene of the attack. Consequently, at the beginning of the decade, feminists sponsored a Rape Speak Out to expose such ineffective and oppressive laws, and the National Organization for Women put together a Rape Task Force.

These efforts caused many states to revise their rape statutes, making it easier to prosecute offenders for sexual violence. New laws, for example, prohibited a tactic used to intimidate women, namely, forcing them on cross-examination to reveal their previous sexual behavior.

Then in 1977, women's groups sponsored a national "Take Back the Night" protest. Across America, women with diverse political views and a number of men who supported their concerns staged marches whereby they insisted that the streets be made safe for women at night and that programs be established to help women who had been victimized by rape and domestic violence.

In this environment, New York City, aided by money from the federal government, set up crisis centers in four of its boroughs. By the end of 1977, the centers had handled more than 1,000 cases, more than half of them dealing with battered women. The crisis centers provided counseling and documented abuses to collect the necessary evidence for court trials. This included taking photographs of any injuries. Women finally felt relieved that someone was listening to them, that someone was willing to help.

Some feminists connected the abuse of women to the expanding popularity of pornography. They complained that pornography presented women as sex objects and encouraged rape and violence. Feminist Robin Morgan called for restrictions on pornographic material; to those who argued that such action would violate freedom of speech, she answered that the "garbage" of pornography could be fought without resorting to censorship. Women could educate others about the negative effects from pornography; they could picket businesses that dealt in pornographic material; and they could expose the "porn czars."

Historian Bruce J. Schulman says that the women's movement "crested" in November 1977 with the convening of the National Women's Conference in Houston. A gathering financed by the federal government at a cost of $5 million, the conference was given the mandate to send to President Carter recommendations on how to end the remaining legal and social inequities between men and women. More than 20,000 women attended (2,000 of them as official delegates), representing a diverse array from radical feminists to prominent moderates. The delegates included first ladies Rosalynn Carter, Lady Bird Johnson, and Betty

Ford, along with former congresswoman Bella Abzug, actress Jean Stapleton, and anthropologist Margaret Mead.

The conference called for the immediate ratification of the ERA, feminist education in the schools, and a federal program to assure "comprehensive" child care. In perhaps their most controversial recommendation, the delegates supported civil rights for lesbians.

Yet, an ominous undercurrent ran through the conference as a minority group of right-wing delegates voiced their objection to the resolutions and, a few miles away, thousands of Christian conservatives staged a "Pro-Family rally," where some 12,000 attendees waved Bibles and American flags and displayed signs reading "God Is a Family Man," "Keep Lesbians Out of Our Schools," and "I Was a Fetus Once." This was the gathering momentum of a conservative reaction to the liberalism and radicalism of the women's movement, a reactionary storm that would gain more strength in the 1980s and 1990s and place feminists on the defensive.

CARTER AND THE CLINCH RIVER BREEDER REACTOR

In a blow to the nuclear power industry, President Jimmy Carter used the first veto of his administration to kill legislation in November that had been passed by Congress and which would have allotted $80 million for a plutonium reactor to be built on the Clinch River in Tennessee. The bill for the reactor had passed Congress after considerable debate, both on Capitol Hill and elsewhere. The controversy stemmed partly from the project's cost—estimated to reach $2 billion ultimately—but mainly from the technology. A breeder reactor produces more fuel than it consumes. Critics said the plutonium fuel would be contaminating and could be stolen by terrorists or by other countries for the making of nuclear weapons.

President Richard Nixon had strongly supported the breeder reactor in the 1960s and helped the nuclear industry promote it. Industry leaders claimed that the breeder reactor was the answer for a shortage of uranium fuel that would materialize in the future, and they said that it would enhance America's ability to produce electric power. Other countries, they pointed out, were already developing the technology and that a failure to act might well leave the United States far behind them. The French had built one breeder reactor and were working on a second. The Russians had built an experimental breeder reactor and were looking toward expanding their program.

In his veto message, Carter called the Clinch River reactor "a large and unnecessarily expensive project which, when completed, would be technically obsolete and economically unsound."[52] He said that the program would make it more difficult for him to fight the proliferation of nuclear weapons.

Nevertheless, the president, a former nuclear engineer, remained committed to nuclear energy. Carter said that he supported "a strong research and development program for advanced nuclear technologies, including base program research on the liquid metal fast breeder, and an accelerated research and development program for advanced non-breeder technologies."[53] He said, "These programs are vital to ensure that energy is available to make the transition over the decades ahead from oil and natural gas to other energy sources."[54]

One congressman, George Brown (Dem., Calif.), called Carter courageous for vetoing the bill. Brown said that the veto was "sound on economic, political, scientific, environmental, and national security grounds."[55] But Senator Frank Church (Dem., Idaho) said, "On this issue I think that the Congress is right and the president is wrong," and predicted: "We are bound to lose our leadership role in shaping a global control system" relating to nuclear energy.[56]

In an interview with several newspaper editors, Carter went to great lengths to qualify his veto. He said his opposition to the Clinch River reactor "is no conclusion at all that I'm against nuclear power nor against the breeder reactor program." He said that the design of the Clinch River project would make the facility quickly obsolete. "We don't need to go into the plutonium society this early," he insisted. "We need to continue our research and development, small pilot project construction, to test the three or four major types of breeder reactors that might ultimately prove to be most feasible when they are needed."[57] It was a view reflecting his background in nuclear engineering, political realities, and his belief that alternatives must be pursued in a country enmeshed in a fuel crisis, where wintertime thermostats had to be lowered to 65 degrees.

ELVIS PRESLEY DIES

The stunning news swept across the country on August 16, 1977, providing another historic benchmark in the evolution of pop culture: Elvis Presley, the King of Rock and Roll, collapsed in the afternoon at his Graceland home in Memphis, Tennessee, and was pronounced dead an hour later at Baptist Memorial Hospital. There were no vital signs when he was taken from Graceland in an ambulance. The initial announcement about his death called it a result of an irregular and ineffective heartbeat. But Presley's doctors said that it would take some time to determine what caused Presley's heart to malfunction.

In the mid-1950's, Elvis Presley met Sam Phillips, who owned Sun Records. Phillips listened to Elvis sing and concluded "Oh, man, that is distinctive. There is something there, something original and different."[58] In 1955, rock and roll had arrived when Bill Haley and the Comets sold 2 million copies of their record "Rock Around the Clock." Now Phillips saw in Elvis a rock and roll star, a white man who sounded black and could thus convey rock and roll's roots in rhythm and blues, or "race music."

From Sun Records, Elvis signed a contract to record for RCA, and in 1956, his first big hit, "Heartbreak Hotel," sold more than 2 million copies. More hits followed quickly—he sold 10 million records by the end of the year—while teenage girls screamed and fainted at his performances, and fan clubs enrolled members by the hundreds of thousands. In 1957, he went to Hollywood, where through the years he made 28 movies—his first one was *Love Me Tender*—innocuous vehicles used primarily to promote his music and his stardom. In fact, many of his albums (he made about 40 of them) were soundtracks from his movies.

Presley appealed to the youth boom of the 1950s. Young people saw in him the music that differentiated them from their parents, and they saw a controlled rebelliousness that they admired and emulated: his leather jacket, his greased hair, his sexually suggestive mannerisms on stage.

The change that occurred in rock music in the 1960s with the invasion of such British bands as the Beatles and the Rolling Stones, and the subsequent shift to performers who largely wrote the material they sang, caused Presley's career to fade. But in the late 1960s and 1970s, he rejuvenated it, first with a television special and then with a series of concerts.

Elvis's reputation took a hit, however, in the summer of 1977, when the book *Elvis: What Happened?* was published by two men formerly in his entourage. The authors told about the singer's immersion in prescription drugs. Lest anyone doubt the truth of the story, they had only to attend Elvis's recent concert in Houston, Texas, where he slurred his words and barely made it through his performance. For Elvis fans, it was a disturbing, sad, and unsettling appearance (and only one of several similar occurrences at the time). Reviewer Bob Claypool wrote: "The man who had given us the original myth of rock 'n roll—the man who created it and *lived* it—was now, for whatever reason, taking it all back."[59]

In August, Elvis prepared to begin another concert tour. Concerned about his weight—he had previously split one of his jumpsuits while moving about the stage—he began an exercise program. He continued to have difficulty sleeping at night and suffered from a range of psychological problems that led his doctor to provide him with a steady and far-ranging supply of depressants, such as Seconal and Demerol. On the afternoon of August 16, Presley took extensive doses of the drugs and then went into his bathroom. There, he keeled over from the toilet and fell on the floor, his gold pajama bottoms down around his ankles. Members of his entourage tried to revive him but failed.

Pathologists later found 14 drugs in Elvis's system, with codeine at 10 times the therapeutic level and methaqualone at, or nearly at, a toxic amount. In the highly acclaimed biography *Careless Love: The Unmaking of Elvis Presley,* author Peter Guralnick writes:

> All one has to do is look at Elvis's life, the accelerating dependence on medications available to him in almost unimaginable quantities, the willing enlistment of doctors who seemed never to give thought to the dangers or likely consequences of what they were prescribing, and the incontrovertible evidence of the medical problems stemming primarily from the use of drugs that Elvis experienced over his last four years, to understand the causes of his death.[60]

Thousands of Elvis's fans appeared at Graceland to view the singer's body. Flowers covered the lawn outside the mansion. One relative sneaked in a small camera and took a picture of Elvis in repose. A few days later, it appeared in a tabloid, the *National Enquirer.*

Guralnick writes:

> The cacophony of voices that have joined together to create a chorus of informed opinion, uninformed speculation, hagiography, symbolism, and blame, can be difficult at times to drown out, but in the end there is only one voice that counts. It is the voice that the world first heard on those bright yellow Sun 78s. . . . It is impossible to silence that voice; you cannot miss it when you listen to "That's All Right" or "Mystery Train" or "Blue Moon of Kentucky" or any of the songs with which Elvis continued to convey his sense of unlimited possibilities almost to the end of his life. . . . In the face of facts, for all that we have come to know, it is necessary to listen unprejudiced

and unencumbered if we are to hear Elvis' message: the proclamation of emotions long suppressed, the embrace of a vulnerability culturally denied, the unabashed striving for freedom. . . . For all of his disappointment, for all of the self-loathing he frequently felt, and all of the disillusionment and fear, he continued to believe in a democratic ideal of redemptive transformation, he continued to seek out a connection with the public that embraced him not for what he was but for what he sought to be.[61]

REGGIE JACKSON AS "MR. OCTOBER"

Brash, some would say egotistical, Reggie Jackson made baseball history with an onslaught of home runs for the New York Yankees during the team's World Series showdown with the Los Angeles Dodgers in October 1977. His feat in those games earned him the nickname "Mr. October."

Prior to joining the Yankees, Jackson played for the Oakland Athletics and, briefly, the Baltimore Orioles. At Oakland, he helped his team win five consecutive division titles and three consecutive World Series championships with power hitting that, in 1973, earned him an MVP award. Jackson became a Yankee in 1977, publicly proclaiming that he would be "the straw that stirs the drink."

In his first weeks with the club, however, he stirred more trouble than many Yankees wanted when he clashed with the team's manager, Billy Martin. In a game against Boston, Martin pulled Jackson from the field after he failed to chase down a fly ball, and in an ensuing argument, the two men nearly came to blows in the dugout while television cameras broadcast the dispute.

But Jackson's hitting proved crucial to the Yankees winning the American League pennant, sending them into the World Series against their historic rivals, the Dodgers. Jackson showed little offensive power in the first two games, but he hit home runs in the fourth and fifth games. Then came game six: If the Yankees could win that one, they would become the world champions.

With the Yankees trailing the Dodgers, Jackson came up to the plate in the fourth inning (he walked his first time up), and on the first pitch from Burt Hooten, he homered to right field, scoring two runs and giving New York a 4-3 lead. In the fifth, on the first pitch from Elias Sosa, he again hit a two-run homer to right, giving the Yankees a commanding 7-3 lead.

Jackson came up to the plate one more time, in the eighth inning. He faced Charlie Hough, and, incredibly, on another first pitch, he hit yet another home run, this one to center field, much deeper than the other two, as deep into the stands as October was into the year. Jackson would forever be known as "Mr. October."

In his major league career, Jackson hit 563 home runs, putting him sixth on the all-time list. He compiled a lifetime slugging percentage of .490. Jackson retired after the 1987 season and was inducted into the Baseball Hall of Fame in 1993.

WALTER PAYTON

Fans and fellow players called Walter Payton "Sweetness," in part for his kind disposition but also because as a running back for the Chicago Bears, he showed incredible moves on the field; he could elude tacklers and yet, when needed, stiff-arm them aside. On November 20, 1977, he added to his list of records by rushing for 275 yards against the Minnesota Vikings.

In 1975, the Bears drafted Payton out of Jackson State University in Mississippi. One year later, he led the National Football Conference (NFC) by rushing for 1,390 yards and 13 touchdowns and earned a place in the Pro Bowl. Then, in 1977, he ran for a career-high 1,852 yards and 14 touchdowns, the most of any runner in the NFC, a feat that included the 275-yard performance against the Vikings, notable as a single-game rushing record which still stands.

Payton continued to play football through the 1987 season, missing only one game. He rushed for more than 1,000 yards every year except 1982 and 1987, accumulating a record 16,726 yards in his career. His 1,500 yards in 1985 helped the Bears win their only Super Bowl championship.

Payton was inducted into the Pro Football Hall of Fame in 1993. He died in 1999, at age 45, the victim of a rare liver disease. One NFL coach, Dennis Green, said Payton had "set a standard for going all out." He was undersized but "he could outwork anybody and he always gave 100 percent. And that was 100 percent to his family, to his friends, to the game of football. . . ."[62] In the record-setting game against the Vikings, he gave a 100 percent effort that football fans would remember for years to come.

CHRONICLE OF EVENTS

1977

January 20: Democrat Jimmy Carter is inaugurated as the 39th president of the United States in a ceremony that is marked by a pledge to pursue humanitarian causes.

January 21: In his first official acts as president, Jimmy Carter pardons Vietnam War draft evaders. His decision affects about 10,000 men.

January 24: President Carter announces that he will seek an agreement with the Soviet Union to end all nuclear testing and reduce the stockpiles of atomic weapons.

January 26: With much of the nation in a deep freeze from severely cold temperatures and a blizzard in the central and eastern states—weather that was pro-

Jimmy Carter entered the White House with the promise of sincerity and honesty. *(Courtesy Jimmy Carter Library)*

ducing a serious strain on natural-gas supplies— President Carter says that he will ask Congress for emergency legislation authorizing a reallocation of natural gas to help the affected regions. In early February, Congress agrees to his request.

January 28: Hispanic comedian Freddie Prinze, age 22, the star of the TV comedy series *Chico and the Man,* commits suicide in Los Angeles.

January 30: The final episode of the eight-part miniseries *Roots,* adapted from Alex Haley's book of the same name, attracts 80 million viewers, the largest ever for a TV show.

February 2: In an attempt to fulfill his campaign pledge of fostering open government, President Carter holds a televised fireside chat in which he outlines many of his proposals, including placing a limit on federal hiring, making federal regulations more understandable, and holding town meetings across the nation.

February 8: A Cincinnati, Ohio, grand jury finds Larry Flynt guilty of engaging in organized crime and selling obscenity for his publishing of the adult magazine *Hustler.* He is fined $10,000 and sentenced to seven to 25 years in jail.

March 5: The North Carolina legislature rejects the Equal Rights Amendment despite a plea from President Carter to ratify it.

March 7: President Carter welcomes Israeli prime minister Yitzhak Rabin to the United States and tells him that any Middle East peace agreement should provide Israel with "defensible borders," a position Israel had long been advocating. The statement angers Arabs and causes Carter to clarify that he was still committed to negotiating an evenhanded agreement.

March 9: The Food and Drug Administration raises a storm of controversy when it proposes that the only artificial sweetener on the marker, saccharin, be banned. The FDA points to tests in Canada showing that saccharin caused cancer in rats. Doctors and groups representing diabetics argue that the ban could lead to obesity, heart disease, and arthritis.

April 7: In an effort to prevent the spread of atomic weapons, President Carter suspends government programs that encourage the use of plutonium in fueling commercial nuclear power plants.

April 11: A California State of Appeals panel orders that five young adult children whose parents had sought to "deprogram" them and separate them from Reverend Sun Myung Moon's Unification Church be allowed to return to the church.

April 18: President Carter announces an energy plan to prevent the shortage of fuel supplies. He says that all citizens must make sacrifices in the effort. His proposal to Congress includes an increase in the gasoline tax, increased taxes on domestically produced oil, penalties on cars that exceed fuel consumption limits, increases in natural gas prices to encourage exploration, the building of more atomic power plants, a change in building standards to encourage efficient energy use, and a decontrol of gasoline prices.

April 28: A prominent spy case comes to an end when Christopher J. Boyce is found guilty of espionage and conspiracy to commit espionage. Boyce formerly worked for defense contractor TRW Systems and passed on or sold to Soviet agents documents containing information about U.S. spy satellites and encryption devices. Boyce admitted his role but claimed that he had been blackmailed into doing what he did by another person. Boyce will received a 40-year sentence for his crime.

May 1: Members of the Clamshell Alliance begin two days of protests at the site of a proposed nuclear power plant in Seabrook, New Hampshire. More than 1,400 demonstrators are arrested.

May 9: A California superior court judge decides to place Patricia Hearst on five-year probation rather than send her to prison for her role in a 1974 robbery and shootout in Los Angeles. Hearst had pleaded no contest to one count of armed robbery and one count of assault with a deadly weapon.

May 16: President Carter achieves a major political victory when Congress passes his proposal to cut income taxes as a way to stimulate the economy. The bill is aimed primarily at middle- and low-income families and will save them about $5 billion.

May 23: The Supreme Court refuses to hear the appeals of Watergate defendants John Mitchell, H. R. Haldeman, and John Ehrlichman. The Court's decision means that the three men will serve time in prison.

June 3: Good news arrives for the Carter administration when the Labor Department reports that unemployment dipped below 7 percent for the first time in more than two years and total employment in May reached a record 90,408,000.

June 3: The United States announces that it will exchange diplomats with Cuba for the first time in 16 years, though the relations between the two countries will fall short of full diplomatic recognition. The U.S. staff in Havana will fly the flag of Switzerland, and the Cuban staff in Washington will fly the flag of Czechoslovakia.

June 7: Voters in Dade County, Florida (greater Miami), repeal a county ordinance that made illegal discrimination on the grounds of sexual preference in employment, housing, and public accommodation. Gay rights advocates condemn the vote. The singer Anita Bryant, head of the group Save Our Children, praises the outcome. Bryant had led the effort to win the repeal, at one point calling homosexuals "human garbage."

June 10: James Earl Ray, convicted of assassinating Martin Luther King, Jr., escapes from Brushy Mountain State Penitentiary in Petros, Tennessee, but is recaptured three days later in a massive manhunt.

June 17: The U.S. Environmental Protection Agency approves a water cooling system for the nuclear power plant in Seabrook, New Hampshire.

June 20: The Supreme Court rules that states can choose to prohibit the spending of Medicaid moneys on abortions. Critics, such as Planned Parenthood, say that the ruling discriminates against the poor by making abortions unaffordable to them.

June 28: The Supreme Court upholds a law that gives the federal government control over Richard Nixon's presidential papers and tape recordings. The court says that there was a real danger that, if left under Nixon's control, some of the papers and tapes might be destroyed.

June 30: In a much-awaited decision, President Carter announces that he will oppose the building and construction of the controversial B-1 bomber. Each of the planes was to have cost $100 million and the entire fleet, including maintenance, about $100 billion. The B-1 was intended to allow air strikes deep within the territory of the Soviet Union, but Carter says that cruise missiles deployed on existing planes would be just as effective.

July 12: Watergate burglar G. Gordon Liddy is granted an early release from prison after President Carter commutes his sentence from 20 to eight years.

July 13: A massive power failure darkens New York City at 9:30 P.M. and leads to widespread looting. The power is partially restored four hours later but not fully restored until 25 hours after the outage began.

July 15: President Carter approves allowing an additional 15,000 refugees from Southeast Asia into the United States in 1977 and 1978, including 7,000 "boat people" who were living on the vessels that they had used to escape from Vietnam.

July 29: Oil from Alaska's North Slope reaches the port of Valdez, marking the successful opening of the Trans-Alaska pipeline.

August 1: The *New York Times* reports that additional documents uncovered by the CIA reveal in more detail the agency's secret program to develop LSD and other drugs as part of a mind control project. The program included drugs administered to prisoners, mental patients, and private citizens without their knowledge.

August 3: President Carter signs into law a bill long desired by environmentalists: the regulation of strip mining. It requires companies to restore land to its approximate original configuration, replant grass and trees, and take measures to prevent the pollution of rivers and streams.

August 3: Two bombs explode in New York City, killing one person and injuring seven more. The FALN, a Puerto Rican independence group, claims credit for the attack.

August 4: President Carter signs an act creating the Department of Energy, the first new cabinet-level department since 1966. On the same day, the Senate confirms Carter's appointment of James Schlesinger as the department's first secretary.

August 10: The United States and Panama announce that they have reached agreement on the terms for a new Panama Canal treaty to return the Canal Zone to Panamanian control by the year 2000.

August 10: David Richard Berkowitz, a 24-year-old postal worker, is arrested as the "Son of Sam" killer at his home near Yonkers, New York. Berkowitz is believed to have murdered six young people and wounded several others in nighttime attacks along the streets of New York City between July 1976 and July 1977.

August 16: Elvis Presley dies at his home, Graceland, in Memphis, Tennessee.

August 20: *Voyager 2* is launched on a flyby mission to Saturn and Jupiter, carrying with it a record album featuring rock and roll and classical music, along with African tribal chants and a message from President Carter.

August 23: Maryland governor Marvin Mandel is found guilty of mail fraud and racketeering in connection with bribes he took to help the owners of a racetrack. In October, he will be sentenced to four years in jail.

September 5: *Voyager 1* is launched and follows *Voyager 2* on a journey toward Saturn and Jupiter.

September 14: Mark Rudd, a radical underground activist from the 1960s, surrenders to the authorities in New York City. Rudd had been a leader during the student uprising at Columbia University in 1968. In October, he will plead guilty to a criminal trespassing charge.

September 21: Bert Lance resigns as President Carter's director of the Office of Management and the Budget amid reports that he had engaged in unacceptable financial practices involving personal loans made to him while he was a bank executive in Georgia.

October 4: Federal District Judge John Sirica reduces the sentences for Watergate figures John Mitchell, H. R. Haldeman, and John Ehrlichman, noting their admission of guilt and their contrition.

October 12: Congress approves a regulation requiring automatic seat belts and air bags in cars by 1984.

The *Voyager I* spacecraft produced this montage of Jupiter and its four moons, Io, Europa, Ganymede, and Callisto. *(National Space Science Data Center)*

The twin Voyager spacecraft, one of which is shown here as a full-scale model, explored Mars. *(National Space Science Data Center)*

October 13: President Carter publicly attacks the oil industry for opposing his energy legislation and engaging in profiteering from the energy crisis. He threatens to impose gasoline rationing or a tax on foreign oil if Congress fails to enact his proposals.

October 17: The Supreme Court lifts a ban on flights by the supersonic Concorde airliner into New York City's John F. Kennedy airport. The jet makes its first test landing there two days later.

October 18: New York Yankees outfielder Reggie Jackson hits four home runs in four consecutive at bats to make baseball history and earn the nickname "Mr. October" as his team beats the Los Angeles Dodgers in six games to win the World Series.

November 5: President Carter uses his veto power for the first time when he rejects legislation authorizing the spending of $80 million on the Clinch River nuclear breeder reactor in Tennessee. Carter says that the facility is too costly, is "economically unnecessary," and, as a plutonium-fueled reactor, will damage his efforts to "curb proliferation of nuclear weapons technology."

November 6: A jury in Phoenix, Arizona, finds contractor Max Dunlap and plumber James Robison guilty of murder and conspiracy in the car bombing that killed Don Bolles, a reporter for the *Arizona Republic*. At the time of his death, Bolles had been investigating land fraud, organized crime, and a scandal involving the Arizona Racing Commission. A third person accused in the crime, John Harvey Adamson, confessed and implicated Dunlap and Robison.

November 18: A jury in Birmingham, Alabama, convicts Ku Klux Klansman Robert E. Chambliss of first-degree murder in the 1963 bombing of a Baptist church that resulted in the death of four young African-American girls. He is sentenced to life in prison.

November 19: The movie *Star Wars* surpasses *Jaws* as the highest-grossing movie to date.

November 20: Chicago Bears running back Walter Payton rushes for 275 yards against the Minnesota Vikings, setting a single-game record.

November 21: The National Women's Conference in Houston, Texas, ends its three-day convention by approving an agenda to advance women's equality. The group advocates passage of the Equal Rights Amendment, the elimination of discrimination in employment, and a pro-choice position.

December 12: The Velsicol Chemical Corporation of Chicago and six of its present and former employees are indicted by a federal grand jury for conspiring to hide test data that show two of its pesticides could cause cancer in human beings.

Rosalynn Carter and Betty Ford appear at a rally to promote passage of the ERA. *(Courtesy Jimmy Carter Library)*

December 14: The movie *Saturday Night Fever* opens in New York City, boosting John Travolta to stardom and bringing the disco fad to greater prominence.

EYEWITNESS TESTIMONY

The Pardoning of Vietnam War Draft Resisters

Presidential Proclamation of Pardon
A Proclamation

Acting pursuant to the grant of authority in Article II, Section 2, of the Constitution of the United States, I, Jimmy Carter, President of the United States, do hereby grant a full, complete and unconditional pardon to: (1) all persons who may have committed any offense between August 4, 1964 and March 28, 1973 in violation of the Military Selective Service Act or any rule or regulation promulgated thereunder; and (2) all persons heretofore convicted, irrespective of the date of conviction, of any offense committed between August 4, 1964 and March 28, 1973 in violation of the Military Selective Service Act, or any rule or regulation promulgated thereunder, restoring to them full political, civil and other rights.

This pardon does not apply to the following who are specifically excluded therefrom:

(1) All persons convicted of or who may have committed any offense in violation of the Military Selective Service Act, or any rule or regulation promulgated thereunder, involving force or violence; and

(2) All persons convicted of or who may have committed any offense in violation of the Military Selective Service Act, or any rule or regulation promulgated thereunder, in connection with duties or responsibilities arising out of employment as agents, officers or employees of the Military Selective Service system.

In witness whereof, I have hereunto set my hand this 21st day of January, in the year of our Lord nineteen hundred and seventy-seven, and of the Independence of the United States of America the two hundred and first.

President Jimmy Carter's proclamation pardoning those who resisted the draft during the Vietnam War, issued January 21, 1977, in Public Papers of the Presidents of the United States: Jimmy Carter, January 20 to June 24, 1977 *(1977), p. 5.*

Executive Order Relating to Proclamation of Pardon
Relating to violations of the Selective Service Act,
August 4, 1964 to March 28, 1973
The following actions shall be taken to facilitate Presidential Proclamation of Pardon of January 21, 1977:

1. The Attorney General shall cause to be dismissed with prejudice to the government all pending indictments for violations of the Military Selective Service Act alleged to have occurred between August 4, 1964 and March 28, 1973 with the exception of the following:

(a) Those cases alleging acts of force or violence deemed to be so serious by the Attorney General as to warrant continued prosecution; and

(b) Those cases alleging acts in violation of the Military Selective Service Act by agents, employees or officers of the Selective Service System arising out of such employment.

2. The Attorney General shall terminate all investigations now pending and shall not initiate further investigations alleging violations of the Military Selective Service Act between August 4, 1964 and March 28, 1973, with the exception of the following:

A refugee woman and her children flee Vietnam aboard the USS *Wabash* in the South China Sea. *(National Archives and Records Administration)*

(a) Those cases involving allegations of force or violence deemed to be so serious by the Attorney General as to warrant continued investigation, or possible prosecution; and

(b) Those cases alleging acts in violation of the Military Selective Service Act by agents, employees or officers of the Selective Service System arising out of such employment.

3. Any person who is or may be precluded from reentering the United States under 8 U.S.C. 1182(a)(22) or under any other law, by reason of having committed or apparently committed any violation of the Military Selective Service Act shall be permitted as any other alien to reenter the United States.

The Attorney General is directed to exercise his discretion under 8 U.S.C. 1182 (d) (5) or other applicable law to permit the reentry of such persons under the same terms and conditions as any other alien.

This shall not include anyone who falls into the exceptions of paragraphs 1(a) and (b) and 2(a) and (b) above.

4. Any individual offered conditional clemency or granted a pardon or other clemency under Executive Order 11803 or Presidential Proclamation 4313, dated September 16, 1974, shall receive the full measure of relief afforded by this program if they are otherwise qualified under the terms of this Executive Order.

President Jimmy Carter's executive order intended to carry out his pardon of those who resisted the draft during the Vietnam War, issued January 21, 1977, in Public Papers of the Presidents of the United States: Jimmy Carter, January 20 to June 24, 1977 *(1977), p. 6.*

The Moonies and Religious Freedom

The ACLU opposes the use of mental incompetency proceedings, temporary conservatorship, or denial of government protection as a method of depriving people of the free exercise of religion, at least with respect to people who have reached the age of majority.

Modes of religious proselytizing or persuasion for a continued adherence that do not employ physical coercion or threat of same are protected by the free exercise of religion clause of the First Amendment against action of state laws or by state officials. The claim of free exercise may not be overcome by the contention that "brainwashing" or "mind control" has

been used, in the absence of evidence that the above standards have been violated.

A statement issued by the American Civil Liberties Union in 1977 condemning forcible deprogramming and cult conservatorships as a violation of freedom of religion, available online at http://bernie.cncfamily.com/aclu1.htm, downloaded August 28, 2004.

You sometimes enjoy watching the full moon rise at night. Is it more moving to see the moon rise over the open plains or over a mountain? Which is more artistic? We in the Unification Church are like the moon rising from way down in the valley. We climb up and up and finally go over the mountain. Even though we are now in the valley do you still believe that we are going to make it over the mountain? Often we are so busy doing some little thing that we do not even see the mountain or the sky. Does your foot or your hip go up first when you jump over the hill? God is almighty; there is nothing He cannot do. When you take off in the normal position your head is up and legs are down, but why not have your head down and your legs up? It does not matter much because we can still jump over the hill.

The Unification Church itself is going to make the jump, not just individuals within the church. Take the San Francisco court case as an example. We are well aware of the hardships and difficulties, but in the meantime our whole church is beginning its take-off, even while you are unaware. Do you feel that the whole church is beginning to rise over the mountain? Do you think I am just trying to tell you something nice because you came so early, or am I simply telling you what is really going on in the world at large? I have a clear sensitivity by which to evaluate events in the world.

One indicator of public opinion is the mail that is sent to me; it is like the pulse of the nation. You have no idea of the interest and attention that was given to the Unification Church after the San Francisco court case. Suddenly many people became sympathetic to our cause and decided, "I'm not a member of Reverend Moon's group, but I can't find anything wrong with him." Perhaps they have also come to a decisive conclusion that there is no one else in the world who can really tame the young people of America and discipline them in a moral, God-centered way. Americans have witnessed the futile efforts of the government and religious leaders to guide young people, and they are beginning to recognize that all these court cases are largely motivated by sheer jealousy. Righteous America is now beginning to stand up for me.

Furthermore, the time is coming when people will begin to admire my courage. Everybody thinks that by this time I must be completely tired and shriveled-looking like a shrimp. But on the contrary I am more courageous and looking forward to even greater accomplishments. Every day I am marching forward more passionately, becoming busier and more respected. People say, "Well, we must give this man credit." They might have thought that I would look bent-over like a shrimp, but this shrimp has wings, and instead of sagging down I am flying upward.

If God is alive and concerned with religion, He must either be giving His concentrated attention to the Unification Church or else He does not really exist. Nowadays the religions of the world are becoming powerless. We are in the minority, no question about it, but even though we are such a small group we are a fearless group, and furthermore, we are intensely anticipating the greatest of all accomplishments: that of liberating even the communists who have already taken over two thirds of the world's population.

The Reverend Sun Myung Moon reacts to the San Francisco court decision concerning the Unification Church, deprogrammers, and freedom of religion in his sermon "The Road of Religion and the Will of God," presented in 1977, available online at http://www.unification.net/1977/770424.html, downloaded August 28, 2004.

My first experience with the anti-cult movement in Maryland was an event in 1976 in Silver Spring. I was leading a performing arts troupe promoting Rev. [Sun Myung] Moon's rally at the Washington Monument, and our team was staying at a motel in Silver Spring. The trumpet player in the band was a man of about 23 years old named Alan Feldsott. One night, without warning, about half a dozen squad cars pulled up in front of the motel. I was called down from my room to negotiate with them. They demanded that I produce Alan Feldsott and showed me a guardianship or "conservatorship" order authorizing them to deliver him into the custody of his relatives and deprogrammers. He had been declared mentally incompetent by a judge who had never seen him, on the basis of the analysis of a psychologist who had never even spoken to him. I told the police I would not cooperate with such a violation of an adult US citizen's civil rights. However, I

had no power to stop them from searching. They searched our sleeping rooms, meeting rooms, and the motel dining room where band members were eating and relaxing at the time. I witnessed one officer use his billy club to smash the window of our bus after the driver simply asked if he had a search warrant. But the Maryland police never found Alan Feldsott. Alan was hiding in the bass drum case. Around midnight, while squad cars continued to stake the place out, we loaded the case in a van, and I smuggled him across the District Line to safety.

A few days later, another young man was not so lucky. During Rev. Moon's Washington Monument Rally to honor America's Bicentennial, in from of a crowd of hundreds of thousands of people, this young man was dragged kicking and screaming from the Washington Monument grounds by National Park Police, another victim of a conservatorship for purposes of deprogramming. We never heard from him again.

Testimony by Dan Fefferman, executive director of the International Coalition for Religious Freedom, about his experience with deprogrammers in 1976 and about the constitutional issue raised by their activities, in Testimony of Dan Fefferman before the Maryland Task Force to Study the Effects of Cult Activities on Public Senior Higher Educational Institutions (1999), available online at http://religiousmovements.lib.virginia.edu/cultsect/mdtaskforce/fefferman_testimony2.htm, downloaded August 28, 2004.

Around [1951] Father first organized the Divine Principle theme. He wrote very fast with a pencil in his notebook. One person beside him would sharpen his pencil, and he couldn't follow his writing speed. By the time Father's pencil got thick, this next person could not sharpen another pencil, [Father] wrote so very fast. That was the beginning of the Divine Principle book; also at that time Father began to teach the Principle.

Kwang Wol Yoo, a Unification Church biographer discussing in 1974 how Sun Myung Moon developed the Divine Principle book, the theological foundation of the church, in George D. Chryssides, The Advent of Sun Myung Moon *(1991), pp. 21–22.*

I was finding value in the wrong things. I used to get high on marijuana, acid, and cocaine very week. . . .

Now I am going in a definite direction instead of constantly changing.

I was drifting. I had no sense of purpose. The major difference in my life since joining the Church is that I have a clearer idea of what I want to accomplish for myself and others.

Comments made in 1977 by two unidentified members of the Unification Church about how their lives had changed since becoming "Moonies," in David G. Bromley and Anson D. Shupe, Moonies in America *(1979), p. 189.*

Q. Of people who came to dinner on Friday night, what percentage would go up to Boonville for a weekend?

A. Maybe twenty-five people would come for dinner and sometimes we'd get as many as half the people, sometimes as few as a quarter of the people (for the weekend seminar).

Q. Of that group, how many would stay for the week-long seminar?

A. There usually would be at least fifteen new people for the week is my recollection. I mean at least that many. . . .

Q. What percentage of those subsequently became members of the group for longer than two or three weeks following the one-week seminar?

A. Well, say thirty people came for the weekend, fifteen people stayed for the week, I guess at the end of that week, ten would probably become members.

Q. And by members, you mean people that would stay with the group longer than two or three weeks?

A. Right.

Q. Of that ten, how many would stay longer than six months?

A. I would say, five.

Barbara Underwood Scharff, a former group leader of the Unification Church at Boonville in northern California, discussing in a court trial on June 21, 1983, the workshops held there by the Moonies between 1975 and 1977, in Eileen Barker, The Making of a Moonie *(1984), p. 284.*

Each case I have worked on is unique. There are some common variables. If I had to reduce what I do to a few words, it would boil down to something like trying to convince young men and women that they can work, they can fight for righteousness, they can make a difference, they needn't prostate themselves before some

divine king in order to be justified. I invite them to leave Eden, to come back into the field of battle, to enter a world of uncertainty where knowledge of the truth does not exempt them from moral responsibility, a world where their successes and failures will be their own.

Former Moonie-turned-deprogrammer Allan Tate Wood discussing in 1979 how he convinces young people to leave the Unification Church, in Allan Tate Wood, Moonstruck *(1979), p. 189.*

The Energy Crisis

Tonight I want to have an unpleasant talk with you about a problem that is unprecedented in our history. With the exception of preventing war, this is the greatest challenge that our country will face during our lifetime.

The energy crisis has not yet overwhelmed us, but it will if we do not act quickly. It's a problem that we will not be able to solve in the next few years, and it's likely to get progressively worse through the rest of this century.

We must not be selfish or timid if we hope to have a decent world for our children and our grandchildren. We simply must balance our demand for energy with our rapidly shrinking resources. By acting now we can control our future instead of letting the future control us. . . .

Our decision about energy will test the character of the America people and the ability of the President and the Congress to govern this Nation. This difficult effort will be the "moral equivalent of war," except that we will be uniting our efforts to build and not to destroy. . . .

The world now uses about 60 million barrels of oil a day, and demand increases each year about 5 percent. This means that just to stay even we need the production of a new Texas every year, an Alaskan North Slope every 9 months, or a new Saudi Arabia every 3 years. Obviously, this cannot continue. . . .

I know that many of you have suspected that some supplies of oil and gas are being withheld from the market. You may be right, but suspicions about the oil companies cannot change the fact that we are running out of petroleum. . . .

Each American uses the energy equivalent of 60 barrels of oil per person each year. Ours is the most wasteful nation on Earth. We waste more energy than we import. With about the same standard of living, we use twice as much energy per person as do other countries like Germany, Japan, and Sweden. . . .

Our national energy plan is based on 10 fundamental principles. The first principle is that we can have an effective and comprehensive energy policy only if the Government takes responsibility for it and if the people understand the seriousness of the challenge and are willing to make sacrifices.

The second principle is that healthy economic growth must continue. Only by saving energy can we maintain our standard of living and keep our people at work. An effective conservation program will create hundreds of thousands of new jobs.

The third principle is that we must protect the environment. Our energy problems have the same cause as our environmental problems—wasteful use of resources. Conservation helps us solve both problems at once.

The fourth principle is that we must reduce our vulnerability to potentially devastating embargoes. We can protect ourselves from uncertain supplies by reducing our demand for oil, by making the most of our abundant resources such as coal, and by developing a strategic petroleum reserve.

The fifth principle is that we must be fair. Our solutions must ask equal sacrifices from every region, every class of people, and every interest group. Industry will have to do its part to conserve just as consumers will. The energy producers deserve fair treatment, but we will not let the oil companies profiteer.

The sixth principle, and the cornerstone of our policy, is to reduce demand through conservation. Our

Jimmy Carter and Energy Secretary James Schlesinger discuss the energy crisis. *(Courtesy Jimmy Carter Library)*

emphasis on conservation is a clear difference between this plan and others which merely encouraged crash production efforts. . . .

The seventh principle is that prices should generally reflect the true replacement cost of energy. We are only cheating ourselves if we make energy artificially cheap and use more than we can really afford.

The eighth principle is that Government policies must be predictable and certain. Both consumers and producers need policies they can count on so they can plan ahead. . . .

The ninth principle is that we must conserve the fuels that are scarcest and make the most of those that are plentiful. We can't continue to use oil and gas for 75 percent of our consumption, as we do now, when they only make up 7 percent of our domestic reserves. We need to shift to plentiful coal, while taking care to protect the environment, and to apply stricter safety standards to nuclear energy.

The tenth and last principle is that we must start now to develop the new, unconventional sources of energy that we will rely on in the next century. . . .

From President Jimmy Carter's address to the nation on April 18, 1977, outlining the challenges facing the United States by an increasingly serious energy crisis, in Public Papers of the Presidents of the United States: Jimmy Carter, January 20 to June 24, 1977 *(1977), pp. 656–662.*

The Clamshell Alliance

A transition to a solar economy is desirable and realizable. It involves neither privation nor social deprivation. Lifestyle changes would be minimal. The rewards would be enormous.

From a statement issued around 1977 by the Oregon Energy Council, in Lee Stephenson and George R. Zachar, Accidents Will Happen *(1979), p. 247.*

Our intention was to occupy the site and stop construction of the plant. We feel Seabrook in particular and nuclear power plants in general are life and death issues. We are acting in self-defense.

Clamshell Alliance spokesman Harvey Wasserman commenting in May 1977 on the recent Seabrook protest, in Time, *May 16, 1977, available online at http://www.time.com/archive/preview/ 0,10987,918965,00.html, downloaded June 30, 2005.*

For all practical purposes, there is a moratorium on building plants. In effect, for the short term, the antinuclear people have won.

Irwin Bupp, a professor at Harvard University, commenting in May 1977 on the effects of the antinuclear protest at Seabrook and elsewhere, in Time, *May 16, 1977, available online at http://www.time.com/ archive/preview/0,10987,918965,00.html, downloaded June 30, 2005.*

A lot of the fellas are unemployed because these projects are tied up in the courts. You're going to see a lot of us out marching on Sundays.

Daniel Tenchara, a pipe fitter, voicing his support in July 1977 for a protest staged by New Hampshire Voice of Energy, a group that advocated the building of the Seabrook nuclear power plant, in Time, *July 11, 1977, available online at http://www.time.com/archive/ preview/0,10987,919085,00.html, downloaded July 1, 2005.*

The B-1 Bomber

Q. Mr. President, in listening to factors involved in your decision, sir, you didn't mention or I didn't hear the fact that you had made a commitment or what many people took to be a commitment during the campaign against the bomber, I think particularly in the submission to the Democratic Platform Committee. Was that a factor, sir?

The President. Well, when I went into office, as I think I said earlier, I tried to take the position of complete open-mindedness, because obviously I've had available to me as President much of the classified analyses and information about weapons systems which I did not have before. And I tried to approach this question with an open mind.

I've spent many hours reading those detailed technical reports, the advice of specialists on both sides, an analysis of ultimate cost of weapons. And although, obviously, opinions are always hard to change, I deliberately tried not to let my campaign statements be the factor in this decision. I've made it, I think, recently with an original, very open mind, after carefully considering all aspects of the question and consulting very closely with the Secretary of Defense. And I might say that with the advent of the cruise missile as a possible alternative, that the Secretary of Defense agrees with me that this is a preferable decision. . . .

Q. Mr. President, is this decision on your part not to go ahead with the B-1 intended as any kind of a signal to the Soviets that you are willing to—that you want to do something quickly in the strategic arms talks?

The President. I can't deny that that's a potential factor. But that has not been a reason for my decision. I think if I had looked upon the B-1 as simply a bargaining chip for the Soviets, then my decision would have been to go ahead with the weapon. But I made my decision on my analysis that, within a given budgetary limit for the defense of our country, which I am sure will always be adequate, that we should have the optimum capability to defend ourselves.

But this is a matter that's of very great importance, and if at the end of a few years the relations with the Soviets should deteriorate drastically, which I don't anticipate, then it may be necessary for me to change my mind. But I don't expect that to occur.

President Carter responds to questions from newspaper reporters about his decision to end funding for the B-1 bomber, from a transcript in Public Papers of the Presidents of the United States: Jimmy Carter, June 25 to December 31, 1977 *(1978), pp. 1,199–1,200.*

The New York City Blackout

Not only has the ability to transmit bulk power to New York City been jeopardized by [the] lack of path diversity, but even the vital northern corridor has been weakened by intentional design compromises. . . . It thus appears that Con Edison and the Pool [other utilities linked to Con Edison] have planned for a transmission system with inadequate strength to withstand foreseeable lightning disturbances.

The refusal to plan for the loss of the . . . double circuit transmission line also led to the design compromise which requires Indian Point 3 to be shut down following a temporary fault on circuits 97 and 98. . . . Had Con Edison kept within established criteria through transmission reinforcement and provided a more reliable design at the Buchanan substation through the installation of additional circuit breakers, the loss of Indian Point 3 would not be a planned occurrence following a double circuit [failure] on 97/98. . . .

In 1974 the Boeing Company, which Con Edison retained to review the adequacy of control facilities, called attention to important deficiencies. The Boeing study concluded that Con Edison system operators depended on "[p]ast experience and extensive exposure to varied load situations to correct impending and actual problems" and that

> [d]uring normal operating conditions the System Operator and District Operators are provided with a minimum amount of data to allow them to maintain cognizance of the system status. At times of overload, or transient change conditions, the operators are not provided with sufficient data, in a readily available form, to allow rapid and reliable decisions.

Despite these conclusions, control room modernization was one of the programs curtailed in Con Edison's 1976 capital budget by reason of the serious financial restraints facing the company.

An excerpt from an investigation into the New York City blackout that places much of the responsibility for the electrical failure on the Con Edison utility company, in Norman Clapp, New York State Investigation of the New York City Blackout, July 13, 1977 *(1978), pp. 34–38, available online at http://blackout.gmu. edu/archive/a_1977.html, downloaded August 27, 2004.*

It's like a fever struck them. They were out there with trucks, vans, trailers, everything that could roll.

Police officer Frank Ross, on July 13, 1977, describing the looting in Bedford-Stuyvesant, Brooklyn, "Night of Terror," in Time, *July 25, 1977, p. 12.*

"All I wanted to know was if he'd seen my kids . . . and he shoved me. They just crazy."

An unidentified woman, on the night of the blackout, describing the police after running into the scene and being shoved away by a sweating cop, July 13, 1977, "Heart of Darkness," in Newsweek, *July 25, 1977, p. 26.*

It's the night of the animals. You grab four or five, and a hundred take their place. We come to a scene, and people who aren't looting whistle to warn the others. All we can do is chase people away from a store, and they just run to the next block, to the next store.

Police sergeant Robert Murphy, on July 13, 1977, describing the looting in Harlem, "Night of Terror," in Time, *July 25, 1977, p. 12.*

The evidence of looting was numbing. As firemen fought blazes from cherry pickers, the looters went about their business virtually unmolested. Occasionally they would step over to one of the fire trucks and drink water from a running outlet. Some of the more enterprising looters parked rented trucks on the side streets, engines running, and loaded up with couches, refrigerators, TV sets—the durable goods that will sell most easily on the black market. Periodically, when a rumor swept through the pack that the police were coming, the looters would break and run. But the police, outnumbered and fatigued, often did not try to chase them. When I left the area, it was burning, the flames taking what little the looters left behind.

Reporter Paul Witteman on July 13, 1977, describing the looting in Bushwick, Brooklyn, "Night of Terror," in Time, July 25, 1977, p. 17.

Streams of black water from broken fire hydrants swept the residue of the looting into the middle of the streets. Burned-out delivery trucks, spilling their seats onto the pavement, blocked doorways. Twisted steel grilles—some yanked from storefronts with trucks that were then filled with loot—lay across sidewalks. In the new Fedco supermarket, shelves gleamed bare and white, while several inches of mashed produce, packages of squashed hamburger, rivers of melted ice cream, and broken bottles covered the floors. The stench was overpowering. Up to 300 stores were cleaned out in the neighborhood, and the next morning sheets of plywood covered most of their smashed windows. Said Policeman John Fitzgerald: "There are only cops and crooks left here now."

Correspondent Mary Cronin, on July 14, 1977, describing the looting in the South Bronx, "Night of Terror," in Time, July 25, 1977, p. 17.

The shop owners don't live here, but the people who work for them do. They run these stores out, and they run out the few jobs in this neighborhood. The lights are gonna come back on, but what about the jobs?

An unidentified black man, on July 14, 1977, complaining about the looting in East Harlem, New York, "Night of Terror," in Time, July 25, 1977, p. 17.

If my mother gets sick in the night and needs her nitroglycerin, where am I gonna go? Maybe you don't care, but where am I supposed to buy my pills?

An unidentified man, on July 14, 1977, shouting at a gang of teenagers who looted a drugstore in East Harlem, New York, "Night of Terror," in Time, July 25, 1977, p 17.

It gets dark here every night. Every night stores get broke into, every night people get mugged, every night you scared on the street. But nobody pays no attention until a blackout comes.

A 14-year-old named Lorraine, on July 14, 1977, describing how she helped loot a drugstore in East Harlem, New York, "Night of Terror," in Time, July 25, 1977, p. 18.

It's really sort of beautiful. Everybody is out on the streets together. There's sort of a party atmosphere.

A young woman named Afreeka Omfree, on July 14, 1977, giving a more positive description of the night's events, "Night of Terror," in Time, July 25, 1977, p. 18.

By all accounts the looting broke out spontaneously and generally in all five boroughs between ten minutes and half an hour after the lights went out at about 9:35 P.M. At police headquarters in Manhattan, the first word that people were breaking into stores did not arrive until 10:00 P.M. But on Utica Avenue in Crown Heights, some reported that the lights had hardly dimmed before the looting began. Brother Ranuas, for instance, a community leader and the owner of Muslim Jewelry on Utica Avenue, said he arrived at his store at 9:45 P.M. to find his gates ripped off and looters pouring out of the door, carrying all his merchandise. In Bedford-Stuyvesant, the owner of Discount Liquors at Throop and Fulton Streets said the looting began five or ten minutes after the blackout. "It was almost like they came out of the air," he said. In the Bronx, police commanders and community people put the starting time at fifteen to twenty minutes after darkness descended; this was just time enough, said Captain Gallagher of the 44th Precinct, "for people to realize the lights weren't going to come back on."

In Bushwick, Aubrey Edmonds, a coordinator for the Bushwick Youth Services, said it was immediately after the blackout that crowds formed, waiting for the first spark. When the lights went out Edmonds was walking back from Broadway on Schaefer Street, and he noticed small knots of people gathering. "There were groups standing on the corners, mumbling and talking to themselves," Edmonds said. "They were trying to get up the energy to do something. They knew something had to be done that night; it was just a question of when someone was going to get it started." He thinks it was twenty minutes before someone got a car and drove through the iron gates of a sporting goods store on Broadway at Decatur Street. At that point a crowd swarmed in, assaulted the white owner and cleaned out the merchandise. Shortly thereafter, the store was set afire. . . .

Our evidence shows that through the night and into the morning, the looting drew in some proportion of people from all strata that live in poor communities. But judging from eyewitness reports and from analyses of data provided by the New York City Criminal Justice Agency and the New York City Police Department on those arrested, the make-up of the looters changed during the course of the blackout. While, obviously, no precise cut-off time can be established for a shift from one type of participant to another, the looting appeared to be divided into three stages that drew in three types of people.

From the time the lights went out until about 10:30 or 11:00 P.M., the looting was overwhelmingly performed by criminal types who opened the stores and swept in quickly to take away the most valuable merchandise. These looters were mainly men between the ages of twenty and thirty. In normal times they virtually command the streets and live by various sorts of dealing, theft and hustling. They need no blackout to engage in crime. . . . It is important to note that in this first stage there was virtually no law enforcement. Initiators of the looting, the street types, were in control of events, even to the extent . . . of keeping other potential looters out of stores until they had cleaned out the best merchandise for themselves.

In the Stage II period, the looters were joined by bands of youths, alienated adolescents who were looking for fun and excitement, but who also seized the opportunity to gain free material goods and money in the chaos they helped to create. . . .

The third stage, which generally began between 11:00 P.M. and midnight, and stretched into the next afternoon, involved the stable poor and working-class members of the community who were caught up by the near hysteria in the streets. Legal constraints against stealing had suddenly been lifted. Social pressure to "dip in" and take something was far greater than the normal pressure to abide by the law. The force loose in the street also drew in a second type of Stage III looter: the better off, employed, neighborhood resident who seemed to be motivated by abject greed. Unlike the Stage I looter, the Stage III person had little or no experience in crime, and was likely to have family and community ties. Stage III looters were encouraged by the early blackout situation,

during which they perceived no risk of arrest. Unfortunately for them, however, the Stage III looters appeared in large numbers at the same time the police were reaching sufficient strength to begin regaining control of the streets.

From a book published in 1979 by the Ford Foundation that analyzed the reasons for and the nature of the looting during the July 1977 power blackout in New York City, in Robert Curvin and Bruce Porter, Blackout Looting! *(1979), available online at http:// blackout.gmu.edu/archive/a_1977.html, downloaded August 27, 2004.*

The Bert Lance Affair

Q. Mr. President, Ernie Schultz, KTVY, Oklahoma City. Because Bert Lance was a personal friend, do you think the checks on his background before his appointment were as thorough as they should have been?

The President. Yes, they were. I have not read the complete FBI file on Bert Lance. But members of my staff have reviewed it in the last few weeks, and I can state to you categorically that the assessment from 85 to 100 different people who were interviewed privately by the FBI, including three representatives from the Department of Justice and three additional people from the Comptroller's Office, all gave Bert Lance an overwhelming endorsement as the future Director of the Office of Management and Budget.

Of course, there were some elements of Bert Lance's past that we didn't have to investigate because I've known Bert for many years. He has built up a reputation in Georgia that is superb as a businessman and as a governmental leader. I worked with him intimately for 4 years when he was the Director of our Transportation Department in Georgia and knew at firsthand his competence and his general attitude toward public service.

So, I don't think that there is any indication that a more thorough scrutiny of Bert Lance's past record or his reputation among those who knew him would have changed my opinion that he was well qualified to be the OMB Director.

Q. Mr. President, Bill Wippel, news director of KIRO News Radio, Seattle. Chris Clark, at WTVF in Nashville, kind of put a question that is the same as mine. You have set the moral standards for your administration. Even though Bert Lance may have done nothing illegal, does his ethical conduct measure up to the standards that you've set for your administration?

The President. Well, of course, there's no way for me to excuse my own or anyone else's overdrafts. This is something that was obviously a mistake. . . .

If I believed all of the charges or allegations against Bert Lance that I have read or heard through the news media. I would have discharged him immediately. Some of those allegations I know to be incorrect, and the ones that prove to be correct, of course, I'll have to make a judgment on them.

But I have no reason to feel that Bert Lance is dishonest or incompetent or that he has acted unethically. The propriety of Bert's loans, overdrafts, and so forth, obviously, will be assessed by me. And I think I can assess the entire series of charges made against Mr. Lance much more accurately and effectively at the conclusion of this week's [Senate] hearings. . . .

President Jimmy Carter's response to questions by reporters about the Bert Lance Affair, from a transcript of his September 15, 1977, press conference, in Public Papers of the Presidents of the United States: Jimmy Carter, June 25 to December 31, 1977 *(1978), p. 1,596.*

Bert Lance is my friend. I know him personally, as well as if he was my own brother. I know him without any doubt in my mind or heart to be a good and an honorable man. He was given, this past weekend, a chance to answer thousands of questions that have been raised about him, unproven allegations that have been raised against him, and he did it well. He told the truth. And I think he proved that our system of government works, because when he was given a chance to testify on his own behalf, he was able to clear his name.

My responsibility, along with Bert's, has been and is to make sure that the American people can have justified confidence in our own Government. And we also have an additional responsibility which is just as difficult, and that is to protect the reputation of decent men and women. Nothing that I have heard or read has shaken my belief in Bert's ability or his integrity. . . .

It was I who insisted that Bert agree to sell his substantial holdings in bank stock. Had he stayed there, in a selfish fashion, and enriched himself and his own family financially, I'm sure he would have been spared any allegations of impropriety. But he wanted to come to Washington and serve his Government because I asked him to, and he did.

I accept Bert's resignation with the greatest sense of regret and sorrow. He's a good man. . . . He's close to me

and always will be, and I think he's made the right decision, because it would be difficult for him to devote full time to his responsibilities in the future. And although I regret his resignation, I do accept it.

An excerpt from President Jimmy Carter's statement at his news conference of September 21, 1977, accepting the resignation of Bert Lance as head of the Office of Management and the Budget, in Public Papers of the Presidents of the United States: Jimmy Carter, June 25 to December 31, 1977 *(1978), pp. 1,636–1,637.*

The practices Lance is supposed to have followed cannot be considered normal or widespread. They just aren't tolerated in most banks.

Edward Smith, spokesman for the American Bankers Association, reacting in September 1977 to charges against Bert Lance, in Time, *September 19, 1977, available online at http://www.time.com/time/ archive/preview/0,10987,915466,00.html, downloaded June 30, 2005.*

The optimism we saw in December has faded and voters see the past, present, and future as quite similar. They are becoming resigned to the idea that problems like inflation, poverty, and war will ever be with us.

Pollster Pat Cadell commenting in September 1977 on the impact of the Bert Lance Affair and other of President Carter's problems, in Burton I. Kaufman, The Presidency of James Earl Carter, Jr. *(1993), p. 64.*

The basic American principle of justice and fair play has been pointedly ignored by certain members of this committee. The rights that I thought that I possessed have, one by one, gone down the drain.

Bert Lance, director of the Office of Management and the Budget, testifying before the Senate's Governmental Affairs Committee, on September 17, 1977, in Burton I. Kaufman, The Presidency of James Earl Carter, Jr. *(1993), p. 62.*

The Son of Sam

Q. What brought you there on that occasion?

A. I had to go and kill somebody—what can I tell you?

Q. Do you recall where you parked your car exactly on the block?

A. Up by a fire hydrant, midway between Cropsey and Shore Parkway.

Q. Did you realize you parked your car by a hydrant?

A. Yes. I saw the police give me a summons.

Q. How did you see that?

A. I was walking away. I saw a police car coming up Shore Parkway turn onto Bay 17th, going up that street. I had a feeling they would go by my car. . . . I saw the policeman give me a summons. Then they went slowly up the block near Cropsey Avenue, and pulled over again. I watched for about ten minutes. They got out of the car. I don't know what they were doing, but I went back to my car. There was a ticket on it. . . .

Q. Then what did you do, David?

A. I saw that couple, Stacy Moskowitz and her boyfriend. They were by the swings; they went back to their car. I don't know how much time elapsed, maybe ten minutes or so. I walked up to their car . . .

Q. Were there other cars parked, or did other cars come eventually?

A. Eventually.

Q. You say you saw this Stacy Moskowitz car and then you saw the one up in front of them?

A. No, the one up front was there before.

Q. Then Stacy Moskowitz came afterwards?

A. Yes.

Q. Did you see them get out of the car?

A. No, I was too far down in the park. I saw them walking. I saw a couple by the swings. I didn't know it was them. I saw them go back to the car.

Q. Then what did you do?

A. I just—I don't know. I waited for a time. I don't know how much time elapsed. I just went up to the car. I just walked up to it, pulled out the gun and put it— you know—I stood a couple of feet from the window.

Q. Were the windows open or closed?

A. Open, and I fired. . . .

Q. Then what did you do?

A. I turned around and I ran out of the park. . . .

Q. You say you ran through the park. You came out of the park eventually?

A. Yes.

Q. Did you go out an exit or hole in the fence?

A. There was a hole in the fence.

From the testimony provided by David Berkowitz (Son of Sam) on August 11, 1977, to Ronald Aiello, head of the Brooklyn District Attorney's homicide bureau, in which Berkowitz discussed his assault on Stacey Moskowitz and Robert Violante, in Maury Terry, The Ultimate Evil, The Truth about the Cult Murders: Son of Sam and Beyond *(1999), pp. 122–123.*

Women Take Back the Night and Hold a National Rights Conference

These are people who were taught to laugh at jokes about faggots and dykes, and they've come to understand that this vote is morally important enough to get over that.

Radical feminist and lesbian rights advocate Kate Millett commenting in November 1977 on the vote by delegates at the National Women's Conference to support lesbian civil rights, in the New York Times, *December 25, 1977, p. 177.*

Can I share something with you? When you were raped last night every other woman was raped with you.

Joseph Burch, a volunteer worker at the crisis center in Queens, New York, responding to a woman who was agonizing over having been raped, in the New York Times, *February 7, 1978, p. 25.*

So we've tried averting our eyes—but where to, these days? Billboards, marquees, and massage-parlor ads are omnipresent. In the act of buying a paper at my corner newsstand, I am surrounded with material contemptuous of my womanhood. My rhetoric may pronounce such material "sexist propaganda"; my nausea rises in simple humiliation. It hurts.

Robin Morgan writing in an essay about the dehumanizing of women through pornography, in the New York Times, *May 24, 1978, p. 27.*

The Clinch River Breeder Reactor

I cannot approve this legislation because:

- It mandates funding for the Clinch River Breeder Reactor Demonstration Plant, that will result in a large and unnecessarily expensive project which, when completed, would be technically obsolete and economically unsound. . . .

- It seriously inhibits the President from pursuing effectively an international policy to prevent the proliferation of nuclear weapons and nuclear explosive capability.

- It puts burdensome limitations on the President and the new Department of Energy in exercising necessary judgment to provide an effective energy research and development program.

- It puts unwise limitations on our ability to implement the new spent fuels policy which I recently announced, to aid our non-proliferation goals.
- It limits the constitutional authority of the President through three one-House veto provisions. One of these provisions could also limit the Administration's ability to recover a fair price for the uranium enrichment service provided by the Federal government.

An excerpt from President Jimmy Carter's message to the Senate on November 5, 1977, vetoing a Department of Energy authorization bill that would have provided funds for the Clinch River Breeder Reactor in Tennessee, in Public Papers of the Presidents of the United States: Jimmy Carter, June 25 to December 31, 1977 *(1978), p. 1972.*

Reggie Jackson

The difference with the Yankees is guys paid attention to what he said. At Oakland nobody listened to him. We just watched him hit. Reggie's really a good guy; down deep he is. I really like him. I always did. He'd give you the shirt off his back. Of course, he'd call a press conference to announce it.

Catfish Hunter, pitcher for the Oakland Athletics, in a comment, likely made in 1977, that reflects on Reggie Jackson, in Maury Allen, Mr. October *(1981), p. 179.*

You see this. This is the Dues Collector. This now helps the Yankees intimidate every other team in baseball. That's what I do just by walking into the clubhouse. Nobody will embarrass the Yankees in the World Series as long as I am carrying the Dues Collector.

Reggie Jackson referring to his black bat in comments to newspaper reporters in 1977, shortly after his trade from the Oakland Athletics to the New York Yankees, in Maury Allen, Mr. October *(1981), p. 181.*

I thought Jackson was dogging it. If I let Jackson get away with it, they all will. I'll lose my team.

New York Yankees manager Billy Martin in a meeting in 1977 with the team's owner, George Steinbrenner, at which Martin explained his dispute with Reggie Jackson, in Roger Kahn, October Men *(2003), p. 155.*

Walter Payton

He conditioned and trained exceptionally hard and well. But he understood that that's what you had to do, what he had to do. And it all shows up in the fourth quarter. Walter worked very hard with his weight training—especially his legs. He had great upper-body strength, but he focused on the legs and back for help. He wanted to do it in the fourth—"Give me the ball," he would say. And he'd wear the other team down. You know, it's hard for a layman, even myself, to stand there on the sideline and understand how he could dish out as much punishment as he took. And he'd wear you out. And then he had that fourth gear, and in the fourth quarter, he used it.

Chicago Bears trainer Fred Caito recalling Walter Payton's football greatness in an undated interview, in Mike Towle, I Remember Walter Payton *(2000), p. 148.*

Probably the best individual performance day I ever had was when I set the single-game rushing record against Minnesota. It was like being in the zone. You know, everybody always talked about how Michael Jordan used to get in a zone. Well, Michael was in the zone very time he got on the court. He was amazing. But for me there are times when you got out on the football field and you never tire. Every move you make is just like the last one, with the same speed, with the same enthusiasm. Every time the play is called, you know exactly what your are supposed to do and you do it. It just happens.

Walter Payton discussing around the year 2000 his record-setting rushing day against the Minnesota Vikings, in Walter Payton and Don Yaeger, Never Die Easy *(2000), p. 86.*

He was pound for pound, he was muscle everywhere. He took a lot of pounding, but he dished out a lot of pounding, just like Jim Brown used to do. He's a solid rock coming at you.

Former Chicago Bears quarterback Jim McMahon recalling around the year 2000 the football career of Walter Payton, in Walter Payton and Don Yaeger, Never Die Easy *(2000), p. 86.*

8

Escapist America
January 1978–December 1978

As Americans struggled with energy shortages and economic stringencies, they found in 1978 challenges in foreign affairs, constitutional issues, an environmental crisis, and a disaster in South America, each of which reflected the continuing impact of the 1960s.

In foreign affairs, President Jimmy Carter concluded negotiations begun with Panama 10 years earlier over the Panama Canal and brokered a peace agreement between Egypt and Israel, which he hoped would be a first step toward a general and long-lasting peace in the Middle East. The economic difficulties expressed themselves in a tax rebellion in California.

Constitutional issues dealt with free speech and affirmative action programs. The environmental crisis echoed warnings about chemicals—warnings that were found in Rachel Carson's book of the 1960s, *Silent Spring*—when residents of Love Canal in upstate New York discovered firsthand the impact of carelessly handled industrial waste. The attraction to alternative religions and churches raised the issue of the danger of cults and resulted in a stunning mass suicide at Jonestown in Guyana.

Taken together, the developments offered little in the way of optimism, little in the way of thinking that America had turned the corner to a better future. To some critics, the popularity of disco confirmed the country's slide into cultural and moral decadence. Others saw in disco not so much decadence as escapism (though these were often seen as intertwined). It was, they claimed, an attempt by the young, especially, to flee the problems that had changed the United States from being a land of opportunity to being a land of limitations.

THE DEATH OF HUBERT H. HUMPHREY

Just days before Christmas 1977, Senator Hubert H. Humphrey of Minnesota looked gaunt and feeble, his body wracked by radiation treatment that he had received for cancer. Speaking to reporters, he told them: "I'm not resigning from anything, I may even join something. The pay is good, the working conditions are good, and I have no intention of resigning. The only way that could happen is if I were totally incapacitated, and I'm a long way from that."[1] Less than a month later, he slipped into a coma, and on January 13, 1978, he died at his home in Waverly, Minnesota, his pelvis decimated by the inoperable cancer.

Humphrey first won election to the U.S. Senate as a Democrat in 1948; he won reelection in 1954 and again in 1960. During those years, he gained a reputation as one of the country's outstanding liberal crusaders. He supported tax benefits for low-income Americans, proposed the Peace Corps and Medicare, and took the lead in advocating civil rights legislation. In fact, he played a prominent role in winning Senate passage of the 1964 Civil Rights Act. His accomplishments caused President Lyndon Johnson to choose him as his running mate in 1964, and Humphrey was subsequently elected vice president.

When Johnson decided against seeking another term in 1968, Humphrey vied for the Democratic presidential nomination. He won it, but his support for the Vietnam War cost him the backing of many of his formerly loyal liberal supporters and earned him the enmity of many young radicals. Still, Humphrey nearly won the presidency, losing to Republican Richard Nixon by the narrowest of margins.

Humphrey returned to the Senate in 1970 and two years later again sought the Democratic presidential nomination. He lost that bid to South Dakota senator George McGovern.

When Humphrey died, the eulogies from both Democrats and Republicans nearly always referred to his concern for the country's disadvantaged:

> "For 30 years, his voice was heard from one end of this country to the other—most often in defense of the oppressed, the hungry, the victims of poverty and discrimination," said President Jimmy Carter.[2]
>
> "He gave unselfishly and unstintingly to all causes for the betterment of mankind, especially the poor, the disadvantaged, and the downtrodden," said former President Gerald Ford.[3]
>
> "He was continuously responsive to calls for help from the weak and defenseless," said New York City mayor Ed Koch.[4]

The senator's body lay in state in the rotunda of the Capitol in Washington, the first senator to be given the honor since Illinois Republican Everett M. Dirksen in 1969, and the first political leader since President Johnson, an architect of the Vietnam policy that had seriously damaged Humphrey's presidential bid, in 1973.

THE SENATE RATIFIES THE PANAMA CANAL TREATIES

When the Senate convened on April 18, 1978, for its roll-call vote on the main Panama Canal Treaty, the document wavered between victory and defeat. The debate over the treaty had been long and bitter, and it continued right up to the final minutes before the scheduled tally. As it turned out, the Senate ratified the agreement under which the United States would relinquish control of the Panama Canal to Panama, by a 68-32 margin, just one more than the required two-thirds majority.

Although negotiations between the United States and Panama over the 40-mile-long Panama Canal had begun long before Jimmy Carter (they had been going on for 13 years), Carter made the issue a test of his administration's ability to conduct foreign policy effectively. During his presidential campaign, he had actually opposed relinquishing control of the canal. But he changed his mind when he concluded that to hold onto the canal would damage the standing of the United States in Latin America and that, in any event, the Panamanians would resort to violence if necessary to end the American presence.

Negotiations with Panama resulted in two treaties, one to make the canal neutral, and another, the main treaty, to turn over operation of the canal to Panama. Many Americans wanted the United States to keep the canal. Since its opening in 1914, it had become an important sea route. With its series of locks, artificial lakes, and channels built among the Panamanian mountains by U.S. companies beginning in 1914, the completed canal enabled ships to travel between the Atlantic and the Pacific Oceans without having to sail around South America.

The United States had gained the land for the canal in the early 1900s, a result of gunboat diplomacy in which President Theodore Roosevelt conspired with Panamanian revolutionaries to wrest Panama from Colombia for the primary purpose, at least from his standpoint, of building a canal that was able to boost the U.S. economy and extend American power by making easier the movement of the country's merchant and naval ships. As the only half-in-jest comment went in the 1970s, the United States had stolen the land fair and square, and now it should keep it. But other Americans believed that the time had come to break away from colonialism and announce a more equitable relationship with Latin America.

In Panama, the canal had long symbolized imperialistic oppression, especially since the Panamanians received only a small percentage of the revenue that was generated by its use. Most galling was the contrast between the poverty in Panama City—the rubbish-strewn streets and ramshackle hovels—and the luxury in which the largely American residents of the Canal Zone—the Zonians—lived, with their comfortable homes surrounded by manicured lawns.

Conservatives in the U.S. Senate so strongly opposed the treaties that both documents at first appeared doomed. Lawmakers battered the White House with complaints about the negotiations as Republicans and Democrats alike vilified even the thought of lowering the American flag over the Canal Zone.

Two developments, however, worked against the treaty's opponents. First, Carter engaged in a masterful campaign to win support among senators and the public. One leading opinion survey found that 45 percent of Americans favored the treaties in the spring of 1978, while 42 percent opposed them, making it the first time supporters outpolled opponents.

Second, the treaty supporters, including Carter, agreed to a reservation pushed by Senator Dennis DeConcini (Dem., Ariz.) and attached to the first treaty, whereby the United States retained the right to intervene in Panama at any time to keep the canal open. The reservation caused several conservative senators to support the treaties, including DeConcini himself. On March 16, the Senate ratified this first treaty, making the Canal Zone neutral territory, by a 68-32 vote.

Knowing the crucial importance of the treaties to their country, Panamanians avidly followed the debates in the Senate. They seethed at the critics when they portrayed Panama as a tinhorn dictatorship and a small backwater, an insult made worse by the DeConcini reservation. They called the reservation a slap at Panamanian sovereignty and charged the United States with wanting to intervene in Panamanian affairs. Panamanian leader General Omar Torrijos said that his country would never approve the treaties without the reservation being removed or mitigated. One Panamanian lawyer called the reservation "unbelievable," and added: "This is worse than anything Teddy Roosevelt could have thought up."[5] In frustration, a Panamanian official said, "We've done all we can. Now it's up to the Senate to decide."[6]

With the protests from Panama growing louder, Carter acted to attach a reservation to the main treaty, while trying to avoid angering DeConcini and his supporters. Under its terms, the United States promised to refrain from interfering in Panama's internal affairs. Many Panamanians opposed Carter's reservation. They wanted nothing less than the DeConcini reservation removed. Lawyers, priests, exiled political leaders, and a former foreign minister called for Panama to reject the treaties and begin new negotiations. A political scientist who had once served on Panama's negotiating team said, "Whatever else is said, DeConcini is still on the books, and that's not acceptable."[7] Student protesters took to the streets and called the DeConcini reservation "the illegitimate child of a bastard treaty."[8]

But Carter's strategy worked. DeConcini accepted the new wording, saying that it "does not do violence" to his own reservation, and the Panamanian government indicated that it would accept the treaties and prevail over those in Panama who opposed them.[9] Panama's ambassador to the United States, Gabriel Lewis, called it "a dignified solution to a difficult problem."[10]

With the ratification on April 18, the United States agreed that Panama would assume full responsibility for the operation of the canal, effective at the end of 1999, and would assume jurisdiction over the Canal Zone. Until 1999, the canal would be operated by a United States agency that was governed by a board consisting of five Americans and four Panamanians. (The board began to operate in 1979 when the treaties started to go into effect.)

General Torrijos said that the treaties made him feel proud. He said that had the U.S. Senate failed to limit the DeConcini reservation, Panama would have rejected further negotiations and instead forcibly seized the canal. He added about the Senate debate: "Never in our republic's life had a Panamanian been

President Jimmy Carter and Panamanian leader General Omar Torrijos shake hands after signing the Panama Canal Treaty on September 7, 1977. *(Courtesy Jimmy Carter Library)*

more insulted than me, never has a country been subject to so much disrespect as Panama; no people has ever seen crude power so closely as we saw it through the conservatives who are a dishonor to a nation of such dignity as the United States."[11]

Historian Burton I. Kaufman has called the ratification of the Panama Canal treaties "a great triumph" for President Carter.[12] The victory reflected the president's intense involvement and the hard work of his secretaries of state and defense, along with Vice President Walter Mondale and the joint chiefs of staff, all of whom lobbied for the agreements. The *New York Times* called the victory "critical" for a president "who had repeatedly told wavering senators that his ability to conduct foreign affairs hung in the balance."[13] With the ratification, Carter said: "These treaties can mark the beginning of a new era in our relations not only with Panama but with all the rest of the world. They symbolize our determination to deal with the developing nations of the world, the small nations of the world, on the basis of mutual respect and partnership."[14]

A REVOLT AGAINST TAXES

By the early 1970s, anger began to build in several states and cities over high taxes. In 1978, the issue exploded in California when voters passed an initiative called Proposition 13 (the Jarvis-Gann Amendment), forcing the state to lower property taxes and limit future increases.

The history behind Proposition 13 went back several years. A law requiring property reevaluations had been raising taxes for businesses and residents. While the taxes increased, the city, county, and state coffers filled with money. These surpluses were spent (some wisely and some wastefully) rather than returned as rebates to the taxpayers. With the higher taxes and with inflation increasing property values—between 1975 and 1978, home values rose 3 percent per *month*—statewide property tax collections jumped from $6.6 billion in 1973 to $12 billion in 1978.

At the same time, Californians paid more in personal and corporate state income taxes and more in federal income taxes and social security. As complaints about the tax burden intensified, the state legislature refused to pass measures aimed at capping property tax increases or more effectively controlling government spending.

Then Democratic governor Edmund G. Brown, Jr., and Democratic legislators angered middle- and upper-income Californians when they proposed that surpluses be returned to taxpayers based on family income. Families with annual incomes below $15,000 would receive most of the money; those making more than $40,000 would receive nothing. Letters of protest over the proposal flooded the capital in Sacramento. Needless to say, the measure never passed the legislature.

Spurred on by the inaction over property taxes, Howard Jarvis and Paul Gann led a campaign to place Proposition 13 on the June 1978 ballot. To do so, they needed to collect about 500,000 signatures. They wound up collecting 1.2 million. Proposition 13 competed with Proposition 8, placed on the ballot by the legislature. Proposition 8 would have allowed the legislature to lower the residential property tax rate, which, in turn, would have reduced homeowners' property taxes by about 30 percent, while also providing some relief for renters.

Proposition 13 provided for an average reduction of 57 percent in both residential and commercial property taxes, and it limited future property tax increases to no more than 2 percent. Additionally, it mandated a two-thirds vote in the legislature before any new taxes could be enacted. The voters defeated Proposition 8 and approved Proposition 13 by a 65 percent–35 percent margin.

Local governments took a big hit when Proposition 13 passed. As they faced a loss of about $7 billion, the legislature stepped in to help by allocating $2.2 billion of the state surplus to school districts, $1.48 billion to county governments, $250 million to city governments, and $125 million to special districts; by creating a $900 million emergency loan fund; and by having the state assume local welfare costs for one year. Despite this assistance, many school districts canceled summer programs, and government agencies laid off about 10,000 workers. Moreover, to receive the moneys, the legislature required local governments to forego any increases in employee salaries.

Governor Brown responded to Proposition 13 by getting the legislature to reduce the state budget for 1978–79, and he interpreted the vote for the proposition as a sign that other taxes should be reduced. Consequently, he supported a one time cut in state income taxes, along with other tax breaks, costing about $1 billion.

If Brown saw his support for lower taxes as necessary for political survival and as accurately reflecting a strong antitax pulse among the voters, he was right. From California to the East Coast, the antitax movement gained momentum. The *New York Times* called it part of a "cantankerous factor," extending beyond a drive for lower taxes to include an effort to kick political incumbents out of office as an expression of frustration with government in general.

Anthony Logalbo, director of the League of Cities and Towns in Massachusetts, said, "For the first time there's a feeling that taxpayers can do something."[15] Campaigns to reduce or limit taxes were underway in Michigan, Nebraska, Texas, Massachusetts, Maryland, Pennsylvania, Colorado, and Wyoming. Tennessee placed a cap on state spending, and although the antitax movement was often portrayed as conservative, it attracted liberals too. *Time* magazine reported:

> Spontaneous taxpayer crusades are popping up from Oregon to Connecticut. In Idaho and Arizona, homeowners are pushing petitions to limit property taxes. In Florida, a proposed state constitutional amendment would force a 29% rollback in local property taxes and require a two-thirds vote of the legislature to increase taxes in the future. Legislatures in at least ten other states are considering property relief of one form or another.[16]

The national implications for what had happened in California appeared evident when Ronald Reagan, the state's former governor, used the vote on Proposition 13 as ammunition for his presidential bid and as support for his platform of lower taxes and smaller government. In Philadelphia, he talked about a "prairie fire" sweeping the country to eliminate "costly, overpowering government."[17] He insisted: "I hope every [Republican] candidate ... will point out the simple truth that tax reduction can actually end recession and create prosperity by broadening the base of the economy."[18] Standing next to Reagan, Republican senator Richard S. Schweiker of Pennsylvania said presciently, "I believe that

Proposition 13 is that cause that will propel Governor Ronald Reagan all the way to the White House in 1980."[19]

NEO-NAZIS IN SKOKIE

As embodied in the First Amendment, freedom of speech has been one of the pedestals on which American liberty has rested, protected even to the point of the Supreme Court ruling it permissible to advocate violence. In the case of *Brandenburg v. Ohio* in 1969, the court overturned the conviction of Clarence Brandenburg, who had been found guilty of violating an Ohio law by advocating violent attacks against blacks and Jews. The court said that the state could only punish speech that created a "tendency toward imminent lawless action."

In 1978, freedom of speech faced another test when members of the National Socialist Party of America, or Nazis or neo-Nazis (as opposed to the Nazis in Germany at about the time of World War II), sought permission to march through the streets of Skokie, Illinois, while wearing their military-style uniforms, passing out anti-Semitic pamphlets, and displaying the swastika. Located north of Chicago, Skokie was a tree-lined community of neat residences and verdant parks, with three high schools that were known for their college-scholarship winners and for a mix of large businesses, corporate headquarters, and small shops. Moreover, the town comprised a large Jewish population, many of whom were survivors of the Holocaust. The Nazis knew this; they wanted to antagonize the Jews, and Skokie's Jews reacted by planning to keep the Nazis out.

Soon after the Nazis announced their plans in 1977, Skokie passed a law banning the display of hate-inspiring symbols, such as swastikas. The Nazis sued, and in their court battle, they gained the support of the American Civil Liberties Union (ACLU). Skokie won a partial victory when an Illinois appellate court ruled that the Nazis could stage their march but must abide by town law and keep the swastika hidden. In January 1978, however, the Illinois Supreme Court decided against Skokie. The Nazis could march and display the swastika, the court said, for the town law infringed on the first amendment.

From there, the controversy went to the federal courts, and Skokie became a national issue, exciting passions among defenders of the First Amendment and haters of the Nazis. The debate split the ACLU, which had a significant Jewish membership. Several thousand members, in fact, quit the organization. The legal director of the ACLU, Bruce Ennis, admitted that a Nazi march in Skokie would cause psychological harm to the townspeople, but, he said, "We cannot establish in this country a new doctrine to prohibit free speech whenever it causes an emotional reaction from an audience."[20]

People talked of bloodshed erupting in peaceful Skokie should the Nazis appear. The radical Jewish Defense League (JDL) threatened to physically attack the Nazis. A spokesperson for the JDL promised to recruit a crowd of thousands and criticized a planned peaceful anti-Nazi demonstration as indicative of those Jews who "sat by in silence" while thousands were sent to Hitler's gas chambers.[21]

In April, a U.S. court of appeals lifted a 45-day injunction previously placed on the Nazi march. Nazi leader Frank Collin said that the march would occur on April 20, a date chosen to coincide with Hitler's birthday. The JDL claimed that it was chosen to coincide with the beginning of Passover.

The continuing court battle, however, postponed the march again. Then in May, the U.S. court of appeals upheld the ruling by the Illinois Supreme Court: The Nazis had the right to march and display their symbols. The following month, the court responded to a petition from Skokie's lawyers by denying their request for a stay against the march. The action left standing the appeals court ruling and cleared the way for the Nazis to demonstrate.

The Nazis, however, decided to cancel their march. Collin had earlier said that he would if his group won in court. On June 22, he said the plan to march had been "pure agitation on our part to restore our free speech," and his group had made its point. He warned: "The minute I suspect that our free speech is being blocked again, I will reschedule the Skokie demonstration."[22] The mayor of Skokie, Albert J. Smith, expressed a different view when he called the Nazi cancellation "a victory for the American way of life" and added, "We look forward to a return to peace and tranquility."[23]

Collin later held two rallies, one at the federal building in Chicago's Loop, which attracted 28 Nazis and about 3,000 counterdemonstrators, and another at Marquette Park, which attracted 22 Nazis and, again, about 3,000 counter-demonstrators. Scuffles between Collin's Nazis and a small group of anti-Nazis led to the arrests of about 21 people. Collin delivered a "white power" speech, and in the charged atmosphere, several whites beat a black man, and others yelled at a group of Jews: "Gas them! Gas them!"[24] The U.S. court of appeals had said in its Skokie ruling: "If . . . civil rights of freedom of speech, expression and assembly are to remain vital for all, they must protect not only those society deems acceptable but also those whose ideas it quite justifiably rejects and despises."[25]

AFFIRMATIVE ACTION AND THE BAKKE CASE

President John Kennedy began to use affirmative action in 1961 when he set policies to increase the number of African Americans working for government contractors. Affirmative action had as its goal integrating the workforce by favoring minorities in employment, hiring and promotion, college admissions, and government contracts. But it was, from the start, a controversial program: Supporters said that it corrected years of discrimination against blacks, women, and others; opponents said that it discriminated against whites, in general, and white men, in particular.

Thus, the case of Alan Bakke received considerable attention and produced a Supreme Court decision that some observers called the most important since *Brown v. Board of Education* in 1954. The case began when, in 1973 and 1974, the University of California at Davis denied Bakke entry into its medical school. The school used a quota system to reserve 16 of its 100 openings for blacks, Hispanics, and Asians and consequently admitted several minority members even though their test scores were lower than Bakke's.

Bakke then sued in the state courts, claiming that his civil rights had been violated by the college's discriminatory program. He won his case in the California Supreme Court, but the university appealed to the U.S. Supreme Court, and in June, the justices issued their opinion, the first ever to deal with the charge of "reverse discrimination." The ruling showed a deeply divided court and offered a triumph for everyone involved. The justices upheld affirmative action and, with it, rejected the argument that educational institutions had to be completely "color blind," but they struck down the Davis quota system as too rigidly discriminatory and ordered Bakke to be admitted.

Four justices—William J. Brennan, Jr., Byron White, Thurgood Marshall, and Harry Blackmun—sided with California. They saw nothing wrong with the Davis quota system. They said that it was necessary to correct past discrimination in the state's schools, and they declared their support for affirmative action in general.

Four other justices—Chief Justice Warren Burger, Potter Stewart, William Rehnquist, and John Paul Stevens—ruled against California. They said that the Davis quota system amounted to racial discrimination.

With the vote tied at 4-4, the final outcome depended on Justice Lewis Powell, and he split his decision, producing the mixed result. Powell sided with the second group when he called the Davis quota system wrong and thus opened the way to Bakke's admission. But he sided with the first group when he declared affirmative action constitutional. In doing so, he validated the cure for past discrimination—namely affirmative action—while rejecting the specific medicine—in this case, a strict quota system.

The case had generated a record 60 briefs, stimulated sharp debates among politicians, and generated hundreds of newspaper editorials. With the decision, each side expressed some relief. Affirmative action, though, remained controversial, and its status had yet to be fully resolved, both in education, to which the ruling directly applied, and in other government programs (along with the private sector).

Several political and social leaders reacted to the court's ruling:

"This is what we thought the law was," said Attorney General Griffin Bell.[26]

"[We are] comforted that, once and for all, the United States Supreme Court has held that racial quotas are flatly illegal," said Arnold Foster, general counsel of the Anti-Defamation League of B'nai B'rith.[27]

"The important thing about the decision is not that Allan Bakke can go to medical school, but that the racists who wanted to run back the clock on minority progress have received a stunning blow," said Joseph Rauh, vice-president of Americans for Democratic Action.[28]

"A bureaucracy that says, 'White teachers get in this line and blacks in this line,' threatened to break up the coalition that worked for affirmative action in the first place. Maybe now we can put the coalition back together," said Senator Daniel Patrick Moynihan (Dem., N.Y.).[29]

Jack Greenberg, director of the NAACP Legal Defense and Education Fund, predicted that the narrowness of the court decision coupled with its confusing content would result in future litigation. He was right. In several cases in the late 1970s and the 1980s, the Supreme Court upheld affirmative action both in and outside of education, such as in *Fullilove v. Klutznick* (1980) when it declared constitutional a plan that set aside for minorities 10 percent of the contracts in federally funded public works projects. In other cases, the court struck down affirmative action programs, such as in *Wygant v. Jackson Board of Education* (1986) when the justices ruled unconstitutional a layoff plan that favored minority teachers over white teachers.

In 2000, the justices, acting in the case of *Johnson v. Georgia,* invalidated an admissions ranking system at the University of Georgia whereby a fixed numerical bonus was applied to minority applicants. In 2003, in the case of *Grutter v. Bollinger,* the justices upheld an affirmative-action program for law school admissions at the University of Michigan, but they struck down such a program for the school's undergraduate admissions because it used point rankings that it said amounted to a quota system. The decision drew heavily on the legacy of the 1978 Bakke case.

A CHEMICAL DISASTER AT LOVE CANAL

The Love Canal neighborhood in Niagara Falls, New York, underwent a drastic change during fall 1978. The once-peaceful residential streets gave way to bulldozers and workers wearing protective suits. They boarded up the emptied lower-middle-class houses and surrounded the 15-acre area with a half-mile-long chain-link fence. That previous August, Love Canal became synonymous with hazardous waste, a tragic example of the tremendous damage done to the environment by industrialization. Eighty-two different chemicals were leaking into basements and contaminating the air in some 200 homes around a landfill (what had been a canal in the 19th century) where, in the late 1940s and 1950s, the Hooker Chemicals and Plastics Corporation had dumped its waste. Now, 30 years later, the price was being paid in misery for the Love Canal residents: The chemicals caused high birth defects and miscarriages and unusually high rates of liver cancer and nervous diseases.

Chemicals began to leak at the Love Canal site in about 1971, unleashing dangerous pesticides that had been buried in 55-gallon metal drums. As the extent of the contamination became known, the New York state government began to buy the houses immediately fronting the canal at a total cost of $10 million and relocating the residents. "It was very hard to leave my home," said Bonnie Snyder. "A lot of firsts happened there. My doctor said it was like I was mourning for my house. When I got the last furniture out, I felt like I'd buried someone."[30]

Officials rejected any attempt to clear the landfill—digging up the drums was considered much too dangerous—so they began an alternative project to contain the leaks. At a cost of about another $10 million (40 percent of which was to be paid for by the federal government), workers built trenches around the landfill, along with drainage pipes to carry polluted water runoff into basins. From there, the water was pumped through special filters, cleansed, and fed into storm sewers.

The size of the Love Canal disaster was enormous. The 82 chemicals weighed 21,800 tons. The list of pollutants included 2,4,5 trichlorphenol that produced dioxin, a poisonous substance, as a by-product.

As it turned out, Love Canal was only one small part of the chemical pollution that faced Niagara Falls. Three other Hooker company dumps contained dangerous contaminants threatening the environment. Two of them were located near the city's drinking-water supply. The 16-acre Hyde Park landfill contained 80,000 tons of hazardous wastes, some of which were polluting a stream, ironically named the Bloody Run. "We've lost six or seven cats," said a resident. "They get down by the stream, and it starts like eating the skin and the fur off their feet. Then they die a few days later."[31] The stream contained dioxin levels of 7.5 parts per billion—thought by some experts to be dangerous enough to threaten human life.

As the cleanup of the Love Canal site continued, nearby residents protested. They complained that their houses had also been contaminated, but government officials had refused to buy their property. The impact of Love Canal spread to other states, as was evident when residents of Borden Township in New Jersey complained about a plan by the state government to locate a hazardous waste dump near a school. One person at a public hearing for the project said, "Nobody learned nothing from Love Canal."[32]

Concerns about hazardous wastes reached across the country and caused Congress, in 1980, to pass the Comprehensive Environmental Response, Compensation, and Liability Act that created the Superfund to clean up contaminated sites. Congress provided $15 billion for the Superfund and stipulated that taxes paid by polluting industries also be put into the project. Yet, the money proved inadequate to the task, and by the early 2000s, many sites remained polluted; moreover, under President George W. Bush, the flow of industry tax dollars ended.

The government used Superfund money to continue the cleanup of Love Canal. In fact, it was the first polluted site listed on the Superfund list. Finally, in March 2004, enough cleanup had been completed for the Environmental Protection Agency to remove Love Canal from the Superfund toxic site category. About 260 homes north of the canal had been renovated, and 150 acres east of the canal had been improved to ready them for light industry.

Nevertheless, hazardous waste remained buried underneath 70 acres in the neighborhood, and critics called the "delisting" of Love Canal as a toxic site premature. Whatever the polluted site's future status, the legacy of Love Canal promised to remain alive for years to come, a legacy expressed poignantly in 1978 by Niagara Falls resident Debra Cerillo: "I have had two miscarriages. My son was diagnosed as hyperactive. I suffer from hypertension. We are typical of the families around Love Canal."[33]

THE CAMP DAVID SUMMIT

When President Jimmy Carter invited Egyptian president Anwar Sadat and Israeli prime minister Menachem Begin to Camp David, Maryland, he hoped to make progress toward a Middle East peace agreement. He did so, but the planned three-day meeting turned into 13 grueling days of shouts, personal attacks, and nerve-wracking arguments.

Carter entered the White House in early 1977 wanting to end the violence between Arabs and Israelis in the Middle East and, at first, events seemed to be working in his favor. Sadat indicated that he was anxious to negotiate a peace agreement, and Yitzhak Rabin, then the prime minister of Israel, signaled his willingness to compromise on Israel's borders, although he rejected a full retreat from the lands that his country conquered in 1967. Even Hafaz-al-Assad, the Syrian president known as most resistant to any agreements with Israel, said he would consider a pact in which the Palestinians received less than full autonomy.

The favorable conditions for peace, however, quickly deteriorated. The Israelis reacted with anger toward statements that were made by Carter about Palestinians needing to have a homeland. Then, in May, Rabin was unseated by Menachem Begin, the leader of the Likud Party, which advocated no compromise with

Arabs. Begin did express his willingness to discuss peace at a meeting in Geneva and said that he would be willing to withdraw troops from occupied lands in exchange for Arab nations' recognizing Israel's right to exist. Yet, at the same time, he announced plans to build new settlements on the West Bank.

The possibility of holding talks in Geneva became more remote when, in October 1977, Carter issued a join communiqué with the Soviet Union calling for such a meeting. The Israelis reacted by accusing Carter of opening the door to increasing the Soviet influence in the Middle East, and they criticized how, in his announcement, he had expressed sympathy with the Palestinians.

Chances for peace appeared to receive a boost in November when Sadat made an unexpected and unprecedented trip to Israel, where he met with Begin. Yet the journey earned Sadat the opprobrium of most Arabs and isolated Egypt from other Arab nations.

In March 1978, Carter met with Begin in Washington. On the calendar, winter was ending, but in the White House, a searing frost could be felt between the two men. Carter condemned Israel's recent invasion of Lebanon. The assault, which was launched by the Israelis in retaliation for an attack by the Palestine Liberation Organization that had killed 35 people, left 1,000 people dead. Carter added further to the chill when he told Begin that Israel should remove all of its troops from the occupied lands, including the West Bank.

Carter's deteriorating relationship with Begin engendered an equally deteriorating relationship with American Jews. Many of them disagreed with Begin's hardliner policies, but they disagreed even more with Carter's blunt criticisms and opposed the president's decision to sell 60 long-range bombers to Saudi Arabia. (Congress approved the sale only after Carter agreed to also sell 20 of the bombers to Israel.)

In early summer, Carter sent Vice President Walter Mondale to meet with Sadat in Egypt and with Begin in Israel. From those talks came an agreement to send representatives to London, but the meeting produced no substantive results.

To Carter, the opening for improved relations between Egypt and Israel that was made possible by Sadat's visit to Jerusalem was about to be squandered. He foresaw the possibility of another war in the Middle East, one perhaps ignited by the current Egyptian military buildup and by continued fighting in Lebanon that threatened to ignite a direct conflict between Israeli and Syrian troops.

The president decided to take a gamble. He would invite Sadat and Begin to meet with him for peace talks. Carter decided to proceed with his plan even though there existed little chance that an agreement could be reached and even though he realized that failure would greatly damage his influence in foreign affairs. Moreover, no preliminary agreement had been arranged, a clear, and some would say foolish, violation of the rule that said lower-level diplomats should make progress on issues before heads of state meet.

In August, Carter sent Sadat a handwritten letter clearly intended to take advantage of the Egyptian leader's trip to Israel and his self-appointed role as leader of the Arab world. He said:

> Because of your dramatic and courageous visit to Jerusalem and its accompanying actions and statements, remarkable progress has been made toward peace in the Middle East. . . . You have . . . the well-deserved confidence of the people of your country and the admiration of the world. . . .

During recent weeks little progress [toward peace] had been made and the relationships [between Egypt and Israel] have deteriorated. A total stalemate is in prospect. Unless we act boldly and constructively now, those of us who now serve as leaders may not again have such a chance to bring peace to the people of your region.

After long discussions with both you and Prime Minister Begin, there is no doubt in my mind that both of you genuinely want peace and have the courage to reach agreement. It is time, therefore, for us to make a renewed effort at the highest level and with the greatest determination.[34]

He sent a similarly worded letter to Begin. Both letters suggested that Camp David be used for the meeting at a time to be determined.

Carter, Sadat, and Begin gathered at Camp David on September 5. With their discussions closed to the press (Carter wanted Sadat and Begin to address each other rather than the media), they began to negotiate the next day. First Lady Rosalynn Carter later described an awkward start to the summit: "Jimmy and I went into our cabin and then an interesting moment—Begin and Sadat both hesitating over who should enter first. Then they both laughed and Begin insisted Sadat enter first. We had watched, as had a handful of people outside, and Jimmy said to me that Begin would never go ahead of Sadat, being perfectly proper according to protocol—President above Prime Minister."[35]

If Carter were looking for frankness, he got more than he could handle. As Sadat and Begin discussed three issues, the Sinai Peninsula, sovereignty in the West Bank and Gaza, and self-government for Palestinians, they engaged in heated exchanges. Sadat forcefully called for Israeli troops to leave the Sinai, and within no time, he and Begin were exchanging personal insults. President Carter wrote in his notes:

First lady Rosalynn Carter poses for her official photograph. *(Courtesy Jimmy Carter Library)*

Sadat announced angrily that a stalemate had been reached. He saw no reason for the discussions to continue. [Begin and Sadat] were moving toward the door, but I got in front of them to partially block the way. I urged them not to break off their talks. . . . Begin agreed . . . Sadat nodded his head. They left without speaking to each other.[36]

Witnessing the animosity between Sadat and Begin, Carter changed the format of the meeting. Rather than have the two men talk face-to-face, Carter began to shuttle between them, exchanging ideas, and prodding them to move forward. Still, the negotiations stalled, and once again, they neared collapse. On September 15, Sadat, frustrated with the lack of progress and angered by an acrimonious meeting with an Israeli official, told Carter that he was leaving. He ordered a helicopter to prepare to take off, and the Egyptian delegation began to pack its bags. But Carter pleaded with Sadat to stay; he told Sadat that if he left, he would be blamed for the failure of Camp David and that his own credibility would be greatly damaged. Convinced by the president's argument, Sadat agreed to stay. Carter later recalled: "I explained to [Sadat] the extremely serious consequences . . . that his action would harm the relationship between Egypt and the United States, he would be violating his promise to me . . . [and] damage one of my most precious possessions—his friendship and our mutual trust."[37]

The departure averted, Begin began to show some willingness to compromise. He agreed to submit to the Israeli Knesset the issue of whether to remove Israeli settlements from the Sinai in exchange for the United States building new airfields in the Negev Desert. Sadat agreed with this arrangement. Begin still refused any specific grant of autonomy to Palestinians living in the West Bank and Gaza Strip, but he and Sadat agreed to a vaguely worded statement providing for Egypt, Israel, and Jordan to negotiate the issue further and to develop some form of self-government for the two regions.

On September 17, Sadat and Begin signed two documents, "A Framework for Peace in the Middle East" and "A Framework for the Conclusion of a Peace Treaty Between Egypt and Israel," together known as the Camp David accords. (Carter signed these documents as a witness.) In effect, the documents established a foundation for future negotiations. The Framework for Peace in the Middle East provided for an end to Israel's military government in the West Bank and Sinai (although Israel could retain forces in some areas to ensure its security) and provided for the residents there to establish self-government within a five-year period. Moreover, it provided for Israel and Egypt, along with Jordanian and Palestinian representatives, to participate in negotiations to resolve the final status of the West Bank and the Gaza Strip, Israel's relations with Jordan, and Israel's right to exist within secure and recognized borders. The Framework for the Conclusion of a Peace Treaty called for Israel's withdrawal from the Sinai Peninsula and the establishment of normal diplomatic relations between Israel and Egypt once the two countries signed a permanent peace treaty later in the year.

Clearly, the accords were limited: They said nothing about Israel building new settlements in the West Bank or Gaza, and there was no guarantee that the Jordanians or the Palestinians would engage in future talks; in fact, the Jordanian government made clear its refusal to discuss anything with Israel until the Israelis returned East Jerusalem to Jordan. Critics derided Carter's failure to obtain a more encompassing peace agreement. The president, however, had accomplished his primary objective: to get the two sides engaged in constructive discussions and to point them in the direction of finalizing and signing a peace agreement.

At the conclusion of the Camp David summit, Carter alluded to the problems encountered and portrayed the negotiations as successful:

> During the last two weeks, the members of all three delegations have spent endless hours, day and night, talking, negotiating, grappling with problems that have divided their people for 30 years. Whenever there was a danger that human energy would fail, or patience would be exhausted or good will would run out—and there were many such moments—these two leaders and the able advisers in all delegations found the resources within them to keep the chances for peace alive. . . .

Anwar Sadat and Menachem Begin greet each other at the beginning of the Camp David Summit. *(Courtesy Jimmy Carter Library)*

I hope that the foresight and the wisdom that have made this session a success will guide these leaders and the leaders of all nations as they continue the progress toward peace.[38]

The president received widespread praise for Camp David. The praise seemed well earned when, in late September, the Knesset agreed to dismantle Israel's settlements in the Sinai.

Another roadblock appeared, however, when Egypt and Israel failed to meet a December deadline for signing their peace agreement. With no progress being made, President Carter decided once again to intervene directly and so traveled to Egypt and Israel to meet with Sadat and Begin. Finally, he secured an agreement by which Israel would follow a schedule for withdrawing its troops from the Sinai and be allowed access to oil from the Sinai oilfields, and Egypt and Israel would exchange ambassadors. The much-delayed and much-heralded Egyptian-Israeli Peace Treaty was signed on the South Lawn of the White House on March 26, 1979.

A Mass Suicide at Jonestown

On November 20, 1978, Guyanese troops arrived at Jonestown, a remote commune 40 miles from the Caribbean Sea and 130 miles from their country's main city of Georgetown; they found, sprawled out on the dirt and along wooden walkways, hundreds of dead bodies—men, women, and children who looked liked they might have fallen asleep but whose remains were rotting in the jungle heat. The dead had come from the United States as followers of Reverend Jim Jones and his People's Temple. At his request, they committed mass suicide by drinking Kool-Aid laced with cyanide. More than 900 died, and Americans searched for answers about cults and what the tragedy said about American society.

The bizarre story had first gained national attention on November 18, when the media reported that Congressman Leo J. Ryan (Dem., Calif.) and several others in his entourage had been shot and killed at a remote airstrip in Fort Kaituma, Guyana, near Jonestown. As the group was preparing to leave the settlement's dirt runway aboard two small planes, a man approached with a gun and began to shoot. Then a tractor suddenly appeared, pulling a trailer. Those aboard the trailer began to fire at the planes. With one plane disabled, four crew members and a passenger boarded the second plane and although it, too, was hit by gunfire, they were able to take off. Others in the Ryan party fled into the surrounding jungle.

In addition to Ryan, the dead included two crew members for NBC News, a photographer for the *San Francisco Examiner,* and a member of the Jonestown commune. Nine cultists had joined Ryan to leave the commune and return to the United States.

Ryan had a reputation as a liberal activist. He had recently protested the hunting of baby seals in Canada and had no compunction about traveling overseas to draw attention to international issues. He flew to Guyana in response to concerns by his constituents in San Francisco about events at Jonestown. They complained about Jim Jones preventing their relatives from leaving the commune and using forced labor there. Ryan decided to check out the stories.

At Jonestown, he spoke with Reverend Jones and briefly addressed a gathering of the cultists. He said:

> I think that all of you know that I'm here to find out more about questions that have been raised about your operation here, but I can tell you right now that, from the few conversations I've had with some of the folks here already this evening, that whatever the comments are, there are some people ... [here who believe this is the best thing] that ever happened to them in their whole life.[39]

Apparently Jones and other leaders of the People's Temple thought Ryan posed a threat to the survival of their commune. By this time, Jones had become increasingly paranoid. He had chosen the site in Guyana, which he named Jonestown, because of its remote location and its distance from his enemies. Jonestown was a difficult place to reach by air or by motor vehicle; it was also a difficult place to escape from, surrounded as it was by a jungle infested with poisonous snakes, piranha, and jaguars. The cultists at Jonestown had become imprisoned by the environment and by Jones's mind. They endured heat, rain, and long, nearly endless hours of the reverend's rambling sermons that often turned into rants against the outside world.

Jones joined the People's Temple, a branch of the Disciples of Christ, in Indianapolis more than 15 years earlier. He was ordained in the church in 1964 and then became a pastor. He soon began to claim that he could perform miracles. He faked "healings" by arranging for members of the congregation to come forward and attest to how they had been supposedly cured by him. Jones required his followers to call him Father, and he convinced them to sign over their real-estate holdings to a group he headed. Yet, he helped the poor by establishing soup kitchens and senior centers.

In 1965, Jones moved the People's Temple to Ukiah, California, in the Redwood Valley, taking about 70 families with him from Indiana. Five years later, he expanded the People's Temple into San Francisco, where he appealed strongly to poor blacks. In a short time, the temple's membership increased to 20,000.

Jones fought for civil rights and social reform. Although most of the People's Temple membership was black, he developed it as an integrated church and spoke out strongly against racism. Attracted to Marxism, he wanted the People's Temple to promote a cooperative ethic as opposed to competitive capitalism, and his preaching often combined this message with an emotional, born-again Christianity.

Although many of Jones's followers came from among the destitute, others came from the middle class, and they included many elderly members. For some, Jones offered redemption from lives of crime and drugs. For the elderly, he provided a sense of place and of value—a feeling that they could still do something with their lives, that they counted. Handsome and personable, Jones was known for his ability to persuade. A colleague of his in Ukiah said about him: "He was an extremely persuasive man who had a different faith and a different message for everyone he dealt with. He was able to hook in with each one in an individual way."[40]

As he "hooked in," he decreed that members of the temple tithe 10 percent of their income and assets. Later, he increased the amount. He acquired more and more money from his members—many of the elderly signed over their social security checks to him—and acquired yet more real estate. One woman gave Jones eight acres of land, her three-bedroom house, and a new pickup truck. A former technician for Standard Oil gave him real property worth $50,000, an automobile, and thousands of dollars in cash.

As Jones promoted civil rights in San Francisco, reached out to help senior citizens, and founded a school for retarded children, his political influence increased. He became a person to whom politicians turned for support in the black community.

Yet, he became increasingly paranoid. He did have enemies, such as racists who vandalized the Ukiah temple and likely set fire to the San Francisco temple. Several defectors began to reveal abuses in the temple and contributed evidence to a magazine article that revealed Jones's fakeries.

But to Jones these people represented only part of a greater menace closing in on him and his mission. He claimed that the U.S. government was out to kill blacks. He claimed that enemies were all around him. To enforce discipline, he ridiculed dissidents at special "confessional" sessions and even beat them with paddles. At the same time, he went into strange revelations about his sexual exploits.

Some say an addiction to prescription drugs fed his delusions and erratic behavior; certainly by the time of his death there was considerable evidence to show his attachment to Valium and other pills.

To escape his enemies, Jones decided to establish a socialist commune in Guyana. About 900 followers settled at Jonestown. When relatives of the cultists accused Jones of violating human rights, he replied with ominous words in a letter:

> Dr. Martin Luther King reaffirmed the validity of ultimate commitment when he told his Freedom Riders: "We must develop the courage of dying for a cause." We likewise affirm that before we will submit quietly to the interminable plotting and persecution of this politically motivated conspiracy, we will resist actively, putting our lives on the line if it comes to that....[41]

When the cultists shot at Ryan and his party at the airport (whether they did so in response to orders by Jones is unclear), they intended to kill them all and thereby kill the latest threat to their settlement. When word reached Jones about the failed attempt, he ordered the mass suicide. He gathered his followers in the pavilion, stood beneath its corrugated metal roof, and told them Guyanese soldiers would soon arrive, destroy all that Jonestown stood for, and kill all the children. He said nothing could save them now.

As he spoke, the Kool-Aid was distributed and given to the children first. Their cries filled the air. He implored:

> Don't be afraid to die. You'll see, there'll be a few people land out here. They'll torture some of our children here. They'll torture our people. They'll torture our seniors. We cannot have this. Are you going to separate yourself from whoever shot the congressman? I don't know who shot him....
>
> Who wants to go with their child has a right to go with their child. I think it's humane. I want to go—I want to see you go, though. I—they can take me and do what they want—whatever they want to do. I want to see you go. I don't want to see you go through this hell no more. No more, no more, no more.... We're trying. If everybody will relax. The best thing you do is to relax, and you will have no problem. You'll have no problem with this thing, if you just relax.[42]

And as some children balked, he said:

> Can't some people assure these children of the relaxation of stepping over to the next plane? They set an example for others. We said—1,000 people who said, we don't like the way the world is.... Take some.... Take our life from us. We laid it down. We got tired.... We didn't commit suicide, we committed an act of revolutionary suicide protesting the conditions of an inhumane world.[43]

Adults had to force-feed some of the children. Some adults, too, resisted and had to be pushed toward the pavilion to take their poison. Some of the temple leaders fled the scene.

As the cyanide took effect, children and adults fell to the ground; their deaths came quickly. A few embraced as they took the cyanide together. When the

Guyanese troops arrived, they found three members of one family sprawled on the ground, their arms wrapped around one another's waists. Most of the bodies lay face down, clothed in red, blue, yellow, white—a morbid mosaic amid the greenery. A reporter who arrived shortly after the troops, wrote: "From the helicopter it looked as if there were a lot of brightly colored specks around the main building. At three hundred feet the smell hit . . . reporters tied handkerchiefs over their faces."[44]

Stunned Americans could barely comprehend the scene. Neither could a stunned world. In the Soviet Union, one newspaper called the tragedy a sign of a "grave illness" in the United States. The *Times of India* described conditions in California, home of the People's Temple, as wealth mixed with "spiritual desolation" and individualism mixed with "hermetic isolation," conditions fertile for cults. A Nigerian newspaper called Jonestown a "sad commentary on American society."[45]

Among the dead, investigators found a suicide note, apparently written by a woman. In reference to Jones, it said, "Dad—I see no way out—I agree with your decision." The writer continued: "For my part—I am more than tired of this wretched, merciless planet & the hell it holds for so many masses of beautiful people—thank you for the only life I've known."[46]

DISCO FLOURISHES

By January 1979, the movie *Saturday Night Fever,* released a year earlier and starring John Travolta, had gained such popularity that the soundtrack became the nation's number one album. This seemed to confirm disco as the reigning king of entertainment and, according to some analysts, the defining form of entertainment for the latter part of the decade.

To many young people, *Saturday Night Fever* reflected their lives as they entered adulthood at a time marked by economic limitations and social uncertainties noted for the decline of 1960s countercultural protest, the jaded attitudes attached to its demise, and the failures of political leaders. In the movie, based on a 1976 magazine article about the rise of disco, John Travolta's character, 19-year-old Tony Manero, works in a paint store in Brooklyn, earning minimum wage. His liberation and his moment of fame comes at the local disco, where he dances his way out of obscurity. Tony and the other young people pop pills, wear gold chains, and display a massive preoccupation with how they look. Director John Badham focused his camera on the dance floor—emphasizing the fervent dance sequences—and producer Robert Stigwood saturated the soundtrack with songs by the Bee Gees.

On its surface, disco seemed like the essence of escapism and a complete disconnect with the social consciousness of the 1960s. But as discos emerged from a revival of dance clubs in the early 1970s, when deejays began to use multiple turntables to keep music going nonstop, the records they played showed a multicultural influence: They combined black rhythm and blues with Latino sounds. Moreover, discos emanated, in part, from gay culture, and they brought together on the dance floor people of different nationalities and races, thus consciously and unconsciously advancing toleration. In doing so, the discos represented more urban than suburban America.

Consequently, disco drew the wrath of suburbanites who disliked its stylishness, of a wide range of white youths who hated its racial and ethnic content, and of black and Latino nationalists who condemned its as a sell-out to whites. Historian Bruce J. Schulman says disco's multidiversity made people hate it "with more intensity than any other form of popular music before or since."[47]

The urbanity, the trendiness, the decadence of disco was evident at the New York City nightspot Studio 54. Among those it attracted, the wealthy and connected took the spotlight, and it quickly became known for its popularity among the glitterati. Studio 54 was the party center for those far removed from Tony Manero's neighborhood: Bianca Jagger, Mick Jagger, Diana Ross, Liza Minnelli, Truman Capote, Andy Warhol, Mikhail Baryshnikov, Elizabeth Taylor, Elton John, Rudolf Nureyev, Salvador Dali, Calvin Klein . . . all made the pilgrimage to Studio 54.

Artist Andy Warhol was among the star guests at the Studio 54 disco. *(Copyright © Diana Mara Henry)*

The disco opened in April 1977. One attendee recalled: "I got there a little late. There were over a thousand people outside. . . . We were three or four layers back, and there were thirty or forty layers behind us. We all took a Quaalude. They took about fifteen or twenty minutes to kick in."[48] That night, "Everywhere there were tranced grins, lighted gizmos rising and falling, the comic book spoon journeying to the lunar nose, cheering, black ties, silver face paint, and famous faces coming into focus for a wink before dissolving into the throng. It was pure theater magic."[49] Confetti drifted down onto the dance floor and on to Bianca Jagger. The next day, the *New York Daily News* carried a front-page picture of Cher at the club. The large crowd on opening night prevented actor Warren Beatty from getting in, as well as Kate Jackson and Henry Winkler.

The famous—part of the emerging celebrity culture—saw Studio 54 as a place where they could party without being hassled. The "sanctuary," however, "would become just another part of the show."[50]

In addition to pills, cocaine flowed at Studio 54, the unisex bathrooms a gathering point for both. The dance floor undulated to the disco beat and to a strange phantasmagoria: topless women; dancers painted in silver and gold; costumed pharaohs; cucumbers; a see-through wedding dress. One partier recalled sitting around a table with friends for hours on end, saying to them: "Oh, this will always last! This will never be over. This is too incredibly bizarre and pushed to the extreme!"[51]

Nothing lasts forever, of course, and by the early 1980s, disco faded from the scene. Yet, elements of the music appeared in new wave and rap, and the disco image, particularly the one presented in *Saturday Night Fever,* continued to serve as a defining moment for the late 1970s, declaring, fairly or unfairly, that mindless escapism was the modus operandi of the era.

RUNNING AND SPIRITUALISM

Between 1977 and 1978, the circulation for *Runner's World* magazine mushroomed from 76,000 to 250,000; at the same time, the Gallup Poll estimated that

15 million people were jogging regularly. A running craze had overtaken America, in part the result of the popularity of *The Complete Book of Running,* written by Jim Fixx.

Fixx himself had been an overweight business executive looking to improve his physical fitness and his attitude. In his book, Fixx likens running to a mystical experience through which a person can achieve individual fulfillment, akin to Zen Buddhism, and obtain happiness along with health benefits. He says that running provides a "sense of enhanced mental energy and concentration" and says that will power and the acceptance of pain—both integral to running—"have a radiating power that subtly influences one's life."[52]

Fixx quotes a runner, David Bradley, who, writing in the *Village Voice,* claimed:

I no longer touch the ground: I am moving through air, floating. The incline is not a hill, it is just air that is a little thicker, and I can breathe deeply and draw myself up without effort. My body is producing draughts of a hormone called epinephrine, which researchers have linked with feelings of euphoria. This, combined with the alpha waves and the repetitive motion of running which acts as a sort of mantra, makes me higher than is legally possible in any other way.[53]

Fixx writes that in interviews with several runners, he found that running made them happier. Throughout their statements ran a strong element of spirituality. He says runners used language akin to mystics and even talked about a religiouslike conversion experience. He concludes: "It is not difficult to find explicit references to the religious quality of running."[54]

MUHAMMAD ALI

Six times Muhammad Ali successfully defended his world heavyweight boxing championship, including a third fight with Joe Frazier. But on February 15, 1978, Ali lost his title to newcomer Leon Spinks in a split decision.

Ali had trained only briefly for the fight, which took place in Las Vegas, Nevada. With his weight up to 242 pounds, Ali moved sluggishly against Spinks, who kept punching Ali in the stomach and arms, tiring the champ and making his movements all the more cumbersome. It was the first time, and as it turned out, the only time, that Ali lost his title in the ring. He later blamed his own lack of preparation more than Spinks's ability for the defeat. He said he felt embarrassed that an opponent with such limited talent could beat him.

But Ali came back. He trained harder, and at age 36, he defeated Spinks in a rematch in New Orleans. Ali dominated most of the rounds and won a unanimous decision. The victory made Ali the first boxer to claim the heavyweight title three times. Shortly after the win, Ali retired. He came out of retirement to fight Larry Holmes in 1980 and Trevor Berbick in 1981. He lost both matches and then retired permanently.

DOUBLE EAGLE II

On August 17, 1978, Maxie Anderson, Ben Abruzzo, and Larry Newman steered their helium-filled balloon *Double Eagle II* to a landing in the town of Miserey,

France. With their touchdown, they completed the first-ever trans-Atlantic balloon flight.

Others had tried before them, and the 14 previous attempts had resulted in five deaths. Anderson and Abruzzo had tried earlier too: In September 1977, they lifted off from Marshfield, Massachusetts, aboard *Double Eagle I,* a 101,000-cubic-foot helium balloon. They nearly crashed into Mt. Katahdin in Maine and then encountered a Canadian storm. While soaked with rain and hampered by ice, they began to drift in the wrong direction, toward Greenland. Finally, they gave up and landed in the Atlantic Ocean amid 25-foot seas. They had to be rescued by a helicopter.

Anderson and Abruzzo decided to try again, and they added Newman as a third pilot. This time they left aboard *Double Eagle II,* a 160,000-cubic foot balloon, from Presque Isle, Maine, on August 11, 1978. Overall, the flight proceeded smoothly, with only two harrowing moments. One occurred when on takeoff they nearly struck a power line. The second occurred over the Atlantic when the balloon descended rapidly from 19,500 feet to 4,000 feet. But they survived the "Big Drop," and as they approached France, they looked for a suitable landing spot. They spotted a field and ended their flight there while securing a heralded place in the history of ballooning.

CHRONICLE OF EVENTS

1978

January 6: President Jimmy Carter returns to Washington from a nine-day tour, having visited Poland, Iran, India, Saudi Arabia, Egypt, France, and Belgium. Carter was embarrassed in Poland when a translator translated the word *desires* into the Polish word for "lusts," making it appear as if he were talking about the "lusts" of the Polish people. In India, an open microphone picked up his comments, meant to be private, about American disagreements with the Indian prime minister over nuclear weapons.

January 13: Senator Hubert H. Humphrey (Dem., Minn.) dies of cancer. Humphrey served as vice president under Lyndon Johnson and nearly defeated Richard Nixon for the presidency in 1968. His career in public office spanned 32 years.

January 19: President Carter delivers his State of the Union speech in which he calls for a tax cut, ratification of the Panama Canal treaty, a new federal Department of Education, and passage of his energy bill.

January 20: An unexpected blizzard engulfs the east from Washington to New England. Some suburbs of New York receive 20 inches of snow. Businesses are forced to close, and motorists are stranded on highways.

January 21: The soundtrack to the movie *Saturday Night Fever* reaches number one on the record charts, confirming the prominence of disco.

February 6: A storm that begins on this day and lasts 40 hours buries New York City in nearly 18 inches of snow, the heaviest amount in 30 years.

February 24: President Carter signs into law the Endangered American Wilderness Act, which designates 1.3 million acres of new wilderness areas in national forests in the West and stipulates that wild areas can still qualify for wilderness designation even though cities or human activities can be seen or heard from them.

March 6: President Carter invokes the Taft-Hartley Act to end a 91-day strike by the United Mine Workers that had been disrupting coal shipments. The miners, however, ignore the order and instead, nearly three weeks later, will reach a settlement with the mine owners.

March 6: Larry Flynt, the owner and publisher of the adult magazine *Hustler,* is shot and left paralyzed

President Carter signs into law the Wilderness Act of 1978. *(Courtesy Jimmy Carter Library)*

from the waist down. He was in Lawrenceville, Georgia, to testify in his own defense at a trial where he was facing charges of distributing obscene materials.

April 3: President Carter returns to Washington from a seven-day journey through Africa and South America. He visited Venezuela, Brazil, Nigeria, and Liberia. While in Venezuela, he won over listeners by presenting two short speeches in Spanish.

April 7: President Carter announces that he will defer production of the controversial neutron bomb, a weapon that uses nuclear radiation to kill people while minimizing the damage to structures.

April 10: Former FBI director L. Patrick Gray and two other ex-FBI officials are indicted on charges of conspiring to deprive U.S. citizens of their civil rights in connection with having authorized illegal entries in the early 1970s against an antiwar group.

April 13: New York state officials and officials with Rockefeller Center announce a deal to keep open the financially troubled Radio City Music Hall, the largest theater in the nation.

April 18: The Senate agrees to turn over the Panama Canal to Panama at the end of 1999. The vote, 68–32, is one more than the two-thirds majority needed to ratify the canal treaty.

April 30: The memoirs of Richard Nixon are published in installments in U.S. newspapers.

May 2: The faculty at Harvard votes to replace its general education program with a core curriculum, part of a shift in colleges away from the liberalized guidelines of the 1960s to stricter curriculum requirements.

May 15: The Supreme Court declines to review and thus leaves standing a North Carolina law that criminalizes homosexual relations between consenting adults.

May 26: The first legal casino gambling outside of Nevada begins in Atlantic City, New Jersey.

May 31: By a vote of 5–3, the Supreme Court rules that the police can obtain warrants to search newspaper offices without prior warning and that newspapers cannot block such searches by filing suits in court.

June 6: California voters approve Proposition 13, a ballot initiative that reduces property taxes by 57 percent. Passage of the proposition causes the governor to cut nearly $400 million from the state budget. The vote is part of a tax revolt spreading across the country.

June 9: The Church of Jesus Christ of Latter-day Saints (Mormons) announces that it will end its exclusion of black men from the priesthood. The change, officials claim, comes after a revelation from God.

June 13: David Berkowitz, the "Son of Sam" killer, is sentenced in New York City to maximum prison terms for the six murders that he had confessed to committing.

June 15: The Supreme Court rules that the Tennessee Valley Authority must halt construction of a dam that threatens an endangered species, a three-inch-long fish called the snail darter.

June 16: President Carter and President Omar Torrijos of Panama exchange the treaties for turning over the Panama Canal to the Panamanians at the end of 1999.

June 22: The National Socialist Party of America (Nazis) cancels its plans for a march through the predominantly Jewish Chicago suburb of Skokie.

June 28: On a 5-4 vote, the Supreme Court rules that colleges can use affirmative action in deciding admissions but not to the point of causing reverse discrimination against whites. The Court thus orders the University of California at Davis to admit Alan Bakke, a 38-year-old white engineer, into its medical college. Bakke had been denied admission because of a quota system that was established to reserve places for members of minorities. The Court says that such quotas are too extreme.

July 3: The Supreme Court upholds fines levied by the Federal Communications Commission against a New York City radio station, WBAI-FM, for broadcasting a routine by comedian George Carlin called "Seven Dirty Words."

July 12: The U.S. ambassador to the United Nations, Andrew Young, ignites a controversy when he equates the plight of dissidents in the Soviet Union with civil rights protesters in the United States. Young later retracts his statement amid protestations from the Carter administration that he had made it more difficult to eradicate oppression in the Soviet Union by allowing the Soviets to claim that the United States also had political prisoners.

July 17: About 1,000 Indians and their supporters complete a cross-country walk from California to the steps of the Capitol in Washington to protest what they call "anti-Indian" legislation in Congress.

Peter Bourne, assistant to President Carter for drugs and mental health, stirred controversy with his statements about legalizing marijuana. *(Courtesy Jimmy Carter Library)*

July 20: President Carter's drug adviser, Dr. Peter G. Bourne, resigns after admitting that he had written a prescription for Quaalude, a powerful sedative, for one of his aides, using a fictitious name for the aide. Bourne will raise a controversy during his departure when he states that there exists among the White House staff a high level of marijuana use. Newspaper columnist Jack Anderson will add to the controversy when he writes that Bourne had used cocaine at a party given by the National Organization for the Reform of Marijuana Laws.

August 2: The New York State health commissioner declares a health emergency for the Love Canal neighborhood near Niagara Falls, a result of chemical wastes dumped into a landfill by the Hooker Chemical company between 1947 and 1952. The chemicals were found to be leaking into backyards and basements, threatening the health of the residents.

August 4: The Environmental Protection Agency approves the building of an open-ocean cooling system for the Seabrook nuclear power plant in New Hampshire.

August 15: The *New York Times* attributes a recent running fad in part to a book by Jim Fixx, *The Complete Book of Running.*

August 17: Three Americans complete the first successful transatlantic balloon flight when they land their craft, the *Double Eagle II,* near Paris.

September 5: President Jimmy Carter begins a historic summit meeting with Egyptian president Anwar Sadat and Israeli prime minister Menachem Begin in an attempt to broker a Middle East peace agreement.

September 15: Thirty-six-year-old Muhammad Ali defeats Leon Spinks in a bout in New Orleans to become the first boxer to claim the heavyweight title three times.

September 17: Egyptian president Anwar Sadat and Israeli prime minister Menachem Begin sign a framework for peace, which President Carter also signs as a witness. Under its terms, Sadat and Begin are to sign a peace agreement in 90 days; Israel is to begin to withdraw its troops from the Sinai Peninsula within several months after the peace agreement is signed and is to complete its troop withdrawal within two to three years; and Israel and Egypt are to establish normal diplomatic relations (making an implicit recognition by Egypt that Israel exists as a state). Moreover, the Camp David Accords provide for the Palestinians to have their own local government and to join Israel, Egypt, and Jordan in negotiating the future status of the West Bank and Gaza Strip.

Many Egyptians will denounce the agreement, and Yasar Arafat, the leader of the Palestine Liberation Organization, will call it a "dirty deal." Most Israelis will support the agreement, but a nationalist group will establish illegal settlements on the West Bank, which Israeli troops will later tear down.

September 21: The leaders of Syria, Algeria, South Yemen, Libya, and the Palestine Liberation Organization meet in Damascus, Syria, and announce that they will seek to block Egyptian president Anwar Sadat's peace policies.

October 3: William and Emily Harris are sentenced to 10 years to life in prison for the kidnapping of newspaper heiress Patricia Hearst.

October 6: Congress votes to extend the deadline for ratification by the states of the Equal Rights Amendment.

October 15: Congress approves Jimmy Carter's energy proposal, much changed from the president's original provisions.

October 15: Congress passes the Humphrey-Hawkins "full employment" bill and sets as a national goal the reduction of unemployment from 6 percent to 4 percent by 1983 and the reduction of inflation to 3 percent by 1983 and zero by 1988.

October 20: The Firestone Tire and Rubber Company agrees to replace 10 million of its "500" brand of steel-belted radial tires after they are found to contain defects that the company hid from consumers.

November 6: An 88-day newspaper strike ends in New York City, allowing the *New York Times* and the *New York Daily News* to resume publishing.

November 20: In Guyana, government soldiers discover the dead bodies of some 900 followers of Reverend Jim Jones and his People's Temple. The followers had committed mass suicide by drinking Kool-Aid spiked with cyanide. Jones is found dead near an alter with a bullet wound in his head.

November 27: San Francisco mayor George Moscone and openly gay city supervisor Harvey Milk are shot dead by Dan White, a disgruntled former supervisor and homophobe.

December 8: U.S. investigators at the site of the People's Temple in Jonestown, Guyana, discover a tape recording of the last minutes of the mass suicide committed by the cult's followers; it includes sounds of children screaming and the voice of Reverend Jim Jones as he exhorts his followers to drink cyanide-laced Kool-Aid.

Civil rights leader Jesse Jackson (center) leads a march in support of the Humphrey-Hawkins bill for full employment. *(Library of Congress, Prints and Photographs Division)*

December 30: The House Assassinations Committee concludes that the shooting of President John Kennedy was likely the result of a conspiracy involving more than one shooter.

EYEWITNESS TESTIMONY

Proposition 13

CALIFORNIA CONSTITUTION
ARTICLE 13A (TAX LIMITATION)
SECTION 1. (a) The maximum amount of any ad valorem tax on real property shall not exceed one percent (1%) of the full cash value of such property. The one percent (1%) tax to be collected by the counties and apportioned according to law to the districts within the counties.

(b) The limitation provided for in subdivision (a) shall not apply to ad valorem taxes or special assessments to pay the interest and redemption charges on any of the following:

(1) Indebtedness approved by the voters prior to July 1, 1978.

(2) Bonded indebtedness for the acquisition or improvement of real property approved on or after July 1, 1978, by two-thirds of the votes cast by the voters voting on the proposition.

(3) Bonded indebtedness incurred by a school district, community college district, or county office of education for the construction, reconstruction, rehabilitation, or replacement of school facilities, including the furnishing and equipping of school facilities, or the acquisition or lease of real property for school facilities, approved by 55 percent of the voters of the district or county, as appropriate, voting on the proposition on or after the effective date of the measure adding this paragraph. . . . that list.

That part of Proposition 13 (the Jarvis-Gann Amendment) dealing with restrictions on property tax rates in California, as approved by the voters on June 6, 1978, available online at http://www.leginfo.ca.gov/.const/ .article_13A, downloaded October 16, 2004.

We are saying that we know [Proposition 13] will severely disrupt state and city governments. We are also saying that we want it to severely disrupt state and city governments. We are not anarchists, we are not radicals, and we do not think we are irresponsible. We are simply fully sick and tired of having our pockets picked at every level of government. . . . We want an end to the countless layers of bureaucracies. We refuse to pay any longer for the parasites who are feathering their own nests directly out of our pockets.

California resident Norman I. Arnold writing a letter to the San Francisco Chronicle *in 1978 in support of Proposition 13, in Joel Fox,* The Legend of Proposition 13 *(2003), p. 72.*

What seemed undeniable . . . was that the California tax revolt had raced the middle-class pulse of the country as feverishly as anything since the invention of the station wagon . . . In Idaho, in Utah—in fact in many of the 23 states that provide for ballot initiatives—the California vote proved an instantaneous shot in the arm for groups seeking to get their own Jarvis-type propositions on the November ballot.

Newsweek magazine commenting on June 17, 1978, *on the impact of the vote to support Proposition 13, in Alvin Rabushka and Pauline Ryan,* The Tax Revolt *(1982), p. 2.*

I opposed [Proposition 13] because I thought there were problems. I think they're still there. . . . But, nevertheless, that [Proposition 13] is the mood. It's an opportunity as well as a problem. And I've tried to fix it. . . . People say, "Well, isn't that a change of mind?" When 65% of the people tell you something, you're a darn fool if you don't listen.

California governor Jerry Brown reacting in September 1978 to accusations that he had flipped-flopped on the Proposition 13 issue, initially opposing it and, with its passage, then supporting it, in Alvin Rabushka and Pauline Ryan, The Tax Revolt *(1982), pp. 44–45.*

We made two quick decisions. We decided to put most of our effort into direct mail, and we decided to build the whole thing around Jarvis. Most people thought Howard Jarvis was a goofy old gadfly who would hurt his own cause. We felt he was somebody ordinary taxpayers could identify with. So we said let's not diffuse this; let's make this one guy and his struggles our entire focus. The other side thought that was great. Well, we were right and they were wrong.

Bill Butcher, of the public relations firm Butcher-Forde, commenting around 1979 on the strategy used by the supporters of Howard Jarvis and his Proposition 13 campaign, in Robert Kuttner, Revolt of the Haves *(1980), p. 71.*

I bought my house in 1974; in 1975 the house was worth $110,000. I was paying approximately $3,400 in property taxes, and as a result of Proposition 13, I paid $1,022. The house is now worth about $400,000.

Without Proposition 13, I would be paying about $13,000 [in property taxes].

Los Angeles resident Harold L. Katz commenting in the early 1980s about the impact of Proposition 13 on him, in Schwadron and Richter, California and the American Tax Revolt (1984), p. 88.

I remember them saying rents would go down, there would be more housing available. But it happened exactly the reverse.

Los Angeles resident Virginia Jimenez commenting in the early 1980s on the impact of Proposition 13 on renters such as herself, in Terry Schwadron and Paul Richter, California and the American Tax Revolt (1984), p. 90.

The point of [Proposition] 13 was to take the fat out of government. But they didn't do that. Where they should have started to cut is at the top.

Thelma Perkins, owner of a bungalow in Los Angeles, commenting in the early 1980s on the failure of Proposition 13 to make the type of budget cuts she had envisioned, in Terry Schwadron and Paul Richter, California and the American Tax Revolt (1984), p. 89.

Proposed Nazi March in Skokie

Another step in the legal process has been taken. However, it is far from the final step as far as the Village of Skokie is concerned. We strongly disagree with today's decision. We are morally, ethically and legally bound to take every recourse at out disposal to have [the U.S. District Court's] decision reversed.

We will appeal. To do less would mean this Village's government is not representing the views and feelings of virtually every Skokie resident, Catholic, Protestant and Jew alike. And, yes, we will ask the courts to forestall any demonstration pending the outcome of our appeal. . . .

As we all know, not all speech is protected by the First Amendment. If there was ever a perfect example of the type of speech which should not be protected, it is the doctrine of Nazism which preaches hatred and violence because of a person's race or national origin. The courts must not be blind to the uniqueness of the Village of Skokie. The court must not be blind to recorded history. The courts must not be blind to the

rights of the citizens of Skokie to be protected from racial slurs. . . .

What Nazism represents is repugnant not just to the people of Skokie, to the people of Illinois, but to virtually every United States citizen and free people everywhere. Nazism has affected people of every creed and national origin and insults the dignity of human beings.

Excerpt from Mayor Albert J. Smith's statement to the media on February 23, 1978, regarding the U.S. District Court ruling that would allow members of the National Socialist Party of America (Nazis) to hold a demonstration in Skokie, Skokie Public Library, available online at http://www.digitalpast.org, downloaded October 17, 2004.

It would be a monstrous tragedy for the courts of this land to rule that an obscene spectacle should be held under the guise of our First Amendment freedoms, which we, of the Jewish community, hold especially dear.

The Jewish community of Chicago hopes the Village of Skokie will continue its efforts to overturn the decision of the U.S. District Court that would enable the Nazis to deliberately provoke the citizens of Skokie and the many others who would be grievously offended by the march.

However, should all legal means fail, the Jewish community will cooperate fully with the Village of Skokie and peoples of other faiths in framing a nonviolent response more in keeping with what our founding fathers had in mind when they drafted the Bill of Rights.

Statement by Raymond Epstein, chairman of the Public Affairs Committee of the Jewish United Fund, made on February 23, 1978, in response to the U.S. District Court ruling that would allow a Nazi march in Skokie, Illinois, Skokie Public Library, available online at http://www.digitalpast.org, downloaded October 17, 2004.

The Alan Bakke Case

It may be assumed that the reservation of a specified number of seats in each class for individuals from the preferred ethnic groups would contribute to the attainment of considerable ethnic diversity in the student body. But petitioner's [i.e., the University of California] argument that this is the only effective means of serving the interest of diversity is seriously flawed. In a most fundamental sense the argument misconceives the nature of the state interest that would justify consideration of race or ethnic background.

It is not an interest in simple ethnic diversity, in which a specified percentage of the student body is in effect guaranteed to be members of selected ethnic groups, with the remaining percentage an undifferentiated aggregation of students. The diversity that furthers a compelling state interest encompasses a far broader array of qualifications and characteristics of which racial or ethnic origin is but a single though important element. Petitioner's special admissions program, focused solely on ethnic diversity, would hinder rather than further attainment of genuine diversity. . . .

In summary, it is evident that the Davis special admissions program involves the use of an explicit racial classification never before countenanced by this Court. It tells applicants who are not Negro, Asian, or Chicano that they are totally excluded from a specific percentage of the seats in an entering class. . . .

The fatal flaw in petitioner's preferential program is its disregard of individual rights as guaranteed by the Fourteenth Amendment. Such rights are not absolute. But when a State's distribution of benefits or imposition of burdens hinges on ancestry or the color of a person's skin, that individual is entitled to a demonstration that the challenged classification is necessary to promote a substantial state interest. Petitioner has failed to carry this burden. For this reason, that portion of the California court's judgment holding petitioner's special admissions program invalid under the Fourteenth Amendment must be affirmed.

In enjoining petitioner from ever considering the race of any applicant, however, the courts below failed to recognize that the State has a substantial interest that legitimately may be served by a properly devised admissions program involving the competitive consideration of race and ethnic origin. For this reason, so much of the California court's judgment as enjoins petitioner from any consideration of the race of any applicant must be reversed.

An excerpt from Justice Lewis Powell's decision, issued June 28, 1978, in University of California v. Alan Bakke, *in which he declared the university's admissions program at its Davis medical school unconstitutional but upheld the right of colleges and schools to establish affirmative action programs. To Powell, the type of program used at Harvard exemplified an acceptable approach to considering race in student admissions, available online at http://caselaw.lp.findlaw.com, downloaded October 16, 2004.*

I believe that admissions quotas based on race are illegal. I am inquiring of friends . . . about the possibility of formally challenging these quotas through the courts.

Alan Bakke writing to George Lowery, chairman of the admissions committee at the University of California Medical School at Davis on July 1, 1973, in Bernard Schwartz, Behind Bakke *(1988), p. 6.*

There is no question here but that Bakke's exclusion from the University of California Medical School at Davis was a result of racial classification. If the Constitution prohibits exclusion of blacks and other minorities on racial grounds it cannot permit the exclusion of whites on racial grounds.

Alan Bakke's lawyer, Reynold Colvin, arguing in California superior court in 1974 that Bakke had been discriminated against, in Bernard Schwartz, Behind Bakke *(1988), p. 16.*

Bakke doesn't dismantle affirmative action and it doesn't take employers off the hook. As a law-enforcement official, I have to say that the *Bakke* case has not left me with any duty to instruct the EEOC staff to do anything different or recommend a change of policy to the Commission.

Eleanor Holmes Norton, chair of the Equal Employment Opportunity Commission (EEOC) reacting in 1978 to the Bakke decision, in Howard Ball, The Bakke Case *(2000), pp. 142–143.*

[The Bakke decision] does not require any drastic shifts in the direction of national policies to assure civil rights.

From an editorial in the Los Angeles Times *in 1978, in Howard Ball,* The Bakke Case *(2000), p. 141.*

Love Canal

We heard he was going to recommend that pregnant women and children under two move . . . no money, just move. I couldn't believe it. I thought, Oh, God, what is going to happen?

An unidentified official with the city of Niagara Falls waterworks commenting in 1978 on the consideration by health commissioner Robert Whalen to move some of the residents of the Love Canal community, in Gordon Levine, Love Canal *(1982), p. 29.*

My daughter already has birth defects. She already has horrible illnesses. She is already sick. What are you going to do for her? She's already over three. Does that mean she has to stay and die? We have chemicals in our basement. You took an air reading. I've got this air reading and I don't even know what it means. Does it mean our lives are in jeopardy?

Love Canal resident Lois Heisner speaking out at a meeting at a public school in August 1978, in Lois Marie Gibbs, Love Canal *(1982), p. 36.*

Gee! It's the miracle of the Love Canal! You live on top of a couple of hundred chemicals for 25 years and nothing's wrong! You just *think* something's wrong! They should really send all of the world's wastes here, because it's the only place on earth such a miracle could happen.

Love Canal resident Marie Pozniak reacting in disdain in 1980 to a report from an investigating scientist that the main impact of the Love Canal contamination would not be physical but psychological, in Adeline Levine, Love Canal *(1982), p. 168.*

We contacted 101 families and asked them if there had been any changes in their health since they had moved from the area (about six months earlier). Of the homes polled, 67 said a family member's health had improved. . . . One of the most frequent responses was that people hadn't had any migraine headaches since moving. . . . It was remarkable how many people had improved. Not one person surveyed told us they had gotten worse.

Love Canal activist Lois Marie Gibbs recalling in 1982 a survey of residents, conducted in 1979, who had relocated from the chemical-laden site, in Lois Marie Gibbs, Love Canal *(1982), p. 93.*

The Camp David Summit

I would appreciate your honoring the confidentiality of this letter, which is private and personal. I want to express myself frankly and directly.

Because of your dramatic and courageous visit to Jerusalem and its accompanying actions and statements, remarkable progress has been made toward peace in the Middle East. The strong leadership qualities exhibited by you and Prime Minister Begin contributed to a better understanding between Egypt and Israel, and opened up the prospect for success in the peace negotiations. In my opinion, you are the leader,

who, in the foreseeable future, can and must continue this progress.

You have a strong hold on the government, loyalty among your associates, the well deserved confidence of the people of your country, and the admiration of the world.

It is imperative that every effort be made to capitalize on this unprecedented opportunity to conclude a peace treaty between Egypt and Israel and to lay the groundwork for a comprehensive and permanent peace agreement for the entire region. The consequences of failure may be very serious.

During recent weeks little progress has been made and the relationships have deteriorated. A total stalemate is in prospect. Unless we act boldly and constructively now, those of us who now serve as leaders may not again have such a chance to bring peace to the people of your region.

After long discussions with both you and Prime Minister Begin, there is no doubt in my mind that both of you genuinely want peace and have the courage to reach agreement. It is time, therefore, for us to make a renewed effort at the highest level and with the greatest determination.

My hope is that, during this visit by Secretary Vance to the Middle East, progress and harmony will be indicated through positive statements and the avoidance of public disputes. Then, as soon as possible, I would like to meet personally with you and Prime Minister Begin to search for additional avenues for peace as we planned at Camp David.

It is important that this proposal be kept completely confidential, that public expectations not be raised too high, and that quiet and material preparation lay the foundation for a successful meeting.

Secretary Vance can discuss with you the details of time and place. Unnecessary delay would be a mistake. I have no strong preference about the location, but Camp David is available. My hope is that the three of us, along with our top advisors, can work together in relative seclusion. Any public announcement of our plans for the meeting can be coordinated among us. Secretary Vance is familiar with my schedule, and I hope that through him you will send me your ideas and advice.

I look forward to an early opportunity to consider with you again one of the most important and challenging issues ever to be decided by political leaders.

Please remember that you have my continuing friendship and personal best wishes as we work together as partners in a common search for peace.

Letter from President Jimmy Carter to President Anwar Sadat of Egypt, August 3, 1978, proposing the peace summit that ultimately was held at Camp David, Jimmy Carter Library, available online at http://www.jimmycarterlibrary.gov/documents/campdavid25/campdavid25_documents.phtml, downloaded October 16, 2004.

In order to achieve peace between them, Israel and Egypt agree to negotiate in good faith with a goal of concluding within three months of the signing of this framework a peace treaty between them. All of the principles of U.N. Resolution 242 will apply in this resolution of the dispute between Israel and Egypt.

Peace Treaty

Unless otherwise mutually agreed terms of the peace treaty will be implemented between two and three years after the peace treaty is signed. In the peace treaty the issues of a) the full exercise of Egyptian sovereignty up to the internationally recognized border between Egypt and mandated Palestine; b) the time of withdrawal of Israeli personnel from the Sinai; c) the use of airfields near El Arish, Rafah, Ras en Naqb, Sharm el Sheikh, Arish, Eitam, Etzion and Ofir for civilian purposes only; d) the

Jimmy Carter and Menachem Begin walk the grounds at Camp David. *(Courtesy Jimmy Carter Library)*

right of free passage of ships of Israel and other nations through the Strait of Tiran, the Gulf of Suez and the Suez Canal; e) the construction of an international highway between the Sinai and Jordan near Elat; and f) the stationing of military forces listed below....

Excerpt from President Carter's September 1978 draft of what became the "Framework for the Conclusion of a Peace Treaty between Egypt and Israel," Jimmy Carter Library, available online at http://www.jimmycarterlibrary.gov/documents/campdavid25/campdavid25_documents.phtml, downloaded October 16, 2004.

Jonestown

To Whomever Finds This Note
Collect all the tapes, all the writing, all the history. The story of this movement, this action, must be examined over and over. It must be understood in all of its incredible dimensions. Words fail. We have pledged our lives to this great cause. We are proud to have something to die for.

We do not fear death. We hope that the world will someday realize the ideals of brotherhood, justice and equality that Jim Jones has lived and died for. We have all chosen to die for this cause. We know there is no way that we can avoid misinterpretation. But Jim Jones and this movement were born too soon. The world was not ready to let us live.

I am sorry there is no eloquence as I write these final words. We are resolved, but grieved that we cannot make the truth of our witness clear.

This is the last day of our lives. May the world find a way to a new birth of social justice. If there is any way that our lives and the life of Jim Jones can ever help that take place, we will not have lived in van [sic].

Jim Jones did not order anyone to attack or kill anyone. It was done by individuals who had too much of seeing people try to destroy this movement, Jim Jones. Their actions have left us no alternative, and rather than see this cause decimated, we have chosen to give our lives. We are proud of that choice.

Please try to understand. Look at all. Look at all in perspective. Look at Jonestown, see what we have tried to do—This was a monument to life, to the [re]newal of the human spirit, broken by capitalism, by a system of exploitation & injustice. Look at all that was built by a beleaguered people. We did not want this kind of ending—we wanted to live, to shine, to bring light to a world that is dying for a little bit of love. To those left behind of our loved ones, many of whom will not understand, who never knew this truth, grieve not, we are grateful for this opportunity to bear witness—a bitter witness—history has chosen our destiny in spite of our own desire to forge our own.

We were at a cross-purpose with history. But we are calm in this hour of our collective leave-taking. As I write these words people are silently amassed, taking a quick potion, inducing sleep, relief.

We are a long-suffering people. Many of us are weary with a long search, a long struggle—going back not only in our own lifetime, but a long painful heritage....

Many of us are now dead. Each moment, another passes over to a peace. We are begging only for some understanding. It will take more than small minds, reporters minds, to fathom these events. Something must come of this.

Beyond all the circumstances surrounding the immediate event, someone can perhaps find the symbolic, the eternal in this moment—the meaning of a people, a struggle—I wish I had time to put it all together, that I had done it. I did not do it. I failed to write the book. Someone else, others will have to do this. Please study this movement, from the very origins of Jim Jones in the rural poverty of Indiana, out from the heart of the America that he later was to stand against for its betrayal of its ideals.

These are a beautiful people, a brave people, not afraid. There is quiet as we leave this world. The sky is gray. People file . . . slowly and take the somewhat bitter drink.

Many more must drink. Our destiny. It is sad that we could not let our light shine in truth, unclouded by the demons of accident, circumstance, miscalculation, error that was not our intent, beyond our intent.

I hope that someone writes this whole story. It is not "news." It is more. We merge with millions of others, we are subsumed in the archetype. People hugging each other, embracing, we are hurrying—we do not want to be captured. We want to bear witness at once.

We did not want it this way. All was going well as Ryan completed [his] first day here. Then a man tried to attack him . . . several set out into [the] jungle wanting to overtake Ryan, [his] aide, and others who left with him. They did, and several [were] killed.

When we heard this, we had no choice. We would be taken. We have to go as one, we want to live as Peoples Temple, or end it. We have chosen. It is finished.

Hugging & kissing & tears & silence & joy in a long line.

Touches and whispered words as this silent line passes. Determination, purpose. A proud people. Only last night, their voices raised in unison, a voice of affirmation and today, a different sort of affirmation, a different dimension of that same victory of the human spirit.

A tiny kitten sits next to me. Watching. A dog barks. The birds gather on the telephone wires. Let all the story of this People[s] Temple be told. Let all the books be opened. This sight . . . o terrible victory. How bitter that we did not, could not, that Jim Jones was crushed by a world that he didn't make—how great the victory.

If nobody understands, it matters not. I am ready to die now. Darkness settles over Jonestown on its last day on earth.

An unsigned note likely written by one of the leaders at Jonestown, Richard Trop, on the day of the mass suicide, November 18, 1978, available online at http:// jonestown.sdsu.edu, downloaded October 14, 2004.

I am 24 years of age right now and don't expect to live through the end of this book. I thought I should at least make some attempt to let the world know what Jim Jones and the Peoples Temple is—OR WAS—all about. It seems that some people and perhaps the majority of people would like to destroy the best thing that ever happened to the 1,200 or so of us who have followed Jim.

I am at a point right now so embittered against the world that I don't know why I am writing this. Someone who finds it will believe I am crazy or believe in the barbed wire that does NOT exist in Jonestown.

It seems that everything good that happens to the world is under constant attack. When I write this, I can expect some mentally deranged fascist person to find it and decide it should be thrown in the trash before anyone gets a chance to hear the truth—which is what I am now writing about.

Where can I begin—JONESTOWN—the most peaceful, loving community that ever existed, JIM JONES—the one who made this paradise possible— much to the contrary of the lies stated about Jim Jones being a power-hungry sadistic, mean person who thought he was God—of all things.

I want you who read this to know that Jim was the most honest, loving, caring concerned person whom I ever met and knew. His love for animals—each creature, poisonous snakes, tarantulas. None of them ever bit him because he was such a gentle person. He knew how mean the world was and he took any and every stray animal and took care of each one.

His love for humans was unsurmountable and it was many of those whom he put his love and trust in that left him and spit in his face. Teresa Buford, Debbie Blakey— they both wanted sex from him which he was too ill to give. Why should he have to give them sex?—And Tim and Grace Stoen—also include them. I should know.

I have spent these last few months taking care of Jim's health. However, it was difficult to take care of anything for him. He always would do it for himself. His hatred of racism, sexism, elitism, and mainly classicism, is what prompted him to make a new world for the people—a paradise in the jungle. The children loved it. So did everyone else.

There were no ugly, mean policemen wanting to beat our heads in, no more racist tears from whites and others who thought they were better. No one was made fun of for their appearance—something no one had control over.

Meanness and making fun were not allowed. Maybe this is why all the lies were started. Besides this fact, no one was allowed to live higher than anyone else.

The United States allowed criticism. The problem being this and not all the side tracks of black power, woman power, Indian power, gay power.

Jim Jones showed us all this—that we could live together with our differences, that we are all the same human beings. Luckily, we are more fortunate than the starving babies of Ethiopia, than the starving babies in the United States.

What a beautiful place this was. The children loved the jungle, learned about animals and plants. There were no cars to run over them; no child-molesters to molest them; nobody to hurt them. They were the freest, most intelligent children I had ever known.

Seniors had dignity. They had whatever they wanted—a plot of land for a garden. Seniors were treated with respect—something they never had in the United States. A rare few were sick, and when they were, they were given the best medical care.

We died because you would not let us live in peace.

A note written by Annie Moore, considered to be the last person to commit suicide at Jonestown. Her body was found in Reverend Jim Jones's cabin. The date of authorship is in dispute: Some believe the note was written shortly before the arrival of Congressman Leo Ryan on November 17, 1978, others believe it was written on November 18, 1978, while the suicides were going on, available online at http://jonestown.sdsu.edu, downloaded October 14, 2004.

Jones: Please get us some medication. It's simple. It's simple. There's no convulsions with it. It's just simple. Just, please get it. Before it's too late. The GDF [Guyana Defense Force] will be here, I tell you. Get movin', get movin', get movin'.

Voices

Woman 6: Now. Do it now!

Jones: Don't be afraid to die. You'll see, there'll be a few people land out here. They'll—they'll torture some of our children here. They'll torture our people. They'll torture our seniors. We cannot have this. Are you going to separate yourself from whoever shot the congressman? I don't know who shot him.

Voices: No. No. No. . . .

Woman 7: Some of the others who endure long enough in a safe place to write about the goodness of Jim Jones.

Jones: I don't know how in the world they're ever going to write about us. It's just too late. It's too late. The congressman's dead. The congressman lays dead. Many of our traitors are dead. They're all layin' out there dead.

Voices

Jones: Hmm? I didn't, but—but my people did. My people did. They're my people, and they—they've been provoked too much. They've been provoked too much. What's happened here's been to—basically been an act of provocation. . . . Please, can we hasten? Can we hasten with that medication? You don't know what you've done. And I tried. . . . They saw it happen and ran into the bush and dropped the machine guns. I never in my life. . . . But we've got to move. Are you gonna get that medication here? . . .

Crying and talking

Woman 10: I just want to uh, say something for everyone that I see that is standing around and—or crying. This is nothing to cry about. This is something we could all rejoice about. We could be happy about this. They always told us that we could cry when you're coming into this world. So when we're leaving, and we're gonna leave it peaceful, I think we should be—we should be happy about this. I was just thinking about Jim Jones. He just has suffered and suffered and suffered. We have—We have the honor guard, and we don't even have a chance to (Unintelligible word) got here. I want to give him one more chance. There's just one more thing I want to say. That's few that's gone, but many more here. (Unintelligible) That's not all of us. That's not all yet. That's just a few that have died. I tried to get to the one that—there's a kid over there (unintelligible)

I'm looking at so many people crying. I wish you would not cry. And just thank Father. . . .

Jones: Please. For God's sake, let's get on with it. We've lived—we've lived as no other people have lived and loved. We've had as much of this world as you're gonna get. Let's just be done with it. Let's be done with the agony of it.

Crowd: Applause

Jones: It's far, far harder to have to walk through every day, die slowly—and from the time you're a child 'til the time you get gray, you're dying. . . . This is a revolutionary suicide. This is not a self-destructive suicide. So they'll pay for this. They brought this upon us. And they'll pay for that. I—leave that destiny to them. . . .

Woman 15: Everything we could have ever done, most loving thing all of us could have done, and it's been a pleasure walking with all of you in this revolutionary struggle. No other way I would rather go to give my life for socialism, communism, and I thank Dad very, very much.

Woman 16: Right. Yes. Dad—Dad's love and nursing, goodness and kindness, and he bring us to this land of freedom. His love—his mother was the advance—the advance guard for socialism. And his love and his principles (unintelligible) will go on forever. . . .

Jones: Where's the vat, the vat, the vat? Where's the vat with the Green C on it? Bring the vat with the Green C in. Please? Bring it here so the adults can begin.

Woman 16: Go on unto the Zion, and thank you, Dad.

Jones: (Unintelligible) Don't, don't fail to follow my advice. You'll be sorry. You'll be sorry—if we do it, than that they do it. Have trust. You mu—You have to step across.

Music

Jones: We used to think this world was—this world was not our home—well, it sure isn't—We were saying—it sure wasn't. He doesn't want to tell me. All he's doing—if they will tell 'em—assure these kids. Can't some people assure these children of the relaxation of stepping over to the next plane? They set an example for others. We said—one thousand people who said, we don't like the way the world is. Take some. Take our life from us. We laid it down. We got tired. We didn't commit suicide, we committed an act of revolutionary suicide protesting the conditions of an inhumane world.

Excerpts from a transcript of the "Death Tape," recorded at Jonestown as Reverend Jim Jones encouraged his followers to commit mass suicide on November 18, 1978. The references to "Dad" and "Father" are to Jones, available online at http://jonestown.sdsu.edu, downloaded October 14, 2004.

Disco

The first time I stepped into Studio 54, I was flooded with a powerful sense of déjà vu. I felt that I was reading a page of *Brave New World*. Far from seeming bizarre or unbelievable, the great industrial theater impressed me as being precisely what discotheques should have always been but never were: a wild part at the River Rouge Plant. Instead of feeling dwarfed under the ninety-foot ceiling, I felt wonderfully elated and composed. The spectacle was exhilarating and beautiful. . . .

Conforming, as it does, so strictly to the "form and pressure" of the present day, disco is a reassuringly familiar phenomenon and a perfectly normal expression of our cockeyed world. Especially, it is emblematic of our divided nature: half lab-coated technician, half dancing savage. Of Disco one could say exactly what Voltaire said of God: "If [He] did not exist, it would be necessary to invent Him."

Writer Albert Goldman observing the disco scene in 1978, in Albert Goldman, Disco *(1978), pp. 158 and 171.*

I'd decided not to do the part. But then I reconsidered. I thought, what's wrong with doing a light musical? Brando did it.

Actor John Travolta commenting on his decision to play the part of Tony Manero in the disco movie Saturday Night Fever, *in* Time, *April 3, 1978, available online at http://www.time.com/time/archive/preview/0,10987,919534,00.html, downloaded June 6, 2005.*

Running and Spiritualism

Someone once said, "For humanity to survive, it will have to invent a new religion." The religion has been invented. It is the religion of the runner.

Bob Anderson, editor of the semimonthly publication On the Run *commenting in September 1978 on America's running craze, in* Time, *September 11, 1978, available online at http://www.time.com/time/archive/printout/0,23657,946077.00.html, downloaded June 1, 2005.*

9

Meltdown America
January 1979–January 1981

The year 1979 provided a fitting end to a decade that was born fitfully in the turmoil of the 1960s and that descended quickly into pessimism, lethargy, even despair. No wonder that, in July 1979, President Jimmy Carter bemoaned a "crisis of spirit" in the United States. While on an individual basis, many Americans worked hard to improve their standing and looked with confidence to the future, collectively the nation still struggled to find prosperity, fortitude, and faith.

A near disaster at the Three Mile Island nuclear power plant in Pennsylvania early in the year only added to the widespread exasperation. But more than any other event, the overrunning of the U.S. embassy in Iran by revolutionary students and the holding of some 50 of the embassy staff as hostages signified America's muddled condition and unleashed a widespread call for new leadership.

A NEAR CATASTROPHE AT THREE MILE ISLAND

In winter 1979, tourists passing through Middletown, Pennsylvania, a small town located 11 miles south of the state capital, Harrisburg, could stop at a visitor's center perched on a bluff overlooking the Susquehanna River and see below a small island that was dominated by four huge cooling stacks. The concrete-and-steel behemoths marked the spot of the Three Mile Island nuclear power plant, which opened in late 1978. The visitor's center offered information lauding the modern plant as a safe, efficient provider of electricity at a time when the country was facing an energy crisis.

In late March 1979, however, the visitor's center was occupied not by tourists but by stern-looking men carrying Geiger counters to measure radiation, for by then a serious accident threatened to release catastrophic levels of radiation into the air and water. The crisis at Three Mile Island called into question the safety of existing nuclear power plants and the viability of building more of them. Moreover, it raised the specter of corporate and government deceit, thus further stoking the decadelong distrust in America's institutions and leaders.

The greening of spring was just unfolding in the Susquehanna Valley on March 28 when the Three Mile Island plant's unit two released above-normal

The Three Mile Island nuclear power plant was the site of a near meltdown. *(National Archives and Records Administration)*

amounts of radiation—significant quantities within the facility and lesser quantities outside. The Nuclear Regulatory Commission (NRC) reported "low levels" of radiation within a mile of the plant and trace levels 16 miles away. The flow of water to the cooling system had been disrupted, causing uranium pellets in several fuel rods to deteriorate and release the radiation. Steam that was vented to relieve pressure in the plant carried the radiation into the air.

As news of the accident spread, a spokesperson for the Metropolitan Edison Company, operators of the plant, assured the public that there was no chance of a meltdown of the nuclear core (which, if it happened, would result in catastrophic contamination). Nevertheless, on March 30, radioactivity was still being released into the air from Three Mile Island, along with the leakage of 400,000 gallons of water containing small amounts of radioactive gases from holding tanks that had reached their capacity.

The NRC reported that the nuclear reactor had been placed into a cooldown to stabilize it and to prevent conditions from worsening. At first, Governor Dick Thornburgh told Pennsylvanians that the accident posed no threat to anyone. Soon afterward, he advised pregnant women and small children to stay at least five miles away from the plant, and he ordered schools closed within that radius. The authorities evacuated several thousand schoolchildren and opened shelters to the public.

Residents in normally serene Middletown and other nearby towns scrambled for food and gas. Long lines formed at service stations and at grocery stores. One attendant said, "Yesterday, I pumped more gas than I've ever pumped in four years."[1] Callers jammed the local phone lines. Government planes flew overhead taking readings to determine the amount of airborne contamination, and the men with the Geiger counters showed up at the town's tourist center.

Making matters worse, Metropolitan Edison admitted that it had initially presented the accident as more limited that it actually was. The company at first said that 180 to 360 of 36,000 fuel rods had melted when the accident disrupted the supply of reactor coolant. Now it said 9,000 of the fuel rods had been damaged. Furthermore, officials admitted that they were having a more difficult time than earlier indicated in shutting down the plant.

Part of the difficulty came from an unexpected gaseous bubble, 1,000 cubic feet in size, composed of hydrogen, oxygen, and xenon. No one had anticipated such a bubble. (One government official called it "a whole new wrinkle."[2]) Expansion of the bubble would cause it to occupy more space and to push away from the fuel rods the water needed to cool them. If they overheated, there might occur a meltdown of the uranium-dioxide fuel elements which would, in turn, shatter the containment vessels and send radioactive elements across the countryside. A member of the NRC said about the bubble: "We are faced with a decision within a few days, rather than hours" about whether the core could be sufficiently cooled. "We face the ultimate risk of a meltdown," he said. "If there is even a small chance of a meltdown we will recommend precautionary evacuation."[3]

So many rumors and conflicting stories flew about from official and unofficial sources that the residents of Middletown became weary and wary. The situation prompted Governor Thornburgh to tell reporters: "There are a number of conflicting versions of every event that seems to occur. I have just got to tell you that we share your frustration. It is a very difficult thing to run these facts down."[4]

With the possibility of worsening conditions hanging over the town and the state as ominously as a cold-war era mushroom cloud, President Jimmy Carter visited the site on April 1, arriving on a yellow school bus. Officials told him that the situation had stabilized, although it was far from secure and could change. At a meeting of local residents, Carter said: "The primary and overriding concern for all of us is the health and the safety of the people of this entire area. As I said before, if we make an error, all of us want to err on the side of extra precautions and extra safety."[5] Carter praised the scientists and technicians who were working hard to resolve the crisis.

As the president spoke, huge trucks arrived at the plant from several other states. They brought with them steel tanks and concrete and lead radiation-containment vessels to handle contaminated material.

During the next few days, conditions at the plant continued to improve, allowing Middletown residents to breathe a little easier. Low-level radiation was still being released, but on April 3, the cooldown was continuing, the bubble crisis was ending, and life in the town was returning to normal, despite jangled nerves. Harold Denton, operations chief for the NRC said, "Today, I want to report that we consider the hydrogen bubble no longer a significant problem in this plant."[6]

Yet, he admitted that, during the nuclear accident, iodine 131 had been released into the air, a particularly dangerous element because even small amounts of it can cause thyroid cancer. (It had been spewed over large parts of the country during atomic-bomb tests.) In the past, iodine 131 had collected on grass, which was then eaten by cows, and then entered the milk that was to be consumed by human beings. Denton said that the release of iodine 131 was continuing during the cleanup.

President Carter departs Three Mile Island after visiting the site of the nuclear crisis. *(National Archives and Records Administration)*

Furthermore, he said that it would take a long time to decontaminate unit two. Estimates ranged from two to four years. Some experts said that the plant would never be in the condition required to be reactivated.

As the cooldown and cleanup continued, investigators researched what had caused the accident. They found a combination of human error and technical failures. Two weeks before the accident, workers turned off two valves on the nuclear reactor's auxiliary water pumps during maintenance and never turned them back on. Consequently, when the accident began, the pumps could not be used to provide the water needed to cool down the fuel rods.

Other valves, that were used to relieve the buildup of water pressure in the reactor, opened as they were supposed to but then malfunctioned and failed to close. Also, the pressure indicator hampered operators by providing inaccurate readings of the water level in the reactor, and the design of the containment vessel made it difficult to isolate all of the water. Finally, operators twice turned off the emergency core cooling system when they should have kept it on (the system was crucial to keeping the uranium in the reactor core from overheating), and they twice allowed uranium pellets in the fuel rods to stand uncovered by the cooling water. A later official investigation emphasized human error and inadequate control-room layout as the culprits in the accident.

Because technical failures related to the plant's design had contributed to the accident, the question arose as to whether or not other plants with similar designs, built by the same company, should be shut down. The NRC initially voted to keep the nine relevant plants open, although subject to added inspection. At a hearing later in the month, the NRC staff recommended that they be shut down until thorough inspections could be completed and technical changes made. The staff members stated: "We conclude that we do not now have reasonable assurance that these . . . plants can continue to operate without undue risk."[7] The commissioners, however, noted the importance of the plants to the country's power supply, so they rejected the staff recommendation and decided to keep them operating.

Three Mile Island raised widespread concern about the safety of nuclear power and galvanized the antinuke movement. In addition to street demonstrations, intense lobbying in Congress began to counteract the previously unbridled power of the nuclear utilities. More members of Congress began to oppose the building of additional nuclear power plants. In California, Governor Edmund Brown, Jr., demanded that the NRC close the Rancho Seco reactor, one of those with a design similar to Three Mile Island, and he urged the nation to switch from nuclear power to alternative sources, such as solar and wind power.

The building of nuclear power plants, however, had been slowing before Three Mile Island, largely a result of costs. They were becoming too expensive to build. Now it was clear that any serious accident would raise the financial stakes even more; it took some $1 billion to clean up Three Mile Island (and unit two was never put back on line).

Three Mile Island led to congressional legislation that required more stringent standards for building nuclear power plants and for more extensive plans to protect the public from any emergency. Several states passed even stricter standards. The costs, the stipulations, the long time required to build a plant all came together to prevent the construction of new facilities. Added to that was the bothersome question of what to do about nuclear waste that was generated by the plants. Sir Crispin Tickell, British permanent representative to the United Nations, observed, "The fact that every year there is waste being produced that will take the next three ice ages and beyond to become harmless is something that has deeply impressed the imagination."[8] Three Mile Island, however, contributed just as much to the overall impressions; it implanted in the public's mind a danger about nuclear power, an emotional, visceral reaction that rational argument found difficult to overcome.

The movie *China Syndrome,* released just weeks before the Three Mile Island incident, only helped to reinforce the fears. In it, an earthquake coupled with human error causes the fuel rods at a nuclear plant in California to lose their water covering and become exposed. The situation threatens to overheat the uranium and cause the core of the reactor to melt into the ground (euphemistically, "all the way to China") and release dangerous radiation. On top of these developments, the movie reveals shoddy work by the contractor in building the plant, evidenced by faulty welds hidden from inspectors by doctored X-rays. Filled with drama and characterized by the excellent acting of Jane Fonda, Jack Lemmon, and Michael Douglas, the movie offers a powerful condemnation of the nuclear power industry. Its coincident release with Three Mile Island only made the movie seem prescient and events surrounding the real crisis eerie.

Then in 1986 came the explosion at Chernobyl in the Soviet Union. That accident sent so much radiation into the air that it contaminated crops, killed dozens of people, and sickened many others. Together, Three Mile Island and Chernobyl crippled nuclear power as a vibrant energy source in the United States. The standstill encountered by the industry through the 1970s and 1980s continued into the beginning of the 21st century.

PRESIDENT CARTER'S "CRISIS OF CONFIDENCE" SPEECH

With America beset by inflation, high unemployment, and an energy crisis, President Jimmy Carter went into retreat for several days and talked privately to leaders from around the nation. When he reappeared, he presented his "crisis of confidence" speech in July 1979. (It is sometimes called the crisis of spirit speech and was popularly called the malaise speech, although he never used the word *malaise.*) "All the legislation in the world can't fix what's wrong with America," he said. "In a nation that was proud of hard work, strong families, close-knit communities, and our faith in God, too many of us now tend to worship self-indulgence and consumption. Human identity is no longer defined by what one does, but by what one owns."[9]

Many people applauded Carter for hitting hard at the underlying causes of America's problems, but others considered it to be excessive sermonizing or, worse yet, a jeremiad. Carter seemed to be taking a cue from Howard Beale, the fictional and embittered television newscaster in an acclaimed movie of the decade, *Network.* His statements, like Beale's, were depressing and something most people did not particularly want to hear. Consequently, with this speech, the president opened himself to charges that he was a defeatist.

Continued bad economic developments added to the country's gloom. A recession had taken hold. With it, inflation and interest rates dropped, but unemployment soared. In July 1979, the jobless numbers hit 8.2 million, nearly

2 million more than at the start of the year. This brought the unemployment rate to 7.8 percent, and President Carter's advisers predicted that it would soon top 8 percent. Pressured by the recession and by pressure from Ronald Reagan, his Republican opponent in the forthcoming presidential campaign, Carter advocated a tax cut. (Reagan advocated a much deeper one.) He unveiled a comprehensive economic recovery program as well. But it was his *third* economic recovery program, a testament to his earlier efforts having accomplished little. He received, in fact, lukewarm reaction to his program. The president appeared to be spinning his wheels, and his crisis of confidence speech only heightened the sense of helplessness, leading more and more Americans to conclude that he was ineffective.

TED BUNDY

Thirty-three-year old Theodore Bundy sat in the courtroom in Miami, Florida, on July 30, 1979. His handsome face, topped by thick black hair, made him appear more the ladies' man than a killer. Confident and smug, he grinned when a jury recommended that he be sentenced to death for murdering two college sorority sisters in Tallahassee. "See you next trial," he said as he waved at the courtroom crowd. He would eventually admit to 40 killings, but he quite possibly killed as many as 100 women, a toll making him one of the most notorious serial killers in American history.

Ted Bundy grew up in Tacoma, Washington. Shy as a young man, his high school classmates nevertheless thought him personable, and he studied hard, earning good grades. In 1967, soon after entering the University of Washington, he fell in love with a beautiful young woman, Stephanie Brooks. They dated for about a year before she decided to end the relationship.

By then, Bundy had transferred to Stanford University. Disheartened by the breakup with Stephanie and overwhelmed by the work at Stanford, his grades suffered, and he decided to drop out of college. He returned to the University of Washington in 1969 and plunged into political activism, working for the Republican Party. At the same time, he began to date Stephanie again. The couple even began to talk about marriage.

But unknown to Stephanie, Bundy was seeing another woman, and, unknown to both women, he began his killing spree. His first victims resembled Stephanie—pretty and slender with hair parted down the middle. Joni Lentz fit the description. An 18-year-old who lived with several roommates in a large house in Seattle, Joni was viciously attacked by Bundy on January 4, 1974. He beat her and sodomized her. Amazingly, Joni survived the attack.

One month later, Bundy broke up with Stephanie—this time, he initiated the rupture—and during the next few months, seven women disappeared in Utah, Oregon, and Washington. Witnesses said that at the scenes they saw a handsome man driving a VW bug (a compact car). Several women said that the man approached them and, with his arm or leg in a cast, asked them for help in getting to his car. He told them that his name was Ted.

Bodies began to turn up, young women who had been murdered in brutal attacks, their bones crushed and their heads smashed from the power behind a blunt instrument, such as a crowbar. In one instance, a woman's teeth were separated from her gums by the force of the blows. Taylor Mountain in Washington state produced several dead bodies. Bundy knew the terrain there well and used it as a burial ground. These first victims, all of them attractive women cut down in their youth, were:

- Lynda Ann Healy, a radio announcer, a singer, and a senior at the University of Washington. She liked to work with mentally handicapped children. Bundy killed her in her bed—while roommates slept nearby oblivious to the crime—and then wrapped her in a bed sheet and carried her from her house.
- Janice Ott, who was last seen helping Bundy attach his boat to his car. He had a cast on his arm and asked for her assistance.
- Denise Naslund, who was last seen walking to a restroom in a park. She, too, helped Bundy with his boat.
- Melissa Smith, only 17 years old and the daughter of the Midvale, Utah, chief of police. Bundy strangled her and raped her.
- Laura Aime, also 17. Bundy beat her with a crowbar and then dumped her dead body near a river in Utah's Wasatch Mountains.

In August 1975, a Utah highway patrolman, Bob Hayward, stopped a tan VW bug. The car's driver was Ted Bundy. On searching the vehicle, Hayward found in it a pair of handcuffs, some rope, a crowbar, a ski mask, an ice pick, and a nylon stocking. He arrested Bundy on suspicion of burglary.

The police then asked three women to view a lineup that included Bundy. One of the women was Carol DaRonch, whom Bundy had tried to kidnap at a Utah mall. Bundy had posed as a security officer and lured DaRonch into his car. When he tried to handcuff her, she managed to escape. Now, DaRonch and the two other women picked Bundy from the lineup. Other evidence surfaced to connect Bundy to the abductions and assaults; primarily the plaster of Paris, which was found in his apartment and that he used to make casts for his arms and legs as well as records of credit-card purchases that he had made at service stations near where several victims had disappeared.

In February 1976, Bundy stood trial in Washington for the attempted kidnapping of DaRonch. That November, he was found guilty and sentenced to 15 years in prison. The following April, he was extradited to Colorado to stand trial for the murder, in 1975, of Caryn Campbell. While in custody in Aspen on June 7, he escaped, jumping from a second-story window at the Pitkin County courthouse to the building's steps 15 feet below after sheriff's deputies left him in a courtroom alone. One witness to the escape reported seeing the fleeing man and saying to a police officer, "Someone just jumped out of a window. Is that normal?"[10]

Bundy remained free for eight days and panicked the town. About 150 people formed a search party. Officials closed schools and banned the sales of guns and ammunition. The police set up road blocks as far as 90 miles from Aspen; they circulated handbills around town, and a search helicopter flew over the roads and hills. Angry and fearful residents locked their windows and doors. A teacher at Colorado Mountain College remarked: "This man is dangerous enough for the police department to warn citizens to stay inside and lock their doors, but he wasn't dangerous enough for them to watch him while he was in the courtroom."[11] The district attorney said, "There's no excuse for what happened yesterday."[12] Relief for Aspen came only when a dirty, unshaven, and hobbled Bundy, limping from an injured leg, was discovered trying to leave town in a stolen Cadillac. When he reappeared in the courthouse, he was accompanied by seven deputies. As to why he had fled, Bundy said, "I didn't want to go back to jail. It was just too pretty outside."[13]

The pretty days apparently remained appealing, and those guarding Bundy remained incompetent. Bundy escaped yet again in December 1977, this time from the Garfield County Jail in Glenwood Springs, Colorado. Ingeniously, he did so by losing enough weight to squeeze through a small hole in the ceiling of his cell. From there, he shimmied through an 18-inch-high crawl space, dropped down into a closet, and then nonchalantly walked out the jailhouse door. It took 15 hours for the authorities to discover that he was missing. The local district attorney called the jailers negligent and said that he was "extremely disappointed" in the escape.[14] A five-day search failed to find the fugitive.

Bundy soon went on another murder spree. He hitchhiked from Glenwood Springs, flew to Chicago, and then on to Florida where he rented an apartment in Tallahassee near the campus of Florida State University. In January 1978, he attacked four women at a sorority house as they slept in bed, killing two of them. Neither of the survivors was able to identify Bundy. One of the dead coeds, Lisa Levy, was clubbed, raped, and strangled, sexually assaulted with a hair-spray can, and severely bitten on the nipples and buttocks. The other, Margaret Bowman, had been clubbed so hard that her skull had been torn away from her brain.

A coed, Nita Neary, entering the sorority house around the time of the assaults hid under a stairway. She saw Bundy in the darkness, wearing a knit blue cap and carrying a log with cloth wrapped around it.

Bundy went from the sorority house to a nearby apartment where he attacked another young woman, clubbing her on the head. She survived the attack, and Bundy, in his rush to flee the scene, left behind a ski mask, similar to the one found in his car in Utah.

One month later, Bundy abducted 12-year-old Kimberly Leach in Lake City, Florida. The police soon discovered her body buried in a state park.

The end to Bundy's rampage came on February 15, 1978, when a policeman in Pensacola, Florida, David Lee, stopped an orange VW bug because it bore stolen license plates. Lee ordered the driver from the car. Out stepped Bundy. When Lee tried to handcuff him, he fled. Lee, however, fired a warning shot with his revolver, and Bundy stopped running.

Bundy stood trial twice. The first trial, held in Miami, began in June 1979 and involved the assaults and murders at the sorority house in Tallahassee. Bundy acted as his own defense attorney. The prosecution had two major pieces of evidence. One was Nita Neary's identification of Bundy as the man whom she saw leaving the sorority house. The other was the bite marks on Lisa Levy's body. They turned out to match the pattern of Bundy's teeth.

The jury deliberated for seven hours. On July 23, it announced its guilty verdict. Bundy showed no emotion and publicly continued to swear to his innocence. Eight days later, he received the death sentence, with the judge calling his murder of the two sorority sisters "heinous, vicious, and cruel."[15] Bundy said he had been convicted by the press, by reporters anxious to find a culprit for the murders.

Bundy's second trial began in January 1980. This time, he was represented by two defense attorneys and pleaded not guilty by reason of insanity to the charge of murdering Kimberly Leach. The prosecution presented as its most damaging evidence fibers from Kimberly Leach's clothes that were found in Bundy's van and on his own clothes. In February, a jury found him guilty.

This trial took a surprise turn when, at his sentencing hearing, Bundy interviewed defense witness Carole Ann Boone, a friend and a divorcee, and then proposed marriage to her. She agreed right there, on the stand, an acceptance that, because she was under oath, meant that the two were immediately legally married. In 1982, she gave birth to their only child.

During the next several years, Bundy pursued numerous appeals. He made his final one to the U.S. Supreme Court, which denied his stay of execution. He was executed in the Florida electric chair on January 24, 1989. Hundreds of people who had gathered outside the prison walls cheered his death.

In the mid-1980s, Bundy met with Bob Keppel, the chief investigator in the criminal division of the Washington state attorney general's office and helped him pursue another murderer, the "Green River killer." In the hours before Bundy was executed, he met with Keppel again and confessed to 40 murders. Keppel recounted his meetings with Bundy in his book, *The Riverman: Ted Bundy and I Hunt for the Green River Killer,* and told how Bundy had kept some of his victims' heads at his home as trophies and had engaged in necrophilia. Keppel called it an extreme perversion. An intelligent, handsome man given to the most horrendous of serial murders, Bundy made his life into an extreme perversion.

THE RESIGNATION OF ANDREW YOUNG

Andrew Young, the first African-American ambassador to the United Nations, was known for being outspoken and impulsive. In July 1979, those qualities got him and the Jimmy Carter administration into trouble when he met with a representative of the Palestine Liberation Organization (PLO) and then denied the nature of the meeting. Before long, Jews were calling for Young to resign, blacks were attacking Jews for their criticism of Young, and U.S. policy in the Middle East was in danger of unraveling.

Carter appointed Young as U.S. ambassador to the UN in 1977, a move that won the president praise from African Americans. Young came into office knowing the sensitive nature of American relations in the Middle East. The United States had a long-standing policy of avoiding contacts with the PLO to avoid any diplomatic recognition that would, in turn, anger Israel.

Nevertheless, Young met on July 26 with PLO representative Zehdi Labib Terzi at the townhouse of the Kuwaiti representative to the UN. When news of the meeting first began to circulate, Young denied that the meeting had been planned. He said that it was nothing more than a chance encounter at which he and Terzi exchanged pleasantries.

But Young later admitted that he had been less than forthright. The meeting with Terzi, he said, had indeed been planned, and he and the PLO representative discussed getting the Security Council to postpone a debate on Palestinian rights. Young added that he acted without first informing the state department.

The meeting came at a particularly bad time for President Carter. During the previous few months, he had been trying to reach out to moderate Arabs in an attempt to forge a new UN resolution relating to the Middle East. His effort was seen by Israel as a threat to its interests. In fact, the Israelis disliked

Carter for shifting U.S. policy toward the Arabs. To them, the shift seemed all the more evident with Carter's recent decision to sell 300 tanks to Jordan.

Carter sought a rapprochement with Arab countries in part because of the threat of another oil boycott. His administration let it be known that such a boycott could occur unless there were progress on the Palestinian issue. But his reaction to the threat only further annoyed Israel. For his part, Carter thought that the Israelis were being obstructionists in their opposition to a new UN resolution.

As much as the brouhaha over Young's meeting hampered Carter's Middle East policy, it hurt him domestically too. The dispute ignited a sharp conflict between two traditional Democratic constituencies: blacks and Jews. Blacks disliked the Jewish pressure to get Young to resign, and Jews disliked the black defense of Young. The animosity reached the stage where African-American leaders began to hurl anti-Semitic epithets at Jewish leaders, and Jewish leaders began to hurl racist epithets at African-American leaders.

Under pressure from Carter, Young finally decided to quit, saying that he had become a liability to the president. He said: "I have chosen to remove myself. It is no longer just my risk. I see myself in some ways continuing to jeopardize the administration."[16] At the same time, he urged African Americans to support Carter for reelection.

Black leaders, though, expressed dismay:

"I had no idea that what appeared to me to be a perfectly logical conversation would be catapulted into this proportion. If we are to have peace, somebody had better talk to [the Palestinians]," said Representative Walter Fauntroy (Dem., Washington, D.C.).[17]

Andrew Young, here shown at his swearing-in ceremony to become U.S. representative to become U.S. representative to the United Nations, was forced to quit after meeting with an official of the PLO. *(Courtesy Jimmy Carter Library)*

"If we have to maintain [Jewish] friendship by refraining from speaking to Arabs, then that friendship must be reassessed," said Reverend Joseph Lowery, the president of the Southern Christian Leadership Conference.[18]

"So the president has apparently decided to sacrifice Africa, the third world, and Black Americans. I think it's tragic," said Reverend Jesse Jackson.[19]

Many Jews expressed remorse about Young having to depart the UN, but they remained wary about Carter's policies in the Middle East. Yaser Arafat, leader of the PLO, condemned the pressure put on Young and called him a believer "in the just cause of the Palestinian people."[20] For Carter, the Young resignation damaged his reelection bid. The decision to pressure Young to quit was a difficult one. A Carter aide said about the president: "He knew he had to take him out. He was heartsick about it."[21]

SHOOTING AT AN ANTI-KLAN RALLY

When leftist radicals decided to stage a "Death to the Klan" march in Greensboro, North Carolina, the KKK reacted with gunfire and killed five protesters in the deadliest civil rights confrontation since the 1960s. The event has since been called the Greensboro Massacre.

Greensboro had earned a place in history in 1960, when black college students staged a sit-in to protest the segregation at the local Woolworth's store. Since then the town had experienced relative quiet as race relations improved. Thus the violence in 1979 took many people within and outside the town by surprise.

Members of the Workers Viewpoint Organization, also known as the Communist Workers Party, put together the Death to the Klan march. The group was active in organizing textile workers in the state and had only recently begun campaigning against the Klan.

Several months before the shooting, on July 8, members of the Workers Viewpoint Organization disrupted a KKK rally. In the ensuing days, they called out the KKK and antagonized them with flyers in which they called the Klansmen "racist cowards."

Then, on November 3, as the anti-Klan protesters began their march through a black neighborhood of Greensboro, about 75 Klansmen and Nazis pulled up in cars and began to shout at them. The protesters reacted by pounding on the cars with their fists. Minutes later, one Klansman opened the trunk of his car and pulled out a gun. Other Klansmen jumped from a van, and with shotguns and semiautomatics in hand, they began to fire at the protesters. A few of the protesters pulled out guns of their own, although most had no protection, and, according to one, the group was unable to get off a shot. The wife of another protester later recalled: "I heard the firing start. I ducked behind a car. I saw the person next to me pull back and he was shot. I think he was dead."[22] A television news reporter recounted: "People were scrambling and ducking and diving for cover. It went on for about two minutes. It was continuous shooting."[23]

In the fusillade, four protesters were killed (three of them white men, the fourth a black woman) and several others were injured. Another protester died from his wounds a few days later.

The police had pulled back from the protest scene before the Death to the Klan march began. As a result, they were absent when the shooting started. But they arrived a short time later and arrested several Klansmen on four counts of murder and one count of conspiring to commit murder. They later arrested a leader of the Workers Viewpoint Organization, based on the incendiary nature of the group's pamphlets, for inciting to riot.

Six Klansmen were placed on trial, and an all-white jury acquitted all but one of them based on self-defense. Many civil rights activists found the jury decision disturbing and charged the jury members with bias against the communists and against blacks. The families of the dead protesters and the survivors filed a civil suit in 1985; as a result, two Greensboro police officers, along with their Klan informant and four of the Klan and Nazi members were found liable for the deaths and injuries.

Today there remain several unanswered questions about the event. They include why the jury at the murder trial reached the decision that it did; why the police failed to protect the marchers; and whether the federal government played any role in encouraging the attack by the Klansmen. Many years later, protester Signe Wallace insisted that the FBI had shown the attackers how to use their guns. She called it a well-planned attack. In spring 2004, Greensboro set up a special group called the Truth and Reconciliation Commission to investigate the circumstances surrounding the tragic event of 25 years earlier.

A REVOLUTION IN IRAN

The U.S. embassy in Tehran, Iran, stood in the center of a revolution whose nature and intensity challenged American power and damaged Jimmy Carter's presidency. Most Westerners found it to be an unfathomable uprising, one marked more by religion than by economics, by ideals more than pragmatism.

Prior to the late 1970s, only occasionally did Iran register on the American consciousness, primarily right after World War II, when the Soviet Union signaled that it might attempt to take over the entire country, and in the early 1950s, when the Iranian parliament voted to nationalize the Anglo-Iranian Oil Company (AIOC).

At that time, the British government had controlling interest in the AIOC and objected strenuously to the nationalization. During the crisis, the shah of Iran, Reza Pahlavi, appointed Mohammad Mossadegh as prime minister.

Mossadegh increasingly relied on communists for support, leading the U.S. president, Dwight Eisenhower, to think that the Soviets might use the oil crisis as an excuse for staging a Marxist coup. Consequently, with the help of the British, the Central Intelligence Agency engineered a plan to overthrow Mossadegh—in effect, an American coup to preempt any Soviet coup. Mossadegh was overthrown in 1953, a move that many Iranians supported, for they disliked his aggrandizement of power at the expense of the shah. Yet, at a later date, Iranians would deride the coup as nothing less than America trampling Iran's sovereignty; ultimately, it made the shah appear to be a mere tool of the United States.

By the 1960s, traditional Muslims were condemning the shah for his promotion of a modern, Westernized society. In 1963, the attacks were led by Ruhollah Khomeini, a *mujtahid,* or religious authority. Khomeini criticized the shah for violating the constitution, called the government and society corrupt, and portrayed Western influence as evil. As protests expanded, the shah cracked down on them, and when riots erupted, he blamed them on Khomeini while ignoring a more widespread dissatisfaction in society. With the riots and the shah's reaction to them, Khomeini grew to hate the United States and came to see the shah as an American puppet.

The Iranian authorities arrested Khomeini, and in 1964 he went into exile, first living in Turkey and then in Iraq. At the same time, the shah reformed landholding in Iran to make it more equitable, extended voting rights to women, and privatized state industries, measures endorsed and hailed by the United States. Iran experienced unprecedented prosperity, but unevenly, with poverty and illiteracy remaining widespread. The country had a dual personality: Many professionals who enjoyed the prosperity supported the shah while many Muslim clerics and the impoverished opposed him. And alongside the progressive reforms stood the repressive tactics that were used by the shah's secret police, SAVAK.

Much of Iran's prosperity came directly from oil, whose revenues increased from $555 million in 1963 to $5 billion in 1973. Iran had become an important supplier of oil to the West and a bulwark against Soviet expansion in the Persian Gulf.

Thus in the late 1960s and early 1970s, President Richard Nixon and his National Security Advisor (later secretary of state), Henry Kissinger, developed close relations with the shah, culminating in 1972 with agreements whereby additional American advisers went to Iran and provided the shah with the most sophisticated conventional U.S. weapons that were available.

In time, Iran's oil revenues allowed the shah to buy almost any military hardware he wanted, and, with Nixon in the White House, the Iranian ruler ordered $9 billion worth of weaponry. Presently, the shah was telling the Americans what weapons he wanted and getting them with no hesitation.

This relationship, including the massive reliance on the shah to protect America's interests in the Persian Gulf, was inherited by President Carter. For a few more months, the arrangement worked. But soon the clerical opposition to the shah found new supporters. When the Iranian economy began to sputter, the professionals and others whose expectations had been raised, now only to be dashed, began to question the legitimacy of the shah.

The first violent episode in the revolution occurred in January 1978 when the government condemned Khomeini. This led to a religious demonstration in Qom (about 100 miles south of Tehran), during which the police fired into the crowd and killed several students. Their deaths caused Ayatollah Shariatmadari, a powerful religious leader in the city, to label the shah's government anti-Islamic.

Other massive demonstrations followed, with the protestors seeking to topple the shah. The crowds included unemployed young men and involved attacks on the symbols of Western society. Clearly, social and religious forces were merging, and as the threat intensified, the government, through SAVAK, reacted with repressive tactics, such as bombing the opposition leaders' houses, declaring martial law, and banning demonstrations.

The United States reacted slowly to these developments, its officials failing to see the peril that was facing the shah and continuing to believe that the status quo would continue. Conditions in Iran, however, only worsened. On September 8, 1978, 20,000 protesters gathered at Jaleh Square in Tehran for a religious rally in defiance of an existing ban against demonstrations. When the crowd refused to disperse, soldiers fired into it. Some of the protesters may have fired back. The violence resulted in several hundred, perhaps several thousand, deaths.

Jaleh Square was an enormous step in the revolution. The bloodshed there shocked the shah, as did other clashes that left hundreds more dead, and a march by one million demonstrators in Tehran. At the same time, Khomeini called for a general strike to overthrow the shah. Within a short time, the turmoil crippled the country's oil industry and the lucrative income that it provided the government.

These developments caused the shah to change course. In a move that was meant in part to quiet those critics who saw his military spending as yet another sellout to the West, he decreased his spending on armaments. The shah used some of the money that he thereby saved to pay for property damaged in the numerous riots and to provide aid to the families of those protesters who had been killed. Additionally, he freed more than 100 political prisoners and partially lifted a curfew.

Still the shah's position deteriorated. To lessen Khomeini's reach from Iraq, the shah had pressured the Iraqis to remove Khomeini from their country. Dictator Saddam Hussein needed little encouragement to do so, for he, too, worried about Khomeini's influence. From Iraq, Khomeini moved to Paris, but the greater distance from Iran did nothing to reduce his influence; in fact, he used the shah's modern, Western-style telephone system to keep in contact with his supporters in Iran.

Few political experts ever thought that the Iranian revolution would become a religious one, and it was indeed likely that only a minority of the revolutionaries themselves embraced religious radicalism. But Khomeini possessed a fiery vision, and he sought to unite church and state to form an Islamic republic that was guided by a supreme religious figure.

Moreover, few political experts thought that the shah's regime would topple as quickly as it did. David Harris writes in *The Crisis: The President, the Prophet, and the Shah—1979 and the Coming of Militant Islam:* "Thanks to a belated warning from Ambassador William Sullivan, President Jimmy Carter finally learned on November 2, 1978, that the shah might actually fall. It was now almost ten months to the day since the Iranian Revolution began, and heretofore . . . the cables from Sullivan had . . . given no hint that His Imperial Majesty's rule was truly in jeopardy."[24] On January 16, 1979, the shah capitulated when he boarded an airliner for Egypt (although he called it a temporary absence). In early February, Khomeini arrived in Tehran to the delight of jubilant Iranians, who turned out in huge numbers to greet him. Within short order, the prime minister resigned, and the military announced that it would not oppose Khomeini. Iran had a new leader.

When the shah left Iran, he found it difficult to arrange asylum. He stayed first in Egypt, and then in Morocco. He wanted to accept an earlier invitation from the United States to make America his home, but the U.S. government was reluctant to accept him while it was involved in delicate negotiations with Iran's revolutionary leaders to secure the safety of American officials in Tehran and elsewhere. The Americans believed that were they to admit the shah, they would ignite retaliatory moves by Iranians against Americans. (President Carter eventually rescinded the invitation.)

Jimmy Carter is seen here meeting with the shah of Iran. *(Courtesy Jimmy Carter Library)*

So the shah went to the Bahamas on a 60-day visa before President Carter arranged asylum for him in Mexico. In May 1979, the Iranian government warned Carter against admitting either the shah or his wife into the United States. The matter became more complicated in October when U.S. officials learned that the shah had cancer. Secretary of state Cyrus Vance then advised President Carter to admit the shah into the United States for medical treatment. On October 21, American officials informed the Iranian prime minister of its decision to do so, though it assured him that the shah would be granted only temporary residence.

Carter had little option but to allow the shah in. To deny the monarch would have invited condemnation for failing to provide a seriously ill man humanitarian aid. Writing in *All Fall Down,* Gary Sick states, "Once the seriousness of the shah's condition became known, there was simply no question of refusing him medical attention."[25] Outside the shah's hospital in New York City, about 200 demonstrators shouted "Death to the shah! The shah is a murderer! Down with U.S. imperialism! Down with the CIA!"[26]

IRANIAN REVOLUTIONARIES TAKE OVER THE U.S. EMBASSY

In their attacks against the West, the revolutionaries aimed primarily at the United States. America became the Great Satan, hated for its past intervention in Iranian affairs. Khomeini stoked the revolutionary flames with his vehemence toward the United States and encouraged and supported a mob of radical students in their takeover of the U.S. embassy in November and in their holding the embassy staff as hostages.

The embassy had been attacked months before, in February. In reaction, officials improved security. They installed surveillance cameras, remote-controlled tear-gas devices, and heavy steel doors. At first, the number of staffers was reduced to the bare bones, but during the summer, the number climbed to about 70. That may well have been a mistake, along with the number of sensitive documents kept in the files. Yet, no one expected that the embassy would actually be invaded. In fact, Americans and revolutionary moderates alike considered it important to keep the embassy open to maintain lines of communication, and when revolutionary students led an anti-American protest near the building on November 1, the government sent police to protect it.

Nevertheless, through his public speeches, Khomeini sent a signal to the revolutionary students: He would support radical assaults on the Americans. He stated: "Students and theological students [must] expand with all their might their attacks against the United States and Israel, so they may force the United States to return the deposed and criminal shah."[27] Three days later, on November 4, 1979, about 3,000 protesters stormed the 27-acre embassy compound. Carrying signs reading "Death To America Is A Beautiful Thought" and "Give Us The Shah," they climbed over the front gates, pried open the windows, surged past the marine guards, and swarmed into the basement and first floor of the chancellery.

For two hours, the embassy staff hid behind the building's steel doors until the students found them and took them as hostages. A statement released by the students confirmed Khomeini's influence. "A few days ago, the [ayatollah] said the Iranian nation must clean up its situation vis-à-vis the United States," it said. "This action is a kind of recognition of that situation. America must know it can not play with the feelings of the Iranian nation."[28] The students called the embassy a center for American spies.

HEIGHTENED TENSION WITH THE TAKEOVER

"Nov. 4, 1979—We were taken back to the Compound, being pushed and hurried along the way and forced to put our hands above our heads and then marched to the Embassy residence. After arriving at the residence I had my hands tied behind my back so tightly with nylon cord that circulation was cut off. I was taken upstairs and put alone in a rear bedroom and after a short time was blindfolded. After protesting strongly that the cord was too tight the cord was removed and the blindfold taken off when they tried to feed me some dates and I refused to eat anything I couldn't see. I strongly protested the violation of my diplomatic immunity, but these protests were ignored. I then was required to sit in a chair facing the bedroom wall. Then another older student came in and when I again protested the violation of my diplomatic immunity he confiscated my U.S. Mission Tehran I.D. card. My hands were again tied and I was taken to the Embassy living room on the ground floor where a number of other hostages were gathered. Some students attempted to talk with us, stating how they didn't hate Americans—only our U.S. Government, President Carter, etc."

—*Robert Ode, hostage*[29]

"The young men and women who participated in the embassy takeover did so based on their conviction that their action was in line with [Khomeini's] policy."

—*Massoumeh Ebtekar, a leader of the revolutionary students*[30]

The assault surprised the Iranian foreign ministry, and it was uncertain how the government would react to it. Then, however, Khomeini's son, Ahmed, arrived at the embassy and joined the students. At that point, the moderate prime minister, Bazargan, resigned, and the radicals consolidated their power on the governing Revolutionary Council.

In taking over the embassy, Iran followed a perilous course. Embassies were sacrosanct in the international community. To allow a mob to commandeer one and hold its staff hostage was unheard of in modern times. By backing the students, Khomeini risked casting revolutionary Iran as an outlaw state: He risked sanctions and other retribution, and he risked consigning Iran to diplomatic oblivion, making it a completely isolated country.

But Khomeini aimed to use the shah's entry into the United States and the embassy takeover as a tool for radicalizing the revolution and using it to create an Islamic state. In *All Fall Down* Gary Sick writes: "The shah, the hostages, and even the students in the embassy became pawns in a high-risk political strategy intended to ensure that the 'second act' of the revolution would be played out according to Khomeini's script."[31]

The students thought that they would hold the embassy hostages for only a few days. Khomeini, however, kept the revolutionary fire blazing by inciting the students to stand fast in the fight against the American devil. He portrayed the admittance of the shah into the United States as part of a foreign plot against the revolution, and he called his opponents in Iran "traitors . . . dependent on the West." He said: "These American-loving rotten brains must be purged from the nation."[32]

In addition to taking the hostages, the students confiscated most of the embassy's documents. They even took those that the staff had shredded and laboriously pasted them together. The documents revealed the names of Iranians in the country who had contacted the embassy, including revolutionaries who had talked with the American officials about limiting violence in the upheaval. The revelations especially damaged moderates, who were subsequently branded as American sympathizers. From the standpoint of the revolutionaries, as Massoumeh Ebtekar later said: "These documents would help all Iranians, from intellectuals to the man and woman on the street, realize the true intentions of the Great Satan toward the Islamic Revolution."[33]

The taking of the hostages made a mockery of the prevailing opinion in Washington that Khomeini would be unable to consolidate his power; that the ayatollah would, in fact, fade into the background as more pragmatic revolutionaries came to the fore. Carter and most Middle East experts believed that the United States could establish a working relationship with moderates. They failed to realize Khomeini's commitment to fighting the Great Satan and his ability to rally Iranians to his cause. Khomeini exhorted his followers: "These days, whenever one asks about his enemy, he says: My enemy is first of all the United States. We demand the return of the great criminal shah from the United States. America must return the great criminal shah from the United States. America must return him to us."[34]

For President Carter, the hostage-taking produced a predicament. If he downplayed the crisis, he might be criticized for being weak. If he reacted with force, he might cause the students to harm their captives. Writing in the *New York Times,* military analyst Drew Middleton said, "Today, force is the last and most dangerous option open to a superpower caught, as the United States now is, in a seeming insoluble situation in Tehran."[35]

President Carter rejected demands by the militant students and Khomeini to return the shah to Iran. Then, in early November, he developed a policy that he would continue to follow for the remainder of his term. First, he launched political, diplomatic, and economic initiatives that combined persuasion with pressure to win the hostages release. Second, he ordered military contingency planning of two types: a rescue mission and a retaliatory or punitive mission planned in such a way as to avoid miring American troops in a protracted fight in Iran from which it would be difficult to extricate them. Gary Sick states: "The U.S. campaign of persuasion and pressure that was mounted in the days and weeks following the hostage seizure was probably the most extensive and sustained effort of its kind ever conducted in peacetime."[36] Pressure came from around the world. Wherever Iran's representatives traveled, they faced criticism for taking hostages. In Cairo, the newspaper *Al Ahram* asked: "Does Islam advocate that one should hunt down a fatally sick man and urge his assassination? Does Islam urge murders, extremism, and autocracy?"[37]

At the same time, the hostage seizure emerged as the leading news story in the United States. The media saturated the public with the crisis—newspaper and television photographs showed the blindfolded hostages being paraded in front of the students—making it all the more difficult for Carter to set the issue aside and providing the radical Iranians with a stage for their views. "Criminal American! Criminal American!" a crowd chanted at Barry Rosen, the embassy spokesperson, as he stood blindfolded, hands tied in front of him, on the embassy grounds.[38]

On November 12, Carter ended all imports of Iranian oil. Two days later, he froze Iranian assets in the United States. On November 20, the Iranians released 13 hostages in response to intervention by the Palestine Liberation Organization. When the hostages arrived in Germany, they told tales that only fueled the outrage in the United States: how they had been forced to remain silent, endure bondage, and undergo brainwashing. Carter reacted to the stories by publicizing the harsh treatment, hoping that it would cause other governments to place more pressure on Iran. The negative publicity influenced Khomeini, who told the students to treat the hostages humanely. As a result, the students ended some of their excessive practices. Captive Robert Ode wrote in his diary:

> December 11, 1979: About 1:30 or 2:00 A.M.—I was awakened, blindfolded and taken to another room in the Residence; a bedroom at the southwest corner. I was given a mattress to lie on. Shortly thereafter two other hostages, Bruce German, B&F Officer, and Robert Blucher, Commercial Attaché, were brought into the room to replace Barry Rosen and another hostage who were taken elsewhere. Although the drapes were drawn at all times and we had the usual guard in the room 24 hours a day and a light burning all night, as usual, it was, in general, a more comfortable room, as we had a bathroom leading off our room that, at first, was fairly clean, and was not used by too many others.[39]

Moreover, Carter tried to get the UN Security Council to impose sanctions on Iran, but the Soviet Union vetoed the measure. Carter then said that the United States would impose its own sanctions, and he asked other countries to do likewise. The European governments, however, refrained, saying that more time was needed to pursue a diplomatic solution to the crisis.

At this stage, most Americans rallied behind Carter. In *The Presidency of James Earl Carter, Jr.,* Burton I. Kaufman observes: "As Americans watched Iranian crowds taunt the United States, the president's prestige soared. According to a Gallup poll, in the four weeks since the hostages had been seized, the public approval of Carter's presidency jumped from 30 percent to 61 percent, the sharpest gain ever in a Gallup survey of presidential popularity."[40] Revolutionary Massoumeh Ebtekar thought otherwise: "Less than a year after the fall of the shah, the taking of the hostages seemed to prove to the world that the idea of 'American leadership' was superficial, and could not prevail against the faith and determination of ordinary people in the millions."[41]

As the 1970s ended, the hostage crisis continued, seemingly impossible to resolve. The media kept a count of the number of days the hostages were in captivity, and with each day that passed, frustration in the United States intensified. A bit of good news came in January 1980. At the time of the embassy takeover, five Americans escaped from the chancellery through an exit, and a sixth diplomat escaped detection in another building. Canadian and other Western families in Iran hid them. The Americans then changed their identity, and on January 29, they took a flight to safety in Europe.

A RESCUE MISSION FAILS

In spring 1980, President Carter decided to use his military option and rescue the hostages. The attempt turned into an embarrassing failure.

As the crisis remained intractable, officials from the United States and Panama had attempted to bargain for a deal that involved a special UN commission whose members would first meet with the hostages to ascertain their condition. The deal looked liked it might work when Iran's new president, Abolhassan Bani-Sadr, elected as a political moderate, in January 1980, expressed his desire to end the crisis. But negotiations collapsed when Khomeini insisted that, before it meet with the hostages, the commission investigate "the crimes committed by the ousted shah and the interferences by the aggressive United States."[42]

Carter then sent a message to Bani-Sadr, noting the Iranian president's earlier comments criticizing the holding of the hostages and reminding Bani-Sadr of a promise that he had made to transfer control of the hostages to the Iranian government by March 15. Carter said that if this were not done by March 31, he would pursue "additional non-belligerent measures that we have withheld until now."[43]

In yet another statement, Bani-Sadr indicated that the Iranian government still wanted to end the students' role in the hostage crisis. Consequently, Carter backed away from the March 31 deadline. At Khomeini's behest, however, the Revolutionary Council vetoed Bani-Sadr's plan.

The American public heaped criticism on Carter for his change of course, and the president reacted to the reversal in Tehran by imposing new sanctions on Iran and breaking diplomatic relations. Importantly, he ordered the rescue mission to be launched, telling his advisers that America's honor was at stake.

Carter's Joint Chiefs of Staff compiled a complex plan, one Gary Sick calls "a grueling and technically difficult operation."[44] Nevertheless, the president's advisers assured Carter that the mission could succeed. In the first stage, men and equipment were gathered in the Middle East and Indian Ocean, and a landing site, called Desert One, was designated southeast of Tehran. In *The Guts to Try*, Colonel James H. Kyle, the deputy commander of the joint task force in charge of the mission, writes: "It is no small undertaking to move thirty-four special-mission aircraft and twenty support aircraft 8,000 miles to a remote corner of the world and set up clandestine operations without slipping up and attracting unwanted attention somewhere along the way—but that's what we did."[45]

Because it was determined that the entire operation must be conducted in darkness, the planners set aside two nights for its completion. On the first night, eight helicopters would depart from the aircraft carrier USS *Nimitz* in the Arabian Sea and join eight C-130 aircraft that were scheduled to depart from several different locations. Together, they were to fly at a low altitude for 500 miles across the Iranian desert, beneath the detection of radar, and land at Desert One. There, the C-130s would refuel the helicopters and load them with soldiers and equipment. The helicopters would then fly to a remote site in the mountains near Tehran and wait through the next day in hiding.

The second night, the helicopters would be flown to Tehran, the troops would disembark, and the hostages would be rescued and flown aboard the helicopters to a deserted airfield. The helicopters would then be abandoned, and the soldiers and hostages would be flown to safety aboard transport aircraft.

But problems arose early in the mission, which began on April 24. A short distance into Iran, a warning light in one of the helicopters indicated a faulty rotor blade. The pilot decided to land, and he and his crew were rescued by one of the other choppers. While the C-130s encountered no problem flying into Iran, two blinding dust clouds forced the helicopters to become separated.

Four hours into the mission, a second helicopter encountered a problem when its flight instruments malfunctioned. The pilot flew back through the dust cloud and returned to the *Nimitz*. The remaining six helicopters continued onward. Then, in the normally desolate desert, they happened across a busload of Iranians, a fuel truck, and a pickup truck. The helicopters attacked and stopped the bus, and they blew up the fuel truck, but the pickup truck escaped.

When the aircraft arrived at Desert One, yet another problem occurred: A hydraulic leak crippled a third helicopter. The squadron was now reduced to five helicopters—according to the plan, one less than the minimum needed to continue the mission. "Just when we thought we had it made," writes Colonel Kyle, "a third helicopter had crapped out, leaving us one short. Never in my wildest nightmares would I have believed that of the eight helicopters launched on the mission, three would abort."[46] Moreover, the dust clouds had caused the helicopters to arrive late, meaning that the cover of darkness would soon be gone. With these new obstacles jeopardizing the entire plan, the commander at Desert One, Colonel Charles Beckwith, decided to end the mission. Colonel Kyle, aboard one of the C-130s, reluctantly agreed, and when President Carter learned of the decision, he, too, agreed with it.

An even bigger tragedy then struck. As the helicopters were refueling to leave Desert One, one chopper kicked up dust with its rotor blades and, in the blinding conditions, collided with a C-130. The accident caused the C-130, loaded with fuel, to explode. "Red-hot chunks of streaking metal painted incandescent lines across the landscape," writes Kyle. "Jet fuel, bullets, grenades, and missiles were the ingredients in this flaming cauldron."[47] The inferno killed eight men and wounded five others. Kyle writes: "There was a sadness gripping all of us . . . sadness and anger at this final catastrophe that was heaped upon our failure."[48]

The survivors boarded the remaining C-130s and fled the scene, abandoning the helicopters and the dead bodies. The failed mission jeopardized the safety of the hostages and likely lengthened their captivity. A saddened President Carter went on national television to explain the disaster to the American people, and although the public at first rallied behind him, his support quickly faded. Gary Sick concludes: "The rescue mission was a failure, but it was a failure of military execution, not of political judgment or command."[49] Yet the tragedy had great political impact. As Burton I. Kaufman observes: "The failure of the rescue attempt probably did more to undermine the Carter presidency than any other single event. . . . As details of the botched plan were revealed, it became another entry in a long list of failures that many Americans attributed to the president."[50]

In the wake of the mission, the Iranian students separated the hostages into groups and dispersed them to different locations. Carter's standing among the American people received another blow when pictures broadcast on television showed Iranians descending on Desert One and poking knives at the charred remains of the American soldiers. Carter stated: "This indicates quite clearly the kinds of people we've been dealing with. They did not bring shame and dishonor on the fallen Americans. They brought shame and dishonor on themselves."[51]

By late summer, Iran was involved in a fierce war with Iraq, which began when Iraqi dictator Saddam Hussein attacked his chaotic neighbor. The American hostages could see the Iraqi planes striking Tehran and cheered the bombardment.

In the United States, Carter turned back a serious challenge to him in the Democratic presidential primaries by Massachusetts senator Edward Kennedy. But he lost the general election in November to Republican Ronald Reagan. Few doubted at the time, and few have doubted since, that the hostage crisis played a crucial role (although far from an absolute one) in determining the outcome of the election. Carter well knew that the release of the hostages before the election would likely allow him to catapult ahead of Reagan in the polls. The Republicans knew this, too, and Reagan's campaign manager, William Casey, set up an elaborate intelligence operation to gather information about any possible deal with Iran that might result in the hostages' release, or what Casey called an October Surprise by the president.

The operation included using retired military officers to look for any unusual movements at air bases and collecting information from informants at the CIA, the National Security Council, and even inside the White House situation room (where strategy was discussed). Moreover, Casey began to plant stories in October about a possible release of the hostages, an action that he undertook to raise the public's expectations. He thought if the hostages were released, his preemptory stories might dilute the impact of the event; if they were not released, the public might become even more disgruntled with Carter.

Casey indeed had something to worry about. His intelligence operation came amid renewed contacts between the United States and Iran over the hostages. Given these discussions and Casey's ambitious efforts, the question was raised after the November election as to whether he and other Republicans had been involved in secret discussions with representatives from Iran to delay the release of the hostages so as to deprive Carter of any "October Surprise." Since 1980, several books and articles have asserted such a scenario. Congress went so far as to establish an October Surprise Task Force to investigate the charges. A final report released in November 1992 by the special counsel found no solid evidence to support the charges. The special counsel stated: "The credible evidence now known falls far short of supporting the allegations of an agreement between the Reagan campaign and Iran to delay the release of the hostages."[52]

But the special counsel added: "The totality of the evidence does suggest that Casey was 'fishing in troubled waters,' and that he conducted informal, clandestine, and potentially dangerous efforts on behalf of the Reagan campaign to gather intelligence on the volatile and unpredictable course of the hostage negotiations between the Carter administration and Iran."[53] Moreover, the special counsel reprimanded Reagan. The report states:

Special Counsel was disappointed by President Reagan's declination of the request for an interview. President Reagan's written reply was wholly inadequate to explain his off-hand but apparently relevant comment to a reporter that he had acted in some fashion as a candidate in connection with the hostage crisis.[54]

Despite the special counsel's conclusion, the evidence remains unsettled. As David Harris writes in *The Crisis: The President, the Prophet, and the Shah*, several Iranian leaders at the time of the hostage crisis and later said that there were discussions with the Republicans. Iranian foreign minister Sadegh Ghotbzadeh claimed that Ronald Reagan, banker David Rockefeller, and former secretary of state Henry Kissinger were all trying to block negotiations. Iranian president Abolhassan Bani-Sadr said that Reagan's envoys wanted to make a deal with him and played him off against his opponents among the Iranian revolutionaries.

In mid-November, the United States and Iran began to exchange notes through an Algerian intermediary. (The death of the shah on July 27 had raised hopes of a break in the impasse over the summer, but nothing had come of it.) Carter said that in exchange for the release of the hostages, he would sign a presidential order promising that the United States would refrain from interfering in Iran's internal affairs. Additionally, he would release all assets to Iran; end all economic and financial sanctions against Iran; give to Iran financial records detailing the shah's property holdings in the United States; and see to it that the federal government did not block Iran's legal claims to the shah's property.

There ensued a lengthy haggling over money. In the end, Iran got much less than it was seeking. The total amounted to $3.67 billion to retire bank loans made by the United States to the shah's government; $1.42 billion placed in escrow to settle disputed claims between American and Iranian banks; and $2.88 billion paid directly to Iran.

The United States and Iran finalized the deal on the morning of January 20, 1981, the day Jimmy Carter left the White House and Ronald Reagan entered it. Carter had worked tirelessly on getting the hostages released, even foregoing sleep during his last two days in office. As he departed Reagan's inauguration and headed back to his home state of Georgia, two planes took off from Tehran with the hostages on board. To Carter's aides, Iran's holding on to the hostages until Reagan had taken the oath of office amounted to just another dig at Carter, denying him the actual release while he was still president of the United States. The hostage crisis had lasted 444 days.

A Crowd Goes Wild against Disco

A half-satirical, half-serious demonstration against disco turned sour on July 12, 1979, when an unruly mob at Chicago's Comiskey Park forced the cancellation of a White Sox baseball game.

Local disc jockey Steve Dahl, of WLUP, an FM rock-and-roll station in Chicago, staged the protest in cooperation with Mike Veeck, the son of White Sox owner Bill Veeck and the team's director of promotions. Dahl had been pretending to blow up disco records on the air and saw the protest as a way to continue his antidisco crusade and enhance his own standing among radio listeners. Mike Veeck saw the protest as more of a promotion and a way to draw a crowd to a twinight doubleheader with the Detroit Tigers. About 60,000 people were in the stadium, some carrying signs declaring "Disco Sucks!," to watch the blowing up of disco records between games. Fans had been told that they would be admitted into the park for just 98 cents if they brought a record with them to be destroyed. So many record-bearing fans showed up that they had to be turned away at the gate. (The crowd outside burned an image of John Travolta, the star of the movie *Saturday Night Fever.*) Little did Dahl and Veeck realize the potential for the records to become flying instruments. Throughout the first game, spectators flung them about the stands and onto the field, endangering the players and people in the crowd. In some instances, the spectators attached cherry bombs to the records so that they would explode in midair. The crowd clearly had little interest in baseball and every interest in mayhem.

The demolition began when Dahl came onto the field and blew up a wooden crate and a dumpster filled with disco records. The dumpster emitted flames and smoke, and shards of disco records hurtled into the air, dropping to the ball field and making a mess of it.

The explosion ignited the crowd. As the White Sox pitcher tried to warm up on the mound, a couple of fans began to slide into second base. Then came more fans. Before long, thousands spilled onto the field, stomping on disco records and tossing firecrackers and cherry bombs. "It looked like medieval times when they go after a castle, pouring over a wall," said Ron Battaglin, a White Sox fan who attended the game.[55] They reignited the smoldering fire of disco records, destroyed the batting cage, tore up the bases, and dug up the grass. Bill Veeck used the PA system to plead for calm but to no avail.

Finally, about 40 minutes later, Chicago's riot police arrived. They cleared the field and arrested some 30 people. In the end, the second game had to be canceled and forfeited by the White Sox.

Demolition Night was part of a larger antidisco movement in the 1970s, part of a protest against the intrinsic nature of the music itself, but also a protest against the gay and black influences in it. These protesters wanted a return to unadulterated rock and roll. Yet, too much can be read into Disco Demolition Night, which came from a combination of factors, not the least of which was rowdy young people encouraged by plentiful drugs, cheap beer, and cheap tickets to go wild. "The worst thing is people calling Disco Demolition homophobic or racist," Dahl later said. "It just wasn't. It's really easy to look at it historically, from this perspective, and attach all those things to it. But we weren't thinking like that."[56] Mike Veeck recollected: "I grew up when people were marching for civil rights, marching against the [Vietnam] war. Exactly 10 years later, I didn't think they would be marching because they hated the Bee Gees."[57]

ELEVEN DIE AT A ROCK CONCERT IN CINCINNATI

Eleven young people died at a rock concert in Cincinnati, Ohio, when a crowd anxious to see the band the Who rushed the doors of Riverfront Coliseum.

All through the afternoon of December 3, 1979, concert-goers gathered outside the coliseum for the show, which was scheduled to begin at eight o'clock that night. By four o'clock, several thousand people were standing on the concourse in front of two entranceways containing eight glass doors each. Twenty-five police supervised the crowd.

As night fell and the air became colder, the crowd became more anxious. Shortly before 7:00 P.M., the Who took the stage for their sound check. The crowd could hear them and began to press against the doors. One concert supervisor asked that the doors be opened to relieve the crush, but his request was denied.

The coliseum was opened as previously planned at 7:05 P.M., but only four doors were unlocked. Those in the back of the crowd kept pushing those in front of them. Fans collapsed to the ground. Others became so packed together that their bodies were lifted from the concourse. Many had to turn their heads straight up to gasp for air.

Some who entered the coliseum did so with blood-stained shoes. It was not until 7:54 P.M., however, just minutes before the start of the concert, that the authorities discovered the first body. The Who's manager was told of the tragedy, but he decided, as did the coliseum management and the fire marshal, to continue with the show. They feared, quite rightly, that a cancellation might send the thousands already in the coliseum into a frenzy and lead to another crush.

Several factors contributed to the deaths, including inadequate police protection and the inexplicable refusal to open more doors or to open them earlier. Most analysts, however, attributed the tragedy to festival seating. A widely used arrangement for rock concerts at the time, under festival seating promoters sold most of their tickets—as they did at Cincinnati—without reserved seats. Fans simply came onto the floor on a first-served, first-come basis, and so they rushed through the doors to be near the stage.

The Who continued their concert tour, although several cities canceled their performances. "Initially, we felt stunned and empty," said lead singer Roger Daltry. "We felt we couldn't go on. But you gotta. There's no point in stopping."[58] One fan whose wife was injured in the crush said the next day, "Last night I realized what happened and just broke down crying."[59]

Many Americans felt like crying about the 1970s. It was, by and large, a bleak and depressing decade filled with disappointments that ranged from the limitations of countercultural efforts, to Watergate, to stagflation, to the hostage crisis in Iran. Whereas the 1950s and much of the 1960s seemed to be decades of limitless possibilities, the 1970s seemed to be a decade that exposed America's limits, be they at home or overseas. Yet, the decade produced some notable advances, arguably the most significant occurring in women's rights and environmental legislation. And it showed the resiliency of Americans and their institutions, holding out the possibility of renewal and advancement in the late 20th and early 21st centuries.

CHRONICLE OF EVENTS

1979

January 1: The United States formally establishes diplomatic relations with communist China and severs ties with Taiwan.

January 16: Shah Mohammed Reza Pahlevi leaves Iran, his departure a result of massive demonstrations that topple his government. He leaves behind a new civilian government headed by Prime Minister Shahpur Bakhtiar, but exiled Muslim leader Ayatollah Ruhollah Khomeini will call successfully for Iranians to remove Bakhtiar from office.

January 19: Former Attorney General John Mitchell is released on parole from a federal prison, making him the last of the Watergate defendants to be freed. He served 19 months of his two-and-one-half-to-eight-year sentence for conspiracy and obstruction of justice.

January 21: The Pittsburgh Steelers become the first football team to win three Super Bowls when they defeat the Dallas Cowboys, 35-31.

January 23: President Jimmy Carter presents his State of the Union speech, in which he promises to pursue an economic policy that will guide the nation between the shoals of inflation and recession and will pursue an arms limitation agreement with the Soviet Union.

January 26: Nelson A. Rockefeller, the former governor of New York and vice president under Gerald Ford, dies of a heart attack.

Anwar Sadat, Jimmy Carter, and Menachem Begin shake hands at the Camp David Accords signing ceremony. *(Courtesy Jimmy Carter Library)*

January 29: San Diego teenager Brenda Spencer walks into an elementary school and begins to shoot, killing two people because, she says, "I don't like Mondays."

January 30: The Iranian government authorizes the return of exiled Muslim leader Ayatollah Ruhollah Khomeini.

February 1: Ayatollah Ruhollah Khomeini returns to Iran and declares his intention to establish an Islamic republic. Continued pressure from Khomeini and from protesters will force Prime Minister Bakhtiar to resign on February 11. Shortly thereafter, a revolutionary council led by Khomeini will gain power.

March 26: President Anwar Sadat of Egypt and Prime Minister Menachem Begin of Israel sign a peace treaty in Washington ending the 31-year state of war between their two countries. The framework for the treaty had been developed at the Camp David summit in 1978.

March 28: An accident at the Three Mile Island nuclear power plant near Middletown, Pennsylvania, results in radioactive gases escaping through a venting system and into the air, endangering the health of residents in surrounding communities. The fuel rods of the reactor are damaged, resulting in a near-meltdown of the plant's core. Moreover, the formation of a hydrogen gas bubble threatens to destroy the plant's containment vessel. By early April, nearly half of the residents within 10 miles of the plant will evacuate their homes. The crisis will end with the planned cold shutdown of one of the reactors in late April.

April 17: Ayatollah Khomeini of Iran accuses the United States and its agents of working to destroy his government.

May 6: Spurred by the Three Mile Island accident, 65,000 protesters march in Washington against nuclear power, the largest such demonstration in the nation's history.

May 25: An American Airlines jetliner crashes shortly after takeoff from Chicago's O'Hare International Airport, killing all 272 people aboard and three on the ground. The tragedy is the worst in the history of U.S. aviation.

June 18: President Jimmy Carter and Soviet President Leonid Brezhnev sign a Strategic Arms Limitation Treaty (SALT II) that limits the United States and the Soviet Union to the same number of long-range bombers and missiles.

July 11: Skylab, the 77-ton orbiting space station which was used during three NASA missions, enters the Earth's atmosphere and breaks apart, its largest pieces falling into the Indian Ocean and across the wilderness of Australia.

July 12: The second half of a Chicago White Sox doubleheader is canceled when a "disco-demolition" rally at Comiskey Park spirals out of control. A crowd rushes the field and refuses to leave.

July 15: In a speech to the nation, President Carter says that the United States is suffering a "crisis of confidence." He claims there is a lack of unity in the country and a loss of faith in the future.

July 17: President Carter shakes up his cabinet and names Hamilton Jordan as his chief of staff. The changes occur as the president's public approval ratings plummet.

July 31: Theodore Bundy is sentenced to die for the murders of two sorority sisters at Florida State University in Tallahassee.

August 15: Andrew Young, the first African-American U.S. ambassador to the United Nations, resigns his post amid revelations that he met with a representative of the Palestine Liberation Organization. The meeting raised serious questions of diplomatic propriety because it was unauthorized and occurred while Egypt and Israel were involved in intense negotiations over Palestine. Many Jewish leaders in the United States had criticized Young for extending de facto recognition to the PLO.

September 14: The FBI admits that, in 1970, its agents tried to slander the reputation of actress Jean Seberg, who had committed suicide. They wanted to discredit her because she had given money to the radical Black Panther party.

September 23: Lou Brock of the St. Louis Cardinals steals his 935th base, making him baseball's all-time leading base stealer.

October 13: Rap music makes its first appearance on the R&B charts with the success of "Rapper's Delight" by the Sugar Hill Gang. The single will sell more than 2 million copies.

October 22: The exiled Shah of Iran arrives in the United States for cancer surgery. His presence stirs vehement anti-American protests in Iran.

November 3: An anti-KKK rally in Greensboro, North Carolina, turns violent when six gunmen kill four of the protesters. Later, an all-white jury will acquit the assailants.

November 4: Iranian students storm the U.S. embassy in Tehran and take 90 hostages. They demand the return of the exiled shah to Iran, whom they want to punish, in exchange for the hostages. They will later release all of the women and the blacks but will hold the remaining hostages for 444 days.

December 3: Eleven rock fans are crushed to death before a Who concert at Riverfront Stadium in Cincinnati, Ohio. The tragedy results when too few doors are opened to let the crowd enter the stadium.

December 4: Jimmy Carter announces that he will seek reelection as president. He faces opposition within the Democratic Party from Senator Edward Kennedy of Massachusetts and former California governor Jerry Brown. Leading Republicans seeking the White House include former California governor Ronald Reagan and Senator Bob Dole of Kansas.

1980

April 24: The United States begins a mission to rescue the American hostages being held in Iran, but it is aborted and results in the death of eight soldiers.

July 27: The shah of Iran dies, raising hopes that the revolutionaries in Tehran will release the Americans whom they are holding as hostages.

1981

January 20: President Carter and the leaders of Iran finalize an agreement, but Iran does not release the hostages being held in Tehran until just as Ronald Reagan is being sworn in as the new U.S. president.

EYEWITNESS TESTIMONY

Three Mile Island

I think as the story unfolds and all these commissions and study groups who have been looking at Three Mile Island for the last 6 months . . . I think we will all learn just how bad a job our public officials did during the crisis. I think it was a pretty bad job. They were talking about calling up the National Guard. Well, the National Guards would have been evacuated as private citizens so they could not be called up. And things like this. Just a big lack of coordination. And I think everybody learned a lot from it. If there is a next time, it might be handled better.

I think Met Ed demonstrated nothing but incompetence and deceit and disregard for the public and customers throughout the incident. The best thing they did was put Denton in charge. I think they did that so that they could avoid having to answer though questions they expected to be asked. My personal feeling is

that Met Ed should be closed down by government order and merged into another utility company. Short of that, I'd be delighted to see the president resign. I'm delighted further that they are using money, as a citizen, as a customer of theirs which I am I wish them nothing but financial success because we are starting to feel it on electric bills, but I think Met Ed botched it. I think the problems can be traced back to lack of supervision and a lack of control on their part and the NRC wasn't doing its job as watchdog etc cetera, et cetera. I don't have a very high opinion of Met Ed.

Comments made in 1979, following the March 1979 nuclear accident, by a newspaper editor who lived near Three Mile Island concerning his views about the handling of the crisis by the government and by the Metropolitan Edison Company, Community Studies Center, Dickinson College, Carlisle, Pennsylvania, available online at http://www.threemileisland.org, downloaded October 17, 2004.

Protesters react to the Three Mile Island crisis by staging an antinuke rally in Harrisburg, Pennsylvania. *(National Archives and Records Administration)*

I thought the company did a lousy job. I think they honestly lied to people. Because they played it down as being almost nothing, and any time there's an escape of radiation into the atmosphere it's a problem. And I think you need to protect the people that its going to come in contact with. They didn't seem to care about that. The only thing they seemed to be caring about was letting the stockholders get their dividends. Let the people who are already paying for the electricity pay an extra money to pay for their plant and the mistake they've made. As far as the company's concerned, I just think they did a terrible job.

Comments made on June 6, 1979, following the March 1979 nuclear accident, by a high school teacher who lived near Three Mile Island concerning her views about how the Metropolitan Edison Company handled the crisis, Community Studies Center, Dickinson College, Carlisle, Pennsylvania, available online at http://www.threemileisland.org, downloaded October 17, 2004.

I would like to see nuclear power completely stopped. I, I can't conceive of how, what can be done with the waste or what with the plutonium that has already been mined. I just. Nuclear weapons it's the same situation. I feel there that it's just futile. It is ridiculous to talk about, you know. We need so many weapons and they need so many weapons just to hold over their heads or to hold over our heads. It just the whole idea of it is just so. It is almost infantile to me. So, but it has been going on for years and years and this is how man has evolved, a wasteful kind of creature. That's how I feel. We have just created these, man is just turning into this kind of futile monster. . . .

Comments made on August 1, 1979, following the March 1979 nuclear accident, by a housewife who lived near Three Mile Island concerning her views about nuclear energy, Community Studies Center, Dickinson College, Carlisle, Pennsylvania, available online at http://www.threemileisland.org, downloaded October 17, 2004.

I feel that energy crisis in which we are right now, on the face of that energy crisis, we need some type of energy we can count upon, count on and I think that nuclear energy at the moment is that answer. But I feel that it has to be very well controlled. I feel that it was not very well controlled at Three Mile Island. I don't know exactly how to control it well, but I think it's

needed and I think it has to be under some strict controls, some strict regulatory control. Just seemed to me, that I guess that the people at Three Mile Island were going to work and pulling the switches and checking the lights and going about it in a dull way and not paying a whole lot of attention to the possibility of having a disaster. I don't think it can be run like that. I think it's got the potential for destroying the countryside and all the living things in that countryside. You have to have people who are on their toes every second of the time. Seemed to me that this is not what was going on there. I do think that we can use nuclear energy and control it and use it to our advantage.

Comments made on October 4, 1979, following the March 1979 nuclear accident, by a doctor who lived near Three Mile Island concerning his views about nuclear energy, Community Studies Center, Dickinson College, Carlisle, Pennsylvania, available online at http://www.threemileisland.org, downloaded October 17, 2004.

Certainty about physical health effects from the accident at Three Mile Island could not be established during the time in which this Commission made its evaluation, but present knowledge provides no reason to disagree with the finding of the President's Commission on the Accident at Three Mile Island that "most of the radiation was contained and the actual release will have a negligible effect on the physical health of individuals.". . .

The Commission also agrees with a related finding by the President's Commission that "the major health effect of the accident appears to have been on the mental health of the people living in the region. . ." The Behavioral Effects Task Force of the President's Commission was given responsibility for examining mental health effects on the public and workers directly involved in the accident. The Task Force technical staff report concluded that "the TMI accident had a pronounced demoralizing effect on the general population of the TMI area . . . However, this effect proved transient in all groups studied except the workers, who continue to show relatively high levels of demoralization. Moreover, the groups in the general population and the workers, in their different ways, have continuing problems of trust that stem directly from the accident."

Results of the Three Mile Island area telephone survey, conducted by Mountain West Research, Inc. for the Nuclear Regulatory Commission (NRC), also indicated there were psychological consequences from the accident. This survey found that one indicator of "the degree of psychological stress experienced by families near TMI is the extent of disagreement regarding the decision to evacuate. Nearly 20% of households over the entire area said there was disagreement over the decision." The Mountain West survey also found that for some, continued stress is evident—22% of respondents perceive TMI to be a continuing threat to their families. However, 28% feel TMI is not a continuing threat.

Excerpt from a 1980 report regarding the health effects following the March 1979 nuclear accident at Three Mile Island, in "Report of the Governor's Commission on Three Mile Island," at Community Studies Center, Dickinson College, Carlisle, Pennsylvania, available online at http://www.threemileisland.org, downloaded October 17, 2004.

The industry evaluation of the TMI accident has been fairly rapid. . . . The human failures have been recognized and the approach being developed to deal with them is a pooling of industry expertise. Four industry groups announced plans on June 28, 1979, for a national institute to establish benchmarks for excellence in nuclear power programs—the Institute for Nuclear Power Operations (INPO). In August a discussion paper by the Electric Power Research Institute (EPRI) further delineated the charter for INPO. From that paper, confirmed by subsequent discussions, it appears that INPO will:

- Establish industry-wide benchmarks for excellence in the management and operation of nuclear power plants.
- Conduct independent evaluations to determine that the benchmarks are being met.
- Review nuclear power operating experience for analysis and feedback to the utilities.
- Incorporate lessons learned into training programs. Coordinate information reporting and analysis with other organizations.
- Establish educational and training requirements for operations and maintenance personnel and develop screening and performance measurement systems.
- Accredit training programs and certify instructors.
- Conduct seminars and generic training for various utility employees, including instructors,

utility executives, and upper management, to ensure quality in the operation of nuclear power programs.
- Perform studies and analyses to support development of criteria for operation, for training, and for the human factors aspects of design and operation.
- Provide emergency preparedness coordination for the nuclear utility industry.
- Exchange information and experience with operators of nuclear power plants in other countries.

All of these activities combined can go to the root of the utility part of the problem for nuclear power plant operations. They promise a degree of self-policing in the industry that alone might ensure the protection of the health and safety of the public. But they promise; they do not ensure. . . .

THE TMI ACTION PLAN

The NRC staff and the Commission are now immersed in the development of the agency-wide action plan referred to earlier. In this process, we do not see a closely knit team forging plans for action. We see instead a task force of staff members drawn from different offices—detailed to work for a lame duck executive director for operations—that is trying to negotiate with each NRC program office and periodically leads a mass pilgrimage to the Commission offices to discuss the action plan with the Commission.

If ever an argument is needed to convince someone of the lack of management in the NRC, one need only attend one of these Commission meetings. The Commission repeatedly insists that it is not deciding, but only taking every matter under advisement. The staff flounders to find a format for the plan that might be acceptable to this enigmatic collegium that is supposed to lead the agency. This is not management in any conventional sense. It appears that the structural problems in the NRC's management persist in the wake of TMI. . . .

THE PROGNOSIS

With every passing day, TMI draws less attention. The crisis in Iran and ever-increasing oil prices push the nuclear safety question into eclipse. Just as the last major reactor accident, the Brown's Ferry fire, slipped beneath the surface of the sea of daily concerns 4 years ago, so can Three Mile Island join it in the coming years. It will take dogged perseverance in the nuclear industry and in the Government to truly learn the lessons of TMI. We are not reassured by what we see so far.

> *An excerpt from a 1980 report by the Nuclear Regulatory Commission's Special Inquiry Group offering a generally pessimistic assessment of corrective procedures in the wake of the Three Mile Island nuclear accident in "Three Mile Island: A Report to the Commissioners and the Public, Vol. I," at Community Studies Center, Dickinson College, Carlisle, Pennsylvania, available online at http://www.threemileisland.org, downloaded October 17, 2004.*

The Crisis of Confidence

I want to speak to you first tonight about a subject even more serious than energy or inflation. I want to talk to you right now about a fundamental threat to American democracy.

I do not mean our political and civil liberties. They will endure. And I do not mean the outward strength of America, a nation that is at peace tonight everywhere in the world, with unmatched economic power and military might.

The threat is nearly invisible in ordinary ways. It is a crisis of confidence. It is a crisis that strikes at the very heart and soul and spirit of our national will. We can see this crisis in the growing doubt about the meaning of our own lives and in the loss of a unity of purpose for our Nation.

The erosion of our confidence in the future is threatening to destroy the social and the political fabric of America.

The confidence that we have always had as a people is not simply some romantic dream or a proverb in a dusty book that we read just on the Fourth of July. It is the idea which founded our Nation and has guided our development as a people. Confidence in the future has supported everything else—public institutions and private enterprise, our own families, and the very Constitution of the United States. Confidence has defined our course and has served as a link between generations. We've always believed in something called progress. We've always had a faith that the days of our children would be better than our own.

Our people are losing that faith, not only in government itself but in the ability as citizens to serve as the ultimate rulers and shapers of our democracy. As a people we know our past and we are proud of it. Our progress has been part of the living history of America,

even the world. We always believed that we were part of a great movement of humanity itself called democracy, involved in the search for freedom and that belief has always strengthened us in our purpose. But just as we are losing our confidence in the future we are also beginning to close the door on our past.

In a nation that was proud of hard work, strong families, close-knit communities, and our faith in God, too many of us now tend to worship self-indulgence and consumption. Human identity is no longer defined by what one does, but by what one owns. But we've discovered that owning things and consuming things does not satisfy our longing for meaning. We've learned that piling up material goods cannot fill the emptiness of lives which have no confidence or purpose. . . .

The symptoms of this crisis of the American spirit are all around us. For the first time in the history of our country a majority of our people believe that the next 5 years will be worse than the past 5 years. Two-thirds of our people do not even vote. The productivity of American workers is actually dropping, and the willingness of Americans to save for the future has fallen below that of all other people in the Western world. As you know, there is a growing disrespect for government and for churches and for schools, the news media, and other institutions. This is not a message of happiness or reassurance, but it is the truth and it is a warning.

Jimmy Carter's press secretary Jody Powell and his chief of staff Hamilton Jordan contributed to the president's contentious relations with Congress. *(Courtesy Jimmy Carter Library)*

These changes did not happen overnight. They've come upon us gradually over the last generation, years that were filled with shocks and tragedy.

We were sure that ours was a nation of the ballot, not the bullet, until the murders of John Kennedy and Robert Kennedy and Martin Luther King, Jr. We were taught that our armies were always invincible and our causes were always just, only to suffer the agony of Vietnam. We respected the Presidency as a place of honor until the shock of Watergate.

We remember when the phrase "sound as a dollar" was an expression of absolute dependability, until 10 years of inflation began to shrink our dollar and our savings. We believed that our Nation's resources were limitless until 1973, when we had to face a growing dependence on foreign oil.

These wounds are still very deep. They have never been healed.

Looking for a way out of this crisis, our people have turned to the Federal Government and found it isolated from the mainstream of our Nation's life. Washington, D.C., has become an island. The gap between our citizens and our Government has never been so wide. The people are looking for honest answers, not easy answers; clear leadership, not false claims and evasiveness and politics as usual.

What you see too often in Washington and elsewhere around the country is a system of government that seems incapable of action. You see a Congress twisted and pulled in every direction by hundreds of well-financed and powerful special interests. You see every extreme position defended to the last vote, almost to the last breath by one unyielding group or another. You often see a balanced and a fair approach that demands sacrifice, a little sacrifice from everyone, abandoned like an orphan without support and without friends.

Often you see paralysis and stagnation and drift. You don't like it, and neither do I. What can we do?

First of all, we must face the truth, and then we can change our course. We simply must have faith in each other, faith in our ability to govern ourselves, and faith in the future of this Nation. Restoring that faith and that confidence to America is now the most important task we face. It is a true challenge of this generation of Americans.

One of the visitors to Camp David last week put it this way: "We've got to stop crying and start sweating, stop talking and start walking, stop cursing and start praying. The strength we need will not come from the White House, but from every house in America."

We know the strength of America. We are strong. We can regain our unity. We can regain our confidence. We are the heirs of generations who survived threats much more powerful and awesome than those that challenge us now. Our fathers and mothers were strong men and women who shaped a new society during the Great Depression, who fought world wars and who carved out a new charter of peace for the world.

We ourselves are the same Americans who just 10 years ago put a man on the Moon. We are the generation that dedicated our society to the pursuit of human rights and equality. And we are the generation that will win the war on the energy problem and in that process rebuild the unity and confidence of America.

We are at a turning point in our history. There are two paths to choose. One is a path I've warned about tonight, the path that leads to fragmentation and self-interest. Down that road lies a mistaken idea of freedom, the right to grasp for ourselves some advantage over others. That path would be one of constant conflict between narrow interests ending in chaos and immobility. It is a certain route to failure.

All the traditions of our past, all the lessons of our heritage, all the promises of our future point to another path, the path of common purpose and the restoration of American values. That path leads to true freedom for our Nation and ourselves. We can take the first steps down that path as we begin to solve our energy problem. . . .

The solution of our energy crisis can also help us to conquer the crisis of the spirit in our country. It can rekindle our sense of unity, our confidence in the future, and give our Nation and all of us individually a new sense of purpose.

You know we can do it. We have the natural resources. We have more oil in our shale alone than several Saudi Arabias. We have more coal than any nation on Earth. We have the world's highest level of technology. We have the most skilled work force, with innovative genius, and I firmly believe that we have the national will to win this war.

I do not promise you that this struggle for freedom will be easy. I do not promise a quick way out of our Nation's problems, when the truth is that the only way out is an all-out effort. What I do promise you is that I will lead our fight, and I will enforce fairness in our struggle, and I will ensure honesty. And above all, I will act.

We can manage the short-term shortages more effectively and we will, but there are no short-term solutions to our long-range problems. There is simply no way to avoid sacrifice. . . .

I will continue to travel this country, to hear the people of America. You can help me to develop a national agenda for the 1980's. I will listen and I will act. These are the promises I made 3 years ago, and I intend to keep them.

Little by little we can and we must rebuild our confidence. We can spend until we empty our treasuries, and we may summon all the wonders of science. But we can succeed only if we tap our greatest resources—America's people, America's values, and America's confidence.

I have seen the strength of America in the inexhaustible resources of our people. In the days to come, let us renew that strength in the struggle for an energy-secure nation.

In closing, let me say this: I will do my best, but I will not do it alone. Let your voice be heard. Whenever you have a chance, say something good about our country. With God's help and for the sake of our Nation, it is time for us to join hands in America. Let us commit ourselves together to a rebirth of the American spirit. Working together with our common faith we cannot fail.

An excerpt from President Jimmy Carter's Crisis of Confidence (or "Malaise") Speech, presented on national television on July 15, 1979, in Public Papers of the Presidents of the United States: Jimmy Carter, *June 23 to December 31, 1979 (1980), pp. 1,235–1,241.*

Ted Bundy

Q. What was Bundy's prime motivation and how did it start?

I think his prime motivation was control and possession. When you look at his earlier attempts and his first experimentations with murder, as he told Steve Michaud, he would go up behind someone and hit them on the head with a two by four just to see what it felt like.

At the time that was something he was horrified about, but when that horrification wore off he felt good about it. That's how it started, he conditioned himself to it and he started early. In the interviews I had with him just before his death, he was talking about three other victims, but after he started talking about one of them

being in 1973 he caught himself and wouldn't talk anymore. We have cases dating back to 1968 that he may be responsible for. There were two stewardesses that were attacked in Queen Ann Hill in Seattle and he used to live across the Fremont Bridge from Queen Ann Hill and used to go right by their apartment on the way to his job in the Safeway store in Queen Ann. I think he was a good suspect for those, and they were also bludgeonings where one girl was murdered and the other lived through it, so he may have been active as early as 1968.

From an undated interview with Robert D. Keppel, president of the Institute for Forensics in Seattle, Washington, and author of The Riverman: Ted Bundy and I Hunt for the Green River Killer, *Court TV's Crime Library, available online at http://www.crimelibrary.com, downloaded October 14, 2004.*

Hostages Held in Iran

It got to the point where we would actually look forward to the bombing raids. If Tehran didn't get hit for several nights in a row, it would depress the hell out of us. We liked the idea of them getting bombed. When the flights came screaming in . . . we'd jump up and start clapping and cheering. . . . Hostages would be shouting, "Give 'em hell!" "Flatten Tehran!" or "Buy Iraqi war bonds!" Things like that. We'd practically shake the prison with our cheering and clapping. . . . When it didn't happen for a few nights in a row we really missed it.

Captive warrant officer Joe Hall recalling the reaction of the American hostages to Iraqi air strikes on Iran. From an undated comment in David Harris, The Crisis: The President, the Prophet, and the Shah—1979 and the Coming of Militant Islam *(2004), p. 395.*

Nov. 4, 1979: Since I wasn't sure whether we were expected to work at the Consular Section, in view of what the Chargé had told me last evening, I went to the office just the same at 7:30 as I had quite a bit of work to do anyway. When I got there, however, I found that everyone was coming to work as usual but we were not open to the general public. About 9:00 I was in my office when a young American woman, apparently the wife of an Iranian, was shown into my office as she wanted to obtain her mother-in-law's Iranian passport that had been left at the Consular Section a day or so before for a non-immigrant visa. Just as I was talking to her in an attempt to find out to whom the passport had been issued, when it was left with us, etc., we were told by the Consul General to drop everything and get up to the second floor of the Consular Section. I really didn't know what was happening but was told that a mob had managed to get into the Embassy Compound and, for our own protection, everyone had to go upstairs immediately.

I noticed that the Consul General was removing the visa plates and locking the visa stamping machines. I went upstairs with the American woman and could see a number of young men in the area between the rear of the Consular Section and the Embassy CO-OP store. We were told to sit on the floor in the outer hall-way offices. A Marine Security Guard was present and was in contact with the main Embassy building (Chancery) by walkie-talkie. After an hour or so we could hear that the mob, which turned out to be student revolutionaries, were also on the walkie-talkie. The Marine Guard then advised that we were going to evacuate the Consular Section.

There were some visitors on the second floor in the Immigrant Visa Unit and the American Services Unit. I was asked to assist an elderly gentleman, either an American of Iranian origin or an Iranian citizen, I don't know, since he was almost blind and was completely terrified, and to be the first one out of the building. When we got outside he was met by a relative who took him away in his car. The students outside the Consular Section appeared to be somewhat confused at that point and the Consul General and about four other American members of the Consular Section, of which I was one, started up the street with the intention of going to his residence. When we were about 1 1/2 blocks from the Consular Section we were surrounded by a group of the students, who were armed, and told to return to the Compound. When we protested a shot was fired into the air above our heads.

It was raining moderately at the time. We were taken back to the Compound, being pushed and hurried along the way and forced to put our hands above our heads and then marched to the Embassy residence. After arriving at the residence I had my hands tied behind my back so tightly with nylon cord that circulation was cut off. I was taken upstairs and put alone in a rear bedroom and after a short time was blindfolded. After protesting strongly that the cord was too tight the cord was removed and the blindfold taken off when

they tried to feed me some dates and I refused to eat anything I couldn't see. I strongly protested the violation of my diplomatic immunity, but these protests were ignored. I then was required to sit in a chair facing the bedroom wall. Then another older student came in and when I again protested the violation of my diplomatic immunity he confiscated my U.S. Mission Tehran I.D. card. My hands were again tied and I was taken to the Embassy living room on the ground floor where a number of other hostages were gathered. Some students attempted to talk with us, stating how they did-n't hate Americans—only our U.S. Government, President Carter, etc. We were given sandwiches, and that night I slept on the living room floor. We were not permitted to talk to our fellow hostages and from then on our hands were tied day and night and only removed while we were eating or had to go to the bathroom.

Nov. 5, 1979: After remaining in the living room the next morning I was taken into the Embassy dining room and forced to sit on a dining room chair around the table with about twelve or so other hostages. Our hands were tied to each side of the chair. We could only rest by leaning on to the dining table and resting our head on a small cushion. The drapes were drawn and we were not permitted to talk with the other hostages. At one point my captors also tried to make me face the wall but I objected since I had no way to rest my head and after considerable objections I was permitted to continue facing the table. Our captors always conversed in stage whispers. We were untied and taken to the toilet as necessary as well as into a small dining room adjacent for meals, then returned to our chairs and again tied to the chair. I slept that night on the floor under the dining table with a piece of drapery for a cover.

Excerpt from a diary kept by captive Robert C. Ode, November 4–5, 1979, Jimmy Carter Library and Museum, available online at http://www. jimmycarterlibrary.org/documents/r_ode/ ode_nov79.phtml, downloaded October 19, 2004.

It's a clear tenet of international law and diplomatic tradition that the host government is fully responsible for the safety and well-being of the property and the legal representatives of another country. Less than a year ago—and this is a fact not generally known or recognized—less than a year ago, 70,000 American citizens were in Iran. As you know, thousands of people were killed during the upheavals there, but almost miraculously and because of the good work of Cyrus Vance and others, our people were brought home safely. I thank God for it. Despite the turmoil, each succeeding Iranian Government—and they were being changed, as you know, quite rapidly—protected the citizens of other countries.

Foreign visitors are often vulnerable to abuse. An embassy is not a fortress. There are no embassies anywhere in the world that can long withstand the attack of a mob if the mob has the support of the host government itself. We had received repeated assurances of protection from the highest officials in the Iranian Government, even a day or two before the mob was incited to attack and before that protection was withdrawn at the last minute The principle of inviolability of embassies is understood and accepted by nations everywhere, and it's particularly important to smaller nations which have no recourse to economic or military power. This is why the United Nations Security Council has also unanimously supported our demand for the release of the American hostages. . . .

No act has so galvanized the American public toward unity in the last decade as has the holding of our people as hostages in Tehran. We stand today as one people. We are dedicated to the principles and the honor of our Nation. We've taken no action which would justify concern among the people or among the Government of Iran. We have done nothing for which any American need apologize. The actions of Iranian leaders and the radicals who invaded our Embassy were completely unjustified. They and all others must know that the United States of America will not yield to international terrorism or to blackmail.

From a speech by President Jimmy Carter at a meeting of the American Federation of Labor and Congress of Industrial Organizations in Washington, D.C., November 15, 1979, in Public Papers of the Presidents of the United States: Jimmy Carter, June 23 to December 31, 1979 *(1980), p. 2,124.*

The Failed Rescue Mission in Iran

Everyone started searching the area surrounding the burning wreckage. We were being as thorough as we could, but had to stay clear of the rear of the flaming mass, where ordnance was still detonating and sending shrapnel ripping into the helicopters. There were no signs of life, and no traces of those we presumed had perished in the fire. There was a sadness gripping all of us . . . sadness and anger at this final catastrophe that was heaped upon our failure.

Colonel James H. Kyle (USAF) recalling the scene at the Desert One site after a helicopter collided with a C-130 refueling plane, in his book The Guts To Try: The Untold Story of the Iran Hostage Rescue Mission by the On-Scene Desert Commander *(1995), p. 338.*

Hostage Release

Back in the United States we were greeted as heroes. We were so isolated that we didn't realize that we had become the center of the American news. In some ways I think the people were celebrating what they believed was American power. They were trying to make a bad situation into something great. . . . I honestly believe that both countries lost. There was a lot of hate on both sides that didn't need to happen.

Excerpt from recollections written in 1981 by captive Barry Rosen, in Peter Jennings and Todd Brewster, The Century *(1998), p. 461.*

The voice came over the Algerian plane's speaker: "You are now leaving Iranian air space!" What a cheer went up from the American hostages on the plane! This was the moment for which we had waited 444 days. Now we knew we were really free! Even though we had been told by the Iranian terrorists that we were being set free, I'm sure all of the hostages didn't really feel that we were on our way to freedom until we actually were out of Iran. So much still could go wrong in the process of obtaining our freedom, but the confirmation that we were actually out of Iran, and the Ayatollah Khomeini's jurisdiction made us finally realize that our ordeal was over! What a magnificent feeling! We were on our way at last! We were going home! . . .

On January 19, 1981, I was taken from my room which I was occupying with five other hostages, Bill Belk and Jerry Miele of the State Department; John Graves of the International Communications Agency; Colonel Thomas Schaeffer, U.S. Air Force who had been the U.S. Defense Attache prior to the takeover of the Embassy; and Donald Hohman, a U.S. Army Medical Specialist who had been sent to Iran to head the embassy Medical Unit until such time as the State Department would send a qualified State Department Nurse for permanent duty.

Ahmad, who I thoroughly detested and I always referred to as "Shovelface" because of his rather flat facial structure was one of the terrorist–supervisors who had control of the "minor league" terrorist guards who controlled us on a daily basis. "Shovelface" spoke English well and, with a newspaper before him, informed me that "some" of the hostages were to be released that evening and flown to Wiesbaden, Germany and that I was "one of the candidates"! While I couldn't seriously believe that our government would permit or accept the release of some, but not all, of the hostages, the thought raced through my mind. . . . "If I am one of the 'candidates'—how do I win this election?"

The next thing I was taken to another room where I was seated before one of the women terrorists . . . a young woman gowned in the usual black chador who had interviewed me on previous occasions. It was my understanding that she had spent several years of her youth as a resident of Philadelphia where she attended school and learned to speak English like an American. In spite of her long residence in the United States she was rabidly anti-American! Perhaps living in Philadelphia makes one that way! I don't know. Since she spoke English so well I later learned that she had appeared frequently on Iranian propaganda TV broadcasts to the United States using the name of "Mary" and was well-known to American TV viewers who were following the hostage situation. Several TV cameras were focused on us and Mary asked me to describe my daily activities while being held hostage. I related how I did calisthenics each morning; then following breakfast I would pursue my daily regimen—pacing rapidly across my room for approximately 1200 times to equate two miles of walking; write letters to my wife, other relatives and friends; read, play Scrabble and other games with other hostages in my room, and study Spanish. Mary queried me as to whether I had been well treated to which I replied, "There was much room for improvement in our treatment" Then she asked me whether I felt there was any justification for having been taken hostage. I replied, "There was absolutely no justification . . . there never was." With that, Mary said, "The interview is over!"

Excerpt from a diary kept by captive Robert C. Ode, January 19, 1981, Jimmy Carter Library, available online at http://www.jimmycarterlibrary.org/ documents/r_ode/ode_rel.phtml, downloaded October 19, 2004.

October Surprise

Special Counsel now turns to the central questions considered in this investigation.

a. Was There a Secret Agreement Between the Reagan Campaign and Representatives of the Ayatollah Khomeini to Delay the Release of the American Hostages Until After the November 1980 Election?

There is not sufficient credible evidence to support this allegation. The primary sources for this allegation—[Oregon businessman Richard] Brenneke, [Israeli national Ari] Ben–Menashe, and [Iranian arms dealer Houshang] Lavi—have proven wholly unreliable. Their claims regarding alleged secret meetings are riddled with inconsistencies, and have been contradicted by irrefutable documentary evidence as well as by the testimony of vastly more credible witnesses. Not one aspect of Ben–Menashe's story, which alleges a series of meetings in Madrid, Amsterdam, Paris and Washington in furtherance of an "October Surprise" conspiracy promoted by Israel, was ever corroborated. There is now reliable evidence (from passports, calendars, credit card receipts, FBI surveillance tapes, etc.) that the men Ben–Menashe claims attended these meetings . . . were definitely not present. Even [Iranian businessman] Jamshid Hashemi, who has testified under oath that Reagan campaign director William Casey met with [Iranian cleric Mehdi] Karrubi in Madrid, also stated that Casey's intent was not to delay, but rather to expedite, the release of the hostages. . . .

In sum, the Special Counsel found that by any standard, the credible evidence now known falls far short of supporting the allegation of an agreement between the Reagan campaign and Iran to delay the release of the hostages.

b. Was Casey Fishing in Troubled Waters?

The evidence supports the conclusion that William Casey, while director of the Reagan campaign, was intensely involved in the hostage crisis and likely was dealing with [banker and international businessman] Cyrus Hashemi, either directly or indirectly, through [New York businessman] John Shaheen.

The Iranian hostage situation was the common denominator in the lives of Casey, Shaheen and Hashemi in 1980. Republican campaign records and the testimony of Reagan campaign operatives establish Casey's keen interest in following every aspect of the hostage crisis. . . .

Casey's hostage-related activities as campaign director may not have stopped at contact with Hashemi. Two disreputable arms dealers . . . place Casey in a London restaurant in the summer of 1980 speaking of hostages and arms. Houshang Lavi may have reached out with his hostage/arms proposals to Casey's aide, Robert Carter, on October 6, 1980.

Finally, numerous witnesses have testified that it was entirely within Casey's character and capabilities to embark on an "extracurricular" hostage mission. Casey's . . . penchant for going outside normal channels are matters of record. . . .

In sum . . . there is no credible evidence that Casey, operating through Hashemi, concluded any infamous agreement or understanding intended to delay the release of the hostages. . . . The totality of the evidence does suggest that Casey was "fishing in troubled waters" and that he conducted informal, clandestine, and potentially dangerous efforts on behalf of the Reagan campaign to gather intelligence on the volatile and unpredictable course of the hostage negotiations between the Carter administration and Iran. . . .

5. Final Remarks

It is the hope of the Special Counsel that this preliminary effort will help shed some light and bring some finality to the "October Surprise" allegations. It is the view of the Special Counsel that this effort has value, both to resolve these serious allegations and to bring to the surface policy issues of importance. Whatever occurred in 1980 in connection with the hostage crisis, it is clear from our investigation that the foreign policy responsibilities and use of intelligence material by an opposition party are subjects that need clarification. Even a Republican effort in 1980 to speed the return of the hostages or simply to gather information on the hostage crisis could have profoundly complicated official negotiations with Iran.

Excerpt from The "October Surprise": Allegations and the Circumstances Surrounding the Release of the American Hostages Held in Iran: Report of the Special Counsel to Senator Terry Sanford and Senator James Jeffords of the Committee on Foreign Relations, United States Senate, November 19, 1992 *(1992), pp. 114–117 and 120–121.*

Appendix A
Documents

1. FBI teletype regarding student protest at Kent State University in Ohio, May 7, 1970, 2:00 P.M.
2. FBI teletype regarding student protest at Kent State University in Ohio, May 7, 1970, 10:07 P.M.
3. Justice Hugo L. Black's concurring opinion in the case of *New York Times Co. v. United States,* June 30, 1971
4. Equal Rights Amendment (ERA) passed by House of Representatives, October 1971
5. McKay Commission Attica prison riot investigation, the examination of Francis Joseph Huen, April 20, 1972
6. Interim agreement between the United States and the Soviet Union to limit strategic nuclear arms (SALT I Treaty), along with the protocol, statements, and understandings, May 26, 1972
7. Paris Peace Accords, Agreement on Ending the War and Restoring Peace in Vietnam, signed in Paris and entered into force January 27, 1973
8. Justice Potter Stewart's concurring opinion in the case of *Roe v. Wade,* January 22, 1973
9. Justice William Rehnquist's dissenting opinion in the case of *Roe v. Wade,* January 22, 1973
10. The War Powers Act, passed by Congress on November 7, 1973
11. Opinion of the Supreme Court delivered by Chief Justice Warren E. Burger in *United States v. Nixon,* July 24, 1974
12. The Articles of Impeachment of Richard M. Nixon, House Judiciary Committee, passed July 27–July 30, 1974
13. Treaty Concerning the Permanent Neutrality and Operation of the Panama Canal, ratified by the U.S. Senate, March 16, 1978
14. The first five articles of the Panama Canal General Treaty with United States Senate modifications, ratified by the Senate, April 18, 1978
15. A Framework for the Conclusion of a Peace Treaty between Egypt and Israel, negotiated at Camp David, September 1978
16. A Framework for Peace in the Middle East, negotiated at Camp David, September 1978
17. President Jimmy Carter's South Lawn Departure Statement for the Middle East, March 7, 1979

1. FBI Teletype Regarding Student Protest at Kent State University in Ohio, May 7, 1970, 2:00 p.m.

Note: Document provided by FBI through Freedom of Information Act has been censored by the FBI where noted.

FBI CLEVELAND
2:00 PM URGENT 5–7–70
TO DIRECTOR, FBI, ALBANY, BALTIMORE, BUF-FALO, CINCINNATI, NEWARK, AND PITTS-BURGH
FROM CLEVELAND (98–2140)
UNSUBS; FIREBOMBING OF ARMY ROTC BUILDING, KENT STATE UNIVERSITY (KSU), KENT OHIO, MAY TWO, SEVENTY. SABOTAGE. 00:CLEVELAND

RE CELVELAND TEL TO THE BUREAU, MAY SIX, SEVENTY.

FOR INFOR OF ALL OFFICES, ABOUT EIGHT PM ON EVENING OF MAY TWO, LAST, ARMY ROTC BUILDING, KSU, WAS DE-STROYED BY FIRE DURING CAMPUS DISRUP-TION. ESTIMATED CROWD OF SIX HUNDRED INDIVIDUALS WERE GATHERED ADJACENT TO BUILDING DURING INCIDENT. PRELIMI-NARY INQUIRIES INDIACTED ABOUT FIFTY TO SEVENTYFIVE OF THESE INDIVIDUALS WERE ACTIVELY ENGAGED IN THROWING ROCKS AND DEBRIS AT BUILDING AND BREAKING WINDOWS IN BUILDING. SOME OF THESE INDIVIDUALS ALSO SET BUILDING ON FIRE.

CLEVELAND OFFICE ATTEMPTING TO LOCATE AND INTERVIEW WITNESSES WHO CAN INDENTIFY UNSUBS. HOWEVER, CAM-PUS WAS CLOSED MAY FOUR LAST BY OHIO NATIONAL GUARD AND STUDENTS WERE EVACUATED. NO DATE HAS BEEN RELEASED FOR REOPENING OF CAMPUS.

CLEVELAND THERFORE SETTING OUT LEADS TO HAVE POSSIBLE WITNESSES LO-CATED AND INTERVIEWED AT HOME ADDRESSES.

THE FOLLOWING STUDENTS ADVISED KSU PD THAT THEY WITNESSED BURNING: [censored]

THE FOLLOWING INDIVIDUALS WERE TREATED AND RELEASED FROM CAMPUS HEALTH CENTER EVENING OF MAY TWO LAST AND WERE POSSIBLY AT BURNING: [censored]

PITTSBURGH, PA., TREATED FOR CUTS ON HAND;

[censored] TOLEDO, OHIO, TREATED FOR CUTS ON HAND.

[censored] NO STREET ADDRESS AVAILABLE, BEVERLY, OHIO, TREATED FOR WOUND TO LEFT KNEE.

THE FOLLOWING INDIVIDUAL WAS TREATED FOR HEARING LOSS ON MAY FOUR LAST AND REPORTEDLY DISCUSSED BURNING AT HEALTH CENTER:

PETER CHARLES BLIEK, THIRTYFOUR HIGHWOOD ROAD, ROCHESTER, NEW YORK.

INQUIRIES WITH ROTC PERSONNEL DETERMINED FOLLOWING ROTC CADETS ON CAMPUS AFTERNOON OF MAY TWO AND WERE PARTICIPATING IN ROTC EXER-CISES, FOLLOWING WHICH THEY WERE CONFRONTED WITH STUDENT HECKLERS:

[censored] COLUMBUS, OHIO;

[censored] PLAINFIELD, NEW JERSEY, A FOR-MER CADET ALSO PRESENT;

[censored] PITTSBURGH, PA.;

[censored] WHO REPORTEDLY HAS INFO ABOUT HIPPIE-TYPE INDIVIDUALS IN VOLK-SWAGEN ON KSU CAMPUS NIGHT OF BURN-ING.

[censored] AKRON, OHIO, TELEPHONICALLY ADVISED THAT [censored], A KSU STUDENT, CAN IDNETIFY A KSU PROFESSOR, WHO ENCOUR-AGED STUDENTS TO DEMONSTRATE AND THREATENED THEM WITH GRADES IF THEY DID NOT. [CENSORED] ADDRESS IS UNKNOWN. HOWEVER, HER MOTHER IS REPORTEDLY EMPLOYED WITH [censored] OHIO.

ABOVE INDIVIDUALS SHOULD BE PROMPT-LY INTERVIEWED RE CAPTIONED MATTER FOR ANY OTHER PERTINENT INFORMA-TION, IT BEING NOTED THE CLEVELAND OFFICE IS ALSO ATTEMPTING TO DEVELOP INFO RE POSSIBLE CONSPIRACY TO BURN BUILDING AND IS CONDUCTING POSSIBLE CIVIL RIGHTS INVESTIGATION RE SHOOT-ING OF KSU STUDENTS ON CAMPUS MAY FOUR LAST.

POSITIVE AND NEGATIVE RESULTS SHOULD BE FURNISHED BY FD-THREE ZERO TWO'S.

END

2. FBI TELETYPE REGARDING STUDENT PROTEST AT KENT STATE UNIVERSITY IN OHIO, MAY 7, 1970, 10:07 P.M.

Note: Document provided by FBI through Freedom of Information Act has been censored by the FBI where noted.

FBI CLEVELAND

1007PM URGENT 5–7–70 GDS

TO DIRECTOR

FROM CLEVELAND (98–2140)

UNSUBS; FIREBOMBING OF ARMY ROTC BLDG., KENT STATE UNIV., KENT, OHIO, MAY TWO, SEVENTY, SABOTAGE. 00: CLEVELAND.

SUMMARY

RE CLEVELAND TEL, MAY SIX, LAST.

INVESTIGATION CONTINUING TO LOCATE WITNESSES RE CAPTIONED MATTER AND IDENTIFY UNSUBS.

[censored] KSU STUDENT AND WITNESS TO FIRE, ADVISED THIS DATE HE OBSERVED TWO WHITE MALES SOAK RAGS IN GASOLINE FROM TANK OF MOTORCYCLE NEAR SCENE AND PROCEED TO START A FIRE IN ROTC BLDG. [censored] HAS TENTATIVELY IDENTIFIED UNKOWN INDIVIDUAL IN PHOTO OF GROUP OF DEMONSTRATORS AS ONE OF ABOVE INDIVIDUALS WHO STARTED FIRE. EFFORTS CONTINUING TO DETERMINE IDENTITY OF UNSUB IN PHOTO.

INQUIRIES THIS DATE DETERMINED THAT FACULTY AND STUDENT DEPUTIES APPOINTED BY KSU ADMINISTRATION ATTEMPTED TO REASON WITH AND DISPERSE CROWD PRIOR TO FIRE. IDENTITIES OF THESE INDIVIDUALS BEING OBTAINED, AND THEY WILL BE INTERVIEWED.

PHOTOS WERE TAKEN THIS DATE OF DOCUMENTS OBTAINED BY KENT PD IN SEARCH OF RESIDENCE AT TWO THREE SEVEN AND ONE-HALF NORTH WATER ST., KENT, ON MAY FOUR, LAST. ATTEMPT WAS MADE TO INTERVIEW ARRESTEES INVOLVED IN THIS SEARCH;

HOWEVER IT WAS LEARNED THEY WERE RELEASED FROM PORTAGE COUNTY JAIL MORNING OF MAY FIVE, LAST.

IT IS NOTED THIS INVESTIGATION IS BEING COORDINATED WITH CIVIL RIGHTS INVESTIGATION AT KSU AND DEATHS OF FOUR STUDENTS, MAY FOUR, LAST.

END

3. JUSTICE HUGO L. BLACK'S CONCURRING OPINION IN THE CASE OF *NEW YORK TIMES CO. V. UNITED STATES*, JUNE 30, 1971

I adhere to the view that the Government's case against the *Washington Post* should have been dismissed and that the injunction against the *New York Times* should have been vacated without oral argument when the cases were first presented to this Court. I believe [403 U.S. 713, 715] that every moment's continuance of the injunctions against these newspapers amounts to a flagrant, indefensible, and continuing violation of the First Amendment. Furthermore, after oral argument, I agree completely that we must affirm the judgment of the Court of Appeals for the District of Columbia Circuit and reverse the judgment of the Court of Appeals for the Second Circuit for the reasons stated by my Brothers DOUGLAS and BRENNAN. In my view it is unfortunate that some of my Brethren are apparently willing to hold that the publication of news may sometimes be enjoined. Such a holding would make a shambles of the First Amendment.

Our Government was launched in 1789 with the adoption of the Constitution. The Bill of Rights, including the First Amendment, followed in 1791. Now, for the first time in the 182 years since the founding of the Republic, the federal courts are asked to hold that the First Amendment does not mean what it says, but rather means that the Government can halt the publication of current news of vital importance to the people of this country.

In seeking injunctions against these newspapers and in its presentation to the Court, the Executive Branch seems to have forgotten the essential purpose and history of the First Amendment. When the Constitution was adopted, many people strongly opposed it because the document contained no Bill of Rights to safeguard certain basic freedoms. They especially feared that the [403 U.S. 713, 716] new powers granted to a central government might be interpreted to permit the government to curtail freedom of religion, press, assembly, and speech. In response to an overwhelming public clamor, James Madison offered a series of amendments to satisfy citizens that these great liberties would remain safe and beyond the power of government to abridge. Madison proposed what later became the First Amendment in three parts, two of which are set out below, and one of which proclaimed: "The people shall not be deprived or abridged of their right to speak, to write, or to publish their sentiments; and the freedom of the press, as one of the great bulwarks of liberty, shall be inviolable." (Emphasis added.) The amendments were offered to curtail and restrict the general powers granted to the Executive, Legislative, and Judicial Branches two years before in the original Constitution. The Bill of Rights changed the original Constitution into a new charter under which no branch of government could abridge the people's freedoms of press, speech, religion, and assembly.

Yet the Solicitor General argues and some members of the Court appear to agree that the general powers of the Government adopted in the original Constitution should be interpreted to limit and restrict the specific and emphatic guarantees of the Bill of Rights adopted later. I can imagine no greater perversion of history. Madison and the other Framers of the First Amendment, able men [403 U.S. 713, 717] that they were, wrote in language they earnestly believed could never be misunderstood: "Congress shall make no law . . . abridging the freedom . . . of the press. . . ." Both the history and language of the First Amendment support the view that the press must be left free to publish news, whatever the source, without censorship, injunctions, or prior restraints.

In the First Amendment the Founding Fathers gave the free press the protection it must have to fulfill its essential role in our democracy. The press was to serve the governed, not the governors. The Government's power to censor the press was abolished so that the press would remain forever free to censure the Government. The press was protected so that it could bare the secrets of government and inform the people. Only a free and unrestrained press can effectively expose deception in government. And paramount among the responsibilities of a free press is the duty to prevent any part of the government from deceiving the people and sending them off to distant lands to die of foreign fevers and foreign shot and shell. In my view, far from deserving condemnation for their courageous reporting, the *New York Times,* the *Washington Post,* and other newspapers should be commended for serving the purpose that the Founding Fathers saw so clearly. In revealing the workings of government that led to the Vietnam war, the newspapers nobly did precisely that which the Founders hoped and trusted they would do.

The Government's case here is based on premises entirely different from those that guided the Framers of the First Amendment. The Solicitor General has carefully and emphatically stated:

"Now, Mr. Justice [BLACK], your construction of . . . [the First Amendment] is well known, and I certainly respect it. You say that no law means no law, and that should be obvious. I can only [403 U.S. 713, 718] say, Mr. Justice, that to me it is equally obvious that 'no law' does not mean 'no law', and I would seek to persuade the Court that is true. . . . [T]here are other parts of the Constitution that grant powers and responsibilities to the Executive, and . . . the First Amendment was not intended to make it impossible for the Executive to function or to protect the security of the United States."

And the Government argues in its brief that in spite of the First Amendment, "[t]he authority of the Executive Department to protect the nation against publication of information whose disclosure would endanger the national security stems from two interrelated sources: the constitutional power of the President over the conduct of foreign affairs and his authority as Commander-in-Chief."

In other words, we are asked to hold that despite the First Amendment's emphatic command, the Executive Branch, the Congress, and the Judiciary can make laws enjoining publication of current news and abridging freedom of the press in the name of "national security." The Government does not even attempt to rely on any act of Congress. Instead it makes the bold and dangerously far-reaching contention that the courts should take it upon themselves to "make" a law abridging freedom of the press in the name of equity, presidential power and national security, even when the representatives of the people in Congress have adhered to the command of the First Amendment and refused to make such a law. See concurring opinion of MR. JUSTICE DOUGLAS, [403 U.S. 713, 719] post, at 721–722. To find that the President has "inherent power" to halt the publication of news by resort to the courts would wipe out the First Amendment and destroy the fundamental liberty and security of the very people the Government hopes to make "secure." No one can read the history of the adoption of the First Amendment without being convinced beyond any doubt that it was injunctions like those sought here that Madison and his collaborators intended to outlaw in this Nation for all time.

The word "security" is a broad, vague generality whose contours should not be invoked to abrogate the fundamental law embodied in the First Amendment. The guarding of military and diplomatic secrets at the expense of informed representative government provides no real security for our Republic. The Framers of the First Amendment, fully aware of both the need to defend a new nation and the abuses of the English and Colonial governments, sought to give this new society strength and security by providing that freedom of speech, press, religion, and assembly should not be abridged. This thought was eloquently expressed in 1937 by Mr. Chief Justice Hughes—great man and great Chief Justice that he was—when the Court held a man could not be punished for attending a meeting run by Communists.

"The greater the importance of safeguarding the community from incitements to the overthrow of our institutions by force and violence, the more imperative is the need to preserve inviolate the constitutional rights of free speech, free press and free [403 U.S. 713, 720] assembly in order to maintain the opportunity for free political discussion, to the end that government may be responsive to the will of the people and that changes, if desired, may be obtained by peaceful means. Therein lies the security of the Republic, the very foundation of constitutional government."

4. EQUAL RIGHTS AMENDMENT (ERA) PASSED BY HOUSE OF REPRESENTATIVES, OCTOBER 1971

Resolved by the Senate and House of Representatives of the United States of America in Congress assembled (two-thirds of each House concurring therein), That the following article is proposed as an amendment to the Constitution of the United States, which shall be valid to all intents and purposes as part of the Constitution when ratified by the legislatures of three-fourths of the several States within seven years from the date of its submission by the Congress:

Section 1. Equality of rights under the law shall not be denied or abridged by the United States or by any State on account of sex.

Section 2. The Congress shall have the power to enforce, by appropriate legislation, the provisions of this article. Section 3. This amendment shall take effect two years after the date of ratification.

5. MCKAY COMMISSION ATTICA PRISON RIOT INVESTIGATION, THE EXAMINATION OF FRANCIS JOSEPH HUEN, APRIL 20, 1972

Note: The New York State Special Commission on Attica was formed to investigate the 1971 riot at Attica State Prison. The commission was headed by Robert B. McKay, dean of the New York University Law School, and thus was more popularly called the McKay Commission. This is the questioning of Francis Joseph Huen, an inmate at Attica.

Examination by [Judge Charles] Willis:

Q   Mr. Huen, how old are you, sir?

A   I will be 36 in August.

Q   Where were you born, sir?

A   Yonkers, New York.

Q   What is your education?

A   Eighth grade.

Q   Are you married?

No, sir.

Q   Presently you are an inmate at Attica, although presently, for purposes of this hearing, I understand that you are being held up in Ossining, New York; is that right?

A   That's true.

Q   When did you go to Attica?

A   September 1, 1970.

Q   What was the offense you were convicted of and the term that you were sentenced to?

A   Well, I was sentenced to concurrent terms of 20 years and 7 years, which because of jail time stipulations, will actually be 22 years and I was sentenced for third degree robbery and second degree robbery.

Q   Now, is this the first time you have been in a correctional institution in New York State?

A   No, sir. I was arrested in 1952 and I was ultimately sentenced to Coxsackie Reformatory.

Q   When, Mr. Huen, will you be eligible for parole?

A   I will be eligible for parole in, I believe, August 1976.

Q   Where were you locked in at the time of the September incident, during that time?

A   I was locked in A block, 6th company.

Q   Where are you presently locked in?

A   In C block, 35 company.

Q   In another area. We will get back to—between those two times, were you locked in any other part of the prison?

A   Oh, I definitely was. Immediately following the riot, in fact September 13, I was placed in HBZ, or the box, as it is usually called and I was there for 4 days.

Q   We will get back to that when you return to us. What presently—what first of all was your work assignment back in September of 1971?

A   The coal gang.

Q   What is your present work assignment?

A   The coal gang.

Q   How do you like your work?

A   Well—

Q   As compared to what's available.

A   Making the best of a bad lot—I'm happy there and I asked to be there.

Q   I think we had an opportunity last week to speak to the officer who heads up that detail. How about the other men who work with you; how do they feel or do you know about that assignment?

A   Well, it's a 7 day a week job and that's a help. It gets you out of the cell and it kills time and Mr. Head—the officer that you just mentioned, he is an easy fellow to get along with and by and large it's the best of a bad lot.

Q   How many men work in that crew?

A   Presently there are 14.

Q   And at the time in September?

A   30.

Q   Just as a matter of record, could you tell me what the racial composition of that crew is? On rough percentages.

A   Right now it's very easy. There are only 2 blacks and the rest are white. At the time I believe there were about 8 whites out of the 30 and the rest were perhaps half black and half Puerto Rican.

Q   Do you believe, prior to the September incidents, that there was any discrimination in job assignments?

A   There was some. It's hard for me to know exactly how much. I did have the impression that there was some.

Q   In what form? When you say discrimination, against blacks and Puerto Ricans or against whites—when you say there was discrimination?

A   Against blacks. I think there was a feeling that blacks were more troublesome and in many jobs, clerk jobs where they had to come in almost constant contact and work with employees, there was a tendency to consider them a bit more troublesome and not to assign them to those jobs, although I really don't know how extensive that was. It is just an impression that I had.

Q   Now, Mr. Huen, to get to some of the more significant parts of the testimony we are trying to elicit, you were in D yard during the period September 9 to 13, 1971; weren't you?

A   Yes, I was.

Q   Did you know, incidentally, anything at that time about the incident in the A block yard the day before where there was a confrontation with the officers?

A   Well, I entered that yard. I came into that yard perhaps within minutes of Lieutenant Maroney and the other officers leaving the yard and I have no direct knowledge of exactly what did happen or what was said, but there was a certain amount of tension and there was a lot of talk about what happened.

Q   And you could feel that tension?

A   Yes. Yes. Definitely.

Q   Incidentally, speaking about tension, say during the summer and the months prior to the September incident, did you—were you aware of any noticeable rise or increase in the tension in Attica?

A   Well, I had been there a year only, so I can't speak about relative tension. There was a great deal of tension. There was a great deal of tension.

Q   Well, would that and your knowledge—either direct or hearsay knowledge of what happened on the 8th, did you believe that anything was to occur on the 9th, the morning of the 9th; did you face that day with any unusual apprehension?

A   No, I did not.

Q   Now, I wonder if you could perhaps trace for us what you were doing on that Thursday morning, September 9.

A   Well, I had a call out from the dentist's office and I was given a pass with a few other inmates and instead of going to my usual work assignment at 8:00, I went to the dentist's office. I was through—the dentist was through with me at just about 8:45, so that within that time, in the next minute or so, a few minutes, I was coming from the hospital and coming through the corridor from C block Times Square area and—

Q   I wonder if you could indicate—there is a pointer here. I know there is some difficulty with inmates because seldom do they get a bird's eye view.

A   This doesn't seem to be a problem. Times Square is here and these are the tunnels going to various blocks [t]his is C-block. The hospital was here. I walked through here, whatever length of time it took to actually get here and when I did, the four gates that are at the end of the tunnels coming in to this Times Square area were locked.

This was very unusual. It's not unheard of, but it's very unusual at that time with the amount of traffic that you have, and there was traffic backed up, inmates, you might say, that were backed up that had to wait to get through and there was an air—a definite air of tension here. You couldn't even get people to talk. I asked what's going on and no one seemed to know what was going on or wanted to say what was going on.

Q   Then what happened?

A   Well, at that point I heard a great deal of screaming—I want to say screaming, but very loud talking, yelling, coming from this tunnel here.

Q   That's A?

A   This is A-block here and this is the A-block tunnel and there was loud noise and there was inmates that could be seen through the bars over here and once again I asked, from guys who had been there a moment or two before me, what was going on and I couldn't get an answer.

Within seconds one of the officer was let—who had been in A-block—was let into Times Square. The gate was opened. There was no attempt by the other inmates on the other side of that gate to follow in through it to Times Square, but he himself had quite a cut on the top of his head and there was blood streaming down all over his shirt and so forth like that. It was sort of a scary moment at that moment for everyone. I thought there was some really definite trouble there.

Q   And then what occurred after that, Mr. Huen?

A   Well, after that, after he had come into the tunnel itself—now, there were two officers stationed right there in Times Square and they didn't seem to be doing anything. They didn't seem to be calling for help or anything like that, although they may have done so, but they didn't seem to be doing anything. They weren't saying anything. They weren't giving any instructions to the prisoners or anything like that, and Mr. Kelsy wasn't talking to them or anything and the screaming and so forth, the yelling, the loud conversations that was going on over here continued.

I noticed inmates trying to peer out windows here and I went over there myself.

I saw officers up on the top of this catwalk, and once Pat was gone, his shirt was out and they hesitated a moment and then ran to this area here, A-block where the hall captain is and where the officers congregate.

Right after that there were—well, the yelling really got excited and these gates here from A-block into Times Square were being pushed against, and I became very apprehensive at this time and I said to myself, "Well, I can't get back to where I'm supposed to be," which is A-block, "Let me try and get back to the hospital." At this point, as I went back towards C-block and in trying to get back to the hospital, the gates in C-block itself were locked up. So, there I was.

I went back mid-way, you might say, between the two gates, and the screaming was getting unbelievable there and the tension and the apprehension on the faces of everyone there at the time was getting pretty—just overwhelming, you might say, and I went back again to the gates of Times Square itself, and I could see the gates being pushed from the A-block side and they were just pushed open like butter, just open.

Q   That's the gate leading from the A-tunnel to Times Square?

A   To Times Square, yes.

Q   All right. Then, Mr. Huen, what did you do and what happened to you?

A   Well, at this time I was nervous about being possibly considered someone that was involved in this. I was thinking about my own neck, you might say.

Q   What was your first impression or your thoughts when you saw this happening; what was part of your apprehension?

A   Well, the whole thing seemed so unreal, especially those gates opening up like that and the inability of the officers to respond in any way whatsoever or even to attempt to. It was just—it was, in a sense, a shock. It's just very, very unreal. Boy, was it unreal. And—

Q   All right, then, you were at last back at the Times Square area.

A   Yes.

Q   And you observed the A-corridor door open. What happened after that?

A   Well, inmates came streaming through—and I'm not sure if I actually saw this—I saw the keys being taken from the officers that were in Times Square to open up the other gates, or whether I just saw them opening up the other gates, I'm not sure, but within seconds all the other gates were opened and inmates were streaming through freely.

Q   Through all the corridors?

A   Yes. Through all the corridors.

Q   Then what happened to you at the time?

A   Again, at this time I went back towards C-block to just get out of the rush. It was like a 42nd Street subway rush, to get out of it.

Now, I could see that the C-block gates were open. There was an officer who—

Q   Well—go ahead.

A   There was an officer that was on the ground. Apparently he had been knocked down, but he was—he was being ignored. They just rushed by him, you might say, and he was getting up sort of in slow motion, and he looked to be in pretty well of a state of shock, more of a state of shock than hurt.

The gate on the opposite side of C-block was still locked and it wasn't able to get—

Q   What were your intentions at that time; your going back and forth?

A   Well, I was just trying to get out of the rush. This had happened very quickly. I hadn't formed any sort of an opinion. It was just reaction. Pure reaction to get out of the way of this. I didn't expect it. I didn't understand it, and I say it was the least likely thing that I ever thought could happen within a structured place such as Attica.

Q   Were you by yourself at the time?

A   By the time that I finally got into C-block itself, one of the fellows—it turned out that all of that yelling that I had heard initially had been from the members of Five Company, and I knew one of the fellows from Five Company, and I asked him what was going on.

Now, I began to get some picture of the correlation between the incident of the day before and the taking out of the cells of one of the fellows that had been involved in the incident of the day before and the troubles that that had caused on Five Company.

Q   Right.

A   And this fellow, if I remember correctly, he said, "It's on. It's on. You know, it's blown. The whole place is going on."

Q   Right. Now, I wonder if you would, at this point, trace your movements and observations from that point until you arrived at the D-yard.

A   Well, as I say, this gate here was still locked. I never saw that gate open. I understand at some point it was open, but I never saw it opened. Myself and this other fellow that I did know, he said, "Come on, let's get out of here. We will get up to the third floor of C-block and get away from this."

I thought there would be a reaction from the guards almost immediately and that would be that.

Q   When you say that, do you mean a reaction on retaking—

A   Yes. They would move right back in. That's what I thought at the time. I didn't know how extensive it was, even though I had seen the other gates open at Times Square, and obviously there were men running all through the other blocks. I didn't think of that at the moment, and I just expected that there would be a reaction, a counter force from the guards that would restore everything to normal within a very short period. And so we went or tried to go up into the third floor. The third floor was locked. We stayed on the second floor in this wing here. There were a number of fellows that I did know fairly well up there at the time, and we intended to just hang around up there until things got straightened out and stay away from the activity that was in the halls. And around the desk.

Q   What happened and how is it that you ended up in D-yard?

A   Well, we saw correction officers massing out here, massing, a dozen at most. They had what appeared to me to be a rifle. They had gas guns. There were brass out there. There was a lieutenant out there. They fired—there is a door right between here—it's not visible—or even a tunnel, the extension of the tunnel that actually connects these tunnels is invisible, but there is a door here and they seemed to be firing gas toward that door, but that was the extent of the effort they made at that time to come back into the prison or to restrict the actions of the inmates. As I say, they were here—they were there for quite a while, perhaps an hour went by. They made no other effort to come back into the prison. They were firing down to this area. I still had some thought that if things get bad I would still get out that way, get away from that. As time went on it was apparent that that wasn't going to happen; that I wasn't going to be allowed to get past that point. There were other inmates exuberant, terrified—in all sorts of conditions, but all very emotional coming in and out of the block that I was in with the fellows I was in, and there was much discussion about what should be done. We were asked by some to go to D-block. They said everybody is going down to D-Block. There is hostages down in D-block and that's the safest point. I, myself, didn't think that was a safe point. I felt, if we went into this open yard, that we would be sitting ducks for whatever was to come.

Q   Was your apprehension and fear of inmates or guards and why?

A   I have to—I would have to describe my own feelings, my own individual feelings as primarily one of shock, one of shock. There were, as I say, a variety of emotions running rampant throughout the place to the people that I saw and one of these that was very real in the minds of a lot of prisoners, that this might be degenerating into a race riot. There were no real indications. There was nothing really done that would support that, but nevertheless there was a feeling that this might happen and, of course, this added to the tension. It let people—they didn't know where to turn.

Q   Subsequently, did you make any determination as to whether it was in fact a race riot?

A   Well, it wasn't until we actually had gotten into the yard itself, and when I got into the yard there seemed to be something bordering on a party atmosphere. It wasn't exuberant, really, totally, but there was—well, there wasn't any fighting going on. At that point all the hostages that ever were going to be collected were collected; they were all together. Some had been hurt, bruised, bloody, so forth, like that. I saw no indications of any real harm that had been done to them, and there seemed to be an effort by some of the wiser heads, you might say, to keep the hotheads away from them and leave them alone. This is our key out of this whole mess, you right say, but while I was still in C-block, it was another story. I didn't really know what to expect. I was in a high state of shock, and the general feeling was still to try, among all the inmates that I saw in C-block, to stay out of D-block yard and stay out of whatever it is that is causing this.

Q   All right, sir. So what happened from the C-block eventually—was it through the request of other inmates—but at any rate, you did go back down and into the D-yard?

A   Yes. Eventually I did, yes.

Q   How long after the initial events that took place in the A corridor—how long after that was it that you got into D yard?

A   Just about 1 hour. Just about 1 hour.

Q   Incidentally, during that period did you hear any whistles or alarms going off?

A   Oh, yes. The power house whistle at some point, it started ringing and blowing and all of that.

Q   Now, when you got in the yard you said your first impression was one of—I will paraphrase. I get the feeling you felt it was like a carnival atmosphere.

A   To some extent, yes. I think there was a sense of relief that while—at least there has got to be—the initial silence, whatever it had been, was not running rampant, and there was guys still running around the halls, they were trying to get to the commissary and try to get candy bars and cartons of cigarettes rather than really, boy, let's kill these hacks or anything like that or "let's start a fight among us."

Q   So that original apprehension you had after you got in the yard was dissipated in itself?

A   Dissipated quite a bit, quite a bit.

Q   Did you feel at that time any threat of danger to yourself?

A   Well, as I say I was in shock primarily. I didn't know what to expect, really, I didn't discount any possibility. I didn't discount the police coming in, the guards or whatever coming in and just opening fire. I didn't discount some hothead just running amok among prisoners, and I didn't know what to expect, but at that time I felt that there would be a breathing space.

Q   Where did you go; where did you locate yourself in D yard?

A   Well, now we are speaking about a five day period, a four day period.

Q   Yes.

A   Eventually, but it wasn't until, I guess, about the second day—eventually a tent was arranged by myself and, I think, 8 or 9 other men right about this spot here. No. I have to right myself. This is the handball court. Right about here.

Q   As close to the center—

A   Yes. Midway between the center here and this corner here. Right about here.

Q   Were you close enough to the leadership table to watch the proceedings over the four day period?

A   Well, I would have to disagree with the characterization of the leadership. One of the most bothersome things that I found throughout the whole period—I didn't feel that there was anyone who had things in control enough to be termed a leadership. If you are speaking about the negotiating people that at various times sat at that table and spoke to Mr. Oswald or the other people that came in, or if you are speaking about the outside people that came in—

Q   No. I'm speaking about the inmates.

A   The inmates—

Q   Who were, to a large degree, the spokesmen.

A   The spokesmen. I don't believe—no, not while actual negotiations were going on. No.

Q   Now, speaking about the spokesmen for the inmates, do you feel that there was any—we have heard testimony concerning the selection of leaders among the various blocks and the election that took place of these representatives from these blocks and who supposedly acted in a leadership capacity or representative capacity. What was your impression of this?

A   Well, you have to understand how structured Attica was and is today. Outside of the men, actually on my gallery that I was working with, those 30 men on a coal gang, it was very difficult to get to know any other inmate, even in your own block, and if they were in other blocks, D block or B block, you didn't know them at all. So, my thought was—and I think because of a lot of people were to say even if you didn't know some of these guys, even if some of the things they said might not be the most practical things that sort, you might say, in order to keep things going in one direction, that I think most people just acquiesced to whoever was nominated.

Q   Do you think—we have heard the activities in the yard characterized everywhere from tyranny to an Athenian democracy. How would you categorize it?

A   Confused.

Q   Confused?

A   Confused.

Q   All right. Now, on the question of demands we have heard that inmates all had an opportunity to get up and speak and to add their request or their demands to the growing list. Did you participate in this?

A   At one point a fellow came around and he said, "This is what has been proposed. Do you have anything to add or do you disagree with anything?" And I felt at the time that the very fact that someone was making an attempt to get a consensus of opinion—that was more than enough for me: as long as everybody would be working together, I thought that it was fine and I didn't even pay too much attention to what the demands were. I wasn't concerned so much with the demands as that there would be a unified group of demands for the outside people to deal with.

Q   Well, do you think that there was a consensus concerning the demands that the majority of inmates were in agreement with in those demands which were being put forth?

A   Well, I think the actual expectations, the actual—what individual inmates wanted varied so—well, take that thing about going to Algeria. Nobody really paid too much attention to that. There were guys in there

that all they wanted was more pink ice cream, we will say, and there were guys in there that were concerned about getting cake in the mess hall, and there were guys that were deeply concerned about improving the parole system and trying to get fresh minds into the institution; to do something about rehabilitation. I got the impression myself that there wasn't any real consensus between any more than 50 people. I don't think you could have gotten 50 people that could have agreed on any one point.

Q   Now subsequently and on that afternoon and evening of the following day, observers began to come to the yard—

A   Yes.

Q   At the request of inmates and/or administration people.

A   Yes.

Q   Were you able to observe or did you listen or pay attention to the things that they said and some of the things that they did, and if so, I would like your impression of what, if any effect, they had upon the men, upon the situation and actually on the eventual outcome of the events.

A   I think they didn't really have too much effect on the total outcome. I think there was an expectation on the part of many prisoners that they would be able to get a note of sanity, you might say, into the proceedings. The obstinate attitude—the real reluctance of the administration to fully negotiate and the confusion that existed among the prisoners themselves, their difficulty of getting agreement about what really, what the—what should be accepted. I thought there was a—I think most prisoners felt that their best hope was that these people, these outside people might possibly be able to get like, as I say, a note of sanity in the proceedings.

Q   Were you hopeful, say, during the first day or two that perhaps there could be an acceptable solution, that there would be a solution other than the ultimate solution?

A   Well, within the first two days, up until the ending of the first day we will say—sometime along that period when the newspaper people came in, when the television people came in, there was a feeling, I think most prisoners had, that the tendency of the administration was to just slap everybody down, lock him up, beat him up, kill him if you have to, wouldn't be able to prevail and that it wouldn't be fair to say that Mr. Tom Wicker over there was going to lead us out of this, because that the combined pressure we might say, the combined exposure of all of the attention that was being focused on Attica would perhaps get us out of there without too much harm, either to us or to the hostages or anyone else.

Q   I would like to ask on that point: do you believe that if it had been continued along those lines, if you heard Mr. Wicker's testimony, that if more time had been given, possibly it could have been otherwise resolved?

A   Well, I think I should say this, that despite all the statements that were made on Sunday concerning the disastrous position we were in, there was still a feeling that public opinion, focused as it was on Attica, would not allow the administration to do what they ultimately did do and just send in people in any way possible, disregarding our lives and the hostages' lives, just get control of the prison.

One of the things I have to mention about that was that there was a feeling—whether this was true or not, and we had no way of knowing whether this was true, but there was a feeling that it was Governor Rockefeller who was going to make the decision to come in or not to come in, to grant amnesty or not to grant amnesty, and there was a feeling that until he did come there and make that decision, that there was always time to negotiate.

I have to elaborate on that again. The only public statement that was made up until the 13th by Governor Rockefeller that we were aware of was a news report, I believe on Sunday night, that came over the television that he would not and could not grant amnesty, which was a core point with the prisoners. Now—

Q   Go ahead.

A   Well, what I'm getting to say is that despite all the testimony, despite Mr. Kunstler's very emotional and very sincere plea to us that if we didn't agree to the demands that had been accepted, that some of us were going to die, and I know that he believed that, because still there was that—there was that statement by Governor Rockefeller which said that he would not and could not grant amnesty; that he explained that Mr. James was the District Attorney of that area and that that was his jurisdiction and he wasn't—he didn't have the power to interfere.

Well, we knew that wasn't true and subsequently, after the riot, Mr. James was superseded, I believe—the word is used by Mr. Fisher to conduct investigations into Attica and so forth and so forth, and we also knew that the governor had the power to replace or take a district attorney in a particular area out of a particular situation and we knew that that could be done.

So, when he said that he would not interfere or grant amnesty, there was a tendency on the prisoners' part not to believe that any more than they believed that he could not act.

Q   May I ask you this: on the sole question, did you think that amnesty was in fact the key issue or the key demand of the men in the yard?

A   I think if the amnesty had been granted or promised—I don't believe myself that it could have been kept. I don't believe that there was any binding way that it could have been offered to us that was enforceable by us in a Court of law, but I very carefully didn't mention that. I didn't want to keep the pot boiling any more than it had to be kept boiling, but I did feel that if Governor Rockefeller had given his personal assurance, whether or not the prisoners would have really relied on his credibility, they would have accepted the fact that there was no more to be done in that area; that he was the last word and, I believe, that there was a good possibility, I don't say a certainty, but there was a good possibility that that would have been the last effort of the inmates to gain any more than what they had been offered.

Q   Let me say this, then, because you felt that the ultimate word and the ultimate credibility would be in the governor, in the event Commissioner Oswald had granted the amnesty; do you think the men would have accepted it coming from him?

A   I don't really know. I think there would have been a serious question about it.

Q   Did amnesty become even more important when you learned of the death of Officer Quinn?

A   Well, Governor—Officer Quinn's death, the announcement of his death had a strong effect on the thinking of everything. Afterward, I think as time went on and men thought about that, I think there was a very strong feeling among a lot of prisoners that, well, a cop has been killed and no matter what you do, they are not going to let that go by the boards; that there is going to be repression; that there are going to be reprisals regardless of what you are going to do, so it made it more difficult.

Getting back to what you said about Mr. Oswald's original amnesty, I think there might possibly still have been a reluctance to accept that after it was known that a cop had been killed.

Now, let me correct myself. I'm saying a cop had been killed, whereas in fact at that time we didn't know. We did not know that he was killed, murdered, in legal sense. It was just that he had died.

Q   At any time were you convinced that the troopers were coming in shooting before it actually happened?

A   I felt myself that there was—that anything was possible. I continued to believe that up until the time that the shots were actually fired. I thought it was possible and probable that if they did come in, that the damage would be a lot worse than it was. I was very aware of that. At the same time I was aware that these negotiations could have gone on for a longer period of time. I really didn't think until shots were fired that that was the end, they were coming in.

Q   Did you want to be in the yard?

A   No, I didn't. It was too scary for me altogether.

Q   Do you think you could have left the yard had you wanted to?

A   Well, it would have been very difficult. As Mr. Carpenter testified yesterday, he was bringing hostages to the gate, I believe he said, of A block or the administration or whatever it was, and he was driven back by guns. So, you had that to contend with and then, of course, you had the feeling of inmates within the yard that, gee, what's wrong with you; who are you with; are you with us or what?

So, that had to be considered and it was also a possibility that if any sizeable amount or even a small amount of inmates had tried to leave the yard, well, it might have caused this corruption between the inmates, and I think the inmates felt very strongly that one of the things the administration was doing was hoping that we would start snarling amongst each other and start to tear each other apart and try to solve the problem that was for them and there was a reluctance to do that.

Q   Now, did you believe that the offer of the 28 demands or the acception of the 28 demands by the Commissioner was all you were going to get?

A   I personally didn't believe that any agreement reached under those circumstances would have been fulfilled. That was my own personal opinion. I think there were quite a few men in the yard that felt that way also. I don't know how prevalent that was.

Q   Do you recall—

A   I would like to add to that. I think one of the confusing things about this whole picture is that the men who were seemingly most violent and most radical nevertheless were people that felt that if they did these things, if they took hostages, if they made a lot of noise and got attention, that something would be done within the prison, and if fellows, like myself, who didn't want any part of the violence and didn't want any part of these confrontations were actually the men that had no faith that any contract would be made and no changes have come.

So, that's a confusing thing for people to see.

On the one hand you have someone making speeches—we want to die, but ultimately this was a guy that thought this would have an effect on prison rehabilitation, let's say.

Q   Do you recall when the so-called ultimatum came in on early Monday?

A   Yes.

Q   Do you recall whether or not the men were asked whether or not they would accept this ultimatum, or at least honor it and give up; do you recall that, that there was—

A   I believe the wording was, "Should we hold out?"

Q   Right.

A   I don't think there was too much of a detailed discussion about whether we should accept what we had been offered. I think there was, at this time—by the time we had gotten to this point, men were weary, men were worn down. The more emotional fellows were starting to lose touch with themselves. It was getting to be a bad moment under any circumstances and there wasn't too much discussion about the demands. It was a question of should we hold out or should we just throw in the towel and let him beat us up or kill us, whatever they wanted to do. I think there was more of that sort of a feeling.

Q   Well, did anyone, in your recollection, agree that they should accept the ultimatum?

A   Well, there was one fellow that questioned whether or not we should accept the ultimatum.

Q   Would you—did you believe you should accept it?

A   Well, you see, this is a difficult thing and it is tempered—my answer has to be tempered by hindsight. I believe—I don't think that this was my personal belief—is that this was one of the 28 demands. I'm not even familiar with the demands. I didn't pay too much attention to them at the time in the yard, but I did feel that whatever the demands were, if you could include a representative of the press who would be there to supervise the overtaking of the prison, whether or not the demands were later kept, whether the agreement was kept later on wasn't too important to me, as long as if we did have someone there from the press, from the outside people who would insure that at least we were not brutalized physically at the actual taking over. I would have been happy, very happy to be out of that yard. But, at that time—at that point, the lack of communication—even between prisoners—had broken down so badly that I didn't even think about proposing such a thing like that, or I don't think anyone would have listened to me, particularly.

Q   So, therefore, you didn't make—at that point you made no statements?

A   No, I made no statements.

Q   Now let me ask you this: when were you—you said something about you weren't convinced that they were going to come in the way they did right up until the last moment. Did you make any preparation yourself for the possibility of an assault?

A   Well, I got as far away from the hostages, who I felt would be a target, and that was the only thing that I thought could be done.

Q   Mr. Huen, we are restricting, as [General Counsel Arthur L.] Liman said, your testimony today to your impressions and your observations of the activities in the yard and, as you know, we have asked that you return next week when we get into that phase of the incidents that led to the assault, the aftermath of the assault, et cetera and, Mr. Chairman, I have no further questions at this time of this witness.

[General Counsel Arthur L.] Liman: Mr. Huen, you can remain until after the luncheon recess so that the Commission can then put some questions to you. I wonder, though, so that they will also have a further basis for questions, if you would describe for them what you described for the staff before this air of what you called unreality in the yard and in particular I refer to the helicopter example.

THE WITNESS: Oh, yes. Just immediately before the actual shooting started, there was an unmarked helicopter. I think it was painted yellow. It wasn't a military type, the big ones that came in later that we had seen on television and knew were outside. It circled over the yard a number of times. To this day I don't know really what it was doing there. While everybody was standing around and beginning to get apprehensive and staring up at this thing circling over their heads, an inmate that I knew to be pretty deranged normally, under normal circumstances, he was coming

to the point of being pretty whacked out at that moment, came to the group and said that was the Young Lords.

The Young Lords have guns. They are going to drop down guns. The cops are going to shoot and then—and as weird as that sounds now, there were men that believed it. There was that air of unreality. There were men standing next to me who'd spent twenty-four years, who knows what to expect, or who you'd think would know what to expect, who turned around and asked me "Is that really the Young Lords?"

MR. LIMAN: Did you also hear inmates say that they thought it was Governor Rockefeller coming in the helicopter?

THE WITNESS: I can't say that I heard that.

MR. LIMAN: We have heard other inmates make that remark.

THE WITNESS: No.

MR. LIMAN: Did this air of unreality manifest itself in other ways during these days?

THE WITNESS: Certainly. I was in a state of shock, I will have to say, throughout the thing, and I was—I felt detached, you might say, from the harshness of it. You speak about was I aware of being—the possibility of being shot at that moment. I felt detached from it. It was just so unreal and so incomprehensible that it was definitely that factor had, I think, an influence throughout everything that did happen in the yard.

MR. WILLIS: One further question I wanted to ask you, Mr. Huen, and that is, for the period of time we have heard testimony to this effect, but I would like to get your impression on this, and that is the treatment of hostages by the inmates over the period of time.

THE WITNESS: Oh, they were handled with kid gloves, except for the first half hour. I didn't see them for an hour afterwards. I did see perhaps three guards being led from G-block and the first two, the inmates and the guards, they sort of stood there and didn't really know it was an unusual situation. So finally one reached out and took a club away from a guy and then just put his hand on him and led him off. Those individual officers never were even beaten or punched or anything like that.

MR. WILLIS: So that your observations were that the hostages were not being mistreated nor were they in danger, at least any imminent danger of any serious injury?

THE WITNESS: Not from the inmates. Definitely not. Definitely not.

6. Interim Agreement between the United States and the Soviet Union to Limit Strategic Nuclear Arms (SALT I Treaty), along with the Protocol, Statements, and Understandings, May 26, 1972

INTERIM AGREEMENT BETWEEN THE UNITED STATES OF AMERICA AND THE UNION OF SOVIET SOCIALIST REPUBLICS ON CERTAIN MEASURES WITH RESPECT TO THE LIMITATION OF STRATEGIC OFFENSIVE ARMS

Signed at Moscow May 26, 1972

Approval authorized by U.S. Congress September 30, 1972

Approved by U.S. President September 30, 1972

Notices of acceptance exchanged October 3, 1972

Entered into force October 3, 1972

The United States of America and the Union of Soviet Socialist Republics, hereinafter referred to as the Parties, Convinced that the Treaty on the Limitation of Anti-Ballistic Missile Systems and this Interim Agreement on Certain Measures with Respect to the Limitation of Strategic Offensive Arms will contribute to the creation of more favorable conditions for active negotiations on limiting strategic arms as well as to the relaxation of international tension and the strengthening of trust between States,

Taking into account the relationship between strategic offensive and defensive arms, Mindful of their obligations under Article VI of the Treaty on the Non-Proliferation of Nuclear Weapons,

Have agreed as follows:

Article I

The Parties undertake not to start construction of additional fixed land-based intercontinental ballistic missile (ICBM) launchers after July 1, 1972.

Article II

The Parties undertake not to convert land-based launchers for light ICBMs, or for ICBMs of older types deployed prior to 1964, into land-based launchers for heavy ICBMs of types deployed after that time.

Article III

The Parties undertake to limit submarine-launched ballistic missile (SLBM) launchers and modern ballistic missile submarines to the numbers operational and under construction on the date of signature of this Interim Agreement, and in addition to launchers and submarines constructed under procedures established by the Parties as replacements for an equal number of ICBM launchers of older types deployed prior to 1964 or for launchers on older submarines.

Article IV

Subject to the provisions of this Interim Agreement, modernization and replacement of strategic offensive ballistic missiles and launchers covered by this Interim Agreement may be undertaken.

Article V

1. For the purpose of providing assurance of compliance with the provisions of this Interim Agreement, each Party shall use national technical means of verification at its disposal in a manner consistent with generally recognized principles of international law.

2. Each Party undertakes not to interfere with the national technical means of verification of the other Party operating in accordance with paragraph 1 of this Article.

3. Each Party undertakes not to use deliberate concealment measures which impede verification by national technical means of compliance with the provisions of this Interim Agreement. This obligation shall not require changes in current construction, assembly, conversion, or overhaul practices.

Article VI

To promote the objectives and implementation of the provisions of this Interim Agreement, the Parties shall use the Standing Consultative Commission established under Article XIII of the Treaty on the Limitation of Anti-Ballistic Missile Systems in accordance with the provisions of that Article.

Article VII

The Parties undertake to continue active negotiations for limitations on strategic offensive arms. The obligations provided for in this Interim Agreement shall not prejudice the scope or terms of the limitations on strategic offensive arms which may be worked out in the course of further negotiations.

Article VIII

1. This Interim Agreement shall enter into force upon exchange of written notices of acceptance by each Party, which exchange shall take place simultaneously with the exchange of instruments of ratification of the

Treaty on the Limitation of Anti-Ballistic Missile Systems.

2. This Interim Agreement shall remain in force for a period of five years unless replaced earlier by an agreement on more complete measures limiting strategic offensive arms. It is the objective of the Parties to conduct active follow-on negotiations with the aim of concluding such an agreement as soon as possible.

3. Each Party shall, in exercising its national sovereignty, have the right to withdraw from this Interim Agreement if it decides that extraordinary events related to the subject matter of this Interim Agreement have jeopardized its supreme interests. It shall give notice of its decision to the other Party six months prior to withdrawal from this Interim Agreement. Such notice shall include a statement of the extraordinary events the notifying Party regards as having jeopardized its supreme interests.

DONE at Moscow on May 26, 1972, in two copies, each in the English and Russian languages, both texts being equally authentic.

FOR THE UNITED STATES OF AMERICA:
RICHARD NIXON
President of the United States of America
FOR THE UNION OF SOVIET SOCIALIST REPUBLICS:
L. I. BREZHNEV
General Secretary of the
Central Committee of the CPSU

PROTOCOL TO THE INTERIM AGREEMENT BETWEEN THE UNITED STATES OF AMERICA AND THE UNION OF SOVIET SOCIALIST REPUBLICS ON CERTAIN MEASURES WITH RESPECT TO THE LIMITATION OF STRATEGIC OFFENSIVE ARMS

The United States of America and the Union of Soviet Socialist Republics, hereinafter referred to as the Parties,

Having agreed on certain limitations relating to submarine-launched ballistic missile launchers and modern ballistic missile submarines, and to replacement procedures, in the Interim Agreement,

Have agreed as follows:

The Parties understand that, under Article III of the Interim Agreement, for the period during which that Agreement remains in force:

The United States may have no more than 710 ballistic missile launchers on submarines (SLBMs) and no more than 44 modern ballistic missile submarines. The Soviet Union may have no more than 950 ballistic missile launchers on submarines and no more than 62 modern ballistic missile submarines.

Additional ballistic missile launchers on submarines up to the above-mentioned levels, in the United States— over 656 ballistic missile launchers on nuclear-powered submarines, and in the USSR—over 740 ballistic missile launchers on nuclear-powered submarines, operational and under construction, may become operational as replacements for equal numbers of ballistic missile launchers of older types deployed prior to 1964 or of ballistic missile launchers on older submarines.

The deployment of modern SLBMs on any submarine, regardless of type, will be counted against the total level of SLBMs permitted for the United States and the USSR. This Protocol shall be considered an integral part of the Interim Agreement.

AGREED STATEMENTS, COMMON UNDERSTANDINGS, AND UNILATERAL STATEMENTS REGARDING THE INTERIM AGREEMENT BETWEEN THE UNITED STATES OF AMERICA AND THE UNION OF SOVIET SOCIALIST REPUBLICS ON CERTAIN MEASURES WITH RESPECT TO THE LIMITATION OF STRATEGIC OFFENSIVE ARMS

1. Agreed Statements

The document set forth below was agreed upon and initialed by the Heads of the Delegations on May 26, 1972 (letter designations added):

AGREED STATEMENTS REGARDING THE INTERIM AGREEMENT BETWEEN THE UNITED STATES OF AMERICA AND THE UNION OF SOVIET SOCIALIST REPUBLICS ON CERTAIN MEASURES WITH RESPECT TO THE LIMITATION OF STRATEGIC OFFENSIVE ARMS

[A]
The Parties understand that land-based ICBM launchers referred to in the Interim Agreement are understood to be launchers for strategic ballistic missiles capable of ranges in excess of the shortest distance between the northeastern border of the continental United States and the northwestern border of the continental USSR.

[B]
The Parties understand that fixed land-based ICBM launchers under active construction as of the date of signature of the Interim Agreement may be completed.

[C]
The Parties understand that in the process of modernization and replacement the dimensions of land-based ICBM silo launchers will not be significantly increased.

[D]
The Parties understand that during the period of the Interim Agreement there shall be no significant increase

in the number of ICBM or SLBM test and training launchers, or in the number of such launchers for modern land-based heavy ICBMs. The Parties further understand that construction or conversion of ICBM launchers at test ranges shall be undertaken only for purposes of testing and training.

[E]

The Parties understand that dismantling or destruction of ICBM launchers of older types deployed prior to 1964 and ballistic missile launchers on older submarines being replaced by new SLBM launchers on modern submarines will be initiated at the time of the beginning of sea trials of a replacement submarine, and will be completed in the shortest possible agreed period of time. Such dismantling or destruction, and timely notification thereof, will be accomplished under procedures to be agreed in the Standing Consultative Commission.

2. Common Understandings

Common understanding of the Parties on the following matters was reached during the negotiations:

A. Increase in ICBM Silo Dimensions

Ambassador Smith made the following statement on May 26, 1972:

The Parties agree that the term "significantly increased" means that an increase will not be greater than 10–15 percent of the present dimensions of land-based ICBM silo launchers.

Minister Semenov replied that this statement corresponded to the Soviet understanding.

B. Standing Consultative Commission

Ambassador Smith made the following statement on May 22, 1972:

The United States proposes that the sides agree that, with regard to initial implementation of the ABM Treaty's Article XIII on the Standing Consultative Commission (SCC) and of the consultation Articles to the Interim Agreement on offensive arms and the Accidents Agreement,

See Article 7 of Agreement to Reduce the Risk of the Outbreak of Nuclear War Between the United States of America and the Union of Soviet Socialist Republics, signed Sept. 30, 1971 agreement establishing the SCC will be worked out early in the follow-on SALT negotiations; until that is completed, the following arrangements will prevail: when SALT is in session, any consultation desired by either side under these Articles can be carried out by the two SALT Delegations; when SALT is not in session, ad hoc arrangements for any desired consultations under these Articles may be made through diplomatic channels.

Minister Semenov replied that, on an ad referendum basis, he could agree that the U.S. statement corresponded to the Soviet understanding.

C. Standstill

On May 6, 1972, Minister Semenov made the following statement:

In an effort to accommodate the wishes of the U.S. side, the Soviet Delegation is prepared to proceed on the basis that the two sides will in fact observe the obligations of both the Interim Agreement and the ABM Treaty beginning from the date of signature of these two documents.

In reply, the U.S. Delegation made the following statement on May 20, 1972:

The United States agrees in principle with the Soviet statement made on May 6 concerning observance of obligations beginning from date of signature but we would like to make clear our understanding that this means that, pending ratification and acceptance, neither side would take any action prohibited by the agreements after they had entered into force. This understanding would continue to apply in the absence of notification by either signatory of its intention not to proceed with ratification or approval.

The Soviet Delegation indicated agreement with the U.S. statement.

3. Unilateral Statements

(a) The following noteworthy unilateral statements were made during the negotiations by the United States Delegation:

A. Withdrawal from the ABM Treaty

On May 9, 1972, Ambassador Smith made the following statement:

The U.S. Delegation has stressed the importance the U.S. Government attaches to achieving agreement on more complete limitations on strategic offensive arms, following agreement on an ABM Treaty and on an Interim Agreement on certain measures with respect to the limitation of strategic offensive arms. The U.S. Delegation believes that an objective of the follow-on negotiations should be to constrain and reduce on a long-term basis threats to the survivability of our respective strategic retaliatory forces. The USSR Delegation has also indicated that the objectives of SALT would remain unfulfilled without the achievement of an agreement providing for more complete limitations on strategic offensive arms. Both sides recognize that the initial agreements would be steps toward the achievement of more complete limitations on strategic arms. If an agreement providing for more complete strategic offensive arms limitations were not achieved within five years, U.S. supreme interests could be jeopardized. Should that occur, it would constitute a basis for withdrawal from the ABM Treaty. The United States does not wish to see such a situation occur, nor do we believe that the USSR does. It is because we wish to prevent such a situation that we emphasize the importance the U.S. Government attaches to achievement of more complete limitations on strategic offensive arms. The U.S. Executive will inform the Congress, in connection with Congressional consideration of the ABM Treaty and the Interim Agreement, of this statement of the U.S. position.

B. Land-Mobile ICBM Launchers

The U.S. Delegation made the following statement on May 20, 1972:

In connection with the important subject of land-mobile ICBM launchers, in the interest of concluding the Interim Agreement the U.S. Delegation now withdraws its proposal that Article I or an agreed statement explicitly prohibit the deployment of mobile land-based ICBM launchers. I have been instructed to inform you that, while agreeing to defer the question of limitation of operational land-mobile ICBM launchers to the subsequent negotiations on more complete limitations on strategic offensive arms, the United States would consider the deployment of operational land-mobile ICBM launchers during the period of the Interim Agreement as inconsistent with the objectives of that Agreement.

C. Covered Facilities

The U.S. Delegation made the following statement on May 20, 1972:

I wish to emphasize the importance that the United States attaches to the provisions of Article V, including in particular their application to fitting out or berthing submarines.

D. "Heavy" ICBMs

The U.S. Delegation made the following statement on May 26, 1972:

The U.S. Delegation regrets that the Soviet Delegation has not been willing to agree on a common definition of a heavy missile. Under these circumstances, the U.S. Delegation believes it necessary to state the following: The United States would consider any ICBM having a volume significantly greater than that of the largest light ICBM now operational on either side to be a heavy ICBM. The United States proceeds on the premise that the Soviet side will give due account to this consideration.

On May 17, 1972, Minister Semenov made the following unilateral "Statement of the Soviet Side":

Taking into account that modern ballistic missile submarines are presently in the possession of not only the United States, but also of its NATO allies, the Soviet Union agrees that for the period of effectiveness of the Interim Freeze Agreement the United States and its NATO allies have up to 50 such submarines with a total of up to 800 ballistic missile launchers thereon (including 41 U.S. submarines with 656 ballistic missile launchers). However, if during the period of effectiveness of the Agreement U.S. allies in NATO should increase the number of their modern submarines to exceed the numbers of submarines they would have operational or under construction on the date of signature of the Agreement, the Soviet Union will have the right to a corresponding increase in the number of its submarines. In the opinion of the Soviet side, the solution of the question of modern ballistic missile submarines provided for in the Interim Agreement only partially compensates for the strategic imbalance in the deployment of the nuclear-powered missile submarines of the USSR and the United States. Therefore, the Soviet side believes that this whole question, and above all the question of liquidating the American missile submarine bases outside the United States, will be appropriately resolved in the course of follow-on negotiations.

On May 24, Ambassador Smith made the following reply to Minister Semenov:

The United States side has studied the "statement made by the Soviet side" of May 17 concerning compensation for submarine basing and SLBM submarines belonging to third countries. The United States does not accept the validity of the considerations in that statement.

On May 26 Minister Semenov repeated the unilateral statement made on May 17. Ambassador Smith also repeated the U.S. rejection on May 26.

7. PARIS PEACE ACCORDS, AGREEMENT ON ENDING THE WAR AND RESTORING PEACE IN VIETNAM, SIGNED IN PARIS AND ENTERED INTO FORCE JANUARY 27, 1973

AGREEMENT ON ENDING THE WAR AND RESTORING PEACE IN VIET-NAM

The Parties participating in the Paris Conference on Viet-Nam,

With a view to ending the war and restoring peace in Viet-Nam on the basis of respect for the Vietnamese people's fundamental national rights and the South Vietnamese people's right to self-determination, and to contributing to the consolidation of peace in Asia and the world,

Have agreed on the following provisions and undertake to respect and to implement them:

Chapter I

THE VIETNAMESE PEOPLE'S FUNDAMENTAL NATIONAL RIGHTS

Article 1

The United States and all other countries respect the independence, sovereignty, unity, and territorial integrity of Viet-Nam as recognized by the 1954 Geneva Agreements on Viet-Nam.

Chapter II

CESSATION OF HOSTILITIES—WITHDRAWAL OF TROOPS,

Article 2

A cease-fire shall be observed throughout South Viet-Nam as of 2400 hours G.M.T. [Greenwich Mean Time], on January 27, 1973.

At the same hour, the United States will stop all its military activities against the territory of the Democratic Republic of Viet-Nam by ground, air and naval forces, wherever they may be based, and end the mining of the territorial waters, ports, harbors, and waterways of the Democratic Republic of Viet-Nam. The United States will remove, permanently deactivate or destroy all the mines in the territorial waters, ports, harbors, and waterways of North Viet-Nam as soon as this Agreement goes into effect.

The complete cessation of hostilities mentioned in this Article shall be durable and without limit of time.

Article 3

The parties undertake to maintain the cease-fire and to ensure a lasting and stable peace.

As soon as the cease-fire goes into effect:

(a) The United States forces and those of the other foreign countries allied with the United States and the Republic of Viet-Nam shall remain in-place pending the implementation of the plan of troop withdrawal.

The Four-Party Joint Military Commission described in Article 16 shall determine the modalities.

(b) The armed forces of the two South Vietnamese parties shall remain in-place. The Two-Party Joint Military Commission described in Article 17 shall determine the areas controlled by each party and the modalities of stationing.

(c) The regular forces of all services and arms and the irregular forces of the parties in South Viet-Nam shall stop all offensive activities against each other and shall strictly abide by the following stipulations:

—All acts of force on the ground, in the air, and on the sea shall be prohibited;

—All hostile acts, terrorism and reprisals by both sides will be banned.

Article 4

The United States will not continue its military involvement or intervene in the internal affairs of South Viet-Nam.

Article 5

Within sixty days of the signing of this Agreement, there will be a total withdrawal from South Viet-Nam of troops, military advisers, and military personnel, including technical military personnel and military personnel associated with the pacification program, armaments, munitions, and war material of the United States and those of the other foreign countries mentioned in Article 3 (a). Advisers from the above-mentioned countries to all paramilitary organizations and the police force will also be withdrawn within the same period of time.

Article 6

The dismantlement of all military bases in South Viet-Nam of the United States and of the other foreign countries mentioned in Article 3 (a) shall be completed within sixty days of the signing of this agreement.

Article 7

From the enforcement of the cease-fire to the formation of the government provided for in Article 9 (b) and 14 of this Agreement, the two South Vietnamese parties shall not accept the introduction of troops, military advisers, and military personnel including technical military personnel, armaments, munitions, and war material into South Viet-Nam.

The two South Vietnamese parties shall be permitted to make periodic replacement of armaments, munitions and war material which have been destroyed, damaged, worn out or used up after the cease-fire, on the basis of piece-for-piece, of the same characteristics and properties, under the supervision of the Joint Military Commission of the two South Vietnamese parties and of the International Commission of Control and Supervision.

THE RETURN OF CAPTURED MILITARY PERSONNEL AND FOREIGN CIVILIANS AND CAPTURED AND DETAINED VIETNAMESE CIVILIAN PERSONNEL

Article 8

(a) The return of captured military personnel and foreign civilians of the parties shall be carried out simultaneously with and completed not later than the same day as the troop withdrawal mentioned in Article 5. The parties shall exchange complete lists of the above-mentioned captured military personnel and foreign civilians on the day of the signing of this Agreement.

(b) The parties shall help each other to get information about those military personnel and foreign civilians of the parties missing in action, to determine the location and take care of the graves of the dead so as to facilitate the exhumation and repatriation of the remains, and to take any such other measures as may be required to get information about those still considered missing in action.

(c) The question of the return of Vietnamese civilian personnel captured and detained in South Viet-Nam will be resolved by the two South Vietnamese parties on the basis of the principles of Article 21 (b) of the Agreement on the Cessation of Hostilities in Viet-Nam of July 20, 1954. The two South Vietnamese parties will do so in a spirit of national reconciliation and concord, with a view to ending hatred and enmity, in order to ease suffering and to reunite families. The two South Vietnamese parties will do their utmost to resolve this question within ninety days after the cease-fire comes into effect.

Chapter IV
THE EXERCISE OF THE SOUTH VIETNAMESE PEOPLE'S RIGHT TO SELF-DETERMINATION

Article 9

The Government of the United States of America and the Government of the Democratic Republic of Viet-Nam undertake to respect the following principles for the exercise of the South Vietnamese people's right to self-determination:

(a) The South Vietnamese people's right to self-determination is sacred, inalienable, and shall be respected by all countries.

(b) The South Vietnamese people shall decide themselves the political future of South Viet-Nam through genuinely free and democratic general elections under international supervision.

(c) Foreign countries shall not impose any political tendency or personality on the South Vietnamese people.

Article 10

The two South Vietnamese parties undertake to respect the cease-fire and maintain peace in South Viet-Nam, settle all matters of contention through negotiations, and avoid all armed conflict.

Article 11

Immediately after the cease-fire, the two South Vietnamese parties will:

—achieve national reconciliation and concord, end hatred and enmity, prohibit all acts of reprisal and discrimination against individuals or organizations that have collaborated with one side or the other;

—ensure the democratic liberties of the people: personal freedom, freedom of speech, freedom of the press, freedom of meeting, freedom of organization, freedom of political activities, freedom of belief, freedom of movement, freedom of residence, freedom of work, right to property ownership, and right to free enterprise.

Article 12

(a) Immediately after the cease-fire, the two South Vietnamese parties shall hold consultations in a spirit of national reconciliation and concord, mutual respect, and mutual non-elimination to set up a National Council of National Reconciliation and Concord of three equal segments. The Council shall operate on the principle of unanimity, after the National Council of National Reconciliation and Concord has assumed its functions, the two South Vietnamese parties will consult about the formation of councils at lower levels. The two South Vietnamese parties shall sign an agreement on the internal matters of South Viet-Nam as soon as possible and do their utmost to accomplish this within ninety days after the cease-fire comes into effect, in keeping with the South Vietnamese people's aspirations for peace, independence and democracy.

(b) The National Council of National Reconciliation and Concord shall have the task of promoting the two South Vietnamese parties' implementation of this Agreement, achievement of national reconciliation and concord and ensurance of democratic liberties. The National Council of National Reconciliation and Concord will organize the free and democratic general elections provided for in Article 9 (b) and decide the procedures and modalities of these general elections. The institutions for which the general elections are to be held will be agreed upon through consultations between the two South Vietnamese parties. The National Council of National Reconciliation and Concord will also decide the procedures and modalities of such local elections as the two South Vietnamese parties agree upon.

Article 13

The question of Vietnamese armed forces in South Viet-Nam shall be settled by the two South Vietnamese parties in a spirit of national reconciliation and concord, equality and mutual respect, without foreign interference, in accordance with the postwar situation. Among the questions to be discussed by the two South Vietnamese parties are steps to reduce their military effectives and to demobilize the troops being reduced. The two South Vietnamese parties will accomplish this as soon as possible.

Article 14

South Viet-Nam will pursue a foreign policy of peace and independence. It will be prepared to establish relations with all countries irrespective of their political and social systems on the basis of mutual respect for independence and sovereignty and accept economic and technical aid from any country with no political conditions attached. The acceptance of military aid by South Viet-Nam in the future shall come under the authority of the government set up after the general elections in South Viet-Nam provided for in Article 9 (b).

Chapter V
THE REUNIFICATION OF VIET-NAM AND THE RELATIONSHIP BETWEEN NORTH AND SOUTH VIET-NAM

Article 15

The reunification of Viet-Nam shall be carried out step by step through peaceful means on the basis of discus-sions and agreements between North and South Viet-Nam, without coercion or annexation by either party, and without foreign interference. The time for reunification will be agreed upon by North and South Viet-Nam

Pending reunification:

(a) The military demarcation line between the two zones at the 17th parallel is only provisional and not a political or territorial boundary, as provided for in paragraph 6 of the Final Declaration of the 1954 Geneva Conference.

(b) North and South Viet-Nam shall respect the Demilitarized Zone on either side of the Provisional Military Demarcation Line.

(c) North and South Viet-Nam shall promptly start negotiations with a view to reestablishing-normal relations in various fields. Among the questions to be negotiated are the modalities of civilian movement across the Provisional Military Demarcation Line.

(d) North and South Viet-Nam shall not join any military alliance or military bloc and shall not allow foreign powers to maintain military bases, troops, military advisers, and military personnel on their respective territories, as stipulated in the 1954 Geneva Agreements on Viet-Nam.

THE JOINT MILITARY COMMISSIONS, THE INTERNATIONAL COMMISSION OF CONTROL AND SUPERVISION, THE INTERNATIONAL CONFERENCE

Article 16

(a) The Parties participating in the Paris Conference on Viet-Nam shall immediately designate representatives to form a Four-Party Joint Military Commission with the task of ensuring joint action by the parties in implementing the following provisions of this Agreement:

—The first paragraph of Article 2, regarding the enforcement of the cease-fire throughout South Viet-Nam;

—Article 3 (a), regarding the cease-fire by U.S. forces and those of the other foreign countries referred to in that Article;

—Article 3 (c), regarding the cease-fire between all parties in South Viet-Nam;

—Article 5, regarding the withdrawal from South Viet-Nam of U.S. troops and those of the other foreign countries mentioned in Article 3 (a);

—Article 6, regarding the dismantlement of military bases in South Viet-Nam of the United States and those of the other foreign countries mentioned in Article 3 (a);
—Article 8 (a), regarding the return of captured military personnel and foreign civilians of the parties;
—Article 8 (b), regarding the mutual assistance of the parties in getting information about those military personnel and foreign civilians of the parties missing in action.
(b) The Four-Party Joint Military Commission shall operate in accordance with the principle of consultations and unanimity. Disagreements shall be referred to the International Commission of Control and Supervision.
(c) The Four-Party Joint Military Commission shall begin operating immediately after the signing of this Agreement and end its activities in sixty days, after the completion of the withdrawal of U.S. troops and those of the other foreign countries mentioned in Article 3 (a) and the completion of the return of captured military personnel and foreign civilians of the parties.
(d) The four parties shall agree immediately on the organization, the working procedure, means of activity, and expenditures of the Four-Party Joint Military Commission.

Article 17

(a) The two South Vietnamese parties shall immediately designate representatives to form a Two-Party Joint Military Commission with the task of ensuring joint action by the two South Vietnamese parties in implementing the following provisions of this Agreement:
—The first paragraph of Article 2, regarding the enforcement of the cease-fire throughout South Viet-Nam, when the Four-Party Joint Military Commission has ended its activities;
—Article 3 (b), regarding the cease-fire between the two South Vietnamese parties;
—Article 3 (c), regarding the cease-fire between all parties in South Viet-Nam, when the Four-Party Joint Military Commission has ended its activities;
—Article 7, regarding the prohibition of the introduction of troops into South Viet-Nam and all other provisions of this Article;
—Article 8 (c), regarding the question of the return of Vietnamese civilian personnel captured and detained in South Viet-Nam;

—Article 13, regarding the reduction of the military effectives of the two South Vietnamese parties and the demobilization of the troops being reduced.
(b) Disagreements shall be referred to the International Commission of Control and Supervision.
(c) After the signing of this Agreement, the Two-Party Joint Military Commission shall agree immediately on the measures and organization aimed at enforcing the cease-fire and preserving peace in South Viet-Nam,

Article 18

(a) After the signing of this Agreement, an International Commission of Control and Supervision shall be established immediately.
(b) Until the International Conference provided for in Article 19 makes definitive arrangements, the International Commission of Control and Supervision will report to the four parties on matters concerning the control and supervision of the implementation of the following provisions of this Agreement:
—The first paragraph of Article 2, regarding the enforcement of the cease-fire throughout South Viet-Nam;
—Article 3 (a), regarding the cease-fire by U.S. forces and those of the other foreign countries referred to in that Article;
—Article 3 (c), regarding the cease-fire between all the parties in South Viet-Nam;
—Article 5, regarding the withdrawal from South Viet-Nam of U.S. troops and those of the other foreign countries mentioned in Article 3 (a);
—Article 6, regarding the dismantlement of military bases in South Viet-Nam of the United States and those of the other foreign countries mentioned in Article 3 (a);
—Article 8 (a), regarding the return of captured military personnel and foreign civilians of the parties.
The International Commission of Control and Supervision shall form control teams for carrying out its tasks. The four parties shall agree immediately on the location and operation of these teams. The parties will facilitate their operation.
(c) Until the International Conference makes definitive arrangements, the International Commission of Control and Supervision will report to the two South Vietnamese parties on matters concerning the control and supervision of the implementation of the following provisions of this Agreement:

—The first paragraph of Article 2, regarding the enforcement of the cease-fire throughout South Viet-Nam, when the Four-Party Joint Military Commission has ended its activities;

—Article 3 (b), regarding the cease-fire between the two South Vietnamese parties;

—Article 3 (c), regarding the cease-fire between all parties in South Viet-Nam, when the Four-Party Joint Military Commission has ended its activities;

—Article 7, regarding the prohibition of the introduction of troops into South Viet-Nam and all other provisions of this Article;

—Article 8 (c), regarding the question of the return of Vietnamese civilian personnel captured and detained in South Viet-Nam;

—Article 9 (b), regarding the free and democratic general elections in South Viet-Nam;

—Article 13, regarding the reduction of the military effectives of the two South Vietnamese parties and the demobilization of the troops being reduced.

The International Commission of Control and Supervision shall form control teams for carrying out its tasks. The two South Vietnamese parties shall agree immediately on the location and operation of these teams. The two South Vietnamese parties will facilitate their operation.

(d) The International Commission of Control and Supervision shall be composed of representatives of four countries: Canada, Hungary, Indonesia and Poland. The chairmanship of this Commission will rotate among the members for specific periods to be determined by the Commission.

(e) The International Commission of Control and Supervision shall carry out its tasks in accordance with the principle of respect for the sovereignty of South Viet-Nam.

(f) The International Commission of Control and Supervision shall operate in accordance with the principle of consultations and unanimity.

(g) The International Commission of Control and Supervision shall begin operating when a cease-fire comes into force in Viet-Nam. As regards the provisions in Article 18 (b) concerning the four parties, the International Commission of Control and Supervision shall end its activities when the Commission's tasks of control and supervision regarding these provisions have been fulfilled. As regards the provisions in Article 18 (c) concerning the two South Vietnamese parties, the International Commission of Control and Supervision

shall end its activities on the request of the government formed after the general elections in South Viet-Nam provided for in Article 9 (b).

(h) The four parties shall agree immediately on the organization, means of activity, and expenditures of the International Commission of Control and Supervision. The relationship between the International Commission and the International Conference will be agreed upon by the International Commission and the International Conference.

Article 19

The parties agree on the convening of an International Conference within thirty days of the signing of this Agreement to acknowledge the signed agreements; to guarantee the ending of the war, the maintenance of peace in Viet-Nam, the respect of the Vietnamese people's fundamental national rights, and the South Vietnamese people's right to self-determination; and to contribute to and guarantee peace in Indochina.

The United States and the Democratic Republic of Viet-Nam, on behalf of the parties participating in the Paris Conference on Viet-Nam will propose to the following parties that they participate in this International Conference: the People's Republic of China, the Republic of France, the Union of Soviet Socialist Republics, the United Kingdom, the four countries of the International Commission of Control and Supervision, and the Secretary General of the United Nations, together with the parties participating in the Paris Conference on Viet-Nam.

Chapter VII
REGARDING CAMBODIA AND LAOS

Article 20

(a) The parties participating in the Paris Conference on Viet-Nam shall strictly respect the 1954 Geneva Agreements on Cambodia and the 1954 Geneva Agreements on Laos, which recognized the Cambodian and the Lao peoples' fundamental national rights, i.e., the independence, sovereignty, unity, and territorial integrity of these countries. The parties shall respect the neutrality of Cambodia and Laos.

The parties participating in the Paris Conference on Viet-Nam undertake to refrain from using the territory of Cambodia and the territory of Laos to encroach on the sovereignty and security of one another and of other countries.

(b) Foreign countries shall put an end to all military activities in Cambodia and Laos, totally withdraw from and refrain from reintroducing into these two countries troops, military advisers and military personnel, armaments, munitions and war material.

(c) The internal affairs of Cambodia and Laos shall be settled by the people of each of these countries without foreign interference.

(d) The problems existing between the Indochinese countries shall be settled by the Indochinese parties on the basis of respect for each other's independence, sovereignty, and territorial integrity, and non-interference in each other's internal affairs.

Chapter VIII
THE RELATIONSHIP BETWEEN THE UNITED STATES AND THE DEMOCRATIC REPUBLIC OF VIET-NAM

Article 21
The United States anticipates that this Agreement will usher in an era of reconciliation with the Democratic Republic of Viet-Nam as with all the peoples of Indochina. In pursuance of its traditional policy, the United States will contribute to healing the wounds of war and to postwar reconstruction of the Democratic Republic of Viet-Nam and throughout Indochina.

Article 22
The ending of the war, the restoration of peace in Viet-Nam, and the strict implementation of this Agreement will create conditions for establishing a new, equal and mutually beneficial relationship between the United States and the Democratic Republic of Viet-Nam on the basis of respect for each other's independence and sovereignty, and non-interference in each other's internal affairs. At the same time this will ensure stable peace in Viet-Nam and contribute to the preservation of lasting peace in Indochina and Southeast Asia.

Chapter IX
OTHER PROVISIONS

Article 23
This Agreement shall enter into force upon signature by plenipotentiary representatives of the parties participating in the Paris Conference on Viet-Nam. All the parties concerned shall strictly implement this Agreement and its Protocols. Done in Paris this twenty-seventh day of January, one thousand nine hundred and seventy-three, in English and Vietnamese. The English and Vietnamese texts are official and equally authentic.

FOR THE GOVERNMENT OF
THE UNITED STATES OF AMERICA: FOR THE
GOVERNMENT OF
THE REPUBLIC OF VIET-NAM:
William P. Rogers, Secretary of State
Tran Van Lam, Secretary of State Minister for Foreign Affairs
FOR THE GOVERNMENT OF
THE DEMOCRATIC REPUBLIC OF VIET-NAM:
FOR THE PROVISIONAL REVOLUTIONARY GOVERNMENT
OF THE REPUBLIC OF SOUTH VIET-NAM:
Nguyen Duy Trinh, Minister for Foreign Affairs
Nguyen Thi Binh, Minister for Foreign Affairs

8. JUSTICE POTTER STEWART'S CONCURRING OPINION IN THE CASE OF *ROE V. WADE*, JANUARY 22, 1973
410 U.S. 113
ROE ET AL. v. WADE, DISTRICT ATTORNEY OF DALLAS COUNTY
APPEAL FROM THE UNITED STATES DISTRICT COURT FOR THE NORTHERN DISTRICT OF TEXAS
No. 70–18.
Argued December 13, 1971 Reargued October 11, 1972
Decided January 22, 1973
In 1963, this Court, in *Ferguson v. Skrupa,* 372 U.S. 726, purported to sound the death knell for the doctrine of substantive due process, a doctrine under which many state laws had in the past been held to violate the Fourteenth Amendment. As Mr. Justice Black's opinion for the Court in Skrupa put it: "We have returned to the original constitutional proposition that courts do not substitute their social and economic beliefs for the judgment of legislative bodies, who are elected to pass laws." Id., at 730. 1

   Barely two years later, in *Griswold v. Connecticut,* 381 U.S. 479, the Court held a Connecticut birth control law unconstitutional. In view of what had been so recently said in Skrupa, the Court's opinion in Griswold understandably did its best to avoid reliance on the Due Process Clause of the Fourteenth Amendment as the ground for decision. Yet, the Connecticut law did not violate any provision of the Bill of Rights, nor any other specific provision of the Constitution. 2 So it was clear [410 U.S. 113, 168] to me then, and it is equally clear to me now, that the Griswold decision can be rationally understood only as a holding that the Connecticut statute substantively invaded the "liberty" that is protected by the Due Process Clause of the Fourteenth Amendment. 3 As so understood, Griswold stands as one in a long line of pre-Skrupa cases decided under the doctrine of substantive due process, and I now accept it as such.

"In a Constitution for a free people, there can be no doubt that the meaning of 'liberty' must be broad indeed." *Board of Regents v. Roth,* 408 U.S. 564, 572. The Constitution nowhere mentions a specific right of personal choice in matters of marriage and family life, but the "liberty" protected by the Due Process Clause of the Fourteenth Amendment covers more than those freedoms explicitly named in the Bill of Rights. See *Schware v. Board of Bar Examiners,* 353 U.S. 232, 238–239; *Pierce v. Society of Sisters,* 268 U.S. 510, 534–535; *Meyer v. Nebraska,* 262 U.S. 390, 399–400. Cf. *Shapiro v. Thompson,* 394 U.S. 618, 629–630; *United States v. Guest,* 383 U.S. 745, 757–758; *Carrington v. Rash,* 380 U.S. 89, 96; *Aptheker v. Secretary of State,* 378 U.S. 500, 505; *Kent v. Dulles,* 357 U.S. 116, 127; *Bolling v. Sharpe,* 347 U.S. 497, 499–500; *Truax v. Raich,* 239 U.S. 33, 41. [410 U.S. 113, 169]

As Mr. Justice Harlan once wrote: "[T]he full scope of the liberty guaranteed by the Due Process Clause cannot be found in or limited by the precise terms of the specific guarantees elsewhere provided in the Constitution. This 'liberty' is not a series of isolated points pricked out in terms of the taking of property; the freedom of speech, press, and religion; the right to keep and bear arms; the freedom from unreasonable searches and seizures; and so on. It is a rational continuum which, broadly speaking, includes a freedom from all substantial arbitrary impositions and purposeless restraints . . . and which also recognizes, what a reasonable and sensitive judgment must, that certain interests require particularly careful scrutiny of the state needs asserted to justify their abridgment." *Poe v. Ullman,* 367 U.S. 497, 543 (opinion dissenting from dismissal of appeal) (citations omitted). In the words of Mr. Justice Frankfurter, "Great concepts like . . . 'liberty'. . . were purposely left to gather meaning from experience. For they relate to the whole domain of social and economic fact, and the statesmen who founded this Nation

knew too well that only a stagnant society remains unchanged." *National Mutual Ins. Co. v. Tidewater Transfer Co.,* 337 U.S. 582, 646 (dissenting opinion).

Several decisions of this Court make clear that freedom of personal choice in matters of marriage and family life is one of the liberties protected by the Due Process Clause of the Fourteenth Amendment. *Loving v. Virginia,* 388 U.S. 1, 12; *Griswold v. Connecticut,* supra; *Pierce v. Society of Sisters,* supra; *Meyer v. Nebraska,* supra. See also *Prince v. Massachusetts,* 321 U.S. 158, 166; *Skinner v. Oklahoma,* 316 U.S. 535, 541. As recently as last Term, in *Eisenstadt v. Baird,* 405 U.S. 438, 453, we recognized "the right of the individual, married or single, to be free from unwarranted governmental intrusion into matters so fundamentally affecting a person [410 U.S. 113, 170] as the decision whether to bear or beget a child." That right necessarily includes the right of a woman to decide whether or not to terminate her pregnancy. "Certainly the interests of a woman in giving of her physical and emotional self during pregnancy and the interests that will be affected throughout her life by the birth and raising of a child are of a far greater degree of significance and personal intimacy than the right to send a child to private school protected in *Pierce v. Society of Sisters,* 268 U.S. 510 (1925), or the right to teach a foreign language protected in *Meyer v. Nebraska,* 262 U.S. 390 (1923)." *Abele v. Markle,* 351 F. Supp. 224, 227 (Conn. 1972).

Clearly, therefore, the Court today is correct in holding that the right asserted by Jane Roe is embraced within the personal liberty protected by the Due Process Clause of the Fourteenth Amendment.

It is evident that the Texas abortion statute infringes that right directly. Indeed, it is difficult to imagine a more complete abridgment of a constitutional freedom than that worked by the inflexible criminal statute now in force in Texas. The question then becomes whether the state interests advanced to justify this abridgment can survive the "particularly careful scrutiny" that the Fourteenth Amendment here requires.

The asserted state interests are protection of the health and safety of the pregnant woman, and protection of the potential future human life within her. These are legitimate objectives, amply sufficient to permit a State to regulate abortions as it does other surgical procedures, and perhaps sufficient to permit a State to regulate abortions more stringently or even to prohibit them in the late stages of pregnancy. But such legislation is not before us, and I think the Court today has thoroughly demonstrated that these state interests cannot constitutionally support the broad abridgment of personal [410 U.S. 113, 171] liberty worked by the existing Texas law. Accordingly, I join the Court's opinion holding that that law is invalid under the Due Process Clause of the Fourteenth Amendment.

9. JUSTICE WILLIAM REHNQUIST'S DISSENTING OPINION IN THE CASE OF *ROE V. WADE*, JANUARY 22, 1973

The Court's opinion brings to the decision of this troubling question both extensive historical fact and a wealth of legal scholarship. While the opinion thus commands my respect, I find myself nonetheless in fundamental disagreement with those parts of it that invalidate the Texas statute in question, and therefore dissent.

I

The Court's opinion decides that a State may impose virtually no restriction on the performance of abortions during the first trimester of pregnancy. Our previous decisions indicate that a necessary predicate for such an opinion is a plaintiff who was in her first trimester of pregnancy at some time during the pendency of her law-suit. While a party may vindicate his own constitutional rights, he may not seek vindication for the rights of others. *Moose Lodge v. Irvis,* 407 U.S. 163 (1972); *Sierra Club v. Morton,* 405 U.S. 727 (1972). The Court's statement of facts in this case makes clear, however, that the record in no way indicates the presence of such a plaintiff. We know only that plaintiff Roe at the time of filing her complaint was a pregnant woman; for aught that appears in this record, she may have been in her last trimester of pregnancy as of the date the complaint was filed.

Nothing in the Court's opinion indicates that Texas might not constitutionally apply its proscription of abortion as written to a woman in that stage of pregnancy. Nonetheless, the Court uses her complaint against the Texas statute as a fulcrum for deciding that States may [410 U.S. 113, 172] impose virtually no restrictions on medical abortions performed during the first trimester of pregnancy. In deciding such a hypothetical lawsuit, the Court departs from the longstanding admonition that it should never "formulate a rule of constitutional law broader than is required by the precise facts to which it is to be applied." *Liverpool, New York & Philadelphia S. S. Co. v. Commissioners of Emigration,* 113 U.S. 33, 39 (1885). See

also *Ashwander v. TVA,* 297 U.S. 288, 345 (1936) (Brandeis, J., concurring).

II

Even if there were a plaintiff in this case capable of litigating the issue which the Court decides, I would reach a conclusion opposite to that reached by the Court. I have difficulty in concluding, as the Court does, that the right of "privacy" is involved in this case. Texas, by the statute here challenged, bars the performance of a medical abortion by a licensed physician on a plaintiff such as Roe. A transaction resulting in an operation such as this is not "private" in the ordinary usage of that word. Nor is the "privacy" that the Court finds here even a distant relative of the freedom from searches and seizures protected by the Fourth Amendment to the Constitution, which the Court has referred to as embodying a right to privacy. *Katz v. United States,* 389 U.S. 347 (1967).

If the Court means by the term "privacy" no more than that the claim of a person to be free from unwanted state regulation of consensual transactions may be a form of "liberty" protected by the Fourteenth Amendment, there is no doubt that similar claims have been upheld in our earlier decisions on the basis of that liberty. I agree with the statement of MR. JUSTICE STEWART in his concurring opinion that the "liberty," against deprivation of which without due process the Fourteenth [410 U.S. 113, 173] Amendment protects, embraces more than the rights found in the Bill of Rights. But that liberty is not guaranteed absolutely against deprivation, only against deprivation without due process of law. The test traditionally applied in the area of social and economic legislation is whether or not a law such as that challenged has a rational relation to a valid state objective. *Williamson v. Lee Optical Co.,* 348 U.S. 483, 491 (1955). The Due Process Clause of the Fourteenth Amendment undoubtedly does place a limit, albeit a broad one, on legislative power to enact laws such as this. If the Texas statute were to prohibit an abortion even where the mother's life is in jeopardy, I have little doubt that such a statute would lack a rational relation to a valid state objective under the test stated in Williamson, supra. But the Court's sweeping invalidation of any restrictions on abortion during the first trimester is impossible to justify under that standard, and the conscious weighing of competing factors that the Court's opinion apparently substitutes for the established test is far more appropriate to a legislative judgment than to a judicial one.

The Court eschews the history of the Fourteenth Amendment in its reliance on the "compelling state interest" test. See *Weber v. Aetna Casualty & Surety Co.,* 406 U.S. 164, 179 (1972) (dissenting opinion). But the Court adds a new wrinkle to this test by transposing it from the legal considerations associated with the Equal Protection Clause of the Fourteenth Amendment to this case arising under the Due Process Clause of the Fourteenth Amendment. Unless I misapprehend the consequences of this transplanting of the "compelling state interest test," the Court's opinion will accomplish the seemingly impossible feat of leaving this area of the law more confused than it found it. [410 U.S. 113, 174]

While the Court's opinion quotes from the dissent of Mr. Justice Holmes in *Lochner v. New York,* 198 U.S. 45, 74 (1905), the result it reaches is more closely attuned to the majority opinion of Mr. Justice Peckham in that case. As in Lochner and similar cases applying substantive due process standards to economic and social welfare legislation, the adoption of the compelling state interest standard will inevitably require this Court to examine the legislative policies and pass on the wisdom of these policies in the very process of deciding whether a particular state interest put forward may or may not be "compelling." The decision here to break pregnancy into three distinct terms and to outline the permissible restrictions the State may impose in each one, for example, partakes more of judicial legislation than it does of a determination of the intent of the drafters of the Fourteenth Amendment.

The fact that a majority of the States reflecting, after all, the majority sentiment in those States, have had restrictions on abortions for at least a century is a strong indication, it seems to me, that the asserted right to an abortion is not "so rooted in the traditions and conscience of our people as to be ranked as fundamental," *Snyder v. Massachusetts,* 291 U.S. 97, 105 (1934). Even today, when society's views on abortion are changing, the very existence of the debate is evidence that the "right" to an abortion is not so universally accepted as the appellant would have us believe.

To reach its result, the Court necessarily has had to find within the scope of the Fourteenth Amendment a right that was apparently completely unknown to the drafters of the Amendment. As early as 1821, the first state law dealing directly with abortion was enacted by the Connecticut Legislature. Conn. Stat., Tit. 22, 14, 16.

By the time of the adoption of the Fourteenth [410 U.S. 113, 175] Amendment in 1868, there were at least 36 laws enacted by state or territorial legislatures limiting abortion. 1 While many States have amended or updated [410 U.S. 113, 176] their laws, 21 of the laws on the books in 1868 remain in effect today. 2 Indeed, the Texas statute struck down today was, as the majority notes, first enacted in 1857 [410 U.S. 113, 177] and "has remained substantially unchanged to the present time." Ante, at 119.

There apparently was no question concerning the validity of this provision or of any of the other state statutes when the Fourteenth Amendment was adopted. The only conclusion possible from this history is that the drafters did not intend to have the Fourteenth Amendment withdraw from the States the power to legislate with respect to this matter.

III

Even if one were to agree that the case that the Court decides were here, and that the enunciation of the substantive constitutional law in the Court's opinion were proper, the actual disposition of the case by the Court is still difficult to justify. The Texas statute is struck down in toto, even though the Court apparently concedes that at later periods of pregnancy Texas might impose these selfsame statutory limitations on abortion. My understanding of past practice is that a statute found [410 U.S. 113, 178] to be invalid as applied to a particular plaintiff, but not unconstitutional as a whole, is not simply "struck down" but is, instead, declared unconstitutional as applied to the fact situation before the Court. *Yick Wo v. Hopkins,* 118 U.S. 356 (1886); *Street v. New York,* 394 U.S. 576 (1969).

For all of the foregoing reasons, I respectfully dissent.

10. THE WAR POWERS ACT, PASSED BY CONGRESS ON NOVEMBER 7, 1973
SECTION 1.

This joint resolution may be cited as the "War Powers Resolution".

Purpose and policy

SEC. 2. (a) It is the purpose of this joint resolution to fulfill the intent of the framers of the Constitution of the United States and insure that the collective judgement of both the Congress and the President will apply to the introduction of United States Armed Forces into hostilities, or into situations where imminent involvement in hostilities is clearly indicated by the circumstances, and to the continued use of such forces in hostilities or in such situations.

SEC. 2. (b) Under article I, section 8, of the Constitution, it is specifically provided that the Congress shall have the power to make all laws necessary and proper for carrying into execution, not only its own powers but also all other powers vested by the Constitution in the Government of the United States, or in any department or officer thereof.

SEC. 2. (c) The constitutional powers of the President as Commander-in-Chief to introduce United States Armed Forces into hostilities, or into situations where imminent involvement in hostilities is clearly indicated by the circumstances, are exercised only pursuant to (1) a declaration of war, (2) specific statutory authorization, or (3) a national emergency created by attack upon the United States, its territories or possessions, or its armed forces.

Consultation

SEC. 3. The President in every possible instance shall consult with Congress before introducing United States Armed Forces into hostilities or into situation where imminent involvement in hostilities is clearly indicated by the circumstances, and after every such introduction shall consult regularly with the Congress until United States Armed Forces are no longer engaged in hostilities or have been removed from such situations.

Reporting

Sec. 4. (a) In the absence of a declaration of war, in any case in which United States Armed Forces are introduced—(1) into hostilities or into situations where imminent involvement in hostilities is clearly indicated by the circumstances; (2) into the territory, airspace or waters of a foreign nation, while equipped for combat, except for deployments which relate solely to supply, replacement, repair, or training of such forces; or (3) (A) the circumstances necessitating the introduction of United States Armed Forces; (B) the constitutional and legislative authority under which such introduction took place; and (C) the estimated scope and duration of the hostilities or involvement.

Sec. 4. (b) The President shall provide such other information as the Congress may request in the fulfillment of its constitutional responsibilities with respect to committing the Nation to war and to the use of United States Armed Forces abroad.

Sec. 4. (c) Whenever United States Armed Forces are introduced into hostilities or into any situation described in subsection (a) of this section, the President shall, so long as such armed forces continue to be engaged in such hostilities or situation, report to the Congress periodically on the status of such hostilities or situation as well as on the scope and duration of such hostilities or situation, but in no event shall he report to the Congress less often than once every six months.

Congressional action

SEC. 5. (a) Each report submitted pursuant to section 4(a)(1) shall be transmitted to the Speaker of the House of Representatives and to the President pro tempore of the Senate on the same calendar day. Each report so transmitted shall be referred to the Committee on Foreign Affairs of the House of Representatives and to the Committee on Foreign Relations of the Senate for appropriate action. If, when the report is transmitted, the Congress has adjourned sine die or has adjourned for any period in excess of three calendar days, the Speaker of the House of Representatives and the President pro tempore of the Senate, if they deem it advisable (or if petitioned by at least 30 percent of the membership of their respective Houses) shall jointly request the President to convene Congress in order that it may consider the report and take appropriate action pursuant to this section.

SEC. 5. (b) Within sixty calendar days after a report is submitted or is required to be submitted pursuant to section 4(a)(1), whichever is earlier, the President shall terminate any use of United States Armed Forces with respect to which such report was submitted (or required to be submitted), unless the Congress (1) has declared war or has enacted a specific authorization for such use of United States Armed Forces, (2) has extended by law such sixty-day period, or (3) is physically unable to meet as a result of an armed attack upon the United States. Such sixty-day period shall be extended for not more than an additional thirty days if the President determines and certifies to the Congress in writing that unavoidable military necessity respecting the safety of United States Armed Forces requires the continued use of such armed forces in the course of bringing about a prompt removal of such forces.

SEC. 5. (c) Notwithstanding subsection (b), at any time that United States Armed Forces are engaged in hostilities outside the territory of the United States, its possessions and territories without a declaration of war or specific statutory authorization, such forces shall be removed by the President if the Congress so directs by concurrent resolution....

SEC. 8. (a) Authority to introduce United States Armed Forces into hostilities or into situations wherein involvement in hostilities is clearly indicated by the circumstances shall not be inferred—(1) from any provision of law (whether or not in effect before the date of the enactment of this joint resolution), including any provision contained in any appropriation Act, unless such provision specifically authorizes the introduction of United States Armed Forces into hostilities or into such situations and stating that it is intended to constitute specific statutory authorization within the meaning of this joint resolution; or (2) from any treaty heretofore or hereafter ratified unless such treaty is implemented by legislation specifically authorizing the introduction of United States Armed Forces into hostilities or into such situations and stating that it is intended to constitute specific statutory authorization within the meaning of this joint resolution.

SEC. 8. (b) Nothing in this joint resolution shall be construed to require any further specific statutory authorization to permit members of United States Armed Forces to participate jointly with members of the armed forces of one or more foreign countries in the headquarters operations of high-level military commands which were established prior to the date of enactment of this joint resolution and pursuant to the United Nations Charter or any treaty ratified by the United States prior to such date.

SEC 8. (c) For purposes of this joint resolution, the term "introduction of United States Armed Forces" includes the assignment of members of such armed forces to command, coordinate, participate in the movement of, or accompany the regular or irregular military forces of any foreign country or government when such military forces are engaged, or there exists an imminent threat that such forces will become engaged, in hostilities.

SEC. 8. (d) Nothing in this joint resolution—(1) is intended to alter the constitutional authority of the Congress or of the President, or the provision of existing treaties; or (2) shall be construed as granting any authority to the President with respect to the introduction of United States Armed Forces into hostilities or into situations wherein involvement in hostilities is clearly indicated by the circumstances which authority he would not have had in the absence of this joint resolution....

Source: The War Powers Act as passed by the 93rd Congress on November 7, 1973, available online at http://www.cs.indiana.edu/statecraft/warpow.html, downloaded May 25, 2004.

11. OPINION OF THE SUPREME COURT DELIVERED BY CHIEF JUSTICE WARREN E. BURGER IN *UNITED STATES V. NIXON,* JULY 24, 1974

This litigation presents for review the denial of a motion, filed in the District Court on behalf of the President of the United States, in the case of *United States v. Mitchell* (D.C. Crim. No. 74–110), to quash a third-party subpoena duces tecum issued by the United States District Court for the District of Columbia, pursuant to Fed. Rule Crim. Proc. 17 (c). The subpoena directed the President to produce certain tape recordings and documents relating to his conversations with aides and advisers. The court rejected the President's claims of absolute executive privilege, of lack of jurisdiction, and of failure to satisfy the requirements of Rule 17 (c). The President appealed to the Court of Appeals. We granted both the United States' petition for certiorari before judgment (No. 73–1766), and also the President's cross-petition for certiorari [418 U.S. 683, 687] before judgment (No. 73–1834), because of the public importance of the issues presented and the need for their prompt resolution. 417 U.S. 927 and 960 (1974).

On March 1, 1974, a grand jury of the United States District Court for the District of Columbia returned an indictment charging seven named individuals 3 with various offenses, including conspiracy to defraud the United States and to obstruct justice. Although he was not designated as such in the indictment, the grand jury named the President, among others, as an unindicted coconspirator. On April 18, 1974, upon motion of the Special [418 U.S. 683, 688] Prosecutor a subpoena duces tecum was issued pursuant to Rule 17 (c) to the President by the United States District Court and made returnable on May 2, 1974. This subpoena required the production, in advance of the September 9 trial date, of certain tapes, memoranda, papers, transcripts, or other writings relating to certain precisely identified meetings between the President and others. 5 The Special Prosecutor was able to fix the time, place, and persons present at these discussions because the White House daily logs and appointment records had been delivered to him. On April 30, the President publicly released edited transcripts of 43 conversations; portions of 20 conversations subject to subpoena in the present case were included. On May 1, 1974, the President's counsel filed a "special appearance" and a motion to quash the subpoena under Rule 17 (c). This motion was accompanied by a formal claim of privilege. At a subsequent hearing, 6 further motions to expunge the grand jury's action naming the President as an unindicted coconspirator and for protective orders against the disclosure of that information were filed or raised orally by counsel for the President.

On May 20, 1974, the District Court denied the motion to quash and the motions to expunge and for protective orders. 377 F. Supp. 1326. It further ordered "the President or any subordinate officer, official, or employee with custody or control of the documents or [418 U.S. 683, 689] objects subpoenaed," id., at 1331, to deliver to the District Court, on or before May 31, 1974, the originals of all subpoenaed items, as well as an index and analysis of those items, together with tape copies of those portions of the subpoenaed recordings for which transcripts had been released to the public by the President on April 30. The District Court rejected jurisdictional challenges based on a contention that the dispute was nonjusticiable because it was between the Special Prosecutor and the Chief Executive and hence "intra-executive" in character; it also rejected the contention that the Judiciary was without authority to review an assertion of executive privilege by the President. The court's rejection of the first challenge was based on the authority and powers vested in the Special Prosecutor by the regulation promulgated by the Attorney General; the court concluded that a justiciable controversy was presented. The second challenge was held to be foreclosed by the decision in *Nixon v. Sirica,* 159 U.S. App. D.C. 58, 487 F.2d 700 (1973).

The District Court held that the judiciary, not the President, was the final arbiter of a claim of executive privilege. The court concluded that, under the circumstances of this case, the presumptive privilege was overcome by the Special Prosecutor's prima facie "demonstration of need sufficiently compelling to warrant judicial examination in chambers...." 377 F. Supp., at 1330. The court held, finally, that the Special Prosecutor had satisfied the requirements of Rule 17 (c). The District Court stayed its order pending appellate review on condition that review was sought before 4 P.M., May 24. The court further provided that matters filed under

seal remain under seal when transmitted as part of the record.

On May 24, 1974, the President filed a timely notice of appeal from the District Court order, and the certified record from the District Court was docketed in the United [418 U.S. 683, 690] States Court of Appeals for the District of Columbia Circuit. On the same day, the President also filed a petition for writ of mandamus in the Court of Appeals seeking review of the District Court order.

Later on May 24, the Special Prosecutor also filed, in this Court, a petition for a writ of certiorari before judgment. On May 31, the petition was granted with an expedited briefing schedule. 417 U.S. 927. On June 6, the President filed, under seal, a cross-petition for writ of certiorari before judgment. This cross-petition was granted June 15, 1974, 417 U.S. 960, and the case was set for argument on July 8, 1974.

I

JURISDICTION

The threshold question presented is whether the May 20, 1974, order of the District Court was an appealable order and whether this case was properly "in" the Court of Appeals when the petition for certiorari was filed in this Court. 28 U.S.C. 1254. The Court of Appeals' jurisdiction under 28 U.S.C. 1291 encompasses only "final decisions of the district courts." Since the appeal was timely filed and all other procedural requirements were met, the petition is properly before this Court for consideration if the District Court order was final. 28 U.S.C. 1254 (1), 2101 (e).

The finality requirements of 28 U.S.C. 1291 embodies a strong congressional policy against piecemeal reviews, and against obstructing or impeding an ongoing judicial proceeding by interlocutory appeals. See, e. g., *Cobbledick v. United States,* 309 U.S. 323, 324–326 (1940). This requirement ordinarily promotes judicial efficiency and hastens the ultimate termination of litigation. In applying this principle to an order denying a motion to quash and requiring the production of evidence pursuant [418 U.S. 683, 691] to a subpoena duces tecum, it has been repeatedly held that the order is not final and hence not appealable. *United States v. Ryan,* 402 U.S. 530, 532 (1971); *Cobbledick v. United States,* supra; *Alexander v. United States,* 201 U.S. 117 (1906). This Court has "consistently held that the necessity for expedition in the administration of the criminal law justifies putting one who seeks to resist the production of desired information to a choice between compliance with a trial court's order to produce prior to any review of that order, and resistance to that order with the concomitant possibility of an adjudication of contempt if his claims are rejected on appeal." *United States v. Ryan,* supra, at 533.

The requirement of submitting to contempt, however, is not without exception and in some instances the purposes underlying the finality rule require a different result. For example, in *Perlman v. United States,* 247 U.S. 7 (1918), a subpoena had been directed to a third party requesting certain exhibits; the appellant, who owned the exhibits, sought to raise a claim of privilege. The Court held an order compelling production was appealable because it was unlikely that the third party would risk a contempt citation in order to allow immediate review of the appellant's claim of privilege. That case fell within the "limited class of cases where denial of immediate review would render impossible any review whatsoever of an individual's claims."

Here too, the traditional contempt avenue to immediate appeal is peculiarly inappropriate due to the unique setting in which the question arises. To require a President of the United States to place himself in the posture of disobeying an order of a court merely to trigger the procedural mechanism for review of the ruling would be [418 U.S. 683, 692] unseemly, and would present an unnecessary occasion for constitutional confrontation between two branches of the Government. Similarly, a federal judge should not be placed in the posture of issuing a citation to a President simply in order to invoke review. The issue whether a President can be cited for contempt could itself engender protracted litigation, and would further delay both review on the merits of his claim of privilege and the ultimate termination of the underlying criminal action for which his evidence is sought. These considerations lead us to conclude that the order of the District Court was an appealable order. The appeal from that order was therefore properly "in" the Court of Appeals, and the case is now properly before this Court on the writ of certiorari before judgment. 28 U.S.C. 1254; 28 U.S.C. 2101 (e). *Gay v. Ruff,* 292 U.S. 25, 30 (1934).

II

JUSTICIABILITY

In the District Court, the President's counsel argued that the court lacked jurisdiction to issue the subpoena because the matter was an intra-branch dispute between a subordinate and superior officer of the Executive Branch and hence not subject to judicial resolution. That argument has been renewed in this Court with emphasis on the contention that the dispute does not present a "case" or "controversy" which can be adjudicated in the federal courts. The President's counsel argues that the federal courts should not intrude into areas committed to the other branches of Government. [418 U.S. 683, 693] He views the present dispute as essentially a "jurisdictional" dispute within the Executive Branch which he analogizes to a dispute between two congressional committees. Since the Executive Branch has exclusive authority and absolute discretion to decide whether to prosecute a case, *Confiscation Cases,* 7 Wall. 454 (1869); *United States v. Cox,* 342 F.2d 167, 171 (CA5), cert. denied sub nom. *Cox v. Hauberg,* 381 U.S. 935 (1965), it is contended that a President's decision is final in determining what evidence is to be used in a given criminal case. Although his counsel concedes that the President has delegated certain specific powers to the Special Prosecutor, he has not "waived nor delegated to the Special Prosecutor the President's duty to claim privilege as to all materials . . . which fall within the President's inherent authority to refuse to disclose to any executive officer." Brief for the President 42. The Special Prosecutor's demand for the items therefore presents, in the view of the President's counsel, a political question under *Baker v. Carr,* 369 U.S. 186 (1962), since it involves a "textually demonstrable" grant of power under Art. II.

The mere assertion of a claim of an "intra-branch dispute," without more, has never operated to defeat federal jurisdiction; justiciability does not depend on such a surface inquiry. In *United States v. ICC,* 337 U.S. 426 (1949), the Court observed, "courts must look behind names that symbolize the parties to determine whether a justiciable case or controversy is presented." See also *Powell v. McCormack,* 395 U.S. 486 (1969); *ICC v. Jersey City,* 322 U.S. 503 (1944); United States ex rel. *Chapman v. FPC,* 345 U.S. 153 (1953); *Secretary of Agriculture v. United States,* 347 U.S. 645 (1954); *FMB v. Isbrandtsen Co.,* 356 U.S. 481, 483 n. 2 (1958); *United States v. Marine Bancorporation;* and *United States v. Connecticut National Bank* [418 U.S. 683, 694] (1974).

Our starting point is the nature of the proceeding for which the evidence is sought—here a pending criminal prosecution. It is a judicial proceeding in a federal court alleging violation of federal laws and is brought in the name of the United States as sovereign. *Berger v. United States,* 295 U.S. 78, 88 (1935). Under the authority of Art. II, 2, Congress has vested in the Attorney General the power to conduct the criminal litigation of the United States Government. 28 U.S.C. 516. It has also vested in him the power to appoint subordinate officers to assist him in the discharge of his duties. 28 U.S.C. 509, 510, 515, 533. Acting pursuant to those statutes, the Attorney General has delegated the authority to represent the United States in these particular matters to a Special Prosecutor with unique authority and tenure. The regulation gives the [418 U.S. 683, 695] Special Prosecutor explicit power to contest the invocation of executive privilege in the process of seeking evidence deemed relevant to the performance of these specially delegated duties. 38 Fed. Reg. 30739, as amended by 38 Fed. Reg. 32805.

So long as this regulation is extant it has the force of law. In United States ex rel. *Accardi v. Shaughnessy,* 347 U.S. 260 (1954), regulations of the Attorney General delegated certain of his discretionary powers to the Board [418 U.S. 683, 696] of Immigration Appeals and required that Board to exercise its own discretion on appeals in deportation cases. The Court held that so long as the Attorney General's regulations remained operative, he denied himself the authority to exercise the discretion delegated to the Board even though the original authority was his and he could reassert it by amending the regulations. *Service v. Dulles,* 354 U.S. 363, 388 (1957), and *Vitarelli v. Seaton,* 359 U.S. 535 (1959), reaffirmed the basic holding of Accardi.

Here, as in Accardi, it is theoretically possible for the Attorney General to amend or revoke the regulation defining the Special Prosecutor's authority. But he has not done so. So long as this regulation remains in force the Executive Branch is bound by it, and indeed the United States as the sovereign composed of the three branches is bound to respect and to enforce it. Moreover, the delegation of authority to the Special Prosecutor in this case is not an ordinary delegation by the Attorney General to a subordinate officer: with the authorization of the President, the Acting Attorney General provided in the regulation that the Special Prosecutor was not to be removed without the "consensus" of eight designated leaders of Congress.

The demands of and the resistance to the subpoena present an obvious controversy in the ordinary sense, but that alone is not sufficient to meet constitutional standards. In the constitutional sense, controversy means more than disagreement and conflict; rather it means the kind of controversy courts traditionally resolve.

Here [418 U.S. 683, 697] at issue is the production or nonproduction of specified evidence deemed by the Special Prosecutor to be relevant and admissible in a pending criminal case. It is sought by one official of the Executive Branch within the scope of his express authority; it is resisted by the Chief Executive on the ground of his duty to preserve the confidentiality of the communications of the President. Whatever the correct answer on the merits, these issues are "of a type which are traditionally justiciable." *United States v. ICC,* 337 U.S., at 430. The independent Special Prosecutor with his asserted need for the subpoenaed material in the underlying criminal prosecution is opposed by the President with his steadfast assertion of privilege against disclosure of the material. This setting assures there is "that concrete adverseness which sharpens the presentation of issues upon which the court so largely depends for illumination of difficult constitutional questions." *Baker v. Carr,* 369 U.S., at 204. Moreover, since the matter is one arising in the regular course of a federal criminal prosecution, it is within the traditional scope of Art. III power.

In light of the uniqueness of the setting in which the conflict arises, the fact that both parties are officers of the Executive Branch cannot be viewed as a barrier to justiciability. It would be inconsistent with the applicable law and regulation, and the unique facts of this case to conclude other than that the Special Prosecutor has standing to bring this action and that a justiciable controversy is presented for decision.

III

RULE 17 (c)
The subpoena duces tecum is challenged on the ground that the Special Prosecutor failed to satisfy the requirements of Fed. Rule Crim. Proc. 17 (c), which governs [418 U.S. 683, 698] the issuance of subpoenas duces tecum in federal criminal proceedings. If we sustained this challenge, there would be no occasion to reach the claim of privilege asserted with respect to the subpoenaed material. Thus we turn to the question whether the requirements of Rule 17 (c) have been satisfied. See *Arkansas Louisiana Gas Co. v. Dept. of Public Utilities,* 304 U.S. 61, 64 (1938); *Ashwander v. TVA,* 297 U.S. 288, 346–347 (1936) (Brandeis, J., concurring).
Rule 17 (c) provides: "A subpoena may also command the person to whom it is directed to produce the books, papers, documents or other objects designated therein. The court on motion made promptly may quash or

modify the subpoena if compliance would be unreasonable or oppressive. The court may direct that books, papers, documents or objects designated in the subpoena be produced before the court at a time prior to the trial or prior to the time when they are to be offered in evidence and may upon their production permit the books, papers, documents or objects or portions thereof to be inspected by the parties and their attorneys."

A subpoena for documents may be quashed if their production would be "unreasonable or oppressive," but not otherwise. The leading case in this Court interpreting this standard is *Bowman Dairy Co. v. United States,* 341 U.S. 214 (1951). This case recognized certain fundamental characteristics of the subpoena duces tecum in criminal cases: (1) it was not intended to provide a means of discovery for criminal cases; (2) its chief innovation was to expedite the trial by providing a time and place before trial for the inspection of [418 U.S. 683, 699] subpoenaed materials. As both parties agree, cases decided in the wake of Bowman have generally followed Judge Weinfeld's formulation in *United States v. Iozia,* 13 F. R. D. 335, 338 (SDNY 1952), as to the required showing. Under this test, in order to require production prior to trial, the moving party must show: (1) that the documents are evidentiary and relevant; (2) that they are not otherwise procurable reasonably in advance of trial by exercise of due diligence; (3) that the party cannot properly prepare for trial without such production and inspection in advance of trial and that the failure to obtain such inspection may tend unreasonably to delay the trial; and (4) that [418 U.S. 683, 700] the application is made in good faith and is not intended as a general "fishing expedition."

Against this background, the Special Prosecutor, in order to carry his burden, must clear three hurdles: (1) relevancy; (2) admissibility; (3) specificity. Our own review of the record necessarily affords a less comprehensive view of the total situation than was available to the trial judge and we are unwilling to conclude that the District Court erred in the evaluation of the Special Prosecutor's showing under Rule 17 (c). Our conclusion is based on the record before us, much of which is under seal. Of course, the contents of the subpoenaed tapes could not at that stage be described fully by the Special Prosecutor, but there was a sufficient likelihood that each of the tapes contains conversations relevant to the offenses charged in the indictment. *United States v. Gross,* 24 F. R. D. 138 (SDNY 1959). With respect to

many of the tapes, the Special Prosecutor offered the sworn testimony or statements of one or more of the participants in the conversations as to what was said at the time. As for the remainder of the tapes, the identity of the participants and the time and place of the conversations, taken in their total context, permit a rational inference that at least part of the conversations relate to the offenses charged in the indictment.

We also conclude there was a sufficient preliminary showing that each of the subpoenaed tapes contains evidence admissible with respect to the offenses charged in the indictment. The most cogent objection to the admissibility of the taped conversations here at issue is that they are a collection of out-of-court statements by declarants who will not be subject to cross-examination and that the statements are therefore inadmissible hearsay. Here, however, most of the tapes apparently contain conversations [418 U.S. 683, 701] to which one or more of the defendants named in the indictment were party. The hearsay rule does not automatically bar all out-of-court statements by a defendant in a criminal case. Declarations by one defendant may also be admissible against other defendants upon a sufficient showing, by independent evidence, of a conspiracy among one or more other defendants and the declarant and if the declarations at issue were in furtherance of that conspiracy. The same is true of declarations of coconspirators who are not defendants in the case on trial. *Dutton v. Evans,* 400 U.S. 74, 81 (1970). Recorded conversations may also be admissible for the limited purpose of impeaching the credibility of any defendant who testifies or any other coconspirator who testifies. Generally, the need for evidence to impeach witnesses is insufficient to require its production in advance of trial. See, e.g., *United States v. Carter,* 15 F. R. D. 367, [418 U.S. 683, 702] 371 (DC 1954). Here, however, there are other valid potential evidentiary uses for the same material, and the analysis and possible transcription of the tapes may take a significant period of time. Accordingly, we cannot conclude that the District Court erred in authorizing the issuance of the subpoena duces tecum.

Enforcement of a pretrial subpoena duces tecum must necessarily be committed to the sound discretion of the trial court since the necessity for the subpoena most often turns upon a determination of factual issues. Without a determination of arbitrariness or that the trial court finding was without record support, an appellate court will not ordinarily disturb a finding that the applicant for a subpoena complied with Rule 17 (c). See, e.g., *Sue v. Chicago Transit Authority,* 279 F.2d 416, 419 (CA7 1960); *Shotkin v. Nelson,* 146 F.2d 402 (CA10 1944).

In a case such as this, however, where a subpoena is directed to a President of the United States, appellate review, in deference to a coordinate branch of Government, should be particularly meticulous to ensure that the standards of Rule 17 (c) have been correctly applied. *United States v. Burr,* 25 F. Cas. 30, 34 (No. 14,692d) (CC Va. 1807). From our examination of the materials submitted by the Special Prosecutor to the District Court in support of his motion for the subpoena, we are persuaded that the District Court's denial of the President's motion to quash the subpoena was consistent with Rule 17 (c). We also conclude that the Special Prosecutor has made a sufficient showing to justify a subpoena for production before trial. The subpoenaed materials are not available from any other source, and their examination and processing should not await trial in the circumstances shown. *Bowman Dairy Co. v. United States,* 341 U.S. 214 (1951); *United States v. Iozia,* 13 F. R. D. 335 (SDNY 1952). [418 U.S. 683, 703]

IV

THE CLAIM OF PRIVILEGE

A

Having determined that the requirements of Rule 17 (c) were satisfied, we turn to the claim that the subpoena should be quashed because it demands "confidential conversations between a President and his close advisors that it would be inconsistent with the public interest to produce." App. 48a. The first contention is a broad claim that the separation of powers doctrine precludes judicial review of a President's claim of privilege. The second contention is that if he does not prevail on the claim of absolute privilege, the court should hold as a matter of constitutional law that the privilege prevails over the subpoena duces tecum.

In the performance of assigned constitutional duties each branch of the Government must initially interpret the Constitution, and the interpretation of its powers by any branch is due great respect from the others. The President's counsel, as we have noted, reads the Constitution as providing an absolute privilege of confidentiality for all Presidential communications. Many decisions of this Court, however, have unequivocally reaffirmed the holding of *Marbury v. Madison,* 1 Cranch

137 (1803), that "[i]t is emphatically the province and duty of the judicial department to say what the law is."

No holding of the Court has defined the scope of judicial power specifically relating to the enforcement of a subpoena for confidential Presidential communications for use in a criminal prosecution, but other exercises of power by the Executive Branch and the Legislative Branch have been found invalid as in conflict with the Constitution. *Powell v. McCormack,* 395 U.S. 486 (1969); *Youngstown Sheet & Tube Co. v. Sawyer,* 343 U.S. 579 (1952). In a [418 U.S. 683, 704] series of cases, the Court interpreted the explicit immunity conferred by express provisions of the Constitution on Members of the House and Senate by the Speech or Debate Clause, U.S. Const. Art. I, 6. *Doe v. McMillan,* 412 U.S. 306 (1973); *Gravel v. United States,* 408 U.S. 606 (1972); *United States v. Brewster,* 408 U.S. 501 (1972); *United States v. Johnson,* 383 U.S. 169 (1966). Since this Court has consistently exercised the power to construe and delineate claims arising under express powers, it must follow that the Court has authority to interpret claims with respect to powers alleged to derive from enumerated powers.

Our system of government "requires that federal courts on occasion interpret the Constitution in a manner at variance with the construction given the document by another branch." *Powell v. McCormack,* supra, at 549. And in *Baker v. Carr,* 369 U.S., at 211, the Court stated: "Deciding whether a matter has in any measure been committed by the Constitution to another branch of government, or whether the action of that branch exceeds whatever authority has been committed, is itself a delicate exercise in constitutional interpretation, and is a responsibility of this Court as ultimate interpreter of the Constitution."

Notwithstanding the deference each branch must accord the others, the "judicial Power of the United States" vested in the federal courts by Art. III, 1, of the Constitution can no more be shared with the Executive Branch than the Chief Executive, for example, can share with the Judiciary the veto power, or the Congress share with the Judiciary the power to override a Presidential veto. Any other conclusion would be contrary to the basic concept of separation of powers and the checks and balances that flow from the scheme of a tripartite government. The Federalist, No. 47, p. 313 (S. Mittell ed. [418 U.S. 683, 705] (1938). We therefore reaffirm that it is the province and duty of this Court "to say what the law is" with respect to the claim of privilege presented in this case. *Marbury v. Madison,* supra, at 177.

B

In support of his claim of absolute privilege, the President's counsel urges two grounds, one of which is common to all governments and one of which is peculiar to our system of separation of powers. The first ground is the valid need for protection of communications between high Government officials and those who advise and assist them in the performance of their manifold duties; the importance of this confidentiality is too plain to require further discussion. Human experience teaches that those who expect public dissemination of their remarks may well temper candor with a concern for appearances and for their own interests to the detriment of the decision-making process. Whatever the nature of the privilege of confidentiality of Presidential communications in the exercise of Art. II powers, the privilege can be said to derive from the supremacy of each branch within its own assigned area of constitutional duties. Certain powers and privileges flow from the nature of enumerated powers; the protection of the confidentiality of [418 U.S. 683, 706] Presidential communications has similar constitutional underpinnings.

The second ground asserted by the President's counsel in support of the claim of absolute privilege rests on the doctrine of separation of powers. Here it is argued that the independence of the Executive Branch within its own sphere, Humphrey's *Executor v. United States,* 295 U.S. 602, 629–630 (1935); *Kilbourn v. Thompson,* 103 U.S. 168, 190–191 (1881), insulates a President from a judicial subpoena in an ongoing criminal prosecution, and thereby protects confidential Presidential communications.

However, neither the doctrine of separation of powers, nor the need for confidentiality of high-level communications, without more, can sustain an absolute, unqualified Presidential privilege of immunity from judicial process under all circumstances. The President's need for complete candor and objectivity from advisers calls for great deference from the courts. However, when the privilege depends solely on the broad, undifferentiated claim of public interest in the confidentiality of such conversations, a confrontation with other values arises. Absent a claim of need to protect military, diplomatic, or sensitive national security secrets, we find it difficult to accept the argument that even the very

important interest in confidentiality of Presidential communications is significantly diminished by production of such material for in camera inspection with all the protection that a district court will be obliged to provide. [418 U.S. 683, 707]

The impediment that an absolute, unqualified privilege would place in the way of the primary constitutional duty of the Judicial Branch to do justice in criminal prosecutions would plainly conflict with the function of the courts under Art. III. In designing the structure of our Government and dividing and allocating the sovereign power among three co-equal branches, the Framers of the Constitution sought to provide a comprehensive system, but the separate powers were not intended to operate with absolute independence.

"While the Constitution diffuses power the better to secure liberty, it also contemplates that practice will integrate the dispersed powers into a workable government. It enjoins upon its branches separateness but interdependence, autonomy but reciprocity." *Youngstown Sheet & Tube Co. v. Sawyer,* 343 U.S., at 635 (Jackson, J., concurring).

To read the Art. II powers of the President as providing an absolute privilege as against a subpoena essential to enforcement of criminal statutes on no more than a generalized claim of the public interest in confidentiality of nonmilitary and non-diplomatic discussions would upset the constitutional balance of "a workable government" and gravely impair the role of the courts under Art. III.

C

Since we conclude that the legitimate needs of the judicial process may outweigh Presidential privilege, it is necessary to resolve those competing interests in a manner that preserves the essential functions of each branch. The right and indeed the duty to resolve that question does not free the Judiciary from according high respect to the representations made on behalf of the President.

The expectation of a President to the confidentiality of his conversations and correspondence, like the claim of confidentiality of judicial deliberations, for example, has all the values to which we accord deference for the privacy of all citizens and, added to those values, is the necessity for protection of the public interest in candid, objective, and even blunt or harsh opinions in Presidential decision-making. A President and those who assist him must be free to explore alternatives in the process of shaping policies and making decisions and to do so in a way many would be unwilling to express except privately. These are the considerations justifying a presumptive privilege for Presidential communications. The privilege is fundamental to the operation of Government and inextricably rooted in the separation of powers under the Constitution. In *Nixon v. Sirica,* 159 U.S. App. D.C. 58, 487 F.2d 700 (1973), the Court of Appeals held that such Presidential communications are "presumptively privileged," and this position is accepted by both parties in the present litigation. We agree with Mr. Chief Justice Marshall's observation, therefore, that "[i]n no case of this kind would a court be required to proceed against the president as against an ordinary individual."

But this presumptive privilege must be considered in light of our historic commitment to the rule of law. This [418 U.S. 683, 709] is nowhere more profoundly manifest than in our view that "the twofold aim [of criminal justice] is that guilt shall not escape or innocence suffer." We have elected to employ an adversary system of criminal justice in which the parties contest all issues before a court of law. The need to develop all relevant facts in the adversary system is both fundamental and comprehensive. The ends of criminal justice would be defeated if judgments were to be founded on a partial or speculative presentation of the facts. The very integrity of the judicial system and public confidence in the system depend on full disclosure of all the facts, within the framework of the rules of evidence. To ensure that justice is done, it is imperative to the function of courts that compulsory process be available for the production of evidence needed either by the prosecution or by the defense.

Only recently the Court restated the ancient proposition of law, albeit in the context of a grand jury inquiry rather than a trial, "that 'the public . . . has a right to every man's evidence,' except for those persons protected by a constitutional, common-law, or statutory privilege, *United States v. Bryan,* 339 U.S. [323, 331 (1950)]; *Blackmer v. United States,* 284 U.S. 421, 438 (1932). . . ." *Branzburg v. Hayes,* 408 U.S. 665, 688 (1972).

The privileges referred to by the Court are designed to protect weighty and legitimate competing interests. Thus, the Fifth Amendment to the Constitution provides that no man "shall be compelled in any criminal case to be a witness against himself." And, generally, an attorney or a priest may not be required to disclose what has been revealed in professional confidence. These and other interests are recognized in law by privileges [418 U.S. 683, 710] against forced disclosure, established in the Constitution, by statute, or at common law. Whatever their origins, these exceptions to the demand for every man's evidence are not lightly created nor expansively construed, for they are in derogation of the search for truth.

In this case the President challenges a subpoena served on him as a third party requiring the production of materials for use in a criminal prosecution; he does so on the claim that he has a privilege against disclosure of confidential communications. He does not place his claim of privilege on the ground they are military or diplomatic secrets. As to these areas of Art. II duties the courts have traditionally shown the utmost deference to Presidential responsibilities. In *C. & S. Air Lines v. Waterman S. S. Corp.,* 333 U.S. 103, 111 (1948), dealing with Presidential authority involving foreign policy considerations, the Court said: "The President, both as Commander-in-Chief and as the Nation's organ for foreign affairs, has available intelligence services whose reports are not and ought not to be published to the world. It would be intolerable that courts, without the relevant information, should review and perhaps nullify actions of the Executive taken on information properly held secret."

In *United States v. Reynolds,* 345 U.S. 1 (1953), dealing [418 U.S. 683, 711] with a claimant's demand for evidence in a Tort Claims Act case against the Government, the Court said: "It may be possible to satisfy the court, from all the circumstances of the case, that there is a reasonable danger that compulsion of the evidence will expose military matters which, in the interest of national security, should not be divulged. When this is the case, the occasion for the privilege is appropriate, and the court should not jeopardize the security which the privilege is meant to protect by insisting upon an examination of the evidence, even by the judge alone, in chambers."

No case of the Court, however, has extended this high degree of deference to a President's generalized interest in confidentiality. Nowhere in the Constitution, as we have noted earlier, is there any explicit reference to a privilege of confidentiality, yet to the extent this interest relates to the effective discharge of a President's powers, it is constitutionally based.

The right to the production of all evidence at a criminal trial similarly has constitutional dimensions. The Sixth Amendment explicitly confers upon every defendant in a criminal trial the right "to be confronted with the witnesses against him" and "to have compulsory process for obtaining witnesses in his favor." Moreover, the Fifth Amendment also guarantees that no person shall be deprived of liberty without due process of law. It is the manifest duty of the courts to vindicate those guarantees, and to accomplish that it is essential that all relevant and admissible evidence be produced.

In this case we must weigh the importance of the general privilege of confidentiality of Presidential communications in performance of the President's responsibilities against the inroads of such a privilege on the fair [418 U.S. 683, 712] administration of criminal justice. The interest in preserving confidentiality is weighty indeed and entitled to great respect. However, we cannot conclude that advisers will be moved to temper the candor of their remarks by the infrequent occasions of disclosure because of the possibility that such conversations will be called for in the context of a criminal prosecution.

On the other hand, the allowance of the privilege to withhold evidence that is demonstrably relevant in a criminal trial would cut deeply into the guarantee of due process of law and gravely impair the basic function of the courts. A President's acknowledged need for confidentiality [418 U.S. 683, 713] in the communications of his office is general in nature, whereas the constitutional need for production of relevant evidence in a criminal proceeding is specific and central to the fair adjudication of a particular criminal case in the administration of justice. Without access to specific facts a criminal prosecution may be totally frustrated. The President's broad interest in confidentiality of communications will not be vitiated by disclosure of a limited number of conversations preliminarily shown to have some bearing on the pending criminal cases.

We conclude that when the ground for asserting privilege as to subpoenaed materials sought for use in a criminal trial is based only on the generalized interest in confidentiality, it cannot prevail over the fundamental demands of due process of law in the fair administration of criminal justice. The generalized assertion of privilege must yield to the demonstrated, specific need for evidence in a pending criminal trial.

D

We have earlier determined that the District Court did not err in authorizing the issuance of the subpoena. If a President concludes that compliance with a subpoena would be injurious to the public interest he may properly, as was done here, invoke a claim of privilege on the return of the subpoena. Upon receiving a claim of privilege from the Chief Executive, it became the further duty of the District Court to treat the subpoenaed material as presumptively privileged and to require the Special Prosecutor to demonstrate that the Presidential material was "essential to the justice of the [pending criminal] case." Here the District Court treated the material as presumptively privileged, proceeded to find that the Special [418 U.S. 683, 714] Prosecutor had made a sufficient showing to rebut the presumption, and ordered an in camera examination of the subpoenaed material. On the basis of our examination of the record we are unable to conclude that the District Court erred in ordering the inspection. Accordingly we affirm the order of the District Court that subpoenaed materials be transmitted to that court. We now turn to the important question of the District Court's responsibilities in conducting the in camera examination of Presidential materials or communications delivered under the compulsion of the subpoena duces tecum.

E

Enforcement of the subpoena duces tecum was stayed pending this Court's resolution of the issues raised by the petitions for certiorari. Those issues now having been disposed of, the matter of implementation will rest with the District Court. "[T]he guard, furnished to [the President] to protect him from being harassed by vexatious and unnecessary subpoenas, is to be looked for in the conduct of a [district] court after those subpoenas have issued; not in any circumstance which is to precede their being issued." *United States v. Burr,* 25 F. Cas., at 34. Statements that meet the test of admissibility and relevance must be isolated; all other material must be excised. At this stage the District Court is not limited to representations of the Special Prosecutor as to the evidence sought by the subpoena; the material will be available to the District Court. It is elementary that in camera inspection of evidence is always a procedure calling for scrupulous protection against any release or publication of material not found by the court, at that stage, probably admissible in evidence and relevant to the issues of the trial for which it is sought. That being true of an ordinary situation, it is obvious that the District Court has [418 U.S. 683, 715] a very heavy responsibility to see to it that Presidential conversations, which are either not relevant or not admissible, are accorded that high degree of respect due the President of the United States. Mr. Chief Justice Marshall, sitting as a trial judge in the Burr case, supra, was extraordinarily careful to point out that "[i]n no case of this kind would a court be required to proceed against the president as against an ordinary individual."

Marshall's statement cannot be read to mean in any sense that a President is above the law, but relates to the singularly unique role under Art. II of a President's communications and activities, related to the performance of duties under that Article. Moreover, a President's communications and activities encompass a vastly wider range of sensitive material than would be true of any "ordinary individual." It is therefore necessary in the public interest to afford Presidential confidentiality the greatest protection consistent with the fair administration of justice. The need for confidentiality even as to idle conversations with associates in which casual reference might be made concerning political leaders within the country or foreign statesmen is too obvious to call for further treatment. We have no doubt that the District Judge will at all times accord to Presidential records that high degree of deference suggested in *United States v. Burr,* supra, and will discharge his responsibility to see to [418 U.S. 683, 716] it that until released to the Special Prosecutor no in camera material is revealed to anyone. This burden applies with even greater force to excised material; once the decision is made to excise, the material is restored to its privileged status and should be returned under seal to its lawful custodian.

Since this matter came before the Court during the pendency of a criminal prosecution, and on representations that time is of the essence, the mandate shall issue forthwith.

12. The Articles of Impeachment of Richard M. Nixon, House Judiciary Committee, Passed July 27–July 30, 1974

RESOLUTION

Impeaching Richard M. Nixon, President of the United States, of high crimes and misdemeanors.

Resolved, that Richard M. Nixon, President of the United States, is impeached for high crimes and misdemeanors, and that the following articles of impeachment be exhibited to the Senate:

Articles of Impeachment exhibited by the House of Representatives of the United States of America in the name of itself and of all of the people of the United States of America, against Richard M. Nixon, President of the United States of America, in maintenance and support of its impeachment against him for high crimes and misdemeanors.

Article I

In his conduct of the office of President of the United States, Richard M. Nixon, in violation of his constitutional oath faithfully to execute the office of President of the United States and, to the best of his ability, preserve, protect, and defend the Constitution of the United States, and in violation of his constitutional duty to take care that the laws be faithfully executed, has prevented, obstructed, and impeded the administration of justice, in that:

On June 17, 1972, and prior thereto, agents of the Committee for the Re-election of the President committed unlawful entry of the headquarters of the Democratic National Committee in Washington, District of Columbia, for the purpose of securing political intelligence. Subsequent thereto, Richard M. Nixon, using the powers of his high office, engaged personally and through his subordinates and agents, in a course of conduct or plan designed to delay, impede, and obstruct the investigation of such unlawful entry; to cover up, conceal and protect those responsible; and to conceal the existence and scope of other unlawful covert activities.

The means used to implement this course of conduct or plan included one or more of the following:

(1) making or causing to be made false or misleading statements to lawfully authorized investigative officers and employees of the United States;

(2) withholding relevant and material evidence or information from lawfully authorized investigative officers and employees of the United States;

(3) approving, condoning, acquiescing in, and counseling witnesses with respect to the giving of false or misleading statements to lawfully authorized investigative officers and employees of the United States and false or misleading testimony in duly instituted judicial and congressional proceedings;

(4) interfering or endeavoring to interfere with the conduct of investigations by the Department of Justice of the United States, the Federal Bureau of Investigation, the Office of Watergate Special Prosecution Force, and Congressional Committees;

(5) approving, condoning, and acquiescing in the surreptitious payment of substantial sums of money for the purpose of obtaining the silence or influencing the testimony of witnesses, potential witness or individuals who participated in such unlawful entry and other illegal activities;

(6) endeavoring to misuse the Central Intelligence Agency, an agency of the United States;

(7) disseminating information received from officers of the Department of Justice of the United States to subjects of investigations conducted by lawfully authorized investigative officers and employees of the United States, for the purpose of aiding and assisting such subjects in their attempts to avoid criminal liability;

(8) making false or misleading public statements for the purpose of deceiving the people of the United States into believing that a thorough and complete investigation had been conducted with respect to allegations of misconduct on the part of personnel of the executive branch of the United States and personnel of the Committee for the Re-election of the President, and that there was no involvement of such personnel in such misconduct; or

(9) endeavoring to cause prospective defendants, and individuals duly tried and convicted, to expect favored treatment and consideration in return for their silence or false testimony, or rewarding individuals for their silence or false testimony.

In all of this, Richard M. Nixon has acted in a manner contrary to his trust as President and subversive of constitutional government, to the great prejudice of the cause of law and justice and to the manifest injury of the people of the United States.

Wherefore Richard M. Nixon, by such conduct, warrants impeachment and trial, and removal from office.

Article II

Using the powers of the office of President of the United States, Richard M. Nixon, in violation of his constitutional oath faithfully to execute the office of President of the United States and, to the best of his ability, preserve, protect, and defend the Constitution of the United States, and in disregard of his constitutional duty to take care that the laws be faithfully executed, has repeatedly engaged in conduct violating the constitutional rights of citizens, impairing the due and proper administration of justice and the conduct of lawful inquiries, or contravening the laws governing agencies of the executive and the purposes of these agencies.

This conduct has included one or more of the following:

(1) He has, acting personally and through his subordinates and agents, endeavored to obtain from the Internal Revenue Service, in violation of the constitutional rights of citizens, confidential information contained in income tax returns for purposes not authorized by law, and to cause, in violation of the constitutional rights of citizens, income tax audits or other income tax investigations to be initiated or conducted in a discriminatory manner.

(2) He misused the Federal Bureau of Investigation, the Secret Service, and other executive personnel, in violation or disregard of the constitutional rights of citizens, by directing or authorizing such agencies or personnel to conduct or continue electronic surveillance or other investigations for purposes unrelated to national security, the enforcement of laws, or any other lawful function of his office; and he did direct the concealment of certain records made by the Federal Bureau of Investigation of electronic surveillance.

(3) He has, acting personally and through his subordinates and agents, in violation or disregard of the constitutional rights of citizens, authorized and permitted to be maintained a secret investigative unit within the office of the President, financed in part with money derived from campaign contributions, which unlawfully utilized the resources of the Central Intelligence Agency, engaged in covert and unlawful activities, and attempted to prejudice the constitutional right of an accused to a fair trial.

(4) He has failed to take care that the laws were faithfully executed by failing to act when he knew or had reason to know that his close subordinates endeavored to impede and frustrate lawful inquiries by duly constituted executive, judicial, and legislative entities concerning the unlawful entry into the headquarters of the Democratic National Committee, and the cover-up thereof, and concerning other unlawful activities, including those relating to the confirmation of Richard Kleindienst as Attorney General of the United States, the electronic surveillance of private citizens, the break-in into the offices of Dr. Lewis Fielding, and the campaign financing practices of the Committee to Re-elect the President.

(5) In disregard of the rule of law, he knowingly misused the executive power by interfering with agencies of

the executive branch, including the Federal Bureau of Investigation, the Criminal Division, and the Office of Special Watergate Prosecution Force, of the Department of Justice, and the Central Intelligence Agency, in violation of his duty to take care that the laws be faithfully executed.

In all of this, Richard M. Nixon has acted in a manner contrary to his trust as President and subversive of constitutional government, to the great prejudice of the cause of law and justice and to the manifest injury of the people of the United States.

Wherefore Richard M. Nixon, by such conduct, warrants impeachment and trial, and removal from office.

Article III

In his conduct of the office of President of the United States, Richard M. Nixon, contrary to his oath faithfully to execute the office of President of the United States and, to the best of his ability, preserve, protect, and defend the Constitution of the United States, and in violation of his duty to take care that the laws be faithfully executed, has failed without lawful cause or excuse to produce papers and things as directed by duly authorized subpoenas issued by the Committee on the Judiciary of the House of Representatives on April 11, 1974, May 15, 1974, May 30, 1974, and June 24, 1974, and willfully disobeyed such subpoenas. The subpoenaed papers and things were deemed necessary by the Committee in order to resolve by direct evidence fundamental, factual questions relating to Presidential direction, knowledge, or approval of actions demonstrated by other evidence to be substantial grounds for impeachment of the President. In refusing to produce these papers and things, Richard M. Nixon, substituting his judgment as to what materials were necessary for the inquiry, interposed the powers of the Presidency against the lawful subpoenas of the House of Representatives, thereby assuming to himself functions and judgments necessary to the exercise of the sole power of impeachment vested by the Constitution in the House of Representatives.

In all of this, Richard M. Nixon has acted in a manner contrary to his trust as President and subversive of constitutional government, to the great prejudice of the cause of law and justice, and to the manifest injury of the people of the United States.

Wherefore Richard M. Nixon, by such conduct, warrants impeachment and trial, and removal from office.

13. Treaty Concerning the Permanent Neutrality and Operation of the Panama Canal, Ratified by the U.S. Senate, March 16, 1978

The United States of America and the Republic of Panama have agreed upon the following:

Article I

The Republic of Panama declares that the Canal, as an international transit waterway, shall be permanently neutral in accordance with the regime established in this Treaty. The same regime of neutrality shall apply to any other international waterway that may be built either partially or wholly in the territory of the Republic of Panama.

Article II

The Republic of Panama declares the neutrality of the Canal in order that both in time of peace and in time of war it shall remain secure and open to peaceful transit by the vessels of all nations on terms of entire equality, so that there will be no discrimination against any nation, or its citizens or subjects, concerning the conditions or charges of transit, or for any other reason, and so that the Canal, and therefore the Isthmus of Panama, shall not be the target of reprisals in any armed conflict between other nations of the world. The foregoing shall be subject to the following requirements:

(a) Payment of tolls and other charges for transit and ancillary services, provided they have been fixed in conformity with the provisions of Article III (c);

(b) Compliance with applicable rules and regulations, provided such rules and regulations are applied in conformity with the provisions of Article III;

(c) The requirement that transiting vessels commit no acts of hostility while in the Canal; and

(d) Such other conditions and restrictions as are established by this Treaty.

Article III

1. For purposes of the security, efficiency and proper maintenance of the Canal the following rules shall apply:

(a) The Canal shall be operated efficiently in accordance with conditions of transit through the Canal, and rules and regulations that shall be just, equitable and reasonable, and limited to those necessary for safe navigation and efficient, sanitary operation of the Canal;

(b) Ancillary services necessary for transit through the Canal shall be provided;

(c) Tolls and other charges for transit and ancillary services shall be just, reasonable, equitable and consistent with the principles of international law;

(d) As a pre-condition of transit, vessels may be required to establish clearly the financial responsibility and guarantees for payment of reasonable and adequate indemnification, consistent with international practice and standards, for damages resulting from acts or omissions of such vessels when passing through the Canal. In the case of vessels owned or operated by a State or for which it has acknowledged responsibility, a certification by that State that it shall observe its obligations under international law to pay for damages resulting from the act or omission of such vessels when passing through the Canal shall be deemed sufficient to establish such financial responsibility;

(e) Vessels of war and auxiliary vessels of all nations shall at all times be entitled to transit the Canal, irrespective of their internal operation, means of propulsion, origin, destination or armament, without being subjected, as a condition of transit, to inspection, search for surveillance. However, such vessels may be required to certify that they have complied with all applicable health, sanitation and quarantine regulations. In addition, such vessels shall be entitled to refuse to disclose their internal operation, origin, armament, cargo or destination. However, auxiliary vessels may be required to present written assurances, certified by an official at a high level of the government of the State requesting the exemption, that they are owned or operated by that government and in this case are being used only on government non-commercial service.

2. For the purposes of this Treaty, the terms "Canal," "vessel of war," "auxiliary vessel," "internal operation," "armament" and "inspection" shall have the meanings assigned them in Annex A to this Treaty.

Article IV

The United States of America and the Republic of Panama agree to maintain the regime of neutrality established in this Treaty, which shall be maintained in order that the Canal shall remain permanently neutral, notwithstanding the termination of any other treaties entered into by the two Contracting Parties.

Article V

After the termination of the Panama Canal Treaty, only the Republic of Panama shall operate the Canal and maintain military forces, defense sites and military installations within its national territory.

Article VI

1. In recognition of the important contributions of the United States of America and of the Republic of Panama to the construction, operation, maintenance, and protection and defense of the Canal, vessels of war and auxiliary vessels of those nations shall, notwithstanding any other provisions of this Treaty, be entitled to transit the Canal irrespective of their internal operation, means of propulsion, origin, destination, armament or cargo carried. Such vessels of war and auxiliary vessels will be entitled to transit the Canal expeditiously.

2. The United States of America, so long as it has responsibility for the operation of the Canal, may continue to provide the Republic of Colombia toll-free transit through the Canal for its troops, vessels and materials of war. Thereafter, the Republic of Panama may provide the Republic of Colombia and the Republic of Costa Rica with the right of toll-free transit.

Article VII

1. The United States of America and the Republic of Panama shall jointly sponsor a resolution in the Organization of American States opening to accession by all nations of the world the Protocol to this Treaty whereby all the signatories will adhere to the objective of this Treaty, agreeing to respect the regime of neutrality set forth herein.

2. The Organization of American States shall act as the depositary for this Treaty and related instruments.

Article VIII

This Treaty shall be subject to ratification in accordance with the constitutional procedures of the two Parties. The instruments of ratification of this Treaty shall be exchanged at Panama at the same time as the instruments of ratification of the Panama Canal Treaty, signed this date, are exchanged. This Treaty shall enter into force, simultaneously with the Panama Canal Treaty, six calendar months from the date of the exchange of the instruments of ratification.

Annex A

1. "Canal" includes the existing Panama Canal, the entrances thereto and the territorial seas of the

Republic of Panama adjacent thereto, as defined on the map annexed hereto (Annex B), and any other interoceanic waterway in which the United States of America is a participant or in which the United States of America has participated in connection with the construction or financing, that may be operated wholly or partially within the territory of the Republic of Panama, the entrances thereto and the territorial seas adjacent thereto.

2. "Vessel of war" means a ship belonging to the naval forces of a State, and bearing the external marks distinguishing warships of its nationality, under the command of an officer duly commissioned by the government and whose name appears in the Navy List, and manned by a crew which is under regular naval discipline.

3. "Auxiliary vessel" means any ship, not a vessel of war, that is owned or operated by a State and used, for the time being, exclusively on government non-commercial service.

4. "Internal operation" encompasses all machinery and propulsion systems, as well as the management and control of the vessel, including its crew. It does not include the measures necessary to transit vessels under the control of pilots while such vessels are in the Canal.

5. "Armament" means arms, ammunition, implements of war and other equipment of a vessel which possesses characteristics appropriate for use for warlike purposes.

6. "Inspection" includes on-board examination of vessel structure, cargo, armament and internal operation. It does not include those measures strictly necessary for measurement, nor those measures strictly necessary to assure safe, sanitary transit and navigation, including examination of deck and visual navigation equipment, nor in the case of live cargoes, such as cattle or other livestock, that may carry communicable diseases, those measures necessary to assure that health and sanitation requirements are satisfied.

14. The First Five Articles of the Panama Canal General Treaty with United States Senate Modifications, Ratified by the Senate, April 18, 1978

The United States of America and the Republic of Panama, Acting in the spirit of the Joint Declaration of April 3, 1964, by the Representatives of the Governments of the United States of America and the Republic of Panama, and of the Joint Statement of Principles of February 7, 1974, initialed by the Secretary of State of the United States of America and the Foreign Minister of the Republic of Panama, and Acknowledging the Republic of Panama's sovereignty over its territory, Have decided to terminate the prior Treaties pertaining to the Panama Canal and to conclude a new Treaty to serve as the basis for a new relationship between them and, accordingly, have agreed upon the following:

Article I

Abrogation of Prior Treaties and Establishment of a New Relationship

1. Upon its entry into force, this Treaty terminates and supersedes:

(a) The Isthmian Canal Convention between the United States of America and the Republic of Panama, signed at Washington, November 18, 1903;

(b) The Treaty of Friendship and Cooperation signed at Washington, March 2, 1936, and the Treaty of Mutual Understanding and Cooperation and the related Memorandum of Understandings Reached, signed at Panama, January 25, 1955, between the United States of America and the Republic of Panama;

(c) All other treaties, conventions, agreements, and exchanges of notes between the United States of America and the Republic of Panama concerning the Panama Canal, which were in force prior to the entry into force of this Treaty; and

(d) Provisions concerning the Panama Canal, which appear in other treaties, conventions, agreements, and exchanges of notes between the United States of America and the Republic of Panama, which were in force prior to the entry into force of this Treaty.

2. In accordance with the terms of this Treaty and related agreements, the Republic of Panama, as territorial sovereign, grants to the United States of America, for the duration of this Treaty, the rights necessary to regulate the transit of ships through the Panama Canal, and to manage, operate, maintain, improve, protect and defend the Canal. The Republic of Panama guarantees to the United States of America the peaceful use of the land and water areas which it has been granted the rights to use for such purposes pursuant to this Treaty and related agreements.

3. The Republic of Panama shall participate increasingly in the management and protection and defense of the Canal, as provided in this Treaty.

4. In view of the special relationship established by this Treaty, the United States of America and the Republic

of Panama shall cooperate to assure the uninterrupted and efficient operation of the Panama Canal.

Article II

Ratification, Entry Into Force, and Termination
1. The Treaty shall be subject to ratification in accordance with the constitutional procedures of the two Parties. The instruments of ratification of this Treaty shall be exchanged at Panama at the same time as the instruments of ratification of the Treaty Concerning the Permanent Neutrality and Operation of the Panama Canal, signed this date, are exchanged. This Treaty shall enter into force, simultaneously with the Treaty Concerning the Permanent Neutrality and Operation of the Panama Canal, six calendar months from the date of the exchange of the instruments of ratification.
2. This Treaty shall terminate at noon, Panama time, December 31, 1999.

Article III

Canal Operation and Management
1. The Republic of Panama, as territorial sovereign, grants to the United States of America the rights to manage, operate, and maintain the Panama Canal, its complementary works, installations, and equipment and to provide for the orderly transit of vessels through the Panama Canal. The United States of America accepts the grant of such rights and undertakes to exercise them in accordance with this Treaty and related agreements.
2. In carrying out the foregoing responsibilities, the United States of America may:

(a) Use for the aforementioned purposes, without cost except as provided in this Treaty, the various installations and areas (including the Panama Canal) and waters, described in the Agreement in Implementation of this Article, signed this date, as well as such other areas and installations as are made available to the United States of America under this Treaty and related agreements, and take the measures necessary to ensure sanitation of such areas;

(b) Make such improvements and alterations to the aforesaid installations and areas as it deems appropriate, consistent with the terms of this Treaty;

(c) Make and enforce all rules pertaining the passage of vessels through the Canal and other rules with respect to navigation and maritime matters, in accordance with this Treaty and related agreements. The Republic of Panama will lend its cooperation, when necessary, in the enforcement of such rules;

(d) Establish, modify, collect and retain tolls for the use of the Panama Canal, and other charges, and establish and modify methods of their assessment;

(e) Regulate relations with employees of the United States Government;

(f) Provide supporting services to facilitate the performance of its responsibilities under this Article;

(g) Issue and enforce regulations for the exercise of the rights and responsibilities of the United States of America under this Treaty and related agreements. The Republic of Panama will lend its cooperation, when necessary, in the enforcement of such rules; and

(h) Exercise any other right granted under this Treaty, or otherwise agreed upon between the two Parties.
3. Pursuant to the foregoing grant of rights, the United States of America shall, in accordance with the terms of this Treaty and the provisions of United States law, carry out its responsibilities by means of a United States Government agency called the Panama Canal Commission, which shall be constituted by and in conformity with the laws of the United States of America.

(a) The Panama Canal Commission shall be supervised by a Board composed of nine members, five of whom shall be nationals of the United States of America, and four of whom shall be Panamanian nationals proposed by the Republic of Panama for appointment to such positions by the United States of America in a timely manner.

(b) Should the Republic of Panama request the United States of America to remove a Panamanian national from membership on the Board, the United States of America shall agree to such request. In that event, the Republic of Panama shall propose another Panamanian national for appointment by the United States of America to such position in a timely manner. In case of removal of a Panamanian member of the Board on the initiative of the United States of America, both Parties will consult in advance in order to reach agreement concerning such removal, and the Republic of Panama shall propose another Panamanian national for appointment by the United States of America in his stead.

(c) The United States of America shall employ a national of the United States of America as Administrator of the Panama Canal Commission, and a Panamanian national as Deputy Administrator, through December 31, 1989. Beginning January 1, 1990, a Panamanian national shall be employed as the Administrator and a national of the United States of America shall occupy the position of Deputy Administrator. Such Panamanian nationals shall be proposed to the United States of America by the Republic of Panama for appointment to such positions by the United States of America.

(d) Should the United States of America remove the Panamanian national from his position as Deputy Administrator, or Administrator, the Republic of Panama shall propose another Panamanian national for appointment to such position by the United States of America.

4. An illustrative description of the activities the Panama Canal Commission will perform in carrying out the responsibilities and rights of the United States of America under this Article is set forth at the Annex. Also set forth in the Annex are procedures for the discontinuance or transfer of those activities performed prior to the entry into force of this Treaty by the Panama Canal Company or the Canal Zone Government which are not to be carried out by the Panama Canal Commission.

5. The Panama Canal Commission shall reimburse the Republic of Panama for the costs incurred by the Republic of Panama in providing the following public services in the Canal operation areas and in housing areas set forth in the Agreement in Implementation of Article III of this Treaty and occupied by both United States and Panamanian citizen employees of the Panama Canal Commission: police, fire protection, street maintenance, street lighting, street cleaning, traffic management and garbage collection. The Panama Canal Commission shall pay the Republic of Panama the sum of ten million United States dollars (US$10,000,000) per annum for the foregoing services. It is agreed that every three years from the date that this Treaty enters into force, the costs involved in furnishing said services shall be reexamined to determine whether adjustment of the annual payment should be made because of inflation and other relevant factors affecting the cost of such services.

6. The Republic of Panama shall be responsible for providing, in all areas comprising the former Canal Zone, services of a general jurisdictional nature such as customs and immigration, postal services, courts and licensing, in accordance with this Treaty and related agreements.

7. The United States of America and the Republic of Panama shall establish a Panama Canal Consultative Committee, composed of an equal number of high-level representatives of the United States of America and the Republic of Panama, and which may appoint such subcommittees as it may deem appropriate. This Committee shall advise the United States of America and the Republic of Panama on matters of policy affecting the Canal's operation. In view of both Parties' special interest in the continuity and efficiency of the Canal operation in the future, the Committee shall advise on matters such as general tolls policy, employment and training policies to increase the participation of Panamanian nationals in the operation of the Canal, and international policies on matters concerning the Canal. The Committee's recommendations shall be transmitted to the two Governments, which shall give such recommendations full consideration in the formulation of such policy decisions.

8. In addition to the participation of Panamanian nationals at high management levels of the Panama Canal Commission, as provided for in paragraph 3 of this Article, there shall be growing participation of Panamanian nationals at all other levels and areas of employment in the aforesaid commission, with the objective of preparing, in an orderly and efficient fashion, for the assumption by the Republic of Panama of full responsibility for the management, operation and maintenance of the Canal upon the termination of this Treaty.

9. The use of the areas, waters and installations with respect to which the United States of America is granted rights pursuant to this Article, and the rights and legal status of United States Government agencies and employees operating in the Republic of Panama pursuant to this Article, shall be governed by Agreement in implementation of this Article, signed this date.

10. Upon entry into force of this Treaty, the United States Government agencies known as the Panama Canal Company and the Canal Zone Government shall cease to operate within the territory of the Republic of Panama that formerly constituted the Canal Zone.

Article IV

Protection and Defense

1. The United States of America and the Republic of Panama commit themselves to protect and defend the Panama Canal. Each Party shall act, in accordance with its constitutional processes, to meet the danger resulting from an armed attack or other actions which threaten the security of the Panama Canal or of ships transiting it.

2. For the duration of this Treaty, the United States of America shall have primary responsibility to protect and defend the Canal. The rights of the United States of America to station, train, and move military forces within the Republic of Panama are described in the Agreement in Implementation of this Article, signed this date. The use of areas and installations and the legal status of the armed forces of the United States of America in the Republic of Panama shall be governed by the aforesaid Agreement.

3. In order to facilitate the participation and cooperation of the armed forces of both Parties in the protection and defense of the Canal, the United States of America and the Republic of Panama shall establish a Combined Board comprised of an equal number of senior military representatives of each Party. These representatives shall be charged by their respective governments with consulting and cooperating on all matters pertaining to the protection and defense of the Canal, and with planning for actions to be taken in concert for that purpose. Such combined protection and defense arrangements shall not inhibit the identity or lines of authority of the armed forces of the United States of America or the Republic of Panama. The Combined Board shall provide for coordination and cooperation concerning such matters as:

(a) The preparation of contingency plans for the protection and defense of the Canal based upon the cooperative efforts of the armed forces of both Parties;

(b) The planning and conduct of combined military exercises; and

(c) The conduct of United States and Panamanian military operations with respect to the protection and defense of the Canal.

4. The Combined Board shall, at five-year intervals throughout the duration of this Treaty, review the resources being made available by the two Parties for the protection and defense of the Canal. Also, the Combined Board shall make appropriate recommendations to the two Governments respecting projected requirements, the efficient utilization of available resources of the two Parties, and other matters of mutual interest with respect to the protection and defense of the Canal.

5. To the extent possible consistent with its primary responsibility for the protection and defense of the Panama Canal, the United States of America will endeavor to maintain its armed forces in the Republic of Panama in normal times at a level not in excess of that of the armed forces of the United States of America in the territory of the former Canal Zone immediately prior to the entry into force of this Treaty.

Article V

Principle of Non-Intervention

Employees of the Panama Canal Commission, their dependents and designated contractors of the Panama Canal Commission, who are nationals of the United States of America, shall respect the laws of the Republic of Panama and shall abstain from any activity incompatible with the spirit of this Treaty. Accordingly, they shall abstain from any political activity in the Republic of Panama as well as from any intervention in the internal affairs of the Republic of Panama. The United States of America shall take all measures within its authority to ensure that the provisions of this Article are fulfilled.

United States Senate Modifications [incorporated into the June 1978 instruments of ratification]

RESERVATIONS:

(1) Pursuant to its adherence to the principle of nonintervention, any action taken by the United States of America in the exercise of its rights to assure that the Panama Canal shall remain open, neutral, secure, and accessible, pursuant to the provisions of the Panama Canal Treaty, the Treaty Concerning the Permanent Neutrality and Operation of the Panama Canal, and the resolutions of ratification thereto, shall be only for the purpose of assuring that the Canal shall remain open, neutral, secure, and accessible, and shall not have as its purpose or be interpreted as a right of intervention in the internal affairs of the Republic of Panama or interference with its political independence or sovereign integrity.

(2) The instruments of ratification of the Panama Canal Treaty to be exchanged by the United States of America and the Republic of Panama shall each include provisions whereby each Party agrees to waive its rights and release the other Party from its obligations under paragraph 2 of Article XII of the Treaty.

(3) Notwithstanding any provision of the Treaty, no funds may be drawn from the Treasury of the United States of America for payments under paragraph 4 of Article XIII without statutory authorization.

(4) Any accumulated unpaid balance under paragraph 4(c) of Article XIII of the Treaty at the date of termination of the Treaty shall be payable only to the extent of any operating surplus in the last year of the

duration of the Treaty, and nothing in such paragraph may be constructed as obligating the United States of America to pay, after the date of the termination of the Treaty, any such unpaid balance which shall have accrued before such date.

(5) Exchange of the instruments of ratification of the Panama Canal Treaty and of the Treaty Concerning the Permanent Neutrality and Operation of the Panama Canal shall not be effective earlier than March 31, 1979, and such Treaties shall not enter into force prior to October 1, 1979, unless legislation necessary to implement the provisions of the Panama Canal Treaty shall have been enacted by the Congress of the United States of America before March 31, 1979.

(6) After the date of entry into force of the Treaty, the Panama Canal Commission shall, unless otherwise provided by legislation enacted by the Congress of the United States of America, be obligated to reimburse the Treasury of the United States of America, as nearly as possible, for the interest cost of the funds or other assets directly invested in the Commission by the Government of the United States of America and for the interest cost of the funds or other assets directly invested in the predecessor Panama Canal Company by the Government of the United States of America and not reimbursed before the date of entry into force of the Treaty. Such reimbursement for such interest costs shall be made at a rate determined by the Secretary of the Treasury of the United States of America and at annual intervals to the extent earned, and if not earned, shall be made from subsequent earnings. For purposes of this reservation, the phrase "funds or other assets directly invested" shall have the same meaning as the phrase "net direct investment" has under section 62 of title 2 of the Canal Zone Code.

15. A Framework for the Conclusion of a Peace Treaty between Egypt and Israel, Negotiated at Camp David, September 1978

A Framework for the Conclusion of a Peace Treaty between Egypt and Israel

In order to achieve peace between them, Israel and Egypt agree to negotiate in good faith with a goal of concluding within three months of the signing of this framework a peace treaty between them:

It is agreed that:

The site of the negotiations will be under a United Nations flag at a location or locations to be mutually agreed.

All of the principles of U.N. Resolution 242 will apply in this resolution of the dispute between Israel and Egypt.

Unless otherwise mutually agreed, terms of the peace treaty will be implemented between two and three years after the peace treaty is signed.

The following matters are agreed between the parties:

the full exercise of Egyptian sovereignty up to the internationally recognized border between Egypt and mandated Palestine;

the withdrawal of Israeli armed forces from the Sinai;

the use of airfields left by the Israelis near al-Arish, Rafah, Ras en-Naqb, and Sharm el-Sheikh for civilian purposes only, including possible commercial use only by all nations;

the right of free passage by ships of Israel through the Gulf of Suez and the Suez Canal on the basis of the Constantinople Convention of 1888 applying to all nations; the Strait of Tiran and Gulf of Aqaba are international waterways to be open to all nations for unimpeded and nonsuspendable freedom of navigation and overflight;

the construction of a highway between the Sinai and Jordan near Eilat with guaranteed free and peaceful passage by Egypt and Jordan; and the stationing of military forces listed below.

Stationing of Forces

No more than one division (mechanized or infantry) of Egyptian armed forces will be stationed within an area lying approximately 50 km. (30 miles) east of the Gulf of Suez and the Suez Canal.

Only United Nations forces and civil police equipped with light weapons to perform normal police functions will be stationed within an area lying west of the international border and the Gulf of Aqaba, varying in width from 20 km. (12 miles) to 40 km. (24 miles).

In the area within 3 km. (1.8 miles) east of the international border there will be Israeli limited military forces not to exceed four infantry battalions and United Nations observers.

Border patrol units not to exceed three battalions will supplement the civil police in maintaining order in the area not included above.

The exact demarcation of the above areas will be as decided during the peace negotiations.

Early warning stations may exist to insure compliance with the terms of the agreement.

United Nations forces will be stationed:

in part of the area in the Sinai lying within about 20 km. of the Mediterranean Sea and adjacent to the international border, and

in the Sharm el-Sheikh area to insure freedom of passage through the Strait of Tiran; and these forces will not be removed unless such removal is approved by the Security Council of the United Nations with a unanimous vote of the five permanent members.

After a peace treaty is signed, and after the interim withdrawal is complete, normal relations will be established between Egypt and Israel, including full recognition, including diplomatic, economic and cultural relations; termination of economic boycotts and barriers to the free movement of goods and people; and mutual protection of citizens by the due process of law.

Interim Withdrawal

Between three months and nine months after the signing of the peace treaty, all Israeli forces will withdraw east of a line extending from a point east of El-Arish to Ras Muhammad, the exact location of this line to be determined by mutual agreement.
For the Government of the Arab Republic of Egypt:
Muhammed Anwar al-Sadat
For the Government of Israel:
Menachem Begin
Witnessed by:
Jimmy Carter,
President of the United States of America

16. A Framework for Peace in the Middle East, Negotiated at Camp David, September 1978

Muhammad Anwar al-Sadat, President of the Arab Republic of Egypt, and Menachem Begin, Prime Minister of Israel, met with Jimmy Carter, President of the United States of America, at Camp David from September 5 to September 17, 1978, and have agreed on the following framework for peace in the Middle East. They invite other parties to the Arab-Israel conflict to adhere to it.

Preamble

The search for peace in the Middle East must be guided by the following:

The agreed basis for a peaceful settlement of the conflict between Israel and its neighbors is United Nations Security Council Resolution 242, in all its parts. After four wars during 30 years, despite intensive human efforts, the Middle East, which is the cradle of civilization and the birthplace of three great religions, does not enjoy the blessings of peace. The people of the Middle East yearn for peace so that the vast human and natural resources of the region can be turned to the pursuits of peace and so that this area can become a model for coexistence and cooperation among nations.

The historic initiative of President Sadat in visiting Jerusalem and the reception accorded to him by the parliament, government and people of Israel, and the reciprocal visit of Prime Minister Begin to Ismailia, the peace proposals made by both leaders, as well as the warm reception of these missions by the peoples of both countries, have created an unprecedented opportunity for peace which must not be lost if this generation and future generations are to be spared the tragedies of war.

The provisions of the Charter of the United Nations and the other accepted norms of international law and legitimacy now provide accepted standards for the conduct of relations among all states.

To achieve a relationship of peace, in the spirit of Article 2 of the United Nations Charter, future negotiations between Israel and any neighbor prepared to negotiate peace and security with it are necessary for the purpose of carrying out all the provisions and principles of Resolutions 242 and 338.

Peace requires respect for the sovereignty, territorial integrity and political independence of every state in the area and their right to live in peace within secure and recognized boundaries free from threats or acts of force. Progress toward that goal can accelerate movement toward a new era of reconciliation in the Middle East marked by cooperation in promoting economic development, in maintaining stability and in assuring security.

Security is enhanced by a relationship of peace and by cooperation between nations which enjoy normal relations. In addition, under the terms of peace treaties, the parties can, on the basis of reciprocity, agree to special security arrangements such as demilitarized zones, limited armaments areas, early warning stations, the presence of international forces, liaison, agreed measures for monitoring and other arrangements that they agree are useful.

Framework

Taking these factors into account, the parties are determined to reach a just, comprehensive, and durable settlement of the Middle East conflict through the conclusion of peace treaties based on Security Council resolutions 242 and 338 in all their parts.

Their purpose is to achieve peace and good neighborly relations. They recognize that for peace to endure, it must involve all those who have been most deeply affected by the conflict. They therefore agree that this framework, as appropriate, is intended by them to constitute a basis for peace not only between Egypt and Israel, but also between Israel and each of its other neighbors which is prepared to negotiate peace with Israel on this basis. With that objective in mind, they have agreed to proceed as follows:

West Bank and Gaza

Egypt, Israel, Jordan and the representatives of the Palestinian people should participate in negotiations on the resolution of the Palestinian problem in all its aspects. To achieve that objective, negotiations relating to the West Bank and Gaza should proceed in three stages:

Egypt and Israel agree that, in order to ensure a peaceful and orderly transfer of authority, and taking into account the security concerns of all the parties, there should be transitional arrangements for the West Bank and Gaza for a period not exceeding five years. In order to provide full autonomy to the inhabitants, under these arrangements the Israeli military government and its civilian administration will be withdrawn as soon as a self-governing authority has been freely elected by the inhabitants of these areas to replace the existing military government. To negotiate the details of a transitional arrangement, Jordan will be invited to join the negotiations on the basis of this framework. These new arrangements should give due consideration both to the principle of self-government by the inhabitants of these territories and to the legitimate security concerns of the parties involved.

Egypt, Israel, and Jordan will agree on the modalities for establishing elected self-governing authority in the West Bank and Gaza. The delegations of Egypt and Jordan may include Palestinians from the West Bank and Gaza or other Palestinians as mutually agreed. The parties will negotiate an agreement which will define the powers and responsibilities of the self-governing authority to be exercised in the West Bank and Gaza. A withdrawal of Israeli armed forces will take place and there will be a redeployment of the remaining Israeli forces into specified security locations. The agreement will also include arrangements for assuring internal and external security and public order. A strong local police force will be established, which may include Jordanian citizens. In addition, Israeli and Jordanian forces will participate in joint patrols and in the manning of control posts to assure the security of the borders.

When the self-governing authority (administrative council) in the West Bank and Gaza is established and inaugurated, the transitional period of five years will begin. As soon as possible, but not later than the third year after the beginning of the transitional period, negotiations will take place to determine the final status of the West Bank and Gaza and its relationship with its neighbors and to conclude a peace treaty between Israel and Jordan by the end of the transitional period. These negotiations will be conducted among Egypt, Israel, Jordan and the elected representatives of the inhabitants of the West Bank and Gaza. Two separate but related committees will be convened, one committee, consisting of representatives of the four parties which will negotiate and agree on the final status of the West Bank and Gaza, and its relationship with its neighbors, and the second committee, consisting of representatives of Israel and representatives of Jordan to be joined by the elected representatives of the inhabitants of the West Bank and Gaza, to negotiate the peace treaty between Israel and Jordan, taking into account the agreement reached in the final status of the West Bank and Gaza. The negotiations shall be based on all the provisions and principles of UN Security Council Resolution 242. The negotiations will resolve, among other matters, the location of the boundaries and the nature of the security arrangements. The solution from the negotiations must also recognize the legitimate right of the Palestinian peoples and their just requirements. In this way, the Palestinians will participate in the determination of their own future through:

The negotiations among Egypt, Israel, Jordan and the representatives of the inhabitants of the West Bank and Gaza to agree on the final status of the West Bank and Gaza and other outstanding issues by the end of the transitional period. Submitting their agreements to a vote by the elected representatives of the inhabitants of the West Bank and Gaza.

Providing for the elected representatives of the inhabitants of the West Bank and Gaza to decide how they shall govern themselves consistent with the provisions of their agreement.

Participating as stated above in the work of the committee negotiating the peace treaty between Israel and Jordan.

All necessary measures will be taken and provisions made to assure the security of Israel and its neighbors during the transitional period and beyond. To assist in providing such security, a strong local police force will be constituted by the self-governing authority. It will be composed of inhabitants of the West Bank and Gaza. The police will maintain liaison on internal security matters with the designated Israeli, Jordanian, and Egyptian officers.

During the transitional period, representatives of Egypt, Israel, Jordan, and the self-governing authority will constitute a continuing committee to decide by agreement on the modalities of admission of persons displaced from the West Bank and Gaza in 1967, together with necessary measures to prevent disruption and disorder. Other matters of common concern may also be dealt with by this committee.

Egypt and Israel will work with each other and with other interested parties to establish agreed procedures for a prompt, just and permanent implementation of the resolution of the refugee problem.

Egypt-Israel

Egypt-Israel undertake not to resort to the threat or the use of force to settle disputes. Any disputes shall be settled by peaceful means in accordance with the provisions of Article 33 of the U.N. Charter.

In order to achieve peace between them, the parties agree to negotiate in good faith with a goal of concluding within three months from the signing of the Framework a peace treaty between them while inviting the other parties to the conflict to proceed simultaneously to negotiate and conclude similar peace treaties with a view to achieving a comprehensive peace in the area. The Framework for the Conclusion of a Peace Treaty between Egypt and Israel will govern the peace negotiations between them. The parties will agree on the modalities and the timetable for the implementation of their obligations under the treaty.

Associated Principles

Egypt and Israel state that the principles and provisions described below should apply to peace treaties between Israel and each of its neighbors—Egypt, Jordan, Syria and Lebanon.

Signatories shall establish among themselves relationships normal to states at peace with one another. To this end, they should undertake to abide by all the provisions of the U.N. Charter. Steps to be taken in this respect include:

full recognition;

abolishing economic boycotts;

guaranteeing that under their jurisdiction the citizens of the other parties shall enjoy the protection of the due process of law.

Signatories should explore possibilities for economic development in the context of final peace treaties, with the objective of contributing to the atmosphere of peace, cooperation and friendship which is their common goal.

Claims commissions may be established for the mutual settlement of all financial claims.

The United States shall be invited to participate in the talks on matters related to the modalities of the implementation of the agreements and working out the timetable for the carrying out of the obligations of the parties.

The United Nations Security Council shall be requested to endorse the peace treaties and ensure that their provisions shall not be violated. The permanent members of the Security Council shall be requested to underwrite the peace treaties and ensure respect for the provisions. They shall be requested to conform their policies and actions with the undertaking contained in this Framework.

17. President Jimmy Carter's South Lawn Departure Statement for the Middle East, March 7, 1979

I leave today on a new mission in the service of the oldest of human dreams—the dream of peace.

Nowhere is the hope for peace more fervent, more alive, than in the Middle East; nowhere is the path to its realization more difficult; nowhere might the price of failure be more terrible.

Peace remains the goal of President Sadat and Prime Minister Begin, and of the great people of Egypt and Israel. I know that they share my determination to see these negotiations bear fruit.

The Middle East has suffered too much and too long from war and the fear of war. Arabs and Israelis alike must now understand that bloodshed and deprivation and death can never settle their differences, can never be the path to renewal and hope.

For the first time in a generation, peace in the Middle East has come within reach. President Sadat's visit to Jerusalem and Prime Minister Begin's warm reception opened the way. At Camp David, we then worked together to forge a political framework in which their differences can be resolved.

Our negotiations are based on the idea that peace can only be achieved when we meet the legitimate need of all who are affected by the conflict. Real peace will not come with a single treaty—important as that would be. But a treaty between Egypt and Israel is an indispensable step toward the broader comprehensive peace we all seek.

Negotiation is a long and tedious process. But there are times when making peace demands more courage than making war. I believe that President Sadat and Prime Minister Begin possess that special kind of courage—and that they possess as well the vision and statesmanship to redeem the great hope they have helped to create.

So it is with hope that I depart, hope tempered by realism. As a friend of Egypt and Israel, we will do our best to help them achieve the peace they have paid for in blood many times over. In doing this—in seeking to lay the basis for a stable and peaceful Middle East—we will also be serving our own deepest national interests, and the interests of all the people of the world.

I know that in this endeavor, I take with me the prayers and good wishes of the American people. In the difficult work that lies ahead, I will draw strength and sustenance from your support.

APPENDIX B
Biographies of Major Personalities

Aaron, Hank (1934–   ) *professional baseball player*
Born into an African-American family on February 5, 1934, in Mobile, Alabama, Hank Aaron rose from dire depression-era poverty to break Babe Ruth's career home run record. Aaron discovered his penchant for baseball when playing the game with neighborhood kids at Carver Recreational Park. In his teens, he played for a semiprofessional team and for a professional team in the Negro League. Recruited by the Milwaukee Braves of the National League, he moved from their Class C to Class A farm club in Jacksonville, Florida, in 1953. While playing shortstop that year, he led the South Atlantic League in batting average, RBIs, runs scored, and hits, despite having to endure racial insults from fans and fellow players. His success earned him promotion to the major leagues, and in 1954, as a right fielder for the Braves, he batted .280 and hit 13 home runs in an injury-shortened season. In 1957, Aaron hit a home run to break a tie game with the St. Louis Cardinals and send the Braves into the World Series against the New York Yankees. His three home runs and a triple in the series contributed greatly to the Braves beating the Yankees. That year he led the NL with 44 home runs, and through the next 16 seasons, he hit 40 or more home runs per season seven more times and batted .300 or higher 11 times. The Braves moved to Atlanta in 1966, and in the early 1970s, as Aaron approached Babe Ruth's career home run record of 714, he began to receive thousands of encouraging letters from around the world and, with them, some hate letters from racists, including a few that threatened his college-age daughter. Undaunted, he came to the plate on April 4, 1974, the opening day of the season and, with his first swing, hit home run number 714. Four days later, he broke Ruth's record off Los Angeles Dodger pitcher Al Downing at Atlanta's Fulton County Stadium. In 1975, Aaron was traded to the Milwaukee Brewers. Before retiring at the end of the 1976 season, he broke Ruth's career RBI record. When his playing days ended, he held several career marks, including most home runs, runs batted in, total bases, and extra-base hits. He then worked as an executive for the Atlanta Braves and in 1982 was elected to the National Baseball Hall of Fame. In 2002, he received the Presidential Medal of Freedom, America's highest civilian honor.

Abzug, Bella (Bella Savitsky) (1920–1998) *politician, lawyer, feminist*
In 1944, while attending law school at Columbia University, Bella Savitsky married Martin Abzug. After her graduation from Columbia, Bella Abzug opened a private law practice. In 1961, she founded Women's Strike for Peace to protest the spread of nuclear weapons. An outspoken critic of the Vietnam War, she tried without success to bring together feminists, peace activists, and labor leaders into an antiwar coalition. Abzug entered politics in 1970 and won election to Congress. A Democrat, she represented a district in Manhattan, New York, and gained national attention for her efforts to advance women's rights. In 1971, she joined Gloria Steinem and others to found the National Women's Political Caucus to encourage more women to get involved in politics. She was also an advocate for black civil rights and for gay rights. Her forceful, and colorful, personality and blunt speeches earned her praise from those who supported her and the enmity of those who opposed her. In 1976, Abzug resigned her congressional seat to run for the U.S. Senate, but she was defeated, and after several unsuccessful campaigns for mayor of New York City and other offices, she left politics. She subsequently worked on environmental issues and advocated breast cancer research. She wrote several books, including, in 1984, *Gender Gap: Bella Abzug's Guide to Political Power for Women.*

Agnew, Spiro (1918–1996) *vice president*
Born in Baltimore, Maryland, on November 9, 1918, the son of a Greek-born father and an American mother, Spiro Agnew attended Johns Hopkins University and then served in the U.S. Army during World War II. In 1947, he graduated from the University of Baltimore with a law degree and entered private practice. In 1962, he was elected Baltimore County Executive as a Republican, and four years later, he won the governorship of Maryland in a year when there was a nationwide rejection of many Democratic candidates in reaction to President Lyndon Johnson's liberal policies. In 1968, Richard Nixon stunned the political world when he chose the rather obscure Agnew—"Agnew who?" was the reaction—as his vice presidential running mate. Agnew won with Nixon that year and again in 1972. He gained prominence as Nixon's point man in attacking student protesters and the media, usually in words filled with vituperation and alliteration: "nattering nabobs of negativism," he called America's critics. But, ironically, while Agnew condemned lawlessness, he broke the law. In October 1973, U.S. Attorney General Elliot Richardson charged him with having accepted bribes while serving as county executive, governor, and vice president. Agnew at first protested his innocence; then on October 10, 1973, he pleaded no contest to falsifying his federal tax returns, paid a fine, accepted a sentence of probation, and resigned the vice presidency, making him the first vice president to quit because of criminal charges. He became an international trade executive and in 1980 published his autobiography, *Go Quietly or Else.* He died in Berlin, Maryland, on September 17, 1996.

Ali, Muhammad (Cassius Clay) (1942–) *boxer*
Muhammad Ali, who became one of the greatest boxers in American history and a symbol of African-American pride and rebelliousness, was born Cassius Clay in Louisville, Kentucky. He first began to box as a teenager when a police officer suggested that he learn the sport. As an amateur, Clay won six Kentucky Golden Glove titles, the 1959 International Golden Gloves heavyweight title, and a gold medal in the light heavyweight division at the 1960 Olympics in Rome. He fought his first professional bout in October 1960 and, shortly thereafter, began to predict when he would score a knockout, often putting his boasts to rhyme. On February 25, 1964, he upset Sonny Liston in a bout at Miami Beach, Florida, to win the world heavyweight

championship. A short time later, he became a Black Muslim and changed his name to Muhammad Ali. His attachment to the black separatist group, noted for its belief in white people being the devil, jolted many Americans. Ali defeated Liston a second time in 1965. He boasted: "Float like a butterfly, sting like a bee, your hands can't hit what your eyes can't see." Adding to his controversial background, in 1967, with the Vietnam War escalating, he announced that he would refuse to serve in the army based on his status as a Black Muslim minister and conscientious objector. The New York State Boxing Commission subsequently stripped him of his title, and a court sentenced him to five years in prison for draft evasion. But a New York court restored his license to fight, and in March 1971, he faced the reigning heavyweight champion, Joe Frazier. Ali lost to Frazier in a 15-round decision. Later that year, the U.S. Supreme Court overturned Ali's conviction. In October 1974, Ali defeated champion George Foreman in Zaire (the "Rumble in the Jungle") by knocking him out in the eighth round. The following year, he defended his title by defeating Frazier in the Philippines in what Ali called "The Thrilla in Manila." He defended his title six more times before losing it in February 1978 to Leon Spinks. In September, the two fighters met in the ring again, and this time Ali won. He retired in 1979, returned to boxing in 1980, and retired for good the following year. He soon suffered body tremors, and, in 1984, doctors diagnosed him with Parkinson syndrome, likely caused by the repeated blows that he received to his head during his boxing career.

Berrigan, Philip (1923–2002) *Catholic priest, political activist*
Philip Berrigan was born on October 5, 1923, in Two Harbors, Minnesota. He served in the army during World War II, an experience that made him detest racism and black poverty, which he witnessed at training bases in the South, and caused him to hate war. In 1955, he was ordained as a Catholic priest and two years later taught at a Josephite-run high school in New Orleans. He obtained an M.S. degree from Xavier University and developed an ever more intense interest in the Civil Rights movement. His activities often ran him afoul of his superiors in the Catholic Church, such as in 1965, when he made a speech in which he linked racial injustice to the injustice of the Vietnam War. In October 1967, he staged a protest at the Baltimore Selective Service office in which he

destroyed files. His most prominent protest occurred on May 17, 1968, when he and his brother, Daniel Berrigan, along with several other colleagues, raided the Selective Service office at Cantonsville, Maryland, and burned files with homemade napalm. The group, known as the Cantonsville Nine, stood trial, and Philip Berrigan was sentenced to three and a half years in prison. In April 1970, while out on bail, he went underground. FBI agents soon captured him, and he was taken to the federal penitentiary in Lewisburg, Pennsylvania. He was later put on trial for engaging in a conspiracy to blow up government buildings and to kidnap presidential adviser Henry Kissinger, but a jury acquitted him. He received parole on the Cantonsville sentence in December 1972. Married, he left the priesthood in 1973. For the rest of his life, he continued to work with peace groups and promote social justice.

Brock, Lou (1939–) *professional baseball player*
Lou Brock once said, "Show me a guy who's afraid to look bad, and I'll show you a guy you can beat every time." Playing for the St. Louis Cardinals, Brock took chances stealing bases, and his chances led to records. Brock was born in El Dorado, Arkansas, grew up in Collinston, Louisiana, and graduated from Southern University in Baton Rouge. In 1960, he signed with the Chicago Cubs. Four years later, the Cubs traded him to the Cardinals, and in 1966, while playing as an outfielder, he led the National League in stolen bases, a feat he would achieve for eight seasons in all. In 1974, he set a major-league record with 118 stolen bases. (Ricky Henderson broke the record in 1982.) In 1977, he surpassed Ty Cobb's lifetime stolen-base record (892), and by the time he retired in 1979, he set a major-league career record of 938. Brock could hit too. He batted more than .300 for seven seasons and retired with a .293 batting average and 900 runs batted in. He was inducted into the National Baseball Hall of Fame in 1985.

Carter, James Earl, Jr. (1924–) *governor, president*
James Earl "Jimmy" Carter, Jr., was born on October 1, 1924, in Plains, a small farming town in southwestern Georgia. In 1946, he graduated from the Naval Academy at Annapolis and later served as the chief engineer of the *Seawolf*, a prototype for a nuclear submarine. In 1953, he returned to Plains to take care of his family's peanut business. He entered politics when he served on the local school board. In 1962, he ran for a seat in the state legislature as a Democrat and lost. He ran for governor in 1966 and again lost. In 1970, he sought the office again and won, largely by submerging his progressive views behind a platform that criticized busing. He had a stormy relationship with the state legislature, engendered in part by his self-righteousness and refusal to compromise. Despite his mixed record, he announced in December 1974 that he would seek the presidency. Most observers gave him little chance of winning; he was, it was said, too obscure. But in an era racked by the lies surrounding the Vietnam War and Watergate, Carter's appeal to truth and virtue struck a strong note, and in July 1976, he accepted the presidential nomination at the Democratic National Convention. During the summer, he built a big lead over the incumbent, Gerald Ford. But Ford closed the gap, causing Carter to win the White House with just 50.1 percent of the popular vote. In terms of accomplishments, his presidency was known for the Panama Canal treaties and the Camp David Accords. In terms of failure, his presidency was known for the Iranian hostage crisis and a generally weak economy encumbered by high oil prices. Those failures contributed to an overall sense that he was indecisive and that, under his leadership, America was moving in the wrong direction. Consequently, he lost his bid for reelection in 1980 to the Republican challenger, Ronald Reagan.

Chisholm, Shirley (1924–2005) *politician*
Shirley Chisholm was the first African-American woman who was elected to Congress. Chisholm received a bachelor's degree from Brooklyn College in 1946 and a master's degree from Columbia University in 1952. As a nursery school teacher and child-care manager, she became well acquainted with poverty in New York, and her desire to help the disadvantaged caused her to enter politics. In 1964, she won a seat in the New York assembly, and in 1968, she was elected as a Democrat to Congress. She supported legislation to expand day care, improve employment and education programs, and help those living in inner cities. In 1972, she sought the Democratic presidential nomination and received 151 delegate votes in a losing cause. Chisholm retired from Congress in 1982 and devoted the rest of her life to teaching and writing. She died on January 1, 2005, in Ormond Beach, Florida.

Clemente, Roberto (1934–1972) *professional baseball player*

Born in Carolina, Puerto Rico, on August 18, 1934, Roberto Clemente won several track-and-field medals in his teens, but he liked playing baseball best. He played amateur baseball and joined a winter league team before signing with the Brooklyn Dodgers in 1953 at age 19. The following year, the Pittsburgh Pirates drafted Clemente from the Dodgers. In 1955, he entered the major leagues, and during the next 18 years with the Pirates, he won the National League Batting championship four times. His World Series batting average of .362 helped his team win two world championships, in 1960 and 1971. He was awarded 12 Gold Gloves as an outfielder and was selected National League MVP in 1966. He excelled in the sport despite suffering chronic back pain from a car accident in 1956. In 1972, he became only the 11th player in major-league history to reach 3,000 hits. Then on December 31, 1972, he died in an airplane crash en route to Nicaragua to provide earthquake victims with medicine, food, and clothing. In 1973, Clemente became the first Hispanic player inducted into the National Baseball Hall of Fame.

Coe, David Allan (1939–) *musician*

Born on September 6, 1939, in Akron, Ohio, David Allan Coe became one of the most controversial of the 1970s-era outlaw country performers. From the age of nine, Coe was in and out of reform schools, correction centers, and prisons. He was paroled from the Ohio State Penitentiary in 1967, and shortly thereafter, Shelby Singleton, an independent producer in Nashville, released two of Coe's record albums. Coe began to call himself The Mysterious Rhinestone Cowboy and to perform on stage in a sequined outfit and a mask. As one of the leaders in the outlaw movement, he challenged the traditional Nashville record industry standards by singing mainly his own songs, using his own band on records (rather than one provided by the record companies), and delving into controversial topics. His music ranged from the tender to the rebellious, from the introspective to the outlandish. In his song "Longhaired Redneck," he warned his critics that he would knock them from their chairs, and when *Rolling Stone* magazine questioned his story about having killed a fellow inmate, he responded with the song, "I'd Like to Kick the Shit Out of You." Coe wrote Tanya Tucker's sentimental 1974 number-one hit, "Would You Lay with Me (In a Field of Stone)?" There followed his cover of Steve Goodman's "You Never Even Called Me by My Name," which became a top-10 song for Coe. His "Take This Job and Shove It" was a big hit for Johnny Paycheck. Coe has also written songs for George Jones, Willie Nelson, Tammy Wynette, the Oakridge Boys, and many others. Despite his success with two cover songs in the 1980s, "The Ride" and "Mona Lisa Lost Her Smile" (and the huge success of his *Greatest Hits Album*), Coe's appearances in the top-10 sales lists have been limited. This has largely been because of his refusal to abandon his rebel approach. Even in the early 21st century, as he continued to record and perform at concerts around the country while in his mid-60s, he took with him the baggage of his musical past and his personality, exuding the toughness of a rough life that was emblazoned as much on the saddle of a Harley Davidson motorcycle as behind the microphone of a recording studio.

Davis, Angela (1944–) *Black Power leader, communist*

A Black Power activist, a communist, and a women's rights advocate, Angela Davis was born on January 26, 1944, in Birmingham, Alabama. She grew up in a middle-class African-American family but, as a young woman, was greatly affected by the white racism then prevalent in the city. Davis entered Brandeis University in Massachusetts in 1961 and, in her senior year, began to study philosophy under the renowned Marxist Herbert Marcuse. In 1967, Davis continued her studies under Marcuse, who had relocated to the University of California at San Diego. That same year, she joined the Black Panther Party. She had become a revolutionary and said, "Revolution is a serious thing, the most serious thing about a revolutionary's life. When one commits oneself to the struggle, it must be for a lifetime." Davis traveled to Cuba in 1969, where she helped harvest sugarcane and proclaimed her admiration for the Cuban revolution. When she returned to San Diego, the University of California hired her to teach philosophy, but after Governor Ronald Reagan and the board of trustees learned that she was a member of the Communist Party, they fired her. In 1970, Davis organized a campaign to help George Jackson and two other men who were imprisoned at Soledad prison. Jackson had been charged with murder, the result of a protest against racism that turned into a prison riot and left one guard dead. That August, Jonathan Jackson, George's brother, led a group in raiding a courthouse. They captured a judge, a district attorney, and several jurors and planned to hold them hostage in exchange for George Jackson's release. A shootout with police ensued, however, and in the gunfire, the judge and Jonathan Jackson were killed. Unfortunately for Angela Davis, two guns used by Jackson were registered in her name. She was charged with murder, conspiracy, and kidnapping and stood trial in 1972. A jury acquitted her on all charges. In the mid-1970s, Davis founded the National Alliance against Racist and Political Repression, a communist-affiliated group with chapters in several states. At the beginning of the 21st century she remained committed to her radical social agenda, as evidenced in her writing and many speaking engagements. In addition to her duties as professor of history and consciousness at the University of California at Santa Cruz, she spent much of her time working for prison reform.

Dean, John (1938–   ) *lawyer, government official*
From 1969 to 1974, John Dean served as White House counsel to President Richard Nixon and became a controversial figure in the Watergate scandal. Dean was born in Akron, Ohio, and, in 1961, obtained a bachelor's degree from Wooster College. He received a graduate fellowship from American University to study government and, in 1965, earned a law degree from Georgetown University. He gained Richard Nixon's attention when, in 1967, he became associate director of the National Commission on the Reform of Federal Criminal Law and, in 1968, wrote position papers on crime for Nixon's presidential campaign. After Nixon won the presidency, Dean became an assistant in the office of the attorney general. He became White House counsel when Nixon appointed the existing counsel, John Ehrlichman, to be his chief domestic adviser. When several Nixon campaign operatives broke into the Democratic National Committee headquarters at Watergate in 1972, Dean helped to cover up the crime. Later, however, he began to provide federal prosecutors with evidence showing White House involvement in the break-in, at which point Nixon fired him. Dean's testimony before the Senate Select Committee on Presidential Campaign Activities implicated Nixon in the Watergate cover-up. Nixon continued to profess his innocence, but the release of taped conversations largely supported Dean's testimony. Dean was ultimately convicted of conspiracy to obstruct justice and to defraud the government and served four months in prison. He

later worked as a private investment banker. In 1976, he published his memoirs, *Blind Ambition*. He has subsequently written many political articles and several other books, including, in 2003, *Worse Than Watergate: The Secret Presidency of George W. Bush*.

Ehrlichman, John (1925–1999) *government official*
A central figure in the Watergate scandal, John Ehrlichman was born in Tacoma, Washington, on March 20, 1925. He attended the University of California at Los Angeles but left before graduating to join the U.S. Army Air Force in 1943. He then returned to UCLA, where he earned a bachelor's degree in 1948. Ehrlichman obtained a law degree from Stanford University in 1951, and from 1952 to 1968, practiced in Seattle, specializing in zoning and land-use law. While he was attending UCLA, he became friends with H. R. Haldeman, and, in 1960, Haldeman recruited him to help with Richard Nixon's presidential campaign. Nixon, a Republican, lost that year to Democrat John Kennedy, but Ehrlichman again joined Nixon in 1962 when Nixon ran unsuccessfully for governor of California. Ehrlichman assisted Nixon yet a third time, in the 1968 presidential race. When Nixon won, Ehrlichman became White House counsel and, later, chief domestic policy adviser. Along with Haldeman, Ehrlichman wielded enormous power in the White House. The two men became known as the Berlin Wall for the way they shielded the president and restricted access to him. In 1971, Ehrlichman authorized the covert and illegal break-in at the office of Dr. Lewis Fielding, who was Dr. Daniel J. Ellsberg's psychiatrist. The burglary was conducted to get information on Ellsberg, who had released the *Pentagon Papers,* a secret study of U.S. involvement in the Vietnam War, to the *New York Times.* Ehrlichman was deeply involved in the Watergate cover-up, and in January 1975, he was convicted on charges of conspiracy, obstruction of justice, and perjury. His sentence ran concurrently with another that was handed down for his role in the Fielding break-in. Ehrlichman served his time at the Federal prison camp in Stafford, Arizona. On his release in 1978, he settled in Santa Fe, New Mexico, and engaged in writing and lecturing. Shortly before his release from prison, he told an interviewer: "I abdicated my moral judgments and turned them over to somebody else. And if I had any advice for my kids, it would be never—to never, ever—defer your moral judgments to anybody: your parents, your wife, anybody." Ehrlichman

died on February 14, 1999, from complications involving diabetes.

Ellsberg, Daniel (1931–) *economist, political scientist*

Known as the man who released the *Pentagon Papers* to the *New York Times* and subsequently suffered government recrimination, Daniel Ellsberg was born on April 7, 1931, in Chicago. He studied at the University of Cambridge and, in 1959, received a doctorate in economics from Harvard. In the early 1960s, he worked as a foreign affairs consultant in the White House. He showed no signs of becoming a dissident and, in fact, ardently supported U.S. cold-war policies. In 1964, he worked in the Pentagon under Secretary of Defense Robert McNamara and then went to Vietnam as an official with the State Department. His experience in Vietnam convinced him that the United States would lose the war. In 1967, McNamara appointed a team of researchers to write a history of relations between the United States and Vietnam since 1945, later called the *Pentagon Papers.* Ellsberg, who at that time was employed by the Rand Corporation, served on the team. He concluded that the United States had been drawn into the war by deceitful actions on the part of several presidents. Ellsberg believed it would be impossible to try to change American policy in Vietnam by working within the Washington bureaucracy, for there were too many entrenched interests whose narrow vision and treacherous practices would defeat any efforts at reform. Consequently, in 1971, he decided to release the *Pentagon Papers* to the *New York Times.* The *Papers* revealed the lies committed by Lyndon Johnson and other presidents in deepening the American involvement in Vietnam. In late June 1971, Ellsberg surrendered to the U.S. attorney in Boston and was charged with theft, conspiracy, and espionage. He thought it likely that he would spend the rest of his life in prison. In September, however, undercover men working for the Nixon administration wiretapped Ellsberg's phone and broke into his psychiatrist's office, hoping to find information that could be used against Ellsberg. Once revealed, the break-in became a part of the Watergate scandal. In May 1972, the White House secretly planned to have Ellsberg assaulted or assassinated. In 1973, a judge dismissed all charges against Ellsberg because of the illegal government activities. Since then, Ellsberg has continued his political activism, condemning the U.S. invasion of Iraq in 2003. His book *Secrets: A Memoir of Vietnam and the Pentagon Papers,* was published in 2002. About the *Pentagon Papers,* Ellsberg said in 1998: "Seven thousand pages of documents of presidential lying did establish forever that presidents all lie."

Ervin, Sam (1896–1985) *U.S. senator*

A native of Morganton, North Carolina, Sam Ervin earned a bachelor's degree from the University of North Carolina in 1917 and a law degree from Harvard University in 1922 before entering politics and holding a seat in the North Carolina general assembly in the 1920s. He served as a judge in the 1930s and early 1940s and, in 1946, won election as a Democrat to the U.S. House of Representatives. He left the House in 1947 to resume his law practice. The following year, he became an associate justice on the North Carolina Supreme Court. Ervin was elected in 1954 to fill a seat left vacant in the U.S. Senate by the death of Clyde R. Hoey, and he won reelection in 1956, 1962, and again in 1968. He served on the Senate select committees that approved the censure of Republican senator Joseph McCarthy. As the Watergate scandal began to unfold early in 1973, Ervin agreed to chair the Senate Select Committee on Presidential Campaign Activities. The Ervin committee, as it was called, reflected his knowledge as a constitutional scholar and his strong belief in principled behavior. During the Watergate hearings, White House counsel John Dean implicated President Richard Nixon in a cover-up, and presidential aide Alexander Butterfield revealed the existence of secret recording machines in the Oval Office and elsewhere. The Watergate tapes exposed the criminal activities of Nixon and his aides, and they were instrumental in causing a House committee to recommend the president's impeachment. Ervin retired from the Senate in 1974 and returned to practicing law in Morganton. He died in Winston-Salem, North Carolina, on April 23, 1985. About Nixon, Ervin once said: "He had the most pronounced, aggravated notion about the powers of the presidency. He envisioned the president as being something of an absolute monarch."

Erving, Julius (1950–) *professional basketball player*

Born in East Meadow, New York, Julius Erving became one of the most prolific and exciting scorers in basketball history. Erving attended the University of Massachusetts, where he excelled on the basketball team in scoring and rebounding. He left college in 1971 to join the Virginia Squires of the American Basketball

Association and as a forward and guard quickly became the fledgling league's greatest star. In 1973, the Squires traded him to the New Jersey Nets, a team that he led to ABA championship titles in 1974 and 1976. The next season, he was with a new team and a new league: the Philadelphia 76ers of the National Basketball Association. He led the 76ers to an NBA championship in 1983 and was an NBA All-Star for 11 consecutive seasons, from 1977 to 1987. By the time he retired in 1987, he had become only the third player in professional basketball history to score more than 30,000 points. In 1993, he was elected to the Basketball Hall of Fame, and in 1996, he was named one of the 50 greatest players in NBA history. After his retirement from the basketball court, he became a business executive, television basketball broadcaster, and, in the late 1990s, executive vice president for the Orlando Magic team in Florida.

Flood, Curt (1938–1997) *professional baseball player*
Curtis Flood was born on January 18, 1938, in Houston, Texas, and began his major-league baseball career in 1956 with the Cincinnati Reds. His season batting average topped .300 six times, and his performance in center field—he set a record by going 223 games without an error—made him a seven-time winner of the Gold Glove award. He was chosen for the All-Star team three times. But despite all of his accomplishments on the field, he became best known for his controversial decision to fight the effort by his ball club, the St. Louis Cardinals, to trade him to the Philadelphia Phillies. At that time, players were subject to a reserve clause that bound them to their clubs. The players had no recourse as to when and where they might be traded—the decision was completely in the hands of the clubs that held their contracts. Flood went to court to overturn the reserve clause, and the court fight lasted from January 1970 to June 1972. Although Flood was an African American, his suit charged major-league baseball not with racism but with violating antitrust laws and with placing baseball players into a condition of "involuntary servitude." He lost when the U.S. Supreme Court ruled against him, but he had set the stage for an end to the reserve system in 1975 when an arbitrator declared two players to be free agents. Flood played a few games for the Washington Senators in 1971 and then retired from the sport. For his career, he batted .293, with 1,861 hits, including 271 doubles, 44

triples, and 85 home runs. He scored 851 runs and had 636 RBI. Flood died in Los Angeles on January 20, 1997, from throat cancer.

Ford, Gerald (1913–   ) *congressman, vice president, president*
Gerald Rudolph Ford, Jr., was born Leslie King, Jr., in Omaha, Nebraska, on July 14, 1913. He was the only child of Leslie Lynch King, a wool dealer, and Dorothy Ayer Gardner King. His parents divorced when he was two years old, and his mother took him to Grand Rapids, Michigan, where he grew up. In 1916, she married Gerald Rudolph Ford, and young Leslie took his stepfather's name. Gerald Ford attended the University of Michigan, where he played on the football team and earned national honors in 1934 as a center. He received contracts to play professionally but instead entered Yale University law school, from where he graduated in 1941. He returned to Grand Rapids to practice law, but in 1942, with World War II underway, he enlisted in the navy. He saw duty in the South Pacific and was discharged in 1945 as a lieutenant with 10 battle stars. Once again practicing law in Grand Rapids, in 1948, he won his first political race when, as a Republican, he defeated a Democratic incumbent to serve in the U.S. House of Representatives. In 1965, his fellow Republicans chose him to serve as minority leader. He earned a reputation in the House as an opponent of President Lyndon Johnson's Great Society social programs, and he advocated the use of more military power in fighting the war in Vietnam. In 1973, when Vice President Spiro Agnew was forced to resign because of criminal charges against him, Nixon chose Ford to become vice president and Congress approved. By then, Nixon was deeply involved in the Watergate scandal, and many believed that Ford could ascend to the presidency. When Nixon resigned in August 1974, Ford did just that. As president, he tried to heal the wounds of Watergate but kept them festering when he pardoned Nixon for any crimes the former president may have committed. Ford tried to restore trust in the White House but kept skepticism alive when he secretly involved the United States in a complex civil war in Angola. In 1976, he turned back a strong attempt by former California governor Ronald Ragan to wrest the Republican presidential nomination from him. Nevertheless, he lost his bid to stay in the White House when Democrat Jimmy Carter defeated him in

a close election. Ford retired to Grand Rapids and, in 1979, published his autobiography, *A Time to Heal.* In 2000, he appeared at the Republican National Convention. Soon thereafter, he suffered a stroke, from which he recovered. Unlike any previous chief executive, Ford had never been elected as part of a national ticket. He was, in essence, a congressional appointee who failed to widen his base effectively beyond Capitol Hill.

Friedan, Betty (Bettye Naomi Goldstein) (1921–2006) *women's rights activist*

A founding member of the National Organization for Women (NOW), Betty Friedan was born Bettye Naomi Goldstein on February 4, 1921, in Peoria, Illinois. In her childhood, two experiences especially affected her and shaped her consciousness, making her question some of her middle-class values: the anti-Semitism she experienced in Peoria and her mother's disappointment with having given up her work as a journalist when she married. Friedan received a B.A. degree in 1942 from Smith College in Massachusetts and, in 1947, married Carl Friedan, a theater producer. (They divorced in 1969.) In 1963, Friedan published her book *The Feminine Mystique,* in which she asserted that the role in the home that society expected women to fulfill both frustrated and oppressed them and represented a male conspiracy to limit competition from them. Friedan used the phrase "the problem that has no name" to indicate the feeling of emptiness gnawing at women. Many women and men applauded Friedan's conclusions, but some reacted negatively to the book and strongly opposed her for undermining traditional middle-class values. At the same time, Friedan declared that advancing women's liberation required political action. So, in 1966, she founded NOW, a group devoted to obtaining equal rights for women. Friedan retired as NOW president in 1970 but continued her activism and, later that year, organized the Women's Strike for Equality. The turnout in Washington, D.C., and in other cities made it the largest women's rights rally in many decades. In the 1970s, Friedan worked through the National Abortion Rights Action League (NARAL), which she had founded in the late 1960s to lead the fight for safe and legal abortions. She organized and directed the First Woman's Bank and Trust Company in New York City and led the campaign to ratify the Equal Rights Amendment. She continued to write and lecture in the 1980s and the 1990s. She died in 2006.

Haldeman, H. R. (Bob Haldeman) (1926–1993) *government official*

As President Richard Nixon's chief of staff, H. R. "Bob" Haldeman (Harry Robbins Haldeman) was extensively involved in illegal activities to cover up Watergate. He was born into a prosperous family in Los Angeles, California, on October 27, 1926, served in the naval reserve during World War II, and graduated from the University of California at Los Angeles in 1948. The following year, he became an account executive with the J. Walter Thompson advertising agency in New York. In 1959, he returned to Los Angeles as vice president of the company's California office. Haldeman first worked for Richard Nixon in 1956 when he helped the then vice president win reelection. He worked also on Nixon's unsuccessful 1960 presidential campaign and his unsuccessful 1962 California gubernatorial campaign. In 1968, he managed Nixon's winning race for the White House. When Nixon took office in 1969, Haldeman became his chief of staff. Other than the president, he wielded the most power in the White House. When operatives for Nixon's reelection organization broke into Watergate in 1972, Haldeman took the lead in covering up the burglary. He destroyed documents and suggested that Nixon use the Central Intelligence Agency to block the FBI from investigating Watergate. As pressure mounted on Nixon in April 1973, the president announced Haldeman's resignation. In 1975, Haldeman was convicted on charges of perjury, conspiracy, and obstruction of justice related to the Watergate break-in. He served 18 months in prison. After his release in 1978, he worked as a real-estate developer and business consultant and owned several restaurants in Florida. He died of cancer in Santa Barbara, California, on November 12, 1993, at which time Nixon hailed him for having "played an indispensable role" in undertaking "a broad range of initiatives at home and abroad."

Hearst, Patty (1954–) *newspaper heiress*

The granddaughter of newspaper publisher William Randolph Hearst, Patty Hearst was born on February 20, 1954, in San Francisco. She came to national attention on February 4, 1974, when members of a leftist group called the Symbionese Liberation Army (SLA) kidnapped her from her apartment in Berkeley, California, where she was living while attending the University of California. On April 15, 1974, Hearst was photographed by surveillance cameras with a rifle in hand, helping the SLA rob a bank. Shortly thereafter, she announced that she had changed her name to Tania and had joined the SLA. In May, she was involved in a shootout at a sporting goods store. In September 1975, she was arrested and charged with armed robbery and assault. At about the same time, a clash between several SLA members and the police resulted in the radicals' deaths. Hearst stood trial in March 1976 and claimed she became sympathetic with the SLA because of the harsh way in which they had treated her. (Called the "Stockholm Syndrome," this is a psychological response by a hostage whereby the hostage becomes loyal to his or her captor for purposes of survival.) A jury found her guilty of bank robbery, and she was sentenced to prison. She pleaded guilty in 1977 to charges surrounding the assault at the sporting goods store and was sentenced to five years probation. President Jimmy Carter commuted her prison sentence after 22 months, and she was released from prison in February 1979. She received a pardon from President Bill Clinton in January 2001.

Hendrix, Jimi (1942–1970) *rock musician*

Jimi Hendrix was born Johnny Allen Hendrix on November 27, 1942, in Seattle, Washington. His name was soon changed to James Marshall Hendrix. When Hendrix was a child, his parents, part black and part Cherokee Indian, took him to a Pentecostal church where he joined them in singing gospel songs. By age eight, he had become obsessed with playing the guitar, and at age 11, his father bought him his first one. Hendrix quit high school during his senior year and, in 1963, joined the army. A back injury led to his early discharge from the service, and he then played with several rhythm-and-blues bands before making his way to New York City and the club scene in Greenwich Village. In 1966, he formed his first band, bought his first Fender Stratocaster guitar, and tried out his material at Café Wha? He got to know other young musicians, such as Bob Dylan and Bruce Springsteen, and developed the technique of playing his Stratocaster while holding it behind his back. In 1966, Hendrix headed to England and with guitarist Noel Chandler and drummer Mitch Mitchell formed the Jimi Hendrix Experience. Hendrix emerged as a star in Europe, and in August 1967, his band made its American debut at the Monterey International Pop Festival in California. The audience sat mesmerized as, at the end of his act, Hendrix set his guitar on fire. Hendrix had presented an electrifying soul and psychedelic performance filled with sensuality or what one observer called "the voodoo child run wild in electric ladyland!" The mixture of blues and psychedelic influences was called acid rock. Hendrix's single "Purple Haze" and album *Are You Experienced?* climbed the record charts, and in 1968, *Rolling Stone* magazine named him Performer of the Year. The following year, Hendrix formed a new band, and he appeared in August at Woodstock. Yet, he grew disenchanted with his music and reformed his band, the Experience. He played with them only sporadically, however. On September 18, 1970, he was found dead in his London apartment, a victim of complications stemming from barbiturates.

Hoover, John Edgar (1895–1972) *FBI director*

A powerful political figure as director of the FBI, J. Edgar Hoover was born in Washington, D.C., on January 1, 1895. Soon after he received a law degree from George Washington University, he was hired in 1917 as a file reviewer for the Justice Department. As special assistant to the attorney general from 1919 to 1924 and assistant director of the Justice Department's Bureau of Investigation from 1921 to 1924, he compiled 60,000 files on radicals and anarchists. In 1924, he was appointed director of the bureau and built it into an investigatory agency that was committed to using modern crime-detecting techniques. He established a fingerprint repository and crime laboratory, and when the bureau became the FBI in 1935, he founded a training academy. He also established programs to track down fraudulent checks, trace the marks peculiar to individual typewriters, and uncover altered automobile identification numbers. With the outbreak of war in Europe in 1939, at the behest of President Franklin Roosevelt, he began internal-security and espionage programs. When the cold war began, he became preoccupied with hunting communists. Critics said this activity detracted from much-needed efforts against organized crime and in support of civil rights. He maintained so many files on politicians in Washington that they avoided crossing him for fear that he might reveal secrets about their lives. In the 1960s, he founded a counterintelligence program called COINTELPRO that used surreptitious, violent, and illegal activities against dissenters—militants, leftists, peace and antiwar activists, women's rights advocates, environmentalists . . . anyone who seemed to challenge what the federal government and Hoover considered to be acceptable behavior. Hoover died in Washington on May 2, 1972.

Jackson, Jesse (1941–   ) *civil rights leader*
An African-American Baptist minister, civil rights leader, and presidential candidate, Jesse Jackson was born on October 8, 1941, in Greenville, South Carolina. In 1963, he joined the Congress of Racial Equality (CORE) and led a 10-month-long protest in Greensboro, North Carolina, that involved marches, sit-ins, and boycotts of businesses that practiced racial segregation. Jackson left the South in 1965 to study at the University of Chicago's theological seminary. That same year, he joined the voting rights protest in Selma, Alabama, that was then being led by Martin Luther King, Jr., and his Southern Christian Leadership Conference (SCLC). Jackson joined the SCLC, quit the seminary, and in 1966 coordinated the SCLC's Operation Breadbasket, a program founded to unite African Americans in placing pressure on manufacturers and retailers to hire more black workers. Jackson was present on the balcony of the Lorraine Hotel on April 4, 1968, when King was slain. With King's death, Jackson, who had been ordained a minister at a Baptist church in 1968, hoped to be named the new leader of the SCLC, but the position went to Ralph Abernathy. In 1971, Jackson ran for mayor of Chicago but lost. Later that year, amid tension with Abernathy, Jackson quit the SCLC and founded People United to Save Humanity (PUSH), intended to help those of many different colors and nationalities. In the early 1970s, Jackson obtained agreements with Burger King and Kentucky Fried Chicken to employ more blacks. Presently, Jackson established PUSH EXCEL to encourage minority students to stay in school. In 1984, Jackson launched a massive voter-registration drive and made his first run for the presidency by entering the Democratic primary. He won a surprising 21 percent of the popular and caucus votes in a losing effort. In 1986, he organized the National Rainbow Coalition to secure social justice, jobs, and education for minorities by electing to office politicians who supported such goals. Jackson ran for president a second time in 1988 but again failed to win the Democratic nomination. In 1997, Jackson began the Wall Street Project, whereby he encouraged blacks to buy stocks and to use their status as shareholders to pressure corporations to provide more jobs and other opportunities for African Americans. About the same time, Jackson merged the PUSH and Rainbow programs, and in the early 21st century, he worked as president of the Rainbow/PUSH Coalition.

Jackson, Reggie (1946–   ) *professional baseball player*
"Mr. October," Reggie Jackson was born Reginald Martinez Jackson in Wyncote, Pennsylvania. Beginning in 1964, he attended Arizona State University, where he played baseball and football. He left college in 1966 when he received a contract from the Kansas City Athletics (later, the Oakland Athletics) baseball team. Following a brief stint in the minor leagues, he began to play for the A's in 1967. Two years later, he hit 47 home runs with 118 runs batted in. Jackson was traded to the Baltimore Orioles in 1976 and, in 1977, signed with the New York Yankees. His power hitting proved instrumental in the Yankees winning three East Division championships, two American league pennants, and, in 1977 and 1978, two World Series. He got the nickname "Mr. October" for the four consecutive home runs that he hit in games five and six of the 1977 World Series against the Los Angeles Dodgers. He retired from baseball after the 1987 season and was inducted into the National Baseball Hall of Fame in 1993.

Jobs, Steve (1955–   ) *business executive*
When Steven Jobs founded the Apple Computer Company, he made computers accessible to teachers, students, and millions of other everyday people. Born in Mountain View, California, Jobs attended high school in Los Altos and dabbled in electronics while working part time at Hewlett-Packard. He met Steven Wozniak, a fellow computer whiz, and they entered into their first moneymaking venture when they manufactured a device that enabled callers to bypass long-distance phone charges illegally. Jobs entered Reed College in Oregon in 1972 but soon quit to work as a video-game developer and, later, to go backpacking in India on a search for spiritual enlightenment. When he returned to California in 1975, he and Wozniak developed a personal computer which they built and marketed from a garage. They called their computer Apple, a name that was likely chosen in memory of the summer that Jobs spent in Oregon working in an orchard. They sold 200 computers their first year and followed it with Apple II, a simple machine which was operable without any knowledge of computer language. (Like Apple I, it had no monitor and so had to be plugged into a TV screen.) Boosted by money from an outside investor, Jobs and Wozniak expanded production, and by 1978, company sales neared $8 million. In 1983, Jobs developed a new computer, the Macintosh;

although it sold well, IBM had also entered the PC market, and by 1985, its sales were exceeding those of Apple. As Apple struggled, Jobs left the company in 1985 and began an educational computer company called NeXt. In 1996, he sold NeXt to Apple and bought Pixar, a computer-animation firm that made *Toy Story,* the first entirely computer-generated full-length movie. Jobs returned to Apple in 1997 as chairman in an attempt to stem its losses. In August of that year, he and Microsoft head Bill Gates formed a partnership between their two companies in which Microsoft invested $150 million in Apple and agreed to let Apple remain largely autonomous.

Joplin, Janis (1943–1970) *rock singer*
Janis Joplin captivated audiences with her hard-driving blues and rock songs that often expressed her inner torture. She was born on January 19, 1943, in Port Arthur, Texas, and at age 17, left home to sing with a country music band in Houston. In 1965, she made her way to San Francisco, where she sang in folk clubs and bars. Joplin returned home to Texas in 1966, dejected by her inability to advance her music career. She soon received a phone call from a rock promoter, Chet Helms, who wanted her to join a new band, Big Brother and the Holding Company, as its lead singer. She agreed, and in 1967, she made a sensational appearance with her rough-hewed blues voice and gained national recognition. She and Big Brother recorded the album *Cheap Thrills* in 1968, which earned a gold record. Later that year, she quit Big Brother and formed another group, the Kozmic Blues Band. In 1969, her album *I Got Dem Ol' Kozmic Blues Again Mama!* went gold. Joplin then began to record *Pearl,* but she never finished it. She died on October 4, 1970, from a heroin overdose. She had for years abused drugs and alcohol in an attempt to obliterate the loneliness and boredom that she felt when away from her music.

Kissinger, Henry (1923–   ) *statesman, political scientist*
Born in Fuerth, Germany, on May 27, 1923, Henry Kissinger came with his parents to the United States in 1938 as they fled the Nazis. He obtained his U.S. citizenship in 1943 and served in the army during World War II. In 1950, he received his bachelor's degree from Harvard and, in 1954, a doctorate in government, also from Harvard. His book *Nuclear Weapons,* published in 1957, gained him widespread recognition in govern-

ment circles. From 1959 to 1969, Kissinger taught at Harvard as professor of government with a specialization in foreign policy. He wrote several books and directed the Harvard Defense Studies Program and the Harvard International Seminar. He was a consultant to the National Security Council during the 1961–62 Berlin crisis. He was also a consultant to the U.S. Arms Control and Disarmament Agency from 1961 to 1968 and to the Department of State from 1965 to 1969. When Richard Nixon won the presidency in 1968, he appointed Kissinger his National Security Advisor and, in 1973, secretary of state. (Kissinger later relinquished his post as National Security Advisor.) He was the chief architect of Nixon's foreign policy, including détente with the Soviet Union, the opening of contacts with communist China, and the signing of a peace agreement to end the Vietnam War (for which he won the Nobel Peace Prize). In his diplomacy, Kissinger used surprise tactics and extensive secrecy, and he stressed objectives over principles. He helped plan the clandestine bombing of Cambodia and the use of illegal domestic wiretaps. Perhaps his most controversial move was his initiative to discredit and topple the government of Salvador Allende, the marxist who had been elected president of Chile. After leaving office, Kissinger joined the faculty of Georgetown University and wrote three books about his White House years. He has since worked as a consultant.

Manson, Charles (1934–   ) *cult leader, murderer*
A psychotic murderer known for the Tate-LaBianca slayings, Charles Manson was born on November 12, 1934, in Cincinnati, Ohio, the illegitimate son of a 16-year-old girl. His mother served time in prison for robbery and placed Manson in a school for boys. Manson committed his first armed robbery at age 13, escaped from the Indiana School for Boys in 1951, and continued his criminal activities in California. He was captured and sentenced to the National Training School for Boys in Washington, D.C., where a counselor described him as antisocial, moody, and restless. In 1952, he assaulted a boy at the school and was transferred to a high-security prison in Chillicothe, Ohio. He received parole in 1954 and returned to California. For the next five years, he stole cars, worked as a pimp, and forged checks. In 1960, he was sentenced to a federal penitentiary in Washington State. While in prison, he obsessed about a rock band, the Beatles. He pleaded for the authorities to deny him parole so that he could avoid

being sent back into society, but they released him in March 1967. At that time, Manson's psychotic personality crossed paths with the counterculture. He began to hang out at Haight-Ashbury, the hippie enclave in San Francisco. Through his pseudoreligious talk he developed a group of followers, the Manson family, who were immersed in drugs and sex and so tightly under his control that, in time, they would carry out his orders to kill. On August 9, 1969, five people were found brutally murdered at the Los Angeles home of movie director Roman Polanski and his wife, actress Sharon Tate. Tate, then eight months pregnant, was one of those killed. On August 10, businessman Leno LaBianca and his wife, Rosemary, were found murdered in much the same grisly way as had been the victims at the Tate house. Manson was placed on trial for the murders on July 24, 1970. Evidence showed that he had ordered the murders to promote a race war, which he hoped would produce an apocalypse. He considered a 1969 record by the Beatles, *The White Album,* to have revealed to him what he must do. The Manson trial ended in 1971, and he and three of his followers were found guilty of the murders and sentenced to death. A fourth family member was sentenced to death in a separate trial. In February 1972, the California Supreme Court abolished the death penalty, a decision that converted the Manson Family convictions to life imprisonment. Manson has applied for parole numerous times, only to be denied.

McGovern, George (1922–   ) *U.S. senator, Democratic presidential nominee*
Born in Avon, South Dakota, on July 19, 1922, George McGovern attended Dakota Wesleyan University from 1940 to 1942 before serving in the U.S. Army Air Corps during World War II. He was discharged from the service in 1945 and returned to Dakota Wesleyan, from where he graduated in 1946. He received his doctorate from Northwestern University in Evanston, Illinois, in 1953 and taught at Dakota Wesleyan. He entered politics when he served as executive secretary of the South Dakota Democratic Party beginning in 1953. In 1956, he won election to the U.S. House of Representatives. He ran for the Senate in 1960 but lost. A few months later, President John Kennedy appointed him director of the Food for Peace Program. In 1962, he again ran for the Senate; this time, he won. He was reelected in 1968 and gained prominence as an outspoken opponent of the Vietnam War. While in the Senate, he chaired the

Democratic Party's reform commission that dismantled many old rules and made the party more receptive to young people, women, and minorities. Those rule changes helped him win his party's presidential nomination in 1972. But his assault on the party's stalwarts and his liberal views alienated many Democrats and caused them to support his Republican opponent for the White House, Richard Nixon. McGovern further weakened his campaign when he first chose Senator Thomas Eagleton of Missouri as his running mate and then dropped him from the ticket when it was revealed that Eagleton had been hospitalized for mental health problems several years earlier. In the general election, Nixon defeated McGovern by a landslide. Two years later, in 1974, McGovern returned to the Senate, but he lost his bid for another term in 1980. He sought the Democratic presidential nomination a second time in 1984 but withdrew from the race when he finished poorly in the Massachusetts primary. He served as U.S. ambassador to the United Nations Food and Agricultural Agencies in Rome from 1998 to 2001, was awarded the Presidential Medal of Freedom in 2000, and was appointed UN Global Ambassador on World Hunger in 2001.

Means, Russell (1940–   ) *American Indian activist*
A leader in the American Indian Movement (AIM), Russell Means worked to promote Indian treaty rights and civil rights against government oppression and exploitation. He was born on the Pine Ridge Reservation of South Dakota and raised near Oakland, California, by his father, part Oglala Lakota and part Irish, and his mother, a Yankton Sioux. He held several jobs, among them rodeo rider and public accountant, before joining AIM in about 1970. In 1972, he led a protest in Gordon, Nebraska, that resulted in the police arresting two white men who were involved in the murder of an Indian. The following year, Means and 200 other AIM protesters held a press conference at Wounded Knee on the Pine Ridge Reservation in the wake of continued injustices against Indians and demanded several reforms. The protest turned into a violent showdown when Indian police, who were allied with the corrupt Sioux tribal president, Dickie Wilson, surrounded the AIM activists. The confrontation between AIM and the combined force of Indian police and federal forces lasted from February to May 1973. Means subsequently stood trial on 10 felony counts, but the government prosecutors so flagrantly violated the

rules of legal conduct that the judge threw out the charges. Means ran against Wilson for the tribal presidency in 1974 but lost in a close election that was marked by Wilson's ballot tampering. Means left AIM in 1988, claiming that it had accomplished its goals, and in 1992, he played the role of Chingachgook in the movie *Last of the Mohicans.* He has since allied with an AIM faction and continues as an activist for Indian rights.

Mitchell, John N. (1913–1988) *attorney general*
The only U.S. attorney general to ever serve prison time, John N. Mitchell was born in Detroit, Michigan, on September 15, 1913, and grew up on Long Island, New York. He received his law degree from Fordham University in New York City and became a successful lawyer with the firm of Caldwell & Raymond, which specialized in bond financing. His work brought him into close contact with Republican political figures, including New York governor Nelson Rockefeller. In 1967, his law firm merged with Richard Nixon's, and the following year, Nixon asked Mitchell to manage his presidential campaign. Mitchell agreed, later explaining, "I did it because I believed in the cause and the individual." When Nixon won, he appointed Mitchell attorney general. A conservative, Mitchell condemned liberals as worse than many communists. He advocated strong measures to fight urban crime, black unrest, and war protesters, including wiretapping without warrants and preventive detention. His numerous efforts against Vietnam dissidents, black militants, and journalists, among others, were later ruled as violations of constitutional rights. While still serving as attorney general, Mitchell oversaw the formation of the Committee for the Re-Election of the President (CREEP) and the acquisition of money used for a variety of "dirty tricks" against Nixon's political opponents, such as forged letters written to destroy the presidential candidacy of Democratic senator Edmund S. Muskie of Maine. Mitchell approved the dirty tricks. In February 1972, Mitchell resigned as attorney general to become the chairman of CREEP. When the Watergate break-in occurred Mitchell—who may, in fact, have approved the burglary—took a leading role in covering up the crime, including providing money to the burglars to keep them silent. On July 1, 1972, Mitchell resigned from CREEP, citing his desire to spend more time with his family. When Nixon blamed Mitchell, among other presidential aides, for Watergate, Mitchell remained loyal to the president. Indeed, his loyalty never wavered. In late 1974, Mitchell went on trial for conspiracy, obstruction of justice, and perjury. He denied the charges but refused to criticize Nixon. He was convicted on January 1, 1975, and received a prison sentence of 30 months to eight years. He entered prison in June 1977 but was paroled and released in January 1979. Disbarred as a lawyer, he lived his remaining years working as a business consultant in relative quiet, refusing most interviews. He died on November 9, 1988, from a heart attack.

Mondale, Walter (1928–   ) *senator, vice president*
Born on January 5, 1928, in Ceylon, Minnesota, Walter Mondale received a bachelor's degree from the University of Minnesota in 1951 and served in the U.S. Army during the Korean War. He received a law degree in 1956, also from the University of Minnesota, and entered private practice in Minneapolis. In 1960, he managed the reelection campaign of Democratic governor Orville Freeman, who then appointed Mondale state attorney general. In 1964, when Hubert Humphrey was elected vice president, Mondale was appointed to fill the remainder of Humphrey's term in the U.S. Senate. He was elected to the seat in 1966 and again in 1972. Mondale established himself as a liberal by concentrating on problems of housing, child welfare, and aging and by advancing civil rights. He chaired the Select Committee on Equal Education Opportunity. When Jimmy Carter campaigned for president in 1976, he chose Mondale as his running mate. With the ticket's victory, Mondale was inaugurated as vice president in January 1977. He became one of Carter's close advisers and an important representative in diplomatic initiatives. In 1980, he again ran with Carter, but the team lost, and Mondale returned to practicing law. In 1984, he won the Democratic presidential nomination and chose Representative Geraldine Ferraro of New York to run with him, making her the first woman to be nominated for vice president by a major political party. Mondale lost, however, to the incumbent, Ronald Reagan, in a landslide. He carried only the District of Columbia and his home state of Minnesota. In 1993, President Bill Clinton appointed Mondale to serve as U.S. ambassador to Japan, a post he held until 1996. He then returned to practicing law in Minnesota. In 2002, the Minnesota Democratic Party chose Mondale to replace Paul Wellstone in the race for the U.S. Senate because Wellstone had been killed in a plane crash. Mondale had less than a week to campaign and was defeated by Republican Norm Coleman.

Morgan, Robin (1941–   ) *feminist, writer*

Robin Morgan described herself in the late 1970s as "one of the women who helped start this wave of feminism back in the Pleistocene age of the middle and late 1960s." She was born on January 29, 1941, in Lake Worth, Florida, and graduated from Columbia University in the early 1960s. She married a poet and worked as a lexicographer for a book publisher while doing freelance editing. Later that decade, she helped organize New York Radical Women, a group that protested the 1968 Miss American Pageant in Atlantic City, New Jersey, for its sexism and racism. In January 1970, Morgan supported a group of feminists who forcibly took over the leftist newspaper *Rat*. She then wrote an article for that publication in which she said "two evils predate capitalism," namely "sexism and racism." Presently, she edited *Sisterhood Is Powerful: An Anthology of Writings from the Women's Liberation Movement,* which included historic documents that were related to feminist activism and articles pertaining to sexism. At various times, she criticized the National Organization for Women (NOW) for its moderate policies and said that only radical feminism could eliminate oppression. In the 1990s, Morgan served briefly as editor of *Ms.* Magazine and wrote *The Anatomy of Freedom,* an exploration of feminist consciousness.

Morrison, Jim (1943–1971) *rock singer*

The lead singer for the rock group the Doors, Jim Morrison was born on December 8, 1943, in Melbourne, Florida. Because his father was in the navy, the family moved frequently during Morrison's childhood. Morrison graduated from high school in Alexandria, Virginia. In the early 1960s, he attended Saint Petersburg Junior College and Florida State University before enrolling in 1966 at the University of California–Los Angeles film school. At UCLA, he met Ray Manzarek, a pianist; Robbie Krieger, a guitarist; and John Densmore, a drummer. Together, they formed a rock band and called themselves the Doors, after the title of Aldous Huxley's book about a mescaline trip, *The Doors of Perception,* and English poet William Blake's words, "If the doors of perception were cleansed, everything would appear as it is, infinite." Morrison once explained: "There's the known. And there's the unknown. And what separates the two is the door, and that's what I want to be." The Doors recorded a demo tape in 1966 and began to play as the house band at the Whisky-A-Go-Go in Los Angeles. In 1967, Elektra Records released their self-titled album,

along with a single, "Light My Fire," both top-10 hits. Counterculture youths liked Morrison's dark, psychological explorations and the band's obvious psychedelic form. Morrison adopted shamanistic tendencies and in the 1968 album, *Waiting for the Sun,* presented himself as the Lizard King. Drugs and alcohol permeated the band, and Morrison became an alcoholic, consuming a fifth of liquor a day. His behavior on and off stage became erratic, and in December 1967, authorities in New Haven, Connecticut, arrested him for public obscenity at a concert there; in 1968, he was arrested for disorderly conduct aboard an airplane headed for Phoenix, Arizona. His most sensational arrest, however, resulted from a concert on March 2, 1969, in Miami, Florida. The police accused him of exposing himself on stage and of public drunkenness. Witnesses disagreed as to whether Morrison did expose himself, but he was found guilty of the charges. He was sentenced to six months of hard labor but was freed pending appeal. In 1971, Morrison took a leave from the band. Emotionally drained and decimated by drugs and alcohol, he traveled to Paris, where he and his wife lived in seclusion. On July 3, 1971, he died in his bathtub from heart failure likely brought on by the drugs.

Nixon, Richard (1913–1994) *senator, vice president, president*

The only president to resign the office, Richard Nixon was born in Yorba Linda, near Los Angeles, on January 9, 1913. He moved with his family to Whittier in 1922 and as a teenager worked in his father's grocery store. In 1934, Nixon graduated from Whittier College with a B.A. in history and earned a scholarship to Duke University Law School. He graduated from there in 1937, third in his class, and returned to Whittier where he practiced law. In 1941, Nixon joined the Office of Price Administration in Washington, D.C., and in 1942, with World War II underway, he enlisted in the navy. Nixon's political career began after he received a letter from a banker in Whittier asking him to run as a Republican for Congress. Nixon defeated Democratic incumbent Jerry Voorhis in 1946, using campaign tactics in which he portrayed his opponent as soft on communism. Once in Congress, Nixon served on the House Un-American Activities Committee (HUAC), investigating communist influences in the United States. He won national attention with his pursuit of Alger Hiss, a former official in the State Department. Nixon accused Hiss of being part of an "underground cell of government employees" who worked for the

Communist Party. The evidence against Hiss proved less than conclusive, but Hiss was convicted for perjury in 1950. That year, Nixon ran for the Senate against Helen Gahagan Douglas, whom he called a communist sympathizer. He won and in the Senate attacked President Harry Truman for failing to win the war in Korea. Nixon's rapid political rise continued in 1952 when presidential nominee Dwight Eisenhower chose him as his running mate. Eisenhower wanted a young candidate and one who could appeal to the conservative wing of the Republican Party. Nixon survived a furor during the campaign over an alleged slush fund that he used for personal expenses and was inaugurated vice president in January 1953. He served a second term, too, that began in 1957. In 1960, Nixon ran against Democrat John F. Kennedy for the White House and lost in a close contest. Some analysts believe that Nixon's poor appearance on television in the first public debate with Kennedy cost him the election. He ran for governor of California in 1962 and again lost. He then vowed that he would never again seek public office, but he began a comeback in 1966 when he campaigned effectively and tirelessly for several congressional candidates. In 1968, he won the Republican presidential nomination and defeated Hubert H. Humphrey in the general election. He promised to get America out of Vietnam and to restore truth to the White House and unity to the nation as a whole. Seeking reelection in 1972, he defeated George S. McGovern in a landslide, but during the campaign, his operatives broke into the headquarters of the Democratic National Committee at Watergate. There followed the cover-up by himself and his aides and the unraveling of the cover-up in 1973 and 1974. His dwindling support in Congress and among the public evaporated early in August 1974 when several Watergate tapes revealed his lies and his role in obstructing justice. Facing impeachment by the House of Representatives, Nixon resigned the presidency, effective August 9, 1974. He avoided prison for his crimes when his successor, Gerald Ford, pardoned him. Disbarred from practicing law, Nixon spent his remaining years writing and trying hard to resurrect his image. He died from a stroke on April 22, 1994, in New York City.

Payton, Walter (1954–1999) *professional football player*
One of the greatest running backs in the history of professional football, Walter Payton was born into an

African-American family in Columbia, Mississippi, on July 25, 1954, and attended Jackson State University. In 1973, he set the NCAA record for most points scored, with 464. His smooth running style and pleasant disposition earned him the nickname "Sweetness." In 1975, the Chicago Bears drafted him, and that fall, he rushed for 679 yards in seven games. The following year, he rushed for 1,390 yards—the beginning of 10 consecutive seasons of more than 1,000 yards rushing. In 1977, he led the league with 1,852 yards rushing, his career high, and helped the Bears make the playoffs for the first time in 14 years. In 1984, he became the NFL's all-time rushing leader when he broke Jim Brown's record of 12,312 yards. He played in the Super Bowl in 1985 in a game in which he failed to score a touchdown, although his team defeated the New England Patriots, 46-10. When he retired at the end of the 1987 season, he had set NFL career records in rushing attempts, with 3,838; rushing yards, with 16,726; and rushing touchdowns, with 110. He was inducted into the Pro Football Hall of Fame in 1993. On February 2, 1999, Payton revealed that he had contracted a rare and fatal liver condition. He died at his home in Chicago on November 1, 1999.

Presley, Elvis (1935–1977) *rock singer, actor*
Born in Tupelo, Mississippi, on January 8, 1935, Elvis Presley began to sing as a boy at the Pentecostal churches that he and his parents attended. He listened extensively to the blues and to country-and-western music and, at age 10, won a school singing contest. Shortly thereafter, he taught himself how to play the guitar. In 1948, Presley moved with his family to Memphis, Tennessee, and five years later, he graduated from high school. He then worked as a truck driver and was discovered by producer Sam Phillips of Sun Records. In July 1954, Elvis recorded his first single for Sun, containing the songs "That's All Right, Mama," and "Blue Moon of Kentucky." Those who heard the record thought Elvis was black, so effectively did he communicate the blues. Presley's fledgling career coincided with the rise of rock and roll, and, in 1955, under the supervision of his personal manager "Colonel" Tom Parker, he moved to RCA records. In 1956, five of his songs reached number one in sales, including "Heartbreak Hotel," "Don't Be Cruel," and "Hound Dog." He also became an actor, appearing in the movie *Love Me Tender*. He would, in all, appear in 33 movies. His service in the army from 1958 to 1960

interrupted his career, but when he returned to civilian life, he resumed his acting and singing with such hit singles as "It's Now or Never," "Good Luck Charm," and "Return to Sender." When the British rock invasion began in 1964 with the Beatles, Presley faded from the music scene. He made a comeback, however, in 1969 with the singles "In the Ghetto" and "Suspicious Minds." Moreover, he made several tours that attracted large audiences, especially in Las Vegas. In his career, he had more singles reach the record charts than any other singer in the history of pop music. By the mid-1970s, Presley was becoming more reclusive, more dependent on drugs, and overweight. His death at age 42 was officially attributed to a heart attack but was likely the result of an overdose of barbiturates.

Reagan, Ronald (1911–2004) *actor, governor, president*
Ronald Reagan was born on February 6, 1911, in Tampico, Illinois, but at age nine, he moved with his parents to Dixon, Illinois. He liked sports at an early age and as a teenager worked as a lifeguard. In 1928, he enrolled at Eureka College (near Peoria, Illinois) and earned average grades while playing on the football team. He graduated in 1932 and began to work as a sports announcer for, first, WOC radio in Davenport and, later, WHO in Des Moines. In 1937, he took a screen test at Warner Brothers Studios in Hollywood and was offered a movie contract. His first substantial role came in 1939 when he starred in a comedy, *Brother Rat*. In 1940, he received excellent reviews for his performance as Notre Dame football player George Gipp in the movie *Knute Rockne, All American*. Reagan spent World War II making films for the military and for Warner Brothers, though he later told people he had fought overseas. In the 1950s, Reagan, a Democrat and for several years head of a union called the Screen Actors Guild, began to shift to the Republican Party, and he made several speeches condemning bureaucratic waste and what he called the dangers of a welfare state. In 1960, he campaigned for Richard Nixon, and in 1966, he ran for governor of California, backed by some of the state's wealthiest and most conservative businessmen. They intended that he eventually become president, and in 1976, the by then former governor sought the Republican nomination. He failed, however, to dislodge the incumbent Republican president, Gerald Ford. Still, he ran a strong race in the primaries and

appealed to conservatives. In 1980, he again sought the nomination. This time he won and went on to defeat the incumbent Democrat, Jimmy Carter. Enormously popular, he easily won reelection in 1984 over his Democratic challenger, Walter Mondale. Reagan's two terms were marked by some notable successes: restored pride in America, an economic revival in the mid-1980s, tax cuts, and policies that contributed to the end of the cold war. They were also marked by some failures: an economic downturn, the promotion of policies that favored the wealthy, and the Iran-contra scandal in which Reagan and his aides violated congressional law. Of 14 persons charged with criminal acts in the scandal, 11 were either convicted of felonies or pleaded guilty to felonies or misdemeanors. Reagan left the White House with a public approval rating of 50 percent, an unusually high number for an exiting president. He retired to his home in Los Angeles, where, in 1990, he wrote his autobiography, *An American Life*. In 1994, in a letter to the American public, he disclosed that he had been diagnosed with Alzheimer's disease. He died on June 5, 2004, at his home in California at age 93, making him the longest-lived president in American history.

Robinson, Frank (1935–) *professional baseball player, manager*
Born in Beaumont, Texas, Frank Robinson joined the Cincinnati Reds in 1956 and made an immediate impression on baseball fans by hitting 38 home runs and leading the National League in runs scored with 122. He won the rookie of the year award. During his career, he played outfield and first base. In 1966, he was traded to the Baltimore Orioles of the American League and won the Triple Crown with a .316 batting average, 49 home runs, and 122 RBIs. He led the league in runs scored and slugging percentage and was designated the most valuable player, complementing the same award that he had won earlier in the National League and making him the first player to be named MVP in both leagues. He was traded to the Los Angeles Dodgers in 1971 and played briefly for the California Angels before being traded to the Cleveland Indians. In 1975, he became player-manager for the Indians, making him the first African American to manage a major league team. He managed the San Francisco Giants from 1981 to 1984 and the Baltimore Orioles from 1988 to 1991. Robinson was inducted into the National Baseball Hall of Fame in 1982 based on his career record of a .294

batting average, with 2,943 hits, 1,829 runs scored, and 1,812 RBIs.

Rockefeller, Nelson (1908–1979) *governor, vice president*

The second son of Abby Aldrich and John D. Rockefeller, Jr., and the grandson of oil tycoon John D. Rockefeller, Nelson Rockefeller was born on July 8, 1908, in Bar Harbor, Maine. In 1930, he graduated from Dartmouth College with a degree in economics. He then managed several of his family's businesses, including banking, real estate, and oil refining. In 1940, President Franklin Roosevelt appointed Rockefeller coordinator of inter-American affairs, and in 1944, he became assistant secretary of state in charge of relations with Latin America. Under President Harry Truman, Rockefeller served as chairman of the Advisory Board on International Development for the Point Four Program, intended to help developing nations with their economies. Rockefeller entered elected politics in 1958 when he ran as a Republican for governor of New York. He won that year and three more times, in 1962, 1966, and 1970. He added several new campuses to the state university system and created 50 state parks. He sought the Republican presidential nomination in 1960, 1964, and 1968, each time losing. His last term as governor was marred by the controversy surrounding the prison riot at Attica, as critics blasted him for the tactics used there. Rockefeller resigned as governor in 1973 to work with two independent commissions. On August 20, 1974, President Gerald Ford nominated him to serve as vice president, and Congress confirmed him. He took office on December 19. In 1975, he investigated the activities of the Central Intelligence Agency. He ran with Ford on the Republican ticket in 1976. When they lost, he returned to New York City and concentrated on collecting art and working for charities. He died from a heart attack on January 26, 1979.

Sirica, John (1904–1992) *judge*

The federal judge who presided over the Watergate trials, John Sirica was born in Waterbury, Connecticut, and received a law degree from Georgetown University in 1926. He engaged in private practice from 1926 until 1934, served as assistant U.S. attorney for the District of Columbia from 1930 to 1934, and then returned to private practice. He was appointed a U.S. district judge for the District of Columbia in 1957 and earned the nickname "Maximum John" for his stringent sentencing. He became chief judge of the district court in 1971, and when the original seven Watergate defendants were brought before his court, because of its importance, he decided to handle the trial himself rather than to assign it to another judge. Five of the defendants pleaded guilty, and two were convicted. One defendant, John McCord, wrote a letter to Sirica revealing that witnesses had lied and that the Watergate break-in involved high ranking officials in the White House. Sirica applied unremitting pressure to get several witnesses to talk and to reveal the facts behind the case. He granted the request by special prosecutor Archibald Cox requiring President Richard Nixon to turn over a number of Watergate tapes. He also granted a request by Cox's successor, Leon Jaworski, requiring Nixon to release an additional 64 tapes. Sirica retired from the bench in 1986.

Steinem, Gloria (1934–) *feminist*

Born on March 25, 1934, in Toledo, Ohio, Gloria Steinem became a leading feminist and journalist, most known as the founding editor of *Ms.* magazine. In 1956, Steinem graduated from Smith College in Massachusetts with a degree in political science. That summer, she traveled to India and discovered there what her biographer, Carolyn G. Heilbrun, calls "the political focus of her life," namely "a strong concern for the disadvantaged." She found also an outlet for her writing when she published freelance articles in Indian newspapers. Steinem returned to the United States in 1958 and, two years later, landed her first job with a magazine. In 1963, Steinem's first article reached print when *Esquire* published her story about the sexual revolution. Her writing gained little recognition, however, until 1968 when her "City Politic" column began to appear in *New York*. In the late 1960s, Steinem became an activist for feminist causes. She joined with Betty Friedan, Bella Abzug, and Shirley Chisholm in 1971 to form the National Women's Political Caucus. A meeting with other feminists later that year gave her the idea to found a feminist magazine. With financing from publisher Clay S. Felker, she published the first issue of *Ms.* in January 1973. It contained a petition that called for the legalization of abortions, and it sold out within eight days. During the following summer, *Ms.* appeared on a regular monthly basis and featured articles such as "Down with Sexist Upbringing" and "Why Women Fear Success." Steinem believed that the oppression of women prevented them from living fuller lives, and she expressed this view in her work at *Ms.* She believed, too, that men and women should share responsibility for child rearing and household chores. In 1972, Steinem campaigned for the Equal Rights Amendment. Three years later, she attended the International Women's Year Conference in Mexico City as an observer. In 1977, she served on President Carter's commission to organize an American Conference on Women. In the 1980s, Steinem worked as a contributing editor at Random House, and in 1998, she and 14 other women purchased *Ms.,* by then a failing magazine, and revived it.

Udall, Morris (1922–1998) *congressman*

A strong protector of the environment and an advocate of congressional reform, Morris Udall was born on June 15, 1922, in St. Johns, Arizona. He served with the U.S. Army Air Force during World War II and graduated from the University of Arizona Law School in 1949, the same year that he and his brother Stewart founded the law firm of Udall & Udall in Tucson. Morris Udall served in local offices before being elected in 1961 to Congress as a Democrat to complete the term of his brother, who had been appointed by President Kennedy as secretary of the Interior. Morris Udall advocated reform of the House seniority system and in 1969 tried, but failed, to replace the incumbent House speaker. In 1977, he became chairman of the Committee on Interior and Insular Affairs. While in that post until he retired from Congress in 1991, he pushed vigorously for environmental legislation. He helped write the 1977 strip-mining legislation, the 1980 Alaska Lands Act, and a 1982 nuclear waste act. Under his guidance, Congress added 8 million acres in 20 states to the federal wilderness system. Udall sought the Democratic presidential nomination in 1976 but lost several close primaries to Jimmy Carter. In 1996, President Bill Clinton awarded Udall the Presidential Medal of Freedom. Udall died on December 12, 1998, from Parkinson's disease.

Wallace, George (1919–1998) *governor*

Segregationist governor of Alabama and three-time candidate for president, George Corley Wallace was born in Clio, Alabama. Educated at the University of Alabama, he served as assistant attorney general of the state, held a seat in the state legislature, and sat on the bench as a district court judge before being elected governor in 1963. Wallace found his electoral niche when he appealed to white segregationists. He vowed

that he would never allow the University of Alabama to admit blacks, and when the federal government ordered him to desegregate the school, he personally stood in a college doorway to block an African American from entering the premises. Federal troops, however, forced him to relent. In 1966, ineligible to succeed himself, Wallace had his wife, Lurleen Burns Wallace, run for governor. Her victory assured George Wallace's continued power in the state house. At the same time, in 1968, he ran for president under the banner of the American Independent Party and received more than 13 percent of the popular vote, along with 46 electoral votes from five southern states, a result of his platform emphasizing law and order, a reduction of federal power, and efforts to block desegregation. He was elected governor in 1970 and, in 1972, decided to seek the Democratic presidential nomination. A would-be assassin shot and partially paralyzed Wallace on May 15, 1972, in Laurel, Maryland. In 1974, Wallace won reelection as governor of Alabama, and in 1976, he again sought the presidency, only to fail for a third time. He left the governor's office in 1979 and then was reelected in 1982. He retired in 1987.

Wolfe, Tom (1931–) *journalist, novelist*

Tom Wolfe, one of the leading practitioners of New Journalism, was born in Richmond, Virginia. In 1951, he graduated from Washington and Lee University, and in 1957, he received a doctorate in American studies from Yale University. He then worked as a reporter at several different newspapers. Two books of his essays were followed by *The Electric Kool-Aid Acid Test,* his 1968 story of novelist Ken Kesey and Kesey's countercultural Merry Pranksters. As a New Journalist, Wolfe believed in making his nonfiction stories read like novels and in communicating feeling as much as factual accuracy. His *The Right Stuff,* published in 1979, chronicled the early days of the American space program. He published his first novel in 1987, titled *The Bonfire of the Vanities,* which was meant to reveal and criticize the materialistic greed of the decade. Other novels followed in 1996, 1998, 2000, and 2004.

Young, Andrew (1932–) *diplomat, civil rights activist*

Andrew Young was born on March 22, 1932, in New Orleans, Louisiana, and graduated in 1951 from Howard University. He also graduated from Hartford Theological Seminary in Connecticut and, in 1955, became the pastor of Bethany Congregational Church in Thomasville, Georgia. In 1961, he joined the Southern Christian Leadership Conference (SCLC), the civil rights group that was founded and led by Martin Luther King, Jr. For the SCLC, he helped organize "citizenship schools," which taught nonviolent protest tactics to African Americans. Young became executive director of the SCLC in 1964 and was a leader in organizing voter-registration drives and desegregation efforts in several Southern cities. In 1972, he ran for Congress in Georgia as a Democrat, and his victory made him the first African American to be elected to the House of Representatives from that state since Reconstruction. As a congressman, he championed programs for poor people and opposed increases in military spending. In 1977, President Carter appointed him U.S. ambassador to the United Nations. He resigned in 1979 over a controversy involving his meeting with a representative of the Palestine Liberation Organization. Two years later, he was elected mayor of Atlanta. He won reelection in 1985 but then lost his 1990 campaign for the Democratic nomination for governor. He subsequently became a professor at Georgia State University's Andrew Young School of Policy Studies and was co-chair of the Atlanta Committee for the 1996 Olympic Games.

APPENDIX C
Maps and Graphs

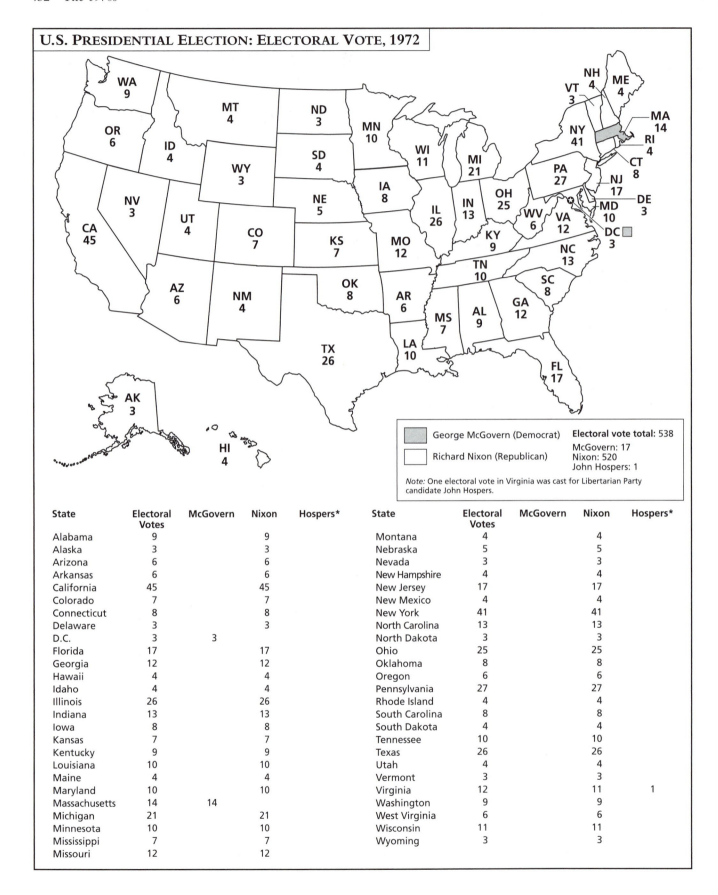

U.S. PRESIDENTIAL ELECTION: ELECTORAL VOTE, 1972

George McGovern (Democrat)	Richard Nixon (Republican)
Electoral vote total: 538	McGovern: 17 / Nixon: 520 / John Hospers: 1

Note: One electoral vote in Virginia was cast for Libertarian Party candidate John Hospers.

State	Electoral Votes	McGovern	Nixon	Hospers*	State	Electoral Votes	McGovern	Nixon	Hospers*
Alabama	9		9		Montana	4		4	
Alaska	3		3		Nebraska	5		5	
Arizona	6		6		Nevada	3		3	
Arkansas	6		6		New Hampshire	4		4	
California	45		45		New Jersey	17		17	
Colorado	7		7		New Mexico	4		4	
Connecticut	8		8		New York	41		41	
Delaware	3		3		North Carolina	13		13	
D.C.	3	3			North Dakota	3		3	
Florida	17		17		Ohio	25		25	
Georgia	12		12		Oklahoma	8		8	
Hawaii	4		4		Oregon	6		6	
Idaho	4		4		Pennsylvania	27		27	
Illinois	26		26		Rhode Island	4		4	
Indiana	13		13		South Carolina	8		8	
Iowa	8		8		South Dakota	4		4	
Kansas	7		7		Tennessee	10		10	
Kentucky	9		9		Texas	26		26	
Louisiana	10		10		Utah	4		4	
Maine	4		4		Vermont	3		3	
Maryland	10		10		Virginia	12		11	1
Massachusetts	14	14			Washington	9		9	
Michigan	21		21		West Virginia	6		6	
Minnesota	10		10		Wisconsin	11		11	
Mississippi	7		7		Wyoming	3		3	
Missouri	12		12						

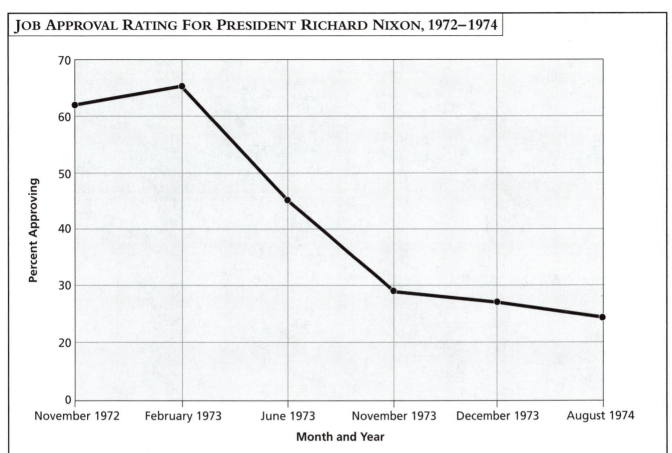

JOB APPROVAL RATING FOR PRESIDENT RICHARD NIXON, 1972–1974

Note: The November 1973 figure is for shortly after President Nixon fired special prosecutor Archibald Cox; December 1973 is for shortly after gap was discovered in a Watergate tape; August 1974 is for shortly after a House committee voted to impeach the president.
Source: Gallup Poll.

U.S. Presidential Election: Electoral Vote, 1976

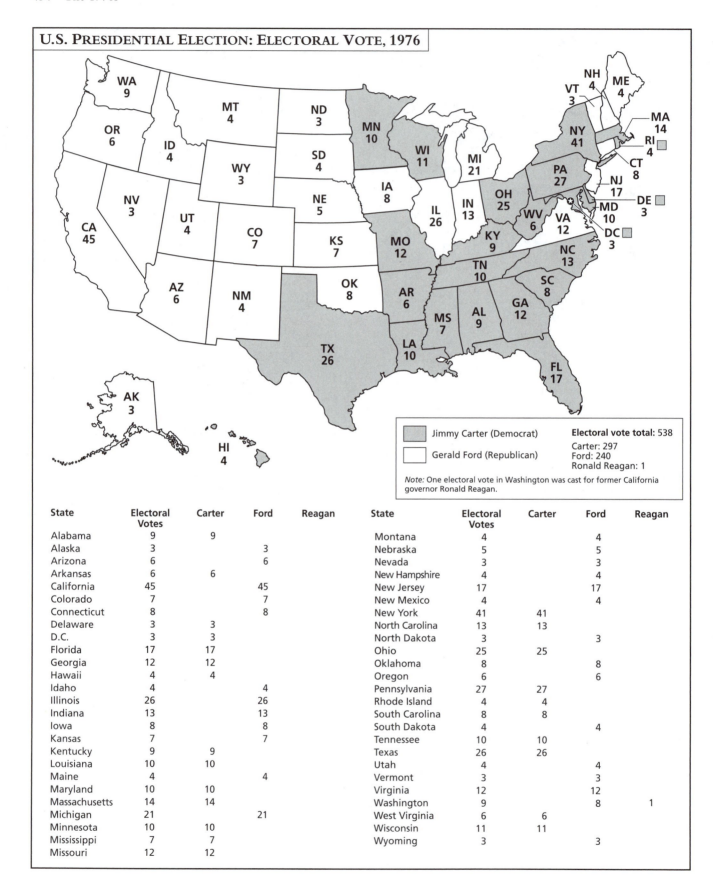

Legend	
▨	Jimmy Carter (Democrat)
☐	Gerald Ford (Republican)

Electoral vote total: 538

Carter: 297
Ford: 240
Ronald Reagan: 1

Note: One electoral vote in Washington was cast for former California governor Ronald Reagan.

State	Electoral Votes	Carter	Ford	Reagan	State	Electoral Votes	Carter	Ford	Reagan
Alabama	9	9			Montana	4		4	
Alaska	3		3		Nebraska	5		5	
Arizona	6		6		Nevada	3		3	
Arkansas	6	6			New Hampshire	4		4	
California	45		45		New Jersey	17		17	
Colorado	7		7		New Mexico	4		4	
Connecticut	8		8		New York	41	41		
Delaware	3	3			North Carolina	13	13		
D.C.	3	3			North Dakota	3		3	
Florida	17	17			Ohio	25	25		
Georgia	12	12			Oklahoma	8		8	
Hawaii	4	4			Oregon	6		6	
Idaho	4		4		Pennsylvania	27	27		
Illinois	26		26		Rhode Island	4	4		
Indiana	13		13		South Carolina	8	8		
Iowa	8		8		South Dakota	4		4	
Kansas	7		7		Tennessee	10	10		
Kentucky	9	9			Texas	26	26		
Louisiana	10	10			Utah	4		4	
Maine	4		4		Vermont	3		3	
Maryland	10	10			Virginia	12		12	
Massachusetts	14	14			Washington	9		8	1
Michigan	21		21		West Virginia	6	6		
Minnesota	10	10			Wisconsin	11	11		
Mississippi	7	7			Wyoming	3		3	
Missouri	12	12							

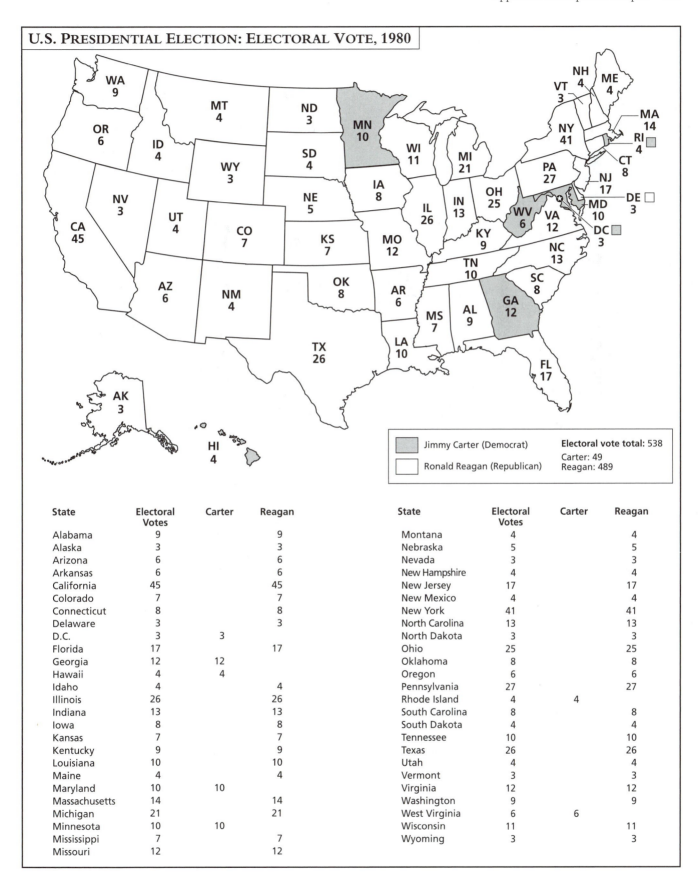

U.S. PRESIDENTIAL ELECTION: ELECTORAL VOTE, 1980

Jimmy Carter (Democrat)

Ronald Reagan (Republican)

Electoral vote total: 538
Carter: 49
Reagan: 489

State	Electoral Votes	Carter	Reagan
Alabama	9		9
Alaska	3		3
Arizona	6		6
Arkansas	6		6
California	45		45
Colorado	7		7
Connecticut	8		8
Delaware	3		3
D.C.	3	3	
Florida	17		17
Georgia	12	12	
Hawaii	4	4	
Idaho	4		4
Illinois	26		26
Indiana	13		13
Iowa	8		8
Kansas	7		7
Kentucky	9		9
Louisiana	10		10
Maine	4		4
Maryland	10	10	
Massachusetts	14		14
Michigan	21		21
Minnesota	10	10	
Mississippi	7		7
Missouri	12		12
Montana	4		4
Nebraska	5		5
Nevada	3		3
New Hampshire	4		4
New Jersey	17		17
New Mexico	4		4
New York	41		41
North Carolina	13		13
North Dakota	3		3
Ohio	25		25
Oklahoma	8		8
Oregon	6		6
Pennsylvania	27		27
Rhode Island	4	4	
South Carolina	8		8
South Dakota	4		4
Tennessee	10		10
Texas	26		26
Utah	4		4
Vermont	3		3
Virginia	12		12
Washington	9		9
West Virginia	6	6	
Wisconsin	11		11
Wyoming	3		3

PUBLIC CONFIDENCE IN INSTITUTIONS, 1966–1979

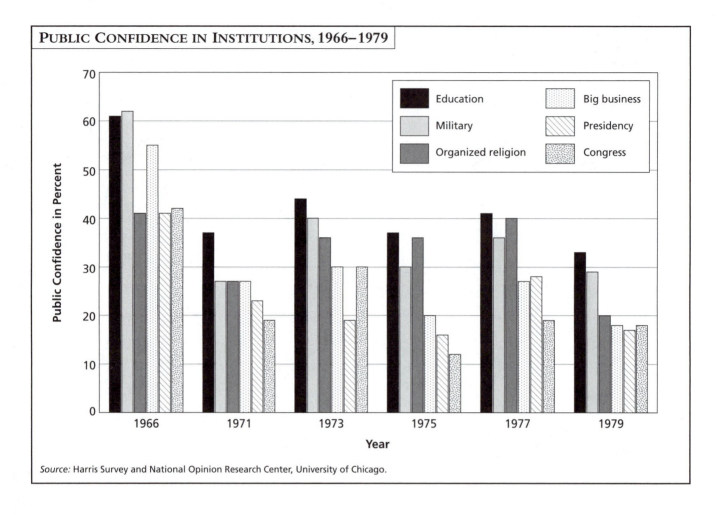

Source: Harris Survey and National Opinion Research Center, University of Chicago.

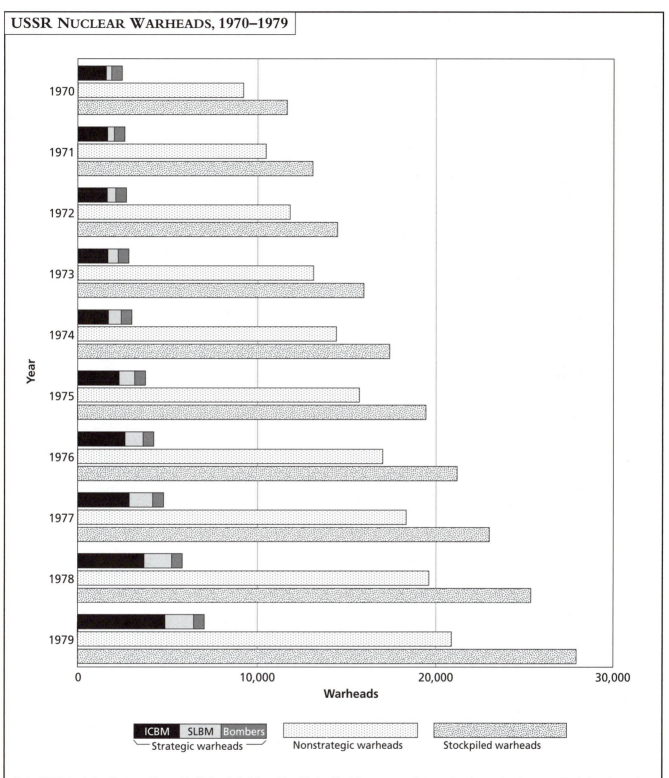

USSR NUCLEAR WARHEADS, 1970–1979

Legend: ICBM | SLBM | Bombers — Strategic warheads | Nonstrategic warheads | Stockpiled warheads

X-axis: Warheads (0, 10,000, 20,000, 30,000)

Y-axis: Year (1970–1979)

Note: ICBM stands for "intercontinental ballistic missile" (capable of being fired from one continent to another, such as between North America and Europe); *SLBM* stands for "strategic long-range ballistic missile" (capable of traveling long distances, generally within a single continent, such as between western and eastern Europe; nonstrategic warheads are nuclear weapons meant primarily to support troops in the field and include certain types of ballistic missiles.
Source: Hamilton, Neil A., *Atlas of the Baby Boom Generation,* New York: Macmillan Reference, 2000.

U.S. NUCLEAR WARHEADS, 1970–1979

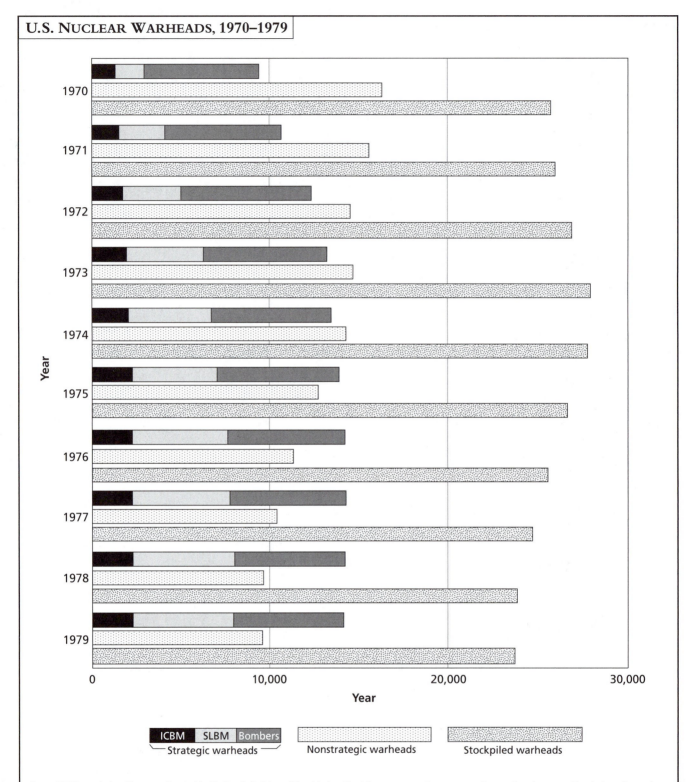

Note: ICBM stands for "intercontinental ballistic missile" (capable of being fired from one continent to another, such as between North America and Europe); SLBM stands for "strategic long-range ballistic missile" (capable of traveling long distances, generally within a single continent, such as between western and eastern Europe; nonstrategic warheads are nuclear weapons meant primarily to support troops in the field and include certain types of ballistic missiles.

Source: Hamilton, Neil A., Atlas of the Baby Boom Generation, New York: Macmillan Reference, 2000.

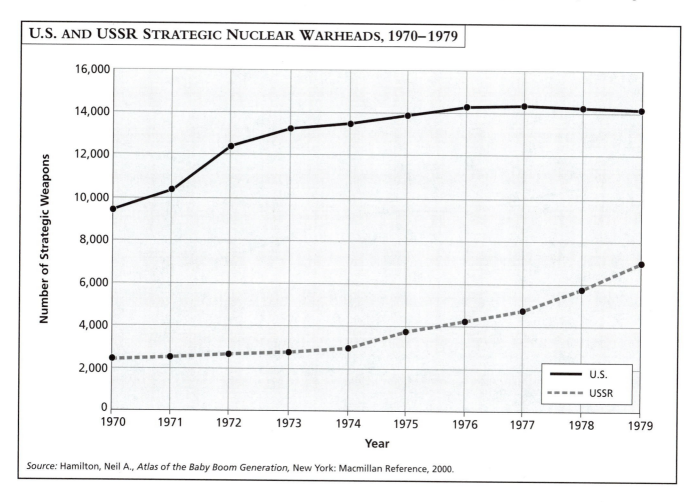

U.S. AND USSR STRATEGIC NUCLEAR WARHEADS, 1970–1979

Source: Hamilton, Neil A., *Atlas of the Baby Boom Generation,* New York: Macmillan Reference, 2000.

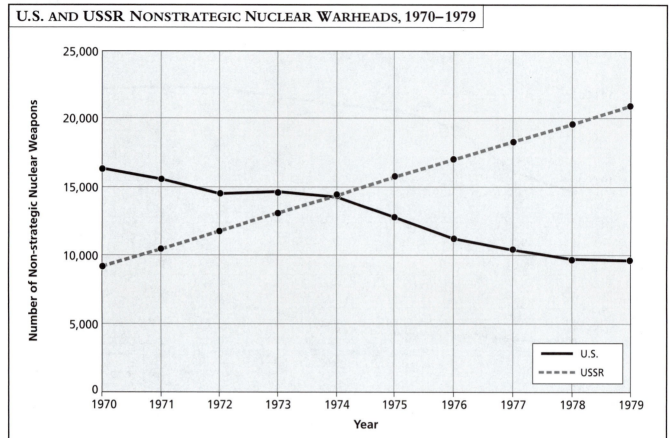

U.S. AND USSR NONSTRATEGIC NUCLEAR WARHEADS, 1970–1979

Note: Nonstrategic warheads are nuclear weapons meant primarily to support troops in the field and include certain types of ballistic missiles.
Source: Hamilton, Neil A., *Atlas of the Baby Boom Generation,* New York: Macmillan Reference, 2000.

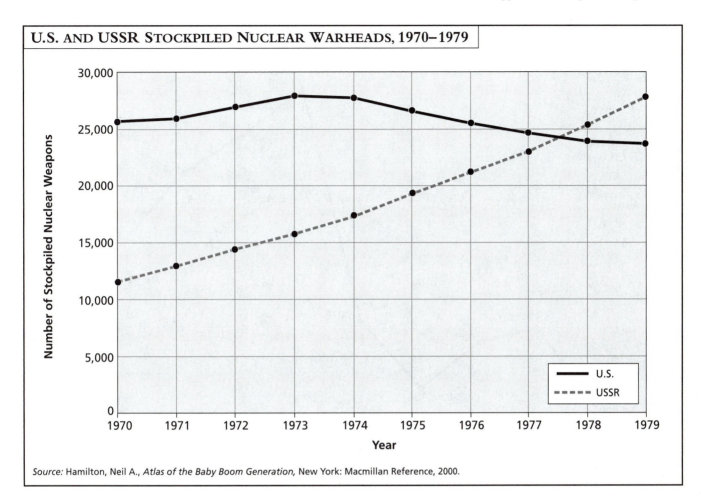

U.S. AND USSR STOCKPILED NUCLEAR WARHEADS, 1970–1979

Source: Hamilton, Neil A., *Atlas of the Baby Boom Generation,* New York: Macmillan Reference, 2000.

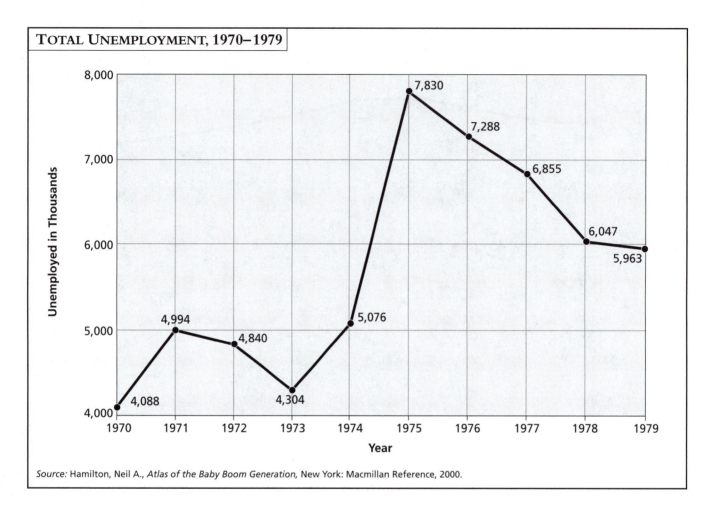

TOTAL UNEMPLOYMENT, 1970–1979

Source: Hamilton, Neil A., *Atlas of the Baby Boom Generation,* New York: Macmillan Reference, 2000.

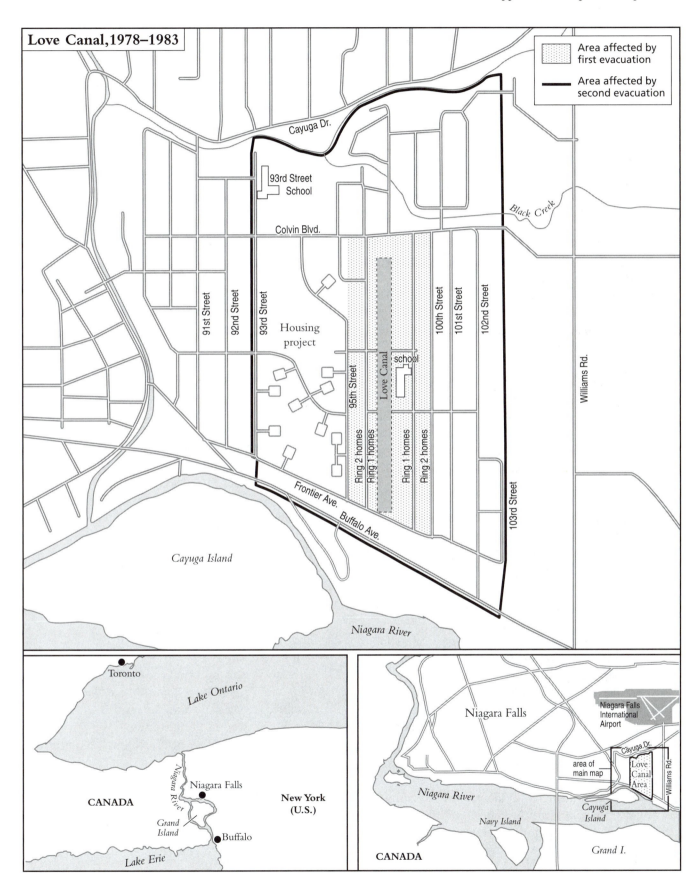

Love Canal, 1978–1983

Area affected by first evacuation

Area affected by second evacuation

Cayuga Dr.

93rd Street School

Colvin Blvd.

Black Creek

91st Street

92nd Street

93rd Street

Housing project

95th Street

Love Canal

school

100th Street

101st Street

102nd Street

Williams Rd.

103rd Street

Ring 2 homes

Ring 1 homes

Ring 1 homes

Ring 2 homes

Frontier Ave.

Buffalo Ave.

Cayuga Island

Niagara River

Toronto

Lake Ontario

Niagara River

Niagara Falls

CANADA

Grand Island

New York (U.S.)

Buffalo

Lake Erie

Niagara Falls

Niagara Falls International Airport

Niagara River

area of main map

Cayuga Dr.

Love Canal Area

Williams Rd.

Cayuga Island

CANADA

Navy Island

Grand I.

NOTES

INTRODUCTION

1. Neil A. Hamilton. *The ABC-CLIO Guide to the 1960s Counterculture in America.* Santa Barbara, Calif.: ABC-CLIO, 1991, p. xiii.
2. Hamilton. *The ABC-CLIO Guide to the 1960s Counterculture in America.* p. xiv.
3. Terry H. Anderson. *The Movement and the Sixties.* New York: Oxford University Press, 1995, p. 251.
4. Tom Wolfe. "The Me Decade and the Third Great Awakening." In *Tom Wolfe: The Purple Decades.* New York: Farrar, Straus, 1982, p. 293.
5. Neil Hamilton. *Atlas of the Baby Boom Generation.* New York: Macmillan Reference, 2000, p. 136.
6. Hamilton. *Atlas of the Baby Boom Generation.* p. 129.
7. Hamilton. *Atlas of the Baby Boom Generation.* p. 123.

1. DIVIDED AMERICA: JANUARY 1970– DECEMBER 1970

1. Anthony Lukas. "Disorder Erupts at Chicago Trial after Judge Jails a Defendant for Using a Vulgarity." *New York Times,* February 3, 1970, p. 18.
2. Lukas. "Disorder Erupts at Chicago Trial after Judge Jails a Defendant for Using a Vulgarity."
3. Anthony Lukas. "Chicago 7 Defense Claims U.S. Concocted Case to Justify Police Violence." *New York Times,* February 12, 1970, p. 20.
4. Todd Gitlin. *The Sixties: Years of Hope, Days of Rage.* New York: Bantam Books, 1993, p. 401.
5. Robert A. Wright. "Youths Battle Police on Coast." *New York Times,* February 27, 1970, p. 1.
6. Bill Ayers. *Fugitive Days: A Memoir.* New York: Penguin Books, 2001, p. 184.
7. Michael T. Kaufman. "Underground Exciting to Gold." *New York Times,* March 13, 1970, p. 27.
8. Kaufman. "Underground Exciting to Gold."
9. Rachel Carson. *Silent Spring.* Boston: Houghton Mifflin, 1994; reprint 1962, pp. 15–16.
10. Joseph Lelyveld. "Millions Join Earth Day Observances across the Nation." *New York Times,* April 23, 1970, p. 1.
11. Lelyveld. "Millions Join Earth Day Observances across the Nation."
12. "The Good Earth." *New York Times,* April 21, 1970, p. 36.
13. Barry Commoner. *The Closing Circle.* New York: Bantam, 1972, p. 293.
14. Commoner. *The Closing Circle.* p. 298.
15. Commoner. *The Closing Circle.* p. 299.
16. Marc Grossman. *The ABC-CLIO Companion to the Environmental Movement.* Santa Barbara, Calif.: ABC-CLIO, 1994, p. 85.
17. Irwin Unger and Debi Unger, eds. *The Times They Were a Changin': The Sixties Reader.* New York: Three Rivers Press, 1998, p. 74.
18. "President Nixon's Speech on Cambodia, April 30, 1970." Available online. URL: http://vietnam.vassar.edu/doc15.html. Downloaded on November 11, 2004.
19. William F. Chafe. *The Unfinished Journey: America since World War II,* 4th ed. New York: Oxford University Press, 1999, p. 397.
20. Linda Charlton. "Big Rallies Are Planned." *New York Times,* May 2, 1970, p. 1.
21. "Protest Season on the Campus." *Time,* May 11, 1970. In *Time Magazine Multimedia Almanac.* Cambridge, Mass.: Softkey International, 1995.
22. "Protest Season on the Campus."
23. Stanley Karnow. *Vietnam.* New York: Viking Press, 1983, p. 611.
24. Milton Viorst. *Fire in the Streets: America in the 1960s.* New York: Simon and Schuster, 1979, p. 507.
25. Chrissie Hynde. "On Kent State." In Ashley Kahn, Holly George Warren, and Shawn Dahl, eds. *Rolling Stone: The Seventies.* Boston: Little, Brown, 1998, p. 24.

26. "Kent State: May 1–4, 1970." May Fourth Task Force. Available online. URL: http://dept.kent.edu/may4/chrono.htm. Downloaded December 15, 2003.

27. Ernie Kosnac. "Three Decades of Remembrance at Kent State." Available online. URL: http://burrkent.edu/archives/may4/brother/brother3.html. Downloaded December 17, 2003.

28. John Kifner. "4 Kent State Students Killed by Troops." *New York Times,* May 5, 1970, p. 1.

29. Douglas T. Miller. *On Our Own: America in the Sixties.* Lexington, Mass.: D. C. Heath, 1996, p. 293.

30. Robert D. McFadden. "College Strife Spreads." *New York Times,* May 8, 1970, p. 1.

31. Jerry M. Flint. "Ohio Guardsmen Defend Shooting of Kent Students." *New York Times,* May 7, 1970, p. 19.

32. Alan King. "Four Dead in Ohio: Memories of Kent State." *Milwaukee Journal Sentinel,* April 30, 2000. Available online. URL: http://www.jsonline.com/news/editorials/apr00/king30042900.asp. Downloaded December 15, 2003.

33. "The South: Death in Two Cities." *Time,* May 25, 1970, p. 22–23.

34. Tom Bates. *Rads: The 1970 Bombing of the Army Math Research Center at the University of Wisconsin and Its Aftermath.* New York: HarperCollins, 1992, photo insert.

35. "Veterans Testify at Blast Hearings." *New York Times,* October 16, 1973, p. 12.

36. "College Bomber Is Sent to Prison." *New York Times,* November 2, 1973, p. 7.

37. "College Bomber Is Sent to Prison."

38. Bates. *Rads: The 1970 Bombing of the Army Math Research Center at the University of Wisconsin and Its Aftermath.* p. 427.

39. Robin Morgan, ed. *Sisterhood Is Powerful: An Anthology of Writing from the Women's Liberation Movement.* New York: Vintage Books, 1970, p. 408.

40. Walter Sullivan. "Apollo 13: Why This Trip Is Necessary." *New York Times,* April 12, 1970, p. E9.

41. Harry Shapiro and Caesar Glebbeck. *Jimi Hendrix: Electric Gypsy.* New York: St. Martin's, 1990, p. 104.

42. "Jimi." *Rolling Stone,* October 15, 1970, p. 8.

43. Shapiro and Glebbeck. *Jimi Hendrix: Electric Gypsy.* p. 475.

44. John Burks. "An Appreciation." *Rolling Stone,* October 15, 1970, p. 8.

45. Donna Gaines. "The Ascension of Led Zeppelin." In *Rolling Stone: The Seventies.* p. 17.

46. Charles A. Reich. *The Greening of America.* New York: Random House, 1970, p. 429.

47. Reich. *The Greening of America.* p. 430.

2. POLARIZED AMERICA: JANUARY 1971–DECEMBER 1971

1. Stephen B. Roberts. "What Made Those Kids Do It?" *New York Times,* January 31, 1971, p. E2.

2. Marilyn Bardsley. "Murder!" Court TVs Crime Library. Available online. URL: http://www.crimelibrary.com/serial_killers/notorious/mansions/prosecution_7.html. Downloaded January 3, 2004.

3. Bardsley. "Murder!"

4. "Charles Manson Quotes." Available online. URL: http://members.tripod.com/mayhem44/mansonquotes/html. Downloaded January 3, 2004.

5. Stanley Karnow. *Vietnam.* New York: Viking Press, 1983, p. 629.

6. Bill Ayers. *Fugitive Days: A Memoir.* New York: Penguin Books, 2001, p. 184.

7. Ayers. *Fugitive Days: A Memoir.* p. 261.

8. William H. Chafe. *The Unfinished Journey: America since World War II.* New York: Oxford University Press, 1999, p. 295.

9. John Kifner. "Brutal Vietnam Campaign Stirs Memories and Questions." *New York Times,* December 28, 2003, p. 16.

10. Chafe. *The Unfinished Journey: America since World War II.* p. 417.

11. Neil Sheehan. *A Bright Shining Lie: John Paul Van and America in Vietnam.* New York: Vintage Books, 1988, p. 690,

12. Kifner. "Brutal Vietnam Campaign Stirs Memories and Questions."

13. Kifner. "Brutal Vietnam Campaign Stirs Memories and Questions."

14. Kifner. "Brutal Vietnam Campaign Stirs Memories and Questions."

15. Kifner. "Brutal Vietnam Campaign Stirs Memories and Questions."

16. Athan G. Theoharis. *The FBI: A Comprehensive Reference Guide.* New York: Checkmark Books, 2000, p. 125.

17. Stanley I. Kutler. *The Wars of Watergate: The Last Crisis of Richard Nixon.* New York: W. W. Norton, 1990, p. 317.

18. Robert M. Smith. "Boggs Sees Peril to U.S. from FBI." *New York Times,* April 7, 1971, p. 21.

19. Robert M. Smith. "Kleindienst Assails Boggs; Invites Inquiry into FBI." *New York Times,* April 8, 1971, p. 1.

20. John W. Finney. "Muskie Says FBI Spied at Rallies on '70s Earth Day." *New York Times,* April 15, 1971, p. 1.

21. Roy Reed. "Agnew Calls Hoover's Critics Politically Motivated." *New York Times,* April 27, 1971, p. 17.

22. Reed. "Agnew Calls Hoover's Critics Politically Motivated."

23. Richard Gid Powers. *Secrecy and Power: The Life of J. Edgar Hoover.* New York: The Free Press, 1987, p. 466.

24. Powers. *Secrecy and Power: The Life of J. Edgar Hoover.*

25. "Boggs Says Father Left FBI Dossiers." *New York Times,* January 31, 1975, p. 27.

26. Powers. *Secrecy and Power: The Life of J. Edgar Hoover.* p. 436.

27. James M. Naughton. "Judge Lets Veterans Sleep on the Mall; Rebukes U.S. Aides." *New York Times,* April 23, 1971, p. 1.

28. Jan Berry. "Why Veterans March against the War." *New York Times,* April 23, 1971, p. 37.

29. Albert L. Hurtado and Peter Iverson. *Major Problems in American Indian History.* Lexington, Mass.: Heath, 1994, p. 523.

30. "1970s Highlights—The Pentagon Papers." *Time,* June 28, 1971. In *Time Magazine Multimedia Almanac.* Cambridge, Mass.: Softkey International, 1995.

31. Hedrick Smith. "Vast Review of War Took a Year." *New York Times,* June 13, 1971, p. 1.

32. "1970s Highlights—The Pentagon Papers."

33. "Reactions Range from Support to a Charge of 'Near Treason.' " *New York Times,* June 17, 1971, p. 19.

34. Max Frankel. "The Lessons of Vietnam." *New York Times,* July 6, 1971, p. 1.

35. Thomas S. Blanton, ed. "The Secret Briefs and the Secret Evidence." National Security Archives. Available online. URL: http://www.gwo.ecu/~nsarchiv/NSAEBB/NSAEBB48. Downloaded January 17, 2004.

36. Fred Ferretti. "Attica Prisoners Win 28 Demands but Still Resist." *New York Times,* September 13, 1971, p. 1.

37. Fred Ferretti. "Like a War Zone." *New York Times,* September 14, 1971, p. 1.

38. Ferretti. "Like a War Zone."

39. Fred Ferretti. "Autopsies Show Shots Killed Nine Attica Guards, Not Knives; State Official Admits Mistake." *New York Times,* September 15, 1971, p. 1.

40. William E. Farrell. "Governor Defends Order to Quell Attica Uprising." *New York Times,* September 16, 1971, p. 1.

41. "The Rockefellers: Attica Prison Riot—September 9–13, 1971." PBS American Experience. URL: http://www.pbs.org/wgbh/amex/rockefellers/peopleevents/e_attica.html. Downloaded January 20, 2004.

42. Ferretti. "Like a War Zone."

43. Tom Wicker. "The Economic Blues." *New York Times,* August 1, 1971, p. E11.

44. *Public Papers of the Presidents of the United States: Richard Nixon, 1971.* Washington, D.C.: United States Government Printing Office, 1972, p. 886.

45. Christopher Lydon. "Reaction Mixed." *New York Times,* August 16, 1971, p. 1.

46. Radicalesbians. "The Woman Identified Woman." Special Collections Library, Duke University, 1970. Available online. URL: http://scriptorium.lib.duke.edu/wlm/womid. Accessed on September 25, 2005.

47. John Noble Wilford. "Astronauts Splash Down Close to Pacific Target to End 12-Day Moon Trip." *New York Times,* August 8, 1971, p. 1.

48. Carol Cooper. "The Soul Nation Climbs Aboard." In Ashley Kahn, Holly George-Warren, and Shawn Dahl, eds. *Rolling Stone: The Seventies.* Boston: Little, Brown, 1998, p. 44.

49. "Ali: It's a Good Feeling to Lose, but I Won." *New York Times,* March 10, 1971, p. 49.

50. Jerry Hopkins and Danny Sugarman. *No One Gets out of Here Alive.* New York: Warner, 1980, p. 373.

51. Paul J. C. Friedlander. "Miami Worries about Disney World." *New York Times,* April 4, 1971, p. XX51.

52. Jon Nordheimer. "Disney World Opens without Expected Crush." *New York Times,* October 2, 1971.

3. RESTLESS AMERICA: JANUARY 1972–DECEMBER 1972

1. *Public Papers of the Presidents of the United States: Richard Nixon, 1972.* Washington, D.C.: United States Government Printing Office, 1974, p. 26.

2. Stanley Karnow. *Vietnam.* New York: Viking Press, 1983, p. 589.
3. *Public Papers of the Presidents of the United States: Richard Nixon, 1972.* p. 104.
4. *Public Papers of the Presidents of the United States: Richard Nixon, 1972.* p. 103.
5. *Public Papers of the Presidents of the United States: Richard Nixon, 1972.* p. 105.
6. John W. Finney. "Reaction Is Mixed." *New York Times,* January 26, 1972, p. 1.
7. Richard J. Barnet and Peter Weiss. "Hanoi Rules out Partial Accord." *New York Times,* February 6, 1972, p. 1.
8. Craig R. Whitney. "Thieu, Criticizing Rogers, Rejects New Concessions." *New York Times,* February 11, 1972, p. 1.
9. Stephen E. Ambrose. *Nixon: The Triumph of a Politician, 1962–1972.* New York: Simon and Schuster, 1989, p. 527.
10. Karnow. *Vietnam.* p. 643.
11. Tad Szulc. "President Leaves on Trip to China; Stops in Hawaii." *New York Times,* February 18, 1972, p. 1.
12. Richard Reeves. *President Nixon: Alone in the White House.* New York: Simon and Schuster, 2001, p. 15.
13. Reeves. *President Nixon: Alone in the White House.* p. 685.
14. Reeves. *President Nixon: Alone in the White House.* p. 698.
15. Richard Nixon. *The Memoirs of Richard Nixon.* New York: Grosset and Dunlap, 1978, p. 559.
16. Nixon. *The Memoirs of Richard Nixon.*
17. Max Frankel. "A Quiet Greeting." *New York Times,* February 21, 1972, p. 1.
18. Stephen E. Ambrose. *Nixon: The Triumph of a Politician, 1962–1972,* vol. 2. New York: Simon and Schuster, 1989, p. 513.
19. Max Frankel. "Nixon Talks Further with Chou and Drives to View Great Wall." *New York Times,* February 24, 1972, p. 1.
20. Ambrose. *Nixon: The Triumph of a Politician, 1962–1972,* vol. 2, p. 514.
21. Max Frankel. "Statement Today by Nixon and Chou Will Define Ties." *New York Times,* February 27, 1972, p. 1.
22. Max Frankel. "China Visit Ends." *New York Times,* February 28, 1972, p. 1.
23. "President Home after China Trip; Reassures Allies." *New York Times,* February 28, 1972, p. 1.
24. "Birch Society Denunciation." *New York Times,* February 29, 1972, p. 16.
25. James Reston. "Mr. Nixon's Finest Hour." *New York Times,* March 1, 1972, p. 39.
26. Reston. "Mr. Nixon's Finest Hour."
27. Nixon. *The Memoirs of Richard Nixon.* p. 565.
28. Freed P. Graham. "Kleindienst Says He Set up Talks on ITT Accord." *New York Times,* March 3, 1972, p. 1.
29. Ambrose. *Nixon: The Triumph of a Politician, 1962–1972,* vol. 2, p. 504.
30. Ambrose. *Nixon: The Triumph of a Politician, 1962–1972,* vol. 2, p. 436.
31. *Public Papers of the Presidents of the United States: Richard Nixon, 1972.* p. 671.
32. William H. Chafe. *The Unfinished Journey: America since World War II.* New York: Oxford University Press, 1999, p. 432.
33. Dan Carter. *The Politics of Rage: George Wallace, the Origins of the New Conservatism, and the Transformation of American Politics.* Baton Rouge: Louisiana State University Press, 1995, p. 388.
34. Dan Carter. *The Politics of Rage: George Wallace, the Origins of the New Conservatism, and the Transformation of American Politics.* p. 437.
35. Dan Carter. *The Politics of Rage: George Wallace, the Origins of the New Conservatism, and the Transformation of American Politics.* p. 437.
36. Stephen Lesher. *George Wallace: American Populist.* Reading, Mass.: Addison-Wesley, 1994, p. 482.
37. James T. Wooten. "Milwaukee Man Held as Suspect." *New York Times,* May 16, 1972, p. 1.
38. Douglas Robinson. "Wallace Supporters and Opponents Denounce High Shooting and Deplore Violence." *New York Times,* May 17, 1972, p. 29.
39. Lesher. *George Wallace: American Populist.* p. 491.
40. Carter. *The Politics of Rage: George Wallace, the Origins of the New Conservatism, and the Transformation of American Politics.* p. 468.
41. Robert B. Semple, Jr. "Nixon in Ottawa Asks Recognition of Differences." *New York Times,* April 15, 1972, p. 1.
42. Ambrose. *Nixon: The Triumph of a Politician, 1962–1972,* vol. 2. p. 537.
43. Ambrose. *Nixon: The Triumph of a Politician, 1962–1972,* vol. 2. p. 539.
44. Henry Kissinger. *White House Years.* Boston: Little, Brown, 1979, p. 1,142.
45. Kissinger. *White House Years.* p. 1,141.

46. Ambrose. *Nixon: The Triumph of a Politician, 1962–1972,* vol. 2. p. 541.

47. Ambrose. *Nixon: The Triumph of a Politician, 1962–1972,* vol. 2. p. 544.

48. Nixon. *The Memoirs of Richard Nixon.* p. 609.

49. Kissinger. *White House Years.* p. 1,141.

50. Nixon. *The Memoirs of Richard Nixon.* p. 613.

51. Nixon. *The Memoirs of Richard Nixon.* p. 614.

52. Hedrick Smith. "Ceilings Are Set." *New York Times,* May 28, 1972, p. 1.

53. Ambrose. *Nixon: The Trimph of a Politician, 1962–1972,* vol. 2. p. 548.

54. Theodore Shabad. "Nixon Talks on TV to Soviet People and Hails Accord." *New York Times,* May 29, 1972, p. 1.

55. Nixon. *The Memoirs of Richard Nixon.* p. 625.

56. *Public Papers of the Presidents of the United States: Richard Nixon, 1972.* p. 363.

57. Tad Szulc. "Democratic Raid Tied to Realtor." *New York Times,* June 19, 1972, p. 1.

58. Reeves. *President Nixon: Alone in the White House.* p. 12.

59. Ambrose. *Nixon: The Triumph of a Politician, 1962–1972,* vol. 2. p. 552.

60. Ambrose. *Nixon: The Triumph of a Politician, 1962–1972,* vol. 2. p. 552.

61. Ambrose. *Nixon: The Triumph of a Politician, 1962–1972,* vol. 2. p. 553.

62. Ambrose. *Nixon: The Triumph of a Politician, 1962–1972,* vol. 2. p. 555.

63. Ambrose. *Nixon: The Triumph of a Politician, 1962–1972,* vol. 2. p. 555.

64. Stanley I. Kutler. *Abuse of Power: The New Nixon Tapes.* New Free Press, 1997, p. 69.

65. Melvin Small. *The Presidency of Richard Nixon.* Lawrence: University Press of Kansas, 1999, p. 277.

66. Small. *The Presidency of Richard Nixon.* p. 111.

67. R. W. Apple, Jr. "McGovern Says Attempt to Bug Office Was Foiled." *New York Times,* September 10, 1972, p. 48.

68. Agis Salpukas. "3 Nixon Aides among 7 Indicted in Raid in Capital." *New York Times,* September 16, 1972, p. 61.

69. "President Backs Bugging Inquiry." *New York Times,* October 6, 1972, p. 27.

70. Douglas E. Kneeland. "McGovern Says Nixon Does Not Respect Rights." *New York Times,* October 20, 1972, p. 21.

71. Stanley I. Kutler. *The Wars of Watergate: The Last Crisis of Richard Nixon.* New York: W. W. Norton, 1990, p. 255.

72. Kissinger. *White House Years.* p. 1,399.

73. Kissinger. *White House Years.* p. 1,403.

74. Kissinger. *White House Years.* p. 1,448.

75. Karnow. *Vietnam.* p. 653.

76. Murray Chass. "Players' Return Depends on Pact." *New York Times,* April 6, 1972, p. 57.

77. C. R. Ways. " 'Nobody Does Anything Better Than Me in Baseball,' Says Roberto Clemente." *New York Times,* April 9, 1972, p. SM38.

78. "Clemente, Pirates' Star, Dies in Crash of Plane Carrying Aid to Nicaragua." *New York Times,* January 2, 1973, p. 73.

79. "Nixon Pays Tribute." *New York Times,* January 3, 1973, p. 32.

4. WATERGATE AMERICA—CRISIS OF CONSCIENCE: JANUARY 1973– AUGUST 1974

1. Melvin Small. *The Presidency of Richard Nixon.* Lawrence University Press of Kansas, 1999, p. 273.

2. R. W. Apple, Jr. "Nixon Inaugurated for His Second Term: Sees World on Threshold of a Peace Era." *New York Times,* January 22, 1973, p. 1.

3. Apple. "Nixon Inaugurated for His Second Term: Sees World on Threshold of a Peace Era."

4. Stanley I. Kutler. *The Wars of Watergate: The Last Crisis of Richard Nixon.* New York: W. W. Norton, 1990, p. 255.

5. Kutler. *The Wars of Watergate: The Last Crisis of Richard Nixon.* p. 4.

6. Larry Berman. *No Peace, No Honor: Nixon, Kissinger. and Betrayal in Vietnam.* New York: The Free Press, 2001, p. 246.

7. Richard Reeves. *President Nixon: Alone in the White House.* New York: Simon and Schuster, 2001, p. 567.

8. "Justice Harry Blackmun Opinion in Roe v. Wade." Abortion Law Homepage. Available online. URL: http://members.aol.com/abtrbng/roefl-o.htm. Downloaded May 14, 2004.

9. "Justice Harry Blackmun Opinion in Roe v. Wade."

10. Small. *The Presidency of Richard Nixon.* p. 280.

11. Richard Nixon. *Six Crises.* Garden City, N. Y.: Doubleday and Company, 1962, p. xiii.

12. "Armed Indians Seize Wounded Knee, Hold Hostages." *New York Times,* March 1, 1973, p. 1.

13. Neil A. Hamilton. *Rebels and Renegades: A Chronology of Social and Political Dissent in the United States.* New York: Routledge, 2002, p. 281.

14. Hamilton. *Rebels and Renegades: A Chronology of Social and Political Dissent in the United States.* p. 282.

15. Walter Rugaber. "Watergate Spy Defendants Were under 'Political Pressure' to Admit Guilt and Keep Silent." *New York Times,* March 24, 1973, p. 1.

16. Kutler. *The Wars of Watergate: The Last Crisis of Richard Nixon.* p. 266.

17. Small. *The Presidency of Richard Nixon.* p. 281.

18. Kutler. *The Wars of Watergate: The Last Crisis of Richard Nixon.* p. 4.

19. Nixon. *Six Crises.* p. xiv.

20. Walter Rugaber. "McCord Testifies His Fellow Plotters Linked High Nixon Aides to Watergate." *New York Times,* March 30, 1973, p. 1.

21. Stephen Ambrose. *Nixon: Ruin and Recovery, 1973–1990.* New York: Simon and Schuster, 1991, pp. 116–117.

22. R. W. Apple, Jr. "Nixon Reports 'Major' Findings In Watergate Inquiry He Made." *New York Times,* April 18, 1973, p. 1.

23. Kutler. *The Wars of Watergate: The Last Crisis of Richard Nixon.* pp. 308–309.

24. William Safire. "Comeback Time." *New York Times,* April 19, 1973, p. 43.

25. Kutler. *The Wars of Watergate: The Last Crisis of Richard Nixon.* p. 319.

26. John Dean III. *Blind Ambition: The White House Years.* New York: Simon and Schuster, 1976, p. 275.

27. Nixon. *Six Crises.* p. xv.

28. "Ellsberg Trial Gave Unusual Insight on Intrusion of Executive Branch into Judicial Process." *New York Times,* May 12, 1973, p. 15.

29. Martin Arnold. "Pentagon Papers Are Dismissed by Court." *New York Times,* May 12, 1973, p. 1.

30. *Public Papers of the Presidents of the United States: Richard Nixon, 1973.* Washington, D.C.: United States Government Printing Office, 1975, p. 549.

31. *Public Papers of the Presidents of the United States: Richard Nixon, 1973.* p. 551.

32. *Public Papers of the Presidents of the United States: Richard Nixon, 1973.* p. 553.

33. Richard Nixon. *The Memoirs of Richard Nixon.* New York: Grosset and Dunlap, 1978, p. 887.

34. Ambrose. *Nixon: Ruin and Recovery, 1973–1990.* p. 178.

35. Douglas E. Kneeland. "Ex-Counsel, Cool and Dogged, Reads 6-Hour Story to the Nation." *New York Times,* June 26, 1973, p. 30.

36. Ambrose. *Nixon: Ruin and Recovery, 1973–1990.* p. 183.

37. Dean. *Blind Ambition: The White House Years.* p. 327.

38. James M. Naughton. "Surprise Witness." *New York Times,* July 17, 1973, p. 1.

39. Kutler. *The Wars of Watergate: The Last Crisis of Richard Nixon.* p. 369.

40. Kutler. *The Wars of Watergate: The Last Crisis of Richard Nixon.* p. 376.

41. Ambrose. *Nixon: Ruin and Recovery, 1973–1990.* p. 201.

42. Nixon. *The Memoirs of Richard Nixon.* p. 490.

43. Ambrose. *Nixon: Ruin and Recovery, 1973–1990.* pp. 240–241.

44. Ambrose. *Nixon: Ruin and Recovery, 1973–1990.* pp. 254–255.

45. Elizabeth Becker. "On New Kissinger Tapes, Crisis in White House and the World." *New York Times,* May 27, 2004, p. 1.

46. Ambrose. *Nixon: Ruin and Recovery, 1973–1990.* p. 257.

47. Ambrose. *Nixon: Ruin and Recovery, 1973–1990.* p. 224.

48. Ambrose. *Nixon: Ruin and Recovery, 1973–1990.*

49. Small. *The Presidency of Richard Nixon.* p. 290.

50. Ambrose. *Nixon: Ruin and Recovery, 1973–1990.* p. 249.

51. Nixon. *Six Crises.* p. xiv.

52. Nixon. *Six Crises.* p. 261.

53. *Public Papers of the Presidents of the United States: Richard Nixon, 1973.* p. 956.

54. Nixon. *Six Crises.* p. xv.

55. "Nixon Resigns." *Time,* August 5, 1974. In *Time Magazine Multimedia Almanac.* Cambridge, Mass.: Softkey International, 1955.

56. Ambrose. *Nixon: Ruin and Recovery, 1973–1990.* p. 395.

57. Ambrose. *Nixon: Ruin and Recovery, 1973–1990.* p. 416.

58. Small. *The Presidency of Richard Nixon.* p. 295.

59. Nixon. *Six Crises.* p. xvi.

60. Nixon. *Six Crises.* p. xvi.

61. *Public Papers of the Presidents of the United States: Richard Nixon, Containing the Public Messages, Speeches, and Statements of the Presidents, January 1 to August 9, 1974.* Washington, D.C.: United States Government Printing Office, 1975, p. 627.

62. John Herbers. "Nixon Resigns the Presidency Effective at Noon Today." *New York Times,* August 9, 1974, p. 1.
63. John Noble Wilford. "Astronauts Back, Weak and Wobbly." *New York Times,* June 23, 1973, p. 1.
64. Joseph Wallace, Neil Hamilton and Marty Appel. *Baseball: 100 Classic Moments in the History of the Game.* New York: Dorling Kindersley, 2000.
65. Al Trautwig. "The Doctor of Dunk." In Ashley Kahn, Holly George-Warren, and Shawn Dahl, eds. *Rolling Stone: The Seventies.* Boston: Little, Brown, 1998, p. 114.
66. Trautwig. "The Doctor of Dunk." p. 115.

5. WATERGATE AMERICA—FAITH NO MORE: AUGUST 1974–1975

1. "Nixon's Final Remarks to the White House Staff." Watergate. info. Available online. URL: http://watergate.info/nixon/74-08-09finalremarks.shtml. Downloaded June 6, 2004.
2. Melvin Small. *The Presidency of Richard Nixon.* Lawrence: University Press of Kansas, 1999, p. 296.
3. Marjorie Hunter. "A Plea to Bind up Watergate Wounds." *New York Times,* August 10, 1974, p. 1.
4. Hunter. "A Plea to Bind up Watergate Wounds."
5. Neil A. Hamilton. *Presidents: A Biographical Dictionary.* New York: Checkmark Books, 2001, p. 322.
6. Stephen Ambrose. *Nixon: Ruin and Recovery, 1973–1990.* New York: Simon and Schuster, 1991, pp. 459–460.
7. Gerald R. Ford. *A Time to Heal.* New York: Harper and Row, 1979, p. 161.
8. John Erlichman. *Witness to Power: The Nixon Years.* New York: Simon and Schuster, 1982, p. 410.
9. Hamilton. *Presidents: A Biographical Dictionary.* p. 326.
10. Ambrose. *Nixon: Ruin and Recovery, 1973–1990.* p. 462.
11. Ambrose. *Nixon: Ruin and Recovery, 1973–1990.* p. 469.
12. Ambrose. *Nixon: Ruin and Recovery, 1973–1990.* p. 476.
13. William H. Chafe. *The Unfinished Journey: America since World War II.* New York: Oxford University Press, 1999, p. 450.
14. John Robert Greene. *The Presidency of Gerald Ford.* Lawrence: University Press of Kansas 1995, p. 73.
15. Green. *The Presidency of Gerald Ford.*
16. Martin Tolchin. "Bailout Barred." *New York Times,* October 30, 1975, p. 1.
17. Tolchin. "Bailout Barred."
18. Tolchin. "Bailout Barred."
19. Francis X. Clines. "Beams and Carey Decry Ford Plan." *New York Times,* October 30, 1975, p. 1.
20. Susan Orlean. "The Outsiders." *New Yorker,* July 26, 2004, p. 47.
21. John Kifner. "Violence Mars Busing in Boston." *New York Times,* September 13, 1974, p. 77.
22. Peter Jennings and Todd Brewster. *The Century.* New York: Doubleday, 1998, p. 44.
23. John Kifner. "Boston School Buses Stoned a 2nd Day, but City Is Mostly Calm: Whites in South Area Press Boycott." *New York Times,* September 14, 1974, p. 13.
24. Lisa Cozzens. "School Integration." African American History. Available online. URL: http://fledge.watson.org/~lisa/blackhistory/schoolintegration/boston/phaseI.html. Downloaded June 14, 2004.
25. Susan Orlean. "The Outsiders." p. 47.
26. "School Integration." *Time,* September 22, 1975. In *Time Magazine Multimedia Almanac.* Cambridge, Mass.: Softkey International, 1995.
27. Jennings and Brewster. *The Century.* p. 443.
28. Richard Rashke. *The Killing of Karen Silkwood.* Ithaca, N.Y.: Cornell Universiy Press, 2000, pp. 21–22.
29. Rashke. *The Killing of Karen Silkwood.* p. 77.
30. Fox Butterfield. "Saigon Defenses Attacked: Airport under Rocket Fire." *New York Times,* April 29, 1975, p. 1.
31. Hamilton. *Presidents: A Biographical Dictionary.* p. 327.
32. Greene. *The Presidency of Gerald Ford.* p. 144.
33. Greene. *The Presidency of Gerald Ford.* p. 150.
34. Greene. *The Presidency of Gerald Ford.* p. 151.
35. Greene. *The Presidency of Gerald Ford.* p. 114.
36. Nicholas M. Horrock. "Ford Acts to Bar Death Plot Data." *New York Times,* November 3, 1975, p. 1.
37. James M. Naughton. "Ford Safe as Guard Seizes a Gun Woman Pointed at Him on Coast." *New York Times,* September 6, 1975, p. 1.
38. Wallace Turner. " 'The Gun Is Pointed,' Miss Fromme Says; Judge Ejects Her." *New York Times,* September 12, 1975, p. 1.
39. Turner. " 'The Gun Is Pointed,' Miss Fromme Says; Judge Ejects Her."
40. Bruce J. Schulman. *The Seventies: The Great Shift in American Culture, Society, and Politics.* Cambridge, Mass.: Da Capo Press, 2002, p. 95.

41. Edward Clinton Ezell and Linda Neuman Ezell. "The Partnership: A History of the Apollo-Soyuz Test Project." Available online. URL: http://www.hq.nasa.gov/office/pao/History/SP-4209/ch11-3.htm. Downloaded June 26, 2004.

42. "Brock Breaks Record." *New York Times,* September 11, 1974, p. 51.

43. George Plimpton. "On Betting Ali." In Ashley Kahn, Holly George-Warren, and Shawn Dahl, eds., *Rolling Stone: The Seventies.* Boston: Little, Brown, 1998, p. 149.

6. BICENTENNIAL AMERICA: JANUARY 1976–DECEMBER 1976

1. Jon Nordheimer. "Americans Finding New Course Is Vital." *New York Times,* July 5, 1976, p. 13.

2. Nordheimer. "Americans Finding New Course Is Vital."

3. Nordheimer. "Americans Finding New Course Is Vital."

4. Nicholas M. Horrock. "Guidelines Due." *New York Times,* February 18, 1973, p. 1.

5. Horrock. "Guidelines Due."

6. Horrock. "Guidelines Due.".

7. Horrock. "Guidelines Due."

8. "Party's Candidate Says Police Aided Break Ins, Providing Security." *New York Times,* March 29, 1976, p. 1.

9. Lesley Oelsner. "High Court Grants Blacks Retroactive Job Seniority." *New York Times,* March 25, 1976, p. 1.

10. Deborah Blum. "A Time to Live, a Time to Die." In Ashley Kahn, Holly George-Warren, and Shawn Dahl, eds., *Rolling Stone: The Seventies.* Boston: Little, Brown, 1998, p. 182.

11. Joseph Sullivan. "Court Rules Karen Quinlan's Father Can Let Her Die by Disconnecting Respirator If Doctors See No Hope." *New York Times,* April 1, 1976, p. 1.

12. Sullivan. "Court Rules Karen Quinlan's Father Can Let Her Die by Disconnecting Respirator If Doctors See No Hope."

13. Sullivan. "Court Rules Karen Quinlan's Father Can Let Her Die by Disconnecting Respirator If Doctors See No Hope."

14. The Quinlan Precedent." *New York Times,* April 2, 1976, p. 25.

15. Robert D. McFadden. "Karen Ann Quinlan, 31, Dies: Focus of '76 Right to Die Case." *New York Times,* June 12, 1985, p. 1.

16. McFadden. "Karen Ann Quinlan, 31, Dies: Focus of '76 Right to Die Case."

17. "Text of Hays's Statement to the House." *New York Times,* May 26, 1976, p. 16.

18. Marian Clark and Rudy Maxa. "Rep. Wayne Hays' $14,000-a-Year Clerk Says She's His Mistress." *Washington Post,* May 23, 1976. Available online. URL: http://www.washingtonpost.com. Downloaded July 14, 2004.

19. Clark and Maxa. "Rep. Wayne Hays' $14,000-a-Year Clerk Says She's His Mistress."

20. Clark and Maxa. "Rep. Wayne Hays' $14,000-a-Year Clerk Says She's His Mistress."

21. Tom Wicker. "Congress, Sex, and the Press." *New York Times,* June 22, 1976, p. 35.

22. James Reston. "Reform by Scandal." *New York Times,* June 4, 1976, p. 19.

23. Helen Prejean. *Dead Man Walking: An Eyewitness Account of the Death Penalty in the United States.* New York: Vintage Books, 1993, pp. 19–20.

24. Lesley Oelsner. "Decision is 7 to 2." *New York Times,* July 3, 1976, p. 1.

25. Tom Goldstein. "Inmates' Lawyers Report Many May Face Execution." *New York Times,* July 3, 1976, p. 1.

26. Goldstein. "Inmates' Lawyers Report Many May Face Execution."

27. Goldstein. "Inmates' Lawyers Report Many May Face Execution."

28. John L. Hess. "A Day of Picnics, Pomp, Pagaentry, and Protest." *New York Times,* July 5, 1976, p. 1.

29. Richard F. Shepard. "Panoply of Sails." *New York Times,* July 5, 1976, p. 1.

30. Hess. "A Day of Picnics, Pomp, Pagaentry, and Protest."

31. *Time,* July 19, 1976. In *Time Magazine Multimedia Almanac.* Cambridge, Mass.: Softkey International, 1993.

32. Robert Lindsey. "3 Abductors Sought as 26 Children Rejoin Families." *New York Times,* July 18, 1976, p. 1.

33. Lindsey. "3 Abductors Sought as 26 Children Rejoin Families."

34. Kevin P. Phillips. *The Emerging Republican Majority.* New Rochelle, N.Y.: Arlington House, 1969, p. 464.

35. Phillips. *The Emerging Republican Majority.* p. 467.

36. Phillips. *The Emerging Republican Majority.* pp. 473–474.
37. Bruce J. Schulman. *The Seventies: The Great Shift in American Culture, Society, and Politics.* Cambridge, Mass.: Da Capo Press, 2002, p. 108.
38. *Time,* March 29, 1976. In *Time Magazine Multimedia Almanac.* Cambridge, Mass.: Softkey International, 1993.
39. *Time,* August 2, 1976. In *Time Magazine Multimedia Almanac.* Cambridge, Mass.: Softkey International, 1993.
40. Burton I. Kaufman. *The Presidency of James Earl Carter, Jr.* Lawrence: University Press of Kansas, 1993, p. 10.
41. Kaufman. *The Presidency of James Earl Carter, Jr.* p. 11.
42. Kaufman. *The Presidency of James Earl Carter, Jr.* p. 16.
43. Tom Wolfe. "The Me Decade and the Third Great Awakening." In *Tom Wolfe: The Purple Decades.* New York: Farrar Straus Giroux, 1982, p. 278.
44. Schulman. *The Seventies.* p. 97.
45. Wolfe. "The Me Decade and the Third Great Awakening." p. 276.
46. Wolfe. "The Me Decade and the Third Great Awakening." p. 277.
47. Wolfe. "The Me Decade and the Third Great Awakening." p. 293.
48. Norman Mailer. *The Executioner's Song.* New York: Books, 1979, p. 255.
49. Mailer. *The Executioner's Song.* p. 777.
50. Utah Court, Granting Killer' Wish, Authorizes Death by Firing Squad." *New York Times,* November 11, 1976, p. 1.
51. Jon Nordheimer. "Gilmore Wins Plea for Execution; Pardons Board Orders Date Set." *New York Times,* December 1, 1976, p. 1.
52. Mailer. *The Executioner's Song.* p. 955.
53. Mailer. *The Executioner's Song.* p. 958.
54. John Noble Wilford. "Viking Robot Sets Down Safely on Mars." *New York Times,* July 21, 1976, p. 1.
55. Wilford. "Viking Robot Sets Down Safely on Mars."

7. FRUSTRATED AMERICA: JANUARY 1977–DECEMBER 1977

1. *Public Papers of the Presidents of the United States: Jimmy Carter, January 20 to June 24, 1977.* Washington, D.C.: United States Government Printing Office, 1975, p. 5.
2. Charles Mohr. "10,000 Affected Now." *New York Times,* January 22, 1977, p. 1.
3. James M. Naughton. "Crowd Delighted as Carters Shun Limousine and Walk to New Home." *New York Times,* January 27, 1977, p. 1.
4. Richard Halloran. "People's Inaugural A Logistics Circus and Extravaganza." *New York Times,* January 21, 1977, p. 27.
5. B. Drummond Ayers, Jr. "The South Rises, Yet Again, on a Big Day." *New York Times,* January 21, 1977, p. 29.
6. *Public Papers of the Presidents of the United States: Jimmy Carter, January 20 to June 24, 1977.* p. 1.
7. Burton I. Kaufman. *The Presidency of James Earl Carter, Jr.* Lawrence: University Press of Kansas, 1993, p. 23.
8. Les Ledbetter. "Moon Church in Court Battle Over Youth's Custody." *New York Times,* March 22, 1977, p. 18.
9. Les Ledbetter. "Parents Win Custody of 5 Members of Moon's Church." *New York Times,* March 25, 1977, p. 1.
10. Les Ledbetter. "Five in Moon Church Win Custody Ruling." *New York Times,* April 12, 1977, p. 1.
11. Ledbetter. "Five in Moon Church Win Custody Ruling."
12. *Public Papers of the Presidents of the United States: Jimmy Carter, January 20 to June 24, 1977.* p. 6.
13. Edward Cowan. "President Urges 65 as Top Heat in Homes to Ease Energy Crisis." *New York Times,* January 22, 1977, p. 1.
14. Cowan. "President Urges 65 as Top Heat in Homes to Ease Energy Crisis."
15. Charles Mohr. "Carter Asks Strict Fuel Savings; Urges "Moral Equivalent of War." *New York Times,* April 19, 1977, p. 1.
16. Kaufman. *The Presidency of James Earl Carter, Jr.* p. 33.
17. James Sterba. "Accusatory Tone in Carter Talk Is Deplored by Oilmen in Houston." *New York Times,* April 20, 1977, p. 18.
18. Sterba. "Accusatory Tone in Carter Talk Is Deplored by Oilmen in Houston."
19. Steven Rattner. "White House Shifts, Says Energy Plans Won't Aid Economy." *New York Times,* April 22, 1977, p. 1.
20. Kaufman. *The Presidency of James Earl Carter, Jr.* p. 108.
21. Christopher Hemann. "Methuen Firm Taking Seabrook Dome Apart." June 19, 2003. Available online. URL http://www.eagletribune.com. Downloaded August 9, 2004.

22. Bernard Weinraub. "House Votes to Build B-1 Bomber as Carter Decision on Plane Nears." *New York Times,* June 29, 1977, p. 1.

23. *Public Papers of the Presidents of the United States: Jimmy Carter, June 25 to December 31, 1977.* Washington, D.C.: United States Government Printing Office, 1978, p. 1,197.

24. Bernard Weinraub. "Cruise Missile Cited." *New York Times,* July 1, 1977, p. 1.

25. *Public Papers of the Presidents of the United States: Jimmy Carter, June 25 to December 31, 1977.*

26. Bernard Weinraub. "Defense Chief Sees a Savings of Billions by Dropping the B-1." *New York Times,* July 2, 1977, p. 1.

27. "Night of Terror." *Time,* July 25, 1977, p. 12.

28. "Night of Terror." p. 17.

29. "Night of Terror." p. 18.

30. "Night of Terror." p. 12.

31. "Night of Terror." p. 17.

32. "Night of Terror." p. 21.

33. "Night of Terror."

34. Stewart L. Udall. *The Quiet Crisis and the Next Generation.* Layton, Utah: Gibbs Smith, 1988, p. 135.

35. Ben A. Franklin. "President Signs Strip-Mining Bill, But Cites Defects." *New York Times,* August 4, 1977, p. 1.

36. *Public Papers of the Presidents of the United States: Jimmy Carter, June 25 to December 31, 1977,* p. 1,408.

37. *Public Papers of the Presidents of the United States: Jimmy Carter, June 25 to December 31, 1977.*

38. *Public Papers of the Presidents of the United States: Jimmy Carter, June 25 to December 31, 1977.* p. 1,409.

39. Charles Mohr. "President Is Somber." *New York Times,* September 22, 1977, p. 1.

40. *Public Papers of the Presidents of the United States: Jimmy Carter, January 20 to June 24, 1977,* p. 2.

41. Maury Terry. *The Ultimate Evil: The Truth about the Cult Murders: Son of Sam & Beyond.* New York: Barnes and Noble Books, 1999, pp. 44–46.

42. Terry. *The Ultimate Evil: The Truth about the Cult Murders: Son of Sam & Beyond.* pp. 48–49.

43. Robert D. McFadden. "Suspect in 'Son of Sam' Murders Arrested in Yonkers." *New York Times,* August 11, 1977, p. 1.

44. Robert D. McFadden. "Suspect in 'Son of Sam' Murders Arrested in Yonkers."

45. Howard Blum. "The Suspect Is Quoted on Killings: 'It Was a Command . . . I Had a Sign.' " *New York Times,* August 12, 1977, p. 1.

46. McFadden. "Suspect in 'Son of Sam' Murders Arrested in Yonkers."

47. Terry. *The Ultimate Evil: The Truth about the Cult Murders: Son of Sam & Beyond.* p. 76.

48. Terry. *The Ultimate Evil: The Truth about the Cult Murders: Son of Sam & Beyond.* p. 528.

49. Terry. *The Ultimate Evil: The Truth about the Cult Murders: Son of Sam & Beyond.* p. 531.

50. Terry. *The Ultimate Evil: The Truth about the Cult Murders: Son of Sam & Beyond.* p. 522.

51. "Berkowitz Interview." ABC News. Available online. URL: http://more.abcnews.go.com/sections/us/berkowitz1113/. Downloaded August 23, 2004.

52. *Public Papers of the Presidents of the United States: Jimmy Carter, June 25 to December 31, 1977.* p. 1,972.

53. *Public Papers of the Presidents of the United States: Jimmy Carter, June 25 to December 31, 1977.* p. 1,973.

54. *Public Papers of the Presidents of the United States: Jimmy Carter, June 25 to December 31, 1977.*

55. "President Uses First Veto to Bar Nuclear Reactor." *New York Times,* November 5, 1977, p. 1.

56. "President Uses First Veto to Bar Nuclear Reactor." *New York Times,* November 5, 1977, p. 1.

57. *Public Papers of the Presidents of the United States: Jimmy Carter, June 25 to December 31, 1977.* p. 2,012.

58. Neil A. Hamilton. *Atlas of the Baby Boom Generation. A Cultural History of Postwar America.* New York: Macmillan, 2000, p. 49.

59. Peter Guralnick. *Careless Love: The Unmaking of Elvis Presley.* Boston: Back Bay Books, 1999, p. 607.

60. Guralnick. *Careless Love: The Unmaking of Elvis Presley.* p. 653.

61. Guralnick. *Careless Love: The Unmaking of Elvis Presley.* pp. 660–661.

62. "Payton Dead at 45." Sporting News: The Vault. Available online. URL: http://www.sportingnews.com/archives/payton/article6.html. Downloaded August 26, 2004.

8. ESCAPIST AMERICA: JANUARY 1978–DECEMBER 1978

1. Douglas E. Kneeland. "Hubert H. Humphrey Is Dead at 66 after 32 Years of Public Service." *New York Times,* January 14, 1978, p. 1.

2. Douglas E. Kneeland. "Hubert H. Humphrey Is Dead at 66 after 32 Years of Public Service."

3. Kneeland. "Hubert H. Humphrey Is Dead at 66 after 32 Years of Public Service."

4. Kneeland. "Hubert H. Humphrey Is Dead at 66 after 32 Years of Public Service."

5. Alan Riding. "Reporter's Notebook: In Panama, a Subdued Sense of Helplessness." *New York Times,* April 12, 1978, p. 9.

6. Riding. "Reporter's Notebook: In Panama, a Subdued Sense of Helplessness."

7. Alan Riding. "Panama Indicates It Can Now Accept Canal Treaties." *New York Times,* April 18, 1978, p. 6.

8. Riding. "Panama Indicates It Can Now Accept Canal Treaties."

9. Adam Clymer. "Key Senator Yields to Party's Leaders on Pledge to Panama." *New York Times,* April 18, 1978, p. 1.

10. Clymer. "Key Senator Yields to Party's Leaders on Pledge to Panama."

11. Alan Riding. "Panamanian Leader Accepts Canal Pacts." *New York Times,* April 19, 1978, p. 1.

12. Burton I. Kaufman. *The Presidency of James Earl Carter, Jr.* Lawrence: University Press of Kansas, 1993, p. 89.

13. Adam Clymer. "Senate Votes to Give up Panama Canal; Carter Foresees 'Beginning of a New Era.'" *New York Times,* April 19, 1978, p. 1.

14. Clymer. "Senate Votes to Give up Panama Canal; Carter Foresees 'Beginning of a New Era.'"

15. Robert Lindsay. "Many States Moving to Limit Spending." *New York Times,* June 26, 1978, p. 9.

16. "Recession and Shortages." *Time,* June 9, 1978. In *Time Magazine Multimedia Almanac.* Cambridge, Mass.: Softkey International, 1995.

17. Adam Clymer. "Reagan Urges Party to Support Tax Cuts." *New York Times,* June 25, 1978, p. 27.

18. Clymer. "Reagan Urges Party to Support Tax Cuts."

19. Clymer. "Reagan Urges Party to Support Tax Cuts."

20. "ACLU Lawyer Defends Nazi Rights." *Chicago Sun-Times,* August 6, 1978. Available online. URL: http://www.digitalpast.org. Downloaded September 1, 2004.

21. "Skokie Streets Will Be Bloody, JDL Declares." *Chicago Sun-Times,* March 3, 1978. Available online. URL: http://www.digitalpast.org. Downloaded September 1, 2004.

22. Douglas Kneeland. "Nazis Call off March in Skokie; Leader Says Drive Was a Success." *New York Times,* June 23, 1978, p. 10.

23. Kneeland. "Nazis Call off March in Skokie; Leader Says Drive Was a Success."

24. "Cops Arrest 21 at Nazi Rally." *Chicago Sun-Times,* July 10, 1978. Available online. URL: http://www.digitalpast.org. Downloaded September 1, 2004.

25. Robert Reinhold. "Justices Clear Skokie Parade by Nazi Group." *New York Times,* June 13, 1978, p. 1.

26. Linda Greenhouse. "Bell Hails Decision." *New York Times,* June 29, 1978, p. 1.

27. Greenhouse. "Bell Hails Decision."

28. Greenhouse. "Bell Hails Decision."

29. Greenhouse. "Bell Hails Decision."

30. Donald G. McNeil, Jr. "Emptied Niagara Neighborhood Now Looks Like a Disaster Area." *New York Times,* November 22, 1978, p. B4.

31. Donald G. McNeil, Jr. "3 Chemical Sites Near Love Canal Possible Hazard." *New York Times,* December 27, 1978, p. B1.

32. Martin Waldron. "Bordentown Fights Toxic Waste Dump." *New York Times,* November 19, 1978, p. 43.

33. Martin Waldron. "Bordentown Fights Toxic Waste Dump."

34. Jimmy Carter to Anwar Sadat, August 3, 1978. Jimmy Carter Library. Available online. URL: http://www.jimmycarterlibrary.org/documents. Downloaded September 5, 2004.

35. "Thirteen Days after Twenty-Five Years." Jimmy Carter Library. Available online. URL: http://www.jimmycarter1ibrary.org/douments/campdavid25. Downloaded September 4, 2004.

36. "Thirteen Days after Twenty-Five Years."

37. "Thirteen Days after Twenty-Five Years."

38. *Public Papers of the Presidents of the United States: Jimmy Carter, June 30 to December 31, 1978.* Washington, D.C.: United States Government Printing Office, 1979, p. 1,520.

39. "Rep. Ryan's Address to Jonestown Community," November 1978, tape Q048.

40. Lacey Fosburgh. "Jones Used Bible-Thumping and Politics of Brotherhood." *New York Times,* November 23, 1978, p. 16.

41. Robert Lindsey. "Jim Jones—From Poverty to Power of Life and Death." *New York Times,* November 26, 1978, p. 1.

42. "Jonestown Death Tape, November 1978." Jonestown Institute. Available online. URL: http://jonestown.sdsu.edu. Downloaded September 8, 2004.

43. "Jonestown Death Tape, November 1978."

44. Tim Cahill. "Paranoia, Panic & Poison." In Ashley Kahn, Holly George-Warren, and Shawn Dahl, eds., *Rolling Stone: The Seventies.* Boston: Little, Brown, 1998, p. 264.

45. Roy Reed. "Cult Killings Yield Criticisms Abroad." *New York Times,* November 30, 1978, p. 17.

46. Nicholas Horrock. "Suicide Note Disclosed." *New York Times,* November 28, 1978, p. 1.

47. Bruce J. Schulman. *The Seventies: The Great Shift in American Culture, Society, and Politics.* Cambridge, Mass.: Da Capo Press, 2002, p. 73.

48. Anthony Haden-Guest. *The Last Party: Studio 54, Disco, and the Culture of the Night.* New York: William Morrow and Company, 1997, p. 45.

49. Haden-Guest. *The Last Party: Studio 54, Disco, and the Culture of the Night.* p. 46.

50. Haden-Guest. *The Last Party: Studio 54, Disco, and the Culture of the Night.* p. 51.

51. Haden-Guest. *The Last Party: Studio 54, Disco, and the Culture of the Night.* p. xv.

52. Jim Fixx. *The Complete Book of Running.* New York: Random House, 1977, p. 14.

53. Fixx. *The Complete Book of Running.* p. 18.

54. Fixx. *The Complete Book of Running.* p. 19.

9. MELTDOWN AMERICA: JANUARY 1979–JANUARY 1981

1. Drummond Ayres, Jr. "A Calm Returns to Midletown but Some Continue to Lie Low." *New York Times,* April 1, 1979, p. 1.

2. Richard D. Lyons. "Carter Visits Nuclear Plant, Urges Cooperation in Crisis." *New York Times,* April 1, 1979, p. 1.

3. Richard D. Lyons. "Children Evacuated." *New York Times,* March 31, 1979, p. 1.

4. Lyons. "Children Evacuated."

5. Lyons. "Carter Visits Nuclear Plant, Urges Cooperation in Crisis."

6. Richard D. Lyons. "Radioactive Plant Faces a Shutdown as Long as 4 Years." *New York Times,* April 4, 1979, p. 1.

7. David Burnham. "Nuclear Commission Gets Plea by Staff to Shut Nine Plants." *New York Times,* April 26, 1979, p. 1.

8. Philip Elmer-Dewitt. "Nuclear Power Plots a Comeback." *Time,* January 2, 1989. In *Time Magazine Multimedia Almanac.* Cambridge, Mass.: Softkey International, 1955.

9. Jimmy Carter. "Crisis of Confidence," Speech. PBS, July 15, 1979. Available online. URL: http://www.pbs.org/wgbh/amex/carter/filmmore/ps_crisis.html. Downloaded May 23, 2005.

10. "Bundy Left Alone in Aspen Courtroom, Leaps out Window, Escapes into Hills." *Salt Lake Tribune,* June 8, 1977, p. B1.

11. "Officials Hunt Aspen Area Hills for Bundy." *Salt Lake Tribune,* June 9, 1977, p. B3.

12. "Officials Hunt Aspen Area Hills for Bundy."

13. "Back in Courtroom, Dead-Tired Bundy Hears New Charges." *Salt Lake Tribune,* June 14, 1977, p. 17.

14. "Jailers Raked in Bundy Escape." *Salt Lake Tribune,* January 5, 1978, p. B8.

15. "Bundy Sentenced to Die in Two Florida Slayings." *New York Times,* August 1, 1979, p. 10.

16. Hedrick Smith. "High Officials Say Young Became Diplomatic and Political Liability." *New York Times,* August 16, 1979, p. 1.

17. Laurie Johnson. "Black Leaders Back Young; Jews Still Fearful On P. L.O." *New York Times,* August 16, 1979, p. 4.

18. Johnson. "Black Leaders Back Young; Jews Still Fearful on P. L.O."

19. Smith. "High Officials Say Young Became Diplomatic and Political Liability."

20. Johnson. "Black Leaders Back Young; Jews Still Fearful on P. L.O."

21. Smith. "High Officials Say Young Became Diplomatic and Political Liability."

22. Tom Stites. "Four Shot to Death at Anti-Klan March." *New New York Times,* November 4, 1979, p. 1.

23. Stites. "Four Shot to Death at Anti Klan March."

24. David Harris. *The Crisis: The President, the Prophet, and the Shah—1979 and the Coming of Militant Islam.* New York: Little, Brown, 2004, p. 95.

25. Gary Sick. *All Fall Down: America's Tragic Encounter with Iran.* Lincoln, Neb.: iUniverse.com, Inc., 2001, p. 218.

26. Lee A. Daniels. "Protestors Shout 'Death to Shah' outside Hospital." *New York Times,* October 25, 1979, p. B14.

27. Daniels. "Protestors Shout 'Death to Shah' outside Hospital." p. 240.

28. "Teheran Students Seize U.S. Embassy and Hold Hostages." *New York Times,* November 5, 1979, p. 1.

29. "Excerpt from An Iran Hostage's Diary." Jimmy Carter Library. Available online. URL: http://www.jimmycarterlibrary.org/documents/r_ode/index.phtml. Downloaded October 11, 2004.

30. Massoumeh Ebtekar. *Takeover in Tehran: The Inside Story of the 1979 U.S. Embassy Capture.* Vancouver, Canada: Talonbooks, 2000, p. 44.

31. Ebtekar. *Takeover in Tehran: The Inside Story of the 1979 U.S. Embassy Capture.* p. 231.

32. Ebtekar. *Takeover in Tehran: The Inside Story of the 1979 U.S. Embassy Capture.* p. 239

33. Ebtekar. *Takeover in Tehran: The Inside Story of the 1979 U.S. Embassy Capture.* p. 81.

34. Bernard Owertzman. "U.S. Rejects Demand of Students in Iran to Send Shah Back." *New York Times,* November 5, 1979, p. 1.

35. Drew Middleton. "In Iran Crisis: Few Choices." *New York Times,* November 7, 1979, p. 14.

36. Middleton. "In Iran Crisis: Few Choices." p. 255.

37. Judith Cummings. "Many Nations Assail Seizure of Embassy." *New York Times,* November 8. 1979, p. 12.

38. John Kifner. "Iranians Bar Hostage Talks, Repeating Demands for Shah." *New York Times,* November 9. 1979, p. 1.

39. "Excerpt from an Iran Hostage's Diary."

40. Burton I. Kaufman. *The Presidency of James Earl Carter, Jr.* Lawrence: University Press of Kansas, 1993, p. 161.

41. Ebtekar. *Takeover in Tehran: The Inside Story of the 1979 U.S. Embassy Capture.* p. 211.

42. Sick. *All Fall Down: America's Tragic Encounter with Iran.* p. 317.

43. Sick. *All Fall Down: America's Tragic Encounter with Iran.* p. 322.

44. Sick. *All Fall Down: America's Tragic Encounter with Iran.* p. 336.

45. Col. James A. Kyle. *The Guts to Try: The Untold Story of the Iran Hostage Rescue Missions by the On-Scene Desert Commander.* New York: Ballantine Books, 1995, p. 227.

46. Kyle. *The Guts to Try: The Untold Story of the Iran Hostage Rescue Missions by the On-Scene Desert Commander.* p. 326.

47. Kyle. *The Guts to Try: The Untold Story of the Iran Hostage Rescue Missions by the On-Scene Desert Commander.* p. 1.

48. Kyle. *The Guts to Try: The Untold Story of the Iran Hostage Rescue Missions by the On-Scene Desert Commander.* p. 338.

49. Sick. *All Fall Down: America's Tragic Encounter with Iran.* p. 356.

50. Burton I. Kaufman. *The Presidency of James Earl Carter, Jr.* p. 175.

51. Kyle. *The Guts to Try: The Untold Story of the Iran Hostage Rescue Missions by the On-Scene Desert Commander.* p. 362.

52. *The "October Surprise" Allegations and the Circumstances Surrounding the Release of the American Hostages Held in Iran: Report of the Special Counsel to Senator Terry Sanford and Senator James Jeffords of the Committee on Foreign Relations, United States Senate, November 19, 1992.* Washington, D.C.: United States Government Printing Office, 1992, p. 115.

53. *The "October Surprise" Allegations and the Circumstances Surrounding the Release of the American Hostages Held in Iran: Report of the Special Counsel to Senator Terry Sanford and Senator James Jeffords of the Committee on Foreign Relations, United States Senate, November 19, 1992.* pp. 116–117.

54. *The "October Surprise" Allegations and the Circumstances Surrounding the Release of the American Hostages Held in Iran: Report of the Special Counsel to Senator Terry Sanford and Senator James Jeffords of the Committee on Foreign Relations, United States Senate, November 19, 1992.* p. 113

55. "The Promotion Night That Ended in Flames." *New York Times,* July 11, 2004, Sports p. 5.

56. Andy Behrens. "Disco Demolition: Bell Bottoms Be Gone!" ESPN Sports. Available online. URL: http://sports.espn.go.com:spn/page3/story?page=behrens/040809. Downloaded October 12, 2004.

57. "The Promotion Night That Ended in Flames."

58. Chet Flippo. "Death of the Cincinnati Eleven." In Ashley Kahn, Holly George-Warren, and Shawn Dahl, eds., *Rolling Stone: The Seventies.* Boston: Little, Brown, 1998, p. 280.

59. Reginald Smart. "For Those Caught in the Crush, Cincinnati's Nightmare Goes On." *New York Times,* December 7, 1979, p. 22.

BIBLIOGRAPHY

BOOKS

Aaron, Hank, and Dick Schaap. *Home Run: My Life in Pictures.* Kingston, N.Y.: Total Sports, 1999.

Aaron, Hank, and Lonnie Wheeler. *I Had a Hammer: The Hank Aaron Story.* New York: HarperCollins Publishers, 1991.

Agnew, Spiro. *Go Quietly . . . Or Else.* New York: Morrow, 1980.

Alexander, Shana. *Anyone's Daughter.* New York: Viking Press, 1979.

Allen, Maury. *Mr. October: The Reggie Jackson Story.* New York: Times Books, 1981.

Ali, Muhammad, with Richard Durham. *The Greatest: My Own Story.* New York: Random House, 1975.

Ambrose, Stephen. *Nixon: Ruin and Recovery, 1973–1990.* New York: Simon and Schuster, 1991.

———. *Nixon: The Triumph of A Politician, 1962–1972.* New York: Simon and Schuster, 1989.

Amburn, Ellis. *Pearl: The Obsessions and Passions of Janis Joplin.* New York: Warner Books, 1992.

Anderson, Terry H. *The Movement and the Sixties.* New York: Oxford University Press, 1995.

Angers, Trent. *The Forgotten Hero of My Lai: The Hugh Thompson Story.* Lafayette, La.: Acadian House, 1999.

Ashby, Leroy. *Fighting the Odds: The Life of Senator Frank Church.* Pullman: Washington State University Press, 1994.

Ayers, Bill. *Fugitive Days: A Memoir.* New York: Penguin Books, 2001.

Ball, Howard. *The Bakke Case: Race, Education, and Affirmative Action.* Lawrence: University Press of Kansas, 2000.

Barker, Eileen. *The Making of a Moonie: Choice or Brainwashing?* Malden, Mass.: Basil Blackwell, 1984.

Bates, Tom. *Rads: The 1970 Bombing of the Army Math Research Center at the University of Wisconsin and Its Aftermath.* New York: HarperCollins, 1992.

Berman, Larry. *No Peace, No Honor: Nixon, Kissinger, and Betrayal in Vietnam.* New York: Free Press, 2001.

Black, Johnny. *Jimi Hendrix: Eyewitness.* London: Carlton, 1999.

Blum, Linda M. *Between Labor and Feminism: The Significance of the Comparable Worth Movement.* Berkeley: University of California Press, 1991.

Boston Women's Health Collective. *Our Bodies, Ourselves.* New York: Simon and Schuster, 1973.

Brinkley, Douglas. *Tour of Duty: John Kerry and the Vietnam War.* New York: William Morrow, 2004.

Brock, Lou, with Franz Schulze. *Stealing Is My Game.* New York: Prentice Hall, 1976.

Bromley, David G., and Anson D. Shupe, Jr. *"Moonies" in America: Cult, Church, and Crusade.* Beverly Hills, Calif.: Sage Publications, 1979.

Buell, Emmett H. *School Desegregation and Defended Neighborhoods: The Boston Controversy.* Lexington, Mass.: Lexington Books, 1982.

Bugliosi, Vincent. *Helter Skelter: The True Story of the Manson Murders.* New York: W. W. Norton, 1994.

Bundy, William P. *A Tangled Web: The Making of Foreign Policy in the Nixon Presidency.* New York: Hill and Wang, 1998.

Butcher, Lee. *Accidental Millionaire: The Rise and Fall of Steve Jobs and Apple Computer.* New York: Paragon House, 1988.

Carter, Dan. *The Politics of Rage: George Wallace, the Origins of the New Conservatism, and the Transformation of American Politics.* Baton Rouge: Louisiana State University Press, 1995.

Carter, Rubin. *The Sixteenth Round: From Number 1 Contender to #45472.* New York: Viking Press, 1974.

Chafe, William H. *The Unfinished Journey: America since World War II.* New York: Oxford University Press, 1999.

Chidester, David. *Salvation and Suicide: Jim Jones, the Peoples Temple, and Jonestown.* Rev. ed. Bloomington: Indiana University Press, 2003.

Chisholm, Shirley. *The Good Fight*. New York: Harper and Row, 1973.

Chomsky, Noam. *Towards a New Cold War: U.S. Foreign Policy from Vietnam to Reagan*. New York: New Press, 2003.

Christofferson, Bill. *The Man from Clear Lake: Earth Day Founder Gaylord Nelson*. Madison: University of Wisconsin Press, 2004.

Chryssides, George D. *The Advent of Sun Myung Moon: The Origins, Beliefs and Practices of the Unification Church*. New York: St. Martin's Press, 1991.

Churchill, Ward, and Jim Vander Wall. *The COINTELPRO Papers: Documents from the FBI's Secret Wars against Domestic Dissent*. Boston: South End Press, 1990.

Cohen, Richard M., and Jules Witcover. *A Heartbeat Away: The Investigation and Resignation of Vice President Spiro T. Agnew*. New York: Viking Press, 1974.

Colen, B. D. *Karen Ann Quinlan: Dying in the Age of Eternal Life*. New York: Nash Publishers, 1976.

Commoner, Barry. *The Closing Circle*. New York: Bantam, 1972.

Curtis, Richard. *The Berrigan Brothers: The Story of Daniel and Philip Berrigan*. New York: Hawthorn Books, 1974.

Dellinger, David. *From Yale to Jail: The Life Story of a Moral Dissenter*. New York: Pantheon Books, 1993.

Douglas, Susan. *Where the Girls Are: Growing up Female with the Mass Media*. New York: Random House, 1994.

Ebtekar, Massoumeh. *Takeover in Tehran: The Inside Story of the 1979 U.S. Embassy Capture*. Vancouver, Canada: Talonbooks, 2000.

Ehrlichman, John. *Witness to Power: The Nixon Years*. New York: Simon and Schuster, 1982.

Ellsberg, Daniel. *Secrets: A Memoir of Vietnam and the Pentagon Papers*. New York: Viking, 2002.

Endleman, Robert. *Jonestown and the Manson Family: Race, Sexuality, and Collective Madness*. New York: Psyche Press, 1993.

Environmental Action Foundation. *Accidents Will Happen: The Case against Nuclear Power*. New York: Harper and Row, 1979.

Faux, Marian. *Roe v. Wade: The Untold Story of the Landmark Supreme Court Decision That Made Abortion Legal*. New York: Cooper Square Press, 2001.

Feinsod, Ethan. *Awake in a Nightmare: Jonestown, the Only Eyewitness Account.* New York: W. W. Norton, 1981.

Ferretti, Fred. *The Year the Big Apple Went Bust.* New York: Putnam, 1976.

Fixx, Jim. *The Complete Book of Running.* New York: Random House, 1977.

Flood, Curt, with Richard Carter. *The Way It Is.* New York: Trident Press, 1971.

Ford, Daniel F. *Three Mile Island: Thirty Minutes to Meltdown.* New York: Penguin Books, 1982.

Ford, Gerald R. *A Time to Heal.* New York: Harper and Row, 1979.

Fox, Joel. *Proposition 13: The Great California Tax Revolt.* Philadelphia: Xlibris, 2003.

Frady, Marshall. *Wallace.* New York: Random House, 1996.

Frazier, Joe, with Phil Berger. *Smokin' Joe: The Autobiography of a Heavyweight Champion, Smokin' Joe Frazier.* New York: Macmillan, 1996.

Friedman, Myra. *Buried Alive: The Biography of Janis Joplin.* New York: Harmony Books, 1992.

Frum, David. *How We Got Here: The 70s, The Decade That Brought You Modern Life (For Better or Worse).* New York: Basic Books, 2000.

Gibbs, Lois Marie, with Murray Levine. *Love Canal: My Story.* Albany: State University of New York Press, 1982.

Gilmore, Mikal. *Shot in the Heart.* New York: Doubleday, 1994.

Goldman, Albert. *Disco.* New York: Hawthorn Books, 1978.

Gordon, William A. *Four Dead in Ohio: Was There a Conspiracy at Kent State?* Laguna Hills, Calif.: North Ridge Books, 1995.

———. *The Fourth of May: Killings and Coverups at Kent State.* Buffalo, N.Y.: Prometheus Books, 1990.

Gray, Mike, and Ira Rosen. *The Warning: Accident at Three Mile Island.* New York: Norton, 2003.

Gitlin, Todd. *The Sixties: Years of Hope, Days of Rage.* New York: Bantam Books, 1987.

Greene, John Robert. *The Presidency of Gerald Ford.* Lawrence: University Press of Kansas, 1995.

Guralnick, Peter. *Careless Love: The Unmaking of Elvis Presley.* Boston: Back Bay Books, 1999.

Haden-Guest, Anthony. *The Last Party: Studio 54, Disco, and the Culture of the Night.* New York: William Morrow and Company, 1997.

Hanhimäki, Jussi M. *The Flawed Architect: Henry Kissinger and American Foreign Policy.* New York: Oxford University Press, 2004.

Harris, David. *The Crisis: The President, the Prophet, and the Shah—1979 and the Coming of Militant Islam.* New York: Little, Brown and Company, 2004.

Hennessee, Judith. *Betty Friedan: Her Life.* New York: Random House, 1999.

Hersh, Seymour M. *The Price of Power: Kissinger in the Nixon White House.* New York: Summit Books, 1983.

Hirsch, James S. *Hurricane: The Miraculous Journey of Rubin Carter.* Boston: Houghton Mifflin, 2000.

Hoff-Wilson, Joan, ed. *Rights of Passage: The Past and Future of the ERA.* Bloomington: Indiana University Press, 1986.

Hopkins, Jerry, and Danny Sugerman. *No One Gets out of Here Alive.* New York: Warner, 1980.

Isaacs, Arnold R. *Vietnam Shadows: The War, Its Ghosts, and Its Legacy.* Baltimore: Johns Hopkins University Press, 1997.

Jackson, Reggie, and Mike Lupica. *Reggie: The Autobiography.* New York: Villard Books, 1984.

Jennings, Peter, and Todd Brewster. *The Century.* New York: Doubleday, 1998.

Johnson, Haynes B. *In the Absence of Power.* New York: Viking Press, 1980.

Kahn, Ashley, Holly George-Warren, and Shawn Dahl, eds. *Rolling Stone: The Seventies.* Boston: Little, Brown, 1998.

Kahn, Roger. *October Men: Reggie Jackson, George Steinbrenner, Billy Martin, and the Yankees' Miraculous Finish in 1978.* Orlando, Fla.: Harcourt, 2003.

Kaufman, Burton I. *The Presidency of James Earl Carter, Jr.* Lawrence: University Press of Kansas, 1993.

Kimball, Jeffrey P. *Nixon's Vietnam War.* Lawrence: University Press of Kansas, 1998.

King, Greg. *Sharon Tate and the Manson Murders.* New York: Barricade Books, 2000.

Kissinger, Henry. *White House Years.* Boston: Little, Brown, 1979.

———. *Years of Renewal.* New York: Simon and Schuster, 1999.

———. *Years of Upheaval.* Boston: Little, Brown, 1982.

Kohn, Howard. *Who Killed Karen Silkwood?* New York: Summit Books, 1991.

Koopmans, Andy. *Charles Manson.* San Diego: Lucent Books, 2005.

Kram, Mark. *Ghosts of Manila: The Fateful Blood Feud between Muhammad Ali and Joe Frazier.* New York: HarperCollins, 2001.

Kurtti, Jeff. *Since the World Began: Walt Disney World, the First 25 Years.* New York: Hyperion, 1996.

Kutler, Stanley I. *Abuse of Power: The New Nixon Tapes.* New York: The Free Press, 1997.

———. *The Wars of Watergate: The Last Crisis of Richard Nixon.* New York: W. W. Norton, 1990.

Kuttner, Robert. *Revolt of the Haves: Tax Rebellions and Hard Times.* New York: Simon and Schuster, 1980.

Kyle, James H. *The Guts to Try: The Untold Story of the Iran Hostage Rescue Mission by the On-Scene Desert Commander.* New York: Ballantine Books, 1995.

Lasch, Christopher. *The Culture of Narcissism: American Life in an Age of Diminishing Expectations.* 1979. Reprint, New York: W. W. Norton, 1991.

Lesher, Stephan. *George Wallace: American Populist.* Reading, Mass.: Addison-Wesley, 1994.

Levine, Adeline. *Love Canal: Science, Politics, and People.* Lexington, Mass.: Lexington Books, 1982.

Lukas, J. Anthony. *Common Ground: A Turbulent Decade in the Lives of Three American Families.* New York: Knopf, 1985.

Maaga, Mary McCormick. *Hearing the Voices of Jonestown.* Syracuse, N.Y.: Syracuse University Press, 1998.

Mailer, Norman. *The Executioner's Song.* New York: Warner Books, 1979.

Mansbridge, Jane. *Why We Lost the ERA.* Chicago: University of Chicago Press, 1986.

Mazur, Allan. *A Hazardous Inquiry: The Rashomon Effect at Love Canal.* Cambridge, Mass.: Harvard University Press, 1998.

McCorvey, Norma, with Andy Meisler. *I Am Roe: My Life, Roe v. Wade, and Freedom of Choice.* New York: HarperCollins, 1994.

Michener, James A. *Kent State: What Happened and Why.* New York: Random House, 1971.

Moore, Rebecca. *In Defense of Peoples Temple and Other Essays.* Lewiston, N.Y.: E. Mellen Press, 1988.

Moore, Rebecca, Anthony B. Pinn, and Mary R. Sawyer, eds. *Peoples Temple and Black Religion in America.* Bloomington: Indiana University Press, 2004.

Morgan, Robin, ed. *Sisterhood Is Powerful: An Anthology of Writings from the Women's Liberation Movement.* New York: Vintage Books, 1970.

Morris, Charles R. *The Cost of Good Intentions: New York City and the Liberal Experiment, 1960–1975.* New York: McGraw-Hill, 1980.

National Staff of Environmental Action, ed. *Earth Day—The Beginning: A Guide for Survival.* New York: Bantam Books, 1970.

Nelson, Gaylord. *Beyond Earth Day: Fulfilling the Promise.* Madison: University of Wisconsin Press, 2002.

Nixon, Richard. *The Memoirs of Richard Nixon.* New York: Grosset and Dunlap, 1978.

The "October Surprise" Allegations and the Circumstances Surrounding the Release of the American Hostages Held in Iran: Report of the Special Counsel to Senator Terry Sanford and Senator James Jeffords of the Committee on Foreign Relations, United States Senate, November 19, 1992. Washington, D.C.: U.S. Government Printing Office, 1992.

Payton, Walter, and Don Yaeger. *Never Die Easy: The Autobiography of Walter Payton.* New York: Villard, 2000.

Persico, Joseph E. *The Imperial Rockefeller: A Biography of Nelson A. Rockefeller.* New York: Simon and Schuster, 1982.

Peterson, Richard E., and John A. Bilorusky. *May 1970: The Campus Aftermath of Cambodia and Kent State.* Berkeley, Calif.: Carnegie Foundation for the Advancement of Teaching, 1971.

Phillips, Gene D., and Rodney Hill, eds. *Francis Ford Coppola: Interviews.* Jackson: University Press of Mississippi, 2004.

Phillips, Kevin P. *The Emerging Republican Majority.* New Rochelle, N.Y.: Arlington House, 1969.

Plimpton, George. *One for the Record: The Inside Story of Hank Aaron's Chase for the Home-run Record.* New York: Harper & Row, 1974.

Powers, Richard Gid. *Secrecy and Power: The Life of J. Edgar Hoover.* New York: The Free Press, 1987.

Public Papers of the Presidents of the United States: Jimmy Carter, Containing the Public Messages, Speeches, and Statements of the President, January 20 to June 24, 1977. Washington, D.C.: United States Government Printing Office, 1977.

Public Papers of the Presidents of the United States: Jimmy Carter, Containing the Public Messages, Speeches, and Statements of the President, June 25 to December 31, 1977. Washington, D.C.: United States Government Printing Office, 1978.

Public Papers of the Presidents of the United States: Jimmy Carter, Containing the Public Messages, Speeches, and Statements of the President, June 30 to December 31, 1978. Washington, D.C.: United States Government Printing Office, 1979.

Public Papers of the Presidents of the United States: Jimmy Carter, Containing the Public Messages, Speeches, and Statements of the President, June 23 to December 31, 1979. Washington, D.C.: United States Government Printing Office, 1980.

Public Papers of the Presidents of the United States: Richard Nixon, Containing the Public Messages, Speeches, and Statements of the President, 1970. Washington, D.C.: United States Government Printing Office, 1971.

Public Papers of the Presidents of the United States: Richard Nixon, Containing the Public Messages, Speeches, and Statements of the President, 1971. Washington, D.C.: United States Government Printing Office, 1972.

Public Papers of the Presidents of the United States: Richard Nixon, Containing the Public Messages, Speeches, and Statements of the President, 1972. Washington, D.C.: United States Government Printing Office, 1974.

Public Papers of the Presidents of the United States: Richard Nixon, Containing the Public Messages, Speeches, and Statements of the President, 1973. Washington, D.C.: United States Government Printing Office, 1975.

Public Papers of the Presidents of the United States: Richard Nixon, Containing the Public Messages, Speeches, and Statements of the President, January 1 to August 9, 1974. Washington, D.C.: United States Government Printing Office, 1975.

Quinlan, Joseph, and Julia Quinlan. *Karen Ann: The Quinlans Tell Their Story.* Garden City, N.Y.: Doubleday, 1977.

Rabushka, Alvin, and Pauline Ryan. *The Tax Revolt.* Stanford, Calif.: Hoover Institution, 1982.

Rashke, Richard. *The Killing of Karen Silkwood.* Ithaca, N.Y.: Cornell University Press, 2000.

Rashke, Richard L. *The Killing of Karen Silkwood: The Story behind the Kerr-McGee Plutonium Case.* New York: Penguin, 1982.

Reeves, Richard. *President Nixon: Alone in the White House.* New York: Simon and Schuster, 2001.

Reich, Cary. *The Life of Nelson A. Rockefeller: Worlds to Conquer, 1908–1958.* New York: Doubleday, 1996.

Rennert, Richard Scott. *Henry Aaron.* New York: Chelsea House Publishers, 1993.

Report of the Department of the Army Review of the Preliminary Investigations into the My Lai Incident: The Report of the Investigation. Vol. 1. Washington, D.C.: U.S. Government Printing Office, 1974.

The Report of the President's Commission on Campus Unrest. Washington, D.C.: U.S. Government Printing Office, 1970.

Robinson, Frank, and Barry Stainback. *Extra Innings.* New York: McGraw-Hill, 1988.

Rohler, Lloyd Earl. *George Wallace: Conservative Populist.* Westport, Conn.: Praeger Publishers, 2004.

Rosen, Ruth. *The World Split Open: How the Modern Women's Movement Changed America.* New York: Penguin Books, 2000.

Rubin, Eva R. *Abortion, Politics, and the Courts:* Roe v. Wade *and Its Aftermath.* Westport, Conn.: Greenwood Press, 1982.

Schram, Martin. *Running for President 1976: The Carter Campaign.* New York: Stein and Day, 1977.

Schulman, Bruce J. *The Seventies: The Great Shift in American Culture, Society, and Politics.* New York: Da Capo Press, 2001.

Schulzinger, Robert D. *Henry Kissinger: Doctor of Diplomacy.* New York: Columbia University Press, 1989.

Schwadron, Terry, ed. *California and the American Tax Revolt: Proposition 13 Five Years Later.* Berkeley: University of California Press, 1984.

Schwartz, Bernard. *Behind Bakke: Affirmative Action and the Supreme Court.* New York: New York University Press, 1988.

Shawcross, William. *Sideshow: Kissinger, Nixon, and the Destruction of Cambodia.* Rev. ed. New York: Simon and Schuster, 1987.

Sick, Gary. *All Fall Down: America's Tragic Encounter with Iran.* Lincoln, Neb.: iUniverse.com, Inc., 2001.

Sills, David L., C. P. Wolf, and Vivien B. Shelanski, eds. *Accident at Three Mile Island: The Human Dimensions.* Boulder, Colo.: Westview Press, 1982.

Skidmore, David. *Reversing Course: Carter's Foreign Policy, Domestic Politics, and the Failure of Reform.* Nashville, Tenn.: Vanderbilt University Press, 1996.

Small, Melvin. *The Presidency of Richard Nixon.* Lawrence: University Press of Kansas, 1999.

Spofford, Tim. *Lynch Street: The May 1970 Slayings at Jackson State College.* Kent, Ohio: Kent State University Press, 1988.

Stephens, Mark. *Three Mile Island.* New York: Random House, 1980.

Stewart, Gail. *The 1970s.* San Diego, Calif.: Lucent Books, 1999.

Stone, I. F. *The Killings at Kent State: How Murder Went Unpunished.* New York: Vintage Books, 1971.

Summers, Anthony. *Official and Confidential: The Secret Life of J. Edgar Hoover.* New York: G. P. Putnam's Sons, 1993.

Terry, Maury. *The Ultimate Evil: The Truth about the Cult Murders: Son of Sam & Beyond.* New York: Barnes & Noble Books, 1999.

Theoharis, Athan G., and John Stuart Cox. *The Boss: J. Edgar Hoover and the Great American Inquisition.* Philadelphia: Temple University Press, 1988.

Thompson, Kenneth W., ed. *The Carter Presidency: Fourteen Intimate Perspectives of Jimmy Carter.* New York: University Press of America, 1990.

Towle, Mike. *I Remember Walter Payton: Personal Memories of Football's "Sweetest" Superstar by the People Who Knew Him Best.* Nashville, Tenn.: Cumberland House, 2000.

Udall, Stewart L. *The Quiet Crisis and the Next Generation.* Layton, Utah: Gibbs Smith, 1988.

Wallace, Joseph, Neil Hamilton, and Marty Appel. *Baseball: 100 Classic Moments in the History of the Game.* New York: Dorling Kindersley, 2000.

Walsh, Edward J. *Democracy in the Shadows: Citizen Mobilization in the Wake of the Accident at Three Mile Island.* New York: Greenwood Press, 1988.

Watkins, Paul. *My Life with Charles Manson.* New York: Bantam Books, 1979.

Weed, Stephen, with Scott Swanton. *My Search for Patty Hearst.* New York: Crown Publishers, 1976.

Wolfe, Tom, ed. *The Purple Decades: A Reader.* New York: Farrar, Straus, 1982.

Wood, Allen Tate. *Moonstruck: A Memoir of My Life in a Cult.* New York: Morrow, 1979.

Young, Jeffrey S. *Steve Jobs: The Journey Is the Reward.* Glenview, Ill.: Scott, Foresman, 1988.

Ziebart, Eve. *The Unofficial Disney Companion: The Inside Story of Walt Disney World and the Man behind the Mouse.* New York: Macmillan, 1997.

ARTICLES

"Ali: It's a Good Feeling to Lose, but I Won." *New York Times,* March 10, 1971, p. 49.

Anderson, Dave. "Ali Regains Title, Flooring Foreman." *New York Times,* October 30, 1974, p. 1.

Apple, R. W., Jr. "McGovern Says Attempt to Bug Office Was Foiled." *New York Times,* September 10, 1972, p. 48.

———. "Nixon Inaugurated for His Second Term: Sees World on Threshold of a Peace Era." *New York Times,* January 22, 1973, p. 1.

———. "Nixon Reports 'Major' Findings in Watergate Inquiry He Made," *New York Times,* April 18, 1973, p. 1.

Arnold, Martin. "Pentagon Papers Charges Are Dismissed by Court." *New York Times,* May 12, 1973, p. 1.

Ayers, B. Drummond, Jr. "A Calm Returns to Middletown But Some Continue to Lie Low." *New York Times,* April 1, 1979, p. 1.

———. "The South Rises, Yet Again, on a Big Day." *New York Times,* January 21, 1977, p. 29.

"Back in Courtroom, Dead-Tired Bundy Hears New Charges." *Salt Lake Tribune,* June 14, 1977, p. 17.

Barnet, Richard J., and Peter Weiss. "Hanoi Rules out a Partial Accord." *New York Times,* February 6, 1972, p. 1.

Becker, Elizabeth. "On New Kissinger Tapes, Crises in White House and the World." *New York Times,* May 27, 2004, p. 1.

Berry, Jan. "Why Veterans March against the War." *New York Times,* April 23, 1971, p. 37.

Bicentennial." *Time*, July 19, 1976. In *Time Magazine Multimedia Almanac*. Cambridge, Mass.: Softkey International, 1995.

Bird, David. "Abuse Victims Get Help at New Crisis Centers." *New York Times*, February 17, 1978, p. 25.

Blum, Howard. "The Suspect Is Quoted on Killings: 'It Was a Command . . . I Had a Sign." *New York Times*, August 12, 1977, p. 1.

"Bundy Left Alone in Aspen Courtroom, Leaps out Window, Escapes into Hills." *Salt Lake Tribune*, June 8, 1977, p. B1.

"Bundy Sentenced to Die in Two Florida Slayings." *New York Times*, August 1, 1979, p. 10.

Burks, John. "An Appreciation." *Rolling Stone*, October 15, 1970, p. 8.

Burnham, David. "Nuclear Commission Gets Plea by Staff to Shut Nine Plants." *New York Times*, April 26, 1979, p. 1.

Butterfield, Fox. "Saigon Defenses Attacked: Airport under Rocket Fire." *New York Times*, April 29, 1975, p. 1.

Charlton, Linda. "Big Rallies Are Planned." *New York Times*, May 2, 1970, p. 1.

Chass, Murray. "Players' Return Depends on Pact." *New York Times*, April 6, 1972, p. 57.

"Clemente, Pirates' Star, Dies in Crash of Plane Carrying Aid to Nicaragua." *New York Times* January 2, 1973, p. 73.

Clines, Francis X. "Beame and Carey Decry Ford Plan." *New York Times*, October 30, 1975, p. 1.

Clymer, Adam. "Key Senator Yields to Party's Leaders on Pledge to Panama." *New York Times*, April 18, 1978, p. 1.

———. "Reagan Urges Party to Support Tax Cuts." *New York Times*, June 25, 1978, p. 27.

———. "Senate Votes to Give up Panama Canal; Carter Foresees 'Beginning of a New Era.' " *New York Times*, April 19, 1978, p. 1.

Cowan, Edward. "President Urges 65 As Top Heat in Homes to Ease Energy Crisis." *New York Times*, January 22, 1977, p. 1.

Cummings, Judith. "Many Nations Assail Seizure of Embassy." *New York Times*, November 8, 1979, p. 12.

Daniels, Lee A. "Protesters Shout 'Death to Shah' outside Hospital." *New York Times,* October 25, 1979, p. B14.

"The Dawning of Earth Day." *Time,* April 27, 1970. In *Time Magazine Multimedia Almanac.* Cambridge, Mass.: Softkey International, 1995.

"Ellsberg Trial Gave Insight on Intrusion of Executive Branch into Judicial Process." *New York Times,* May 12, 1973, p. 15.

Elmer-Dewitt, Philip. "Nuclear Power Plots a Comeback." *Time,* January 2, 1989. In *Time Magazine Multimedia Almanac.* Cambridge, Mass.: Softkey International, 1995.

"Excerpts from Kissinger's News Conference on the President's Peace Proposals." *New York Times,* January 27, 1972, p. 14.

Farrell, William E. "Governor Defends Order to Quell Attica Uprising." *New York Times,* September 16, 1971, p. 1.

Ferretti, Fred. "Attica Prisoners Win 28 Demands but Still Resist." *New York Times,* September 13, 1971, p. 1.

————. "Autopsies Show Shots Killed Nine Attica Guards, Not Knives; State Official Admits Mistake." *New York Times,* September 15, 1971, p. 1.

————. "Like a War Zone." *New York Times,* September 14, 1971, p. 1.

Finney, John W. "Muskie Says FBI Spied at Rallies on '70s Earth Day." *New York Times,* April 15, 1971, p. 1.

————. "Reaction Is Mixed." *New York Times,* January 26, 1972, p. 1.

Fleming, Anne Tylor. "That Week in Houston." *New York Times,* December 25, 1977, p. 127.

Flint, Jerry M. "Ohio Guardsmen Defend Shooting of Kent Students." *New York Times,* May 7, 1970, p. 19.

Fosburgh, Lacey. "Jones Used Bible-Thumping and Politics of Brotherhood." *New York Times,* November 23, 1978, p. 16.

Frankel, Max. "China Visit Ends." *New York Times,* February 28, 1972, p. 1.

————. "The Lessons of Vietnam." *New York Times,* July 6, 1971, p. 1.

————. "Nixon Talks Further with Chou and Drives to View Great Wall." *New York Times,* February 24, 1972, p. 1.

————. "A Quiet Greeting." *New York Times,* February 21, 1972, p. 1.

———. "Statement Today by Nixon and Chou Will Define Ties." *New York Times,* February 27, 1972, p. 1.

Franklin, Ben A. "President Signs Strip-Mining Bill, but Cites Defects." *New York Times,* August 4, 1977, p. 1.

Friedlander, Paul J. C. "Miami: Worries about Disney World." *New York Times,* April 4, 1971, p. XX51.

Gelb, Leslie H. "Should We Play Dirty Tricks in the World?" *New York Times,* December 21, 1975, p. 209.

Goldstein, Tom. "Inmates' Lawyers Report Many May Face Execution." *New York Times,* July 3, 1976, p. 1.

Graham, Freed P. "Kleindienst Says He Set up Talks on ITT Accord." *New York Times,* March 3, 1972, p. 1.

Greenhouse, Linda. "Bell Hails Decision." *New York Times,* June 29, 1978, p. 1.

Gwertzman, Bernard. "U.S. Rejects Demands of Students in Iran to Send Shah Back." *New York Times,* November 5, 1979, p. 1.

Halloran, Richard. "People's Inaugural a Logistics Circus and Extravaganza." *New York Times,* January 21, 1977, p. 27.

Herbers, John. "Nixon Resigns the Presidency Effective at Noon Today." *New York Times,* August 9, 1974, p. 1.

Hess, John L. "A Day of Picnics, Pomp, Pageantry, and Protest." *New York Times,* July 5, 1976, p. 1.

Horrock, Nicholas M. "Ford Acts to Bar Death Plot Data." *New York Times,* November 3, 1975, p. 1.

———. "Guidelines Due." *New York Times,* February 18, 1973, p. 1.

———. "Suicide Note Disclosed." *New York Times,* November 28, 1978, p. 1.

Hunter, Marjorie. "Most Congressional Leaders Applaud Court Decision: The White House Is Silent." *New York Times,* July 1, 1971, p. 16.

———. "A Plea to Bind up Watergate Wounds." *New York Times,* August 10, 1974, p. 1.

"Jailers Raked in Bundy Escape." *Salt Lake Tribune,* January 5, 1978, p. B8.

"Jimi." *Rolling Stone,* October 15, 1970, p. 8.

Johnson, Laurie. "Black Leaders Back Young: Jews Still Fearful on P. L.O." *New York Times,* August 16, 1979, p. 14.

Kaufman, Michael T. "Underground Exciting to Gold." *New York Times,* March 13, 1970, p. 27.

Kifner, John. "Boston School Buses Stoned a 2nd Day, but City Is Mostly Calm: Whites in South Area Press Boycott." *New York Times,* September 14, 1974, p. 13.

———. "Brutal Vietnam Campaign Stirs Memories and Questions." *New York Times,* December 28, 2003, p. 16.

———. "Iranian Bar Hostage Talks, Repeating Demands for Shah." *New York Times,* November 9, 1979, p. 1.

———. "Violence Mars Busing in Boston." *New York Times,* September 13, 1974, p. 77.

Kneeland, Douglas, E. "Ex-Counsel, Cool and Dogged, Reads 6-Hour Story to the Nation." *New York Times,* June 26, 1973, p. 30.

———. "Hubert H. Humphrey Is Dead at 66 after 32 Years of Public Service." *New York Times,* January 14, 1978, p. 1.

———. "McGovern Says Nixon Does Not Respect Rights." *New York Times,* October 20, 1972, p. 21.

Kneeland, Douglas. "Nazis Call off March in Skokie; Leader Says Drive Was a Success." *New York Times,* p. 10.

Ledbetter, Les. "Five in Moon Church Win Custody Ruling." *New York Times,* April 12, 1977, p. 1.

———. "Moon Church in Court Battle Over Youths' Custody." *New York Times,* March 22, 1977, p. 18.

———. "Parents Win Custody of 5 Members of Moon's Church." *New York Times,* March 25, 1977, p. 1.

Lelyveld, Joseph. "Millions Join Earth Day Observances across the Nation." *New York Times,* April 23, 1970, p. 1.

Lindsey, Robert. "Jim Jones—From Poverty to Power of Life and Death." *New York Times,* November 26, 1978, p. 1.

———. "Many States Moving to Limit Spending." *New York Times,* June 26, 1978, p. 9.

———. "3 Abductors Sought as 26 Children Rejoin Families." *New York Times,* July 18, 1976, p. 1.

Lukas, J. Anthony. "Chicago 7 Defense Claims U.S. Concocted Case to Justify Police Violence." *New York Times,* February 12, 1970, p. 20.

———. "Disorder Erupts at Chicago Trial after Judge Jails a Defendant for Using a Vulgarity." *New York Times,* February 5, 1970, p. 18.

Lyons, Richard D. "Carter Visits Nuclear Plant, Urges Cooperation in Crisis." *New York Times,* April 2, 1979, p. 1.

———. "Children Evacuated." *New York Times,* March 31, 1979, p. 1.

———. "Radioactive Plant Faces a Shutdown as Long as 4 Years." *New York Times,* April 4, 1979, p. 1.

Maitland, Leslie. "Rubin Carter Is Convicted with Artis in 3 Murders." *New York Times,* December 22, 1976, p. 1.

McFadden, Robert D. "College Strife Spreads." *New York Times,* May 8, 1970, p. 1.

———. "Karen Ann Quinlan, 31, Dies: Focus of '76 Right to Die Case." *New York Times,* June 12, 1985, p. 1.

———. "Suspect in 'Son of Sam' Murders Arrested in Yonkers." *New York Times,* August 11, 1977, p. 1.

McNeil, Donald G., Jr. "Emptied Niagara Neighborhood Now Looks Like a Disaster Area." *New York Times,* November 22, 1978, p. B4.

———. "3 Chemical Sites Near Love Canal Possible Hazard." *New York Times,* December 27, 1978, p. B1.

Middleton, Drew. "In Iran Crisis: Few Choices." *New York Times,* November 7, 1979, p. 14.

Mohr, Charles. "Carter Asks Strict Fuel Saving; Urges 'Moral Equivalent of War'." *New York Times,* April 19, 1977, p. 1.

———. "President Is Somber." *New York Times,* September 22, 1977, p. 1.

———. "10,000 Affected Now." *New York Times,* January 22, 1977, p. 1.

Morgan, Robin. "Check It Out: Porn, No. But Free Speech, Yes." *New York Times,* March 24, 1978, p. 27.

Naughton, James M. "Crowd Delighted as Carters Shun Limousine and Walk to New Home." *New York Times,* January 27, 1977, p. 1.

———. "Ford Safe as Guard Seizes a Gun Woman Pointed at Him on Coast." *New York Times,* September 6, 1975, p. 1.

———. "Judge Lets Veterans Sleep on the Mall; Rebukes U.S. Aides." *New York Times,* April 23, 1971, p. 1.

———. "Surprise Witness." *New York Times,* July 17, 1973, p. 1.

"Night of Terror." *Time,* July 25, 1977, p. 12.

"Nixon Resigns." *Time,* August 5, 1974, in *Time Magazine Multimedia Almanac.* Cambridge, Mass.: Softkey International, 1995.

"Nixon Resigns." *Time,* September 16, 1974, in *Time Magazine Multimedia Almanac.* Cambridge, Mass.: Softkey International, 1995.

Nordheimer, Jon. "Americans Finding New Course Is Vital." *New York Times,* July 5, 1976, p. 13.

———. "Disney World Opens without Expected Crush." *New York Times,* October 2, 1971, p. 33.

———. "Gilmore Wins Plea for Execution; Pardons Board Orders Date Set." *New York Times,* December 1, 1976, p. 1.

Oelsner, Lesley. "Decision Is 7 to 2." *New York Times,* July 3, 1973, p. 1.

———. "High Court Grants Blacks Retroactive Job Seniority." *New York Times,* March 25, 1976, p. 1.

"Officials Hunt Aspen Area Hills for Bundy." *Salt Lake Tribune,* June 9, 1977, p. B3.

Orlean, Susan. "The Outsiders." *The New Yorker,* July 26, 2004, p. 47.

Palmer, Laura. "Goodbye, Vietnam." In Ashley Kahn, Holly George-Warren, and Shawn Dahl, eds. *Rolling Stone: The Seventies.* Boston: Little, Brown, 1998.

"President Uses First Veto to Bar Nuclear Reactor." *New York Times,* November 5, 1977, p. 1.

"The Promotion Night That Ended in Flames." *New York Times,* July 11, 2004, Sports p. 5.

"Protest Season on the Campus." *Time,* May 11, 1970. In *Time Magazine Multimedia Almanac.* Cambridge, Mass.: Softkey International, 1995.

"Public Reaction to Agnew Talk Is Found to Be Mostly Negative." *New York Times,* October 17, 1973, p. 32.

"The Quinlan Precedent." *New York Times,* April 2, 1976, p. 25.

Rattner, Steven. "White House Shifts, Says Energy Plans Won't Aid Economy." *New York Times,* April 22, 1977, p. 1.

"Recession and Shortages." *Time,* June 19, 1978. In *Time Magazine Multimedia Almanac.* Cambridge, Mass.: Softkey International, 1995.

Reed, Roy. "Agnew Calls Hoover's Critics Politically Motivated." *New York Times,* April 27, 1971, p. 17.

———. "Cult Killing Yield Criticisms Abroad." *New York Times,* November 30, 1978, p. 17.

Reinhold, Robert. "Justices Clear Skokie Parade by Nazi Group." *New York Times,* June 13, 1978, p. 1.

Reston, James. "Mr. Nixon's Finest Hour." *New York Times,* March 1, 1972, p. 39.

———. "Reform by Scandal." *New York Times,* June 4, 1976, p. 19.

Riding, Alan. "Panama Indicates It Can Now Accept Canal Treaties." *New York Times,* April 18, 1978, p. 6.

———. "Panamanian Leader Accepts Canal Pacts." *New York Times,* April 19, 1978, p. 1.

———. "Reporter's Notebook: In Panama, a Subdued Sense of Helplessness." *New York Times,* April 12, 1978, p. 1.

Roberts, Steven V. "G.O.P. Women Hurt by Agnew Action." *New York Times,* October 12, 1973, p. 29.

———. "What Made Those Kids Do It?" *New York Times,* January 31, 1971, p. E2.

Robinson, Douglas. "Wallace Opponents and Supporters Denounce His Shooting and Deplore Violence." *New York Times,* May 17, 1972, p. 29.

Rugaber, Walter. "McCord Testifies His Fellow Plotters Linked High Nixon Aides to Watergate." *New York Times,* March 30, 1973, p. 1.

———. "Watergate Spy Defendants Were under 'Political Pressure' to Admit Guilt and Keep Silent." *New York Times,* March 24, 1973, p. 1.

Salpukas, Agis. "2 Nixon Aides among 7 Indicted in Raid in Capital." *New York Times,* September 16, 1972, p. 1.

"School Integration." *Time,* September 22, 1975. In *Time Magazine Multimedia Almanac.* Cambridge, Mass.: Softkey International, 1995.

Semple, Robert B., Jr. "Nixon in Ottawa Asks Recognition of Differences." *New York Times,* April 15, 1972, p. 1.

———. "Nixon Says Violence Invites Tragedy." *New York Times,* May 5, 1970, p. 17.S

Shabad, Theodore. "Nixon Talks on TV to Soviet People and Hails Accord." *New York Times,* May 29, 1972, p. 1.

Shepard, Richard F. "Panoply of Sails." *New York Times,* July 5, 1976, p. 1.

Sibley, John. "Rap Brown and 3 Convicted of Robbery and Assault." *New York Times,* March 30, 1973, p. 14.

Smith, Hedrick. "High Officials Say Young Became Diplomatic and Political Liability." *New York Times,* August 16, 1979, p. 1.

Smith, Robert M. "Boggs Sees Peril to U.S. from FBI." *New York Times,* April 7, 1971, p. 21.

"The South: Death in Two Cities." *Time,* May 25, 1970, pp. 22–23.

Sterba, James. "Accusatory Tone in Carter Talk Is Deplored by Oilmen in Houston." *New York Times,* April 20, 1977, p. 18.

Stites, Tom. "Four Shot to Death at Anti-Klan March." *New York Times,* November 4, 1979, p. 1.

Stuart, Reginald. "For Those Caught in the Crush, Cincinnati's Nightmare Goes On." *New York Times,* December 7, 1979, p. 22.

Sullivan, Joseph F. "Court Rules Karen Quinlan's Father Can Let Her Die by Disconnecting Respirator If Doctors See No Hope." *New York Times,* April 1, 1976, p. 1.

Sullivan, Walter. "Apollo 13: Why This Trip Is Necessary." *New York Times,* April 12, 1970, p. E9.

Szulc, Ted. "Democratic Raid Tied to Realtor." *New York Times,* June 19, 1972, p. 1.

———. "President Leaves on Trip to China; Stops in Hawaii." *New York Times,* February 18, 1972, p. 1.

Teheran Students Seize U.S. Embassy and Hold Hostages." *New York Times,* November 5, 1979, p. 1.

"Text of Ford's Letter to Senator Church." *New York Times,* November 5, 1975, p. 18.

"Text of Hanoi Communiqué Disclosing Peace Plans Offered at Private Sessions." *New York Times,* February 1, 1972, p. 12.

"Text of Hays' Statement to the House." *New York Times,* May 26, 1976, p. 16.

"Text of Hyland Statement on Karen Ann Quinlan." *New York Times,* April 7, 1976, p. 89.

"Text of the Walter J. Hickel Letter." *New York Times,* May 7, 1970, p. 18.

Tolchin, Martin. "Bailout Barred." *New York Times,* October 30, 1975, p. 1.

Turner, Wallace. " 'The Gun Is Pointed,' Miss Fromme Says; Judge Ejects Her." *New York Times,* September 12, 1975, p. 1.

"Utah Court, Granting Killer's Wish, Authorizes Death by Firing Squad." *New York Times,* November 11, 1976, p. 1.

Waldron, Martin. "Bordentown Fights Toxic Waste Dam." *New York Times,* November 19, 1978, p. 43.

"Watergate Hearings." *Time,* July 9, 1973. In *Time Magazine Multimedia Almanac.* Cambridge, Mass.: Softkey International, 1995.

Ways, C. R. " 'Nobody Does Anything Better Than Me in Baseball,' Says Roberto Clemente." *New York Times,* April 9, 1972, p. SM38.

Wenner, Jann S. "Leaking the Truth." In Ashley Kahn, Holly George-Warren, and Shawn Dahl, eds. *Rolling Stone: The Seventies.* Boston: Little, Brown, 1998.

Weinraub, Bernard. "Cruise Missile Cited." *New York Times,* July 1, 1977, p. 1.

————. "Defense Chief Sees a Savings of Billions by Dropping the B-1." *New York Times,* July 2, 1977, p. 1.

————. "House Votes to Build B-1 Bomber as Carter Decision on Plane Nears." *New York Times,* June 29, 1977, p. 1.

Whitney, Craig R. "Thieu, Criticizing Rogers, Rejects New Concessions." *New York Times,* February 11, 1972, p. 1.

Wicker, Tom. "Congress, Sex, and the Press." *New York Times,* June 22, 1976, p. 35.

Wilford, John Noble. "Astronauts Back, Weak and Wobbly." *New York Times,* June 23, 1973, p. 1.

————. "Astronauts Splash Down Close to Pacific Target to End 12-Day Moon Trip." *New York Times,* August 8, 1971, p. 1.

————. "Viking Robot Sets down Safely on Mars." *New York Times,* July 21, 1976, p. 1.

Wooten, James T. "Milwaukee Man Held as Suspect." *New York Times,* May 16, 1972, p. 1.

Wright, Robert A. "Youths Battle Police on Coast." *New York Times,* February 27, 1970, p. 1.

WEB DOCUMENTS

"ACLU Lawyer Defends Nazi Rights." *Chicago Sun-Times,* August 6, 1978. Available online. URL: http://www.digitalpast.org. Downloaded September 1, 2004.

"AIM Statement on Wounded Knee November 1973." Michigan State University. Available online. URL: http://www.aics.org/WK/wk011.html. Downloaded May 24, 2004.

Armstrong, Paul W. "Karen Ann Quinlan." Available online. URL: http://imc.gsm.com/demos/dddemo/consult/karenann.htm. Downloaded July 27, 2004.

Bardsley, Marilyn. "Murder!" Court TV's Crime Library. Available online. URL: http://www.crimelibrary.com/serial_killers/notorious/manson/prosecution_7.html. Downloaded January 3, 2004.

Behrens, Andy. "Disco Demolition: Bell Bottoms Be Gone!" ESPN Sports. Available online. URL: http://sports.espn.go.com/espn/page3/story?page=behrens/040809. Downloaded October 12, 2004.

Blanton, Thomas S., ed. "The Secret Briefs and the Secret Evidence." National Security Archives. Available online. URL: http://www.gwu.edu/~nsarchiv/NSAEBB/NSAEBB48. Downloaded January 17, 2004.

"Briscoe Statement to the Press, September 8, 1974." Texas State Library & Archives Commission. Available online. URL: http://www.tsl.state.tx.us/governors/modern/briscoe-nixon-1.html. Downloaded: June 28, 2004.

"California Constitution, Amendment 13A." Available online. URL: http://www.leginfo.ca.gov/.const/.article_13A. Downloaded October 16, 2004.

Carter, Jimmy. "Crisis of Confidence" Speech. July 15, 1979. PBS. Available online. URL: http://www.pbs.org/wgbh/annex/carter/filmmore/PS_crisis.html. Downloaded May 23, 2005.

"Charles Manson Quotes." Available online. URL: http://members.tripod.com/mayhem44/mansonquotes.html. Downloaded January 3, 2004.

Clapp, Norman. *New York State Investigation of the New York City Blackout, July 13, 1977.* Blackout History Project. Available online. URL: http://blackout.gmu.edu/archive/a_1977.html. Downloaded: August 27, 2004.

Clark, Marion, and Rudy Maxa. "Rep. Wayne Hays' $14,000-a-Year Clerk Says She's His Mistress." *Washington Post,* May 23, 1976. Available online. URL: http://www.washingtonpost.com. Downloaded July 24, 2003.

"Closing remarks by Defense Attorney William Kunstler at the Trial of the Chicago Seven, February 13, 1970." Available online. URL: http://www.law.umkc.edu/faculty/projects/ftrials/Chicago7/Closing.html. Downloaded January 25, 2004.

"Cops Arrest 21 at Nazi Rally." *Chicago Sun-Times,* July 10, 1978. Available online. URL: http://www.digitalpast.org. Downloaded September 1, 2004.

"Counterattack for Seabrook." *Time,* July 11, 1977. Available online. URL: http://www.time.com/time/archive/preview/0,10987,919085,00.html. Downloaded June 29, 2005.

Cozzens, Lisa. "School Integration." African American History. Available online. URL: http://fledge.watson.org/~lisa/blackhistory/school-integration/boston/phaseI.html. Downloaded June 14, 2004.

Curvin, Robert, and Bruce Porter. *Blackout Looting!* Blackout History Project. Available online. URL: http://blackout.gmu.edu/archive/a_1977.html. Downloaded August 27, 2004.

"Death Tape" transcript. Alternative Considerations of Jonestown and Peoples Temple. Department of Religious Studies. San Diego State University. Available online. URL: http://jonestown.sdsu.edu. Downloaded October 14, 2004.

"Department of Defense, U.S. Milgroup, Situation Report #2, October 1, 1973." Chile and the United States: Declassified Documents Relating to the Military Coup, 1970–1976. National Security Archive Electronic Briefing Books. Available online. URL: http://www.gwu.edu/~nsarchiv/NSAEBB/NSAEBB8/ch21-01.htm. Downloaded May 24, 2004.

"Department of State, Chilean Executions, November 16, 1973." Chile and the United States: Declassified Documents Relating to the Military Coup, 1970–1976. National Security Archive Electronic Briefing Books. Available online. URL: http://www.gwu.edu/~nsarchiv/NSAEBB/NSAEBB8/ch10-01.htm. Downloaded May 25, 2004.

"Excerpt from An Iran Hostage's Diary." Jimmy Carter Library. Available online. URL: http://www.jimmycarterlibrary.org/documents/r_ode/index.phtml. Downloaded October 11, 2004.

Ezell, Edward Clinton, and Linda Neuman Ezell. "The Partnership: A History of the Apollo–Soyuz Test Project." Available online. URL: http://www.hq.nasa.gov/office/pao/History/SP-4209/ch11-3.htm. Downloaded June 26, 2004.

"Gerald R. Ford's Remarks on Taking the Oath of Office as President." Gerald R. Ford Library and Museum. Available online. URL: http://www.ford.utexas.edu/library/speeches/740001.htm. Downloaded June 28, 2004.

Hemann, Christopher. "Methuen Firm Taking Seabrook Dome Apart." June 19, 2003. Available online. URL: http://www.eagletribune.com. Downloaded August 9, 2004.

"High Steppin' to Stardom." *Time,* April 3, 1978. Available online. URL: http://www.time.com/archive/preview/0,10987,919534,00.html. Downloaded June 6, 2005.

"How Bankers View Bert." *Time,* September 19, 1977. Available online. URL: http://www.time. com/time/archive/preview/0,10987,915466,00.html. Downloaded June 30, 2005.

"Indecent Exposure on Capitol Hill." *Time,* June 7, 1976. Available online. URL: http://www.time.com/time/archive/preview/0,10987,947699,00. html. Downloaded: June 6, 2005.

"Interim Report: Alleged Assassination Plots Involving Foreign Leaders." History Matters. Available online. URL: http://history-matters.com/archive/church/reports/ir/html/ChurchIR_0008a.htm. Downloaded June 29, 2004.

"Interview with Daniel Ellsberg." 1999. Available online URL: http://www.cnn.com/SPECIALS/cold.war/guides/debate/chats/Ellsberg/. Downloaded May 5, 2005.

"Interview with a Doctor, October 4, 1979." Three Mile Island 1979 Emergency. Community Studies Center. Dickinson College. Available online. URL: http://www.threemileisland.org. Downloaded October 17, 2004.

"Interview with a High School Teacher, June 6, 1979." Three Mile Island 1979 Emergency. Community Studies Center. Dickinson College. Available online. URL: http://www.threemileisland.org. Downloaded October 17, 2004.

"Interview with a Housewife, August 1, 1979." Three Mile Island 1979 Emergency. Dickinson College. Available online. URL: http://www.threemileisland.org. Downloaded October 17, 2004.

"Interview with a Newspaper Editor, 1979." Three Mile Island 1979 Emergency. Dickinson College. Available online. URL: http://www.threemileisland.org. Downloaded October 17, 2004.

"Interview with Robert D. Keppel." Court TV's Crime Library. Available online. URL: http://www.crimelibrary.com. Downloaded October 14, 2004.

Jewell, Larry W., ed. "News Conference Statement by Dr. Henry A. Kissinger, Assistant to the President for National Security Affairs, January 24, 1973." Available online. URL: http://www.ibiblio.org/pub/academic/history/marshall/military/vietnam/policies.and.politics/paris _peace_1973.txt. Downloaded May 24, 2004.

"Jimmy Carter Acceptance Speech." Selected Speeches of Jimmy Carter. Jimmy Carter Library and Museum. Available online. URL: http://jimmycarterlibrary.org/documents/speeches/acceptance_speech.pdf. Downloaded July 27, 2004.

Jimmy Carter to President Anwar Sadat, August 3, 1978. The Camp David Accords after Twenty-Five Years. Jimmy Carter Library and Museum. Available online. URL: http://www.jimmycarterlibrary.gov/documents/campdavid25/campdavid25_documents.phtml. Downloaded October 16, 2004.

"Joint U.S.-U.S.S.R. Communiqué, San Clemente, June 24, 1973." Washington Post.Com. Available online. URL: http://www.washingtonpost.com/wp-srv/inatl/longterm/summit/archive/com1973-1.htm. Downloaded May 24, 2004.

"Jonestown Death Tape, November 1978." Jonestown Institute. Available online. URL: http://jonestown.sdsu.edu. Downloaded September 8, 2004.

Jones, Eric M., ed. "Apollo 17 Lunar Surface Journal." National Aeronautics and Space Administration. Available online. URL: http://www.hq.nasa.gov/alsj/a17/a17j.html. Downloaded April 8, 2004.

———. "Down the Ladder for EVA-1." Apollo 14 Lunar Surface Journal. National Aeronautics and Space Administration. Available online. URL: http://www.hq.nasa.gov/alsj/a14/a14-prelim1.html. Downloaded February 15, 2004.

———. "The Hammer and the Feather." Apollo 15 Lunar Surface Journal. National Aeronautics and Space Administration. Available online. URL: http://www.hq.nasa.gov/alsj/a15/a15.clsout3.html. Downloaded February 15, 2004.

"The Justice Department's Summary of FBI Reports." May Fourth Task Force. Available online. URL: http://dept.kent.edu/may4/justice_fbi_summary.htm. Downloaded January 25, 2004.

"Justice Harry Blackmun Opinion in Roe v. Wade." Abortion Law Homepage. Available online. URL: http://members.aol.com/abtrbng/roefl-o.htm. Downloaded May 14, 2004.

"Kent State: May 1–4, 1970." May Fourth Task Force. Available online. URL: http://dept.kent.edu/may4/chrono.htm. Downloaded December 15, 2003.

King, Alan. "Four Dead in Ohio: Memories of Kent State." *Milwaukee Journal Sentinel,* April 30, 2000. Available online. URL: http://www.jsonline.com/news/editorials/apr00/king30042900.asp. Downloaded December 15, 2003.

Kosnac, Ernie. "Three Decades of Remembrance at Kent State." Available online. URL: http://www.burr.kent.edu/archives/may4/brother/brother3.html. Downloaded December 17, 2003.

"Kozmic Blues." Janis Joplin Net. Available online. URL: http://www.janisjoplin.net/kozmic/quotesll.html. Downloaded January 30, 2004.

Linder, Doug, ed. "United States v Nixon (1974)." Exploring Constitutional Law. Available online. URL: http://www.law.umkc.edu/faculty/projects/ftrials/conlaw/separationofpowers.htm. Downloaded May 24, 2004.

Lovell, James. "Houston, We've Had a Problem." National Aeronautics and Space Administration History Homepage. Available online. URL: http://www.hq.nasa.gov/office/pao/History/SP-350/ch-13-1.html. Downloaded January 29, 2004.

"Matter of Quinlan." California State University. Available online. URL: http://www.csulb.edu/~jvancamp/452_r6.html. Downloaded: July 27, 2004.

"Mayor's Response to Court Ruling." Skokie Public Library. Available online. URL: http://www.digitalpast.org. Downloaded October 17, 2004.

"Memorable Quotes from *All in the Family.*" IMDB. Available online. URL: http://www.imdb.com/title/tt0066626/quotes. Downloaded February 16, 2004.

Meyer, Lawrence. "President Taped Talks, Phone Calls." *Washington Post,* July 17, 1973. Available online. URL: http://www.washingtonpost.com/wp-srv/orpolitics/watergate/chronology.htm. Downloaded May 5, 2005.

Moon, Sun Myung. "The Road of Religion and the Will of God." Available online. URL: http://www.unification.net/1977/770424.html. Downloaded August 28, 2004.

"New York Times Co. v. United States." Basic Readings in U.S. Democracy. Available online. URL: http://usinfo.state.gov/usa/infousa/facts/democrac/48.htm. Downloaded November 17, 2004.

"Nixon's Final Remarks to the White House Staff." Watergate.info. Available online. URL: http://watergate.info/nixon/74-08-09final-remarks.shtml. Downloaded June 6, 2004.

"Nixon's Response." Watergate.info. Available online. URL: http://www.watergate.info/ford/pardon.shtml. Downloaded June 28, 2004.

Note written by Anita Moore. Alternative Considerations of Jonestown and Peoples Temple. Department of Religious Studies. San Diego State University. Available online. URL: http://jonestown.sdsu.edu. Downloaded October 14, 2004.

"Payton Dead at 45." Sporting News: The Vault. Available online. URL: www.sportingnews.com/archives/payton/article6.html. Downloaded August 26, 2004.

Pentagon Papers. Documents Relating to American Foreign Policy: Vietnam. Vincent Ferraro, Mt. Holyoke College. Available online. URL: http://www.mtholyoke.edu/acad/intrel/pentagon/pent11.htm. Downloaded February 14, 2004.

"President Carter's Draft of What Became the 'Framework for the Conclusion of a Peace Treaty Between Egypt and Israel.' " The Camp David Accord after Twenty-Five Years. Jimmy Carter Library and Museum. Available online. URL: http://www.jimmycarterlibrary.gov/documents/campdavid25/campdavid25_documents.phtml. Downloaded October 16, 2004.

"President Ford's Pardon of Richard Nixon." Watergate.info. Available online. URL: http://www.watergate.info/ford/pardon.shtml. Downloaded June 28, 2004.

"President Gerald R. Ford's Remarks in Kansas City upon Accepting the 1976 Republican Presidential Nomination." Selected President Gerald R. Ford Speeches and Writings. Gerald R. Ford Library and Museum. Available online. URL: http://www.ford.utexas.edu/library/speeches/760733.htm. Downloaded July 28, 2004.

"President Nixon's Speech on Cambodia, April 30, 1970." Available online. URL: http://vietnam.vassar.edu/doc15.html. Downloaded November 11, 2004.

Prichard, Anne, ed. "ACLU Report." The Anti-Cult Movement. Available online. URL: http://bernie.cncfamily.com/aclu1.htm. Downloaded August 28, 2004.

"Regents of the University of California v. Bakke." FindLaw. Available online. URL: http://caselaw.lp.findlaw.com. Downloaded October 16, 2004.

"Report of the Governor's Commission on Three Mile Island," 1980. Three Mile Island 1979 Emergency. Community Studies Center. Dickinson College. Available online. URL: http://www.threemileisland.org. Downloaded October 17, 2004.

"Robert C. Ode Diary," August 4–5 1979. "Jimmy Carter Library and Museum. Available online. URL: http://www.jimmycarterlibrary.org/documents/r_ode/ode_nov79.phtml. Downloaded October 19, 2004.

"The Rockefellers: Attica Prison Riot—September 9–13, 1971." PBS American Experience. Available online. URL: http://www.pbs.org/wgbh/amex/rockefellers/peopleevents/e_attica.html. Downloaded January 20, 2004.

"Sex Scandal Shakes up Washington." *Time,* June 14, 1976. Available online. URL: http://www.time.com/time/archive/preview/0,10987,914210,00.html. Downloaded June 6, 2005.

"The Siege of Seabrook." *Time,* May 16, 1977. Available online. URL: http://www.time.com/time/archives/preview/0,10987,918965,00. html. Downloaded June 29, 2005.

Simmons, Gene. *On the Moon with Apollo 16.* National Aeronautics and Space Administration History Office. Available online. URL: http://history.nasa.gov/EP-95/ep95.htm. Downloaded April 8, 2004.

"Skokie Streets Will Be Bloody, JDL Declares." *Chicago Sun-Times,* March 3, 1978. Available online. URL: http://www.digitalpast.org. Downloaded September 1, 2004.

"Speech of Ohio Governor James A. Rhodes." May Fourth Task Force. Available online. URL: http://dept.kent.edu/may4/rhodes_speech_05031970.htm. Downloaded January 28, 2004.

"Statement by Raymond Epstein." Skokie Public Library. Available online. URL: http://www.digitalpast.org. Downloaded October 17, 2004.

"Summation of Aubrey Daniels for the Prosecution." The My Lai Courts Martial. Available online. URL: http://www.law.umkc.edu/faculty/projects/ftrials/mylai/defense.html. Downloaded February 14, 2004.

"Summation of George Latimer for the Defense." The My Lai Courts Martial. Available online. URL: http://www.law.umkc.edu/faculty/projects/ftrials/mylai/defense.html. Downloaded February 14, 2004.

"Testimony of Charles Manson in the Tate-LaBianca Murder Trial." The Trial of Charles Manson. Available online. URL: http://www.law.umkc.edu/faculty/projects/ftrials/manson/mansontestimony-m.html Downloaded February 13, 2004.

"Testimony of Dan Fefferman before the Maryland Task Force to Study the Effects of Cult Activities on Public Senior Higher Educational Institutions." Religious Movements Home Page Project. University of Virginia. Available online. URL: http://religiousmovements.lib.virginia.edu/cultsect/mdtaskforce/fefferman_testimony2. Downloaded August 28, 2004.

"Testimony of Linda Kasabian in the Charles Manson Trial." The Trial of Charles Manson. Available online. URL: http://www.law.umkc.edu/faculty/projects/ftrials/manson/mansontestimony-k.html. Downloaded February 13, 2004.

"Texts of the Panama Canal Treaties with U.S. Senate Modifications." CZBrats. Available online. URL: http://www.czbrats.com/treaty77/trtext.htm. Downloaded October 16, 2004.

"Thirteen Days after Twenty-Five Years." Jimmy Carter Library. Available online. URL: http://www.jimmycarterlibrary.org/documents/campdavid25. Downloaded September 4, 2004.

"Three Mile Island: A Report to the Commissioners and the Public, Vol. I," 1980. Three Mile Island 1979 Emergency. Community Studies Center. Dickinson College. Available online. URL: http://www.threemileisland.org. Downloaded October 17, 2004.

Trippet, Frank. "Running a Good Thing into the Ground." *Time,* September 11, 1978. Available online. URL: http://www.time.com/archive/printou/ 0,23657,946007,00. html.

"Unsigned Note, Richard Trop." Alternative Considerations of Jonestown and Peoples Temple. Department of Religious Studies. San Diego State University. Available online. URL: http://jonestown.sdsu.edu. Downloaded October 14, 2005.

"The War Powers Act of 1973." Available online. URL: http://www.cs.indiana. edu/statecraft/warpow.html. Downloaded May 25, 2004.

"The Woman-Identified Woman." 1970. Available online. URL: http://www. cwluherstory.com/cwluarchive/womidwom.html. Downloaded April 16, 2005.

INDEX

Locators in *italic* indicate illustrations. Locators in **boldface** indicate main entries/topics and biographies. Locators followed by *m* indicate maps. Locators followed by *g* indicate graphs. Locators followed by *c* indicate chronology entries.